ALSO BY GLORIA KAUFER GREENE

Don't Tell 'Em It's Good for 'Em
(with Nancy Baggett and Ruth Glick)

Eat Your Vegetables!
(with Nancy Baggett and Ruth Glick)

THE NEW
Jewish
Holiday
Cookbook

THE NEW
Jewish
Holiday
Cookbook

AN INTERNATIONAL COLLECTION
OF RECIPES AND CUSTOMS

GLORIA KAUFER GREENE

TIMES BOOKS

RANDOM HOUSE

All rights reserved under International and Pan-American Copyright Conventions.
Published in the United States by Times Books, a division of Random House, Inc., New
York, and simultaneously in Canada by Random House of Canada Limited, Toronto.

Some of the recipes contained in this book previously appeared in modified form
in the *Baltimore Jewish Times.*

This is a revised edition of *The Jewish Holiday Cookbook,* published
in 1985 by Times Books, a division of Random House, Inc.

Library of Congress Cataloging-in-Publication Data
Greene, Gloria Kaufer.
The new Jewish holiday cookbook: an international collection of
recipes and customs / Gloria Kaufer Greene.—Completely rev. and
updated with more than 100 new recipes
p.   cm.
Rev. and updated ed. of: The Jewish holiday cookbook. c1985.
ISBN 0-8129-2977-2
1. Cookery, Jewish.   2. Fasts and feasts—Judaism.   I. Greene,
Gloria Kaufer.   Jewish holiday cookbook.   II. Title.
TX724.G723   1999
641.5′676—dc21   98-55721

Random House website address: www.atrandom.com

Printed in the United States of America on acid-free paper

24689753

Revised Edition

Book design by Helene Berinsky

Times Books are available at special discounts for bulk purchases for sales
promotions or premiums. Special editions, including personalized covers,
excerpts of existing books, and corporate imprints, can be created in large
quantities for special needs. For more information, write to Special Markets,
Times Books, 201 East 50th Street, New York, N.Y. 10022, or call 800-800-3246.

*This book is dedicated to my husband, Geoffrey, and
our four wonderful children, Dylan, Trevor, Jared, and Stacey,
whose love and constant support sustain me always.*

୭ଓ

*It is also dedicated to my parents, Hindy and Irv Kaufer,
for lovingly passing down to me the Jewish culinary heritage
that they inherited from their own parents and grandparents.
May the chain continue unbroken for many generations to come.*

ACKNOWLEDGMENTS

Several people have given of themselves in one way or another to help make this revised edition, as well as the original edition, of this book a reality.

I especially want to thank those wonderful acquaintances and relatives who talked with me for hours in preparation for the first edition, and generously shared with me some of their most cherished possessions—their family histories and their heirloom recipes.

Ida Revah Dana, her husband, Leon, son Silvio, and daughter-in-law Dulcie Drazin Dana enlightened me with the delights of Turkish-Jewish food, and treated me to many wonderful dishes in their homes. Mrs. Dana taught me more about Sephardic cooking than anyone else I interviewed, and she told me about some delightful holiday customs that my Ashkenazic family has adopted as our own. The Danas also paved the way for my visit (during a trip to Istanbul) with the warm and memorable Salfati family, who taught me about Turkish-Jewish cuisine in situ. Sharon Cantor Gordon told me about her husband Michael's upbringing in Cuba, and about the tasty dishes that her late mother-in-law, Regina Gordon, used to prepare for the family. Denise Saville Zandman, native of Wales and citizen of Israel, and her sabra husband, Dov Zandman, helped me with many Hebrew food terms, and described in detail the Israeli celebration of many Jewish holidays. They also introduced me to two excellent Jewish cooks—Denise's mother, Pauline Rubens Saville of Wales, and Dov's mother, Liora Ben-Chaim Zand-

man, originally from Libya. Kibbutzniks Jill Cohen Schein and David Schein, Americans who made aliyah to Israel, told me about meals in the kibbutz dining room, where Jill worked as manager. Rabbi Joshua Toledano spent many hours describing his youth in Morocco and also Sephardic holiday customs in general. Both Ralph Ohayon and Ginette Rosilio Spier told me about their Jewish upbringings in Morocco, as did Danielle El-Maleh Mosse, who also lived in Algeria and France. In addition, Mrs. Spier taught me how to make several Moroccan-Jewish dishes. Rachel Muallem Gabes and her son, Marc Muallem, shared details of Jewish life in Iraq and Persia. Bellah Ini, her daughter-in-law Willma Bross Iny, and son, Tzadok Iny, let me in on more secrets of Iraqi-Jewish cuisine. Judith and Morris Erger recalled for me their early lives in Czechoslovakia, where they once owned a delicatessen, and taught me some of the delicious Ashkenazic cuisine they first learned there. I discovered much about Syrian-Jewish culinary culture and tasted many fantastic examples of it at the New Jersey home of Ginger Kassin, where I also spoke with Rachelle Cohen, Shelly Djmal, Poopa Dweck, Sarine Kattan, Nina Shamah, and Jackie Esses. Sandra Waldman Kahane and her sister-in-law, Ida Kahane, told me about Jewish food in their native Colombia, South America, and in their new home, Israel. Lily Livne also described Israeli customs and cuisine, as well as those of her birthplace, Egypt. Rianne Melmed, from Capetown, South Africa, gave me fascinating information about South African–Jewish food, as well as a few hints on Scottish-Jewish cookery, which she learned from her mother-in-law, Ethel Melmed. Leia Derera taught me about delectable Romanian-Jewish specialties. Edith Jeuda Donnenberg described the fascinating customs of her family's Greek-Jewish Seders.

My mother, Helene ("Hindy") Kaplan Kaufer, not only taught me several of the recipes that appear in this book, but also told me wonderful family stories, especially those about her late maternal grandparents, Bubby Rose and Zaida Harry Levine. My father, Irving Kaufer, reminded me of the culinary prowess of my late grandfather, Joseph Kaufer. My paternal aunt, Hannah Kaufer Hafetz, and my cousin, Linda Kaufer Newirth, filled me in with details of family history and recipes. Over the years, my cousin Gail Sandler Nathanson shared many of her best recipes and memories with me.

Whenever I needed expert advice on Yiddish wording, my mother-in-law, Freda Michaelson Greene Cantor, and her husband, Samuel Cantor, were always helpful. My mother-in-law also provided me with recipes for my husband's favorite dishes.

Nancy Baggett, who wrote two cookbooks with me and Ruth Glick, and who continues to write wonderful cookbooks, was an inspiration with her professionalism and perfectionist attitude toward recipes. She developed several recipes for our books together that continue to be my favorites.

Linda Hayes, of Columbia Literary Associates, provided support from the moment the idea for this book was conceived through the anguishing moments as deadline approached.

Rabbi Susan Grossman, religious leader of Beth Shalom Congregation in Columbia, Maryland, read over this revised edition's Pesach introduction, and gave me excellent advice so that I could revise it even better. She also motivated me with inspiring words of encouragement as I toiled through the revisions.

Our previous religious leader, Rabbi Kenneth Cohen, now executive director of the Seaboard Region of the United Synagogues of Conservative Judaism, also answered many of my kashrut questions and those related to other food issues.

While I was working on the revised edition, many members of Beth Shalom Congregation (my "home away from home") provided warm support and constant encouragement as I struggled to balance the demands of a large family, synagogue commitments, and work. In addition, Jacalyn Ely and her mother, Sylvia Ely, shared recipes and stories with me. My close friend—and an excellent cook—Susan Kohler Groman not only gave me ideas for recipes, but often provided delicious sustenance including dishes that she learned from her Sephardic mother-in-law. Over the years, my family of six and Susan's family of five have shared many Shabbat dinners and Jewish holidays together. As I recall, it was Susan who took the first step and warmly invited all of us to her home for the first Shabbat dinner together.

Both our families are members of a wonderful Havurah (friendship group) that has also been the source of much of my enjoyment on the Jewish holidays. The dozen families in our Havurah join together to break the fast of Yom Kippur, share a bountiful meal in a sukkah, eat our first *hametz* after Pesach, and do many other holiday-related activities with our numerous children.

Finally, and most of all, I want to thank those who were closest to me throughout both the ecstasies and difficulties of working on a project of this dimension—my husband, Geoff, and our children, Dylan, Trevor, Jared, and Stacey. Their love and total support made this book possible. It is with my family that I derive the most joy in celebrating the Jewish holidays.

CONTENTS

xiv

PREFACE TO THE SECOND EDITION

In March of 1998, when I was deep into work on this new edition of my book, Harold Kushner spoke to some members of my synagogue, Beth Shalom Congregation, shortly before the installation ceremony for our new rabbi. One particular point really touched me. Rabbi Kushner said that when he is asked by non-Jews to succinctly define Judaism, he says it is "the science of making the mundane holy." For instance, he explained, kashrut and other food-related Jewish laws transform the basic necessity of eating into a sacred act, which spiritually elevates humans above animals.

Later, when I discussed this point with Rabbi Susan Grossman, our newly installed religious leader, she provided me with even more inspiration. Rabbi Grossman noted that cooking Jewish recipes and passing them down to others could also be considered sacred acts because they connect modern Jews with the customs of their ancestors. She said that by writing a Jewish cookbook, I am helping others bring the sacred into their own homes.

Rabbi Grossman's comments were meaningful for me personally. When I first wrote *The Jewish Holiday Cookbook* almost fifteen years ago, I was primarily a food writer who happened to celebrate Jewish holidays. As food editor of the *Baltimore Jewish Times* for many years, I had done a lot of research and knew a significant amount about each holiday. And, as you might expect, I always prepared special foods on the appropriate calendar date. Nevertheless, our family holiday celebrations were, for the most part,

superficial. I cooked and we all ate, but our holidays were not filled with the unique joy that comes from really caring about the customs.

I know this in retrospect because of the many changes that have taken place in my life in the past decade and a half. Probably the most significant is that my husband and I decided to expand our family. We now have four children with an age difference of more than thirteen years from oldest to youngest. When our oldest son became bar mitzvah in the late 1980s, I realized how important it was to pass on a positive attitude about our Jewish heritage to him and his younger siblings. In order to interest every member of our large family (from toddler to teen), I had to be creative.

I began by reviving a tradition that had been one of my own favorites while I was growing up—chicken soup on the Shabbat table every Friday night. (It was my mother's chicken soup that brought me home from college and tempted my nice Jewish boy-friend to join us for Shabbat dinner when we first started dating more than thirty years ago.) Homemade challah and knaidlach soon became Shabbat regulars along with the very successful soup. I also instituted my mother's Friday-evening "rule"—the whole family would always eat Shabbat dinner together.

When a friend bravely invited my entire family of six to her home for Shabbat dinner, I discovered a custom that had not been part of my childhood—sharing this special meal with another family. What fun for us all! I soon began inviting others to our home on a regular basis. Cooking for ten or more people several times a month was difficult at first, but several new Shabbat recipes made it easier and more enjoyable.

My success with Shabbat inspired me to delve into all the holidays more fully, and my family began to look forward to each celebration with great enthusiasm. We now regularly build a sukkah, deliver *shalach manos* (food gifts) for Purim, and have elaborate Seders for both Pesach and Tu B'Shevat. We also enjoy observing many other Jewish holiday customs. The yearly cycle has taken on new meaning for us.

Of course, our Jewish celebrations continue to revolve around food. Many recipes in the first edition of *The Jewish Holiday Cookbook* were mainstays and loved by our guests. Nevertheless, I found that my personal copy of the book was becoming increasingly marked up due to changes I had made in recipes, either to simplify the technique, make the dish more healthful, or just improve the taste. Also, I had added many quick and easy recipes to my holiday repertoire.

When an editor at Times Books asked me if I would like to update *The Jewish Holiday Cookbook,* I knew that the time was right. I had become a food writer who really understood what it meant to celebrate and cook for the Jewish holidays. Furthermore, I had received fantastic feedback from many readers and cooking students who told me

what they loved in the first edition, what confused them, and what "new" recipes they wanted that were not included previously. I'd also learned how certain "innovative" recipes in my book had become "traditional" for some families. My book had inspired new Jewish customs!

Because of this feedback and my own experience, I have made several improvements in this edition. There are more than one hundred completely new recipes—most of them quick and easy to prepare, with many in the popular chapters on Shabbat, Rosh Hashanah, and Pesach. Also, I have revised the directions in almost every recipe to make them clearer and to take advantage of modern cooking equipment. Where possible, the recipes have been adjusted to make them more healthful while still retaining excellent flavor. Basically, I have tried to keep everything that was really good in the original edition and make it even better in this one.

Due to space limitations, however, I did find it necessary to omit some recipes. Since I first wrote *The Jewish Holiday Cookbook,* many other food writers have joined me in my desire to preserve Jewish recipes and customs. Some have written encyclopedic works that feature every Jewish dish imaginable. Because of this, I no longer felt that it was necessary to include less popular recipes in my own book simply to prevent them from being lost to Jewish culture. While I assume that a few of my readers may miss a certain favorite dish that does not appear in this edition, I expect that they will find plenty of wonderful new recipes to take its place.

This exciting new edition of *The Jewish Holiday Cookbook* is a collection of recipes that really work for the holidays, recipes that have been very successful with my own family and our many guests. As in the first edition, not all have historic Jewish origins. But like other Jewish dishes throughout the ages, all have become "Jewish" by virtue of being served on the holiday table. Using these recipes has added much pleasure to my celebration of the Jewish holidays. I hope that this book will do the same for you.

Gloria Kaufer Greene
Columbia, Maryland

PREFACE TO THE FIRST EDITION

When I first became cooking editor of the *Baltimore Jewish Times* in 1980, I had no intention of writing a Jewish cookbook. I thought that the subject was already well covered. But during the next few years, my extensive research on the subject of Jewish food taught me otherwise.

I found it necessary to peruse many volumes whenever I wanted to write an indepth article about the culinary customs of any particular Jewish holiday. What I was able to glean from the available literature was often scanty or inconsistent; and most "traditional" holiday recipes were so vaguely written that they could hardly be followed by the uninitiated expert, let alone the novice cook.

Furthermore, the information was almost always about Ashkenazic (Eastern European–Jewish) cuisine. There was very little material available on the culinary heritage of the Sephardim (those Jews whose ancestors had once lived in Spain or Portugal) or the foods cooked by Jews from the Middle East and other areas.

I began to interview Jewish cooks who had immigrated to the United States from many different countries. Furthermore, whenever I traveled—to Israel, Turkey, Canada, and many other places—I made it a point to contact Jewish cooks.

During my trips and at home, I searched bookstores for obscure, out-of-print Jewish cookbooks. I also mail-ordered unusual cookbooks published by synagogues and Jewish women's groups.

I tested and adapted a multitude of Jewish recipes from all over the world, and wrote out the very best with clear and precise directions, so that even the complicated techniques did not have to be learned at one's mother's knee.

When the results of all these endeavors began to appear in my cooking columns, the reader response was overwhelmingly positive and satisfying. I was told repeatedly that my articles were interesting and informative—even by those who never touched a skillet.

Thus, I was inspired to collect and organize enough material for a comprehensive Jewish cookbook. This book is a fascinating reference for both Jews and non-Jews who want information on Jewish culinary culture. And it provides practical, delectable recipes that can bring this culture to life in your own dining room. I hope it will fill a gap in current Jewish culinary literature and give pleasure to all.

Gloria Kaufer Greene
Columbia, Maryland

THE NEW
Jewish
Holiday
Cookbook

INTRODUCTION

In recent decades, international cooking and dining have become very chic among Americans. More and more people are adding a whole world of ethnic foods to their culinary and gustatory repertoires.

Yet, Jewish cuisine has had an international flavor for more than two thousand years, ever since the beginning of the Diaspora. Early Jews were exiled from their homeland in Judea, first by the Assyrians and Babylonians, and later by Roman conquerors. By the year 300, Jews, who then numbered about three million, had settled in almost every part of the immense Roman Empire. From there, a constant succession of expulsions and dispersions, as well as voluntary migrations, eventually scattered Jews to most areas of the civilized world.

Throughout history, religious dietary laws, local customs, and limited resources have often put severe limitations on the types of foods available to Jews. Rather than stifling their culinary creativity, however, these restrictions have stimulated the Jewish people to develop an international kosher cuisine that is as delicious as it is diversified. No other single "nation" or ethnic group can claim such fantastic variety!

Indeed, Jewish cooks have always been resourceful. When they couldn't prepare a desirable dish, for whatever reason, they invariably found a way to make something else do. Thus, wherever they have lived, Jews have adapted the best and most available local foods in such a way as to make them distinctly Jewish. And, many times, they carried these specialties to other lands, where further modifications and improvements made the dish barely recognizable from the original.

So, then, just what is "Jewish cuisine"?

Before I began to write extensively about Jewish cooking, I thought it meant only the Ashkenazic foods that were the mainstay of my Jewish upbringing. *Ashkenazim*—those Jews whose ancestors dwelled primarily in Eastern and Central Europe—now comprise the vast majority of American Jewry. Thus, their cuisine is what most Americans, Jew and Gentile alike, think of as "Jewish food." It includes chopped liver, pot-roasted brisket, chicken soup with matzah balls, kreplach, mandlen, kugel, tzimmes, blintzes, and latkes—to name just a few favorites. Most Ashkenazic dishes have Yiddish names because that was once the common language spoken by all those who prepared them.

The term "Ashkenazim" comes from *Ashkenaz,* which is an old Hebrew word for "Germany." By the tenth century, Jews who had settled along the southern borders of Germany during Roman rule had migrated northward across the Alps and established the Ashkenazic tradition in Jewish centers along the Rhine River.

During the next several hundred years, however, periodic expulsions or flights from persecution, as well as migrations necessary for economic survival, brought the majority of these Jews to Poland and such nearby areas as Lithuania, Bohemia, and Russia. Yiddish—medieval German with some Hebrew and local vernacular thrown in—developed during this period.

The climate was, for the most part, cold and uncompromising, and food supplies in the *shtetls* (small villages) where most Ashkenazic Jews lived were often quite meager. Nevertheless, they found ingenious ways to stretch whatever they had into tasty dishes that not only satisfied and sustained, but made life a bit more pleasant as well.

When times were better, the Ashkenazim refined their cuisine and indulged in the luxuries of fresh fish, fruits, vegetables, sweets, and more. Migrations to the Austro-Hungarian Empire further influenced Ashkenazic cooking and introduced, among other things, elegant pastries and tortes.

When I became seriously involved in food writing, I began to learn about the "other type" of Jewish food—the kind prepared and prized by Sephardim. I did not, however, delve deeply into its mysteries until 1980, when I became food editor of the *Baltimore Jewish Times.*

In my weekly columns, particularly those about the Jewish holidays, I decided it would be interesting and culturally valuable to discuss not only Ashkenazic culinary customs, which most of my readers already knew about, but also those of Sephardic origin.

Naturally, I wanted to include traditional recipes from both heritages. This led to much research and recipe testing, during which I discovered a bounty of fascinating information about the foods eaten by the Sephardim.

Sephardic Jews form a far more heterogeneous group than their Ashkenazic brethren. Though they are often considered to be "any Jews who are not Ashkenazic," this definition is really too simplistic.

The Hebrew word *Sepharad* originally referred to an area of Asia where some exiled Jerusalemites went after the destruction of the First Holy Temple. During the Middle Ages, however, it came to mean the Iberian Peninsula, and Sephardim were the Jews who lived there peacefully under Muslim rule for many centuries. After the heinous Spanish Inquisition, those Jews who had been expelled from Spain and Portugal, and also all their descendants, became generally known as Sephardim—no matter where they eventually resettled.

Most of the deported Sephardim sailed eastward to the Balkans and central areas of the Ottoman Turkish Empire, where they and their extensive talents were needed and welcomed. Another large group made new homes along the northern coast of Africa, particularly in Morocco. Smaller numbers went to Italy and some Middle Eastern areas. Later, new Sephardic communities were established in other parts of the world, such as Holland and its colonies, several major cities of Europe, and even North America, whose first Jews were Sephardim.

During their brilliant "Golden Age" in Iberia, Sephardic Jewry had developed a sophisticated culture, complete with elaborate culinary skills. Throughout their exile, the Sephardim maintained many of these skills, while adapting their cuisine to local ingredients, and adding native cooking techniques to their own repertoire. In return, the Sephardim often had a positive influence on the cooking of the countries in which they resided.

As with Ashkenazic cooking, climate played an important role in the types of foods eaten. Sephardim generally have lived in warm areas with long, abundant growing seasons, and so an amazing variety of fresh vegetables and fruits is prominent in their cuisine. Also, foods typically are cooked in olive oil, not the rendered animal fat (called schmaltz) that was, of necessity, usually used by Ashkenazim.

The names of most Sephardic dishes reflect their conglomerate origins. Many are Judeo-Spanish, or *Judezmo,* as it is sometimes called. *Ladino*—the liturgical form of this language—is basically Castilian Spanish with some Hebrew mixed in. Like Yiddish, it is written in Hebrew characters. Over the centuries, conversational Judeo-Spanish has picked up many words from local languages, particularly Turkish. Thus, the transliter-

ated Judeo-Spanish names of dishes often include words that resemble Spanish or Turkish words, but have slightly different spellings or pronunciations.

In addition to the true Sephardim, there is another group of non-Ashkenazic Jews, sometimes referred to as "Oriental Jews," whose ancestors never lived on the Iberian Peninsula or any part of Europe, but stayed in the Middle East or returned to it after they were deported from ancient Judea. Because this area has long been dominated by Arabs, the Jewish cuisine took on an Arabic flavor, and many of the dishes have Arabic names. The Jews from these communities spoke Arabic as their everyday language.

Small early communities of Jews were also established in the Balkans, Morocco, Italy, the Near East, India, and even Asia, as well as in some other obscure regions such as Ethiopia. And, in each place, the local cuisine was absorbed and adapted along with the local language.

The non-Ashkenazic Jews who have Iberian ancestors actually far outnumber those who don't. Thus, to simplify matters and avoid confusion, all of them are often grouped together, in modern parlance, as "Sephardim." (With the recipes of this book, however, I have tried to make a distinction whenever it was possible.)

Although Jews from different countries have different culinary customs, they all share the ancient Hebrews as their common ancestors and the Torah as their immutable guide. Their cuisines, therefore, have the same primary basis—namely, the dietary rules called the laws of kashrut.

The word "kosher" (*kasher* in Hebrew) means "ritually fit." Thus, kosher food is simply fit for consumption according to Jewish law. The laws of kashrut are based on biblical injunctions, and any health value is considered to be coincidental. They have been followed by Jews, without question, for millennia, and have shaped Jewish cuisine in a truly unique fashion.

The laws specifically state which types of animals may be eaten and which may not. According to Leviticus, ". . . any animal that has true hoofs, with clefts through the hoofs, and that chews the cud—such you may eat." Cattle and sheep are thus permitted, for example, but pigs, rabbits, and horses are not. Also, ". . . anything in water, whether in the seas or in the streams, that has fins and scales—those you may eat." Thus, most vertebrate fish are permitted, but not shellfish.

Almost all "crawling" and "swarming" things, such as reptiles and insects, are also forbidden, as are certain birds (and their eggs), "animals that walk on paws," and any animal that has died of disease or natural causes.

Permitted animals and poultry (but not fish) must be ritually slaughtered in a manner that ensures both that the animal dies as quickly and as painlessly as possible and that

most of the blood drains from the animal's carcass. After being slaughtered, the carcass is examined to certify that the animal was healthy.

The consumption of blood is absolutely forbidden. Therefore, shortly after butchering, raw meat must be soaked in water, treated with coarse salt, and drained well; then it must be rinsed thoroughly to ensure that all possible blood has been removed. This process is called, in the English vernacular, "kashering." Because it is impossible to kasher liver in this manner, it must be broiled instead. Broiling is considered an alternative to salt kashering, and may also be used with other cuts of meat. (Fish does not need kashering of any type.)

Also forbidden are certain fats and the sciatic nerves and connected tendons in the hindquarters of permitted animals. Dissecting these parts out of the meat is difficult and time-consuming; therefore, in the United States, the hindquarters are virtually always sold to nonkosher butchers. However, in Israel and some other countries, where meat is relatively scarce and expensive, the tedious dissection is done, and kosher cuts from the hindquarters are thus available.

A strict prohibition against eating meat and dairy (that is, milk products) together in any form comes from the biblical statement "You shall not boil a kid in its mother's milk." This injunction is repeated twice in Exodus and once in Deuteronomy. To ensure that the law will not be violated, all kitchen equipment, utensils, and dishes used to prepare and eat meat must be kept completely separate from those used for dairy.

Certain foods are considered to be neither meat nor dairy, and are "neutral" or *pareve* (a Yiddish word that is pronounced "'pahr-eh-vuh" or, in the English vernacular, "'pahr-ev"). This category includes all fruits, vegetables, and grains—that is, anything that grows from the earth—as well as eggs and fish. Because they are "neutral," pareve foods may be eaten with either meat or dairy products. (However, the early rabbis determined that fish and meat should not be cooked together or eaten on the same dish, though they may be included in separate courses of the same meal. A small minority of Jews observe a similar separation of fish and dairy products.)

For convenience, all the recipes in this book have been marked P for pareve, M for meat, or D for dairy.

In addition, the recipes have been categorized, in chapters, according to the Jewish holiday when they would be served most appropriately. Of course, it is unnecessary to restrict the recipes *only* to certain holidays. They can be used throughout the year for various occasions.

I chose to arrange the recipes by holidays because, throughout the ages, many Jewish foods have been traditionally identified with religious rituals, and thus symbolically

came to be associated with specific holidays. More important, in many modern Jewish households, holidays seem to be the major focus for culinary endeavors revolving around ethnic foods. Even "nonobservant" Jews celebrate many holidays with a special family meal. Holidays are the time when many Jewish families take particular pride in their roots and want to pass on this heritage to their children.

The traditional Jewish foods served on holidays need not be limited to those from one's own culinary background. Though my husband and I are both Ashkenazic Jews, it has become our family custom to enjoy at least one traditional Sephardic dish (and usually more) at each holiday meal. Holidays in our home have thus become adventures in international dining. And because we make a point of discussing with our children the origin of each dish and any symbolism connected to it, our meals are also tasty lessons in worldwide Judaic culture.

The recipes in this book are an international collection of culinary treasures awaiting discovery and delectation by both Jews and non-Jews alike. They have been culled and adapted from a number of sources. Several of the Ashkenazic recipes (though not all) were taught to me by expert cooks in my own family. I had to look elsewhere for the other recipes, which turned out to be a fascinating experience that was deliciously worthwhile. While researching this book, I interviewed Jewish cooks from all over the world, most of whom now live in the United States, Canada, or Israel.

The majority of these people create wonderful dishes by instinct and memory alone—their only measurements being "a handful of this" or "a pinch of that." Consequently, I had to test every recipe a number of times in my own kitchen. Often, I adjusted ingredients to increase flavor or nutritional value, and I sometimes simplified technique. Yet, I always tried to retain the basic integrity and authenticity of each dish.

Other recipes in this book, such as a Gingerbread Sukkah, Soft Pretzels for Hanukkah, Ricotta Latkes, and a special layered Cheese Blintz Casserole, were completely my own innovations, devised specifically with a certain holiday in mind. Sometimes, I adapted recipes from non-Jewish cuisines to make them kosher and appropriate for my holiday table.

In so doing, I followed in the footsteps of other Jewish cooks throughout the ages, who have constantly modified and improved Jewish cooking. The process is a continuous one, and is especially evident in modern-day Israel, where the multifaceted cuisines of immigrants are gradually being transformed by a brand-new style of imaginative local cooking that takes superb advantage of indigenous foods.

Jewish cooking has thus come full circle. The ancient birthplace of Jewish cuisine is where its newest dishes are currently being created.

9

Jewish food is, of course, inseparable from the traditions, customs, history, and lore of the people who cook it. Thus, I have attempted to make this cookbook as rich in culinary culture as it is replete with recipes. It has been designed to provide sustenance for the mind and soul, as well as the body. And it can help carry on a culinary legacy that began more than two thousand years ago.

So, as they say in Israel, "*B'tayavon!*" "Good appetite!"

Introduction

A NOTE ON TRANSLITERATIONS USED IN THIS BOOK

Hebrew, Yiddish, and Ladino (or Judeo-Spanish) are all customarily written in Hebrew characters. Therefore, words from these languages must be transliterated for English-speaking readers. Because there is no universal standard, transliterations are quite inconsistent from source to source.

In this book, I have tried to spell words from the above languages as they sound, except for one major exception. Because the "ch" designation for the Hebrew-Yiddish guttural "h" sound is so confusing, and is often misunderstood to be the "ch" of "chair," I have decided to use a plain "h" instead when it comes at the beginning of a word. (For example, I say "Hanukkah," not "Chanukah.") However, I have left the guttural "ch" at the beginning of a very few words (such as "challah") where it is virtually always used, or where leaving it out makes a word incomprehensible. Also, I generally left the "ch" at the *end* of a word, such as in "kreplach," or "Pesach," where it is less likely to be mispronounced.

Occasionally, I have included a phonetic pronunciation, when I felt this would be helpful.

Transliterations of Hebrew words generally are based on the Sephardic pronunciations commonly used in modern Israel.

A COMMENT ON THE NOTATION
P , M , OR D

For the convenience of those who observe the dietary laws of kashrut, all recipes have been designated either P for pareve, M for meat, or D for dairy. In a few cases where there is a choice of ingredients (such as butter or margarine), the recipe may be designated D or P.

GLOSSARY OF INGREDIENTS

This brief glossary includes only those ingredients that are called for in more than one recipe, and may need more explanation than that which is given in the text.

ALMONDS. Almost all the almonds called for in this book are blanched almonds, meaning that the brown skin has been removed from the almond kernel. Raw, blanched almonds usually can be purchased either whole or slivered. (Sliced almonds are *not* blanched.) Sometimes, blanched almonds are available finely ground. For freshest taste, store almonds in the freezer, but be sure to let them come to room temperature before chopping or finely grinding them. When the measurement of almonds is critical to a recipe, the following can be used as a guide:

Blanched whole almonds
   1 cup = 5⅓ ounces
   8 ounces = 1½ cups
   10 ounces = 1⅞ cups

Blanched slivered almonds
   1 cup = 4 ounces
   8 ounces = 2 cups
   10 ounces = 2½ cups

Blanched finely ground almonds
    1 cup = 3¾ ounces
    10 ounces = 2⅔ cups
    Commercially ground powdery almonds
    7 ounces = about 2 cups

BULGUR WHEAT. This is made from kernels (or "berries") of whole wheat that have been parboiled, dried, and cracked into small pieces. Bulgur is available at most health food stores, and some supermarkets. For best keeping, store it in the freezer. (Note: Cracked wheat, which looks like bulgur, has not been parboiled.)

BUTTER, MARGARINE, OR OIL. In this book, I have tried to replace butter and margarine with heart-healthy oil (olive, canola, or safflower) wherever possible. When the harder fats are necessary for the proper flavor or texture, I left them. Sometimes, I have given the option of butter or pareve margarine when a recipe could be used with either meat or dairy meals. However, when a recipe is undeniably "dairy" or when butter is essential for flavor (as in butter cookies), I favor butter over margarine. Butter not only tastes much better, it may also be preferable for health reasons. The oils in margarine are hardened by a process called "hydrogenation," which produces trans fatty acids. The latest studies indicate that these fats may be more harmful to the body than the saturated fat in real butter. When pareve margarine must be used for religious reasons, the most healthful kosher brands will list a liquid oil as one of the first ingredients. Avoid those with cottonseed oil (which may be almost impossible at Pesach), as it is rather high in saturated fat. Some Jews have the custom that most other oils are *kitniyot* and should be avoided at Pesach. Ashkenazic kashrut supervisors tend to follow these strict guidelines.

CANOLA OIL. This "heart-healthy" oil is high in monounsaturated fat (which lowers "bad" cholesterol while not affecting or possibly even raising "good" cholesterol), and is very low in harmful saturated fat. It has a high "smoking point" (when frying) and is bland-tasting, making it an excellent all-purpose oil for baking and cooking. Many authorities consider it to be acceptable for Pesach.

CARDAMOM. This sweet-smelling spice is available at most supermarkets in its ground form. It comes from small seed pods, which are sold whole at some specialty stores.

CHICKPEAS. These are also known as *garbanzo beans, humus, nahit, bub, arbus, ceci,* and other names. They are used extensively in Jewish cooking—particularly Middle Eastern Sephardic cuisine. Chickpeas are available precooked and canned at most supermarkets. Dried chickpeas may also be available there, or they may be found at health food stores or specialty stores.

CILANTRO OR CILANTRO LEAVES. This herb is sometimes used in Moroccan and Middle Eastern cooking. It is the leaf of the coriander plant, and cannot be used interchangeably with ground coriander spice, which comes from the seeds.

CORIANDER OR CORIANDER SEED. This spice is often used in Middle Eastern cuisine. It is available ground in most supermarkets and some specialty stores. (Note: The herb cilantro is the leaf of the coriander plant. It cannot be used interchangeably with ground coriander.)

CUMIN. This brownish-gold spice is used quite often in Middle Eastern cuisine. (For instance, it gives Israeli falafel a deliciously distinctive taste.) It is available ground in most supermarkets.

EGG SUBSTITUTE. In this book, the term "egg substitute" means egg whites mixed with natural coloring and other natural ingredients to make a pasteurized yellow liquid that can be used in recipes instead of beaten whole eggs. With any recipe that is not already dairy due to other ingredients, and always with meat recipes, I call for pareve egg substitute. (Some egg substitutes contain milk products; check the classification to make sure.) I use the type that is refrigerated (rather than frozen) and comes in 8-ounce or 2-ounce containers. For a long time, I resisted this product as an ersatz replacement, but I have embraced it in recent years for several reasons: (1) The major brands have been greatly improved, and there are many foods, especially baked goods, in which a good-quality egg substitute is hardly discernible from real eggs. (2) Egg substitute is much lower in cholesterol and fat than the real thing (the impetus for its invention, after all), allowing me to prepare "guilt-free" egg-laden kugels. (3) It is pasteurized, a real bonus that means: my children can lick the cake batter from the bowl, I don't have to disinfect my countertop after I have rolled out cookie dough, we can have moist French toast, and I can adjust seasonings in my casseroles *before* they are baked—with nary a fret about salmonella contamination. (4) It is already well beaten, making it much more convenient

to use in a hurry than real eggs and an excellent glaze for yeast breads and other baked goods. And (5) It is measured (¼ cup = 1 large egg), so the amount used is consistent every time a recipe is prepared, unlike real eggs, whose size can vary greatly, even among eggs in the same carton because egg "size" is determined by the *total* number of ounces in a dozen eggs. (Note: One 8-ounce carton of egg substitute contains about 1 cup.)

FARMER CHEESE. Though it occasionally has other meanings, in this cookbook, farmer cheese always refers to a soft, unripened cheese that is similar to fine, dry cottage cheese. This type of farmer cheese is usually sold in rectangular, soft plastic packages that contain about 7½ to 8 ounces each. It may also be sold loose, in bulk, at some stores. It is used instead of cottage cheese, because it is finer and drier, and does not release liquid when cooked. It is traditionally used in many Ashkenazic Jewish recipes.

FETA CHEESE. This "salt-cured" white cheese is available at most supermarkets. It is used in Sephardic savory pastries and other dishes, particularly those with a Greek influence.

FILO (pronounced "'fee-low"). This is a very thin dough that looks and feels remarkably like white tissue paper. Filo (also spelled "fillo," "phyllo," or "fila," and sometimes called "strudel leaves") usually comes in a long, narrow box that contains several sheets folded together and sealed inside a plastic bag. Filo can be purchased in the frozen food sections of some supermarkets, as well as in most Greek or Middle Eastern ethnic grocery stores and gourmet specialty stores. The packaged sheets should always be brought to room temperature before unwrapping, unfolding, and using. If they have been frozen, they must first be thawed in the refrigerator overnight.

The delicate sheets of filo dry out extremely quickly. Therefore, whenever they are removed from their sealed plastic bag, they should be kept in a stack between two slightly damp (but not wet) dish towels, and used as soon as possible for best results. If filo is handled correctly, it is easy and fun to use. However, if thawed improperly or allowed to dry out, it may crumble and become impossible to work with. Any unused sheets of filo should be folded and returned to their plastic bag. Seal the bag well with tape, and store the filo in the refrigerator (for a week or two) or freezer.

FLOUR. In this book, I have clearly denoted the type of white flour that works best for each recipe. The types that I call for, in order based on increasing protein content, are all-purpose flour, unbleached flour, and bread flour. Whenever I say all-purpose flour, I

mean bleached flour with a relatively low protein content. It produces the best cookies, cakes, muffins, and piecrusts. Unbleached flour (sometimes called all-purpose un-bleached flour) has a higher protein content, making it better for breads, soft pretzels, strudel, and other baked goods where a "strong" rather than "delicate" dough texture is desired. Bread flour has the highest protein content of all, making it excellent for gluten development in breads. However, this also makes the dough very difficult to knead; therefore, I have sometimes combined unbleached and bread flour in recipes.

KASHA. This word can mean almost any type of cereal; however, to Ashkenazic Jews, it almost invariably means buckwheat groats. Although buckwheat is botanically not a grain, it is usually cooked like one. Buckwheat kasha can be purchased in most super-markets as whole groats, coarsely cracked, or finely ground.

KASHKAVAL CHEESE. Also called *kaskaval,* this Balkan cheese is made from sheep's milk. It is very popular among Sephardic Jews who hail from Turkey, Greece, and nearby areas, and has become commonplace in Israel, although it still tends to be a specialty cheese in the United States. Very similar cheeses that are sometimes used are Greek *kasseri* and Ital-ian *caciocavallo.* (According to *Eat and Be Satisfied: A Social History of Jewish Food,* by John Cooper, the word *kaskaval* is derived from *caciocavallo.* Cooper says that this cheese was so popular with Near Eastern Jews that the Greeks called it *casheri,* meaning "kosher" cheese. It seems that casheri, which could be spelled *kasheri,* must be a variant form of the more common word, *kasseri.*) These cheeses may be available at specialty stores, and some of them may also be special-ordered from a few distributors of kosher cheese in New York City.

MARGARINE. See "Butter, Margarine, or Oil."

OIL. See "Canola Oil," "Olive Oil," and "Safflower Oil," and "Butter, Margarine, or Oil."

OLIVE OIL. When used for salads or sautéing, olive oil should be "extra-virgin" (from the first pressing) with a rich, fruity taste that adds to the flavor of food. The best olive oil is richly tinted green. ("Light" olive oil is a lower-quality oil that is "light" in color and flavor, but not in fat or calories, and may be preferable for baking due to its bland taste.) Store olive oil in a dark place, and, if you do not use it frequently, buy it in rela-tively small quantities to keep it from becoming rancid during long storage. It is low in

saturated fat, and very high in heart-healthy monounsaturated fat. Extra-virgin olive oil is acceptable for Pesach.

PASTEURIZED DRIED EGG WHITES. This soft white powder is reconstituted with warm water following the package directions, and then is used exactly like fresh egg whites. The foam produced by beating pasteurized egg whites to peaks is actually more stable than with fresh whites, making it harder to inadvertently overbeat the pasteurized whites. While pasteurized dried egg whites may be used in any recipes calling for egg whites, they are particularly useful in recipes in which egg whites are not cooked, such as dessert mousses and high-protein frothy "shakes," to avoid any potential problems with salmonella bacterial contamination. (See the recipe for Quick Chocolate Mousse, page 406.) This product is also convenient for recipes that call for a lot of egg whites, such as angel food cake.

In my area, there is an excellent brand of this product, "Just Whites," available in small containers in supermarkets. The dry powder does not need to be refrigerated. Just Whites is composed solely of pasteurized dried egg whites and is currently certified by the Orthodox Union (O-U). It is distributed by Deb-El Foods Corporation, 2 Papetti Plaza, Elizabeth, NJ 07206-1421 (Phone: 908-351-0330). Other brands of pasteurized dried egg whites may also be available.

PINE NUTS. Often called by their Italian name, *pignoli,* these are used frequently in Mediterranean and Middle Eastern cuisine. There are basically two types: the European ones are cylindrical and slightly resemble slivered almonds; the southwestern American type (which is less expensive) is more triangular-shaped. Both are soft and very rich-tasting; however, gourmets generally prefer the European type. Pine nuts can be purchased at some supermarkets, as well as health food and specialty stores. Though they are expensive, a few go a long way to make a dish especially appealing and "exotic." Store pine nuts in the freezer, where they will stay fresh-tasting for a long time. They do not need to be thawed before use.

ROSE WATER. This unusual flavoring, which is extracted from rose petals, is occasionally used in Middle Eastern and Near Eastern cooking. It can be purchased at many specialty stores.

SAFFLOWER OIL. This oil is high in polyunsaturated fat, and very low in harmful saturated fat. It has a high "smoking point" (when frying) and is bland-tasting, making it a

good all-purpose oil for baking and cooking. (However, some experts say that it may lower "good" cholesterol along with the "bad" type. Canola oil, which is monounsaturated, lowers bad cholesterol, but not good.) Many authorities consider it to be acceptable for Pesach.

SEEDS (ANISE, CARAWAY, POPPY, AND SESAME). Although all these seeds are usually available at supermarkets, large quantities are often much less expensive at health food stores and ethnic grocery stores. Store seeds in the freezer, where they will keep at least a year. See also "Sesame Seeds."

SESAME SEEDS. Sesame seeds should always be the hulled, "white" type. (There are also black sesame seeds, which are used in Asian cooking.) Unhulled white seeds may be called "brown sesame seeds" because they are tan or very pale brown; this is not the same as "toasted" sesame seeds. Hulled white sesame seeds usually are toasted in a dry skillet to bring out their richest flavor and aroma. For best results, this should be done just before they are used. To toast sesame seeds, put them into a large, ungreased skillet, and cook them over medium to medium-high heat, stirring frequently, for about 5 to 10 minutes, or until they are light brown and very aromatic. They will be uneven shades of brown. Do not let them burn. If the seeds start to "pop" and bounce out of the pan, the heat is too high. See also, "Seeds."

SPINACH, FROZEN. For any recipe in which spinach is to be cooked, frozen spinach works as well as fresh, and it may even taste better than fresh spinach past its prime. To quickly defrost a box of frozen spinach, use a small knife to stab some holes in the top of the box right through the wrap; then place the box on several layers of paper towels (to absorb drips) in the microwave oven. Cook it on "high" for about 3 to 4 minutes, or until most of the box—except the very center—feels soft. Let it rest for 5 minutes to continue to defrost. Then open the box, remove the spinach, and use your hands to squeeze out excess moisture. (A potato ricer can also be used for this task.) It does not matter if the center of the spinach is still slightly frozen. Do not microwave the spinach too long or it may start to cook in the box and become rather messy.

TAHINI. This is a plain paste ground from hulled sesame seeds, just as peanut butter is made from peanuts. Tahini is available at most health food and specialty stores, as well as many supermarkets. Once opened, it will keep for several months in the refrigerator if the plastic lid is tightly resealed on the can. A newly opened can of tahini should always

be stirred very well before using it, to resuspend the separated sesame oil. This task is most easily done in a food processor. The refrigerated tahini should then stay mixed for a while. Be sure to always stir in any separated oil before using tahini. Do not discard the oil. In Israel, both the pure sesame seed paste and a dressing made from it are called *tahina*—the only difference being that the latter is sometimes described as "prepared" tahina.

YEAST. There are two basic types of dry yeast currently on the market. "Active dry yeast" has been available for many years, and was the first alternative to compressed fresh yeast (which still may be available in some areas, but is too difficult for most home cooks to store and use).

More recently, several strains of fine, resilient dry yeasts have been produced that do not need advanced "proofing" in water, and can be used to produce delicious baked goods with only one quick rising. Depending on the brand, they may be called "fast-acting," "quick," "bread machine," or "instant" yeast (the names keep changing). The recipes in this book that call for yeast specify which type of dry yeast to use. For the most part, they are not interchangeable if the recipes are followed as directed.

Shabbat

What is Shabbat? Shabbat is taste:

The warm flavor of homemade soup;

The rich taste of Challah;

The sweetness of Shabbat cake,

And, perhaps, the taste of the world to come.

This is Shabbat.

—From a poem by Yochanan ben Avraham

 SHABBAT, OR "SABBATH" IN ENGLISH, IS THE MOST IMPORTANT holiday of the Jewish calendar. In the Torah, God commands that the seventh day of every week be kept a "day of rest" as a perpetual covenant between God and the Jewish people. Shabbat reminds us that God rested on the seventh day after creating the world. Jews observe this holiday each week from Friday evening at sundown until after nightfall on Saturday.

Throughout Jewish history, the best foods and the nicest clothes have always been reserved for Shabbat, the most splendid day of the week. New fruits and vegetables of the season were sometimes not eaten on weekdays so that they could be relished on Shabbat. And poor Jews often scrimped throughout the rest of the week just to have a decent Shabbat meal.

Shabbat is ushered in with the kindling of special candles. A minimum of two candles is traditionally used because, in the Torah, God exhorts us to "remember" and "observe" the Sabbath. However, many families light a candle for each member (or sometimes one for each child, as we do). Because it is against Jewish law to kindle a flame during Shabbat, the candles must be lit *before* the blessing is said. Then we briefly

cover our eyes with our hands so as not to derive "benefit" from the flame until after we have completed the blessing and the holiday has begun. After lighting the candles, many parents bless their children.

On Shabbat, unlike other days and holidays, it is considered a *mitzvah*—a religious obligation—to eat three main meals (not including breakfast). These are the Friday-evening or *Erev Shabbat* meal, the midday meal on Saturday, and an early evening meal on Saturday known as *Shalosh Se'udot* (meaning "three meals") or *Se'udah Shelisheet* (meaning "the third meal"). This tradition is said to have come about because of a verse in Exodus that quotes Moses saying the word "today" three times in referring to eating manna on Shabbat. The Talmud tells us that one who partakes of these three meals will receive favorable judgment in the world to come.

The first two meals of Shabbat (and sometimes the third) begin with the *Kiddush*—a special prayer said over a cup of wine or grape juice. This is followed by the blessing for challah (pages 32 and 39), two loaves of which are always on the Shabbat table (except during Pesach, when leavened bread is forbidden). The bread is dipped into or sprinkled with salt before it is eaten to recall the ancient Temple in Jerusalem, where salt was always present on the sacrificial altar. (For more details about challah, see "The Symbolism and Shaping of Challah," page 26.)

It is customary for the main course on Friday evening to be meat or poultry. In times past, when many Jews were impoverished, these foods were luxuries and thus were served in relatively large quantities only on Shabbat.

Fish is also usually on the menu. In fact, the Talmud says that fish, at the very least, must be eaten on Shabbat. And a Yiddish proverb says, "Shabbat without fish is like a wedding without dancing." Jewish sages determined several symbolic reasons for this custom. Some said that since God created fish on the fifth day, and humankind on the sixth, and the Sabbath followed on the seventh, the three should be kept together, with people eating fish on Shabbat. Others noted that the Hebrew letters in the word for fish, *dag,* numerically add up to seven, the day of the week on which we observe Shabbat. Also, in Genesis, God repeatedly blesses people and fish, and tells both to "be fruitful and multiply"; therefore, fish has also come to stand for fertility and immortality. In the past, some pious Jews refrained from eating fish during the week just so that it would be particularly enjoyable on Shabbat.

Gefilte fish became quite traditional for Ashkenazic Jews on Shabbat for an interesting, nonculinary reason. Removing bones from fish constitutes "borer," the act of separating the inedible part of food from that which is edible. Since religious law prohibits

this activity on the seventh day, most fish to be served on Shabbat was boned and prepared in advance. This particular dish had the added benefit of stretching a small amount of fish to feed a whole family. The word *gefilte* is Yiddish for "stuffed," and the dish is so named because, at one time, the boned, minced fish paste was stuffed back into the fish skin before it was cooked. The method was simplified by forming the fish mixture into balls or oval shapes.

For the Friday-evening meal, Ashkenazic Jews also typically serve soup—usually rich, golden chicken broth, while Sephardic Jews often prefer a large selection of cooked and chilled vegetable salads. After such a large, multicourse holiday meal, dessert is often kept light, and may feature egg cookies, sponge cake, or fresh fruit.

As a fire may not be kindled and no work is permitted on Shabbat, the observant Jewish cook must prepare all food for the entire day ahead of time. However, it is also important to have at least two hot, cooked meals for the holiday. For many centuries, this seeming dilemma has been deliciously solved by serving as the midday dinner on Saturday a hearty stew that is assembled and partially cooked on Friday before sundown, and then allowed to slowly simmer overnight. (For more details, see the recipes for Cholent, page 50, and Dafina, page 52.)

The late-Saturday-afternoon meal is usually lighter than the other two. It is generally a nonmeat meal with bread, smoked or pickled fish, hard-boiled eggs, kugel, and cakes. After eating, Orthodox Jews known as *Hasidim* sometimes gather to discuss nuances of the Torah and to sing Shabbat songs.

Because Shabbat is a day exalted above all others in the week, pious Jews are always very unhappy to see it come to an end. Therefore, after *Havdalah,* the lovely ceremony held at the conclusion of Shabbat, Hasidim often have yet another light meal (or snack) called *Melavah Malkah,* in which they honor the departing Sabbath Queen. The occasion may be used to celebrate any recent joyous events, such as a bar mitzvah or betrothal. (For more details, see the recipe for Spiced Apple Coffee Cake, page 91.)

Many of the recipes in this chapter have been chosen because of their traditional symbolism with regard to Shabbat. Others are simply in keeping with the spirit of the holiday. My family often welcomes guests to our Erev Shabbat dinner, and I have included several tried-and-true company favorites. Most of the dishes served during other Jewish holidays are also very appropriate for Erev Shabbat, so be sure to look through the rest of this cookbook for more ideas. By the same token, many of the recipes in this chapter can be used for other holidays as well.

The Symbolism and Shaping of Challah

The bread now called *challah* is prominent at almost every Jewish festival and celebration (except, of course, during Pesach). In ancient times, the ceremonial loaf more likely had a flat, round shape similar to the Pita (page 454) that is still very popular in the Middle East.

During hundreds of years in the Diaspora (particularly in Eastern Europe), challah evolved into the rich, egg-laden, beautifully shaped bread with which we are now so familiar. Jewish scholars, as is their wont, have ascribed symbolism to every bump and cranny in this "staff of life," as well as to the way it is presented on the table.

Thus, much challah tradition is related to the perfect food—manna—which the Israelites collected and ate as they wandered in the Sinai desert before entering the Promised Land. For instance, there are always *two* loaves on the Shabbat table (and at other festivals) to remind us of the double portion of manna given to our ancestors on Friday so they would not have to profane the Sabbath by gathering and carrying food. In addition, it was customary in ancient times for joyous and abundant Shabbat meals to feature two main dishes (unlike ordinary weekday meals, which had only one), and a loaf of bread always accompanied each course. During the *motzi* blessing for bread, the two loaves are held together as one. Both loaves must be *whole* (not sliced), because every Israelite gathered two *full* measures of manna prior to Shabbat.

The seeds often sprinkled on top of a challah just before it is baked are supposed to be similar to manna as it is described in Exodus. When the Shabbat table is set, the twin *challot* (the plural of *challah*) are usually covered with a beautifully decorated cloth, which represents the dew that covered the manna. The tablecloth or plate *under* the bread symbolizes the layer of dew that was below the manna. Both the challah cover and tablecloth are often white, as were the manna and the desert sands upon which it fell. White is also symbolic of the purity of Shabbat.

Another explanation for the covering is that the challot are hidden so they will not be "offended" that the Kiddush prayer for wine is recited before their own blessing. At weekday meals (when Kiddush is not said), the *motzi* for bread is the premier blessing. The covering thus preserves the "honor" of the challot on Shabbat and festivals, and its dramatic removal draws special attention to the loaves when the *motzi* is said.

In many households (including my own), the Sabbath challah is not sliced for serving, but is pulled apart by diners instead. Some say that this custom developed because a knife, like a sword, is considered to be an instrument of violence and war, whereas Shabbat is a time of peace.

Another prevalent custom is to place a piece of challah in front of each diner (or let each diner individually pull a piece from the challot on the table), rather than handing the challah from person to person. This is done because bread is placed directly into the hands of a mourner at a meal of condolence, which is not appropriate for joyful Shabbat. Also, it is a reminder that bread comes from God, and not from the hands of people. Some Jews, especially among Sephardim, gently toss a piece of bread to diners who are beyond easy reach.

Before it is eaten, the challah traditionally is dipped into or sprinkled with salt as a reminder of the salt always used on the sacrificial altar of the Holy Temple. Because of its necessity during sacrifices to God, salt came to represent the covenant between God and the Jews. Also, in ancient times, salt was very important as a food preservative. Rabbi Susan Grossman says that the salt on our modern "ceremonial" table may thus serve to symbolize the "preservation" of the Jewish people since Temple times. During the Days of Awe, challah is dipped into honey instead of salt, symbolic of our hope for a "sweet" year.

The Torah says that a portion of the raw dough from each large batch of bread must be separated and offered to God (through the priests of the Holy Temple). The special portion was called "challah." Since the destruction of the Second Temple, observant Jewish bakers have symbolically carried out this offering by removing an olive-sized piece of dough from large batches, and burning it in the oven as they say a special blessing. This act is known as "taking challah." In time, challah became the customary name for the entire holiday loaf.

NOTE: None of the bread recipes in this cookbook uses enough flour to require "taking challah."

Braiding Challah

It is written that twelve loaves of *shew-bread,* representing the twelve tribes of ancient Israel, were continually displayed in two rows in the portable Tabernacle and later on the altar of the Holy Temple in Jerusalem. Each Shabbat, the loaves were replenished, and the previous week's bread given to the priests for sustenance.

The twelve loaves are sometimes symbolized by braiding two challot so that six "humps" show on top of each one, or by braiding each loaf with six individual strands of dough. The latter is sometimes accomplished by capping a large three-strand braid

with a smaller three-strand braid, then baking the two together as one loaf. However, some bakers prefer to weave six equal strands into a magnificent single braid.

Four-strand loaves have become commonplace simply because they look more attractive, rise higher, and are thus often lighter than standard three-strand loaves, yet are easier to braid than the six-strand type. Challot from bakeries are often made with four or sometimes five strands.

There are many ways to form slightly different braids using the same number of strands. Offered here are those with steps that are particularly simple, logical, and easy to remember. Before you try these techniques on bread dough, it is best to practice them with even lengths of thick yarn knotted together at one end. That way, you can determine which method works best for you.

Before braiding the bread dough, roll out very smooth, evenly sized strands that are about twelve inches long. For a loaf that tapers at both ends, make the strands slightly thicker in the center. Lay out the strands parallel to each other, and tightly pinch them together at one end. As you work, keep the braid even and compact. Be careful not to stretch or tear the strands, or the surface of the loaf may develop pits as it rises and bakes. When the braiding is completed, pinch the dough strands tightly at the bottom end to keep them from unraveling. Neatly tuck under both ends of the loaf, and place it on a prepared baking sheet to rise.

NOTE: For details on handling and baking challah dough, see the recipe for Gloria's Glorious Challah on page 32.

To Braid Three Strands

A three-strand challah is relatively flat, but very easy to braid. It is braided the same way that most people braid hair. You may go *over* or *under* the center strand, as long as you are consistent. "Under" produces a slightly higher loaf than "over." Keep repeating steps A and B.

A. Pass the strand on the right over (or under) the one in the center.
B. Pass the strand on the left over (or under) the one now in the center.

NOTE: Some prefer to use three parallel strands that are not pinched together. Begin the braiding in the center of the loaf, and go to one end and then to the other, finally pinching the ends.

The New Jewish Holiday Cookbook

To Braid Four Strands

1. After much experimentation, I've decided that this is my favorite method of braiding. It is easy, yet makes a very high, attractive challah. It is the method described in detail in Gloria's Glorious Challah. Keep repeating steps A and B.

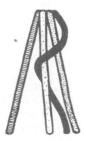 

A. Pass the strand on the far right over the two to the left of it, then back under the one now on its immediate right.

B. Pass the strand on the far left over the two to the right of it, then back under the one now on its immediate left.

2. This challah is a bit flatter than the one in the first method. The technique is quite simple, though the loaf tends to move toward one side as it is being braided. Keep repeating step A, always beginning on the same side (your choice) and moving in the same direction.

A. Pass the strand on the far left (or right) over the one next to it, under the one after that, and over the last strand.

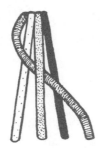 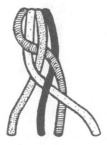

3. This version is slightly more difficult than the first two, but it makes a high, beautiful challah. Keep repeating steps A and B.

A. Pass the second strand from the right over to the far-left position; then pass the strand on the far right over the one now on its immediate left.

B. Pass the strand second from the left over to the far-right position; then pass the strand on the far left over the one now on its immediate right.

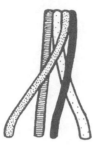 

To Braid Five Strands

Keep repeating steps A, B, and C.

A. Pass the second strand from the left over the one on its immediate right.

B. Pass the strand on the far right over the strand that is now second from the left.

C. Pass the strand on the far left over the two strands to its immediate right.

To Braid Six Strands

1. Many six-stranded braids are much more complicated and confusing than this impressive-looking one. Keep repeating steps A, B, C, and D.

A. Pass the second strand from the right to the far-left position.

B. Pass the strand on the far right over the two strands now on its immediate left.

The New Jewish Holiday Cookbook

C. Pass the second strand from the left over to the far-right position.

D. Pass the strand on the far left over the two strands now on its immediate right.

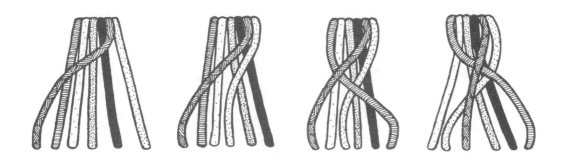

2. This is actually composed of two three-stranded braids (for a total of six strands), which are baked together as one loaf.

Divide the dough into four pieces—three that are equal and one slightly larger. Braid the three equal pieces as described above in "To Braid Three Strands." Then divide the remaining larger piece of dough into three equal strands, and braid them. Lay the small braid over the large one; then let the two braids rise and bake together.

Creating Other Shapes

Throughout the ages, imaginative Jewish bakers all over the world have lovingly pounded, bent, squeezed, and rolled their challah dough into many other innovative and interesting designs. On Rosh Hashanah, for instance, Spiral Challah (page 103) and loaves shaped like ladders are quite popular.

Small pieces of the dough can also be shaped into rolls (page 38). Simple round rolls—made from balls of dough—can be baked on cookie sheets or in muffin tins. Or the dough can be formed into short strands, and each one tied into a double knot with the bottom end tucked under. For rolls that resemble birds, tie a short dough strand into a single knot, and lift up the top end for a head. Just before baking, notch the bottom end of the strand a few times to resemble tail feathers.

Tiny individual loaves, which are each braided from three very small strands of dough, can be great fun for children to shape. In some households, two of these miniature challot are put near each child's place setting on the Shabbat table. Or twelve tiny challot may be placed on the table to symbolize the breads of the Holy Temple.

Gloria's Glorious Challah

QUICK AND EASY NO-CHOLESTEROL SABBATH BRAID

$\boxed{\text{P}}$

Almost every Friday, I use this recipe to make a pair of gorgeous, tasty *challot* (plural of *challah*). I have developed it after years of experimentation. The directions include my favorite method for using a large heavy-duty mixer with a dough hook, with an alternative method for kneading by hand. It includes many hints for quick and easy challah baking. Read over the entire recipe before beginning. It takes only about two hours to produce the finished challot, much less time than most standard recipes.

For the dough and glaze, I prefer to use egg substitute rather than fresh eggs because it is pasteurized and cannot cause food poisoning even if hands and equipment are not washed perfectly well after touching the raw dough. Also, the kosher pareve egg substitute that I use is fat-free and cholesterol-free, and can be conveniently stored in the refrigerator. (Some egg substitutes contain milk products and are not pareve; others must be stored in the freezer.)

The new strains of "fast-acting" instant yeast do not need to be proofed (i.e., dissolved beforehand) and can be added directly to the dry ingredients, speeding up the mixing. Moreover, the dough does not require rising before shaping. Because risen bread dough can be very difficult to roll into strands due to bubbles and elasticity, shaping dough that has not risen also expedites the process in this recipe.

The shaped braids are immediately glazed with egg substitute *before* they rise. Glazing risen dough may cause it to deflate or become misshapen. In addition, the glaze keeps the loaves from drying out while they rise. They are put into a barely warm, turned-off oven to rise until they nearly double. Then, the oven is simply turned on to bake the loaves. This process helps increase the loaves' "oven spring," so they rise high during baking.

This recipe is fun to do with children (who can freely touch the dough without fear of accidental food poisoning), and I have successfully taught it to many adults in hands-on cooking classes.

The four-braid technique described below makes high, beautiful challot, and it is very easy to execute. For details on this and other shaping techniques, see "The Symbolism and Shaping of Challah" (page 26).

NOTES: Fast-acting yeast costs less if purchased in bulk, and it can be stored in the freezer well beyond its printed room-temperature "pull date." It may also be called "instant," "quick-rising," or "bread machine" yeast, depending on the manufacturer.

Regarding flour, I have found a combination of bread and unbleached flours to work best in this recipe, and the dough is not too difficult to knead by hand. All bread flour may be used with a heavy-duty mixer and dough hook (I use a large KitchenAid), though it is more difficult to hand-knead this dough due to its very high gluten content. A high-gluten unbleached flour, such as King Arthur's brand, may be used for the entire recipe in lieu of bread flour, and will produce excellent results. Bleached all-purpose flour will work, but will produce much less desirable results; it is better for cookies, cakes, and pastry.

4 cups bread flour (see Notes)

2 to 3 cups unbleached flour, divided (see Notes)

2 packets (4½ teaspoons) fast-acting dry yeast (see Notes and the Glossary of Ingredients)

⅓ cup sugar

2 teaspoons salt

1 (8-ounce) carton (1 cup) pareve egg substitute or 4 large eggs, divided

⅓ cup canola oil

1½ cups hot (120 to 130 degrees) tap water (no hotter than this or it may kill the yeast)

Approximately 1 teaspoon poppy or sesame seeds (optional)

MIXER METHOD

In the large (about 5-quart) bowl of a heavy-duty electric mixer that has a dough-kneading hook, put the 4 cups bread flour, 1 cup of the unbleached flour, the yeast, sugar, and salt. Mix the dry ingredients by holding the hook in your hand and using it to stir (this saves washing another utensil). Measure out ¾ cup of the egg substitute, and save the rest in the carton to glaze the challah. Add the ¾ cup egg substitute (or add 3 large eggs, lightly beaten) and the oil to the flour mixture, and stir in with the hook. It is not necessary to mix well. Finally, add the hot water, and stir in.

Set the bowl into the mixer, and attach the dough hook. Turn the mixer to kneading speed. As the dough kneads, lightly sprinkle just enough unbleached flour around the inside surface of the bowl so that the dough stays on the hook and does not come down off the hook into the bottom of the bowl. You will probably need to use more flour in the beginning, and less as the dough kneads. Let the dough knead for about 5 to 10 minutes, or until it is very smooth. When it is almost done kneading, it should need very little or no more flour and should almost clean the inner surface of the bowl.

NOTE: If the dough rides over the top of the hook, scrape it down and add more flour. This may happen if the bowl is smaller than 5 quarts. In the future, consider reducing the recipe by one-third and making smaller loaves.

Remove the dough hook from the dough, but leave the dough in the mixer bowl. Cover the bowl with a plastic lid or a piece of plastic wrap so the dough does not dry out and let it rest for about 15 to 30 minutes. This is not a rising period, but time to let the gluten ease so the dough can be shaped. If the room is warm, the dough may rise slightly.

HAND METHOD

In a large bowl, combine the 4 cups bread flour, yeast, sugar, and salt, and mix to combine using a sturdy mixing spoon (such as a wooden one). Measure out ¾ cup of the egg substitute, and save the rest in the carton to glaze the challah. Add the ¾ cup egg substitute (or add 3 eggs, lightly beaten) and the oil to the flour mixture, and stir in lightly. Add the hot water and stir in, mixing very well for several minutes.

NOTE: A strong electric stand mixer with standard beaters may be used for mixing to this point, but the rest must be done by hand if there is no dough hook.

Stir in about 1½ cups unbleached flour, and mix to make a soft, sticky dough. Let the dough rest, covered, for about 5 minutes to allow the flour to absorb some moisture (so that less flour will be required during kneading).

Turn out the dough onto a well-floured surface (board, countertop, etc.) and knead by repeatedly folding and turning the dough, adding small sprinkles of flour as needed to keep the dough from sticking to hands or surface. Try to keep the hands free of sticky dough, as this will make even more dough stick. To "clean" the hands, sprinkle them lightly with flour and rub them together.

Knead for about 10 to 15 minutes, or until the dough is very smooth and silky feeling, and is no longer sticky. To keep the dough from drying out, put it into an ungreased covered bowl, or turn a bowl over the dough on the kneading surface, or cover the dough with plastic, and let it rest for about 15

to 30 minutes. This is not a rising period, but time to let the gluten ease so the dough can be shaped. If the room is warm, the dough may rise slightly.

BOTH METHODS

To easily remove the dough from the bowl, sprinkle a little extra flour over the dough, and use a spatula to push the flour all the way down the sides of the bowl while completely loosening the dough at the same time. Turn out the dough onto a lightly floured board, and press it gently into a large rectangle (about 10 by 14 inches) of even thickness. For two four-braid large challot, use a knife or sharp-edged dough scraper to cut the dough in half; then cut each half in half again to make four; then cut each piece in half once more to produce eight equal pieces. Handling the dough as little as possible, form each piece into a ball. (This can be done by gently stretching the top of a piece of dough to its underside all around.) Very lightly coat each ball with flour so it does not stick to the cutting board.

Form the first four dough balls into thick 12-inch "strands" by holding up a ball in your hands and gently squeezing it between your thumb and other fingers to elongate it into a thick snake. When it is almost the right size, roll it out on a board or directly on the countertop to smooth its sides and slightly lengthen it. If possible, use no flour for rolling, as floured dough is slippery and will slide rather than roll. Each strand should be either of even thickness its entire length or slightly thicker in the middle and tapering to the ends.

When each strand is finished, coat it completely with a dusting of flour, brushing off any excess. The flour prevents the strands from sticking to the countertop during braiding. It also helps the braided strands keep their definition and not blend together during rising and baking, so the finished challot have nicely separated "bumps."

Lay the four strands on the countertop, parallel to each other and about ½ inch apart. Squeeze the strands together very tightly at one end so they cannot unravel during rising and baking. Braid them by starting with the first strand on the right. Lift it over the two strands next to it and then put it back under the strand on its immediate right (lift the strand on its right with your other hand, as you place the first strand under it). Do this "compactly" so the overlapping strands stay close to the pinched end.

Then do the same on the opposite side, beginning with the far-left strand. (Lift it over the two to its right—which are now overlapping each other—back under the one on its immediate left.) Continue alternating sides until the strands are completely braided. Handle the strands gently; do not stretch or pull them as you braid or you'll end up with a long, narrow loaf with stretch marks when it bakes. When the ends of the strands are too short to braid anymore, pinch them very tightly together so that the loaf cannot unravel during baking.

Tuck both ends of the loaf slightly under so you cannot see where the strands were pinched, and push the ends of the loaf together gently to slightly compact it and make it higher in the center. The loaf should appear relatively short and fat. (The finished challah will be much larger.)

Gently transfer the braided loaf to a large, heavy, flat, shiny aluminum baking sheet (cookie sheet) that has been greased, or coated with nonstick cooking spray, or topped with special parchment paper used for baking.

NOTE: I prefer to use a 13 by 16-inch *insulated* baking sheet lined with parchment. Both loaves fit on this if they are placed across the width of the sheet a few inches apart. If your baking sheets are smaller, use one for each loaf, and place the loaf lengthwise on the sheet. If the baking sheets are not the insulated type, use two stacked together to produce a more evenly baked loaf that does not brown too quickly on the bottom.

Repeat all shaping directions to make a second braided loaf from the remaining four dough balls.

When both loaves are formed and on the baking sheet, use a pastry brush to coat them well with the reserved egg substitute (just leave it in the carton, and open both sides of the top for easy access) or with the remaining whole egg beaten with 1 teaspoon water. Sprinkle the tops lightly with poppy or sesame seeds, as desired. Turn your oven on to 200 degrees (or the lowest setting above this) and immediately set a timer for 1 minute. Turn off the oven after exactly 1 minute. Then quickly place the baking sheet with the loaves on a middle rack of the barely warm oven, and let the loaves rise for 30 minutes.

Leave the loaves in the oven, and turn the temperature up to 350 degrees. Bake the loaves for 45 to 50 minutes, or until they are golden brown (they

will not be as dark with egg substitute glaze as they are with whole egg or egg yolk glaze). The loaves should make a hollow sound when thumped on the bottom (or be 190 to 205 degrees when an instant-read thermometer is inserted into the bottom). If egg substitute has been used, underdone loaves will not make anyone ill; they just might be a little dense. Slightly overdone loaves will be a bit too dry, with a crumbly crust. Neither is that bad; after all, it's homemade challah!

Immediately remove the loaves from the baking sheet, and cool them on wire racks for at least 1 hour before eating them. If you're not using the loaves within a few hours, cool them *completely;* then put each one in an airtight plastic bag and store at room temperature for up to 24 hours. For longer storage, seal each loaf well in an airtight plastic bag or use plastic wrap (they may go stale in foil wrap) and freeze them. Thaw the frozen loaves in their wrappers. Thawed loaves may be warmed, wrapped in foil, in a low oven for a few minutes. It's best not to use a microwave oven to thaw or warm the loaves, as most microwave ovens are rather uneven in these tasks, and they may "petrify" the bread.

Makes 2 large (about 1½ pounds each) four-braided challot.

Variations

RICH EGG CHALLAH

Use whole eggs (not egg substitute), and increase the sugar and oil to ½ cup each. The top may be glazed with 1 or 2 egg yolks beaten with a few teaspoons of water. (For an even sweeter, more cakelike challah, see the Spiral Challah on page 103 in the Rosh Hashanah chapter.)

"WATER" CHALLAH (CHALLAH DOUGH WITH NO EGGS)

Omit the eggs or egg substitute in the above dough mixture, and increase the hot water to 2 cups. If desired, ¹⁄₁₆ teaspoon turmeric may be added to give the dough a pale yellow color. The shaped loaves should be glazed with egg or egg substitute if a shiny golden crust is desired. Egg white may be used for shine, but it does not give much color.

ROUND ROLLS

Challah dough makes great rolls. For rolls, shape the rested dough into balls about a third of the desired final size, and let them rise at room temperature on the baking sheet (leave plenty of room between the balls) until almost double. It is not necessary to glaze them. Bake the rolls in a preheated 350-degree oven until the bottoms sound hollow, about 15 to 20 minutes depending on the size of each roll. Makes 20 or more rolls, depending on the size.

CHALLAH-DOUGH "FOCACCIA" (ITALIAN-STYLE FLATBREAD)

Focaccia (pronounced "foh-kah′-tchuh") is a relatively flat loaf that is eaten by cutting it into wedges or breaking it apart. My family loves when I bake challah dough into this style of bread as an occasional variation on our usual braided loaf, and it is very quick to shape when I'm in a hurry or for weekday use. Even though the same dough is used as for challah, focaccia tastes rather different because of the baking technique. Sometimes, I substitute 1 cup oat bran for 1 cup flour in the initial mixture. This gives an intriguing, delicious taste and adds healthful fiber.

For each large focaccia, cut the rested challah dough in half. Use your fingertips to press one piece of the dough into a large flat oval or circle about ½ to ¾ inch thick directly on a large baking sheet that has been parchment-lined, or greased, or coated with nonstick spray. (For smaller baking sheets, cut the dough into thirds and make 3 smaller loaves.) It is traditional to brush or spray the top with olive oil and sprinkle it lightly with herbs (rosemary is a typical choice). Or the dough may be egg-glazed as with challah and sprinkled with seeds. Let it rise at room temperature until puffy, then use your index finger to gently poke several dimples or dents in the top. Bake in a preheated 400-degree oven about 20 to 25 minutes, or until lightly browned. Cool on a wire rack, but serve while still warm if desired. To serve, slice or break off chunks. Makes 2 very large focaccia (or more smaller ones if desired).

NOTE: This version of focaccia is not "traditional" for Italians.

POPPY SEED YEAST CAKE

This delicious cake is made from the above challah dough. See the recipe on page 95.

SWEET CROWNS FOR THE SHABBAT QUEEN

These miniatures can be made using the above challah dough. See the recipe on page 93.

Grandpa's Challah

When I was a child, my paternal grandfather, Joseph Kaufer, was renowned throughout the Jewish community of Wilkes-Barre, Pennsylvania, as an amateur baker par excellence. As far back as my dad—the youngest of thirteen children—can remember, his father was the best baker in the family and remained so almost until his death in 1966 at age eighty-three.

Grandpa's specialties were yeast-raised breads and cakes. For Shabbat dinner at home, he always made rich *challot* (the plural of *challah*) like those included here. For bar mitzvah and wedding celebrations, he prepared gorgeous, perfectly braided, glazed challot that were so huge they had to be baked in a professional oven at a bakery. Grandpa's giant challah was so wonderful that it was even used as a top raffle prize to raise money for our synagogue.

My dad fondly recalls how, many decades ago, Grandpa would mix up an enormous batch of dough on Saturday evening, then set it out on the porch in a bucket covered with a towel to rise slowly during the night. Any of his children who went out on a date was expected, upon returning home, to punch down the dough and knead it a few times before going to bed. Grandpa would then get up in the wee hours of Sunday morning to concoct wonderful doughnuts, cinnamon buns, onion-laden flat breads called *pletzels,* and more, so all would be ready in time for a delectable family breakfast.

After some of my father's older brothers and sisters married and left home, Grandpa awoke even earlier so that he would have time to personally deliver his warm, oven-fresh baked goods to them—sometimes with young Irving (my dad) in tow.

As with many expert bakers, Grandpa rarely measured ingredients, and most of his recipes are gone forever. However, in his later years, Grandpa lived with one of my aunts, Hannah Kaufer Hafetz, an able baker in her own right, who gave me a list of ingredients for challah on which the following recipe is based.

NOTE: This recipe was created before the advent of instant yeast. For a new, quicker challah variation that features such yeast, see Gloria's Glorious Challah on page 32. It includes many details to make challah baking easier.

2 packets (about 4½ teaspoons) active dry yeast (see the Glossary of Ingredients)

1½ cups warm (105 to 115 degrees) water, divided

½ cup sugar

About 6 to 6½ cups white bread flour or unbleached white flour (or a combination)

2 teaspoons salt

½ cup softened pareve margarine or canola oil

3 large eggs

GLAZE

1 egg beaten with 1 teaspoon water
Poppy seeds (optional)

Mix the yeast with ½ cup of the water and 1 teaspoon of the sugar, and let the mixture rest for 5 to 10 minutes, or until it begins to foam.

Meanwhile, put about 4 cups of the flour into a large bowl with the remaining sugar, the salt, and the margarine or oil. Use an electric mixer or a pastry blender to combine the ingredients until they form coarse crumbs. Add the yeast mixture, the remaining 1 cup of water, and the eggs, and beat the loose dough with the mixer or a wooden spoon for about 3 minutes. By hand (or with a heavy-duty mixer), slowly stir in just enough of the remaining flour to form a soft, slightly sticky dough. Cover the dough with plastic wrap, and let it rest for about 5 minutes.

Turn out the dough onto a lightly floured surface and knead it, adding sprinkles of flour as necessary to keep the dough from sticking to your fingers and the surface, for about 10 minutes, or until it is very smooth and satiny. Put the dough into an oiled bowl, and turn the dough so that all sides are oiled. Cover the bowl with a plastic lid or with a piece of plastic wrap and a dish towel, to keep the dough moist and dark. Let the dough rise until doubled in bulk, about 1 to 2 hours depending on the room temperature.

Punch down the dough, and knead it very gently a few times to remove bubbles. Divide the dough in half, for two loaves. Then divide each half into three, four, five, or six pieces, depending on the number of strands desired for each loaf. Cover the dough pieces loosely with plastic wrap, and let them rest for 10 minutes to relax the gluten and make them easier to shape.

Use lightly floured hands to squeeze each dough piece into a log; then roll it out into a smooth strand. Coat each strand lightly with flour just before braiding. (This helps to define the shape of the risen braid.) Braid the strands following the directions in the section on "The Symbolism and Shaping of Challah" (page 26). Carefully set the loaves several inches apart on a very large (at least 13 by 16 inches), greased or nonstick spray-coated baking sheet (or put one on each of two smaller sheets). Gently brush the loaves well with the egg glaze and, if desired, sprinkle them lightly with poppy seeds. (It is easier to glaze before rising, rather than after, as is conventionally done.) Let the loaves rise at room temperature until almost doubled in bulk, about 1 hour or longer. (Braided bread dough tends to hold its shape better if allowed to rise slowly at room temperature, rather than in a warm place. Do not let the braided loaves rise too much, or they may become distorted during baking.) Meanwhile, preheat the oven to 350 degrees.

Bake the loaves in a 350-degree oven for 40 to 45 minutes, or until the crust has browned and the bottom of each loaf sounds hollow when tapped. Remove the loaves from the baking sheet, and cool them on wire racks.

Makes 2 large challot, about 1½ pounds each.

My Mother's Incredible Chicken Soup

During my childhood, my mother, Helene "Hindy" Kaplan Kaufer, prepared this richly flavored, golden-yellow soup just about every Erev Shabbat. As sure as Friday followed Thursday, Mom would begin her day by plucking any stray feathers from the chicken and cleaning the onions and carrots. She would also clean the chicken feet and delicate "unlaid" eggs that we all loved as special culinary treats.

On rare occasions, however, Mom would yearn for variety, and cook up a different pottage. No matter how delicious and lavish her creation might be, there would be

mutiny on our bounty. Somehow, my father, my two sisters, and I all felt that the only way Shabbat could begin properly was by eating Mom's delectable chicken soup.

And so it is with my own husband and four children. They consider this wonderful "golden chicken broth," or *goldena yoich* in Yiddish, to be the only "authentic" Jewish soup for Friday night, Rosh Hashanah, the meal before Yom Kippur, and Pesach. I prepare it very frequently, sometimes weekly, even on some of the hottest days of summer. When my youngest child walks in from school on Friday, she shrieks for joy when the fragrant aroma of chicken soup fills the air. And her older brother will come home from college just for chicken soup on Shabbat. All my children rate it as their "number one" favorite food! And it is always a hit with our guests.

I usually load each serving of soup with noodles, Knaidlach ("matzah balls," page 356), and plenty of boned soup chicken. For certain holidays and special occasions, I prepare other soup accompaniments (see suggestions with the recipe). For many Shabbat dinners, a laden bowl of chicken soup served with my special homemade Challah (page 32) for "dunking" suffices as our very satisfying main course.

Following is the recipe that my mother developed, and I have adapted. Mom taught me some essential "tricks" to having an intensely flavored, translucent golden broth that is rich-tasting but not at all fatty. These are: (1) skim the soup well at the beginning of the cooking process to remove all foam and debris, (2) use plenty of meaty chicken pieces (not just backs and wings), preferably from a kosher pullet, (3) very slowly simmer the soup for at least 7 or 8 hours (yes, that's right) to develop intense chicken flavor and golden color, and (4) do not stir at all during the long cooking period so that the fat will gently rise to the surface of the broth and stay there for easy removal afterward. (Rapid boiling and stirring cause the fat to emulsify in the broth, making the soup cloudy and greasy-tasting.) If time is an issue, the soup can be prepared ahead for convenience, and refrigerated or even frozen.

NOTES: In this recipe, I've found that coarse kosher salt gives the best flavor, and it is better to add it at the beginning of the cooking process rather than at the end. Teaspoon for teaspoon, kosher salt is less "salty" than table salt, so more is required. While the amount of salt may be decreased if desired, keep in mind that chicken soup without enough salt is bland. You can start out with less salt if you prefer, and add more later if necessary. Pepper is also essential for good flavor.

It is not necessary to use completely thawed chicken to make this soup. If chicken pieces are frozen together in a package, use a microwave oven to thaw the package only

enough to separate the pieces and slightly soften exterior fat for easy removal. Also, be sure to wash your hands and any equipment that comes in contact with the raw chicken very carefully in hot, sudsy water to avoid possible bacterial contamination.

14 cups water

2 teaspoons kosher salt or 1¼ teaspoons table salt, or to taste

½ teaspoon ground black pepper, or to taste

4 or 5 small or 3 medium onions, peeled but left whole

Up to 1 pound carrots, peeled and cut into 1- to 2-inch sections (ready-peeled whole small carrots may be used and are a great convenience)

2 or 3 celery stalks, trimmed and cut in half (optional)

1 large chicken (about 4 pounds), preferably a pullet, quartered

TO SERVE (YOUR CHOICE)

Cooked noodles, rice, Knaidlach (page 356), Mandlen (page 109), Farfel (page 111), Triflach (page 45), or Meat Kreplach (page 112)

Put the water into a sturdy 8-quart soup pot or stockpot, stir in the salt and pepper, and bring it to a boil. Meanwhile, prepare the onions, carrots, and celery (if used), and set them aside.

Run very hot tap water over the chicken pieces and rinse them well. Use a small, sharp knife to remove all exterior fat and any feathers. Leave the skin on the chicken; it adds significantly to the flavor of the soup. Clean the chicken neck and gizzard (*pupik*), and add them to the pot of boiling water along with the cleaned chicken pieces.

Lower the heat so that the water just boils, and cook the chicken, uncovered, for about 10 to 15 minutes. Use a wide, fine strainer (or a spoon) to remove and discard the foam and other particles that rise to the surface of the soup. When there is no more foam, gently stir in the onions, carrots, and celery (if used).

Cover the soup, and adjust the heat so that it simmers (i.e., boils very gently with small bubbles—not large ones—continually, but slowly, rising to the surface). It may be necessary to check the soup occasionally and readjust the heat. Cook the soup for about 7 to 8 hours (see the above comments) without stirring. The soup should stay translucent (not cloudy) if it does not boil rapidly and is not vigorously stirred.

Before serving, use a wide, slotted spoon to gently remove and discard the onion and celery (I personally enjoy eating these "braised" vegetables as a snack). Very carefully transfer the chicken (it will be falling apart) to platters to cool, and reserve the carrots in a bowl.

Let the broth cool slightly, then skim off and discard all the fat that has risen to the surface. (I use a "fat mop" that sops up all the fat, or a special fat-removal ladle. Or the broth may be chilled overnight to partially solidify the fat and make removal easier.) After removing the fat, use a wide, shallow strainer to remove any bones or other debris that may be left in the rich soup broth, or pour the broth through a large strainer.

While the chicken is still warm, but not too hot to touch, carefully remove all the chicken meat from the bones, and shred the meat into small chunks. Set the chicken aside to be added to each portion of soup. Have any other soup garnishes ready to add to the soup.

Put the reserved carrots back into the soup, along with knaidlach if they are to be served. (Do not add noodles or rice directly to the soup, or they will soak up the broth and become "soggy.") If desired, the boned chicken may be added back to the soup, or it may be put into each bowl. Shortly before serving the soup, heat it just to a light simmer. Taste it, and add seasonings if necessary.

To serve the soup, set out individual bowls on the counter. Into each bowl, put accompaniments such as noodles, rice, kreplach, etc., as well as some boned chicken if it is not in the soup. Ladle plenty of soup broth and some carrots into each bowl, and serve the soup immediately while it is still piping hot. If serving mandlen, offer them on the side for each diner to add.

The soup and chicken freeze very well (as do the knaidlach), but the carrots and noodles get mushy, so remove them before freezing.

Makes about 12 servings.

Triflach

TINY NOODLE DUMPLINGS

As my mother-in-law, Freda Michaelson Greene Cantor, watched me prepare these delicate, irregularly shaped, Eastern European dumplings, she exclaimed in surprise, "You're making *triflach,* like my mother used to make!" A friend's mother told me her Jewish-Polish grandmother used to call them *cloiskeh.* They are also called *galushka, spaetzle,* or *nockerl.* Apparently, there are many names for these easy-to-prepare little "trifles." They are delicious as a soup garnish and can be served with stews. Or they may be tossed with butter and grated cheese for a nice dairy side dish.

2 cups unbleached white flour	*2 large eggs*
¹/₂ teaspoon salt	*About 5 to 6 tablespoons water*

In a medium bowl, combine the flour and salt. Make a well in the center of the flour. Put the eggs and 4 tablespoons of the water into the well, and beat them together gently with a fork. Then gradually mix in the flour. Stir in just enough additional water to make a soft, slightly sticky dough. Gather the dough into a ball, and wrap it in plastic wrap. Let it rest at least 10 minutes or up to overnight in the refrigerator.

In a large pot, over high heat, bring about 3 quarts of water to a boil. Spread a third of the dough on a small plate (see Note). Dip a small spoon into the boiling water; then use it to scoop a tiny bit of the dough off the plate into the water. Continue until all the dough on the plate has been used. Boil the triflach for 3 to 6 minutes, or until they are just tender throughout. If overcooked, they become mushy. Remove the triflach with a slotted spoon, and transfer them to a bowl. Repeat until all the dough is used. For best flavor and texture, serve the triflach as soon as possible. If necessary, they may be reheated quickly in boiling water.

Makes about 3¹/₂ cups of cooked triflach.

NOTE: If desired, the dough may be formed into triflach by pressing it through a special "spaetzle machine" or a grater or ricer with large holes. Cook as directed above.

Ground Beef and Vegetable Soup

This is very easy to prepare and does not take a long time to cook. It is perfect for a cold winter Shabbat when you want a change from chicken soup. The taste of the soup can be varied easily by changing the frozen vegetable mix.

1 pound lean ground beef	4 carrots, peeled and cut into ⅜-inch
1 large onion, finely chopped	slices
2 garlic cloves, minced	1 teaspoon dried basil leaves
2 celery stalks, trimmed and cut into	1 teaspoon dried marjoram leaves
¼-inch slices (optional)	2 packets or cubes beef bouillon
6 cups boiling water	(optional)
1 (14- to 16-ounce) can tomatoes,	1 (12- to 16-ounce) package frozen
including juice, chopped	mixed vegetables or frozen peas
½ cup pearl barley	Salt and ground black pepper to taste

In a medium soup pot or Dutch oven, brown the ground beef with the onion, garlic, and celery (if used). Add the boiling water, tomatoes and their juice, barley, carrots, basil, marjoram, and dried bouillon (if used). Bring to a boil while stirring (make sure bouillon is dissolved), lower the heat, and simmer, covered, for 40 to 45 minutes or until the barley is almost tender. Stir in the frozen vegetables, and simmer about 5 minutes longer, or until all the vegetables are tender. Season to taste with salt and pepper.

Makes about 6 to 8 servings.

Red Lentil Soup

Various types of lentil soup are popular among Sephardim, who often call it *sopa de lentejas* in Judeo-Spanish. The recipes sometimes use brown lentils instead of red, and may substitute tomato sauce or paste for canned tomatoes. Also, the seasonings vary greatly.

Jews of Egyptian heritage are particularly fond of soup made with red lentils. "Red" lentils, which are smaller than the more common brown ones and actually bright orange in color, are available at many specialty and health food stores. They partially disintegrate during cooking, making the soup thick and giving it a lovely color.

I recently learned that a very similar recipe for red lentil soup appears in *The Five Books of Miriam,* by Ellen Frankel, in the chapter called "Toledot." That is the portion of the Torah in which Esau exchanges his birthright for a pottage of lentils made by his brother, Jacob. Ms. Frankel theorizes that Jacob's stew was probably made with red lentils.

In a footnote, Besty Platkin Teutch (who shared the recipe with Ms. Frankel) explains that she makes this soup for Shabbat Toledot, which, she says, "mysteriously, always seems to come at the perfect seasonal moment to shift to hot soup on Friday night in the Northeast where I live." It's an interesting coincidence that our oldest son and his younger cousin each became bar mitzvah on Shabbat Toledot, as did the oldest son of our very good friends. I plan to follow Ms. Teutch's example, and serve this soup on Shabbat Toledot as a way to reminisce about the boys' Torah portion.

1 ½ tablespoons olive oil
1 medium onion, finely chopped
1 garlic clove, minced
2 carrots, peeled and diced
5 to 6 cups beef, chicken, or vegetable broth
2 cups (about ¾ pound) red lentils, sorted and rinsed

1 (14- to 16-ounce) can tomatoes, finely chopped, including juice
½ teaspoon ground cumin
¼ teaspoon ground coriander
1 tablespoon lemon juice
Salt and ground black pepper, to taste

Put the oil into a large saucepan or 4-quart soup pot over medium-high heat; then sauté the onion and garlic until they are tender. Add the carrots, and stir for a minute longer. Add 5 cups of broth, the lentils, tomatoes, cumin, coriander, and lemon juice. Bring to a boil; then reduce the heat, and simmer the soup, covered, about 40 minutes or until the lentils are very tender and the soup is thick. If the soup becomes too thick, add more broth or hot water. Season the soup to taste with salt and pepper.

Makes about 6 servings.

Heraimeh

LIBYAN-STYLE FISH IN TOMATO SAUCE

P

I originally learned about this dish several years ago from Denise Saville Zandman, a Welsh Jew who went to visit Israel in the early 1970s. It wasn't long before she fell in love with the country and also with one of its sabras (native Israelis), Dov Zandman. They married and made their home in Haifa.

Although Mrs. Zandman was primarily familiar with the British-style, Ashkenazic cuisine of her birthplace, she found that many of her husband's favorite foods were the exotic Libyan-Jewish dishes that his mother often prepared. After several lessons from her mother-in-law, Mrs. Zandman learned how to expertly cook—and, indeed, to prefer—the wonderfully spicy dishes for which many of the Sephardic Jews of Israel are justly famed.

This "make-ahead" garlicky fish dish is easy yet exotic and, for those who like a little spice in their meals, an interesting alternative to the usual Erev Shabbat gefilte fish. It's also perfect for lunch after *shul* (Yiddish for "synagogue") on Saturday, as it requires no heating. This version has been adapted to contemporary tastes. For instance, it calls for fillets rather than the more traditional fish steaks, uses more tomato paste to make a thicker sauce, and is very conservative on the amount of hot pepper. This dish is usually served at room temperature or slightly chilled, several hours or even the day after it is cooked. And it is always accompanied by plenty of bread to sop up the luscious, rich sauce.

NOTE: "Thick" fillets of firm-fleshed fish that will not easily fall apart while simmering in a sauce work the best. Even if the fish does fall apart, it still can be spooned onto pieces of bread like a fish "spread" and is quite tasty.

3 tablespoons good-quality olive oil

2 medium onions, finely chopped

4 large garlic cloves, pressed or very finely minced

1/4 cup (4 tablespoons) tomato paste

3 tablespoons lemon juice

1/2 teaspoon salt

1/2 teaspoon ground cumin

1/2 teaspoon paprika

1/8 to 1/4 teaspoon cayenne pepper or 1/2 teaspoon ground black pepper

About 1 cup water

1 to 1 1/2 pounds fish fillets (any firm-fleshed, mild-flavored fish)

TO SERVE

Challah, Italian-style bread, or French-style bread, thickly sliced

Put the oil into a large, heavy, preferably nonstick, skillet, over medium-high heat, and sauté the onions and garlic until they are tender. Add the tomato paste, lemon juice, salt, cumin, paprika, cayenne, and about ½ cup of the water. Mix well. Cook the thick sauce for 15 to 20 minutes, stirring often and adding water as needed to keep it from sticking to the pan, to give the flavors a chance to mingle and further soften the onion. Stir in ½ cup more water until it is well combined, and bring the sauce to a simmer.

Add the fish fillets in one layer or slightly overlapping; then spoon some of the sauce over them. Cover the skillet, and gently simmer the fish in the sauce, stirring occasionally, for about 10 to 12 minutes or just until the fish is cooked through. (If the fish is overcooked, it may fall apart in the sauce. Not to worry—it's still delicious!) During the cooking period, add water to the sauce if it becomes so thick that it is sticking to the bottom of the pan.

Transfer the cooked fish and sauce to a serving dish or casserole. Chill the fish in the refrigerator but, for best flavor, take it out about an hour before serving so it will be only slightly chilled or at room temperature. Serve it with bread to dip in the sauce. Or spoon the fish mixture onto a slice of bread to eat it.

Makes about 6 to 10 servings as a first course; about 4 to 6 as a main course.

Fish in Tarragon-Tomato Sauce

A good first course for the Shabbat evening meal, this is also tasty as a main dish on other nights of the week.

1 ½ tablespoons olive or canola oil
1 medium onion, finely chopped
1 large garlic clove, minced
1 (14- to 16-ounce) can tomatoes, chopped, including juice
½ cup dry white table wine
2 tablespoons finely chopped fresh parsley leaves

2 teaspoons dried chives or 1 ½ tablespoons chopped fresh chives
2 teaspoons dried tarragon leaves
½ teaspoon salt
⅛ teaspoon ground black pepper
1 pound skinless fish fillets, such as cod, haddock, or a similar white-fleshed fish

Put the oil into a large, deep skillet, over medium-high heat; then sauté the onion and garlic until tender. Stir in the tomatoes, wine, parsley, chives, tarragon, salt, and pepper. Simmer, uncovered, stirring often, about 15 minutes.

Add the fish fillets to the skillet, and spoon a little sauce over each one. Simmer, uncovered, about 8 to 10 minutes longer, or until fish is cooked through, and the sauce is thickened. Serve hot, or at room temperature.

Makes about 6 to 8 servings as a first course for Shabbat dinner, or about 4 main-dish servings.

Cholent

LONG-COOKED MEAT STEW

Although Jewish law prohibits kindling a fire on Shabbat, it is nevertheless considered a *mitzvah*—a religious obligation—to eat a hot meal at midday on Saturday. Over the centuries, Jews throughout the world have worked out a number of ingenious solutions for this dilemma. All involve cooking food overnight in very low heat that is not adjusted once Shabbat has begun.

Among Ashkenazic Jews, the Sabbath food is a meat stew called *cholent*. The medieval word *cholent* (with "ch" pronounced as in "chair") may have come from the French *chaud-lent*, meaning "warm slowly," or, less likely, from the Yiddish *shul ende*, which describes when the cholent is eaten—at "synagogue end."

In the past, a hot fire was started in the community's bakery oven before Shabbat, and then left to slowly burn itself out over a long period of time. On Friday afternoon, a member of each Jewish household would bring to the oven a filled pot that was tightly sealed with flour-water paste. The cooked cholent would be retrieved on Saturday for a palatable warm repast.

Despite its early origins, cholent (in its various international forms) is still very popular among observant Jews, with so many different versions that whole books have been written on it. In 1998, a "Cholent Olympics" cooking contest in Tel Aviv drew several hundred entries, with 150 finalists bringing in their pots for a mass tasting at the Dan Panorama Hotel.

Nowadays, cholent is almost always cooked at home. It may be placed in an oven at very low temperature, in an electric slow-cooker, or in a stovetop pot on a *blekh* (a nonflammable metal pad that keeps the burner temperature very low and steady).

The "standard" Eastern European cholent, as described below, usually contains meat, lima beans, barley, and potatoes, and sometimes also a piece of *kishka* ("stuffed derma") put on top of the other ingredients just before the cholent is put into the oven.

In Israel, a similar stew (which is often made with chicken instead of red meat, due to the high cost and relative scarcity of the latter) is usually called *hameem* or *hamin,* from the Hebrew word for "hot." Similarly, the Sephardic version of the stew is known as *hamin.* Both typically contain several whole eggs, as in the Moroccan variation called Dafina (page 52). (See also Huevos Haminados on page 354.)

Iraqi Jews have an unusual long-cooked Shabbat dish called *pacha,* which is tripe stuffed with lamb and an assortment of seasonings, including cardamom, cinnamon, cloves, turmeric, and rose petals. A similar filling (without the lamb) is used for Tabeet (page 62), an Iraqi Sabbath specialty made with a whole chicken. Persian Jews have a different version of stuffed tripe called *geepa,* which features dried yellow peas, rice, leeks, herbs, and spices.

There is nothing like waking up to the wonderful aroma of cholent simmering in the oven. Though this recipe makes a lot, the leftovers reheat quite well. Read the recipe throughly before beginning.

1 cup dry baby lima beans, sorted and rinsed	²⁄₃ cup pearl barley
1 cup dry white beans, such as navy beans or great northern beans, sorted and rinsed	¹⁄₂ cup dry lentils, sorted and rinsed
	3 garlic cloves, minced
	1¹⁄₂ teaspoons paprika
About 2¹⁄₂ pounds chuck roast, brisket, top of the rib, or other pot roast	1 teaspoon salt
	¹⁄₄ to ¹⁄₂ teaspoon ground black pepper
2 tablespoons canola oil	¹⁄₂ teaspoon ground ginger
2 large onions, finely chopped	About 6 small, thin-skinned "new" red or white potatoes, well scrubbed

Begin the cholent the day before serving it. Put the lima beans and white beans into a large saucepan with water to cover them by at least 2 inches. Cover, and bring to a boil. Boil for 2 minutes; then remove from the heat. Let the beans soak in the water for 1 to 3 hours. (Alternatively, soak unboiled beans in water overnight.) Drain the beans well before using them. Trim the meat of all visible fat, and cut it into four to six large chunks.

Put the oil into a 6- to 8-quart nonaluminum, ovenproof Dutch oven or stewpot over medium-high heat; then sauté the onions until they just begin

to brown. Add the meat to the pot, and brown the pieces on all sides. Add the soaked and drained beans, barley, lentils, garlic, paprika, salt, pepper, and ginger. Put the potatoes on top. Add enough boiling water so that everything is almost covered, but there is at least 1 inch headroom at the top of the pot. Preheat the oven to 350 degrees.

Over medium heat, bring the cholent to a boil; then cover the pot tightly and place it in the 350-degree oven. Bake it for 1 hour; then reduce the heat to 225 to 250 degrees, and bake it overnight (12 to 20 hours). The cholent can be served any time, after the minimal 12 hours. Do not stir the cholent while it is cooking.

Serve the cholent in soup bowls, giving each diner a portion of each of the ingredients. Spoon the broth on top.

Makes about 8 hearty servings.

NOTE: If desired, cholent can be cooked overnight in a very large slow-cooker. After browning the onions and meat, transfer them and the remaining ingredients to the slow-cooker. Cook on high heat for 1 hour; then turn the heat to low and cook overnight.

Dafina

NORTH AFRICAN–STYLE LONG-COOKED MEAT STEW

North African Jews have a variation of Cholent (page 50) that is called *dafina* or *adafina* (meaning "hidden," as in the burning embers) or *t'fina, s'kheena, sefrina,* or *frackh,* depending on the cook and the city of origin. Like many other Shabbat stews, it has meat, potatoes, and beans (usually chickpeas), but differs from them in that it traditionally included a calf's foot, a cloth bag of rice or wheat berries, and a giant meatball or dumpling called *coclo* or *kouclas.* The dumpling could be stuffed into a chicken neck, packed into a cloth bag, or partially poached or browned ahead so it would hold its shape without any covering. (Interestingly, both the name and the dumpling are similar to the Ashkenazic kugel that is occasionally cooked with cholent.)

Almost all *dafinas* also include delicious eggs cooked in their shells atop the stew. Called Huevos Haminados (see page 354 in the Pesach chapter for directions on how to cook the eggs alone), the eggs are sometimes removed from the stew on Saturday morning and eaten as a hot breakfast.

Another type of Shabbat stew eaten in North Africa is called *orissa* and usually features wheat berries. In some areas, *orissa* may be made with sweet potatoes, honey, and cinnamon.

I based the following recipe for *dafina* on those of several Moroccan Jews who came from different parts of that country. All the recipes had the basics in common, with each person adding his or her own special touch. One told me that dates were the secret, adding flavor and color but not sweetness. (He was right! They are included below.) Others used brown sugar or caramelized white sugar for the same purpose.

The dumplings added to the stew were all different—most made with meat and rice and herbs, but others with just seasoned bread crumbs and fat. At any rate, I decided to forgo the dumpling, as the stew is quite filling without it. Also, since most of the Moroccans lamented the difficulty of getting kosher calves' feet in the United States, I omitted them as well. However, I was careful to retain the special combination of seasonings that makes *dafina* so special.

One devotee of *dafina* who enthusiastically shared his recipe with me several years ago was Rabbi Joshua Toledano, religious leader of Philadelphia's Congregation Mikveh Israel, one of the oldest Sephardic synagogues in the United States. Rabbi Toledano, descendant of a long line of rabbis that he traced back to pre-Inquisition Spain, also carried on the heritage of the family's *dafina,* which became famous in Morocco in the early 1960s.

According to Rabbi Toledano, King Hassan II had just come into power and was touring Morocco to officially proclaim his reign. Rabbi Toledano's maternal grandfather, a wealthy businessman of Meknes, was among those who welcomed the king at the gates of the city. He was also a good friend of the governor of Meknes, who happened to be the king's uncle.

The king arrived on a Friday afternoon and, during an audience with his uncle, demanded to have "the Jewish *dafina*" for his evening meal. The governor went to his Jewish friend and explained the situation. Ten prominent rabbis got together and decided that the Jewish community could profane the Shabbat, just this once, for the king. Together, many people prepared a huge *dafina* that they were able to cook for only three to four hours because of the time limitation.

The king loved it. In fact, he enjoyed it so much that the next day he requested *dafina* for his midday meal. Again, the governor came to see his Jewish friend. This time, Rabbi Toledano's grandfather called upon the families of all nine of his children, who combined their own individual *dafinas*, already prepared for Shabbat, into a magnificent one fit for a king.

King Hassan II left Meknes happy and satisfied, and the governor was forever indebted to Rabbi Toledano's family.

Read the following recipe through before beginning.

1½ cups dry chickpeas (garbanzo beans), sorted and rinsed	¼ teaspoon ground ginger
About 2½ pounds chuck roast, brisket, top of the rib, or other pot roast	¼ teaspoon ground turmeric
	1 teaspoon salt
2 medium onions, finely chopped	¼ teaspoon ground black pepper
3 garlic cloves, finely minced	1 cup uncooked white or brown rice or whole wheat "berries" (kernels)
¼ cup chopped pitted dates	
½ teaspoon ground cinnamon	6 to 8 small, thin-skinned "new" red or white potatoes, well scrubbed
½ teaspoon ground allspice	
	6 to 8 unshelled raw eggs, any size

Begin the *dafina* the day before serving it. Put the chickpeas into a medium saucepan with water to cover them by at least 2 inches. Cover, and bring to a boil. Boil 2 minutes; then remove from the heat. Let the beans soak in the water for 1 to 3 hours. (Alternatively, soak unboiled beans in water overnight.) Drain the beans well before using them. Trim the meat of all visible fat, and cut it into four to six large chunks.

In the bottom of a 6- to 8-quart nonaluminum, ovenproof Dutch oven or stewpot, spread the soaked chickpeas. Put the meat on top of the beans. Scatter the onions, garlic, dates, spices, and seasonings around the meat. Cut a very large square from a double thickness of cheesecloth. Put the rice or wheat berries in the center of the square. Then bring up the edges of the cloth, and tie them tightly at the top with clean, heavy, white cord to form a loose bag. There should be enough room in the bag for the grains to at least double in size. Put the bag in the center of the pot, on top of the meat. Surround it with potatoes and eggs, alternating them so the potatoes "cushion" the eggs. Add enough boiling water so that everything is almost covered, but there is at least 1 inch of headroom at the top of the pot. Preheat the oven to 350 degrees.

Over medium heat, bring the dafina to a boil; then cover the pot tightly, and place it in the 350-degree oven. Bake it for 1 hour; then reduce the heat to 225 to 250 degrees, and bake it overnight (12 to 20 hours). The dafina can be served at any time after the minimal 12 hours. Do not stir the dafina while it is cooking.

The dafina is usually served in "courses." First, the eggs are shelled and served with the potatoes and a little broth. (Some Moroccans like to chop the eggs and potatoes together.) This is followed by the rice or wheat, and then the rest of the dafina. Sometimes, the meat and grain are eaten on a plate, and the beans are served in the rich broth as a "soup."

Makes about 8 hearty servings.

NOTE: If desired, the *dafina* can be cooked in a very large slow-cooker. Put all the ingredients in the cooker in the order listed above. Cook on high heat for 1 hour; then turn the heat to low and cook overnight.

Zippy Cranberry Pot Roast

This combination of ingredients may seem a little unusual, but the sweet-and-sour sauce tastes fabulous, a bit like a barbecue sauce. This family favorite—which is perfect for company—is great to prepare ahead, and tastes even better when reheated the second day.

NOTE: I prefer to use an "apple roast" or similar lean pot roast to prepare this. The roast shrinks considerably during the cooking process, but is entirely edible with almost no fat.

SAUCE
1 (16-ounce) can tomato sauce
1 (16-ounce) can whole cranberry
   sauce
1 tablespoon prepared horseradish
1 teaspoon ground (powdered) mustard

3 tablespoons apple cider vinegar

MEAT
1 3- to 5-pound boneless, lean, beef
   pot roast, trimmed of all fat

Shabbat

Combine all the sauce ingredients in a 6- to 8-quart (depending on the size of the roast) nonaluminum (noncorrosive) Dutch oven or stewpot. Over high heat, bring the sauce to a boil; then lower the heat and simmer the sauce, uncovered, for about 5 minutes. Put the roast into the sauce, and cover the pot tightly. Simmer the pot roast over low heat, basting it often with the sauce, for 2 to 3 hours, or until the meat is very tender. (If the roast is very thick, turn it over once or twice during the cooking period.)

Carefully transfer the cooked roast to a cutting board. Raise the heat, and cook down the uncovered sauce, stirring often, until it has thickened considerably (and is like barbecue sauce). Meanwhile, cut the roast into ½-inch slices against the grain of the meat, and transfer it to a serving platter. Spoon some of the sauce over the roast, and put the remainder in a bowl to serve on the side.

If preparing the roast ahead of time, let it cool slightly on the cutting board (it will be easier to cut); then cut it into slices as above. Spoon some of the thickened sauce into an ovenproof casserole dish. Arrange partially overlapping meat slices on top of the sauce. Pour the remainder of the sauce on top. Cover and refrigerate until needed. Warm the covered casserole in a 325-degree oven or in a microwave oven until the roast and sauce are heated through completely. Serve directly from the casserole.

Makes 8 to 12 servings, depending on the size of the roast.

Beef and Broccoli, Chinese-Style

Although this is not a traditionally Jewish dish, it has become a favorite of my children for Erev Shabbat dinner. I find it quick and easy to prepare thanks to thinly sliced, very lean, raw beef that is called "pepper steak" at kosher supermarkets in my area. I suppose this interesting labeling reflects the legendary Jewish fondness for Chinese-style food.

Although my family prefers broccoli to the usual green bell peppers, this flexible recipe also can be used to make "pepper steak" (i.e., beef and peppers), or even a version with frozen vegetables (quick and easy in a pinch). Chicken may be substituted for beef, if desired. (See Variations below.) With the addition of rice, each version is a complete dinner.

NOTES: A Chinese wok is not necessary to cook this; I use a very wide, shallow pot (Dutch oven). To more easily slice large pieces of raw beef at home, freeze it slightly and use a sharp knife and cutting board (which should be washed very well in hot, sudsy water) to cut across the "grain" of the meat. Medium-grain rice, which is "stickier" than long-grain rice, is typically served with Chinese-style dishes.

MARINADE AND BEEF

2 tablespoons soy sauce

2 tablespoons dry white wine or sherry

1 tablespoon water

1 teaspoon canola oil

1 garlic clove, minced or pressed

¼ teaspoon ground ginger

¼ teaspoon sugar

1¼ pounds lean beef, very thinly sliced ⅛ to ¼ inch thick, or presliced raw "pepper steak" (see comments above)

TO SERVE

1½ cups raw medium- or long-grain rice, cooked as directed on package

VEGETABLES AND SAUCE

1 large onion, peeled

1 large bunch of broccoli (about 3 stems with full tops)

2 tablespoons canola oil

¼ cup water

½ cup beef broth or bouillon (may be reconstituted from cubes or granules) or water

1 tablespoon cornstarch

Combine all marinade ingredients in a medium nonaluminum bowl. Add the sliced beef and use a fork to gently move it around so that all the pieces are separated and coated with marinade. Allow the meat to marinate for 15 to 30 minutes, covered, in the refrigerator. Put the rice on to cook.

Meanwhile, cut the onion in half through the stem end, and then into ¼ to ⅜ inch thick semicircular slices. Cut off the broccoli stems; then cut each top into small florets. Peel the stems, and cut them into slices.

Put the oil into a large, deep skillet, Dutch oven, or wok over medium-high heat. Add the onion, and sauté until it is tender. Add the broccoli florets and stem slices, and stir for about 2 minutes. Add the water to the skillet, cover, and steam the broccoli for about 3 to 5 minutes, or just until it is crisp-tender.

Meanwhile, mix the beef broth with the cornstarch so it is completely combined. Set aside.

When the broccoli is ready, transfer the entire contents of the skillet to a large serving bowl. Add the beef and all its marinade to the skillet. Cook,

Shabbat

stirring often and turning over the pieces as necessary, until the beef is cooked through and not pink. Move the beef to the edge of the skillet, so that the juices are in the center. Give the cornstarch mixture a stir, and add it to the pan juices while stirring. Continue stirring until the sauce thickens. Add the broccoli-onion mixture back to the skillet, and cook, stirring, so that all the meat and vegetables become coated with the sauce and heated through.

Serve immediately over the hot, cooked rice.

NOTE: This dish can be kept warm or reheated if necessary; however, the broccoli may soften somewhat. The rice will stay hot in the pot for a while after cooking if removed from the heat and the cover left in place.

Makes 5 to 6 servings.

Variations

BEEF WITH MIXED VEGETABLES, CHINESE-STYLE

For the broccoli florets in the main recipe, substitute 1 (1-pound) bag frozen vegetables that includes one or more types, such as broccoli, cauliflower, snow peas, sugar snap peas, miniature corn on the cob, carrots, water chestnuts, and/or whole green beans. There are many appealing, colorful mixes available. Follow the above recipe, steaming the vegetables just until they are crisp-tender.

PEPPER STEAK

For this classic Chinese dish, substitute 3 sweet green bell peppers for the broccoli (if desired, one red or yellow pepper may be used for additional color). Remove the seeds and stem from the peppers, and cut them into 1-inch squares. Cut the onion into wedges (not slices) and separate the pieces. Follow the above directions, but when the onion is partially cooked, add the pepper and stir-fry it with the onion until it is crisp-tender. Do not add water, or steam the vegetables.

CHICKEN AND VEGETABLES, CHINESE-STYLE

Use any recipe above, and substitute 1¼ pounds boneless, skinless chicken breasts for the beef. Cut the chicken into 1-inch squares. Cook the chicken until is opaque and not at all pink. It will be tinted brown from the marinade.

Mafroum

LIBYAN-STYLE STUFFED VEGETABLES

This tasty dish is often served on Shabbat by Libyan Jews such as Liora Ben-Chaim Zandman, a resident of Jerusalem. Just a year after Israel became a state, Mrs. Zandman and her family left their home in Tripoli and "made *aliyah*" (immigrated to Israel). In her adopted country, she married and raised a family, but still kept cooking the delicious dishes of her native land.

Though many of her favorite foods are obviously Middle Eastern in style and taste, they have distinctively Jewish touches, such as the matzah meal in the following meat stuffing.

In this recipe, potato and eggplant slices are stuffed, then fried in a tasty coating that helps hold them together, and finally simmered in a flavorful tomato sauce. If desired, *mafroum* can be prepared using only eggplant *or* potatoes.

STUFFING

1 pound very lean ground beef or lamb

1 to 2 medium onions, grated

2 to 3 garlic cloves, minced

1/4 cup finely chopped fresh parsley
    leaves

2 large eggs or 1/2 cup pareve egg
    substitute

1 teaspoon ground cinnamon

1/2 to 1 teaspoon salt

1/4 to 1/2 teaspoon black pepper,
    preferably freshly ground

About 1/4 cup matzah meal

VEGETABLES

1 medium eggplant (about 1 pound)

2 to 3 large boiling or all-purpose
    potatoes

Vegetable oil for frying

All-purpose or unbleached white flour

1 to 2 large eggs, lightly beaten

SAUCE

1 large onion, thinly sliced

1 6-ounce can tomato paste

3 cups water

Salt, ground black pepper, and
    cinnamon to taste

For the stuffing, combine all the stuffing ingredients in a large bowl, and mix very well with your hands until the mixture is quite smooth and well blended. (A food processor may be used for this step.) Set the stuffing aside.

Prepare the vegetables as follows: Use a sharp knife to cut off the ends of the eggplant; then cut it crosswise into 3/4-inch-thick slices. Carefully slit each slice almost in half to form two thin slices that are connected at one end. (It may be easier to do this by cutting 3/8-inch crosswise slices from the whole eggplant, but only slicing every other one completely through.)

Peel the potatoes; then cut them lengthwise into 1/2-inch slices. Slit the slices almost in half, as with the eggplant.

To stuff the vegetables, use your fingers to firmly pack the meat stuffing inside each slit slice, forming "sandwiches" that look like partially open clamshells. The stuffing layer should be about ⅜ to ½ inch thick. It will be slightly more difficult to stuff the potatoes, as they do not give as easily as the eggplant.

In a large Dutch oven, soup pot, or very large, deep skillet, heat about 2 to 3 tablespoons of oil. Lightly coat each sandwich with flour, then the beaten egg. Fry the sandwiches in the oil, in batches, until they are golden brown on both sides. Set them aside on a plate. (If desired, the recipe may be prepared ahead of time up to this point, and the sandwiches refrigerated until about an hour before serving time.)

For the sauce, pour all the oil from the pot except about 1 tablespoon (or add more oil, if necessary). Add the onion and cook, stirring, until it is tender. Stir in the tomato paste, water, and seasonings to taste. Bring the sauce to a simmer. Carefully add all the fried sandwiches to the sauce, trying to have no more than two layers. The sauce should almost, but not completely, cover them. Add a bit more water, if necessary.

Cover the pot, and simmer the vegetable sandwiches for about 1 hour, or until they are tender and the meat is cooked through. Occasionally baste the top vegetables with some of the sauce.

To serve, use a slotted spoon to remove the stuffed vegetables from the pot to a serving platter. If the sauce seems too watery, quickly boil it down until it reaches a thicker consistency. Adjust the seasonings to taste. Pour some of the sauce over the vegetables, and serve the rest on the side.

Makes about 6 servings.

Tabeet

IRAQI-STYLE WHOLE CHICKEN AND RICE

Years ago in Baghdad, this dish was prepared as a type of cholent to be served after services on Shabbat. Rachel Muallem Gabes, a native of Iraq, recalled that it was cooked very slowly overnight on a stove fired with fine charcoal and wood.

In 1942, when the German army was about to enter Egypt, Mrs. Gabes and her family fled to Iran. In 1950, the family again became endangered because of her father-in-law's participation in an underground movement to help Russian Jews escape to Israel. This time, they traveled to the United States, and eventually became naturalized citizens.

In this country, Mrs. Gabes no longer prepared *tabeet* as an overnight dish. Instead, she would cook it for several hours during the day, and serve it on Friday night or at a dinner party. For added flavor and color, she sometimes steamed some vegetables and fruit, such as turnips, fresh beets, and apples, on top of the rice surrounding the chicken.

The following simplified version of *tabeet* is an amalgam of recipes I learned from Mrs. Gabes and other Iraqi Jews. As in traditional versions, the chicken contains a rice stuffing that is seasoned differently from the rice that surrounds the chicken. Also, it forms the "crust" on the bottom of the pan that is so prized by both Iraqis and Persians. However, it takes only about 2 hours to cook.

NOTE: The rice in this dish is parboiled, then rinsed to remove excess starch that may cause stickiness. All the seasonings can be adjusted to taste.

2 cups uncooked long-grain white rice
4 cups water

STUFFING SEASONINGS
Generous ¼ teaspoon each ground
*   cardamom and salt*
⅛ teaspoon each cinnamon, cloves,
*   turmeric, and ground black pepper*
1 tablespoon tomato paste

2 tablespoons water
1 teaspoon crumbled, dried rose petals
*   (optional)*

CHICKEN
1 whole, 4-pound (approximately)
*   chicken, cleaned to remove as much*
*   fat as possible*
½ teaspoon ground turmeric

RICE SEASONINGS
2 tablespoons olive oil
1 medium onion, finely chopped
3 tablespoons tomato paste
$\frac{1}{2}$ teaspoon ground cinnamon

Pinch of ground allspice or cloves
$\frac{1}{2}$ teaspoon salt
$\frac{1}{8}$ teaspoon black pepper
$1\frac{1}{2}$ cups water

Put the rice and 4 cups water in a large saucepan over high heat. Bring to a boil; then reduce the heat, and simmer for 5 minutes. Remove the saucepan from the heat, and drain the rice in a colander. Rinse the rice with cool water, and drain it well.

Put ¾ cup of the parboiled rice in a small bowl. (Reserve the remainder.) Add all the stuffing seasonings including the rose petals (if used) and water, and mix well. Loosely stuff the chicken with the rice mixture, and close both ends by sewing together the skin flaps, or skewer them closed with round wooden toothpicks (the sturdy type that are pointed at both ends).

Put the chicken, breast side up, in a 6- to 8-quart soup pot or Dutch oven (a nonstick one will make removal of the rice easiest) with about 1 inch of water. Sprinkle the turmeric over the chicken and into the water to give extra color. Bring the water to a boil over high heat; then reduce the heat, cover the pot tightly, and steam the chicken for about 45 minutes or until it is almost tender but not falling apart. During the cooking period, baste the chicken often with the cooking water, and poke a few deep holes through the breast with a metal skewer to release fat and to allow some juices to enter the cavity containing the stuffing.

Use two large spoons to carefully remove the cooked chicken from the pot, and set it aside on a platter. Discard the cooking liquid (it will be greasy), and wipe out the pot. To season the rice, put the 2 tablespoons oil into the pot, and sauté the onion until it is tender but not brown. Add all the rice seasonings and water; then stir well. Stir in the reserved parboiled rice. Put the chicken on top, and push it down a bit into the rice. Bring to a boil over medium-high heat, cover tightly, and lower the heat so the rice barely simmers. Steam the rice and chicken about 1 hour without disturbing the rice. It will form a crust on the bottom.

To serve, carefully transfer the chicken to a serving dish. If desired, remove and discard the skin. Use a flexible spatula or pancake turner to remove

the rice in the pot, turning the rice over so the crust is on top. Serve it with the chicken and stuffing. (For ease in removing the rice crust, sprinkle a tablespoon of water over the rice, cover the pot, and set it aside for a few minutes.)

Makes about 6 servings.

Chicken and Spaghetti, Syrian-Style

Jews of Syrian ancestry often enjoy this dish, which they may call *djaja macaruni,* as part of their Friday-evening meal. Some Egyptian Jews, using spices such as cardamom and ginger, prepare a similar chicken-and-pasta dinner called *trayah.*

In the following recipe, chicken pieces are braised instead of the more traditional method of roasting a whole chicken. My family prefers boneless breasts, although thighs tend to stay moister during the final baking process. Boneless chicken saves time and effort later in the recipe. Other pasta may be substituted for the spaghetti (for instance, some use elbow macaroni or ziti), and all the seasonings can be adjusted to taste.

NOTE: Individually frozen, boneless or bone-in chicken pieces may be used in this recipe without defrosting; simply cook them about 10 minutes longer, or until they are tender and cooked through.

1 cup cold water
1 medium onion, grated
2 to 3 garlic cloves, minced
½ teaspoon paprika
½ teaspoon salt
⅛ to ¼ teaspoon ground black pepper
2½ to 3½ pounds meaty chicken pieces,
*   skin removed, or 1½ to 2 pounds*
*   boneless, skinless chicken breasts*
*   and/or thighs*

1 pound thin spaghetti
1 tablespoon canola or olive oil
1 (16-ounce) can tomato sauce
1 teaspoon ground cinnamon
½ teaspoon ground allspice

Put the water, onion, garlic, paprika, salt, and pepper into an ovenproof, 5- to 6-quart Dutch oven or soup pot, and bring to a simmer. Add the chicken pieces, turning them so that all sides are coated with the seasoning mixture. Bring the mixture back to a simmer; then cover the pot. Simmer meaty chicken pieces for 30 to 45 minutes, or just until cooked through; boneless chicken will take only about 10 to 15 minutes. Turn the chicken pieces occasionally so all sides are immersed in the seasoned liquid.

Meanwhile, bring a large pot of salted water to a boil for the spaghetti. Take a handful of the spaghetti, and break the strands in half before adding to the pot. Continue until all the spaghetti is broken. Stir so that all the strands are separated. Cook the spaghetti according to the package directions, but about 3 minutes less than indicated, so that it is still quite firm. Drain the spaghetti, rinse it briefly under cold water to stop the cooking; then drain it again. Put the drained spaghetti back into its pot, and toss it well with the oil so the strands do not stick together. Set aside.

When the chicken is ready, remove the pot from the heat. Use tongs or a slotted spoon to transfer the chicken to a platter or cutting board. Reserve the broth in the pot. Preheat the oven to 325 degrees. When the chicken is cool enough to handle, remove it from the bones and cut it into chunks. (Boneless chicken may be cut up as soon as it is removed from the pot.) Add the tomato sauce, cinnamon, and allspice to the broth reserved in the pot, and stir until they are mixed in completely. Bring the sauce to a light simmer; then remove it from the heat. Stir the parboiled spaghetti into the sauce; then bury all the chicken in the spaghetti.

Bake, uncovered, at 325 degrees for about 30 minutes, or until the sauce is absorbed and the top is firm and dry.

ALTERNATIVE METHOD: A quicker though less authentic way to prepare this dish is to not bake it, but simply finish it by heating the spaghetti, sauce, and chicken together, uncovered, for a few minutes on top of the stove. Stir often until the spaghetti has absorbed most of the sauce and has softened to a desirable consistency. (The top obviously will not be firm, as when baked.)

Makes 6 to 8 servings.

Shabbat

Easy Chicken and Chickpeas, Moroccan-Style

This is typical of Moroccan-style stews or *tagines* in that it has an unusual, yet delectable combination of sweet and savory spices and it features poultry with dried fruit. The chickpea sauce is so tasty and nutritious that it could easily be a vegetarian dish on its own.

Individually frozen, boneless, skinless chicken breasts do not have to be thawed before use in this recipe. Just cook them about 10 minutes longer than indicated until they are no longer pink in the center.

This stew is wonderful served over Quick Couscous (page 126), which is very easily prepared using the instant varieties on the market. Orzo (rice-shaped pasta) or any other fine, small pasta such as barley-shaped noodles would also be an excellent accompaniment.

2 tablespoons extra-virgin olive oil
1 large onion, finely chopped
2 garlic cloves, minced
½ teaspoon ground cinnamon
½ teaspoon ground ginger
¼ teaspoon ground cumin
⅛ teaspoon ground black pepper
⅛ teaspoon salt, or to taste
1 (14- to 16-ounce) can tomatoes, including juice, diced or finely chopped

2½ to 3½ pounds meaty chicken pieces, skin removed, or 1½ to 2 pounds boneless, skinless chicken breasts
1 (15- to 16-ounce) can chickpeas, drained and rinsed well in a colander
¼ cup dark or light raisins

To Serve
Quick Couscous (page 126) or about 12 ounces small-type pasta, cooked as directed on the package

Put the oil into a large, deep skillet or Dutch oven over medium-high heat; then sauté the onion and garlic until tender. Add the spices, and stir until they are completely incorporated. Stir in the chopped tomatoes and juice. Add the chicken pieces in one layer, spooning some of the sauce over the top of each piece.

Lower the heat, and simmer the chicken, covered, just until it is cooked through. Turn chicken pieces occasionally during cooking. Boneless chicken

breasts will take only about 10 to 15 minutes; pieces with bones about 30 to 45 minutes. Use tongs to remove the chicken pieces, and reserve them.

Stir the chickpeas and raisins into the sauce. If necessary, raise the heat slightly, and briefly cook the sauce, uncovered, until it has reduced to a desired consistency. Return the chicken to the sauce and continue cooking, basting the chicken with sauce, for just a few minutes until the chicken is hot.

Serve the chicken and sauce over a bed of couscous or pasta.

Makes 6 to 8 servings.

Chicken Harikebab
INDIAN-STYLE SPICED CHICKEN AND POTATOES

This deliciously spiced dish originated with the Jews of Calcutta, India. Most of the founders of this unusual community emigrated from Baghdad, Iraq, during the eighteenth century. Their cuisine is a curious combination of Middle Eastern–style dishes and Indian spices and vegetables. The Calcutta Jewish community flourished until the latter half of the twentieth century, when most members left to go to England and Australia, as well as the United States due to political unrest in India. The gradual dispersion of this unique group is now almost complete.

Though there are a number of spices in this currylike *harikebab,* it is not "hot" like many other Indian stews, just very flavorful. The turmeric tints the chicken and potatoes a brilliant yellow color (and will do the same to light-colored plastic cooking utensils).

Although this dish is usually prepared with chicken, the same spices are sometimes used for a similar lamb or beef stew. Following is my adaptation of this dish based on several different recipes. Traditionally, several whole spices would be used, but I have used only ground spices for convenience.

This stew is usually cooked on top of the stove. I have also given a technique for using the oven based on directions for this dish in *Indian-Jewish Cooking,* by Mavis Hyman, a Calcutta-born Jew who now lives in England. Her book contains one of the most unusual collections of Jewish recipes that I have ever seen.

Shabbat

3 tablespoons olive or canola oil
1 large onion, finely chopped
1 to 2 garlic cloves, finely minced
$\frac{1}{2}$ teaspoon ground ginger or 1
    teaspoon grated fresh ginger
$\frac{1}{2}$ teaspoon turmeric
$\frac{1}{2}$ teaspoon ground cardamom
$\frac{1}{4}$ teaspoon ground cinnamon
$\frac{1}{8}$ teaspoon ground cloves
$\frac{1}{2}$ teaspoon salt, or to taste

$\frac{1}{8}$ to $\frac{1}{4}$ teaspoon black pepper
1 cup water
About 4 pounds meaty chicken pieces,
    skin removed
About 2 to 2$\frac{1}{2}$ pounds small red or
    white potatoes, peeled

TO SERVE (OPTIONAL)
Hot, cooked rice
Chutney

This dish can be made on top of the stove or in the oven.

For the stove, put the oil into a 6- to 8-quart Dutch oven or 12-inch-wide deep skillet over medium heat, and sauté the onion and garlic until tender. Add the ginger, turmeric, cardamom, cinnamon, cloves, salt, and pepper to the onions in the skillet, and stir to mix well. Then stir in the water, and bring the sauce to a boil. Add the chicken and potatoes to the skillet and simmer, covered, turning the pieces occasionally, for about 40 minutes, or until all is cooked through. Remove the cover for the last few several minutes of cooking to thicken the sauce.

For the oven, grease well a large roasting pan or line it with heavy-duty aluminum foil, and place the chicken pieces and potatoes in it in one layer. Preheat the oven to 350 degrees. Prepare the above onion-spice sauce in a skillet or medium saucepan. Pour the heated sauce mixture over the chicken and potatoes, and gently turn them so that they are coated. Cover the pan with foil, and place it in a 350-degree oven. Bake for 40 minutes; then remove the foil and baste the chicken and potatoes with sauce. Continue baking, uncovered, basting and turning the chicken and potatoes occasionally, about 10 to 20 minutes longer, or until the chicken is cooked through and the potatoes are tender (but not mushy), and the sauce has thickened. If the sauce gets too dry before the end of the cooking period, add small amounts of water as needed. If necessary, adjust spices or seasonings before serving.

Makes about 6 to 8 servings.

NOTE: This recipe can be prepared on top of the stove with 2 pounds boneless, skinless chicken breasts instead of the meaty chicken pieces. Cut the potatoes in half or fourths so that they will cook faster. Prepare as directed above, but cook for only about 20 minutes, or until the chicken is cooked through and the potatoes are tender but not mushy. Uncover the skillet toward the end of the cooking period to allow the sauce to thicken.

Quick Cranberry-Orange Chicken

This is a dish that has become a favorite of mine for two reasons: it is delicious and I can assemble it in just minutes using individually frozen boneless, skinless chicken breasts.

When I am really in a rush, such as in winter when Shabbat comes so early, I don't bother to cut up and sauté a fresh onion. I just put all the sauce ingredients directly into a pan, stir in a few tablespoons of onion flakes, and bring the sauce to a boil. Then I add the frozen boneless, skinless chicken breasts, and simmer them for about 20 to 25 minutes, or until they are cooked through. Meanwhile, I cook the noodles and prepare a salad and side-dish vegetable. Shabbat dinner is ready in less than half an hour!

SAUCE
1 (16-ounce) can whole cranberry
    sauce
1 cup orange juice
1/4 teaspoon ground cinnamon
1/4 teaspoon ground ginger

CHICKEN
2 tablespoons canola oil
1 medium onion, finely chopped
2 pounds boneless, skinless chicken
    breast halves

TO SERVE
1 pound egg noodles, linguine, or other
    pasta, cooked

In a small bowl or measuring cup, combine the cranberry sauce, orange juice, cinnamon, and ginger. Set aside.

Put the oil into a wide, deep skillet or Dutch oven over medium-high heat; then sauté the onion until it is tender. Push the onion to the edges of the

Shabbat

pan, and add the chicken in one layer. Brown the chicken lightly on both sides, and mix with the sautéed onions.

Pour the cranberry-orange mixture over the chicken and onions. Bring to a boil. Cover the pan, lower the heat, and simmer the chicken for about 10 to 15 minutes, or just until it is cooked through and tender. Use tongs to remove the chicken, and quickly boil down the sauce until it has thickened to a desired consistency. Return the chicken to the skillet for a few minutes to coat it with sauce and heat it through. Serve over cooked noodles.

Makes about 6 servings.

Chicken in White Wine Sauce

This elegant yet very easy dish has a wonderful flavor and seems appropriate for Shabbat, as wine plays a prominent role in the Friday-evening Kiddush. The onions become very soft and are the basis for a delectable sauce that is a favorite in our household.

For recipes such as this and others that call for small amounts of wine, I keep an inexpensive bottle of dry white table wine in my refrigerator. There are now many kosher wines that work wonderfully. I have found that replacing the cork so it can be easily removed by hand, or tightly covering the bottle with several layers of plastic wrap held in place by a rubber band, keeps the refrigerated wine sufficiently fresh for cooking for several months. (A wine connoisseur might disagree, but this has been suitable for me.)

NOTE: White grape juice is much too sweet to be substituted for the white wine in this dish. Furthermore, just about all the alcohol in the wine evaporates during cooking, making this dish appropriate for all family members.

3 tablespoons extra-virgin olive oil, or as needed
2 medium onions, finely chopped
1 garlic clove, pressed, crushed, or minced

1 1/2 to 2 pounds boneless, skinless chicken breast halves
1/2 cup dry or slightly sweet white table wine
1 teaspoon dried tarragon

¹/₄ *teaspoon ground black pepper*
Salt to taste

2 tablespoons finely chopped fresh
parsley (optional)

Put the oil into a deep 12-inch skillet or a Dutch oven over medium-high heat; then sauté the onions and garlic until they are tender and just beginning to brown. Either remove the onion mixture to a plate or push it to the perimeter of the pan. If the pan is not nonstick and seems very dry, add a little oil. Add the chicken breasts in one layer, and brown them lightly on both sides. Add the wine, tarragon, and black pepper to the skillet, and spoon the sautéed onions over and around the chicken.

Bring the liquid to a simmer, and cover the skillet. Simmer gently, turning the chicken pieces once, just until the chicken is cooked through and tender, about 10 to 15 minutes. The total time will depend on the size of the chicken pieces.

Transfer the chicken to a serving dish. Stir the bottom of the pan gently to scrape up any tasty, browned (not burned) bits. If the onion-wine sauce remaining in the skillet seems too watery, quickly boil it down a bit while stirring. Add salt to taste. Spoon the sauce over the chicken breasts so each has a generous amount of onions. If desired, sprinkle the chicken with chopped parsley (or garnish the platter with parsley sprigs) before serving.

Makes about 6 to 8 servings.

Chicken with Brandied Cherry Sauce

Loosely adapted from a popular entrée served many years ago at the Holland Glory Restaurant in Amsterdam, this quick and easy dish is sure to be a hit among cherry fanciers. Brandy, wine, or cream sherry (which contains no cream and is my personal preference) gives the sauce a wonderful flavor, while the alcohol evaporates during cooking. Canned cherries sometimes contain hidden pits; you may wish to check that all pits have been removed.

1 (16-ounce) can dark sweet cherries,
    including liquid

2 tablespoons canola oil

6 medium boneless chicken breast
    halves (about 1 1/2 pounds)

1/3 cup cherry-flavored brandy, sweet
    cherry wine, or cream sherry

1 tablespoon cornstarch

2 teaspoons sugar

1 1/2 tablespoons cool water

Drain the liquid from the cherries into a small measuring cup. There should be at least 2/3 cup; add water, if necessary. (Reserve the well-drained cherries.)

Put the oil into a large skillet over medium-high heat; then lightly brown the chicken pieces on both sides. Pour the cherry liquid over the chicken in the skillet along with the brandy (or wine or sherry). Cover the skillet, lower the heat, and simmer the chicken in the cherry juice, turning once, for 15 to 20 minutes, or just until the chicken is tender and cooked through. Meanwhile, in a custard cup or very small bowl, stir the cornstarch and sugar with the water, and set aside. Use tongs or a slotted spoon to remove the cooked chicken from the skillet to a serving platter.

Stir the cornstarch mixture to make sure that no cornstarch is stuck to the bottom, and add it to the juice in the skillet while stirring. Simmer the sauce until it thickens and is not cloudy, about 1 minute, stirring constantly and scraping up any browned bits on the bottom of the pan. Gently stir in the reserved drained cherries for about 1 minute, or until they are heated through. Spoon the cherries and sauce over the chicken breasts. (If desired, the cooked chicken breasts may be warmed in the sauce in the skillet for a few minutes immediately before serving.)

NOTE: To make this dish ahead, cook the chicken as directed, but do not thicken the liquid with the cornstarch mixture. Refrigerate the chicken in its pan juices, and the drained cherries in a separate container. Shortly before serving, reheat the chicken and juice by simmering them together in a covered skillet. Prepare the cornstarch mixture, and proceed as above to make the cherry sauce, simmering the cherries a little longer to make sure that they are heated through.

Makes about 6 servings.

Ensalada de Pimiento y Tomat

ROASTED PEPPER AND TOMATO SALAD

P

Vegetables salads such as this are very popular for Sephardim from the Middle East and Morocco. Several salads are always on the Friday-evening Shabbat table, and are served at most other holidays as well. They are usually accompanied by fresh bread for dipping into the salad.

Charring the peppers cooks them so they are soft, and gives them a lovely, smoky flavor. It also makes them very easy to peel, leaving behind beautiful (unmarked) pepper flesh. In the past, the peppers for this salad were always roasted over an open fire. Here, the technique has been simplified using a broiler, gas grill, or gas flame.

If desired, unseasoned, peeled, roasted pepper pieces may be frozen and used at a later time. A combination of red and green peppers provides a colorful salad; however, the red (ripe) peppers take less time to char than the green ones, so they should be watched carefully. Yellow bell peppers may also be used, and take about the same time to char as red.

2 or 3 medium sweet green bell peppers	*1 tablespoon finely chopped fresh*
2 or 3 medium sweet red bell peppers	* parsley leaves*
2 medium tomatoes, preferably vine-	*2 tablespoons extra-virgin olive oil*
* ripened, peeled (if desired), seeded,*	*2 tablespoons lemon juice*
* and cut into small pieces*	*¼ teaspoon salt*
2 thin scallions, including green tops,	*¼ teaspoon ground cumin*
* thinly sliced*	*¼ teaspoon paprika*
2 garlic cloves, finely minced	*Ground black pepper to taste*

Preheat your broiler. Put the peppers in a foil-lined baking pan (such as a jelly roll pan), and place the pan about 6 inches under the heated element. Broil the peppers, rotating them occasionally with tongs, for about 15 to 20 minutes, or until the skins are completely blistered and charred. Alternatively, place the peppers on a hot gas grill, and rotate them occasionally as above.

Use tongs or a large spoon to transfer the hot, roasted peppers to a covered container or closed heavy plastic bag, and let the peppers cool for about 15 minutes. The trapped steam helps loosen the skins. Rinse each pepper

under cool running water, while you remove and discard the skin, stem, and seeds. (Be careful of hot steam that may remain inside the peppers.) Drain the peppers very well, and blot them on paper towels. Cut the peppers into small pieces.

Combine the remaining salad ingredients in a serving bowl, and mix in the pepper pieces. Chill the salad several hours or overnight to give the flavors a chance to blend. For the best taste, remove the salad from the refrigerator about 1 hour before serving time. Serve slightly chilled or at room temperature. Stir the salad before serving.

Makes about 6 servings.

Bamia

OKRA IN TOMATO SAUCE

Okra, which is very popular among Sephardim, appears on the table at most festive meals. Those who are unfamiliar with this vegetable will be pleasantly surprised at how tasty it can be when prepared using Sephardic techniques. Sometimes, the okra is part of a large vegetable stew, which contains such varied vegetables as green pepper, eggplant, green beans, and tomatoes. On other occasions, the preparation is simpler.

Following is one of the most popular and easiest okra dishes. It is tasty both hot as a side dish, or cold as a salad, and can be varied by using tomato sauce or fresh tomatoes instead of canned ones.

For best flavor, okra should be very fresh and not withered or brown. I have bought the very best okra at local farmers' markets during the summer.

1 to 1½ pounds fresh small okra, each approximately 3 inches long	1 (14- to 16-ounce) can tomatoes, including juice, chopped
2 tablespoons extra-virgin olive oil	2 tablespoons lemon juice
1 large onion, finely chopped	⅛ teaspoon black pepper, preferably
2 garlic cloves, minced	freshly ground

Rinse the okra in a colander. Use a paring knife to trim off each stem just above where it meets the pod, being careful not to expose any seeds. (Discard

any fibrous pods that are not easily trimmed.) If the tips of the okra are brown or bruised, cut them off, but no more than ¼ inch so as not to expose seeds. (Loose seeds may produce a gelatinous texture that is undesirable in this dish.)

In a medium saucepan, heat the oil over medium-high heat. Cook the onion and garlic, stirring, until tender. Add the okra, tomatoes and their juice, lemon juice, and pepper. Bring to a boil; then reduce the heat, and simmer, covered, for about 5 minutes. Remove the cover, and continue simmering until the okra is tender and most of the liquid has evaporated to form a thick sauce, about 5 to 10 minutes longer. Serve hot as a side dish, or chill and serve cold or at room temperature as an appetizer or salad.

Makes 6 to 8 servings.

Browned-Onion Lokshen Kugel

SAVORY NOODLE PUDDING

Lokshen kugel, literally "noodle pudding" in Yiddish, is a very popular Ashkenazic side dish that is often served on Shabbat and holidays. It has been reasoned that we eat a lot of lokshen kugel on Shabbat because it symbolizes the Jewish people. Like Jews, the noodles in kugel become so entangled with each other that they can never be completely separated.

In this kugel, *lots* of onions are cooked until they become a rich golden brown and have a wonderful aroma. A tiny bit of sugar is added, which helps to caramelize the onions and to make them slightly darker. As the onions cook, they compact into a much smaller volume than when they were raw.

I developed this recipe because one of my sons has always loved fried onions but was not too enthusiastic about lokshen kugel. With this delicious combination, he can't resist!

Shabbat

About 5 medium onions (or more
    smaller ones)
¼ cup canola or olive oil
1 teaspoon sugar
1 (12-ounce) package medium-wide
    egg noodles

½ teaspoon salt
¼ teaspoon ground black pepper
4 large eggs, beaten or 1 cup pareve
    egg substitute

Peel the onions, cut them in half through the root end, and cut them crosswise into ½-inch semicircular slices. Put the oil into a large, deep skillet or Dutch oven over medium heat. Add the onions, and sauté them, separating the "rings," for about 20 minutes, or until they are lightly browned. Sprinkle the sugar on the top; then continue cooking and stirring the onions until they are greatly reduced in volume and are richly browned and very aromatic. (Do not let them burn.) Remove them from the heat, and set them aside to cool.

Using a 5-quart or similar pot, cook the noodles according to the package directions, using the shorter time listed. While the noodles are cooking, coat a 10-inch square (or similar) baking dish or pan with nonstick cooking spray or grease it well. Preheat the oven to 350 degrees.

Drain the noodles well; then stir in the reserved onions until they are completely mixed in. Break up any clumps of cooked onions so that they are evenly distributed. Stir in the salt and pepper. Finally, add the eggs and stir them in well. Turn out the noodle mixture into the prepared pan, and smooth the top with the back of a spoon. Cover the baking dish with a piece of foil (or a lid), and bake the kugel at 350 degrees for 30 minutes. Remove the cover, and continue baking the kugel for about 20 minutes longer, or until it is lightly browned and cooked through. Serve hot or at room temperature, cut into squares.

Makes about 8 servings.

Frijoles Negros
CUBAN-STYLE BLACK BEANS

At the beginning of the twentieth century, when she was only two, Regina Korenstein Gordon and her family left their native home in Poland with hopes of immigrating to the United States. However, U.S. quota restrictions made this impossible, and so they decided to live in Cuba. There, they became part of a large, active Jewish community. Regina grew up in Cuba, and married another Jewish immigrant, David Gershgorn, who had left Russia (and his family) to escape conscription into the army.

During the late 1940s, an American tourist visiting Cuba mistook David Gershgorn for a friend of hers who lived in the United States. It was indeed an incredible coincidence that the woman's friend turned out to be Mr. Gershgorn's brother, Morris Gordon, whom he hadn't seen or heard of since childhood. The "Yankee" brother eventually persuaded Mr. Gershgorn and his entire family to move to the United States, and adopt the Americanized version of their surname—just a few years before the Communist takeover of Cuba.

In Philadelphia, Mrs. Regina Gordon continued to cook the unique Cuban-European cuisine that she had learned during her youth, and that her family favored. Mrs. Gordon passed away in the 1980s, but loving memories of her linger on in recipes, such as the one here. It comes by way of her daughter-in-law, Sharon Gordon, who enthusiastically carries on the family's culinary traditions.

On Friday nights, Sharon recalled, Mrs. Regina Gordon often served this dish with chicken soup, East European–style brisket or rib roast, avocado salad, and thinly sliced, fried *plátano* (or plantain), a bananalike vegetable that is popular in the Caribbean.

The bean mixture typically is served over perfectly cooked, long-grain white rice. However, the combination of beans with a whole grain like brown rice actually provides enough complete protein to serve as a delicious main course.

NOTES: If you cannot find black beans with the other dry beans in the supermarket, look in the specialty section featuring Spanish foods.

To use canned beans, substitute 2 (15- to 16-ounce) cans plain black beans for the cooked dry beans. Drain the canned beans well in a colander, and rinse them with cold water until it is clear. Sauté the vegetables as directed below; then add the drained beans to the vegetables with about ¼ cup water. Cook, stirring often, as directed.

1 pound (2½ cups) dry black (turtle)
   beans, sorted and rinsed well (see
   Notes)
1 large bay leaf
2 tablespoons olive or canola oil
1 large onion, finely chopped
4 to 5 garlic cloves, minced
1 large green bell pepper, finely chopped

1 teaspoon salt, or to taste
⅛ teaspoon black pepper

To Serve
4 to 5 cups hot, cooked white or brown
   rice, preferably "converted" rice
Finely chopped onions to taste
   (optional)

Put the dry beans and bay leaf into a very large saucepan or small Dutch oven, and add about 6 cups cold water or enough to cover the beans by approximately 1 inch. Bring the water to a boil over high heat; then cover the saucepan and lower the heat. Simmer the beans, covered, for 1 hour. Then continue cooking them for about 1 hour longer, periodically adding small amounts of very hot or boiling water, as necessary, to keep the level of liquid just as high as the beans but not higher.

Meanwhile, heat the oil in a large skillet over medium-high heat; then sauté the onion, garlic, and green pepper until they are tender. Set the vegetables aside.

When the beans are very soft, stir in the sautéed vegetables. Continue cooking the beans over low heat, uncovered, stirring often, for about 30 minutes longer, or until they become slightly mashed and form a creamy sauce, and the vegetables are blended into the beans. Season the bean mixture with the salt and pepper, adjusting them to taste. Serve the beans over hot, cooked rice. If desired, top them with freshly chopped onion.

Makes 8 to 10 servings as a side dish.

Brown Rice Pilaf

This dish is a great way to introduce brown rice to a skeptical family.

1½ tablespoons canola oil
1½ cups uncooked brown rice
3 cups hot chicken or vegetable broth or
    bouillon made from cubes or
    powder
½ teaspoon ground allspice
¼ teaspoon ground cinnamon

⅛ teaspoon ground cloves
1 teaspoon lemon juice
¼ teaspoon salt
⅛ teaspoon black pepper
½ cup slivered almonds
½ cup raisins

Heat the oil in a medium-sized saucepan over medium heat. Add the uncooked rice, and stir constantly for about 2 minutes. Slowly add the hot broth while stirring. Then stir in the remaining ingredients. Bring to a boil; then lower the heat and cover the pan tightly.

Simmer the rice for 45 to 50 minutes, or until all the liquid is absorbed. (For drier rice, remove the lid during last 5 minutes of cooking.) Use a fork to fluff and stir the rice once before serving, making sure the raisins and almonds are distributed evenly.

Makes 6 to 8 servings.

Herbed Kasha-Mushroom Pilaf

"Kasha" is another name for toasted buckwheat groats. Though botanically not a grain, kasha is usually cooked and eaten just like one. It is a favorite of those Jews with Russian backgrounds, and is often served with "bow tie" noodles and gravy. Following is a different way to cook kasha. Serve it as a side dish, or use it to stuff poultry before roasting.

¼ cup canola oil
1 large onion, finely chopped
2 celery stalks, diced
1½ cups chopped fresh mushrooms
1½ cups whole or coarse kasha
* (buckwheat groats)*
1 large egg, lightly beaten
3 cups chicken or vegetable broth or
* bouillon made from cubes or powder*

3 tablespoons finely chopped fresh
* parsley leaves*
½ teaspoon ground sage
½ teaspoon dried thyme leaves
Salt and freshly ground black pepper to
* taste*

Put the oil into a saucepan over medium-high heat; then sauté the onion and celery until tender. Add the mushrooms and cook, stirring, 1 minute longer. Mix the kasha with the egg, and add this to the saucepan. Cook, stirring, 1 to 2 minutes longer or until the kasha seems dry. Then stir in the remaining ingredients.

Bring the broth to a boil; then cover the saucepan, and reduce the heat. Simmer the pilaf for 15 to 20 minutes, or until all the liquid is absorbed and the kasha is tender.

Makes 6 to 8 servings.

Eir Kichelach

EGG COOKIES OR BOW TIES

There are dozens of variations on these very popular light cookies. Some are made with a stiff, rolled dough, others with a softer dough that is "dropped" onto the baking sheet. Some use copious amounts of oil, others use none at all. Some call for baking powder, others don't. Some are barely sweet, others are very sweet. Some are cut into simple squares, rectangles, or circles; others are cut into fancier diamonds or twisted into bow ties.

With their Yiddish name, *eir kichelach* (*kichel* is singular) are obviously Ashkenazic. But Sephardic Jews of Turkish and Greek origins use a very similar dough to make ring-

shaped cookies called Biscochos de Huevo (page 82), which literally translates to "egg cookies," just like *eir kichelach*. And Jews in the Sephardic community on the island of Curaçao serve a similar crisp sponge cookie called Panlevi (page 83) on holidays and other special occasions.

The following *eir kichel* recipe is my own combination of many versions. The cookies are light, pleasantly but not excessively sweet, and easy to make. Since the first edition of this book was published, this recipe has become one of my mother's favorites. In fact, she often makes *eir kichelach* to take as gifts to delighted friends. It has given me great pleasure to be able to pass "up" a recipe to my first cooking mentor.

On my mother's suggestion, I have doubled the original recipe. She says that you can never have too many, and they keep very well.

NOTE: If desired, 1 cup egg substitute can be used for the eggs, or 3 egg whites substituted for 2 of the whole eggs, or 5 egg whites for 3 of the whole eggs.

4 large eggs (see Note)
½ cup sugar, plus more for rolling and topping
7 tablespoons vegetable oil (½ cup less 1 tablespoon)

½ teaspoon vanilla extract
3½ cups all-purpose flour
2 teaspoons baking powder

Use an electric mixer to beat the eggs with the sugar for several minutes until very light and fluffy; then beat in the oil and vanilla. Stir in the flour and baking powder, and mix until combined. If the dough is still very sticky, add a little more flour. Divide the dough into two pieces, shape each into a fat disk, and wrap it in plastic or wax paper. Let the disks rest for 5 to 10 minutes. Line some cookie sheets with baking parchment, or coat them with nonstick cooking spray. Preheat the oven to 350 degrees.

Using extra sugar (instead of flour) to keep the dough from sticking, roll out each disk of dough to about ¼ inch thick. Sprinkle more sugar on top, and gently press it in with the rolling pin. Using a sharp knife or pastry wheel, cut the dough into small squares, rectangles, or diamonds. To make bow ties, cut the dough into rectangles about 1 inch wide by 2½ to 3 inches long. Carefully twist each rectangle twice in the center so that the sugared surface faces upward.

Place the cookies on the prepared sheets, keeping them at least ½ inch apart. Bake the cookies at 350 degrees for about 20 minutes, or until they are lightly browned. Remove the cookies from the sheets, and cool them completely on wire racks. Store them in airtight containers. They will keep for about 2 weeks at room temperature, or they may be frozen for longer storage.

Makes about 72 small, flat cookies or about 48 bow ties.

NOTE: These are not the very puffy type of *eir kichelach* found at some Jewish bakeries.

Biscochos de Huevo
RING-SHAPED EGG COOKIES

These crunchy, sesame-coated cookies are very popular among Sephardim whose ancestors hail from Turkey and Greece. They are frequently served for Shabbat and most holidays, and are often kept in tins to have around for a quick snack for unexpected guests.

Sometimes the term *biscocho* (also spelled *bizcocho* and *biskotcho*), which means "biscuit" or "cookie," is also used to describe a ringed yeast-raised snack that is more salty than sweet. For this variation, see the recipe for Ka'ak (page 160).

DOUGH
4 large eggs or 1 cup pareve egg
  substitute
²/₃ to 1 cup sugar (use larger amount for
  sweeter cookies)
¹/₂ cup canola oil
¹/₂ to 1 teaspoon vanilla extract
  (optional)
4 cups all-purpose flour

1 tablespoon baking powder
¹/₂ teaspoon salt

TOPPING
About ¹/₂ cup hulled raw sesame seeds

EGG WASH
1 egg beaten with 1 teaspoon water or
  ¹/₄ cup egg substitute

Line two large cookie sheets with baking parchment, or coat them with nonstick cooking spray.

For the dough, use an electric mixer to beat the 4 eggs (or egg substitute) with the sugar for several minutes until very light and fluffy; then beat in the oil and vanilla (if used). Stir in the flour, baking powder, and salt until combined. If the dough is still very sticky, add a little more flour. Allow the dough to rest for 5 minutes. Preheat the oven to 375 degrees. Put the sesame seeds into a small bowl. Prepare the egg wash.

Pinch off a walnut-sized piece of dough and roll it into a rope that is ⅜ inch thick and about 5 inches long, using small amounts of extra flour if necessary to avoid sticking. (Or divide the dough in half, and form each half into a thick log. Cut off a section of the log as in making refrigerator cookies, and roll the section to a rope as directed above.) Pinch the ends of the rope together to form a ring. Repeat until all the dough has been formed into rings.

Brush the top surface of each ring with the egg-water mixture; then immediately dip the ring into the sesame seeds. Place the rings on a baking sheet at least 1 inch apart with the seeds facing upward.

Bake at 375 degrees for about 15 to 20 minutes, or until lightly browned. Cool the rings completely on wire racks before storing in airtight containers.

Makes about 48 cookies.

Panlevi

CRISP EGG COOKIES

Five centuries ago, during the period of the heinous Inquisition, many Jews fled from Spain and Portugal to countries that were more tolerant. A number of Jews went to live in Holland and, from there, small groups eventually settled in almost all the Dutch colonies.

One such settlement was on the island of Curaçao, part of the Netherlands Antilles in the Caribbean. The oldest surviving synagogue and Jewish cemetery in the Western Hemisphere are located there, along with an extant Jewish community.

Cookies like those that follow have been served for centuries by the Sephardim of Curaçao on holidays and other special occasions. Interestingly, it became a "New World" tradition to accompany them with a drink of hot chocolate at the celebration of a *Brit Milah* (ritual circumcision).

Shabbat

4 large eggs

²⁄₃ cup sugar

¹⁄₄ teaspoon ground cinnamon

¹⁄₄ teaspoon ground nutmeg

1 teaspoon vanilla extract

1¹⁄₂ cups all-purpose flour

¹⁄₂ teaspoon baking powder

In a medium bowl, use an electric mixer to beat the eggs with the sugar until very thick and light. Beat in the cinnamon, nutmeg, and vanilla. Beat in the flour and baking powder. The batter will be loose.

Preheat the oven to 350 degrees. Line some cookie sheets with baking parchment, or coat them with nonstick cooking spray. Drop the batter by generous teaspoonfuls, pushing it off the spoon with your fingertip. Leave at least 1½ inches between each cookie.

Bake at 350 degrees for about 18 to 20 minutes, or until the edges of the cookies are browned. If using parchment, let the cookies cool on the paper on a wire rack (slide the parchment with the cookies onto the rack). Otherwise, immediately use a metal spatula to remove the cookies from the baking sheet to the cooling rack. They should become crisp as they cool. If the cookies are too soft, return them to a 200-degree oven for a few minutes to crisp. When the cookies on the parchment can be easily handled, peel them from the parchment and let them cool completely on the rack.

Makes about 40 (2-inch) cookies.

Linzertorte

RASPBERRY JAM TART

Jews of Austro-Hungarian heritage are justly proud of delectable pastries such as this. A linzertorte is actually a jam-filled tart with an unusual almond-flavored cookie-dough bottom crust and lattice top.

Several years ago, at Erev Shabbat dinner, I served this dessert to a Jewish family who had just moved to our community. They were delighted by my choice. It turned out the woman's parents were both originally from Austria, and linzertorte is one of her favorite pastries. It was the perfect beginning to a long friendship.

NOTES: Raspberry jam with seeds is the traditional filling for linzertorte; however, seedless raspberry jam may be substituted. If using a food processor to prepare the dough for the crust, finely grind or chop the almonds first, remove them from the food processor bowl, and proceed with the recipe.

½ cup butter or margarine, softened	1 large egg
¾ cup sugar	2 tablespoons lemon juice
1⅔ cups all-purpose flour	1 teaspoon grated lemon peel, yellow
1 cup (about 4 ounces) very finely	part only
ground almonds	½ teaspoon almond extract
1 teaspoon baking powder	1 cup (1 10-ounce jar) red or black
¾ teaspoon ground cinnamon	raspberry jam
¼ teaspoon ground cloves	Confectioners' sugar to sprinkle

Mix the butter or margarine with the sugar until very smooth. Do this by hand with a wooden spoon, or use a heavy-duty electric mixer or a food processor fitted with a steel blade. Add the flour, almonds, baking powder, cinnamon, and cloves, and mix or lightly process until fine crumbs are formed. Add the egg, lemon juice, peel, and almond extract, and mix well or gently pulse-process to form a stiff dough. Form the dough into a flat oval, wrap it in plastic wrap or wax paper, and chill it for about 30 minutes, or until it is slightly firm. (The dough may be made ahead to this point and chilled until needed. In this case, let it warm a few minutes at room temperature before using it.)

Cut off one-third of the dough, and roll it out between two sheets of wax paper to form a 9½ by 5-inch rectangle of even thickness. Leave the dough in the paper, and chill it in the freezer for 5 to 10 minutes, or until it is quite firm. It will be used for the lattice top.

Meanwhile, roll out the remaining two-thirds of the dough between two sheets of heavy plastic wrap or wax paper to form a circle about 11 inches in diameter. Peel off the top sheet of plastic or paper, and invert the circle over a nonstick spray-coated 9-inch tart pan (preferably with a removable bottom) or 9-inch springform pan. With the wrap or paper on top, gently press the dough into the pan and 1 inch up the sides. Carefully peel off the plastic or paper. (An alternative method to form the bottom crust is to press small pieces of the dough into the pan using your fingertips.)

Shabbat

Use a narrow, long-handled spoon to stir the jam in the jar to soften it. Spread it evenly in the bottom of the crust. Remove the chilled rectangle from the freezer. Preheat the oven to 350 degrees.

Lay the chilled, rolled-out dough on a cutting board, and use a sharp knife or kitchen scissors to cut it lengthwise into eight strips (each about ½ inch wide) right through the paper and dough. Peel the paper off one side of a strip; then lay the strip, paper side up, across the filled pastry shell. Peel off the second piece of paper. Continue with the remaining strips, alternately placing one strip horizontally, the next vertically, to form a lattice with four strips in each direction. *Be sure to remove all wax paper.* Press the ends of the strips against the perimeter of the bottom crust, and trim off any overhanging pieces.

Bake the linzertorte at 350 degrees for 40 to 45 minutes, or until the crust is lightly browned and firm. Cool the torte in the pan on a wire rack for about 30 minutes; then remove the sides of the pan, and slide the torte off the pan base onto the rack to cool completely. (If using a tart pan without a removable bottom, cool and serve the torte in the pan.) Shortly before serving, sprinkle the completely cooled torte *very lightly* with sieved confectioners' sugar so that the lattice shows through. To serve, cut into wedges.

The linzertorte can be made ahead, and keeps very well for several days. It also freezes nicely. Defrost, wrapped, at room temperature. Do not sprinkle with confectioners' sugar until shortly before serving.

Makes about 8 servings.

Orange Chiffon Cake

Chiffon cakes are light like sponge cakes, but they tend to be moister and stay fresh longer thanks to the addition of oil. I started baking this particular cake several years ago when a Jewish exchange student from Italy lived with our family. He was rather particular about baked goods, and I was having a hard time pleasing him with a Shabbat

dessert until I tried this recipe. It reminded him very much of his mother's delicious Sephardic cakes. In fact, he liked the cake so much that I decided to make it for his seventeenth birthday. As usual, I sprinkled the top with confectioners' sugar.

It wasn't until the candles were lit and blown out that I realized my folly. The sugar was blown all over me! Now, when I bake this for a birthday, I top it with Orange Drizzle Icing (page 88) instead of powdered sugar.

The following cake is very similar to the very popular Pan de Espanya that the Sephardim frequently serve on Shabbat. (For a Pesach version, see page 398.)

5 large eggs
3 extra egg whites
½ cup canola oil
¾ cup orange juice
1 tablespoon grated orange peel, colored part only (optional)
1 teaspoon vanilla extract
2 cups all-purpose flour

1½ cups sugar, divided
1 tablespoon baking powder
½ teaspoon cream of tartar

To Serve (Optional)
Confectioners' sugar
1 recipe Orange Drizzle Icing (page 88)

Preheat the oven to 350 degrees. Have an ungreased 10-inch tube pan ready. If it is not the two-piece type with a removable tube insert, grease the bottom only and cut a doughnut-shaped piece of wax paper to fit in the bottom. (This will make it easier to remove the cake from the pan.)

Separate the eggs, putting the 8 whites into a large, very clean, nonplastic mixing bowl, and the 5 yolks into another large bowl. To the bowl with the yolks, add the oil, orange juice, peel (if used), and vanilla. Mix well. Then add the flour, 1 cup of the sugar, and baking powder. Beat with an electric mixer or by hand until the orange batter is well blended and light and fluffy.

To the whites in the large mixing bowl, add the cream of tartar. Use an electric mixer with very clean beaters to beat the whites and the cream of tartar until frothy; then gradually but deliberately add the remaining ½ cup sugar while continuing to beat the whites until they are very thick with stiff peaks. This will take from 5 to 10 minutes depending on the type of mixer. Stir about one-fourth of the whites into the orange batter to lighten it. Then add the orange batter to the whites and gently, but thoroughly, fold to combine completely. Make sure no lumps of egg white remain.

Turn out the batter into the tube pan, and smooth the top. Tap the pan against the countertop to release any large air bubbles. Bake at 350 degrees for about 60 minutes, or until the top of the cake springs back when lightly pressed with a fingertip.

Remove the pan from the oven and immediately invert it on its "legs," or fit the tube over the neck of a bottle to cool upside down. Cool the cake completely before removing it from the pan. Run a knife around the outer and inner edges of the cake, and lift out the tube insert if used. Invert the cake onto a platter. (If the pan was lined with paper, peel it off the bottom of the cake.)

If desired, sprinkle the cake lightly with sieved confectioners' sugar shortly before serving, or top it with some Orange Drizzle Icing.

Makes about 12 servings.

Orange Drizzle Icing

This may be used to top the Orange Chiffon Cake (page 86) if desired.

NOTE: For Vanilla Drizzle Icing, increase the vanilla extract to 1 teaspoon and omit the orange juice and peel. For the liquid, use milk, water, or pareve milk substitute.

2 cups confectioners' sugar
2 tablespoons softened pareve stick margarine or butter
½ teaspoon vanilla extract

2 to 4 tablespoons orange juice
1 teaspoon grated orange peel, colored part only (optional)

In a medium bowl, combine the confectioners' sugar, margarine, and vanilla extract. Mix well with a spoon, gradually adding very small amounts of juice until a "drizzling" consistency is reached; that is, when a spoonful of icing is gently tipped, the icing drips out in a narrow stream. If the icing is too thin, stir in extra confectioners' sugar. As soon as the icing is ready, use a

spoon to drizzle it over the cake top and sides in a random pattern. Or spoon the icing into a freezer bag, snip a bottom corner to make a small hole, and gently squeeze the icing over the top of the cake. If desired, sprinkle with grated peel.

Makes enough to decorate 1 large cake in a drizzle pattern.

Pareve Pound Cake with Drizzle Icing

The "pound" cake got its name because it used to contain a pound each of eggs, butter, sugar, and flour. Most modern pound cakes imitate the original more in texture and versatility than in specific amounts of ingredients.

Unfortunately, most pound cake recipes still call for butter and milk, and result in cakes that are not only incompatible with a Shabbat meat dinner, but also high in saturated fat. As I have been trying to limit my family's consumption of margarine (due to the possible health hazards of the trans fatty acids it contains), I developed this very easy pareve (neither meat nor dairy) recipe that uses heart-healthy monounsaturated canola oil instead. In addition, I have found that egg substitute works quite well in this delicious cake.

It is perfect for Shabbat, and also makes an excellent birthday cake. To make it particularly festive for parties, you can stir about ¼ to ⅓ cup colorful sprinkles into the batter just before pouring it into the baking pan. I usually put sprinkles on *top* of the baked cake (as suggested below) instead of inside it. Most people love almond flavoring in the cake and icing, but you can leave it out if you prefer.

The chocolate-marbled variation (below) has also been a big hit with my family and friends. The first time I made it, my youngest son sampled it and came running to tell me, "This cake is fabulous!" I was touched. I had never before heard him utter such an effusive adjective.

1 cup canola or safflower oil

2 cups sugar

1 cup pareve egg substitute or 4 large
eggs

2 teaspoons vanilla extract

1 teaspoon almond extract (optional)

3 cups all-purpose flour

4 teaspoons baking powder

1/2 teaspoon salt

3/4 cup pareve nonfat milk substitute,
orange juice, or, water

DRIZZLE ICING (OPTIONAL)

2 cups confectioners' sugar

2 tablespoons softened pareve stick
margarine

1/2 teaspoon vanilla extract

1/2 teaspoon almond extract (optional)

2 to 4 tablespoons pareve nonfat milk
substitute or water

TOPPING (OPTIONAL)

Colorful sprinkles

Coat a 12-cup fluted tube pan (Bundt pan) with nonstick cooking spray or grease it well. Set aside. Preheat the oven to 325 degrees.

In a large mixing bowl, put the oil, sugar, eggs, and both extracts, and beat with an electric mixer about 2 minutes, or until thoroughly combined. Add the flour, baking powder, salt, and liquid, and blend at low speed until all the dry ingredients are moistened. Then increase the mixer speed, and beat for 2 to 3 minutes, or until very well mixed. (The batter will not be very thick.)

Pour the batter into the prepared pan. Bake at 325 degrees for 55 to 65 minutes, or until a wooden pick inserted in the center comes out clean. (A large crack may form in the top of cake; it will not be visible when the cake is inverted.) Cool the cake in the pan on a cake rack for 30 minutes. Invert the cake onto a platter and cool completely before serving. The cake may be glazed while it is still slightly warm, though it should not be hot.

If drizzle icing is desired, combine all the ingredients except the milk substitute in a small bowl, mixing well. Slowly add very small amounts of the liquid, stirring constantly, until a "drizzling" consistency is reached; that is, when a spoonful of icing is gently tipped, the icing drips out in a narrow stream. If the icing is too thin, stir in extra confectioners' sugar. As soon as the icing is ready, use a spoon to drizzle it over the cake in a random pattern. Or spoon the icing into a freezer bag, snip a bottom corner to make a small hole, and gently squeeze the icing over the top of the cake. (You do not have to use all the icing.) If desired, the icing can be sprinkled with sprinkles while it is still moist.

Let the cake rest, uncovered, until the icing firms up. To store the cake for more than a few hours before serving it, do not put on the icing and wrap the cake in plastic wrap. Store it at room temperature for a day or two. For longer storage, freeze the cake. Shortly before serving, prepare the icing and drizzle it on the defrosted cake.

Makes 12 to 16 servings.

Variation

MARBLE POUND CAKE

Prepare the batter as directed above. Put 1 ounce unsweetened baking chocolate into a 2-cup Pyrex measuring cup. Melt the chocolate in a microwave oven (1 to 2½ minutes on "high"—check every 30 seconds after the first minute) or place the measuring cup in a small skillet of water on the stove, and heat, stirring occasionally, until the chocolate melts. Stir a small amount of batter into the chocolate to loosen it from the bottom of the cup; then add more batter to the 1¼-cup mark, and mix very well until completely combined. Pour all the remaining light batter into the prepared pan. Pour the chocolate batter on top. Use a scooping motion with a spoon (it works better than a knife) to gently swirl the batters together. Bake as directed above.

Spiced Apple Coffee Cake

During the *Havdalah* service, which signifies the end of Shabbat, all participants smell a mixture of pleasant spices (or *basamim*). The spices represent the wonderful "fragrance" of Shabbat, and are said to help us get over our disappointment that the symbolic "Shabbat Queen" is departing.

Some Jews, particularly Hasidim, give her a royal send-off with a special meal called *Melavah Malkah* ("Accompanying the Queen"). This may be a large feast, or simply an assortment of cake and cookies. The following delicious cake contains the same spices often used for Havdalah, and would be perfect for Melavah Malkah or any time during Shabbat.

FILLING AND TOPPING

²/₃ cup finely chopped walnuts or pecans

¹/₄ cup sugar

1 teaspoon ground cinnamon

1 large Golden Delicious apple, peeled, cored, and thinly sliced

BATTER

¹/₂ cup butter or margarine, softened

³/₄ cup sugar

3 large eggs or ³/₄ cup pareve egg substitute

1 teaspoon ground cinnamon

¹/₄ teaspoon ground allspice

¹/₄ teaspoon ground cloves

1 cup apple cider or richly flavored apple juice

2 cups all-purpose flour (may be half whole wheat, if desired)

1 teaspoon baking powder

1 teaspoon baking soda

In a small bowl, make the filling and topping by mixing together the nuts, sugar, and cinnamon. Set the mixture aside with the apple slices. Preheat the oven to 375 degrees.

For the batter, use an electric mixer to cream the butter and sugar until light and fluffy. Beat in the eggs, one by one, and stir until well combined. Beat in the cinnamon, allspice, and cloves. Alternately add the cider and flour, mixing after each addition. Then mix in the baking powder and soda until completely combined.

Pour half the batter into a nonstick-spray-coated or well-greased 9-inch square baking pan. Sprinkle the batter with half of the nut mixture. Arrange the apple slices on top. Spread the remaining batter over the apples, and sprinkle it with the remaining nut mixture. Use your fingertips to lightly press the topping into the batter.

Bake the cake at 375 degrees for 30 to 40 minutes, or until a toothpick inserted in the center comes out clean. Cool in the pan on rack. Cut into large squares to serve.

Makes about 9 servings.

Sweet Crowns for the Shabbat Queen

MINIATURE FILLED CHALLAH ROLLS

P

Shabbat is often likened to a beautiful bride or queen who makes a regal appearance only once each week. The Shabbat Queen's crown is occasionally symbolized by forming a long, narrow challah braid into a circular, doughnutlike shape. The challah may be filled with confections that represent the sweetness of the day.

Following is a simple recipe for a miniature crown bread, which is baked in a muffin tin. It is a perfect project for young children (see special Notes following the recipe). In fact, I originally developed the recipe and technique for a group of four-year-olds at Bet Yeladim Preschool in Columbia, Maryland.

NOTES: The crowns can be produced with either homemade challah dough, such as Gloria's Glorious Challah (page 32), or already prepared dough that can sometimes be purchased from Jewish bakeries. The dough should be ready for shaping.

Listed below are instructions for one crown. For more, simply repeat the steps. Please feel free to vary the filling as you wish; the following are only suggestions. All amounts of filling ingredients are approximate. For the glaze, ingredient amounts may be multiplied to have enough for several crowns.

FOR EACH INDIVIDUAL CROWN

1 (2-ounce) piece challah dough (about the size of a small plum) (see Notes above)

1 teaspoon pareve tub margarine or very soft stick margarine

1 teaspoon granulated brown sugar or regular dark or light brown sugar

1/8 teaspoon ground cinnamon

2 to 3 teaspoons of some of the following fillings: raisins, dried currants, dried cranberries, diced dried apricots, chopped dates, chopped walnuts or pecans, sunflower seeds, shredded coconut, and/or chocolate chips

GLAZE (PER CROWN)

2 tablespoons confectioners' sugar

1 drop vanilla extract

Colored sprinkles (optional)

On a very lightly floured board, pat or roll out the dough to a 3 by 6-inch rectangle. If the dough is sticky, use small amounts of flour as needed. Spread the margarine over the top surface of the dough. Sprinkle the brown sugar, cinnamon, and your choice of filling(s) evenly over the margarine. Roll up the rectangle, as for a jelly roll, beginning at one of the 6-inch sides. With the seam on the inside, bring the ends of the roll around to form a doughnut shape, and pinch the ends together very tightly. Put the crown in a nonstick-spray-coated or well-greased standard-sized muffin tin or 6-ounce custard cup. Repeat the procedure for as many crowns as desired. Let the crowns rise until almost doubled in bulk. Meanwhile, preheat the oven to 350 degrees.

Bake the crowns at 350 degrees for 15 to 18 minutes, or until one sounds hollow when tapped. Remove from the pan, and cool on a wire rack. The crowns may be glazed while they are lukewarm, but not when they are hot. (The glaze will melt and drip off.)

For the glaze, mix together confectioners' sugar, vanilla, and just enough water to make a spreading consistency. Spoon or spread the glaze over the crown. If desired, decorate the top with colored sprinkles.

Makes 1 miniature crown.

Notes for Adults Working with a Group of Young Children

With a bit of advance planning, this can be an enjoyable, very successful project. Ahead of time, use a dark marker to draw a 3 by 6-inch rectangle on the center of a sheet of construction paper or cardboard, making one for each child. Cut heavy-duty plastic wrap into 12-inch pieces, making one for each child. To keep each finished crown separate and identifiable, cut disposable foil muffin tins into individual cups and use a permanent marking pen to put the name of each child on the outside of a cup. Measure out 2-ounce balls of dough, lightly flour each one, and place each in a sealed plastic sandwich bag (one per child). Chill (or freeze) the dough until using it so it won't rise too much. (Thaw frozen dough balls overnight in the refrigerator.)

Just before starting the project, open a few tubs of soft margarine, and put a few wooden tongue depressors or plastic knives in each one (for spreading). Put granulated brown sugar in several small bowls, and put each type of fill-

ing in its own bowl. Place a plastic spoon in each bowl. (Disposable bowls may be used for easy cleanup.) Open one or two small containers of cinnamon so that the sprinkle holes are visible. Spray the inside of each foil cup with nonstick cooking spray, and set aside. Put a little flour in a bowl in case any of the dough pieces become sticky.

Give each child a rectangle, a piece of plastic wrap, and a bag of dough. Instruct the children to place the plastic wrap on top of their rectangles. Tell them to remove the dough from the bag, and use their fingers to press out the dough on top of the wrap until it fills the rectangle that is visible through the plastic. Then have the children spread a small amount of very soft margarine over the dough, using a tongue depressor or plastic knife. Next, have them use a spoon to lightly sprinkle the dough with granulated brown sugar (it sprinkles easier than the regular kind). They can shake on a bit of cinnamon right from the container. Let them choose and add the other fillings that they want.

Assist the children in rolling up the dough as directed in the recipe and connecting the ends to form a circle. Have the children put their crowns into the labeled foil cups. Let the crowns rise; then bake as directed, and cool them to lukewarm in the foil cup on a rack. If desired, let each child spoon some icing on top of his or her crown, and decorate it. They can take them home in the foil cups, or eat them immediately. (The paper rectangles may be reused to repeat the project.)

Poppy Seed Yeast Cake

Once you have made the dough for Gloria's Glorious Challah (page 32), this beautiful yeast-dough cake is a cinch because it is filled with very tasty ready-to-use canned poppy seed filling. I simply remove a third of my Shabbat challah dough for the dessert cake, and use the remaining dough for a pair of smaller-than-usual challot. My family of poppy seed fans absolutely loves this cake, and insisted that I include it in this book.

This cake reminds me of the poppy-seed-laden yeast cakes that are sold at Jewish delicatessens and bakeries "by the pound." I first fell in love with such a cake many years ago at a Jewish restaurant-deli in Los Angeles and was delighted to figure out such an easy way to make it at home. My version has a very attractive woven ladder top.

NOTES: If desired, you can use the Rich Egg Challah variation (page 37) when you are planning to use some of the dough for this cake. The challah dough should have "rested" for 15 to 30 minutes and be ready to shape, as directed in the challah recipe, before it is used to make this cake.

The cake is glazed before baking to give it a shiny top. The three glaze suggestions are listed in order of the amount of browning they provide. Egg substitute produces the lightest color, while egg yolk results in a dark brown color.

DOUGH
1/3 of the kneaded dough for Gloria's Glorious Challah (page 32) (see Notes)

GLAZE
1/4 cup pareve egg substitute or 1 beaten egg or 1 egg yolk beaten with 1 teaspoon water (see Notes)

FILLING
1 (12 1/2-ounce or similar size) can pareve poppy seed filling for cakes and pastries

DRIZZLE ICING
1 recipe Drizzle Icing for the Pareve Pound Cake (page 89)

Line a large, heavy, flat shiny metal baking sheet with baking parchment, coat it with nonstick cooking spray or grease it. Press the dough into a rectangle in the middle of the baking sheet; then roll it out to a 9 by 14-inch rectangle of even thickness. (It may go past the edges of some baking sheets. The finished cake will be about 4 by 12 inches.)

Use the edge of a ruler to lightly mark the dough lengthwise into three sections that are each 3 inches wide and 14 inches long. Evenly spread all the poppy seed filling in the center section, keeping it 1 inch from each narrow end. Use a pastry wheel or sharp knife to cut each side section of the dough into 14 parallel 1-inch-wide and 3-inch-long strips that look like fringe coming out from the center section. Cut off and discard (or use for another purpose) the 1 by 3-inch strip on each corner, leaving 12 strips on each side of the dough.

A small piece of dough should now be jutting out from each short side of the poppy seed filling. Fold each piece of dough over the filling. Then, beginning at one narrow end and alternating from side to side, fold each strip of

fringe over the filling on a slight diagonal, so that opposite strips of fringe cross each other on top of the cake. When all the strips have been folded, the filling will be covered with a sort of woven ladder or lattice. The ends of the last few strips may hang off the cake; either cut them off or tuck them under the cake. Do not be concerned if some of the poppy seed filling is visible between the folded strips.

Brush the entire cake well with glaze, then let it rest in a warm place for 20 minutes. Meanwhile, preheat the oven to 350 degrees. Bake the cake at 350 degrees for about 25 to 30 minutes, or until the top is browned (see Notes) and sounds hollow when it is tapped lightly. Transfer the cake to a wire rack to cool to room temperature, and then top it with drizzle icing. If desired, the drizzle icing may be applied while the cake is lukewarm, though it may melt slightly.

To serve the cake, use a serrated knife to cut it crosswise into thick slices about 1 to 1½ inches wide.

Makes 8 to 12 servings.

Ja'alah
MIXED FRUIT AND NUTS

Before and after the Shabbat meal (and other festive meals), Yemenite Jews partake of this delicious mixture so they can say blessings thanking God for the fruit of the tree, the vine, the earth, and other foods.

Their main course on Shabbat is likely to be *shawayeh,* meat roasted on a grill and flavored with *hawayiz* (a seasoning mix of black pepper, caraway seeds, cardamom, and turmeric). The bread may be *lakhuah* (a very flat sourdough loaf made on a griddle like a pancake). Also likely to be included are *hilbuh* (a paste of fenugreek seeds, garlic, coriander leaves, and cumin), *zhoog* (a spicy-hot mixture of chili peppers, garlic, coriander, cumin, cardamom, and water), or a relish made by combining the two with tomatoes. Yemenite Jews claim that all these seasonings help prevent heart disease and gastrointestinal problems.

After such a spicy meal, one is sure to welcome the sweet mixture that follows. *Ja'alah* is also served to postpartum mothers to help them regain strength. Sometimes, soaked and toasted beans—such as chickpeas—are added to it.

Shelled roasted peanuts	*Raisins*
Whole shelled almonds	*Dried apricots or similar dried fruit*
Hulled sunflower seeds	*Assorted candy or candied fruit*

Mix the above in any proportions desired, and put the mixture in a bowl on the Shabbat table, perhaps with some fresh fruit.

The Days of Awe:

ROSH HASHANAH THROUGH YOM KIPPUR

 "L'SHANAH TOVAH!" "TO A GOOD YEAR!" DURING THE "DAYS of Awe" (*Yamim Nora'im* in Hebrew), from Rosh Hashanah through Yom Kippur, this optimistic greeting is exchanged frequently by Jews all around the world. According to traditional Judaism, divine judgment on each person's life is made and rendered during this time. The ten days that begin with Rosh Hashanah and end with Yom Kippur are also called the "Ten Days of Repentance" (*Aseret Yemay Teshuvah*).

Rosh Hashanah (literally, "head of the year"), is the Jewish religious "New Year." It takes place on the first and second days of the Hebrew month of Tishri, which usually occur in September or early October. *Yom Kippur* ("Day of Atonement"), is on the tenth of Tishri.

As Tishri is the seventh month of the Hebrew calendar, Rosh Hashanah is not a "new year" in the simple secular sense. In fact, the Torah refers to the holiday as *Yom Teruah* ("Day of Shofar Sounding") and *Yom Ha'Zikaron* ("Day of Remembering"). Rather, it is the time each year when Jews consider anew their obligations to God and to other people. The Talmud actually discusses four different "new years" on the Hebrew calendar, and notes that Rosh Hashanah is the New Year for "years," marking the anniversary of creation. Thus the *years* on a Hebrew calendar (though not the months) are counted from each Rosh Hashanah to the next.

Various Jewish communities celebrate the "High Holy Days" (as they are sometimes called in the English vernacular) in many similar ways. During services for Rosh Hashanah, the *shofar* (ram's horn) is sounded while those in the congregation reflect on the past and on their hopes for a bright future.

On Yom Kippur, practically the entire holiday is spent in solemn prayer at the synagogue, as each Jew attempts to atone for sins of the past year and prepare for the upcoming year. In addition to not eating and drinking, Jews must also abstain from certain other activities that are considered to be personally pleasurable.

The meals of Rosh Hashanah and those before and after the fast of Yom Kippur are times for feasting, and there are many culinary customs associated with them. One of the oldest and most widespread is the eating of sweet foods, particularly honey, to symbolize a universal hope that our lives will be sweet in the coming year.

Both Ashkenazic and Sephardic Jews dip apples and challah into honey. Dried fruit, sugar, and honey are used to sweeten many dishes, including main courses and vegetables. And, of course, several types of honey-laden desserts are favored for the Days of Awe. The challah also may be honey-sweetened, and is usually formed into a spiraling round loaf. (See the recipe on page 103 for more details.)

Fish is often on the holiday table as a symbol of fertility and immortality. Among Sephardic Jews, a whole fish may be served with its head intact as a reminder that we should strive to be at the "head" of our peers, and an example of righteousness to all. With this same idea in mind, it was the custom for some Italian Jews to eat ravioli filled with calves' brains, and for Moroccans to cook the brains into fritters. Greeks have preferred savory pastries filled with hard-boiled eggs and brains. Jews from several different cultures have partaken of calves' or lambs' tongue in a variety of sauces. Yemenites and Afghans have even served a whole sheep's head, highly seasoned with fenugreek, which also recalls the ram sacrificed by Abraham in place of his son.

Many Sephardim (and some Ashkenazim) perform a special ceremony during the main meals of Rosh Hashanah in which they say prayers of hope over seven specified foods. The number seven is considered lucky (or even holy, by some) because, among other reasons, Shabbat takes place on the seventh day of each week, and Rosh Hashanah occurs on the first day of the seventh month.

Seasonal vegetables that are plentiful and grow rapidly are always featured, because they are considered symbols of abundance. Leeks are also sometimes eaten for luck, and large winter squash express the hope that the participants may "grow in fullness of blessing."

Some foods are included because their Hebrew names are puns on words in holiday prayers. For instance, the Hebrew word for "leek" sounds like the one meaning "to cut off our enemies," and the word for "dates" sounds like part of the blessing in which we ask for our enemies to be eliminated. Dates are also eaten because they are sweet, and because some consider them symbols of beauty and peace.

Both Ashkenazim and Sephardim eat other foods, such as sweetened carrots and beets, for similar reasons. Details are included with the holiday recipes for these foods in this chapter.

On the second night of Rosh Hashanah, at least one "new" fruit—that is, a fruit not yet sampled that season—is usually eaten. Unlike other Jewish holidays, the two days of Rosh Hashanah are considered to be one extended day (thus *both* days are celebrated in Israel and the Diaspora). Therefore, the *sheheheyanu* prayer for new experiences, in which we thank God for allowing us to reach this important moment of life in peace and health, might be "wasted" if it were repeated on the second evening without the "experience" of enjoying something "new."

In many Jewish households, this fruit is either grapes or a pomegranate, two favorites of both ancient and modern-day Israel. The exotic and succulent pomegranate also represents the hope that we will be privileged in the coming year to perform as many worthy deeds and pious acts as the pomegranate is replete with seeds.

Shortly before Rosh Hashanah, plump red pomegranates usually become plentiful in Jewish markets both here and abroad. Each year, my children look forward to a specially chosen, leathery-skinned pomegranate that we display on our holiday table, and then cut open to share as part of our dessert on the second night of Rosh Hashanah. On a trip to Israel several years ago, we were delighted to actually find a pomegranate tree growing right in front of our kibbutz guesthouse.

The abundant seeds of the pomegranate, with their potential for new growth, also symbolize fertility and fruitfulness, as do sesame seeds and many other types of edible seeds enjoyed on Rosh Hashanah. Yemenites, for example, always eat a sauce made of fenugreek seeds, and many Moroccans dip dates in aniseeds and/or sesame seeds.

Although the vast majority of culinary customs associated with this holiday are positive, optimistic ones, there are a few in which certain foods are deliberately avoided. For instance, sour and bitter foods usually are not eaten (unless combined in a sweet-sour sauce that is predominantly sweet), and some Jews avoid black-colored food, such as black olives and eggplant, as well. Iraqi Jews may not eat fish on Rosh Hashanah because the Hebrew word for "fish" (*dag*) is very similar to the word for "worry" (*da'ag*). And

certain Ashkenazic Jews avoid nuts because the total numerical value of the letters in the Hebrew word for "nut" is quite close to that of the word for "sin."

As mentioned earlier, the ceremonial challah is dipped in honey—not salt as during the rest of the year. In fact, in some homes, all the salt on the holiday table is replaced with sugar.

Most of the culinary traditions are followed throughout the Days of Awe. However, there are a few special ones for the meals that immediately precede and follow the twenty-five-hour Yom Kippur fast. It's actually considered a *mitzvah*—a religious obligation—to feast on the day before Yom Kippur. When we fast, we are supposed to feel hunger pangs, to be acutely aware of how difficult it is to atone for our sins. This is all the more obvious if we have dined well beforehand. Thus, in biblical times, Jews sometimes held great banquets prior to fasting.

More recently, it has become very traditional for Jews worldwide to partake of chicken soup at the prefast dinner. Boiled chicken—like all the foods usually eaten at this meal—is bland and easily digested, thus preventing undue thirst and indigestion during the long hours of prayer in the coming day. Ashkenazic Jews usually serve *kreplach* (meat-filled dumplings) in the soup.

For the festive meal following Yom Kippur—the "break-fast," as it is often called—Ashkenazim typically enjoy a light, dairy meal, which invariably includes pickled and/or smoked fish. The latter custom apparently came about because such fish supposedly helps to restore the salts and minerals lost from the body during fasting. Many of the dairy dishes at this meal, such as sweet *lokshen kugel* and cheese *blintzes,* are the same as those served during the holiday of Shavuot (see that chapter).

Italian Jews often break their fast with fried doughnuts coated with sugar. The round shape, like that of the round challah eaten during Days of Awe, symbolizes hope for a well-rounded year, as well as good luck the whole year round. Since the doughnuts actually have a "double round" form, they additionally symbolize a hope for happiness all around the world. Similarly, Syrian Jews eat Ka'ak (page 160), doughnut-shaped snacks that are coated with sesame seeds.

Some Moroccan Jews and also those from the island of Curaçao in the Netherlands Antilles break the fast by drinking coffee topped with a fluffy mixture of beaten egg yolks and sugar. Iraqi Jews prefer to sip *hariri,* a sweet nondairy "milk" made from almonds.

At the postfast meal, Moroccan and other North African Jews often partake of a hearty meat, bean, and vegetable soup called *harirah*—a custom adapted from local

Arabs, who eat the soup to break the Muslim fast of Ramadan. Also enjoyed is Djaja M'kalli (page 131), a marvelous dish of chicken cooked with green olives and pickled lemons. And Greek and Turkish Jews are fond of eating a very light lemon-flavored chicken soup called Avgolemono (page 108), which usually is preceded by a sweet drink made of melon seeds, called *pepitada*.

It is also customary for Jews of all cultural backgrounds to break their fasts with many of the same sweet, spicy cakes and cookies that are traditional for Rosh Hashanah. Recipes for several of these, as well as many other symbolic holiday dishes, are included in this chapter. In addition, the chapter on Hanukkah and the chapter on Shavuot contain several dairy casseroles and other dishes that would be quite appropriate for an Ashkenazic "break-fast."

"Yom Tov" Spiral Challah

HOLIDAY EGG BREAD

Two beautiful loaves of challah are customary at almost every Jewish holiday meal. For the Days of Awe, many Jews all over the world form a sweet challah into a round shape instead of the usual straight braid. The roundness symbolizes a universal wish for a well-rounded and full year, abundant in peace, happiness, and prosperity. And the round loaves typically spiral upward in the center, to show that we want our prayers to ascend to heaven.

More elaborate breads may be shaped into ladders or birds for the same reason. Occasionally, the dough is braided into a long, narrow strip, and the ends looped together to make a circular loaf. Or the dough may be formed into a ball that is crowned with a small braid, ladder, or bird.

During the Days of Awe, when the blessing for the bread is said, it is dipped into honey (not salt, as usual), in hope of a sweet year to come. Similarly, extra sugar and honey, as well as raisins, are often mixed into a rich dough, giving the challah a cakelike taste and texture. Light raisins are often used in keeping with the white "purity" of the holiday, and because some prefer to avoid "black" foods.

Sephardic Jews, particularly those from the Mediterranean area, may add aniseeds and/or sesame seeds for flavor and because they represent fruitfulness. Italian Jews some-

times use a combination of fruity olive oil and aniseeds to produce a loaf with a deliciously exotic flavor. Unlike the Shabbat braid, seeds are used only *inside* the round loaf and are generally not sprinkled on the smooth exterior of the brilliantly glazed spiral.

The following is an amalgam of sweet egg bread recipes from both Ashkenazic and Sephardic cultures. It is traditionally eaten throughout the Days of Awe and also during Sukkot, when God's final decree is said to be "sealed."

This recipe differs from the one in the original edition of this book in that it calls for fast-acting "quick" yeast. Like many other cooks, my time in the kitchen has become limited, yet I always make homemade challah for holidays. This faster version has received raves from family and friends. (For more details, see the comments with Gloria's Glorious Challah on page 32.)

Also, I found it very frustrating that my spiral challot would often tip to one side as they baked, so I tried a number of different ways of shaping the dough. None worked that well, although using high-gluten bread flour certainly helped. Then, one day, after forgetting to mix the raisins into the dough as usual, I put them into the challah using a cinnamon bun technique. I was delighted to discover that my emergency trick made the most beautiful spiral challah ever. It also distributed the raisins very well, with none poking out of the loaf and burning. Now, I always use this technique, even without raisins! See the directions for details.

NOTES: This recipe makes two spiral loaves. I usually put raisins in one and keep one plain, to satisfy every taste at my table. If desired, this dough may be shaped into two or three braided loaves following the directions in the Shabbat chapter.

If you do not have two ovens or one very large oven, put one formed spiral loaf in the refrigerator, while the other rises. When the first loaf is baking, remove the second from the refrigerator, and let it finish rising at room temperature. It should be ready for baking when the first loaf is done. Before putting it into the oven, turn off the oven and open the door, so that it can cool somewhat. It does not have to be "cold," as the slightly chilled loaf will take longer to "warm up" when it is baking than did the first loaf.

About 6½ to 7½ cups white bread flour or high-gluten unbleached flour or a mixture

2 tablespoons (2½ packets) fast-acting dry yeast (see the Glossary of Ingredients).

⅓ cup sugar

2 teaspoons salt

1 tablespoon each aniseeds and sesame seeds (or 2 tablespoons of either one) (optional)

4 large or extra-large eggs or 1 cup pareve egg substitute, divided

¼ cup canola oil

¼ cup extra-virgin olive oil or additional canola oil

⅓ cup honey

1½ cups hot (120 to 130 degrees) tap water (no hotter than this or it may kill the yeast)

½ to 1 cup light or dark raisins (optional)

MIXER METHOD

In the large (about 5-quart) bowl of a heavy-duty electric mixer that has a dough-kneading hook, put about 5 cups of the bread flour, yeast, sugar, salt, and seeds. Mix the dry ingredients by holding the hook in your hand and using it to stir (this saves washing another utensil). Add 3 eggs (or ¾ cup egg substitute) and the oil and honey (use an oiled measuring cup for the honey and it will slide right out) to the flour mixture, and stir in with the hook. It is not necessary to mix well. Finally, add the hot water and stir in.

Set the bowl into the mixer, and attach the dough hook. Turn the mixer to kneading speed. If the dough is very wet and soft, add about ½ cup flour or enough so that the dough begins to gather around the hook. As the dough kneads, lightly sprinkle just enough flour around the inside surface of the bowl so that the dough stays on the hook and does not come down off the hook into the bottom of the bowl. You will probably need to use more flour in the beginning, and less as the dough kneads. Let the dough knead for about 5 to 10 minutes, or until it is very smooth. When it is almost done kneading, it should need very little or no more flour and should almost clean the inner surface of the bowl.

NOTE: If the dough rides over the top of the hook, scrape it down and add more flour. This may happen if the bowl is too small for the recipe. Consider reducing the recipe by one-third in the future.

Remove the dough hook from the dough, but leave the dough in the mixer bowl. Cover the bowl with a plastic lid or a piece of plastic wrap so the dough does not dry out, and let it rest for 20 minutes. It will probably not rise very much.

The Days of Awe: Rosh Hashanah Through Yom Kippur

HAND METHOD

In a large bowl, combine 4 cups of the bread flour, yeast, sugar, and salt, and mix to combine using a sturdy mixing spoon (such as a wooden one). Add 3 eggs (or ¾ cup egg substitute) and the oil and honey (use an oiled measuring cup for the honey and it will slide right out) to the flour mixture, and stir in lightly. Finally, add the hot water, and stir it in very well.

NOTE: A strong electric stand mixer with standard beaters may be used for mixing to this point, but the rest must be done by hand if there is no dough hook.

Stir in about 1½ cups more flour, and mix to make a soft, sticky dough. Let the dough rest, covered, for about 5 minutes to allow the flour to absorb some moisture (so that less flour will be required during kneading).

Turn out the dough onto a well-floured surface (board, countertop, etc.), and knead, adding small sprinkles of flour as needed to keep the dough from sticking to your hands or the surface. Try to keep your hands free of sticky dough, as this will make even more dough stick. To "clean" your hands, sprinkle them lightly with flour and rub them together.

Knead for about 10 to 15 minutes, or until the dough is very smooth and silky, and is no longer sticky. To keep the dough from drying out, put it into an ungreased covered bowl, or turn a bowl over the dough on the kneading surface, or cover the dough with plastic. Let it rest for 20 minutes. It will probably not rise very much.

BOTH METHODS

While the dough is resting, prepare the baking sheets. Use large, heavy, flat, shiny aluminum baking sheets (cookie sheets) and coat them with non-stick cooking spray or top them with special parchment paper used for baking.

NOTE: I prefer to use 13 by 16-inch insulated-style baking sheets lined with parchment. If your baking sheets are not this type, use two stacked together to produce a more evenly baked loaf that does not brown too quickly on the bottom.

To easily remove the dough from a bowl, sprinkle a little extra flour over the dough, and use a spatula to push the flour all the way down the sides of the bowl while completely loosening the dough at the same time. Turn out the dough onto a lightly floured board, and press it gently into a rough mound of even thickness. Cut the dough in half. Shape each half into a spiral loaf adding raisins, if desired, as directed below. Be careful not to stretch or tear the dough as you shape it, or the surface of the loaf may develop holes when it rises and bakes.

For a Spiral

With very lightly floured hands, gently squeeze the dough into a snake of even thickness that is about 36 inches long. Place the snake horizontally on a lightly floured countertop or other surface. Use your fingertips to press the snake very flat, making a rectangle that is about 4 inches wide and 36 inches long. If using raisins, press about ½ cup of them into the top of the dough, arranging them so that none are touching and the whole surface is covered.

Beginning with the long edge closest to you, tightly roll up the dough like a very long jelly roll, forming a neat log (and enclosing the raisins, if they are used). Pinch the remaining long edge of the dough tightly against the log so that it cannot unroll, and pinch both ends of the log closed. Gently roll the log on a floured surface to smooth down the pinched long edge and to coat the log completely with flour. Brush off any excess flour.

With your hand, raise one end of the log so it points upward. Fold it over about 2 inches so the rough end of the log will not show at the top of the loaf, but still keep this end slightly raised so it will be the highest part of the loaf. Use your other hand to neatly wind the rest of the log around the bent end in a spiral fashion, keeping the seam side down. Tuck the final end neatly under the bottom of the round loaf, and pinch it against the loaf so that the spiral cannot unravel. Carefully transfer the loaf to the center of a prepared baking sheet.

Repeat with the second half of the dough to form another round loaf. These are large challot, and each must be placed on its own baking sheet. As soon as the loaves are shaped, brush them heavily with egg glaze. For the glaze, beat the remaining egg with a teaspoon of water until the egg is barely frothy. Or use the remaining ¼ cup egg substitute directly from the carton.

Let the loaves rise at room temperature until they are almost, but not quite, double. Put each loaf on the middle rack of a cold oven. (See the Notes if you have only one oven that cannot fit both loaves at the same time. I use

two ovens.) Raise the heat to 350 degrees. Bake for 45 to 50 minutes, or until the loaves sound hollow when tapped on the bottom, or when an instant-read thermometer inserted into the bottom of the loaf reads 190 to 205 degrees. Immediately remove the loaves from the baking sheets, and cool them completely on wire racks.

Makes 2 large loaves, about 1¾ pounds each.

Avgolemono or Sopa de Huevo y Limon
EGG-LEMON SOUP

Whether they call it by its Greek or Judeo-Spanish name, Sephardic Jews, particularly those with Turkish or Greek backgrounds, often break the Yom Kippur fast with this light, elegant soup. It is very quick and easy to prepare, and is a great way to perk up leftover homemade chicken broth or good-quality canned broth.

6 cups strained chicken broth, seasoned
    to taste with salt and pepper
Dillweed to taste (optional)
½ cup uncooked medium-grain or long-
    grain white rice

3 large eggs (no substitutes)
2 to 4 tablespoons lemon juice, or to
    taste

Put the broth into a 3- to 4-quart saucepan, and bring it to a simmer over medium-high heat, adding dillweed if desired. Add the rice and gently simmer, covered, for about 20 minutes, or just until the rice is tender. Adjust the heat so that the broth stays quite hot but does not boil at all.

In a medium bowl, beat the eggs with a wire whisk or fork until they are light; then beat in the lemon juice. Slowly add about ¾ cup of the hot broth to the egg-lemon mixture while constantly stirring. Gradually add this mixture back to the broth remaining in the pan, stirring constantly. Continue stirring and heating for about 2 minutes longer, or until the soup thickens slightly and the eggs are cooked. Do not boil the soup, or the eggs will curdle.

Makes 4 to 6 servings.

Mandlen

SOUP "NUTS"

Though the Yiddish name of this soup garnish translates literally to "almonds," nuts are not among the ingredients. It's just that the little nuggets of pastry are said to resemble them. I think they look more like tiny, puffed-up pillows. Some say they are popular for Rosh Hashanah because the "round" shape has the same symbolism as a round Spiral Challah (see page 103).

More than almost any other Jewish food, the taste of mandlen in My Mother's Incredible Chicken Soup (page 41) warms me with a flood of wonderful gustatory memories from my youth. When I was a child, my mother always made mandlen for Rosh Hashanah and many other holidays including Shabbat. My sisters and I considered them to be the most delectable treats. In fact, Mom's biggest problem was keeping enough mandlen around until dinnertime because my sisters and I would sneak into the kitchen and snitch a few whenever she wasn't looking.

My mother always deep-fried the tiny pieces of dough, but I prefer to bake them because it is quicker and easier. Furthermore, baked mandlen are decidedly lower in fat, yet still quite tasty. Fried mandlen may be somewhat lighter and more delicate than baked ones, but my own children are just as quick to snitch my baked ones as I used to be with my mom's. The same dough can be used for either method.

2 large eggs or ½ cup pareve egg
    substitute
1 tablespoon canola oil
½ teaspoon salt
½ teaspoon baking powder (optional;
    omit with fried mandlen)

About 1¼ cups unbleached flour
Canola oil, if you will be frying and not
    baking the mandlen

Use a fork to beat the eggs or egg substitute with 1 tablespoon oil in a medium bowl. Add the salt, baking powder (if used), and about 1 cup of the flour, and mix well. Add just enough additional flour so the dough is not sticky when handled. Knead gently in the bowl for a few minutes to smooth out the dough, adding bits of flour as needed. If you will be baking the mandlen, preheat the oven to 375 degrees.

Divide the dough into six to eight pieces. On a lightly floured plastic or wooden cutting board, use your hand to roll each piece of dough into a rope

The Days of Awe: Rosh Hashanah Through Yom Kippur

that is ⅜ to ½ inch thick. (If there is not enough flour on the board, the dough will stick to your hands and the board; if there is too much flour, the dough will slide and not roll out properly to thin ropes.) Very lightly coat each rope with flour and cut it into ½-inch-long "nuggets," using a sharp knife. If the knife sticks to the dough, flour it occasionally. The nuggets may be either baked or fried, as follows:

BAKING METHOD

Place the nuggets, one at a time, on a large nonstick-spray-coated or well-greased large jelly roll pan or other shallow baking pan. The nuggets should be in one layer and not touching each other. All the nuggets will fit on one jelly roll pan. Bake them at 375 degrees for 20 to 25 minutes, or until they are lightly browned and quite firm. (Shake the pan occasionally, so that the mandlen move around and bake evenly.) Remove the pan from the oven, and place it on a wire rack to let the mandlen cool to room temperature before storing them.

FRYING METHOD

Toss all the cut dough nuggets with just enough flour so that they do not stick together. Put enough oil into a saucepan so that it is about 1½ inches deep. Heat the oil until it is very hot, about 375 degrees. Gently drop a handful of the nuggets into the oil so they are not too crowded. Fry them until they are slightly puffed and golden on all sides. Remove the mandlen with a slotted spoon, and drain them on paper towels. Repeat until all the dough nuggets have been fried. Cool them to room temperature before storing.

Store all mandlen in an airtight container (hidden from the children!).

Makes about 80 to 90 mandlen, about 2½ cups.

Homemade Noodle Farfel

Egg Barley

For the same reason that we have round challah during the Days of Awe—our desire to have a well-rounded, fulfilled year—Hasidic Jews often eat "round" (barley-shaped) farfel in soup. Also, there is a play on the word "farfel"; it represents a hope that any misdeeds of the past year will "fall" away in the future.

These tiny noodle dumplings, which are not as "round" as store-bought, are very tasty and surprisingly easy to prepare. Serve them with soup or stew.

2 cups unbleached flour　　　　　*2 large eggs (no substitutes)*
½ teaspoon salt

Combine the flour and salt in a medium bowl, and make a well in the center. Break the eggs into the well, and beat them with a fork. Gradually beat in the flour from around the edges of the well until the dough is too stiff to use a fork. Then work the flour in with your hands until a very stiff dough is formed. Roll the dough into a thick log about 1-inch wide; then let it air-dry for at least 1 hour, or until it is stiff enough to grate.

Rub the dough across a coarse grater to form pieces the size of barley. Or finely chop the dough using a food processor fitted with a steel blade. (First cut the dough into chunks, coat them with flour, and let them dry for a short time. Pulse-process just until the dough is finely chopped.) If the farfel is at all sticky, toss it with a bit more flour. Then spread it on a dish towel to dry until you are ready to cook it.

Cook the farfel in salted boiling water or soup for about 10 minutes, or until it is tender.

Makes about 8 servings.

Meat Kreplach

TRIANGULAR NOODLE DUMPLINGS

It is very traditional for Ashkenazic Jews to include kreplach in the chicken soup at the prefast Yom Kippur meal. According to one interpretation of this custom, the meat covered with dough symbolizes our hope that on the Day of Atonement, God's strict justice will be "covered" with compassion and mercy.

Kreplach are eaten also on *Hoshanah Rabbah* (the seventh day of Succot) and Purim. Some say that we eat kreplach on the three holidays in which someone or something is "beaten," because the meat inside the kreplach is prepared by chopping, which is sort of like beating. On the day before Yom Kippur, men may be symbolically flogged while they ask forgiveness for their sins; on Hoshanah Rabbah, willow branches are beaten; and during the reading of the *Megillah* on Purim, we stamp or beat our feet against the floor whenever the name of the wicked Haman is said.

Be that as it may, tasty kreplach (Jewish wontons?) were a good way to use up leftover cooked meat. In fact, when I was growing up, my mother always made the filling from extra pieces of roast beef and steak that she had saved in the freezer. When she collected enough for a batch of kreplach, she thawed the cooked meat, ground it in a meat grinder, and added the remaining filling ingredients.

In this age of cutting down on red meat, I rarely serve roast beef or steak and don't often have leftovers. That's why I worked out a technique to use fresh ground beef for the filling, as in the recipe below. I make them every year for the meal before Yom Kippur because my family loves them so. This recipe makes plenty for the rest of the Days of Awe.

I use a large food processor and hand-cranked chrome pasta machine (the type that looks like a wringer washing machine) to make this recipe especially easy and fun. However, it can be made without these conveniences. Read it completely through before beginning. It has been significantly improved since the original version appeared in the first edition of this book.

FILLING
¾ pound lean ground beef
1 small onion, finely chopped
1 garlic clove, minced (optional)

1 large egg, lightly beaten or ¼ cup
pareve egg substitute
Salt and ground black pepper to taste

DOUGH

3 cups unbleached flour

¾ teaspoon salt

3 large eggs (no substitutes)

About 3 to 5 tablespoons water

For the filling, put the ground beef, onion, and garlic (if used) into a large skillet over medium-high heat. Cook the meat, pressing it often with a potato masher or fork to keep the pieces as small as possible. When the meat is completely cooked through, drain off all excess fat. Continue cooking the meat until any remaining moisture has evaporated. Set the meat aside to cool.

The dough may be made in a food processor or by hand. When a food processor is used, it kneads the dough in less than a minute.

NOTE: With a small food processor, you may need to divide the recipe in half and process it in two batches.

For the food processor, combine the flour and salt in the bowl fitted with a steel blade. Pulse-process a few times. Add the eggs and pulse-process a few more times until crumbly. With the machine running, add the water through the tube, using just enough water so that the dough forms a ball. (If too much water is added, the dough will become sticky. Add a bit more flour, and process a few seconds longer.) Continue processing about 30 seconds longer to knead the dough. It should be very smooth.

To make the dough by hand, put the flour and salt into a medium bowl. Make a well in the center of the flour. Add the eggs and the smaller amount of water to the well, and beat them with a fork. Gradually beat the flour into the egg mixture to form a stiff dough. If the dough is dry and crumbly, add water; if it is wet and sticky, add flour. Knead the dough in the bowl or on a board for about 5 to 8 minutes, or until it is very smooth and silky.

Wrap the dough well in plastic wrap so it does not dry out, and let it rest at room temperature for 20 minutes to 1 hour to relax the gluten and make it easier to roll out.

While the dough is resting, complete the meat filling. For a traditional, fine-textured filling, finely mince the cooked meat mixture in a food processor or put it through a meat grinder. Stir in the egg, salt, and pepper (or add to the processor and pulse-process a few times). The filling should hold to-

The Days of Awe: Rosh Hashanah Through Yom Kippur

gether when put into a teaspoon, and not crumble apart. If necessary, stir a few extra teaspoons of beaten egg into the filling.

To roll out the dough by hand, divide it into three pieces, and rewrap the pieces not being used so they do not dry out. On a lightly floured board, roll out the first piece of dough to a very thin 9 by 12-inch rectangle that is as neat as possible. Make sure the bottom of the dough is floured and not sticking to the board. Let the dough rest a few minutes so it does not shrink a lot when cut. Cut the dough into twelve 3-inch squares using a pastry wheel or a sharp knife. Have a small bowl of water handy. Put a generous teaspoon of filling on each square. Use your finger to rub a little water along two perpendicular edges of a square. (This will help glue the folded kreplach closed.) Fold over the dough on the diagonal to form a triangle, so that the two wet edges meet the two dry edges. (Do not wet all four edges, or the dough won't stick together.) Press the top and bottom edges together with your fingers; then press on the edges with the tines of a fork to tightly seal them closed. Place the kreplach on a lightly floured surface. Repeat until all the kreplach are formed, using the remaining pieces of dough. If you have a little extra dough or filling, don't worry about it. You'll still have plenty of kreplach!

To roll out the dough using an Italian pasta machine with rollers, divide the dough into four pieces. Shape one piece of dough into a log and flatten the log. (Keep the remaining dough wrapped.) Flour the dough, then put it through the widest roller setting, narrow end first. Flour the dough again and repeat, using the same setting. Raise the setting one notch (i.e., make the rollers a bit closer together), and roll the strip of dough through twice, using tiny bits of flour if necessary to prevent sticking. The dough should be getting much longer and a bit wider. Repeat for one or two more settings, until the dough is thin but still has body and is about 2½ to 3 inches wide (I finish on #3 on my machine). Flour the bottom of the dough "ribbon" so it doesn't stick to a board, and cut it crosswise into about nine squares. Fill as directed above. Repeat for the remaining dough pieces.

NOTE: If desired, the kreplach may be frozen at this point. Freeze them in a single layer, uncovered, on a baking sheet; then place them into a sealed plastic bag for storage. Do not thaw them before cooking; just cook them for about 5 minutes longer, or just until they are done.

To cook the kreplach, gently drop one-third to one-half of them into a large pot of lightly salted boiling water, and simmer them for 5 to 10 minutes, or until they are just tender but not at all mushy. (They will increase greatly in size as they cook.) Remove them from the water with a slotted spoon. Repeat with the remaining kreplach. Store them in a covered bowl. They should not stick together after they have been cooked.

To serve the kreplach, reheat them in hot chicken soup. (Or, if desired, drain the kreplach very well; then fry them in a small amount of hot oil, margarine, or rendered chicken fat until they are golden on both sides. Then serve them hot as hors d'oeuvres or a side dish.)

Makes about 36 large kreplach.

Fried Gefilte Fish, British-Style

When I asked Pauline Rubens Saville, a native of Birmingham, England, and a long-time resident of South Wales, for a typical British-Jewish recipe, she wasn't sure how to respond. Having an Ashkenazic background similar to my own, she assumed that both of us prepared traditional foods in the same manner. But when we compared recipes, I was surprised to learn that she—and, indeed, most British Jews—prefer their gefilte fish fried, not poached, as do Americans.

In fact, Mrs. Saville told me that poached gefilte fish is usually eaten only when fried fish might be too heavy, such as to break the fast on Yom Kippur, or by people who are ill. She was indeed quite astonished to find out that American Jews actually favor it.

Another difference is that Mrs. Saville's recipe calls for cod combined with either haddock or hake in the minced fish mixture, rather than carp and pike. She explained that the British combination is more subtle-tasting and lighter in texture and color than its American–East European counterpart. (White gefilte fish is also in keeping with the "purity" of the Days of Awe.)

The following tasty gefilte fish mixture is actually quite versatile. It can be made with any combination of cod, haddock, and/or hake, and in any proportions desired, depending on the fish that is available. Sometimes, British-Jewish cooks add a bit of ground almonds to the mixture, particularly if it seems to be rather wet. They shape the

mixture into large patties for meals, or small balls for hors d'oeuvres (see Note). They may coat the patties or balls with seasoned matzah meal or just leave them "bare." No matter how it's prepared, the fried gefilte fish is always served with plenty of grated horseradish, or *chrain* (with a guttural "ch,") in Yiddish.

NOTE: For gefilte fish hors d'oeuvres, form the fish mixture into 1-inch balls. If desired, coat them with matzah meal. To preserve their round shape, deep-fry the balls in hot oil. Drain them on paper towels. Serve them chilled, on toothpicks.

FISH MIXTURE
1½ pounds skinless fillets of cod
½ pound skinless haddock or hake (steakfish) fillets
2 medium onions, peeled and cut into eighths
2 large eggs or ½ cup pareve egg substitute
1 tablespoon canola oil
1½ teaspoons sugar
1 teaspoon salt
⅛ teaspoon ground white pepper
1 to 2 tablespoons finely ground almonds (optional)

About 4 to 6 tablespoons matzah meal
Vegetable oil for frying

COATING (OPTIONAL)
½ cup matzah meal
1 tablespoon all-purpose flour, preferably unbleached (or very fine matzah cake meal)
Salt and ground white or black pepper to taste

TO SERVE (OPTIONAL)
Prepared horseradish condiment, preferably the "red" type with beets

Cut the fish into pieces, and finely grind it in a food processor fitted with a steel blade, or with a food grinder. Grind the onions in the same manner, and add them to the fish. Mix in the eggs, 1 tablespoon oil, sugar, salt, and pepper. Add the ground almonds (if used), and just enough matzah meal so that the fish mixture can be easily handled and is not sticky. Form the fish mixture into plump patties, using about ¼ cup to ⅓ cup of the mixture for each one.

If a coating is desired, put the coating ingredients into a large plastic bag, close the top, and shake until mixed. To coat each patty, put it into the bag, close the bag, and shake gently until the patty is lightly coated.

To fry coated or uncoated patties, heat oil that is about ⅛ to ¼ inch deep in a large skillet over medium-high heat. Fry the patties until they are browned

on both sides. Drain them on paper towels. Refrigerate the patties until serving time, and serve them chilled, with horseradish if desired.

Makes 16 to 20 patties; about 8 servings as a first course.

Pesce all'Ebraica
ITALIAN-STYLE SWEET-AND-SOUR FISH

The Italian name of this interesting dish means "Jewish-style fish." The combination of raisins and pine nuts is quite popular among Italian Jews, who traditionally serve this dish for Rosh Hashanah and to break the Yom Kippur fast.

Small whole fish are fried, and then gently simmered in a delicate sweet-and-sour sauce. The head of each fish is left intact, in keeping with holiday custom. For a baked version that uses fillets instead of whole fish, see the variation below.

About 6 whole small dressed fish, such as rainbow trout
All-purpose flour
Canola oil or light olive oil, for frying
⅓ cup water
1 to 2 tablespoons honey
3 tablespoons red wine vinegar or lemon juice

2 tablespoons extra-virgin olive oil
⅓ cup light or dark raisins
2 to 4 tablespoons pine nuts (pignoli) or slivered almonds, preferably lightly toasted
1 teaspoon dried mint leaves or 1 tablespoon chopped fresh spearmint leaves

Lightly dredge the fish in the flour. Put oil that is ⅛ to ¼ inch deep into a very large skillet over medium-high heat. Fry the dredged fish in the hot oil, in batches if necessary, until they are golden brown on both sides. Remove the fish from the skillet, and drain them on paper toweling. Discard any oil remaining in the skillet.

Add to the skillet the water, honey, vinegar, 2 tablespoons olive oil, raisins, pine nuts, and mint leaves. Bring the mixture to a simmer and cook, stirring, for 1 to 2 minutes to blend the flavors. Return the fish to the skillet, and spoon the sauce over it. Simmer the fish, basting often, about 5 minutes longer.

Makes about 6 servings as a first course.

The Days of Awe: Rosh Hashanah Through Yom Kippur

Variation

BAKED PESCA ALL'EBRAICA

For this version, substitute 1¼ pounds skinless fillets of firm, white-fleshed fish, such as flounder, perch, haddock, or cod for the whole fish. Omit the dredging with flour and frying in oil. Preheat the oven to 400 degrees. Put the fillets, in one layer, in a greased or nonstick spray-coated baking dish. Decrease the water to 1 tablespoon (baked fillets usually give off plenty of liquid). Combine the water, honey, vinegar, and 2 tablespoons olive oil, and mix very well. Pour the mixture evenly over the fillets. Sprinkle the raisins and nuts over the fish. Bake the fish, uncovered, at 400 degrees for about 10 to 15 minutes, or until it is cooked through but not falling apart. Baste it once or twice during the cooking period. Serve hot or lukewarm.

Makes about 6 servings as a first course.

Quick Chopped Herring

The spread known as "chopped herring" is very popular among Ashkenazic Jews, and has always been one of my own personal favorites. I can still remember watching my maternal grandmother, Lillian Levine Kaplan, prepare it years ago when I was a young child. In those days, "Mama Lil" (as she was affectionately known by her grandchildren and great-grandchildren) would purchase a special selection of whole pickled herrings, which she boned and put through a hand-operated grinder along with onions and other ingredients. The process took over her whole kitchen.

I personally thought that this smelled wonderful, but not everyone agreed. And as Mama Lil's kitchen was in an apartment located at the back of my grandparents' furniture store, it wasn't always good for business!

Very few people make chopped herring from scratch any longer. Most buy it at the delicatessen or supermarket. However, with a food processor, the following "modernized" version can be prepared in seconds. And it tastes great.

2 slices toasted rye or whole wheat
    bread, torn into pieces
1 16-ounce jar (or 2 8-ounce jars)
    herring fillets in wine sauce
2 hard-boiled eggs, shelled and
    quartered
2 large apples, peeled, cored, and cut
    into eighths

2 tablespoons sweet red wine (optional)

TO SERVE
Lettuce leaves
Challah, other bread such as rye or
    pita, or crackers

Put the bread into a food-processor bowl fitted with a steel blade, and process until the bread becomes fine crumbs. Drain the herring, reserving the onions and some of the liquid. Add the drained herring fillets, onions from the jar, eggs, and apples to the food processor, and process until the mixture is almost smooth. If it is too thick, add a little of the reserved liquid or the wine. If it is too wet, add more bread crumbs. Process until the mixture is smooth.

Put the chopped herring into a covered bowl or container, and refrigerate it for several hours or until serving time to allow the flavors to mingle. (It can be stored in the refrigerator for up to 3 days.) Serve it on a bed of lettuce accompanied with bread or crackers.

Makes about 8 servings.

Easy Wine-Marinated Brisket

This is an absolutely delicious yet very easy recipe that my mother often uses for her holiday brisket or top-of-the-rib roast. My sister likes to include whole baby mushrooms, and she always uses white wine. I personally have had great success using very lean pot roasts with red wine in the marinade. No matter how we make this roast, everyone always loves it!

My mother taught me a neat trick to save time when marinating the roast. If it does not need to be trimmed at all, the frozen roast can be added to the marinade and left to thaw in the refrigerator overnight.

MARINADE

1 cup dry red or white table wine

2 tablespoons soy sauce

1 small onion, peeled and grated

2 garlic cloves, finely minced

MEAT

1 (3 to 3½-pound) brisket, top-of-the-rib roast, or other beef roast,

trimmed of all excess fat and any membranes

1 to 2 medium onions, peeled, halved, and thinly sliced

1 to 2 cups fresh or canned whole baby mushrooms, rinsed well and stems cut off at the base (optional)

In a nonaluminum (noncorrosive) ovenproof pot or deep roasting pan large enough to hold the roast, mix together all the marinade ingredients. Add the roast, and turn it over in the marinade so that it is completely coated. If time is available, let the meat marinate for a few hours up to overnight in the refrigerator, turning it occasionally. (A frozen, trimmed brisket can be defrosted overnight in the marinade in the refrigerator.) In a pinch, the roast may be immediately cooked in the marinade.

Preheat the oven to 325 degrees. Scatter the sliced onion and mushrooms (if used) around the roast. Cover the pot or pan tightly with a lid or foil wrap. Pot-roast the brisket at 325 degrees, basting it occasionally with the pan juices, for 2½ to 3 hours, or until it is very tender.

When the roast is ready, remove it from the oven and carefully lift it out of the pot to a cutting board. Reserve the juice and onion in the pot. Let the roast cool for about 10 minutes. Thinly slice it against the grain, and transfer the slices to a serving casserole. Skim any fat from the pan juices, and pour the juices, onions, and mushrooms (if used) over the brisket.

The roast may be prepared 2 to 3 days ahead, sliced, and refrigerated, covered, in its pan juices (with onions and mushrooms). Reheat it, covered, in a microwave oven or regular oven shortly before serving.

Makes about 8 to 10 servings.

Tzimmes

MEAT STEW WITH SWEET VEGETABLES AND FRUIT

The Yiddish word *tzimmes* has come to mean anything that is a fuss or all mixed up. Well, this wonderful one-pot meal is certainly "all mixed up" with meat, fruit, and vegetables, but it's not really that much of a fuss. The following sweet version is a very traditional Ashkenazic dish not only for Rosh Hashanah, but also for Sukkot, when hot one-pot meals are quite useful. The long cooking time is necessary to tenderize the meat and blend all the delicious flavors.

This can be made ahead, and some even prefer it on the second day.

1 cup hot water

1 cup orange juice

2 tablespoons honey

2 tablespoons packed dark brown sugar

1 (4- to 5-pound) boneless chuck roast or brisket, trimmed of all surface fat

1/4 to 1/2 teaspoon ground cinnamon

1/4 to 1/2 teaspoon ground ginger

4 carrots, peeled and cut into 2-inch pieces, or 10 to 15 peeled baby carrots

3 medium sweet potatoes, peeled and cut into 1-inch chunks

1 medium butternut squash (about 1 1/2 pounds), peeled, seeded, and cut into 1-inch chunks

6 ounces pitted prunes (about 20 large)

5 ounces dried apricots (about 20 large)

Cornstarch and cold water (optional)

In a nonaluminum 6- to 8-quart ovenproof pot or deep, large roasting pan, combine the water, juice, honey, and brown sugar. Add the roast, turning it so it is coated with the sweet liquid. Let the meat marinate in the mixture while you preheat the oven to 325 degrees. Cover the pot tightly with a lid or foil wrap. Pot-roast the meat at 325 degrees, basting it occasionally, for about 3 hours, or until it is just tender.

Stir the cinnamon and ginger into the broth. Randomly arrange the carrots, sweet potatoes, squash, prunes, and apricots around the roast, and spoon some broth over all. Cover the pot, and place it back in the oven. Pot-roast, basting occasionally, for 45 minutes, or until the vegetables and roast are fork-tender.

The Days of Awe: Rosh Hashanah Through Yom Kippur

Carefully transfer the cooked roast to a cutting board. Thinly slice it against the grain of the meat, and transfer it to a serving platter. Use a slotted spoon to remove the vegetables and fruit from the pot, and put them around the roast. Spoon some of its pan juices over the roast and vegetables.

If preparing the roast ahead of time, let it cool slightly on the cutting board (it will be easier to cut); then cut it into slices as above. Spoon some of its pan juices into a large ovenproof casserole dish. Arrange partially overlapping meat slices on top of the sauce. Arrange the vegetables around the meat. Pour the remainder of the juices on top. Cover and refrigerate until needed. Warm the covered casserole in a 325-degree oven or in a microwave oven until the roast and sauce are completely heated through. Serve directly from the casserole.

Makes 10 to 12 servings, depending on the size of the roast.

Lamb and Brown Rice Pilaf

Middle Eastern Jews and those from the Balkan countries often serve lamb for Rosh Hashanah to recall how God tested Abraham's faith by asking him to sacrifice his son, Isaac, but ultimately allowed him to substitute a ram. Some popular dishes include stuffed breast of lamb, lamb shoulder roast, and lamb pilaf. I based the following one on various Middle Eastern pilafs. The raisins, apple, and spices give it a slightly sweet flavor, making it perfect for this holiday. I used brown rice in this version because it has a rich taste that goes well with lamb, and a longer cooking time than white rice, which allows the lamb to become tender.

In her interesting commentary on women of the Torah, *The Five Books of Miriam,* author Ellen Frankel gives a different, intriguing reason to serve this dish. She characterizes my pilaf as "Rebecca's Stew," and suggests that it is probably close to the type of dish Rebecca prepared for her husband, Isaac, in helping her son Jacob to acquire his father's blessing. One might imagine that perhaps Rebecca learned from her mother-in-law, Sarah, how to prepare it.

2 to 3 pounds lean boneless lamb

3 tablespoons extra-virgin olive oil

2 large onions, finely chopped

3 to 4 garlic cloves, finely minced

4 celery stalks, finely chopped

3 cups uncooked long-grain brown rice

6 cups beef broth, or bouillon made
    from cubes or powder

2 (15- to 16-ounce) cans chickpeas
    (garbanzo beans), drained and
    rinsed

1 1/2 cups dark or light raisins

1 apple, peeled, cored, and finely
    chopped

1 cup finely chopped fresh parsley
    leaves

1 teaspoon ground allspice

1/4 teaspoon ground cinnamon

1/2 teaspoon dried thyme leaves

1/2 teaspoon black pepper

1/4 teaspoon salt, or to taste

Trim the lamb of all fat and gristle, and cut it into 1/2-inch cubes. Set it aside.

Put the oil into a very large saucepan or Dutch oven over medium-high heat; then sauté the onions, garlic, and celery until tender. Add the rice and cook, stirring, 1 minute longer. Add the lamb cubes and stir until they are browned on all sides. Stir in the broth, chickpeas, raisins, apple, parsley, allspice, cinnamon, thyme, pepper, and salt.

Bring to a boil; then cover, and lower the heat. Simmer, covered, about 45 minutes, or until all the liquid is absorbed. Toss with a fork before serving.

Makes about 8 servings.

Couscous aux Légumes Sucrés

CHICKEN OR BEEF STEW WITH SWEET VEGETABLES

*C*ouscous, a rich stew that is always served with the tiny semolina wheat pasta also called *Couscous* (page 126), is one of the most popular dishes of Jews with North African ancestry. They serve it on festive holidays, Shabbat, and other happy occasions such as weddings and the naming of babies.

Couscous is very versatile and often varies with the country, city, or even the household in which it originated. It can be subtle or fiery hot; it can be made with meat,

chicken, or fish; it can be vegetarian. Sometimes, elaborately spiced meatballs or stuffed vegetables are added to the main course stew—a custom that is particularly Jewish. The pasta can even be used for a Sweet Couscous (page 232), featuring nuts, dried fruits, and cinnamon.

The following recipe is for a marvelous couscous that is perfect for Rosh Hashanah, and very healthful as well (it has a generous amount of carotene and fiber). Loosely based on a dish in *The Book of Jewish Food* by Claudia Roden, it features the brightly colored sweet vegetables and raisins that are often included in High Holiday couscous. It is typical in that the emphasis is on the vegetables and pasta, not the meat. Please feel free to use other vegetables that suit your taste. Some that are often included in Jewish couscous are zucchini, turnips, leeks, celery, and tomatoes.

The recipe is not difficult, and every step is carefully explained. Most of the vegetables can be peeled and cut up while the chicken or meat is cooking. Chicken meat is removed from the bones for easy serving and eating (and because the pieces take up too much room in the pot) and then returned to the pot with the vegetables. Beef does not require this step.

NOTE: The amounts and types of vegetables in the following recipe can be altered as desired. Put longer-cooking ones in first, and quicker-cooking ones in later.

3½ to 4 pounds meaty chicken pieces or
   2½ to 3 pounds lean beef pot roast
4 small whole onions
8 cups water
3 large carrots
3 medium sweet potatoes (about 2½
   pounds)
1 medium butternut squash (2½ to 3
   pounds)
1 very small green ("white") cabbage or
   cabbage heart (about 1 pound)
1 (15- to 16-ounce) can chickpeas
   (garbanzo beans)
1 cup light raisins

1 teaspoon salt
½ teaspoon ground black or white
   pepper
¼ teaspoon ground turmeric
¼ cup finely chopped fresh parsley
   leaves
2 teaspoons dried cilantro (coriander)
   leaves or 2 tablespoons finely
   chopped fresh leaves

TO SERVE
Quick Couscous (page 126)
Ground cinnamon (optional)

If using chicken, remove any surface fat. If using beef, trim off all the excess fat and cut the meat into eight to ten chunks. Carefully peel each onion so that the root end stays intact and holds the onion together. Leave the onions whole, and set them aside.

Put the 8 cups water into an 8-quart stew or soup pot or Dutch oven, and bring to a boil over high heat. Add the chicken or beef to the water. Lower the heat so that the water just boils, and cook the chicken or beef, uncovered, for about 10 minutes. Use a wide, fine strainer (or a spoon) to remove and discard the foam and other particles that rise to the surface of the soup. When there is no more foam, cover and simmer.

For chicken, add the onions and simmer for 1¼ hours, or until the chicken is very tender and is easily removed from the bones. For beef, simmer for about 1 hour, then add the onions. Simmer for an additional 1 hour, or until the meat is very tender.

While the chicken or beef is cooking, prepare the remaining ingredients, and set them aside.

Peel the carrots (or lightly scrape them) and cut them into 2-inch chunks. Peel the sweet potatoes, and cut them into fourths (it doesn't matter how). Cut the "neck" (top) off the butternut squash close to where it flares into the round bottom, and discard the bottom or reserve it for another use (it is filled with seeds and fibers). Peel the neck of the squash, and cut it into 1½-inch chunks.

Remove and discard the outer leaves of the cabbage. If the cabbage is larger than about 5 inches in diameter, peel off several outer leaves and reserve them for another use. (A cabbage that is too large will fill the pot!) Cut the cabbage into eight wedges directly through the core so that the pieces stay intact. Drain the chickpeas into a colander, and rinse them well. Measure out the raisins.

If chicken is used, remove the pot from the heat when it is done cooking. Carefully transfer the chicken pieces to platters, using a large slotted spoon. Reserve the broth with the onions, making sure no bones are left in the broth. (If desired, any fat that rises to the surface of the broth may be skimmed off.) Discard the chicken skin, then use two forks to remove all the chicken meat from the bones, in large chunks if possible, and return the meat to the broth. Bring the broth to a simmer. (Leave beef in its broth.)

Stir the salt, pepper, turmeric, parsley, and cilantro into the broth with the cooked, boned chicken or beef chunks. Add the prepared carrots, sweet potatoes, squash, cabbage, chickpeas, and raisins in a random fashion, immersing them as much as possible into the broth. (Some may be reserved for another use if there is not enough room in your pot.) Simmer the vegetables for about 30 minutes, or until the sweet potato and squash are cooked through and tender but not falling apart. Adjust any seasonings in the stew, if necessary.

While the vegetables are cooking, prepare Quick Couscous as directed.

To serve the stew in the traditional manner, spread the couscous pasta on a large serving platter or tray. Use a slotted spoon to remove the meat and vegetables from the pot, and place them on top of the pasta. Spoon a small amount of the broth from the pot over the stew, and serve the remainder of the broth on the side for the diners to ladle on their portions as they wish. Some like the couscous rather dry; others prefer it to be more soupy.

An alternative method, which may be preferable because it is easier to serve several people, is to leave the couscous pasta in the bowl in which it was prepared. Put the couscous meat and vegetables on a plate, and the broth in a bowl as suggested above. If desired, the couscous pasta may be decorated with a light sprinkling of cinnamon.

Makes 8 to 10 servings.

Quick Couscous

TINY PASTA PELLETS

*C*ouscous is a tiny pasta, not a grain, that is prominent in North African–Jewish cuisine. It used to be made at home by rolling ground semolina into tiny pellets that then had to be soaked and steamed and rubbed in the hands several times to make the couscous light and tender. Later couscous was sold "rolled," but not cooked or steamed.

It was traditionally prepared in a *couscousière*—a special two-section pot that looks like an enormous double boiler. A rich stew, also called *couscous,* simmered in the bulbous bottom section, while the pasta was repeatedly steamed in a smaller top section

with tiny holes in its base. The complete preparation involved several steps that could take hours, and would result in fluffy, tender couscous.

Nowadays, processed couscous—also called precooked, ready-to-cook, or quick couscous—is available in most American supermarkets. Some brands are imported from France, where many Jews from North Africa now live. Processed couscous is definitely quicker and easier to prepare than previous types; the method on the box typically takes only 5 minutes. This "quick" couscous is so convenient that it has become a staple in many homes, and is even available with a variety of seasonings.

Although some cooks still insist on steaming processed couscous in the old laborious manner, it really is not necessary if certain techniques are used to keep the couscous light and fluffy. I personally don't like the sticky, compact results I get when I follow the directions on most boxes. So I have worked out a technique that uses a microwave oven to steam quick couscous in just a few minutes directly in its serving bowl. Its wonderful texture and lightness are very similar to couscous steamed in the traditional way.

I happened upon this technique quite accidentally while reheating some leftover couscous in the microwave oven. It was better than when I had originally made it! Couscous can be reheated several times in this manner, simply by adding a few sprinkles of water each time. (If a microwave oven is not available, couscous can be prepared in a regular oven as directed below.)

NOTE: This couscous is not the same as the large "Israeli couscous" that resembles large egg barley and is sold in some kosher supermarkets and Jewish specialty stores.

FOR 5 TO 6 SERVINGS
1½ cups (10 ounces) plain dry quick-
   cooking couscous
Generous ¼ teaspoon salt
1½ cups boiling water
2 tablespoons olive oil, divided
2 to 4 tablespoons warm water, plus
   more if needed

FOR 8 TO 10 SERVINGS
2½ cups (1 pound) plain dry quick-
   cooking couscous
½ teaspoon salt
2½ cups boiling water
3 tablespoons olive oil, divided
¼ to ½ cup warm water, plus more if
   needed

Put the dry couscous into a large microwaveproof or ovenproof bowl or casserole. (The couscous will increase in size several times.) Toss the couscous with the salt. Add the boiling water and 1 tablespoon of oil, and immediately

The Days of Awe: Rosh Hashanah Through Yom Kippur

stir with a fork, lifting and separating the grains, for about 5 minutes, or until the water is completely absorbed. Stir in the remaining oil. Use the fork or your fingers to break apart any lumps.

Stir in the warm water, and cover the couscous tightly. If using a microwave oven, immediately heat the couscous on "high" for about 2 to 3 minutes, or until it is heated through and all the water is absorbed. If using a regular oven, put the couscous into a 325- to 375-degree oven (whatever is most convenient for you), and warm it just until it is heated through and the water is absorbed. In either case, when the couscous is hot, immediately fluff it up with a fork, breaking up any lumps. It should taste tender with just a little bite, and all the pellets should be separated. (Couscous should not be gummy or sticky.) If it is still too hard, add a few tablespoons of water and repeat the above heating procedure until the couscous is tender. (Different brands of couscous may require slightly different amounts of water.)

The couscous may be served immediately, or it may be set aside until the accompanying dinner is almost ready to be served. To reheat the couscous, add 1 or 2 tablespoons warm water, and heat as directed above. Immediately fluff it up with a fork as before, and serve.

Makes 5 to 10 servings, depending on amount of dry couscous used.

Fricasada

CHICKEN BRAISED IN TOMATOES AND HONEY

This cinnamon-scented chicken has become one of my family's favorite dishes for Rosh Hashanah and year round. Based on North African–Jewish cuisine, it features honey for a sweet New Year. A very similar Sephardic dish is traditionally served at the meal before Yom Kippur.

Toasted sesame seeds or almonds may be used as a garnish on top of the chicken and sauce. Some cooks actually prefer to use both, while other cooks use neither. The choice is yours. Toasting brings out the flavor of the sesame seeds or almonds, and it is not very difficult. For directions, see the Note below.

There are two ways to prepare *fricasada*. Either way, a delicious sweet tomato sauce is produced. For the more traditional "Jewish" version, chopped onion is sautéed in oil and then the other sauce ingredients are added. In another version (see Variation), puréed onion is combined with the other sauce ingredients to make a smoother sauce in which pieces of onion are not visible. Sometimes, I vary the technique for a change.

This is a very easy dish, which can be made even quicker by using flash-frozen individual boneless, skinless chicken breasts directly from the freezer. Just simmer them about 10 minutes longer to be certain that they are cooked through completely.

NOTE: To toast sesame seeds, put them into an ungreased skillet, and stir them over medium-high heat for about 5 to 10 minutes, or until they are lightly browned and very aromatic. To toast slivered almonds, spread them on a cookie sheet and put them in a 350-degree oven for 5 to 10 minutes, or until golden and flavorful. If both almonds and sesame seeds are used, they can be toasted together in a skillet as for seeds.

1 (14- to 16-ounce) can tomatoes, including juice, diced or finely chopped
2 tablespoons honey
1 teaspoon ground cinnamon
1/4 teaspoon black pepper
2 tablespoons good-quality olive oil
1 medium onion, finely chopped
2 garlic cloves, minced
About 3 pounds meaty chicken pieces, skin removed, or 2 pounds boneless, skinless chicken breast halves

GARNISH (OPTIONAL)
2 to 3 tablespoons raw hulled sesame seeds or 1/3 cup slivered almonds (or a mixture), preferably toasted (see Note)

TO SERVE (OPTIONAL)
Quick Couscous (page 126)

In a small bowl or measuring cup, combine the tomatoes and their juice, honey, cinnamon, and pepper. Set aside.

Put the oil into a wide, deep skillet or Dutch oven over medium-high heat; then sauté the onion and garlic until they are tender. Push the onion to the edges of the pan. If the pan is very dry, add a bit more oil. Put the chicken pieces in the pan and brown them lightly on all sides. Pour the reserved

The Days of Awe: Rosh Hashanah Through Yom Kippur

tomato mixture over the browned chicken. Stir the bottom of the pan gently to loosen any browned bits into the sauce and to mix in the cooked onion. Bring the sauce to a boil. Cover the pan tightly, and lower the heat so the chicken gently simmers.

Simmer the chicken, basting and turning the pieces occasionally, for 10 to 15 minutes for boneless breasts or about 45 minutes for bone-in pieces, or until the chicken is cooked through. Meanwhile, if using sesame seeds and/or almonds, toast them as directed in the Note.

When the chicken is done, transfer it to a serving plate. Raise the heat under the tomato sauce, and quickly boil the sauce down, stirring constantly, to thicken it. It should be the texture of thick spaghetti sauce. Spoon the sauce over the chicken pieces. Sprinkle the sesame seeds and/or almonds on top. Serve immediately, over hot couscous if desired.

To make this dish ahead, place the cooked chicken into a large, covered casserole and spoon the thickened sauce on top. Do not sprinkle on the seeds or nuts. Cover and refrigerate. Before serving, reheat the chicken in a 325-degree oven or a microwave oven until hot but not dry. Spoon some of the sauce from the bottom of the casserole over the top of the chicken, and sprinkle the sauce with seeds and/or nuts. Serve directly from the casserole.

Makes about 6 servings.

Variation

EASY FRICASADA

This produces a smoother sauce than the version above, and is very quick and easy to prepare because a food processor (fitted with a steel blade) is used and it is not necessary to finely chop the tomatoes, onion, or garlic by hand. Also, the onions are not sautéed.

With the food processor running, drop the garlic cloves though the hole in the lid so that the garlic becomes minced. Turn off the food processor and add to its bowl the peeled onion, cut into eighths with the root end removed, the tomatoes and their juice, honey, cinnamon, and pepper. Process until the onion and tomatoes are coarsely puréed. Set aside.

Put the oil into a wide, deep skillet or a Dutch oven over medium-high heat; then brown the chicken pieces lightly on all sides. Pour the tomato-

onion mixture over the browned chicken, and bring the sauce to a boil. Cover the pan tightly, and lower the heat so the chicken gently simmers. Follow the cooking and serving directions in the main recipe.

Djaja M'kalli

MOROCCAN-STYLE LEMON CHICKEN WITH OLIVES

Moroccan Jews often break the fast of Yom Kippur with this wonderfully exotic dish, which they also call *djaja zetoon* or *pollo con olivos y limón* in Judeo-Spanish. They usually make it with pickled lemons, which have been preserved in salt and oil. Although almost all North Africans make and eat pickled lemons, only the Jewish cooks use oil in the pickling process.

For the lemons to be pickled in the Jewish manner, several of them are cut lengthwise into fourths or into slices, and salted very well. Sometimes, they are also sprinkled with paprika (another Jewish touch). Then they are tightly packed into very clean jars and covered with oil. The tightly covered jars are kept at room temperature. After about 2 or 3 weeks, the lemon peels lose most of their bitterness and become softened and translucent. The entire lemon, peel and all, can then be used whenever needed, or stored for up to a year. When used, preserved lemons are usually rinsed and chopped into small pieces.

The following recipe employs a different, "shortcut" technique to soften and mellow the peel of a whole lemon in only 30 minutes (while the chicken is cooking). Although the lemon is not pickled, it looks and tastes something like one that has been, and it can be used in this easy, delicious dish without weeks of advance planning. (Of course, an authentic pickled lemon can be substituted, if desired. Chop it into small pieces, and add it to the skillet toward the end of the cooking period, in place of the boiled lemon described below.)

This dish is one of my personal favorites.

1 cup water

1 small onion, grated

1 small onion, finely chopped

2 to 3 garlic cloves, finely minced

¼ cup finely chopped fresh parsley leaves

2 teaspoons dried cilantro leaves or 2 tablespoons finely chopped fresh cilantro leaves

½ teaspoon ground ginger

¼ teaspoon ground turmeric

¼ teaspoon ground black pepper

About 3½ pounds meaty chicken pieces, skin removed

1 medium fresh lemon

1 cup green olives, whole or pitted (with any pimiento removed and discarded)

2 tablespoons lemon juice, preferably fresh

GARNISH (OPTIONAL)

1 fresh lemon, cut into narrow wedges

In a very large, deep skillet or a Dutch oven, mix together the water, grated onion, chopped onion, garlic, parsley, cilantro, ginger, turmeric, and pepper. Add the chicken, and bring the liquid to a boil over medium-high heat. Lower the heat, and simmer the chicken, covered, for about 1 hour, or until it is very tender. Rotate the chicken occasionally with tongs, so that all sides are in the liquid for part of the cooking period.

While the chicken is cooking, use a small, sharp knife to score four or five very shallow 1-inch cuts in the surface of the lemon peel. Put the lemon into a saucepan, and cover it with water. Bring it to a boil over high heat; then reduce the heat and simmer it, covered, for about 30 minutes. The peel should be very tender. Rinse the lemon under cool running water to stop the cooking process, and let it cool until it can be handled. If water has gotten into the lemon, squeeze it out. Cut open the lemon along one of the scored marks (if it hasn't already opened during cooking). Discard seeds and any loose lemon pulp that has come free from the peel. Cut the peel (with any attached pulp) into small pieces. Set aside.

While the lemon is cooking, bring the olives to a boil in plain water, and simmer them for 3 minutes; discard the water, and let the olives soak in cool, clean water until needed. This helps remove excess saltiness and bitterness from the olives.

When the chicken is tender, stir the 2 tablespoons lemon juice into the sauce. If the chicken has given off a lot of liquid and the sauce is thin, raise the heat, and quickly boil the sauce down until it has thickened to the desired

consistency. Reduce the heat to low, and stir in the olives and reserved pieces of cooked lemon peel. Simmer gently about 5 minutes longer, stirring occasionally and rotating the chicken pieces in the rich sauce.

To serve, put the chicken on a large platter, and spoon the sauce with the olives and lemon pieces over the top. If desired, garnish with the lemon wedges.

Makes about 6 servings.

Chicken and Sweet Potatoes in Orange Sauce

The sweet potatoes cook right along with the chicken in this easy and flavorful skillet dinner that is perfect for a midweek dinner during the Days of Awe. For company, the recipe can be doubled and cooked in a large Dutch oven. (It could even be baked in a casserole at 350 degrees for about the same amount of time.)

2 to 3 medium sweet potatoes
1 pound boneless, skinless, chicken
   breast halves or thighs
2 tablespoons all-purpose flour
2 tablespoons canola oil
1¼ cups orange juice
¼ teaspoon ground cinnamon

⅛ teaspoon ground ginger
⅛ teaspoon ground black pepper
½ cup light or dark raisins (optional)

TO SERVE
Hot cooked white or brown rice

Peel the sweet potatoes, and cut them into ½-inch cubes. Set aside. Cut the chicken into small pieces, about 1 to 1½ inches square, and toss the chicken with the flour. Put the oil into a large, deep skillet over medium-high heat; then lightly brown the chicken pieces on both sides.

While they are browning, mix the orange juice with the cinnamon, ginger, and pepper. Add the juice to the skillet along with the sweet potato cubes and raisins (if used). Bring to a boil; then cover and reduce the heat. Simmer, stirring occasionally, for about 30 to 35 minutes, or until the poultry and sweet potatoes are tender, and the sauce is thickened. (If the sauce be-

comes too thick, stir in a few teaspoons of juice or water. If it's too thin, un-cover the skillet, and simmer the mixture about 5 minutes longer, or until some liquid has evaporated and the sauce has thickened.) Serve over a bed of hot rice.

Makes about 4 to 5 servings.

Apple-Raisin Lokshen Kugel
Fruity Noodle "Pudding"

This classic lokshen kugel is very easy to prepare and goes with a variety of foods. It is slightly sweet, with chunks of baked apple. Tender pears, such as Bartlett or Anjou, may be substituted for the apples. If desired, ½ cup chopped walnuts may be added with the apples or pears.

NOTES: Just about any type of apple can be used in this kugel. I like Golden Delicious because it holds its shape well during baking, and the light peel is not obvious to diners.

If a Pyrex baking dish is used, this kugel can be prepared ahead, refrigerated covered with heavy plastic wrap, and reheated in a microwave oven shortly before serving.

1 (12-ounce) package medium or wide egg noodles	½ cup light or dark raisins
¼ cup canola oil or melted pareve margarine	⅓ cup sugar
	1½ teaspoons cinnamon
	¼ teaspoon salt
3 medium apples, such as Golden Delicious (see Notes)	4 large eggs, lightly beaten, or 1 cup pareve egg substitute

Using a 5-quart or similar pot, cook the noodles according to package di-rections, using the shorter time listed. While the noodles are cooking, coat a 9 by 13-inch baking dish with nonstick cooking spray or grease it well. Pre-heat the oven to 350 degrees.

The New Jewish Holiday Cookbook

Drain the noodles well; then return them to the cooking pot off the heat (so as not to dirty another bowl). Stir in the oil so that the noodles don't stick together.

Peel the apples if desired. (This is really not necessary with light-skinned apples, and the peel adds fiber and nutrients.) Cut the apples into fourths, and remove the core and seeds; then slice the apples into small pieces.

Add the apples to the noodles in the pot, along with the raisins, sugar, cinnamon, and salt, and mix well. Add the eggs and stir so that all the noodles are coated. Transfer the mixture to the prepared baking dish. Cover tightly with aluminum foil that has been coated with nonstick spray or greased, so the noodles on top don't stick to it.

Bake at 350 degrees for 35 minutes; then remove the foil and bake for another 15 to 20 minutes, or until the top is firm and the apples are soft. Serve warm or at room temperature, cut into squares or spooned out of the dish.

Makes about 10 servings.

Honey-Sweetened Carrot Salad

This North African–style salad is one of my favorites, and is always a hit with guests who are surprised by its intriguing taste. Similar Jewish carrot salads have many different names, depending on the community. Most seem to include garlic, cumin, paprika, and parsley, although the proportions vary with the cook and city of origin. Sometimes, hot pepper is added to make a more piquant salad. This honey-sweetened version is my adaptation of several different recipes. An almost identical salad without honey is quite popular in Israel (see Variation).

NOTE: In cooking the carrots, I have employed a little trick that I learned from my first cooking teacher, my mother. Mom always adds a little honey to the water when cooking fresh carrots to give them a nice sweet touch. Plain carrots cooked this way are delicious when served hot as a side dish.

CARROTS

2 pounds carrots

²/₃ cup water

1 tablespoon honey

DRESSING

¹/₄ cup lemon juice or cider vinegar

2 to 4 tablespoons honey, or to taste

1 tablespoon olive or canola oil

2 garlic cloves, finely minced or pressed

¹/₂ teaspoon sweet paprika

¹/₂ to 1 teaspoon ground cumin

¹/₂ teaspoon ground cinnamon (optional)

¹/₂ cup finely chopped fresh parsley
    leaves

Peel and thinly slice the carrots. (This will be especially quick and easy if you use the small, peeled carrots available in most supermarkets, and a food processor fitted with a slicing blade.) If preferred, the carrots may be diced.

Put the water and 1 tablespoon honey into a medium saucepan over medium-high heat. Bring to a boil, add the carrots, and stir until they are all moistened. Lower the heat, and simmer, covered, until the carrots are just crisp-tender, about 5 to 8 minutes. (Do not overcook the carrots, or they will get mushy.)

Meanwhile, combine the dressing ingredients in a medium bowl. Drain the cooked carrots well, and immediately add them to the dressing mixture. Mix well, cover, and chill for at least 1 to 2 hours up to overnight to give the flavors a chance to mingle. Stir occasionally to coat the carrots with the dressing. Serve chilled or at room temperature. This keeps well for several days in the refrigerator.

Makes about 8 servings.

Variation

MOROCCAN CARROT SALAD, ISRAELI-STYLE

Follow the above recipe, but omit all honey and cinnamon. Add salt and finely chopped chili peppers (fresh or flakes) or cayenne pepper to taste, if desired.

Glazed Carrot Sticks with Apricots

Sweet carrots are always popular for Rosh Hashanah. To quickly prepare this dish, use the peeled small carrots that are available at most supermarkets. Cut each one in half lengthwise. Then lay all the halves down on the flat side, and cut them lengthwise in half again. Each thin carrot stick will look almost triangular in cross section.

1½ tablespoons pareve margarine or
    canola oil
1 medium onion, peeled, halved and
    thinly sliced
1 pound carrots, peeled and cut into
    small sticks (see above)
About 15 dried apricots, cut lengthwise
    into thirds

½ cup orange juice
¼ teaspoon ground cinnamon
¼ teaspoon ground ginger
1 tablespoon packed dark or light
    brown sugar

Put the margarine or oil into a medium saucepan over medium-high heat. When it is hot, sauté the onion until it is tender but not brown. Add the remaining ingredients and bring to boil, stirring occasionally. Lower the heat, cover the saucepan, and simmer the carrots, stirring occasionally to distribute the sauce evenly. Cook the carrots for about 10 to 12 minutes, or until they are barely crisp-tender. Remove the cover, raise the heat, and stir constantly until the sauce boils down and forms a rich glaze on the carrots.

Makes 4 to 6 servings.

Sunshine Carrot Coins

Among the vegetables favored for Rosh Hashanah, carrots are probably the most popular in Ashkenazic households. Because the Yiddish word *mehren* can mean either "carrots" or "increase," carrots have come to represent the wish that our merits will be increased in the coming year.

Furthermore, carrots cut into thin, round slices resemble gold coins, and symbolize a hope for future prosperity. And, of course, carrots are sweet—especially when cooked with fruit, as in the following recipe—for a sweet year.

1 pound carrots
1/2 cup orange juice
1 tablespoon honey
1/4 cup light or dark raisins
2 tablespoons finely chopped fresh
    spearmint leaves or 2 teaspoons
    dried mint leaves
1 tablespoon shredded orange peel,
    colored part only

Pinch each of ground ginger and
    nutmeg
1 medium orange, peeled and cut into
    chunks
1 teaspoon cornstarch (optional)
2 teaspoons water (optional)

Peel the carrots and thinly slice them into circles. Put the carrots, orange juice, honey, raisins, mint leaves, orange peel, ginger, and nutmeg into a medium saucepan over high heat. Cover and bring to a boil; lower the heat, and simmer the carrots for about 8 minutes, or until they are crisp-tender.

Add the orange pieces and cook, stirring, about 1 minute longer, or until the orange pieces are heated through. To thicken the sauce slightly, thoroughly combine the cornstarch and water; then add the mixture to the pan. Cook, stirring, only until the sauce thickens slightly and comes to a boil. Remove from the heat and serve.

Makes 4 to 5 servings.

Acorn Squash with Streusel

The small, dark green acorn squash, with its bright orange flesh, is another sweet fall vegetable that is perfect for Rosh Hashanah. Winter squash is one of the vegetables blessed by Sephardim on this holiday as part of their *Yehi Ratsones,* or "May it be thy will . . ." prayers, in which they ask God for a good year. Ashkenazim may serve this colorful squash as an alternative to carrots or sweet potatoes.

NOTES: In the following dish, acorn squash halves are filled with a delicious nutty streusel. For an even easier way to serve them, bake the inverted squash halves for a total of 45 minutes to 1 hour, or until the orange flesh is very soft when pierced with a fork. Coat the cavity of each plain baked half with a tablespoon of real maple syrup and sprinkle it with finely chopped walnuts or pecans. Serve in the green shell. This easy variation is a favorite of my children.

There are now many miniature varieties of winter (hard) squash. Any other small winter squash (about 1 to 1¼ pounds each) may be substituted for the acorn squash. Choose those that feel heavy for their size. If acorn squash are larger than 1 pound each, buy the smallest ones available for a total of about 4 to 5 pounds, cut them in half as directed, and divide the filling among them. Bake them a little longer if necessary. When they are done baking, cut each half lengthwise in half again to make smaller servings.

(Some Jews do not eat nuts during the Days of Awe. If that is your preference, simply omit the nuts.)

4 small (1 to 1¼ pounds each) acorn squash (see Notes)
¼ cup packed dark brown sugar
3 tablespoons all-purpose flour
½ teaspoon ground cinnamon

½ teaspoon ground nutmeg
½ cup finely chopped walnuts or pecans
3 tablespoons softened pareve margarine

Preheat the oven to 375 degrees. Do not peel the squash. Use a sharp, heavy knife and cutting board to cut each squash in half lengthwise through the stem end. Scoop out all the seeds and fibers (a serrated grapefruit spoon works great). Place the halves, cut side down, in a large foil-lined baking pan containing about ¼ inch water. Tightly cover the pan with another piece of foil. Bake at 375 degrees for 30 minutes.

Meanwhile, prepare the filling. Combine the brown sugar, flour, cinnamon, nutmeg, and nuts in a small bowl. Cut in the margarine with a pastry blender, your fingertips, or two knives, until the mixture is crumbly and completely mixed. Set aside.

Remove the partially baked squash halves from the oven, and carefully turn each one over so the cut side is facing up. Sprinkle the nut filling into the cavities, dividing it evenly. Re-cover the pan, and continue baking the

squash halves for about 20 to 30 minutes longer, or until the flesh is quite tender and very easily pierced with a fork.

Serve each squash half, intact, as one serving. Diners can spoon the filling and squash flesh directly from the shell.

This dish can be prepared ahead, and rewarmed in a covered baking dish (so the squash don't dry out) until the squash are hot throughout. A microwave oven may be used.

Makes 8 servings.

Layered Sweet Potato and Pear Casserole

This side dish is perfect for Rosh Hashanah, and is also well suited for Thanksgiving. The brown sugar and spices bring out the naturally sweet flavors of ripe pears and carotene-rich sweet potatoes, an Ashkenazic favorite for this holiday.

NOTES: To save time, a very large (about 40-ounce) can of sweet potatoes in syrup may be substituted for the cooked fresh sweet potatoes below. Drain the canned sweet potatoes well before using them, and cut off any fibrous areas. Cut them into thick slices before using. They will be somewhat softer than fresh sweet potatoes.

(Some Jews do not eat nuts during the Days of Awe. If that is your preference, simply omit the nuts.)

2¹/₂ to 3 pounds sweet potatoes, peeled and thickly sliced (about 5 cups)
¹/₂ cup finely chopped walnuts or pecans
3 tablespoons dark brown sugar
3¹/₂ tablespoons all-purpose flour
¹/₂ teaspoon ground cinnamon

¹/₄ teaspoon ground nutmeg
¹/₄ teaspoon ground ginger
3 tablespoons pareve margarine
3 medium soft, ripe pears, such as Bartlett or Anjou

Put the sliced raw sweet potatoes into a medium saucepan and add water to a depth of about 1 inch. Cover the pot, and bring the sweet potatoes to a boil over high heat. Lower the heat, and steam the sweet potatoes for about

20 minutes, or until they are fork-tender but not at all mushy. Remove them from the heat and drain well.

Meanwhile, combine the nuts, brown sugar, flour, and spices in a small bowl. Cut in the margarine with a pastry blender, fork, or your fingertips until the mixture resembles very coarse crumbs. Set aside the nut mixture until the sweet potatoes are ready. Core and thinly slice the pears. (It is not necessary to peel them.)

Coat with nonstick cooking spray or grease a 2- to 2½-quart oven-to-table casserole. Preheat the oven to 350 degrees. Layer a third of the cooked sweet potatoes in the bottom. Top with a third of the pears, and then a third of the nut mixture. Repeat the layers two more times so that the nut mixture is on top.

Bake the casserole, covered, at 350 degrees for about 40 minutes, or until the pears are very tender. Serve warm or at room temperature. (This may be prepared ahead up to the baking point and refrigerated. After refrigerating, bake for a slightly longer time.) The casserole may be baked ahead and reheated in a 325-degree oven or a microwave oven until hot completely through.

Makes about 6 servings.

Mashed Sweet Potatoes with Pineapple

One of the vegetables Ashkenazic Jews particularly enjoy during the Days of Awe is sweet potatoes, as they represent a hope for a sweet year. This easy casserole can be assembled ahead of time, and baked just before serving.

5 medium sweet potatoes (about 2½ pounds)
2 to 3 tablespoons pareve margarine, cut into small pieces
½ cup orange juice
1 teaspoon grated orange peel, colored part only

1 (8-ounce) can juice-pack crushed pineapple, including juice
½ cup light raisins
2 tablespoons packed dark brown sugar

Peel the sweet potatoes, and coarsely cut them into chunks. Put them in a large saucepan with about 2 inches of water. Bring the water to a boil over high heat; then cover the pan tightly, and lower the heat. Simmer the sweet potatoes for about 35 minutes, or until they are quite tender. Immediately drain them well.

Coarsely mash the hot sweet potatoes with a fork; then stir in the margarine until it is melted. Add the orange juice, peel, pineapple with its juice, and raisins, and stir until well combined. Turn out the mixture into a greased 1½- to 2-quart casserole, and sprinkle the brown sugar on top. (The casserole may be prepared ahead to this point.) Bake the casserole in a 350-degree oven for about 40 minutes, or until it is hot throughout.

Makes about 5 to 6 servings.

Easy Beet Salad

At every festive meal, Moroccan Jews follow the custom of their native land and serve many seasonal vegetable salads. They often serve this salad, called *salada barba,* on Rosh Hashanah.

Sephardic Jews eat a very similar salad called *salata de panjar.* Naturally sweet beets are eaten, not only for a sweet year, but also because the Hebrew word for "beet" sounds like a word in the New Year blessing in which Sephardim ask that their enemies be "removed" (or "beaten" back).

This salad is traditionally prepared with fresh beets (though it is much quicker and easier with canned beets, as below). Sephardim use the beetroots for this dish, and reserve the green tops for a different holiday salad. They partake of beet greens on Rosh Hashanah in the hope that any enemies will wither and shrink as the fresh greens do when they are cooked.

3 tablespoons lemon juice

2 tablespoons extra-virgin olive oil

1 garlic clove, finely minced or pressed
   (optional)

2 to 4 tablespoons finely chopped fresh
   parsley leaves

2 teaspoons sugar

1/8 teaspoon ground cumin

1/8 teaspoon ground cinnamon

Pinch of salt

1 (15- to 16-ounce) can sliced red
   beets, drained

In a medium bowl, combine all the ingredients except the beets. Dice the beets or cut them into strips, and add them to the bowl. Chill the salad until serving time, mixing occasionally. Serve it chilled or at room temperature.

Makes about 4 servings.

Green Beans with Leeks and Carrots, Turkish-Style

During the Days of Awe, Turkish Jews and many other Sephardim eat leeks as a symbolic pun in the hope that they will "never lack in luck" during the coming year. Also, the Hebrew word for "leek," *karti*, sounds like *yikaretu*, part of a Rosh Hashanah blessing in which they ask that our enemies "be cut off."

Sephardim may serve the following colorful dish slightly chilled or at room temperature with an assortment of other cooked vegetable salads at the beginning of festive meals. Or they may prefer to serve it warm, as a side dish. Either way, it tastes great.

NOTE: If you cannot find flat, "Italian" green beans—the Sephardic preference—use regular whole green beans instead.

4 medium to large fresh leeks

3 medium carrots

1 medium onion, peeled

2 tablespoons good-quality olive oil

1/2 cup water

1 1/2 tablespoons lemon juice

2 tablespoons finely chopped parsley
   leaves

1/4 teaspoon sugar

1/8 teaspoon salt

1 (9- to 10-ounce) package frozen
   Italian (flat) green beans, slightly
   thawed (see Note)

The Days of Awe: Rosh Hashanah Through Yom Kippur

To clean the leeks, cut off and discard the roots and all but 1 to 2 inches of the green tops. Slit the top of each leek in half lengthwise down to the point where the green part meets the white. Gently spread the leaves, and rinse the leeks very well under running water to remove any sand or grit. Drain them well. Slice the cleaned leeks crosswise into ½-inch-thick pieces, and set aside. Peel the carrots (if desired) and cut them into ¼-inch-thick slices. Set aside.

Cut the onion in half, and then into ½-inch-thick semicircular slices. Put the oil into a medium saucepan over medium-high heat. Add the onion and cook, breaking up the slices. When the onion is tender, add the reserved leeks and cook, stirring often, for about 5 minutes longer. Then add the carrots, ½ cup water, lemon juice, parsley, sugar, and salt, and stir gently to combine.

Bring the mixture to a boil; then lower the heat, cover, and simmer for 20 minutes. Gently stir in the green beans. Simmer, covered, for 10 minutes longer, or until all the vegetables are tender. Serve warm. Or to serve in the Turkish manner, chill completely (several hours or overnight), and serve chilled or at room temperature.

Makes 4 to 6 servings.

Lubiya or Fijones Frescos

BLACK-EYED PEAS IN TOMATO SAUCE

Because beans are so abundant, they are one of the special foods eaten by many Sephardic Jews on Rosh Hashanah to express symbolically a desire for a fruitful year. Black-eyed peas are a type of cowpea, a bean that is particularly plentiful in the Middle East. In the following recipe, the beans are cooked in a style favored by Turkish Jews.

1 tablespoon olive oil
1 medium onion, finely chopped
1 (14- to 16-ounce) can tomatoes, including juice, chopped
1 (10-ounce) package frozen black-eyed peas (cowpeas), slightly thawed

⅛ teaspoon ground black pepper
Salt to taste (optional)

TO SERVE (OPTIONAL)
Hot cooked white or brown rice

Put the oil into a large saucepan over medium-high heat; then sauté the onion until it is tender. Add the tomatoes and their juice, the black-eyed peas, and pepper. Cover, and bring to a boil; then lower the heat, and simmer about 30 minutes. Remove the cover, raise the heat slightly, and lightly boil the beans, stirring often, for 15 to 20 minutes longer, or until they are tender and the liquid has reduced to a thick sauce. Season to taste with salt. If desired, serve over hot cooked rice.

Makes 4 to 5 servings.

Okra with Prunes and Apricots, Syrian-Style

I first tasted this unusual yet very delicious dish at a fascinating prenuptial Syrian-Jewish celebration called a *sweeneh*. The word means "tray," and it represents the tray of goodies traditionally presented by the groom's mother at the bride's premarital ritual bath or *mikvah*. In recent years, the *sweeneh* has often become an elaborate party held at the home of the groom's mother, where exquisite gifts for the bride from her future mother-in-law are elegantly displayed for all to see. Guests are treated to a luncheon of delectable Syrian-Jewish dishes.

The following mixture is so tasty that even those who may be wary of okra will enjoy it. It has been adapted from a recipe in *Deal Delights,* by the Sisterhood of the Deal Synagogue in New Jersey. The original calls for *temerhindi,* a sweet-sour sauce made from tamarind pods and seeds, sugar, lemon juice, sour salt, and water. This unusual Syrian-Jewish condiment tastes a bit like thickened, unsweetened prune juice mixed with lemon juice, ingredients that are much more commonly available and thus have been substituted below.

The combination of sweet dried fruit and a popular (among Sephardim) fall vegetable makes this recipe perfectly suited to the New Year. I've also enjoyed making this in summer, using wonderful homegrown okra available at our local farmers' market.

About 12 ounces fresh, small, whole
    okra or 1 (10-ounce) package
    frozen whole okra, thawed and
    patted dry
$^2/_3$ cup unsweetened prune juice
1 $^1/_2$ to 2 tablespoons lemon juice

1 tablespoon tomato paste
$^1/_8$ teaspoon salt
1 tablespoon extra-virgin olive oil
$^1/_2$ cup (about 3 ounces) pitted prunes
$^1/_2$ cup (about 3 ounces) dried apricot
    halves

Wash the okra well, and very carefully trim off the tough stem ends so as
not to expose any seeds. If the tips are brown, very carefully trim them as
well. (Exposing the seeds results in a gelatinous texture that is unappealing to
many people.) Combine the prune juice, lemon juice, tomato paste, and salt,
and mix very well. Set aside.

Put the oil into a large skillet (preferably nonstick) over medium-high
heat; then sauté the okra until it is lightly browned, about 3 to 5 minutes.
Pour the prune juice mixture over the okra. Distribute the prunes and apricots among the okra.

Bring the liquid to a boil; cover the skillet, and lower the heat. Simmer
the okra and fruit, stirring occasionally, for 5 to 15 minutes, or until they are
tender and the liquid has formed a thick, rich glaze. If necessary, at the end of
the cooking time, remove the cover from the skillet and cook down the liquid, stirring often, until it forms a glaze.

Makes 4 to 6 servings.

Tayglach or Pinyonati

CRUNCHY DOUGH NUGGETS IN HONEY

This sticky, crunchy confection is popular for Rosh Hashanah and the Yom Kippur
"break-fast" among both Ashkenazic Jews (who call it *tayglach*, with a guttural "ch") and
Sephardic Jews (who call it *pinyonati*), because its honey syrup symbolizes a hope for a
sweet year. Both groups also enjoy it for Purim. On these same holidays, Italian Jews
may have a similar pastry that they call *ceciarchiata* because the pieces of dough vaguely
resemble chickpeas (*ceci*, in Italian). In more elaborate versions of tayglach, the dough is

shaped into tiny snails or knots. Sometimes, a nut or raisins are placed in the center of each one.

Whatever its origin, the dessert is prepared in basically the same manner. Small nuggets of baked, fried, or raw dough are added to a honey syrup and simmered or baked until the syrup darkens and thickens to a soft candy consistency. Nuts are typically added to the syrup. Candied fruits, such as cherries, are sometimes added at the end of the cooking process. The finished product may be left in one large slab to be cut up as needed, or it may be divided into individual servings.

Be wary when eating tayglach; it has been known to pull apart dental work!

DOUGH

2 large eggs or ½ cup pareve egg
    substitute
2 tablespoons canola oil
½ teaspoon baking powder
1¼ to 1½ cups unbleached flour

SYRUP AND NUTS

⅔ cup honey
⅓ cup packed light or dark brown sugar
½ to 1 teaspoon ground ginger
¼ teaspoon ground cinnamon
½ to 1 cup coarsely broken walnuts or
    pecans, or slivered almonds

For the dough, use a fork to beat the eggs or egg substitute with the oil in a medium bowl. Add the baking powder and about 1 cup of the flour, and mix well. Add just enough additional flour so the dough is not sticky when handled. Knead gently in the bowl for a few minutes to smooth out the dough, adding bits of flour if needed. Preheat the oven to 350 degrees.

Divide the dough into six to eight pieces. On a lightly floured plastic or wooden cutting board, use your hands to roll each piece of dough into a rope that is ⅜ to ½ inch thick. (If there is not enough flour on the board, the dough will stick to your hands and the board; if there is too much flour, the dough will slide and not roll properly into thin ropes.) Very lightly coat each rope with flour and cut it into ⅜- to ½-inch-long "nuggets," using a sharp knife. If the knife sticks to the dough, flour it occasionally.

As soon as each piece of dough is cut into nuggets, place the nuggets, one at a time, on a large nonstick-spray-coated or well-greased large jelly roll pan or other shallow baking pan. The nuggets should be in one layer and not touching each other. All the nuggets will fit on one jelly roll pan. Bake them at 350 degrees for 15 to 20 minutes, or until they are very lightly browned.

The Days of Awe: Rosh Hashanah Through Yom Kippur

(Shake the pan occasionally, so that the nuggets bake evenly.) Remove them from the oven, and let them cool slightly on the baking sheet.

Meanwhile, prepare the syrup. In a heavy 2½- to 3½-quart saucepan, combine the honey, brown sugar, ginger, and cinnamon, and bring to a boil over medium-high heat. Lower the heat, and very gently simmer the syrup for 10 minutes. Add the warm dough pieces to the syrup. Simmer, stirring frequently but gently with a wooden spoon, for 15 minutes. Stir in the nuts. Continue simmering, while stirring, an additional 5 minutes. Remove the saucepan from the heat and cool the tayglach in the pan, stirring occasionally, for 5 to 10 minutes, or until the syrup becomes very thick and the dough pieces hold together. Turn out all the mixture onto a lightly oiled or nonstick-spray-coated jelly roll pan (such as the one used to bake the nuggets) or heat-proof platter, and let it cool slightly.

Dip your hands (or a spoon) into ice water and use barely wet fingers (or spoon) to form the warm mixture into small mounds or balls containing about three or four pieces of dough and some nuts in each. (The water helps to prevent sticking.) Let the tayglach cool completely before storing. Keep the portions of tayglach separated or they will stick to each other. (Alternatively, the tayglach may be stored in one large mound, and pieces pulled off as desired.)

Tayglach will keep for at least 2 weeks if stored in an airtight container at room temperature. (Pots and pans used for preparation are easily cleaned by soaking them in very hot water.)

Makes 24 to 30 portions of tayglach.

Hadgi Badam

ALMOND-CARDAMOM COOKIES

Jews of Iraqi heritage like to break the Yom Kippur fast with these tasty treats. For Pesach, they sometimes prepare a slightly different version that does not call for flour, egg yolks, or baking powder (page 346). *Hadgi badam* are also widely eaten on Purim. When

shaping the dough, Iraqi Jews sometimes moisten their hands with fragrant rose water to give the cookies a bit of added flavor.

Cardamom (called *hel* in both Hebrew and Arabic) is a sweet-smelling spice that is very popular in Asia and the Middle East, as well as in Scandinavia. For some obscure reason, it is still relatively unknown in the United States. The following cookies are a nice way to give cardamom a try.

NOTE: I've worked out an easy way to make these cookies using a food processor and a very small ice cream scoop that is called a "disher." Small, stainless steel dishers are available at most cookware stores and some supermarkets. They are great for quickly shaping cookie dough before baking.

1 cup blanched slivered or whole almonds (about 4 ounces)	*⅛ teaspoon baking powder*
⅔ cup sugar	*2 large eggs or ½ cup pareve egg substitute*
1 cup all-purpose flour	*About 30 shelled whole almonds or pistachios (optional)*
½ teaspoon ground cardamom	

In a food processor fitted with a steel blade, grind the almonds with the sugar. Add the flour, cardamom, and baking powder, and pulse-process just to mix in. Add the eggs and pulse-process to make a stiff, slightly sticky dough. Preheat the oven to 350 degrees.

Drop generous teaspoonfuls of the dough about 2 inches apart on parchment-lined, or nonstick-spray-coated, cookie sheets. Or for more perfectly shaped cookies, use a very small (#70) disher (see Note), or wet your hands with water, and form the paste into 1-inch balls. Press an almond or pistachio into the top of each ball to slightly flatten it.

Bake the cookies at 350 degrees for 12 to 15 minutes, or until they are firm and very lightly browned. Remove the cookies from the baking sheets, and cool them on wire racks.

Makes about 30 cookies.

Zimsterne or Erste-Steren

SPICY STAR COOKIES

These cookies, adapted from German-Jewish cuisine, are a tasty reminder that we must wait for the "first stars" of the evening to appear before we can break the fast of Yom Kippur. (*Zimsterne* is German for "to the stars"; *Erste Steren* is Yiddish for "first stars.") Furthermore, they are shaped like the six-pointed Star of David.

A small nosh of these crunchy, honey-sweetened treats helps to alleviate hunger pangs while the rest of the postfast meal is being readied. As the cookies keep well, they can be made several days (or even weeks) ahead.

DOUGH
1/4 cup butter or margarine
2/3 cup sugar
1/2 cup honey
3 large eggs or 3/4 cup pareve egg
    substitute
About 3 3/4 cups all-purpose flour
2 teaspoons baking powder

1/2 teaspoon baking soda
1 1/2 to 2 teaspoons ground cinnamon
1/2 teaspoon ground nutmeg
1/4 teaspoon ground cloves

GLAZE (OPTIONAL)
1 large egg, beaten with 1 teaspoon
    water

In a large mixing bowl, use a heavy-duty mixer or a wooden spoon to cream the butter with the sugar and honey until smooth and fluffy. Beat in the eggs. Combine the remaining ingredients, and add to the butter-egg mixture. Mix until well combined. If the dough seems very sticky, add a little extra flour. Divide the dough into three pieces, flatten each one into a disk, and wrap them separately in plastic wrap. Refrigerate the dough several hours (or overnight) until it is quite firm.

Preheat the oven to 375 degrees. Remove one piece of dough from the refrigerator, and roll it out on a lightly floured surface until it is about ⅛ inch thick. Cut out the dough with a small, six-pointed star-shaped cutter, and carefully transfer the cookies to nonstick, spray-coated, parchment-lined, or greased cookie sheets, placing them about 1 inch apart. Reroll the scraps, and cut out as above. (Refrigerate any dough that becomes too soft to work with easily.) Repeat the procedure for the remaining dough.

To give the cookies an attractive, shiny top, brush them lightly with the egg glaze just before baking. Bake the cookies at 375 degrees for 8 to 10 minutes, or until they are lightly browned. Cool them on wire racks. (The cookies get crisper as they cool.)

Makes about 50 cookies; the exact number depends on the size of the cookie cutter.

Orange Honey Cake

During the Days of Awe, as well as Sukkot, one of the most prevalent desserts on the Ashkenazic table is a rich, dense honey cake usually known as *lekach*.

Not a single Rosh Hashanah, Yom Kippur "break-fast," or Brit Milah in our family goes by without this wonderfully fragrant, dark loaf cake. My mother has made it as long as I can remember, and I have carried on the tradition. It differs from most other Ashkenazic honey cakes in that it contains orange juice concentrate, which gives it a wonderfully appealing flavor.

This honey cake develops its best taste and texture a day or two after it is made, so it can be done ahead. Also, this recipe makes two loaf cakes because it is just as easy to make two as one. I usually serve one for Rosh Hashanah and save the second one to break our fast after Yom Kippur. The cake freezes remarkably well and can be saved for Sukkot, when honey cake is also traditional. It is also perfect for Shabbat.

NOTES: If a little bit of oil is poured into the measuring cup before the honey, the honey will slide right out.

The cakes will take less time to bake in dull or dark loaf pans than in shiny ones, as dark pans absorb more heat. You can substitute 1 cup cooled strong coffee for the hot water and instant granules.

1 cup hot water (see Notes)

1 tablespoon instant coffee granules (see Notes)

1 (6-ounce) can (²/₃ cup) frozen orange juice concentrate, thawed

1 teaspoon ground cinnamon

1 teaspoon ground allspice

¼ teaspoon salt

2 teaspoons baking powder

2 teaspoons baking soda

3½ cups all-purpose flour

4 large eggs (no substitutes)

⅓ cup canola oil

1¼ cups sugar

1 cup honey

Coat with nonstick spray or grease two 9 by 5-inch loaf pans. Line the bottom of each pan with a small piece of wax paper cut to fit; then spray or grease the paper. Set the pans aside. Preheat the oven to 325 degrees.

Put the hot water into a 2-cup measuring cup or a small bowl. Add the instant coffee granules, and stir until they are dissolved. Stir in the orange juice concentrate to cool the coffee. Set aside.

Measure out the cinnamon, allspice, salt, baking powder, and baking soda and place in a small custard cup or on a piece of wax paper. Set aside.

Measure the flour by spooning it into the proper-size measuring cups, and leveling off the top. After measuring the flour, sift it onto a large piece of wax paper or into an extra bowl. (Sifting is necessary as tiny lumps may not beat out during the mixing process and will appear in the finished cake.)

Put the eggs, oil, sugar, and honey into a large mixer bowl. With an electric mixer at medium speed, beat them together until completely combined, about 2 minutes. Add the spice mixture, and beat until combined. Beat in about a third of the flour, then a third of the orange-coffee mixture, repeating twice until all the ingredients are added. Beat on low speed until the flour is completely mixed in, scraping the bowl if necessary. Then beat the batter on high speed for 1 to 2 minutes or until it is very smooth. The batter will be thin.

Pour the batter into the prepared pans, dividing it evenly. Bake the cakes at 325 degrees for about 60 to 70 minutes, or until a toothpick inserted into the center of each cake comes out completely clean (test *both* cakes). If there is a wet spot in the center of the top of a cake, bake it a few minutes longer. Remove the cakes from the oven, and let them cool for 1 hour in their pans on a wire rack. The sides of the cakes should shrink away from the pans a little.

Run a knife around the sides of each cake to loosen it; then turn the cake out of its pan, and peel the wax paper from the bottom. Invert the cakes so that the tops are facing upward. Cool the cakes completely on the wire rack. Wrap the cooled cakes well for storage (use sturdy plastic wrap and/or heavy-duty foil).

If the wrapped cakes are allowed to "mellow" overnight, their taste and texture will improve, and they will be easier to slice (a serrated bread knife works best). The tightly wrapped loaves can be kept at room temperature for up to 4 days, or they may be frozen for several months. (Defrost, wrapped, at room temperature, before slicing and serving.) To serve, cut each loaf cross-wise into slices, and arrange the slices, slightly overlapping, on a tray or platter.

Makes 2 loaf cakes; about 10 slices from each.

Honey-Spice Chiffon Cake

This light, high, tube cake is much like a rich sponge cake, and thus quite different from most dense honey cakes typically served on Rosh Hashanah.

A relatively recent invention, chiffon cakes were originated in the late 1920s by a baker—coincidentally named Henry Baker—who kept his formula a secret until the 1940s, when he sold it to General Mills. Once the basic recipe was made known to the public, easy-to-make, delicious chiffon cakes immediately became popular.

As so many chiffon cake variations are pareve, they are particularly convenient for those of us who observe kashrut, because they can be served at both meat and dairy meals.

Chiffon cakes differ from sponge cakes in that they contain oil, which helps keep them fresh-tasting longer. This particular one stays quite moist, and can be baked 2 or 3 days ahead of time if it is well wrapped.

7 large eggs, separated
²/₃ cup sugar, divided
²/₃ cup honey
¹/₂ cup canola oil
2 cups all-purpose flour
1 tablespoon baking powder
¹/₄ teaspoon baking soda

2 teaspoons ground cinnamon
1 teaspoon ground allspice
¹/₂ teaspoon ground cloves
¹/₄ teaspoon ground nutmeg
¹/₄ teaspoon salt
²/₃ cup water
Confectioners' sugar (optional)

Have an ungreased 10-inch angel food tube pan handy. If it is not the two-piece type with a removable tube insert, grease the bottom only and cut a doughnut-shaped piece of wax paper to fit in the bottom. (This will make it easier to remove the cake from the pan.)

Put the egg yolks, ⅓ cup of the sugar, and the honey into a large mixing bowl, and beat with an electric mixer until light. Beat in the oil until well combined. In a bowl, or on a piece of wax paper, sift together the flour, baking powder, baking soda, cinnamon, allspice, cloves, nutmeg, and salt, and add these dry ingredients to the batter alternately with the water. Mix until well blended. Preheat the oven to 325 degrees.

In a clean bowl, with clean beaters, beat the egg whites until frothy; then gradually add the remaining ⅓ cup sugar while continuing to beat just until stiff peaks form. Do not overbeat the whites or they will be difficult to fold into the batter. Stir about a fourth of the whites into the batter to lighten it. Then gently but thoroughly fold all the batter back into the remaining whites. Make sure no lumps of egg white remain.

Pour the batter into the tube pan, and smooth the top. Tap the pan against the countertop to release any large air bubbles. Bake at 325 degrees for 60 to 70 minutes, or until the top of the cake springs back when lightly pressed with a fingertip.

Remove the pan from the oven, and immediately invert it on its "legs," or fit the tube over the top of a bottle to cool upside down. Cool the cake completely before removing it from the pan. Run a knife around the outer and inner edges of the cake, and lift out the tube insert if used. Invert the cake onto a platter. (If the pan was lined with paper, peel it off the bottom of the cake.)

If desired, sprinkle the cake lightly with sieved confectioners' sugar shortly before serving.

Makes about 12 servings.

Apple Crumb Pie

Ever since I was a child, homemade apple pie has been one of my favorites. My mother makes an excellent two-crust pie, but I personally prefer a streusel crumb top. Since the development of kosher vegetable shortening to replace lard in the crust, fruit pies have been popular with Jewish cooks because they are pareve and can be served with a meat meal by those who observe kashrut. As apples are so popular during the Days of Awe, this delicious pie would be a great holiday dessert.

NOTES: Whole wheat flour is used in the crust for its interesting taste and texture; however, all white flour may be used instead. Although pie dough can be made by hand, a food processor is the quickest, easiest way to make excellent pie dough if it is not over-processed. An electric peeler for the apples saves time as well as wear and tear on hands and it wastes less apple than a manual peeler or knife. A glass pie plate is recommended because it browns the bottom crust better than a shiny metal pan. The combination of apples for the filling was chosen for a nice mixture of sweet and tart, firm and soft. Please read the recipe through before beginning. I have designed the recipe to be as quick and foolproof as possible, using modern equipment and special methods.

PIE DOUGH (FOR 1 10-INCH CRUST)
1 cup all-purpose white flour
½ cup whole wheat flour (not bread flour) or all-purpose white flour
1 tablespoon granulated sugar
½ teaspoon salt
½ cup vegetable shortening
1 tablespoon canola oil
3 to 4 tablespoons cold water, or as needed
Pareve nonstick cooking spray or canola oil

APPLE FILLING
10 medium apples (4 Golden Delicious, 4 McIntosh, and 2 Granny Smith)

⅓ cup packed dark or light brown sugar
1 ½ tablespoons cornstarch
1 teaspoon ground cinnamon
½ teaspoon ground nutmeg
⅛ teaspoon salt
¼ cup rich apple juice or cider

STREUSEL TOPPING
⅔ cup all-purpose flour
¼ cup granulated sugar
¼ cup packed dark or light brown sugar
¼ teaspoon ground cinnamon
¼ teaspoon ground nutmeg
¼ teaspoon vanilla extract
4 tablespoons (½ stick) softened pareve margarine

To make the dough in a food processor: Put the white flour, whole wheat flour, sugar, and salt in a food processor fitted with a steel blade, and pulse-process once or twice. Add shortening and 1 tablespoon oil, and process very briefly to cut them in. Add 3 tablespoons water to the processor and process very briefly. The dough should begin to hold together, but *not* form a ball. If the dough is still very dry, add dribbles of water and pulse-process a few more seconds just until it is holding together in large clumps. Remove the blade from the food processor bowl, and invert a 12-inch plastic bag over the top. Turn over the bowl, and tap out all dough into the bag. Squeeze the dough in the bag into a ball. Press it flat into a round disk. Place in the refrigerator while preparing the apples.

To make the dough by hand: Combine the flours, sugar, and salt in a medium bowl, and cut in the shortening and oil using a pastry cutter, fingertips, or knives. Add 3 tablespoons of water and mix with a fork to make a cohesive dough. If the dough is too dry, add sprinkles of water as needed. Gather the dough into a ball. Press it flat into a disk, and wrap in plastic. Place in the refrigerator while preparing the apples.

Peel the apples (using an electric peeler, if desired). Cut the apples into eighths and remove the seeds. (A metal "apple wedger" gadget may be used to cut and core the apples in one push.) Cut the wedges into ¼-inch slices. Put all the slices into a very large bowl. In a small bowl, combine the brown sugar, cornstarch, cinnamon, nutmeg and salt, and mix well. Slowly add the apple juice, while stirring, and mix well to make a sauce. Pour the sauce over the apples, and mix well with a rubber scraper. Set aside.

Coat with nonstick cooking spray or grease a 10-inch glass pie plate (not the deep-dish style). Set aside. Preheat the oven to 425 degrees.

To roll out the dough: Put the disk of dough between two large pieces of heavy plastic wrap. Roll the dough from the center out toward the perimeter until it makes a 13-inch-diameter circle (or large enough for your pie plate) of even thickness. Peel off the top sheet of plastic. Turn the crust over onto the pie plate, center it exactly to fit, and press it into place through the plastic; then carefully peel off the second sheet of plastic. Fold under any excess dough on the edges of the pie plate, and crimp the edges by pressing the dough between the index finger of one hand and the thumb and index finger of the other hand. To keep the crust from becoming soggy when it bakes,

spray the inside with olive oil spray or nonstick cooking spray, or brush it very lightly with canola oil.

Stir the apples so all are coated with sauce. Carefully spoon all the apples into the crust, heaping them very high in the center. Pour any sauce left in the bowl evenly over the top. Bake the pie at 425 degrees for 15 minutes. Meanwhile, prepare the streusel topping.

In a medium bowl, use a fork to mix together the flour, granulated and brown sugars, cinnamon, and nutmeg. Stir in the vanilla; then cut the margarine into the dry mixture by mashing it with a fork. Mix (using fingertips if necessary) until the mixture is moist and can be squeezed in the hand to form small lumps. After the pie has baked as directed above, remove it from the oven to a rack. Very carefully hand-sprinkle the streusel crumbs on top, leaving some of it in small lumps. Be sure to cover the entire top. Turn down the heat to 350 degrees, and bake for an additional 55 to 60 minutes (to ensure soft apples). Cool the pie on a rack. Refrigerate it if overnight storage is necessary. It may be eaten slightly warm, at room temperature, or chilled.

Makes 8 to 10 servings.

Whole Wheat "Jewish Apple Cake"

I've had several versions of "Jewish Apple Cake" in my files for a long time, but I got the first one more than twenty-five years ago at a hospital bake sale in downtown Baltimore shortly after I was married. The ladies' auxiliary was cleverly selling handwritten recipe cards along with baked goods. I was very curious as to just what made the particular cake "Jewish"—I had never seen that nomenclature before—but none of the volunteers had a clue.

Later, I saw other recipes for Jewish Apple Cake, all of which called for oil rather than butter, as in most cakes. The use of oil makes the cake pareve, meaning it can be served at either meat or dairy meals by Jewish cooks who observe kashrut. As apples have always been popular in Eastern European cuisine, it's possible that Ashkenazic American bakers invented oil-based apple cakes that eventually got the ethnic appellation.

Whole wheat flour gives an appealing texture to this cake, which is especially high in fiber and low in saturated fat. Furthermore, this version is relatively easy to prepare because unpeeled apples are coarsely chopped (in a food processor, if desired) and then are folded into the batter with the walnuts. Other versions require neatly sliced apples to be tediously layered with the batter.

NOTES: Golden Delicious apples are recommended because they hold their shape well during baking and do not exude too much juice; however, other firm-baking apples may be used. If desired, diced pears may be substituted for the apples. Nuts are nontraditional for a Jewish Apple Cake, but they fit very well in this version. They may be omitted if desired.

4 medium Golden Delicious apples	1/2 teaspoon ground nutmeg
4 large eggs or 1 cup pareve egg substitute or 2 large eggs plus 3 egg whites	2 cups all-purpose flour
	1 cup whole wheat flour (not bread flour)
1 cup granulated sugar	2 teaspoons baking soda
1 cup packed dark brown sugar	1 cup coarsely chopped walnuts (optional)
1 cup canola oil	Confectioners' sugar (optional)
2 teaspoons vanilla extract	
1 teaspoon ground cinnamon	

Coat well with nonstick cooking spray or grease a 12-cup Bundt pan or tube pan. Coarsely chop the apples into 1/2-inch pieces by hand or with a food processor. It is not necessary to peel the apples unless you prefer not to have bits of peel in the cake. Set the apples aside momentarily. Preheat the oven to 350 degrees.

Put the eggs, granulated sugar, brown sugar, and oil into a large mixer bowl, and beat with an electric mixer until light. Beat in the vanilla, cinnamon, and nutmeg. Mix in the all-purpose and whole wheat flours and baking soda just until combined. The batter will be very thick. Stir in the apples and nuts by hand. There will seem to be a lot of fruit and nuts for the amount of batter.

Turn out the batter into the prepared pan, and bake at 350 degrees for 70 to 80 minutes, or until a toothpick inserted into the center comes out clean. Cool in the pan on a rack for 15 minutes; then turn the cake out of the pan

to cool completely on a wire rack. If desired, just before serving, sprinkle the top lightly with sieved confectioners' sugar.

Makes 1 large round cake, about 16 slices.

Pear-Raspberry Tart

This very quick and easy dessert pastry is quite suitable for a Rosh Hashanah dinner or a Yom Kippur "break-fast," when delectable, sweet pears are in season. I also prepare this tasty treat for Shabbat dinner. A Golden Delicious apple may be substituted for the pear, if desired.

CRUST AND TOPPING
1 1/4 cups all-purpose flour
1 cup quick rolled oats
1/3 cup granulated sugar
1/3 cup packed dark brown sugar
1 teaspoon baking powder
1/4 cup canola oil

1/4 cup water
1/2 teaspoon almond extract

FILLING
1 large ripe pear, such as Bartlett or
    Anjou
1/2 cup seedless raspberry preserves

Coat with nonstick cooking spray or grease a 9-inch round tart or cake pan or an 8-inch square pan. Preheat the oven to 375 degrees.

For the crust and topping, put the flour, oats, granulated and brown sugars, and baking powder into a medium bowl, and mix with a fork to combine. Add the oil, water, and almond extract, and mix to make moist crumbs. Remove 1 cup of the mixture, and set aside. Press the rest into the bottom of the prepared pan.

Core and thinly slice the pear. Spread the preserves on top of the crust, and top with the sliced pear. Sprinkle the reserved crust mixture on top. Bake at 375 degrees for about 35 minutes, or until the pear is tender and the crust is firm. Cool completely before cutting into wedges to serve.

Makes 6 to 8 servings.

The Days of Awe: Rosh Hashanah Through Yom Kippur

Ka'ak

SAVORY SESAME-ANISE RINGS

P

*K*a'ak are among the foods mentioned in the Talmud. These crunchy snacks—which are like anise-flavored pretzel rings—are staples in the households of Syrian Jews. I first tasted them at the Deal, New Jersey, home of Ginger Kassin, whose ancestors hail from Aleppo, Syria.

Many Syrian Jews still follow culinary customs that have been practiced for generations. For instance, *ka'ak* are served at just about every festival (except, of course, Pesach), and are also featured at religious occasions such as Oneg Shabbat and Brit Milah. Furthermore, a guest in any Syrian-Jewish home is always offered *ka'ak* as a courtesy.

Ka'ak are also eaten to break the fast after Yom Kippur. They are perfectly suited for this, as they are not sweet, but are subtly flavored with a variety of refreshing spices. The sesame seeds on top represent the hope that the coming year will be fruitful and replete with good deeds.

Similar sesame "rings" are also eaten by Jews from other Middle Eastern countries such as Iraq and Egypt, and they are popular in Israel. Depending on the background of the baker, they may be seasoned with anise, cumin, coriander, or other spices, or simply salt. Sephardic Jews make a yeast-raised form of *biscocho* that is very similar to *ka'ak*. These may also be called *rozkitas, roscas, rosefuettes,* or *rosquettes*. These are usually baked in a slightly different manner than the following *ka'ak* (see Note below).

This is my adaptation of a recipe for *ka'ak* that appeared in *Deal Delights,* a cookbook compiled by the Sisterhood of the Deal Synagogue. The *ka'ak* are baked twice, to dry them out and make them crunchy. They keep quite well, and thus can be made in advance and stored at room temperature for a week or longer. Or they can be frozen for several months.

NOTE: There is an alternative method of baking the rings that makes them crunchy but not quite as hard as those below, and does not require a second baking. Preheat the oven to 350 degrees. Bake the prepared dough rings for 25 to 30 minutes, or until they are lightly browned. Cool them completely on wire racks.

1 package (2¼ teaspoons) active dry
   yeast

1 teaspoon sugar

1¼ cups warm (105 to 115 degrees)
   water

4 to 4½ cups unbleached flour (may be
   half whole wheat flour)

2 tablespoons aniseeds

½ teaspoon ground cumin

½ teaspoon ground coriander seeds
   (optional)

2 teaspoons salt

⅔ cup vegetable shortening

1 tablespoon canola oil

GLAZE AND TOPPING

1 large egg, lightly beaten with 1
   teaspoon water, or ¼ cup egg
   substitute

About ⅓ cup sesame seeds

In a small bowl, dissolve the yeast and sugar in the warm water, and let the mixture rest for 5 to 10 minutes or until it is foamy.

In a large bowl, combine 4 cups of the flour, the aniseeds, cumin, coriander (if used), and salt. Cut in the shortening and oil with a pastry blender or electric mixer until the mixture resembles coarse crumbs. Add the yeast mixture, and mix to make a firm dough. If using a heavy-duty mixer with a dough hook, knead the dough in the mixer. Otherwise, turn out the dough onto a lightly floured surface, and knead it for 5 to 10 minutes, or until it is smooth and elastic. Add sprinkles of flour, as necessary, to keep the dough from sticking.

Put the dough into an oiled bowl, and turn it so that all surfaces are oiled. Cover the bowl loosely with plastic wrap and a dish towel, and let the dough rise until it has doubled in bulk, about 1½ hours. Preheat the oven to 400 degrees.

Punch down the dough; then divide it in half. Form one-half into a log that is about 2 inches in diameter and 15 inches long. Crosswise cut the log into ½-inch wide pieces. Roll each piece into a rope that is ½-inch thick and about 5 inches long. Bring the ends of each rope together to form a small ring, and pinch the ends tightly together.

Dip the top (only) of each ring into the egg glaze, and then into the sesame seeds. Place the rings, seeded side up, about 1 inch apart on a large, parchment-lined, lightly greased, or nonstick-spray-coated heavy baking

The Days of Awe: Rosh Hashanah Through Yom Kippur

sheet. (For a "fancy" look, use a small, sharp knife to cut notches about ½ inch apart around the outside of each ring.) Immediately bake the rings at 400 degrees for 10 minutes. Meanwhile, shape the remaining dough into rings, place on another baking sheet, and bake as above. When both batches of rings are done baking, make sure they are loosened from the baking sheets, but leave them in place. Lower the oven temperature to 300 degrees.

Return the rings to the oven. (One baking sheet can be put on the top oven shelf, and the other on the middle.) Bake the rings for an additional 20 to 30 minutes, rotating the two sheets every 10 minutes for more-even baking, or until they are dried out and crisp, like pretzels. Cool them completely on wire racks; then store them in an airtight container.

Makes about 50 to 60 rings.

Sukkot, Shemini Atzeret, and Simhat Torah

THREE TIMES DURING THE YEAR, AT SUKKOT, PESACH, AND Shavuot, early Jews made festive pilgrimage to the Holy Temple in Jerusalem. Sukkot, the most jubilant and splendid of these thanksgiving festivals, occurred at the conclusion of the autumn harvest. This holiday was so prominent in ancient times that any reference simply to "The Festival" always meant Sukkot.

As with many Jewish holidays, it actually had a number of names. It was called *Hag Ha'Asif* ("Festival of the Ingathering"), referring to the gathering of crops, as well as *Zeman Simhatenu* ("Season of Our Gladness"). It was also called *Hag Ha'Sukkot* or "Festival of the Tabernacles." The latter name eventually became shortened to *Sukkot.*

Tabernacles, booths, huts, or cabanas, as the word *sukkot* is variously translated, became an important part of the festival due to its agricultural nature. In earlier times, families banded together in villages for protection, and went back and forth to farms that were scattered on the outskirts. During the busy fall harvest season, however, there was no time for such travels. So farmers built rough-hewn huts with foliage roofs as temporary on-site residences. Pilgrims traveling to Jerusalem also used such huts.

The sukkot were given biblical importance with the following commandment from Leviticus: "You shall live in booths seven days . . . in order that future generations may

know that I made the Israelite people live in booths when I brought them out of the land of Egypt. I am the Lord your God." Thus, sukkot came to commemorate the temporary abodes of those who wandered through the desert with Moses after the Exodus.

To this day, Jews all over the world build impermanent foliage-topped booths to celebrate the holiday of Sukkot, which begins on the fifteenth day of the Hebrew month of Tishri, exactly two weeks after the first day of Rosh Hashanah, and occurs in September or October. One is supposed to begin construction shortly after Yom Kippur, and the completed *sukkah* (the singular form of *sukkot*) should be beautifully decorated to reflect the joyous nature of the holiday.

The festival of Sukkot lasts seven days. During that time, Jewish families are supposed to eat all their main meals in a sukkah, particularly on the first day. Feasting is the keynote; indeed, it is forbidden to fast during this happy festival. Also, we are encouraged to use the sukkah for other relaxing activities, such as reading, conversation, or entertaining guests.

However, because one should always rejoice in the sukkah and not suffer in it, we are not supposed to be in the sukkah when it is raining or conditions are otherwise uncomfortable. It is for this reason that those of us in colder climates do not usually sleep in the sukkah, though in Israel this practice is more commonplace.

According to Jewish law, a sukkah should have at least three sides. Although the sukkah is supposed to be a temporary structure, it may use a permanent building as one or more of its sides. In Israel, where most of the Jewish population live in apartments, sukkot proliferate well above street level on tiny balconies, terraces, and rooftops. In suburban America (where the practice of building a sukkah appears to be on the increase), porches, wooden decks, and grassy backyards are likely locations.

The top of the sukkah should be open enough to allow a view of the stars at night, yet still provide more shade than sunlight during the day. The roof covering, called *sechach* (pronounced with guttural "ch"s) in Hebrew, must be something in its natural state, which once grew but is now cut down. Evergreen branches, bamboo poles (which can be saved for many years), and dried cornstalks are commonly used. For our sukkah, we trim overgrown bushes and trees in our yard and in the wooded area behind our house.

Sukkah-building is a family project in our household, enjoyed by all. My husband and our older sons clean and assemble the plastic-pipe frame, and cut and place the *sechach*. I attach a wooden lattice top that supports the greenery and hang plastic tarps for the sides. And our two younger children gaily decorate the inside walls with their own artwork and other items.

The New Jewish Holiday Cookbook

In celebration of the harvest, the sukkah decoration almost always includes some fruits and vegetables that reach maturity in autumn. As these vary greatly from place to place, so do the sukkot. For instance, a typical American sukkah might have apples, pears, gourds, strings of cranberries, and Indian corn hanging from its roof and walls. An Israeli sukkah would more likely be adorned with pomegranates, persimmons, oranges, avocados, grapes, figs, and dates.

Because fresh produce tends to attract bees and wasps at this time of year—which definitely can have a detrimental effect on one's joy while dining—many modern sukkot (including my own) are gaily decorated with *plastic* fruit and vegetables. These have the added benefit of being reusable from year to year, and they don't wither or spoil.

For all sukkot, wherever they are located, a fresh *etrog* and *lulav* are essential. These comprise the four species of plants that must be held together in a specific manner and shaken in daylight (so we can see them) during the holiday, except for Shabbat. They are waved in the four compass directions, as well as up toward the heavens and down toward earth, to acknowledge God's encompassing presence. In addition, the four species are carried around the synagogue during the morning service on each day of Sukkot (except Shabbat), while a *hoshanah* ("save us") hymn is recited.

The *etrog* (or citron), an ancient citrus fruit considered by some to be the biblical fruit eaten by Adam and Eve, is the most important of the symbolic plants because it is the only one having both taste and smell. This sour-tasting yellow fruit has a surprisingly lovely aroma. (When we keep our etrog indoors overnight, displayed in its special holder, it perfumes our house with a wonderful fragrance.) An etrog looks like a very large elongated lemon but, when cut open, has much more rind with hardly any flesh. Unlike most citrus, the blossom end of an etrog frequently forms a distinctive point called a *pitom,* which many Jews find desirable, partially because it clearly designates the "top" of the fruit. After Sukkot is over, the etrog is sometimes cooked into preserves or candy with the addition of much sugar.

The *lulav* is composed of a palm branch (its fruit has taste but no smell) in the center, three myrtle branches (smell but no taste) on the right, and two willow branches (no taste or smell) on the left. The branches are all tied together or placed in a natural woven holder so they can be held in one hand.

Sometimes, the four species are said to represent parts of a person's body—the etrog is similar to a heart, the palm branch is straight but bendable like a spine, myrtle leaves are shaped like eyes, and willow leaves like lips. There are many additional symbolic and mystical interpretations.

Sukkot, Shemini Atzeret, and Simhat Torah

The foods eaten during Sukkot reflect the bounty of a harvest celebration, and are frequently shared with guests in the sukkah. In fact, it is a holiday custom to symbolically welcome biblical patriarchs (and, for some, matriarchs) as honorary guests, or *ushpizin,* each day. Lavish casseroles, rich stews, and filled pastries are typical, especially those featuring autumnal vegetables and fruits. In the past, fresh produce was available only during the brief harvest period when it was in season. Thus, it became favored for use in special holiday fare. A wide variety of savory and sweet "stuffed foods" is served because their extravagance is in keeping with the opulent atmosphere of celebration. Sweet-and-sour stuffed cabbage called Holishkes or Prakkes (page 170) is particularly popular among Ashkenazim.

One-dish casseroles are popular for a more pragmatic reason. They are easy to transport from kitchen to sukkah, and stay hot and palatable throughout a meal eaten outdoors. Even on cool nights, they help keep the family warm and satisfied.

On *Hoshanah Rabbah,* the seventh and last day of Sukkot, the etrog and lulav are carried around the synagogue seven times, rather than just once as on the six previous days. Each person present then takes a willow branch and beats it on the floor until most of its leaves have fallen off. The fallen leaves symbolize many things, including the falling away of sins, the falling of rain, and renewed life in the spring (when leaves will grow again).

Hoshanah Rabbah is considered the last day when any unfavorable divine judgments of Yom Kippur may be reversed, and when God's final verdict is sealed and "written." Therefore, round challah and honey-sweetened treats are eaten for the same reasons as during the Days of Awe. Sometimes, the *challah* (holiday bread) is shaped like an outreaching hand to receive the divine decree. As on Yom Kippur and Purim, Meat Kreplach (see page 112) are also a traditional part of the meal served after the synagogue service.

In Israel, a sweet dish made with a giant, pumpkinlike squash called *dla'at* may also be served on this day. The size and abundance of the squash make it a symbol of plenty, and its pleasing taste expresses hope for a sweet year. Also, Jews from the Germanic countries often eat a dish made with cabbage cooked in water (*kohl mit wasser*), as a play on the Hebrew words *kol me'vasser* from a prayer recited when the willow branches are beaten.

Hoshanah Rabbah is followed immediately by *Shemini Atzeret* ("Eighth Day of Assembly"), which is linked to the Sukkot festival but is a separate, independent holiday. On this day, it has become customary to say a solemn prayer for rain. According to tra-

dition, this is when God judges the world's water, so the prayer asks for enough rain to support life but not so much as to cause flooding and famine.

As with several other Jewish holidays, Shemini Atzeret was extended to two days in the Diaspora, to allow for a "margin of error" should the exact date of celebration be slightly miscalculated by those far away from the Land of Israel. The second day eventually became known as *Simhat Torah* ("Rejoicing in the Law") because this is when the last verses of the sacred Torah (the Five Books of Moses) are read in the synagogue, and the cyclical reading of the Torah begins anew with Genesis.

The synagogue service for Simhat Torah (which is pronounced with a guttural "h" in the first word) is one of the happiest and most exuberant of the entire year. All the scrolls of the Torah are removed from the Ark and lovingly paraded around the sanctuary while members of the congregation joyfully dance and sing Hebrew songs. Children often wave colorful paper flags. In many places, it was once customary for an apple or beet holding a lit candle to be stuck on the top of each miniature flagpole. Nowadays, youngsters are often given bags containing candy, fruit, and nuts.

All over Israel (where Shemini Atzeret and Simhat Torah are celebrated on the same day), and in many other places, the Torah procession continues outside into the streets surrounding the synagogue, where observers typically get caught up in the merriment and join in the dancing and singing.

For Simhat Torah, Israeli bakers sometimes add a fruity candy called "Turkish delight" to the fillings for pastries such as strudel and fluden, and street vendors sell candy-coated apples. Worldwide, spicy honey cookies and small cakes filled with fruits and nuts are popular treats, as are etrog preserves and candied etrog peel. Also, seasonal fruits and vegetables are traditionally preserved or dried at this time, for the year ahead.

In keeping with the opulent spirit of Sukkot and the holidays that immediately follow it, this chapter is "stuffed" with recipes for delectable fall dishes. It also includes detailed directions for constructing a miniature gingerbread sukkah.

In addition, many of the sweet pastries and desserts served during the Days of Awe continue to be enjoyed during Sukkot. They are frequently offered at popular "open houses," where guests happily nosh their way from one sukkah to another throughout an intermediate day of the holiday.

Note also that many Sukkot recipes would also be perfect for Thanksgiving. After all, it is generally understood that the American Pilgrims, who based many of their customs on the Hebrew Bible, patterned their 1621 celebration after Sukkot.

Mitzapuny

MEATY SPLIT PEA, BEAN, AND BARLEY SOUP

The first time my maternal great-grandparents, Rose Dublin and Harry Levine, met was on the day they wed. As with most turn-of-the-century marriages in Russian shtetls, theirs had been arranged. Fortunately for them, it was love at first sight. Unfortunately, however, my great-grandfather was about to be conscripted into the Russian army for many years.

So, when they said their good-byes to family and friends and ostensibly left on a short honeymoon, Bubby Rose and Zaida Harry walked out of the country with only the belongings they could carry. They eventually made their way to England, where they planned to settle. Because the cold, damp weather repeatedly left them ill, they decided to head for America and the "golden opportunities" of New York City, where they eventually settled in Brooklyn and had four children, including my mother's mother.

All through her travels, Bubby Rose carried this recipe in her mind. When times were difficult, she used a few soup bones to make a version that filled the stomach without emptying the purse. In better times, chunks of meat and some fresh vegetables were added (as below) to make it very rich. No matter what, it was always thick and hearty enough to be a very satisfying one-dish meal—more like a stew than a soup.

With its variety of important nutrients, *mitzapuny* is also healthful, a fact not lost on my mother, who learned how to make it from her beloved bubby. Mom prepared it for me the day I came home from the hospital with my first baby. One of my favorite childhood dishes, the delicious pottage nourished my spirit as well as my body. It was just what the doctor ordered.

In trying to track down the meaning of the soup's name, I learned about the Yiddish word *martzapunis*. The word, I was told, literally translates as the name of an exotic fruit, but it has come to mean anything special and extraordinary. Whether or not that was what Bubby Rose meant years ago when she used to make this soup for my mother, it is indeed quite special. When the weather is chilly and the wind howls, nothing warms like a big bowl of *mitzapuny*. It's the perfect one-dish dinner for Sukkot.

12 cups water

2 to 3 pounds soup beef, trimmed of all surface fat and cut into large chunks

3 small onions, peeled and left whole

4 to 5 medium carrots or about 1 pound peeled baby carrots, cut into ½-inch chunks

2 celery stalks, thinly sliced

1¼ cups dry green split peas, sorted and rinsed

1 cup dry baby lima beans, sorted and rinsed

½ cup uncooked pearl barley, rinsed

1 teaspoon salt

¼ teaspoon ground black pepper

Bring the water to a boil in a 6-quart or larger soup pot over high heat. Add the meat, and lower the heat so the water simmers. Gently cook the meat for 30 minutes, skimming off and discarding all the foam that rises to the surface. Meanwhile, prepare the remaining ingredients.

Add the remaining ingredients, cover the pot, and simmer the soup, stirring occasionally (especially during the end of the cooking period), for about 3 hours longer, or until the split peas have disintegrated, the meat is very tender, and the soup is thick. If it becomes too thick, stir in some hot water. Remove and discard the onions before serving. Adjust the seasonings to taste.

Makes about 8 to 10 servings.

NOTE: Leftovers can be frozen. Defrost the soup before reheating, and add water if the soup has become too thick. Stir the soup often when reheating it, so it does not stick to the bottom of the pot. This problem can be avoided by reheating individual servings of the soup in a microwave oven.

Variation

BEEF AND BARLEY SOUP (WITH MUSHROOMS)

If mushrooms are desired, pour 1 cup boiling water over 1 ounce of dried mushrooms, and let them soak for 30 minutes. Drain the mushrooms well, and cut up any very large pieces. Set aside the mushrooms. (The mushroom liquid may be poured through a coffee filter to remove any grit, and added to the soup.) Finely chop 1 medium onion, and sauté it in 1 to 2 tablespoons canola oil. Add the water and meat, and simmer as directed above. Omit the split peas, and increase the barley to 1¼ cups. Add the soaked mushrooms

Sukkot, Shemini Atzeret, and Simhat Torah

with the remaining ingredients. Add ½ to 1 teaspoon each dried thyme and marjoram leaves. Cook until the meat and lima beans are tender. Adjust seasonings to taste.

Holishkes or Prakkes
SWEET-AND-SOUR STUFFED CABBAGE

For many Ashkenazic Jews, stuffed cabbage—that is, meat-stuffed cabbage rolls simmered in sweet-and-sour sauce—is essential for Sukkot. It is one of the many dishes that were developed in the shtetls of Eastern and Central Europe to transform mundane ingredients like cabbage into rich-tasting delicacies. At the same time, precious meat was stretched to serve a few more.

This dish probably became traditional for Sukkot because cabbage is plentiful during the harvest season, and stuffed foods are customarily eaten on the holiday to symbolize abundance.

Jews of varying backgrounds have many different appellations for the ever-popular "stuffed cabbage" (a common American-Jewish term). Some of the more familiar Ashkenazic ones include *holishkes, prakkes* (pronounced "prah'-kuss"), *holoptches,* and *galuptzes.* Sephardic Jews make a very similar type of stuffed cabbage, occasionally using ground lamb instead of beef. Those from Turkey and nearby areas generally call the dish *dolmas de col* or *yaprakis* (which sounds sort of like *prakkes*). Middle Eastern Jews spice it differently, and sometimes call it *sarmas* or *mishi malfouf.*

As with many other Jewish recipes that have been carried around the world, stuffed cabbage has innumerable variations. To give the following Ashkenazic variation a delicious, satisfying taste, I have added a few innovative ingredients, including applesauce and mustard powder.

This recipe makes lots more than the one in my original book. When you are using a large cabbage (it is much easier and quicker to stuff large cabbage leaves than small ones), you may as well make enough for holiday company and other meals. Besides, many people think that this stuffed cabbage tastes even better when it is left over.

NOTE: Green (also called "white") cabbage is the firm cabbage with smooth leaves that is commonly found in supermarkets. If time allows, it may be softened by freezing

it for 2 to 3 days, and then defrosting it in the refrigerator overnight. Boiling the leaves, as directed below, is then not necessary.

1 large head green (white) cabbage (see Note)

SAUCE

1 (28- to 29-ounce) can tomato purée
3¾ cups water
1 cup applesauce
1 large onion, finely chopped
½ cup packed dark brown sugar
½ cup apple cider vinegar
2 tablespoons lemon juice
1 teaspoon powdered mustard
Salt and ground black pepper to taste
½ cup raisins

FILLING

2½ to 3 pounds very lean ground beef
1 large onion, grated
1¼ cups uncooked long-grain white rice
¾ cup applesauce
3 large eggs or ¾ cup pareve egg substitute
1½ teaspoons salt
½ teaspoon black pepper, preferably freshly ground
¼ teaspoon ground allspice (optional)

Cut out and discard the core and any discolored outer leaves from the cabbage. Boil the entire head of cabbage in a large pot of water for about 10 minutes, or until the outer leaves soften. Remove the cabbage to a colander and carefully peel off the leaves so that they do not tear. (Don't worry about little tears or holes on the edges of the leaves.) When the inner leaves become too hard to peel, return the cabbage to the boiling water, and repeat the process until most of the cabbage leaves are removed. Stack the curved leaves so they look like little "bowls."

While the cabbage is boiling, begin the sauce. Put all the ingredients in a heavy, wide, deep pot such as a large (6- to 8-quart) Dutch oven. Stir well to mix the ingredients, making sure that the brown sugar is dissolved. Bring the sauce to a simmer over medium-high heat; then reduce the heat, cover, and gently simmer, stirring occasionally.

Meanwhile, prepare the filling and stuff the cabbage. For the filling, mix together all the ingredients very well with your hands or a fork until they are well combined and smooth. To stuff the cabbage, mound about ¼ to ½ cup filling in the center of a leaf (the exact amount depends on the size of the leaf; the filling should be completely enclosed with none showing). Fold up the

Sukkot, Shemini Atzeret, and Simhat Torah

thick edge of the leaf that was nearest the core to partially cover the filling. Next, fold in one side and then the other. Finally, roll up the leaf to enclose the filling. Put the roll, seam side down, into the simmering sauce. Continue until all the filling is used. (There may be extra leaves.) Try to arrange the cabbage rolls in no more than two layers in the pot.

Spoon some sauce over any rolls that are not already covered with it, and cover the pan. Gently simmer the rolls so they do not come apart, basting them occasionally, for 60 to 75 minutes, or until the meat and rice in the filling are cooked through, and the sauce is thick. Occasionally use a spoon to make sure that the rolls are not sticking on the bottom of the pot and burning. If the sauce gets too thick during the cooking period, add a little water to the pot.

Serve each cabbage roll with plenty of sweet-and-sour sauce because the meat filling is rather plain without it.

Stuffed cabbage can be made ahead and reheated, and has a deserved reputation for being "even better the next day." It can also be frozen.

Makes 10 to 12 servings.

Quick "Unstuffed" Sweet-and-Sour Cabbage and Beef

Stuffed Cabbage (page 170) made the old-fashioned way is a favorite dish of mine, but I don't always have the time to fuss with it. Also, my children sometimes peel off the cabbage wrappers and don't eat them. As cabbage is a very healthful vegetable, I was determined to find a way to prepare the dish in a quick and easy way that would encourage my kids to eat the cabbage. The following has been a great success with my family.

NOTE: The recipe calls for a small amount of cooked rice. Instant rice may be used.

1 to 1¼ pounds lean ground beef
1 medium onion, finely chopped

1 (15- to 16-ounce) can plain tomato sauce

½ cup unsweetened applesauce

¼ cup water

3 tablespoons cider vinegar

2 tablespoons packed dark brown sugar

⅛ teaspoon ground black pepper

4 cups (about 1 pound) finely chopped
 green (white) cabbage

1 cup cooked rice (see Note)

In a 12-inch-wide deep skillet or a Dutch oven, cook the ground beef and onion over medium heat, breaking up the meat with a spoon or S-shaped potato masher. When the meat has browned and the onion is tender, spoon off and discard any fat in the skillet.

Add the tomato sauce, applesauce, water, vinegar, brown sugar, and pepper. Bring the mixture to a boil, stirring constantly. Stir in the cabbage, which will wilt as it cooks and become more compact.

Lower the heat and simmer, covered, stirring occasionally, for 25 to 30 minutes, or until the cabbage is very tender. Stir in the cooked rice, and heat a few minutes longer until it is cooked through. This is most easily served in bowls.

Makes about 4 to 5 servings.

Freda's Stuffed Peppers

Many years ago, when I first started cooking for my (then) new husband, I discovered that he had a favorite dish—his mother's stuffed peppers. My mother-in-law, Freda, graciously obliged when I asked for the recipe, never telling me about her son's little quirk. I soon discovered that my hubby loved the filling and sauce, but would have nothing to do with the softened peppers, which he peeled off and discarded.

It turned out that my dear spouse loves the delicious flavor instilled into the sauce from the peppers, but not their cooked texture. As I enjoy almost every vegetable no matter how it is cooked, this is not a problem. I just add his "peelings" to my plate!

My mother-in-law had another solution. Fresh peppers used to be very expensive, and my husband didn't eat them anyway, so Freda didn't put all the meat mixture into peppers. She would use about a third of it to make giant meatballs that cooked with the

peppers and picked up their flavor. This is an alternative way of making this dish, which is very easy to prepare and requires no unusual ingredients.

NOTE: When buying green peppers for this dish, choose those that are short and wide rather than tall and narrow, as they will be easier to clean and fill.

6 to 8 green peppers (see Note)

About 2 pounds very lean ground beef

²⁄₃ cup uncooked long-grain white rice

1 large egg or ¹⁄₄ cup pareve egg substitute

About 1¹⁄₄ cups water, divided

³⁄₄ teaspoon salt

¹⁄₄ teaspoon ground black pepper

2 (16-ounce) cans plain tomato sauce

Clean the peppers by carefully cutting out and removing the stem, core, and all seeds, leaving the peppers whole. Use your fingers or a fork to mix the meat, rice, egg, ¼ cup water, salt, and pepper very well. Fill each pepper with some of the mixture. If there is any extra meat filling, form it into large meatballs. Put the tomato sauce and 1 cup water into a large, heavy, deep skillet or a Dutch oven, and bring it to a simmer. Gently add the stuffed peppers to the sauce, standing them upright in one layer if possible. Arrange any meatballs around the peppers. Spoon some sauce over the top of each pepper and the meatballs.

Cover, and gently simmer the peppers for about 1½ hours (the long cooking time makes the pepper flesh somewhat mushy, but gives the sauce a great flavor). Occasionally, push the peppers and meatballs around with a spoon so they don't stick to the bottom of the pan, and baste them with some sauce. If the sauce gets too thick, stir in a little water. Serve peppers and meatballs with some sauce spooned over them.

Makes about 6 servings.

Kibbeh

MEAT LOAF WITH BULGUR WHEAT AND PINE NUTS

This classical Middle Eastern meat dish is popular in Israel, particularly among those Jews who emigrated from Syria, Lebanon, Iraq, and Kurdistan. There are actually several types of kibbeh, all made from basically the same ingredients. The following version is baked in layers in a pan, and may be called *kibbeh bil saniyeh,* meaning "kibbeh in a tray."

More time-consuming and difficult to prepare is the kibbeh that is formed into torpedo or pear shapes, filled with a precooked meat mixture, and deep-fried. The outer layer is usually made from ground meat kneaded with bulgur wheat. However, some Jews use matzah meal or rice instead of bulgur, or a meatless mixture made with matzah meal and/or rice. Occasionally, pomegranate seeds are added to the meat filling.

Sometimes, kibbeh is eaten raw in the same manner as steak tartare, and is considered a delicacy. Syrian Jews make a vegetarian variation of this type of kibbeh, using red lentils in place of meat.

Baked *kibbeh bil saniyeh* can be made ahead and reheated, and is a great company dish. The flavor is subtle—even a bit mysterious. In the following version, a layer of cooked ground beef and pine nuts is placed between two layers of finely ground raw beef and bulgur. The layers are baked together as a meat loaf.

Kibbeh is traditionally made with lamb, the most common meat in the Middle East. However, it is also excellent with beef, which is my preference because kosher ground beef is more available and less expensive than ground lamb, and it generally is lower in fat.

2 cups fine bulgur wheat

FILLING
1 pound lean ground beef or lamb
1 large onion, finely chopped
1 teaspoon ground cinnamon
1/4 teaspoon ground allspice
1/4 teaspoon salt
1/4 teaspoon ground black pepper
1/2 cup pine nuts (pignoli) or slivered almonds (or a mixture)

BULGUR-MEAT LAYERS
2 medium onions, peeled
1/2 teaspoon ground allspice
1/2 teaspoon ground cinnamon
1 teaspoon salt
1/4 teaspoon ground black pepper
1 1/2 pounds lean ground beef or lamb
1/2 cup very cold water

FOR BAKING
3 tablespoons canola oil
2 tablespoons water

Sukkot, Shemini Atzeret, and Simhat Torah

Put the bulgur in a large bowl and cover it with water. Let it soak for 15 to 20 minutes. Coat a 9 by 13-inch baking dish with nonstick cooking spray or grease it well. Set aside.

For the filling, cook the ground meat with the onion in a large skillet over medium-high heat. Use an S-shaped potato masher or similar utensil to repeatedly press against the meat and onion, so that the meat breaks down into very small pieces. Stir in the cinnamon, allspice, salt, and pepper. Continue cooking the meat mixture until most of the liquid in the skillet evaporates. Add the pine nuts, and stir 1 to 2 minutes, or until they are lightly toasted. Drain off and discard any excess fat in the skillet. Adjust seasonings to taste. Set the meat filling aside to cool while you prepare the bulgur-meat layers.

For the bulgur-meat layers, it is easiest to use a food processor fitted with a steel blade, or a meat grinder may be used.

For a food processor, cut the onions into quarters and finely chop them in the food processor. Transfer the onions to a medium bowl, and stir in the allspice, cinnamon, salt, and pepper. Drain the water from the reserved bulgur wheat, pressing out any excess. Add the bulgur to the onion mixture, and mix well. Put about one-fourth of the raw ground meat into the food processor bowl with about one-fourth of the bulgur mixture and process, adding 2 tablespoons of the cold water while the machine is running. Process the mixture until it forms a smooth paste. Transfer the paste to a large bowl. Repeat the process until all the meat and bulgur mixture has been used. Mix the batches together so they are well combined.

For a meat grinder, mix together all the raw ground meat, drained and squeezed bulgur, and the ½ cup cold water; then put the combination through the fine blade of the grinder to form a paste. Put the onions through the grinder, pushing out the last bits of meat. Add all the spices and seasonings to the meat and onion mixture. Knead the mixture with your hands or mix it with a sturdy spoon until it is a smooth paste.

Preheat the oven to 375 degrees.

Press half of the bulgur-meat paste into the bottom of the prepared baking dish. Keep your hands or spatula wet so the mixture does not stick. Top the bulgur-meat layer with the cooled, precooked meat and pine nut filling, spreading it evenly, and lightly pressing it in place. Top the filling with the remaining bulgur-meat paste. This is easiest to do if you press a portion of the paste into a flat patty on your wet hand, then place several of these patties on

top of the filling, like the pieces of a puzzle. Use a wet spatula to blend them together so that the filling does not show and the top is smooth.

Deeply score the kibbeh into large diamonds or squares. (To cut diamonds, first cut the kibbeh lengthwise into 4 even strips; then make parallel, diagonal cuts across the kibbeh, forming diamonds.) Mix together the oil and water, and spoon the mixture over the top so every piece of kibbeh is coated. Bake the kibbeh at 375 degrees for about 35 to 45 minutes, or until the top is well browned and the meat is cooked completely through. Carefully drain off and discard any fat that has accumulated around the edges of the meat. Let the kibbeh cool in the pan for about 5 minutes. Cut along the score marks, and serve hot or lukewarm.

Makes 18 to 20 large diamonds or squares; about 8 main-dish servings.

Papas Rellenas
MEAT-STUFFED MASHED POTATO CROQUETTES

Michael Gordon was born in Cuba and spent his early childhood there before immigrating to the United States. Though his family had Ashkenazic roots, they adopted many Spanish customs while in Cuba, just as other Jews have done wherever they have lived in the Diaspora. Thus, Mr. Gordon was known as "Miguel" during his youth, and his mother often prepared dishes that were popular in Cuba. But she always added a special Jewish touch.

Her version of *papas rellenas,* for example, uses matzah meal. This variation is made not only by Cuban Jews, but by those from other parts of Latin America as well.

South American Jews also make the dish, often with their own variations. For instance, Peruvian Jews may use a more elaborate meat filling with raisins, almonds, and olives. And those from Chile and other countries may use chicken instead of red meat. Sometimes, the dish is called *patatas rellenos.*

Interestingly, the following recipe is almost identical to one called *urug batata* or *batata charp,* which is made by Iraqi Jews. The only difference is that the Iraqis omit the green pepper in the filling and add, instead, lots of chopped parsley and such ground spices as cinnamon, cloves, cumin, turmeric, and coriander.

Sukkot, Shemini Atzeret, and Simhat Torah

I have included *papas rellenas* in this chapter because they are in keeping with the tradition of eating stuffed foods on Sukkot. However, they are also very popular for Shabbat.

FILLING
1 pound lean ground beef
1 medium onion, finely chopped
4 to 5 garlic cloves, minced
1 medium green pepper, finely chopped
Salt and pepper to taste

MASHED POTATO COVERING
About 2½ pounds boiling or all-purpose
    potatoes, well scrubbed

1 large egg

COATING, ETC.
1 large egg, lightly beaten with 1
    teaspoon water
Matzah meal
Vegetable or canola oil for frying

For the filling, cook the ground beef with the onion, garlic, and green pepper in a large skillet over medium-high heat, until the meat is browned and the vegetables are tender. While cooking the meat, break it up and mash it with an *S*-shaped potato masher or similar utensil so that the mixture is as fine as possible. Drain off and discard any excess fat in the skillet. Set the meat mixture aside to cool. Season to taste with salt and pepper.

For the mashed potatoes, put the potatoes into a large saucepan, and add enough water so it is about 2 inches deep. Bring to a boil over high heat; then cover the pan, and lower the heat. Simmer the potatoes for 30 to 40 minutes, or until they are quite tender. Immediately drain off the cooking water, and let the potatoes cool until they can be handled. Peel the potatoes; then mash them well with a potato masher or fork. Stir in salt and pepper to taste, and then one of the eggs, and mix very well to make a soft sticky mixture that holds its shape. (If the potato mixture is extremely loose and wet, stir in a few tablespoons of flour or matzah meal.) Put some matzah meal into a bowl.

While shaping the papas rellenas, be sure to keep your hands clean and wet, as this will keep the potato dough from sticking. Put about a 2-inch-diameter ball of the potato mixture on the moistened palm of one hand; then use your other hand to pat it out to a small saucer shape. Put about 1 tablespoon of the filling in the center; then fold up the potato around the filling, completely enclosing it. Form the papa rellena into a ball (for deep-frying) or

a flat patty (for pan-frying); then coat it lightly, first with the beaten egg-water mixture, and next with the matzah meal. Set on a platter. Repeat until all the potatoes and filling are used up.

Deep-fry the balls in a saucepan of hot oil, or pan-fry the patties in oil about ¼ inch deep in a large skillet over medium-high heat, until they are golden brown and crisp on all sides. Drain on paper toweling.

Makes about 20 papas rellenas.

Pastilla
RICHLY FLAVORED CHICKEN AND ALMOND PIE IN FILO

M

This wonder of Moroccan-Jewish cuisine, which may be called *pastiya* or *bestila,* is one of my family's favorite dishes. *Pastilla* not only tastes wonderful, but the decorated finished pie also looks beautiful, making it excellent for entertaining. In fact, it is served at most Moroccan-Jewish festive celebrations, including weddings and bar mitzvah parties, due to its richness and extravagance.

Although it is not traditional for Sukkot, it is perfectly suited for this holiday because it is lavishly stuffed. Also, it tends to stay warm inside its filo "crust" even in a chilly sukkah. It has been a great success with our Sukkot guests, who are delighted with the unusual combination of flavors and textures in the filling. And my children request it every Sukkot.

Pastilla traditionally is prepared with pigeons (squab), but chicken is almost always substituted in the United States. Also, packaged, ultrathin sheets of filo (also spelled "phyllo" and sometimes called "strudel leaves") dough are used instead of *warka,* very thin pastry leaves that are handmade in Morocco by dexterous cooks.

Preparation of *pastilla* is a bit complicated because there are several steps required. However, none is that difficult, and the three fillings can be made one or two days in advance of the assembly, which should be done on the day that the pie is served.

NOTES: Filo is available at many supermarkets, ethnic groceries, and gourmet stores. For details on using filo dough, see the Glossary of Ingredients. This *pastilla* does not call for an entire 1-pound package, only some of the sheets. Those remaining should be

returned immediately to the package, tightly sealed, and refrigerated or frozen for another use.

Filo is typically brushed with melted butter to separate and flavor the layers, but Moroccan Jews use pareve margarine or mild-flavored olive oil when the filo is to be filled with meat. I usually use a combination of both. However, I have found that olive oil in a spray can (sold as a kosher cooking spray) is really convenient, saves time, and requires less total fat. Keep in mind that the filo should be barely moistened, not drenched, with fat.

If no large round pan is available, a large shallow rectangular roasting pan may be used. Stack the sheets of filo in the pan, arranging a few on the bottom so that they overlap the sides of the pan and may be brought up over the filling to enclose it as directed below.

FOR THE CHICKEN
2 medium onions, grated
1 cup finely chopped fresh parsley
  leaves
1 teaspoon dried cilantro leaves or 1
  tablespoon chopped fresh cilantro
  leaves
1 teaspoon ground ginger
¾ teaspoon ground cinnamon
½ teaspoon ground black pepper
¼ teaspoon ground turmeric
½ teaspoon salt
2 cups water
4 to 5 pounds meaty chicken pieces

FOR THE OTHER FILLINGS
2 cups (about 10 ounces) blanched
  slivered or whole almonds
2 tablespoons granulated sugar
1 teaspoon ground cinnamon
8 large eggs (no substitutes)

FOR ASSEMBLING AND TOPPING
¼ cup unsalted pareve margarine plus
  ¼ cup light olive oil or ½ cup light
  olive oil or 1 (5- to 6-ounce can)
  olive oil cooking spray
11 large filo sheets (about ½ pound), at
  room temperature
Confectioners' sugar
Ground cinnamon (optional)

For the chicken, put all the ingredients except the chicken into a 5- to 6-quart pot or Dutch oven, and bring to a boil over high heat. Add the chicken, and spoon some liquid over every piece. Lower the heat, cover, and simmer the chicken for 1 to 1¼ hours, or until it is very tender. Occasionally rotate the chicken pieces so that each is immersed in the broth for part of the cooking period. (Moroccan cooks use potholders to lift the pot while holding the

lid on tightly with both hands; then they give the pot a few quick shakes to mix everything.)

While the chicken is cooking, preheat the oven to 350 degrees. Spread the almonds in a shallow pan and toast them in the oven for about 5 to 10 minutes, or until they are very lightly browned. Let them cool completely. Then put the almonds and the sugar and cinnamon into a food processor fitted with the steel blade. Pulse-process the almonds until they are finely ground. (If a food processor is not available, finely grind the almonds in another device, and mix them with the sugar and cinnamon.) Set the almond mixture aside.

Remove the cooked chicken pieces from the pot with tongs (reserving the broth), and set them aside to cool. While the chicken is cooling, beat the eggs in a bowl until the yolks and whites are completely mixed together and smooth.

Prepare the egg filling as follows: Increase the heat under the broth so that it comes to a boil; then boil it, uncovered, until it has reduced to about 1 to 1½ cups. (Watch carefully so that the broth does not completely boil away!) Lower the heat so that the broth simmers; then slowly add the beaten eggs while constantly stirring. Stir the mixture continuously, scraping the bottom of the pan, until the eggs are scrambled and completely cooked into soft, solid curds with lots of green specks. (This will look strange, but it tastes great in the pie.) Set the egg mixture aside to cool.

When the chicken is cool enough to handle, discard the skin, remove the meat from the bones, and shred it. Set the shredded chicken aside.

(To this point, the pastilla can be prepared ahead. You can refrigerate the chicken, egg mixture, and almond mixture in separate containers for up to 2 days.)

To assemble the pastilla, preheat the oven to 400 degrees. (The pastilla may be assembled a few hours before baking it, and kept in the refrigerator until baking time.) Melt the margarine with the oil in a microwave oven or in a small saucepan over medium heat. (If the margarine starts to solidify during the assembly, reheat it slightly.) Or use plain light olive oil or olive oil spray.

Have all the fillings ready. Use a pastry brush to completely coat the inside of a 13- to 14-inch round pizza pan (or similar pan such as a paella pan; see Notes) with some of the oil-margarine mixture or oil, or spray it with oil. Working as quickly as possible so the filo dough does not dry out, unwrap it

and lay it out flat on a countertop. Lay a sheet of filo in the center of the pan. (Some of it may hang over the edges.) *Lightly* brush or spray the sheet (it does not have to be completely covered) with oil or oil-margarine. Top it with a second sheet, and brush or spray as above. Then place six sheets around the edge of the pan like the spokes of a wheel, arranging them so that about half of each sheet is in the pan, and the remainder hangs over the side. Brush or spray the sheets. Place one more sheet in the center of the pan, and brush or spray it well.

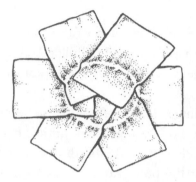

Arrange the pieces of shredded chicken over the filo in the pan. Use a slotted spoon or strainer to remove the egg curds from the broth, and spread them over the chicken. Top with the almond mixture.

Drizzle 2 tablespoons of any broth remaining from the eggs over the filling to keep it moist. One by one, smoothly fold the overhanging filo sheets over the filling, completely enclosing it; then brush or spray the top with oil-margarine or oil. Top off the pie with two more sheets of filo, brushing or spraying each. Tuck in any overhanging edges. Brush or spray the top well.

Bake the pastilla at 400 degrees for 30 to 35 minutes, or until the top is golden brown. If the baked pastilla is left whole after its removal from the oven, it will stay hot for 15 to 30 minutes. Before serving, lightly sift confectioners' sugar on the top of the pie to coat it completely. (It is an Arabic custom, adopted by some Jews, to sprinkle cinnamon over the sugar. This is usually done in narrow, intersecting lines to form a diamond or square pattern. Or you can be creative, and make a Star of David or use a stencil to produce an interesting design.)

Serve the pastilla hot or lukewarm in the pan, with the whole pie presented at the table. For individual portions, cut the pie into approximate squares as neatly as possible (the crispy filo top will flake apart).

Makes 8 to 12 servings.

Chicken with Cabbage and Noodles

Cabbage was one of the few vegetables available to impoverished Jews living in a rural *shtetl* (village). They became very clever at finding different ways to cook it. Noodles and cabbage, or *lokshen mit kroit* in Yiddish, is a popular Ashkenazic vegetarian side dish. In this "modernized" recipe, I have transformed it into an elegant chicken entreé.

2 medium leeks

1 medium onion

1 pound green (white) cabbage

1½ pounds boneless, skinless, chicken breasts or boneless turkey breast

5 tablespoons dry sherry or dry white table wine, divided

2 tablespoons olive oil

1 teaspoon caraway seeds (optional)

½ teaspoon dried thyme leaves

¼ teaspoon salt

⅛ teaspoon ground black pepper

2 tablespoons water

1 (12-ounce) package medium-wide flat noodles

Clean the leeks carefully to remove any sand inside them. (To do this, cut off and discard the root and all the green except for 1 inch. Then cut the leek in half lengthwise, and separate the layers. Rinse the layers well under cold running water; then drain the leeks on paper towels.) Chop the leeks finely, and set aside.

Peel the onion and cut it in half; then cut it into very thin slices. Set it aside with the leeks.

Finely chop the cabbage and set it aside separately.

Cut the chicken (or turkey) into ¾- to 1-inch pieces, and toss it with 2 tablespoons of the sherry. Set aside.

Put the oil into a deep 12-inch skillet or a Dutch oven over medium-high heat; then add the onion and reserved leeks, and cook until they are tender. Add the cabbage, and stir until it is wilted. Then mix in the chicken and its marinade, the remaining 3 tablespoons sherry, caraway seeds (if used), thyme, salt, pepper, and water. Bring to a simmer; then reduce the heat and cover the skillet tightly. Steam the chicken and vegetables for about 10 minutes, or until they are tender.

Meanwhile, cook the noodles according to the package directions, and drain them well. When the chicken mixture is cooked through, stir in the noodles and serve.

Makes about 4 to 6 servings.

Glazed Turkey with Fruit-Nut Stuffing

As the Pilgrims were fond of following customs in the Hebrew Bible, it is likely that the American holiday of Thanksgiving was patterned after the Jewish one of Sukkot. Both celebrate an abundant fall harvest. Interestingly, modern American Jews have turned the tables (so to speak) on the Pilgrims, and now serve many typical Thanksgiving foods, including stuffed turkey, during Sukkot.

Actually, this is quite fitting. When Columbus first brought the turkey back from the New World, Sephardic Jewish merchants who dealt in rarities began selling the birds as delicacies and thus helped spread the turkey throughout Europe. After the fowl was domesticated almost beyond recognition, it was brought back to the Americas to be crossbred with its wild cousins, and eventually became the turkey we have today.

It is likely that our name for the bird came from a Hebrew word for parrot, *tuki.* Some say that Luis de Torres, a Crypto-Jew (Marrano) who was a member of Columbus's crew, dubbed it with the misnomer when he first saw the wild turkey strutting about and flaunting its plumage.

Interestingly, not all Jews consider turkey to be a kosher bird. The Torah does not specifically list permitted birds, only those that are forbidden. The rabbis of the Talmud established certain characteristics that kosher fowl must have, and then further decided that "tradition" should determine what birds are allowed. Thus, domesticated chickens,

ducks, geese, and pigeons are permitted, though not wild species of these birds. In many communities, pheasant is allowed, but not in others. The domesticated turkey is a relatively new breed that eventually became a part of the "tradition" of most Jews (because of its similarity to kosher fowl), but not all. Kosher turkey is actually very popular in Israel, where it often substitutes for other meats in recipes.

The following turkey recipe is quite in keeping with the Sukkot tradition of eating "stuffed" foods and harvest fruits.

NOTES: Be sure to take sanitary precautions when dealing with raw poultry, and use a meat thermometer to ensure that the turkey is completely cooked. If desired, the stuffing may be baked separately in a covered casserole (for about 1 hour at 325 degrees) and basted with turkey juices when the turkey is done cooking. The turkey will take about 3¼ to 3¾ hours if roasted without stuffing. Apply the glaze during the last hour of roasting.

FRUIT-NUT STUFFING
2 tablespoons canola oil
1 large onion, finely chopped
2 celery stalks, diced
1 cup orange juice
⅓ cup sugar
1½ cups fresh or fresh-frozen
    cranberries (about 6 ounces)
12 pitted prunes, coarsely chopped
6 dried apricots, coarsely chopped
1 cup raisins
3 medium apples, cored and diced
1½ cups slivered almonds or chopped
    nuts
½ cup finely chopped fresh parsley
    leaves
1 teaspoon ground cinnamon

¼ teaspoon ground cloves
⅛ teaspoon ground ginger
Salt and ground black pepper to taste
2 large eggs, lightly beaten, or ½ cup
    pareve egg substitute

TURKEY
1 (12- to 14-pound) turkey, completely
    defrosted in the refrigerator (at least
    48 hours)
Canola oil

ORANGE-HONEY GLAZE (OPTIONAL)
½ cup orange juice
¼ cup honey
2 tablespoons canola oil
⅛ teaspoon ground ginger

For the fruit-nut stuffing, put the oil into a medium saucepan over medium-high heat; then cook the onion and celery, stirring, until they are tender. Transfer them to a large bowl. Set aside.

Sukkot, Shemini Atzeret, and Simhat Torah

In the same pan, combine the orange juice and sugar, and bring the mixture to a boil over medium-high heat. Stir in the cranberries, and bring to a boil. Reduce the heat, and simmer the cranberries, stirring occasionally, for about 10 minutes, or until the berry skins pop. Mix in the prunes, apricots, and raisins, and remove the fruit mixture from the heat. Transfer it to the bowl containing the cooked onions and celery. Add all the remaining stuffing ingredients except the eggs, and mix well. Adjust the seasonings to taste. Stir in the eggs. Set aside while preparing the turkey. Preheat oven to 325 degrees.

Remove the turkey from its wrapper. Clean the turkey well, and discard the giblets (or reserve them for another use). Cut off any large pockets of fat around the tail area. Brush the skin lightly with canola oil.

Fill the body and neck cavities of the turkey with the stuffing, allowing some room for expansion. Tuck the legs under the band of skin or the trussing wire at the tail, or tie the legs together with heavy cord. Skewer or sew the neck skin closed against the body. Place the turkey, breast side up on a rack in a shallow roasting pan (lined with foil for easy cleanup, if desired). Roast at 325 degrees for 3 hours.

Meanwhile, if the orange-honey glaze is desired, prepare it by beating together all the glaze ingredients with a fork until they are well combined. After the turkey has roasted for 3 hours, spoon the glaze over it. Roast the turkey for about 1 to 1½ hours longer, or until the juices released when the thigh is pricked with a fork are clear, not pink, and the internal temperature of the thickest part of the thigh reaches 180 degrees according to a meat thermometer. If the breast gets browned before the rest of the turkey is done, cover it loosely with a foil tent. For easier cutting and juicier meat, let the turkey rest about 15 minutes before carving it.

Makes 12 or more servings.

Fruit-and-Vegetable Tzimmes
AUTUMN CASSEROLE

The sweet, "mixed-up" stew known as *tzimmes* is just as popular for Sukkot as it is for Rosh Hashanah. The following version is meatless, and meant to be served as a side dish. It uses popular fall vegetables and dried fruits.

3 large sweet potatoes, peeled and
    thinly sliced
4 large carrots, peeled and thinly sliced
1 small butternut squash, peeled,
    seeded, and thinly sliced
¼ cup dark raisins
¼ cup light raisins

¼ cup pitted prunes
¼ cup chopped dates
Grated peel of 1 orange, colored part
    only
Juice of 1 orange
2 tablespoons packed brown sugar
¼ cup honey or real maple syrup

In a greased or nonstick spray-coated 9 by 13-inch pan, layer the sweet potatoes, carrots, squash, and dried fruit. Sprinkle the top with the orange peel, juice, brown sugar, and honey.

Cover the pan with foil or a lid, and bake it in a preheated 350-degree oven for about 1 to 1½ hours, or until all vegetables and fruits are very tender.

Makes 8 to 10 servings.

Shlishkes
FINGER-SIZED POTATO DUMPLINGS

When I was a child, my favorite buffet selection at family bar mitzvah celebrations was buttery, crumb-coated *shlishkes*. My cousin Gail and I would meet at the *shlishke* chafing dish, and together we would eagerly devour the toothsome treats to our hearts' content.

I had never attempted to make these tiny Ashkenazic potato dumplings until I realized how easy they would be if I used Mrs. Erger's easy potato dough for Plum Knedliky (see page 192). After a little experimentation, the *shlishkes* were right on target—just

how I remembered them. When I served them to my father, he couldn't get enough, and suggested that I "double the recipe next time." I knew that I had a winner.

Interestingly, a very similar potato dough is also used for the Italian favorite, potato gnocchi. However, gnocchi (which actually means "knuckles") are usually pressed against a rough surface such as a grater or the tines of a fork before they're cooked, so that rich sauces, based on tomatoes or cheese, cling to them.

The following slightly chewy, miniature dumplings make a great side dish and, of course, they're perfect for a buffet meal.

EASY POTATO DOUGH
2 cups instant potato flakes
2 cups boiling water
2 tablespoons canola oil
1/2 teaspoon salt
2 large eggs or 1/2 cup egg substitute
Approximately 2 to 2 1/2 cups unbleached
    flour

COATING
1/4 cup butter, margarine, or canola oil
1 1/2 cups fine cornflake crumbs or dry
    plain bread crumbs

Put the potato flakes into a large mixing bowl; then add the boiling water, and mix well to make stiff mashed potatoes. Stir in the oil and salt, and set the mixture aside to cool to lukewarm, stirring occasionally.

When the potato mixture is cool, beat in the eggs until completely combined; then gradually add the flour while mixing. Add just enough flour to form a soft dough that is not sticky. Lightly knead the dough in the bowl for 1 to 2 minutes, or until it is springy. Let the dough rest briefly.

Keeping the dough, your hands, and a cutting board well floured, roll the dough into ropes that are 1/2 to 3/4 inch thick. Cut each rope into 1- to 1 1/2-inch-long pieces. If necessary, toss the dough pieces with flour so they do not stick to each other or to the surface. When all the dough has been cut, drop the pieces into a large pot of boiling, salted water. (You may need to cook them in two batches.) Stir gently to make sure that none of the shlishkes stick to the bottom. After they rise to the top, boil them, uncovered or partially covered, for 4 to 8 minutes longer, or until they are chewy and firm, but not doughy. (Overcooking can make them gummy. Taste to check doneness.) Immediately remove them with a slotted spoon, and drain them well in a colander.

While the shlishkes are cooking, heat the butter, margarine, or oil in a large skillet over medium heat; then stir in the cornflake crumbs until they are completely coated and hot. Remove the skillet from the heat. (If using bread crumbs, sauté them until they are golden brown.)

Toss the well-drained shlishkes in the crumbs. Serve them warm. If necessary, they may be reheated, covered, in the microwave oven or in a conventional oven at 350 degrees until hot.

Makes 6 to 8 servings as a side dish.

Cran-Apple-Pear Sauce

This dark red fruit sauce, one of my personal favorites for many years, is a lovely change from the usual plain applesauce. It has the zippy taste of cranberries mingled with the subtle flavors of other fall fruits, making it a side dish that is perfect for Sukkot and Thanksgiving. Fresh cranberries can be frozen right in their bag for use in this recipe later in the year.

This recipe makes lots of sauce, but it keeps quite well in the refrigerator for up to a week (the recipe may be cut in half for a smaller amount). It is not necessary to peel the fruit unless you mind the small bits of peel in the sauce. The "lumpy" texture of the small pieces of fruit adds to this dish's appeal.

2 (12-ounce) bags fresh or fresh-frozen cranberries (6 cups)	1 cup water
	1½ to 2 cups sugar, or to taste
4 medium apples	1 teaspoon ground cinnamon
4 medium pears	½ teaspoon ground nutmeg
1 cup orange juice	

Rinse the cranberries well in a colander, and discard any that are shriveled, spoiled, or discolored. Discard any stems. Cut the apples and pears into quarters, remove the cores, and cut each section into ½-inch pieces.

Put the fruit into a large (at least 5-quart), heavy, nonaluminum pot. Add the orange juice, water, 1½ cups sugar, cinnamon, and nutmeg. Stir all the ingredients so they are evenly distributed. Bring the mixture to a boil over

Sukkot, Shemini Atzeret, and Simhat Torah

medium-high heat. Lower the heat and simmer, covered, stirring occasion-ally, until the mixture has thickened and the fruit is soft (about 30 minutes).

Remove the mixture from the heat and let it cool slightly; then mix it with a spoon to make a very lumpy "sauce." Taste the sauce and add sugar as needed (the amount will depend on the sweetness of the fruit and your own taste preference; the sauce should be slightly tart). Stir so that any added sugar is completely dissolved in the sauce. Let the sauce cool to room temperature, then transfer it to a noncorrosive bowl, and chill it, covered, in the refrigera-tor. (It will thicken even more as it chills.) Serve cold or at room temperature. The sauce will keep well for up to a week in the refrigerator.

Makes 7 to 8 cups; 10 or more servings.

Harvesttime Cranberry Relish

Because cranberries are a seasonal fall fruit and so brightly colored, they have become a popular decoration for many American sukkot. Children love to string them on threads, and hang up the chains from the roof of the sukkah.

As a food, cranberries go well with many of the fall "harvest" dishes on the holiday table. The following slightly tart relish differs from cranberry sauce in that it requires no cooking, and can be quickly made in a food processor. If necessary, the ingredients can even be put through a food grinder.

Also, the relish features an assortment of other fall fruits with the cranberries. It makes an excellent accompaniment to poultry or meat, or it can be used as a side dish with other foods.

NOTES: It is not necessary to peel the apple or pear for this recipe. The peels add color, texture, and nutritional value. (Do not use previously frozen cranberries.)

1 medium navel orange
1 (12-ounce) bag very fresh cranberries
  (3 cups), rinsed, drained, and
  sorted

1 medium apple, cored and cut into
  eighths
1 medium pear, cored and cut into
  eighths

¼ cup walnut or pecan pieces

¼ cup dark raisins

½ cup packed dark brown sugar

2 to 3 tablespoons granulated sugar, or
   to taste

1 tablespoon lemon juice

Wash the orange well. Use a vegetable peeler or sharp knife to remove the thin, colored part of the peel from the orange. Set it aside. Remove and discard all the white pith from the orange; then cut the orange pulp into chunks. Put the orange peel and pulp into a food processor fitted with a steel blade, and add the remaining relish ingredients. Pulse-process the mixture until the ingredients are finely chopped but not at all smoothly puréed. (If necessary, process the ingredients in batches; then combine all the batches and mix well.) Or put the ingredients through the coarse blade of a food grinder.

Chill the relish at least several hours or overnight, stirring occasionally, until the sugar has completely dissolved and the flavors have blended. If the relish is not sweet enough (it should be a little tart), stir in granulated sugar to taste, making sure it is completely dissolved.

Makes about 3½ cups.

Red Cabbage and Apple Slaw

This raw salad is very similar to a cooked Ashkenazic sweet-and-sour cabbage and apples side dish. Immigrants to America may have adapted it into a salad when they became comfortable with the use of a common American ingredient—mayonnaise. This salad not only tastes great but looks very "appealing" as well. One reason is that the "peel" is left on the apples.

1 small head red cabbage (about 1¼
   pounds)

4 large, firm, and tart apples, such as
   Granny Smith

2 to 3 tablespoons sugar, or to taste

¼ cup apple cider vinegar or red wine
   vinegar

½ cup mayonnaise

Pinch of ground cloves, or to taste

Sukkot, Shemini Atzeret, and Simhat Torah

Cut the cabbage and apples into fourths, and remove and discard the cores. Use a food processor or a hand grater to finely shred the cabbage and apples. Put the cabbage and apple shreds into a large bowl, and stir in the sugar, vinegar, mayonnaise, and cloves until well combined. Refrigerate the salad several hours, stirring occasionally, to give the flavors time to develop.

Makes about 8 servings.

Plum Knedliky or Knaidlach
FRUIT-FILLED POTATO DUMPLINGS

These delectable plum dumplings make a great dessert or teatime snack. They are very popular in many parts of the Czech Republic, Slovakia, and Hungary, where the choicest small, purple plums grow.

In the United States, fresh Italian prune-plums, which are usually available in early fall, seem to work best in this recipe. The firm, oval prune-plums are only about the size of a walnut, and are very easily pitted. The cavity from which the pit is removed is sprinkled with sugar or cinnamon-sugar, which melts into a tasty sauce as the dumplings cook.

Other fruits, such as peeled, quartered peaches and well-drained canned apricot halves, can be used as well. In a pinch, even a spoonful of fruit preserves can be used for the filling.

The dough that surrounds the fruit contains mashed potatoes, giving it a very good flavor and wonderfully chewy texture. The following "modernized" version of this potato dough came from Judith Erger, a Jewish native of Sinover, Czechoslovakia, who immigrated to the United States.

When Mrs. Erger first showed me how to make plum dumplings using instant potato flakes, I was a bit astounded to see such an expert Old World cook using a convenience food. But when I tasted the results, I had to agree with Mrs. Erger that she had indeed found a very suitable and delightfully quick substitute for the time-consuming job of boiling, peeling, and ricing potatoes. (What's more, fresh potatoes can be a bit tricky to work with because the water content may vary considerably.)

Mrs. Erger's use of cornflake crumbs instead of the usual bread crumbs in the coating is another tasty and modern substitution that also works quite well.

In many classic recipes for plum knedliky, the dough is rolled out and cut into squares before filling. But I think Mrs. Erger's technique, which follows, is easier and foolproof.

EASY POTATO DOUGH
1 cup instant potato flakes
1 cup boiling water
1 tablespoon canola oil
¼ teaspoon salt
1 large egg
Approximately 1 to 1¼ cups unbleached flour

FILLING
About 12 small, fresh Italian prune-plums
3 tablespoons sugar
½ teaspoon ground cinnamon

COATING
2 tablespoons butter, margarine, or canola oil
¾ cup fine cornflake crumbs or dry plain bread crumbs

TO SERVE (OPTIONAL)
Preserves or jam, such as apricot or plum, warmed in a small saucepan over low heat or in a heatproof bowl in the microwave oven

Put the potato flakes into a large mixing bowl; then add the boiling water and mix well to make stiff mashed potatoes. Stir in the oil and salt, and set the mixture aside to cool to lukewarm, stirring occasionally.

When the potato mixture is cool, beat in the egg until completely combined; then gradually add the flour while mixing. Add just enough flour to form a soft dough that is not sticky. Lightly knead the dough in the bowl for 1 to 2 minutes, or until it is springy. (At this point, if necessary, the dough can be covered well with plastic wrap and set aside for a short while. It can even be refrigerated overnight.)

Let the dough rest briefly while you prepare the plums. Cut each plum in half lengthwise, along the "groove"; then remove and discard the pit. Keep the mated halves of each plum together, so they can be reassembled later. In a small bowl, combine the cinnamon and sugar.

Fill a 6- to 8-quart wide pot three-fourths full with lightly salted water and bring it to a boil while you shape the dumplings.

If the dough has become very sticky while resting, knead in a bit more flour. With well-floured hands, form the dough into about twelve balls, ap-

Sukkot, Shemini Atzeret, and Simhat Torah

proximately the size of golf balls (exact size depends on the size of the plums). Place the balls on a well-floured surface, not touching one another.

In the floured palm of one hand (or on a floured surface), use your other hand to pat out one of the balls into a circle about ¼ inch thick. In the center, place one plum half with its cut side up. Sprinkle the plum's cavity with a generous ½ teaspoon of cinnamon-sugar. Top it with the matching half, re-assembling the plum. Bring the dough up and around the plum, and pinch it tightly closed so that the plum is completely covered. Roll the dumpling in flour, and shape it in your hands to form a neat ball. Place it seam side down on a floured surface. Repeat the steps for the remaining dumplings.

When all the dumplings are shaped, gently drop them into the rapidly boiling water. After about 1 minute, nudge the dumplings gently with a wooden spoon to make sure they don't stick to the bottom of the pot. Angle the cover on the pot so it is not tightly closed. Adjust the heat so that the water boils gently. Boil the dumplings for 12 to 15 minutes. To test for doneness, taste one. The dough should be chewy, but not doughy or gummy.

When the dumplings are almost done cooking, heat the butter, margarine, or oil in a large skillet over medium heat; then stir in the cornflake crumbs until they are completely coated and hot. Remove the skillet from the heat. (If using bread crumbs, sauté them until they are golden brown.)

When the dumplings are cooked through, carefully remove each one from the pot with a slotted spoon, drain it very well, and gently roll it in the crumbs until lightly coated. Serve the dumplings warm, topped with a little heated jam if desired.

Refrigerate leftover dumplings and reheat them, covered, in a microwave oven or in a 350-degree conventional oven until they are hot.

Makes about 12 large dumplings.

Cranberry-Walnut Muffins

These easy muffins are always a hit in my house for Sukkot and Thanksgiving. I quickly make the batter in a food processor, which coarsely chops the nuts and cranberries right into the batter, saving extra steps. It can also be mixed by hand.

Several years ago, I invited a family of Russian–Jewish immigrants to my home to celebrate their first Thanksgiving. While they adored all the traditional American foods that I served, they were especially fascinated with the taste and bright natural color of cranberries. These muffins were among their favorites of the day.

1 cup all-purpose flour
1 cup whole wheat flour
½ cup packed dark brown sugar
¼ cup granulated sugar
1 teaspoon ground cinnamon
1 teaspoon ground nutmeg
½ teaspoon ground ginger
1½ teaspoons baking powder
½ teaspoon baking soda

¼ cup canola oil
2 large eggs or ½ cup pareve egg
    substitute
¾ cup orange juice
1½ cups walnut or pecan pieces
1½ cups fresh or fresh-frozen (and
    slightly thawed) cranberries (about
    6 ounces)

Preheat the oven to 375 degrees. Coat twelve cups in a muffin tin and the top of the tin with nonstick cooking spray or grease the tin well.

For the food processor: Put all the dry ingredients into the bowl fitted with a steel blade. Pulse-process a few times to mix. Add the oil, and pulse-process a few more times. Add the eggs and juice, and pulse-process one or two times to begin the mixing. Add the nuts and cranberries. Pulse-process only until they are coarsely chopped and the batter is completely moistened. Do not overprocess or the muffins will be tough.

By hand: Put all the dry ingredients into a medium bowl. Add the oil, eggs, and orange juice, and stir just until moistened. Coarsely chop the nuts and cranberries, and stir them into the batter.

Divide the batter evenly among the twelve muffin cups. Bake at 375 degrees for about 25 minutes, or until a wooden pick comes out clean. Cool the muffins in the pan on a wire rack for 5 minutes, then tap the side of the pan against the countertop to loosen the muffins. These muffins taste best shortly

after baking, but, they may be made ahead and served at room temperature or reheated if desired.

Makes 12 large muffins.

Double-Corn Bread

This corn bread is soft and quite moist, almost like a corn pudding (or kugel?). It contains both cornmeal and corn kernels, making it doubly "corny" and tasty. Unlike most corn bread, it is pareve and therefore suitable for meat meals. (Cream-style canned corn does not contain any cream; it just looks creamy.) As an added bonus, it takes only minutes to mix up. Its soft texture makes it easiest to eat with a fork; and it tastes best when hot.

1 cup yellow or white cornmeal, preferably stone-ground	2 large eggs or ½ cup pareve egg substitute
1 cup all-purpose flour	⅓ cup canola oil
3 tablespoons sugar	1 (about 15-ounce) can cream-style corn, including all liquid
4 teaspoons baking powder	Pareve margarine to spread (optional)
½ teaspoon salt	

Preheat the oven to 400 degrees. Coat an 8-inch square baking dish or pan with nonstick cooking spray or grease it well. In a medium bowl, combine the cornmeal, flour, sugar, baking powder, and salt. Make a well in the center, and add the eggs, oil, and canned corn. Beat the wet ingredients with a fork to combine them, then incorporate the dry ingredients. Stir with a fork only until all the ingredients are completely moistened and combined.

Spoon the mixture into the prepared pan. Bake at 400 degrees for about 20 to 25 minutes, or until a knife inserted in the center comes out clean. Cut into squares, and serve directly from the baking dish. This corn bread tastes best shortly after baking, but it can be made a day ahead and reheated in a microwave oven. (It is not as tasty at room temperature.) Serve with margarine if desired.

Makes about 9 servings.

Easy Apple-Nut Strudel

Strudel is very traditional for Sukkot because of its lavish use of fruit and nuts. Also, it is "stuffed," like many other holiday foods. This quick version takes advantage of the packaged filo dough available refrigerated or frozen at many supermarkets, ethnic groceries, and gourmet stores. The large ultra-thin sheets of dough are also often called "strudel leaves."

The following recipe does not use a whole 1-pound package, just some of the sheets. Those remaining should be returned immediately to the package, tightly sealed, and refrigerated or frozen for another use.

NOTE: See the Glossary of Ingredients for details on purchasing and using filo. For a classic stretched-dough strudel, see the recipe for Dried-Fruit Strudel, page 284.)

½ cup dark or light raisins
⅓ cup wine, fruit juice, or water
5 medium Golden Delicious apples
1 cup chopped walnuts or pecans
1 teaspoon ground cinnamon
¼ cup granulated sugar
2 tablespoons packed dark brown sugar
2 tablespoons canola oil
About ½ cup apricot preserves

12 large filo sheets, at room temperature (see Note)
Canola oil or olive oil cooking spray, as needed (see Notes with Pastilla, page 179)
About 1 cup fine, dry bread crumbs or cake crumbs
Confectioners' sugar (optional)

Soak the raisins in the wine or other liquid until plumped. (To hasten the soaking process, heat the raisins and liquid in a microwave oven for about 30 seconds.) Core and dice the apples (it is not necessary to peel them unless desired). You should have about 5 cups of diced apples.

Mix together the apples, nuts, cinnamon, granulated and brown sugars, and 2 tablespoons oil. Drain the raisins, reserving 1 tablespoon of the soaking liquid. Add the raisins to the apple mixture.

In a small saucepan or in a small cup in the microwave oven, heat the apricot preserves with the 1 tablespoon reserved liquid until the preserves are warmed and thinned. Preheat the oven to 350 degrees.

Lay one filo sheet on a slightly damp, but not wet, dish towel, and brush it very lightly with oil, or spray it lightly with olive oil cooking spray. Evenly sprinkle the sheet with 1 tablespoon of crumbs. Top with another coated sheet, and more crumbs. Repeat the layering procedure with three more sheets. Put a plain filo sheet on top. Brush its entire surface with half of the thinned apricot preserves. Then sprinkle it with 2 tablespoons of crumbs.

Compactly place half of the apple mixture on the top sheet, keeping it in a narrow strip parallel to one longer side and 4 inches in from that edge. Leave a 1-inch margin on each of the shorter sides. Fold over the 4-inch edge to cover the apples, then fold in the sides to keep the apples from falling out the ends. Continue rolling up, jelly roll fashion, using the towel as an aid if necessary.

Place the strudel seam side down in a parchment-lined, nonstick-spray-coated, or greased jelly roll (or similar 15 by 10-inch) pan. Brush or spray the entire outer surface of the strudel with oil. To make a second strudel, repeat the layering, filling, and rolling process. Keep the strudels about 2 inches apart in the jelly roll pan.

Score the top of each strudel diagonally, through a few leaves only, into about eight even pieces. Bake the strudels at 350 degrees for about 35 to 40 minutes, or until the strudel surface is browned and crisp. Remove the strudels from the oven, and let them cool slightly in the pan on a rack. Use a spatula to loosen the bottoms of the strudels from the parchment or the pan. Cool to at least lukewarm before serving. Carefully transfer the strudels to a serving tray. Serve lukewarm or at room temperature. Just before serving, very lightly sprinkle the top with sieved confectioners' sugar, if desired. Cut through the scored marks to divide the strudel into serving pieces. (Or, if preferred, the cooled strudels may be sliced before they are served, and the slices arranged on a platter.)

Makes 2 strudels; about 16 pieces.

Raised-Dough Cake
FRUIT-AND-NUT-FILLED YEAST PASTRY

At the end of the nineteenth century, my paternal grandparents separately immigrated to this country from Galicia, then a part of Austria-Hungary. My grandfather met my grandmother in 1905 when he stopped by her Exeter, Pennsylvania, house as a door-to-door salesman. They were the first couple to be married in a nearby small *shul* (synagogue) that had just been built by Jewish immigrants, and my great-grandfather, Rabbi Benjamin Bransdorf, officiated at the wedding of his daughter.

I always think of my grandmother, Gussie Bransdorf Kaufer (for whom I am named), whenever I make this delicious "cake," which is really a filled, rolled pastry. For a long time, I was under the impression that this was her old, family recipe. After the first edition of this book appeared, some relatives told me that I misunderstood the recipe's origins, and that it actually had a different source. It doesn't matter. For me, this sweet Old World pastry will remain a way to remember my sweet grandmother who passed away before I was born.

It also brings back wonderful memories of the Brit Milah of each of my three sons, when family members or friends made sure that this treasured treat of my youth was on the dessert table.

My mother, who taught me how to make this pastry, and my paternal aunts have always called it nothing more than "raised-dough cake," probably because the original name was forgotten and they all knew what the simple title meant. After all, in the modern kitchens of the fifties and sixties, very few cakes were still made with dough raised by yeast.

NOTES: The following recipe makes three long pastries, which freeze quite well. The recipe should be started at least one day ahead of serving because the dough must be refrigerated overnight. The original recipe called for fresh yeast; if desired, 1 small cake (about 0.6 ounces) of fresh compressed yeast may be substituted for the dry yeast. However, fresh yeast can be rather finicky, so be sure that it is *very* fresh and not near its expiration date. The milk used to dissolve fresh yeast should be only 80 to 90 degrees, as it is much more sensitive to higher temperatures than is dry yeast.

DOUGH

1 packet (2¼ teaspoons) active dry
    yeast (see the Glossary of
    Ingredients)
½ cup warm (105 to 115 degrees) milk
1 cup butter
2 tablespoons sugar
3 large egg yolks (reserve the whites for
    the filling)
3 to 3½ cups unbleached flour

FILLING

1 cup coarsely chopped walnuts
1 cup light or dark raisins (or a
    mixture)
1 cup shredded sweetened coconut
1 tablespoon ground cinnamon
3 large egg whites (reserved from the
    dough)
½ cup sugar

Make the dough the day before baking the cake. Stir the yeast into the milk, and set the mixture aside for the yeast to soften. In a large mixing bowl, use a heavy-duty mixer or a wooden spoon to cream the butter with the sugar; then mix in the egg yolks. Stir in the flour alternately with the yeast mixture, mixing well after each addition. Add just enough flour so the dough comes away from the sides of the bowl but is still slightly sticky. Cover the bowl with plastic wrap, and refrigerate the dough at least 8 hours, or overnight. It will rise slightly in the refrigerator. (Save the 3 egg whites in a covered container in the refrigerator.)

Remove the egg whites and dough from the refrigerator. Divide the chilled dough into three equal parts, and allow it to rest for a few minutes at room temperature to soften slightly. Then roll out each piece of dough on a separate sheet of wax paper to a 9 by 11-inch rectangle.

For the filling, mix together the walnuts, raisins, coconut, and cinnamon. In a large bowl, use an electric mixer to beat the egg whites until foamy; then gradually add the sugar, and continue beating until the whites form stiff, shiny peaks. Spread a third of the beaten whites over each rectangle of dough, leaving a 1½-inch border all around. Then sprinkle a third of the nut mixture over the egg whites on each rectangle.

Using the wax paper as an aid, and beginning with an 11-inch side, roll up each rectangle of dough like a jelly roll. (Make sure the wax paper does not stay attached to the dough.) Neatly pinch the long edge and ends of each cake roll tightly closed; then set each roll, seam side down, on a nonstick-spray-coated, baking-parchment lined, or greased and floured baking sheet (preferably the

insulated type). (Two cakes may fit on one large sheet; leave plenty of space between them for rising.)

Let the cake rolls rise at room temperature until they are not quite doubled in bulk, about 1 to 1½ hours. Meanwhile, preheat the oven to 350 degrees. Bake the cakes for about 30 to 35 minutes, or until the tops are golden brown, rotating the sheets about halfway though the baking. Use a spatula to carefully slide the cakes from the baking sheets to wire racks to cool completely. Cut them into slices at serving time. (If freezing the cakes, cool them completely before wrapping for the freezer. Defrost them wrapped.)

Makes 3 rolled cakes; about 8 servings each.

Hot Mulled Cider

When guests come to visit your sukkah, a mug of this delicious and soothing hot drink will help keep them warm. For best flavor, it should be made with unfiltered (dark brown) pasteurized apple cider. Formerly available only during the fall, this type of fresh-tasting cider can now be bought year-round in many supermarkets.

I recently discovered that the English word "cider" has Hebrew origins. According to *Webster's,* it comes from the Hebrew word *shekar,* a sweet fermented drink, which is derived from *shakar,* meaning "to be intoxicated." In modern Hebrew, *sheekor* means a drunkard, which is very similar to the familiar Yiddish term *shikker.*

According to John D. Jacobson, in his little book of unusual food facts called *Eatioms,* the Hebrew source word for "cider" is related to another word, *shagah,* that was adopted into Yiddish as *meshuggeh,* meaning "crazy" or "insane" (how one acts when drunk). As the following mulled cider is nonalcoholic, you don't have to worry about becoming *meshuggeh* when you drink it!

8 to 10 cups apple cider	*About 20 whole, dried allspice berries*
6 cups cranberry juice cocktail	*1 large navel orange*
4 cups apricot nectar	*20 whole cloves*
3 or 4 sticks rolled cinnamon bark	

Sukkot, Shemini Atzeret, and Simhat Torah

Put the cider, cranberry juice, and apricot nectar into a large pot over medium heat. Stir in the cinnamon sticks. Put the allspice into a tea ball or tie them together in a cheesecloth bag. (They will give more flavor if allowed to float freely in the pot, but in this case you must filter the drink through a strainer before serving.) Wash the orange and cut it in half; then stick 10 cloves into the peel of each half. Float the orange halves in the juice with their cut side up.

Cover the pot, and slowly heat the juice mixture until it simmers. Reduce the heat so the juice stays just below the simmering point, and let it mull for 1 hour. Remove the cinnamon sticks, allspice, and orange halves. Count the cloves, and retrieve any that may have fallen out of the oranges. Leave the pot on the burner over very low heat, and ladle the mulled cider right from the pot into mugs.

Makes 12 to 14 mug-size servings, or about 20 smaller ones.

Gingerbread Sukkah

Many Jews take the commandment to "dwell in" a sukkah very seriously—that is, they at least eat, if not sleep, in one during the Sukkot holiday. (Please see the chapter introduction for more details.) As a miniature symbol, a gaily decorated gingerbread sukkah can be the impetus for provocative holiday discussions, especially when the whole family shares in the joy and creativity of baking and "building" it.

I first created a gingerbread sukkah many years ago because our family did not yet have a life-size sukkah of our own. My young children were very curious about the holiday, and wanted to know how a sukkah is built. As someone who has always found cooking to be a wonderful educational medium, I adapted the idea for an edible sukkah from the classic gingerbread house. I figured that if my family couldn't eat *in* a sukkah, at least we could *eat* a sukkah. The gingerbread model was successful beyond my imagination.

Eventually, my husband and I were inspired to put together a real sukkah that has brought much pleasure to our family every year when we rebuild it. Nevertheless, there is still a special thrill to be found in producing an edible model.

Like any worthwhile construction project, a gingerbread sukkah takes some time and effort. But the preparation can be divided into two separate sessions (baking and assembly) of only 1 or 2 hours each. The gingerbread pieces may be baked up to 3 weeks before assembly.

And at the end of the Sukkot celebration, the structure can be eaten, providing a tasty feast for joyous Simhat Torah!

The following detailed directions are for a finished sukkah that is about 5 inches high, 7 inches wide, and 4½ inches deep. (Be sure to read all directions before beginning.)

Patterns

To easily cut out the raw gingerbread dough for the sukkah, cardboard patterns must be made first. These can then be used repeatedly to make many sukkot year after year. Make the patterns as follows, drawing them on the cardboard before cutting them out. Label each pattern for easy identification. Even though some patterns are duplicates, there must be one for each piece of the sukkah so that all the patterns can be arranged on the dough before cutting it.

1. *Front and back walls.* Cut out two 7-inch-wide by 5-inch-high rectangles. In the lower center of the pattern piece you will use for the front wall, cut out a door opening that is 1½ inches wide by 2½ inches high. In the center of the back wall pattern, cut out a window that is 2½ inches wide by 2 inches high.

2. *Side walls.* Cut out two 4-inch-wide by 5-inch-high rectangles. In the center of each one, cut out a window that is 1½ inches square.

3. *Roof.* The lattice roof is made from strips of dough that are cut from rectangular sections. For the patterns, cut out one rectangular piece of cardboard that is 9 by 2½ inches, and one that is 6¼ by 3¾ inches. (To give the assembled roof extra support, you will need six thin wooden skewers or craft sticks or drinking straws that are 5¾ inches long.)

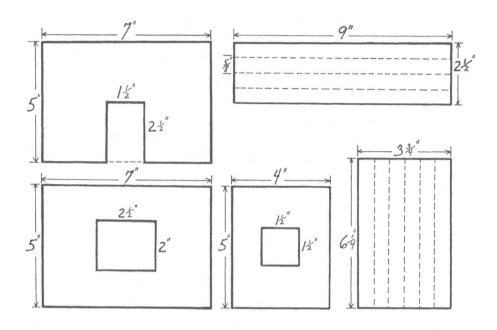

Special Gingerbread Dough

1 1/2 teaspoons ground ginger
1/2 teaspoon ground cinnamon
1/2 teaspoon ground nutmeg
1/2 teaspoon baking soda
1/4 teaspoon salt
2 1/2 cups all-purpose flour (to measure
    the flour, spoon it into a measuring
    cup; then level the top with a knife)

1/2 cup sugar
1/2 cup solid white vegetable shortening
    such as Crisco (NO substitutes)
1/2 cup light or dark molasses

Put the ginger, cinnamon, nutmeg, baking soda, and salt into a small cup, and set aside. Measure out the flour into a bowl or onto a large piece of wax paper, and have it handy. Have a ruler handy to measure the edges of the rolled dough.

NOTE: Once the following procedure is begun, it cannot be interrupted until the dough has been rolled out.

Put the sugar, shortening, and molasses into a 2½- to 3-quart saucepan, and mix them together with a wooden spoon just until combined. Set the saucepan over medium-high heat, and stir the mixture occasionally until it comes to a full rolling boil. Immediately remove it from the heat and stir in about ½ cup of the flour. Then stir in the spice mixture until completely combined. Add the remaining flour all at once, and mix the dough with the wooden spoon until all the flour is incorporated and the dough can be easily scraped away from the sides of the pan. Be sure to reach into the corners and bottom of the pan as you mix. The dough will be very stiff.

Turn out the warm dough onto a lightly oiled cutting board, flat cookie sheet, or other flat surface. As soon as it has cooled enough to touch, use your hands to press the dough into a smooth, rectangular-shaped mound. Flatten the mound; then immediately use a rolling pin to roll the dough out to a very neat 12½ by 15-inch rectangle of even thickness (about ⅛ inch). Use the ruler to measure the dimensions of the rectangle and to make sure the sides and corners are straight. Then use a pastry wheel or sharp knife to cut off any uneven edges, and reattach them as needed to fill in the rectangle. (The rolled-out dough must be the correct size for all the pattern pieces to fit properly.) The warm dough will not be sticky, and will be very easy to roll. However, it must be rolled out while warm, as it becomes impossibly stiff once it cools. (In a pinch, the dough can sometimes be slightly rewarmed for a few seconds in a microwave oven. But be sure not to heat it so much that it cooks.)

CUTTING THE DOUGH

Let the rolled-out dough rest for 5 to 10 minutes, or until it is completely cool, so it will be easier to cut and maneuver the pieces. Very lightly flour the top surface of the dough so that the patterns won't stick. Arrange all the patterns on the dough, placing them adjacent to each other and along the edge of the dough so there is as little waste as possible. Trace each pattern with a small pastry wheel or small knife; then lift off the pattern so that you can see what has been traced. Carefully cut out and remove the windows from the walls. Cut out the door piece, but reserve it for the finished sukkah. (The leftover window pieces may be baked into edible "samples.") Cut the 9-inch-long roof rectangle lengthwise into four strips that are 9- by ⅜-inch each. Cut the 6¼-inch-long roof rectangle into six strips that are 6¼- by ⅜-inch each.

Sukkot, Shemini Atzeret, and Simhat Torah

BAKING THE WALLS

Preheat the oven to 350 degrees. After all the patterns have been cut, use a large metal pancake turner or spatula to transfer the wall pieces and the door cut from the doorway (but *not* the roof strips) to a large nonstick-spray-coated or well-greased shiny baking sheet (or two smaller sheets). Leave about 1 inch between each piece. Bake the pieces at 350 degrees for 11 to 13 minutes, or until a light touch does not leave an imprint in the dough.

Remove the baking sheet from the oven, and immediately retrace each pattern, one at a time, by placing it over the corresponding cookie wall, and using the pastry wheel or knife to cut off any excess edges that have expanded during baking. This will be easy while the dough is still hot and soft. (It gets quite firm as it cools.)

Leave the pieces on the baking sheet to cool slightly; then carefully loosen them with the pancake turner and transfer them to a flat surface (not a wire rack) to cool completely. (The three window hole pieces and any wall trimmings may now provide sustenance for hardworking cooks who are being driven crazy by the wonderful aroma!)

BAKING THE LATTICE ROOF

Generously coat with nonstick spray or grease well or line with baking parchment a clean, cool baking sheet. Lay the four 9-inch strips of dough on it so that they are parallel to each other and there is a ¾-inch space between each one. Basket-weave the 6¼-inch strips over and under the longer strips (beginning with one over, the next under, and so forth), keeping the shorter strips parallel to each other and evenly spaced to form an open lattice. The ends of all the strips should stick out exactly ¾-inch from the main part of the lattice; adjust the strips if necessary. (This is not only for appearance, but so the roof will fit correctly on top of the sukkah walls. Use a ruler for measurements.)

Bake the lattice in a preheated 350-degree oven for about 11 to 14 minutes, or until browned and a firm touch does not leave an imprint. Cool it on the baking sheet about 5 minutes, or until stiff. Then very carefully use the pancake turner to loosen the edges and then the middle of the lattice. Transfer the roof to a flat surface to cool completely.

STORING THE BAKED PIECES

Once the gingerbread pieces are completely cool, they may be assembled, or they may be stored in an airtight container for up to 3 weeks. Store them carefully so they do not break.

Decorating and Assembling the Sukkah

SUGGESTIONS FOR SUKKAH DECORATIONS

Collect an assortment of the following edible "decorations" to attach to the outside of the sukkah.

> *Shelled nuts (such as walnut halves, pecan halves, whole almonds, whole cashews, whole hazelnuts)*
>
> *Hulled large seeds (such as sunflower seeds and/or pumpkin seeds, which are green and look like little leaves)*
>
> *Small dried fruits (such as apricot halves, raisins, small wedges of dried pineapple, chunks of dried papaya, banana chips, dates, etc.)*

A BASE TO HOLD THE SUKKAH

Make a base for the sukkah by wrapping a rectangular piece of thick, heavy cardboard approximately 8 by 12 inches (or a circular one about 11 inches in diameter) with heavy-duty foil or white freezer paper. Use tape to secure the edges of the wrap to the underside of the cardboard. A serving tray may be used instead.

DECORATING THE WALLS

Just before assembling the sukkah, prepare the Brown Icing "Glue" as directed in the recipe below. Fill a cake-decorating bag (fitted with a ³⁄₁₆- to ¼-

inch plain round tip) about three-fourths full with icing. Twist or fold the top of the bag over very tightly, and be sure to hold the top closed while squeezing the bag, or icing may leak out.

First, decorate the outsides of the walls with some of the suggested decorations before the walls are assembled. (It is very easy to do this while the walls are lying flat on a table. The side of the wall that was facing up during baking should be the outside of the sukkah. Remember that no one will see the inside.) To make window trim, squeeze a thick continuous bead of icing all around a window hole. Press seeds or raisins into the icing. Larger fruit and nuts look good along the bottom of the wall. Squeeze small but thick dollops to attach any desired larger decorations. Use enough icing to hold each item securely in place. (Enjoy the decorating, but be careful not to overdo it; let some gingerbread show!) Allow the decorated walls to dry flat for about 20 to 30 minutes, or until the decorations are secure, and their icing is almost dry. (Keep the remaining icing at room temperature and covered. Keep the decorating bag tightly closed at the top, and the icing in it will be fine.)

BUILDING THE SIDES OF THE SUKKAH

When the wall decorations are set, the sukkah can be assembled. (NOTE: It is helpful to have an assistant for this part.) Have the base ready, and plan where to put the sukkah on it. You will begin the assembly with one of the smaller side walls (they are interchangeable). Use the decorating bag to squeeze a thick continuous bead of icing on the short bottom edge and on both long side edges of one of the side wall pieces. Stand the wall in place on its short "glued" bottom edge on the prepared cardboard base. Make sure that its decorated side is facing out. Have an assistant temporarily hold the wall steady, or lean the inside of the wall against a small can or bottle.

Second, put a continuous bead of icing on the long bottom edge (only) of the back wall. Stand it on its "glued" edge and place it perpendicular to the side wall, with one short end (not the very edge) leaning against one of the "glued" side edges of the side wall to form an *L*. If correctly placed with enough icing, these two walls should be able to stand alone without support.

Third, put a continuous bead of icing on the short bottom edge and both long side edges of the second side wall, and set it in place with one "glued" side edge touching the remaining end of the back wall just like the first side wall.

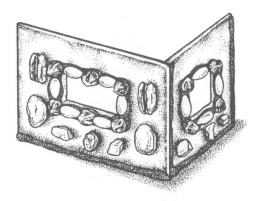

Finally, put icing on the bottom edge (only) of the front wall, and lean it against the iced edges of the two side walls. You should have a very stable, neat rectangular "box" that is 7 inches long, 4½ inches wide, and 5 inches high.

Reinforce the corners of the box, both inside and out, by "caulking" them with a thin bead of icing. You can use a moistened finger to smooth the bead of icing into the joints. If the sukkah seems at all unsteady on the base, caulk the sukkah where it meets the base as well.

ASSEMBLING THE LATTICE ROOF

Let the walls dry for several minutes while you prepare the lattice roof for placement. To give the roof extra support so that it will not sag at all during an extended period, use six thin wooden skewers or craft sticks or cut drinking straws as supports. The supports should be about 5¾ inches long, so that they will reach from the front wall to the back wall of the sukkah when the roof is in place, but are not obviously seen. To attach the supports, carefully turn the lattice over and use icing to glue a support onto the flat underside of each of the 6¼-inch crossbeams of the lattice. (Be sure to remove the supports before eating the roof.)

To attach the roof to the sukkah, squeeze a thick bead of icing all around the top edge of the walls. Center the roof in place (with the supporting sticks concealed underneath), and press down very gently so it becomes firmly attached. It will make the structure of the sukkah secure. Check where the roof meets the walls and caulk any gaps.

If desired, use icing to attach food decorations to the roof where the lattice beams cross each other. (Or use a few sprigs of plastic or silk greenery to look more like the *sechach* [natural covering] on a real sukkah.) Also, the door can be glued against the doorway so it is ajar, in an inviting sort of way. Before the door is glued on, it can be decorated with seeds or a Star of David piped from the icing bag (you may need to use a smaller tip).

Allow the completed sukkah to rest for several hours before moving it. The icing will dry rock hard, (it's still edible), and the sukkah will be relatively sturdy. Once the icing is completely dry, the sukkah can be very loosely covered with plastic wrap to keep off dust. It should stay edible and tasty for up to 2 weeks.

Brown Icing "Glue"

The original recipe for this icing called for raw egg whites that were not cooked. Because of the slight risk of bacterial contamination from raw eggs, I now use pasteurized dried egg whites, (such as Just Whites) for this icing. It can be substituted for raw egg whites in any recipe, and actually beats up better than fresh whites. (For more information, see Glossary of Ingredients.) If Just Whites is not available, meringue powder, which is available where cake-decorating supplies are sold, may be used.

To apply the icing, you will need a cake-decorating bag and one ³⁄₁₆- to ¼-inch plain round tip. (If a decorating bag is not available, you can try using a sturdy plastic freezer bag with a zipper top. Use scissors to snip off one bottom corner, making a small hole. Put the icing in the bag, zip it closed, and squeeze the icing out the hole.)

*Pasteurized dried egg white powder,
    such as Just Whites (see comments
    above), plus warm water to equal 3
    egg whites*
¹⁄₂ teaspoon cream of tartar

*3³⁄₄ cups sifted confectioners' sugar
    (measure after sifting)*
*¹⁄₄ cup sifted unsweetened cocoa powder
    (or carob powder) (measure after
    sifting)*

In a medium mixing bowl, dissolve the dried egg white powder in the warm water as directed on the package. Add the cream of tartar. Beat with an

electric mixer until well mixed and quite foamy. Gradually add the confectioners' sugar and cocoa while beating. Beat at medium to high speed for several minutes until the icing increases slightly in volume, lightens slightly in color, and is like very thick whipped cream. (This may take 10 to 12 minutes with a handheld mixer.)

Since individual measuring techniques may vary slightly, the icing consistency may have to be adjusted. If the icing is very loose even after several minutes of beating, beat in a little extra confectioners' sugar. If it is so stiff that it is not sticky like a "glue," beat in a few more drops of water.

Keep the bowl of icing loosely covered with a damp towel (or a tight lid) so the icing does not dry out, and use the icing soon for best results.

Makes 1 gingerbread sukkah, about 7 inches wide, 5 inches high, and 4½ inches deep.

Sukkot, Shemini Atzeret, and Simhat Torah

Hanukkah

THE FIRST HANUKKAH WAS CELEBRATED IN THE SECOND CEN-
tury B.C.E. by Judah the Maccabee and his followers. A few years earlier,
the Syrian king, Antiochus IV, had decreed that all his subjects must become totally Hellenized, that is, adopt the dominant Greek culture. He
instituted pagan practices in the Holy Temple of Jerusalem and expressly forbade all Jewish ritual on penalty of death.

In the village of Modi'in, the Hasmonean family of Mattathias (a Jewish priest) and
his five sons initiated a revolt against the oppressors. When Mattathias died a short while
later, his son Judah took over as leader of a small but determined group of rebels.

Judah, who was known as Maccabee (meaning "hammer"), probably because of his
persistence or strength, was a brilliant strategist who, after many courageous battles,
brought victory to the Jews and an end to tyranny. The Hasmoneans cleansed the dese-
crated Holy Temple and, on the twenty-fifth day of the Hebrew month of Kislev, they
rededicated it. (The Hebrew word *chanukah*—pronounced with a guttural "ch"—means
"dedication.")

During the pagan occupation of the Holy Temple, its sacred seven-branched *menorah* (candelabrum), which was supposed to continuously burn ritually pure oil, had been
extinguished. When the Temple menorah was rekindled at the dedication, only enough

undefiled oil for one day could be found. According to tradition, this small amount miraculously burned for eight days and nights until more purified oil could be obtained.

To commemorate the miracle of the oil and the inspiring events surrounding it, we celebrate *Chanukah* (or *Hanukkah,* as it is more commonly spelled in the English vernacular)—the only major Jewish holiday that is not based on the canonized Hebrew Bible. During an eight-day period that begins on the twenty-fifth of Kislev, which occurs in December or possibly late November, Jews all over the world burn oil or candles in a special nine-branched menorah that is often placed near a window for all passersby to see. The holiday menorah is called a *hanukkiyah,* to distinguish it from the Temple menorah or any other candelabrum.

In some households, each family member has his or her own *hanukkiyah* to fulfill the *mitzvah*—religious obligation—of kindling the Hanukkah lights and singing the special blessings. During the holiday, my family's front window is aglow in the candlelight of our six beautiful *hanukkiyot,* which we have collected over many years. The first was an Israeli-made one that I received as a special merit award in Jewish day school when I was a young child. Now, our two youngest children take special pride in setting up all the *hanukkiyot* each afternoon. (They enjoy using a crayon sharpener to shave the bottom of any candle that won't fit properly—a technique that I devised long ago.) In doing this task, they have become keenly aware of the kindling laws.

On each night, a servant candle, or *shamash,* is lit first. It is then used to light the cups of oil or other candles. On the first night, one cup or candle is lit, two on the second night, and so forth, until eight cups of oil or candles are brilliantly glowing on the last night. Thus, the holiday is also known as the *Festival of Lights.*

Over the years, the relevance of using oil during Hanukkah was further substantiated by Jewish mystics who pointed out that the Hebrew words for "eight" (*shemoneh*) and "Hasmoneans" (*Hashmonayim*) each contains all the letters of the word for "oil" (*shemen*).

Due to its importance, oil is also prevalent in holiday cooking. Indeed, a variety of foods fried in oil are traditional for Hanukkah meals. Among Ashkenazic Jews, pancakes (*latkes,* in Yiddish)—particularly those made with grated potatoes and onions—have long been a holiday favorite. In the past, when oil was scarce and very expensive, Potato Latkes (page 215) were usually fried in melted goose fat. Geese that had been fattened during the summer and fall were slaughtered shortly before Hanukkah. Most of the rendered fat (schmaltz) was put aside for Passover, but some was always used for Hanukkah latkes. The latkes were often served with roasted goose and sometimes the *gribeness* (skin cracklings) left over from rendering the fat.

For their edible holiday symbols, Sephardic Jews prefer to fry in oil a variety of delectable pastries, many of which are dipped in sweet syrup. In Israel, Soofganiyot (page 248)—jelly-filled doughnuts coated with sugar—are the popular choice.

A lesser-known Hanukkah culinary custom is the partaking of cheese and all sorts of dairy dishes in honor of the brave Jewish heroine Judith. It is written in the Apocrypha that the beautiful widow Judith arranged to dine with an enemy general who intended to destroy her town. During the meal, she fed him great quantities of cheese, and then encouraged him to drink much wine to quench his subsequent thirst. As soon as he fell drunkenly asleep, Judith beheaded him. When his soldiers found out that their general had been slain by a woman, they fled in fear, and the town and its people were spared. Judith's valor is said to have inspired Judah the Maccabee and his followers.

Often, the two culinary traditions of Hanukkah—dairy dishes and oil-fried foods—are combined to produce holiday specialties such as cheese latkes, dairy doughnuts, and potato latkes topped with sour cream. Dairy main dishes eaten on Hanukkah include those that are also popular on Shavuot (see that chapter). These are often served at informal family "open house" celebrations.

The sixth night of Hanukkah is also *Rosh Hodesh,* the beginning of a month on the lunar Hebrew calendar. Moroccan Jews celebrate this minor holiday by gathering together for a festive meal that often features a delicious dish of Sweet Couscous (page 232), which may be served with buttermilk or yogurt.

On the last day of Hanukkah, some Turkish Jews enjoy a special meal called *merenda,* at which many relatives and friends gather, each bringing a portion of the food to be shared by everyone present.

In the United States, as elsewhere, new holiday customs are still evolving. For instance, it has become popular to make Butter Cookies (page 241) shaped like many of the Hanukkah symbols. In that vein, this chapter also includes a recipe for Soft Pretzels (page 264) that have been designed especially for Hanukkah celebrations, and can be used to teach children about the holiday. It also features several types of latkes, an assortment of Sephardic fried pastries, a collection of cookies, and a variety of tasty cheese dishes.

Potato Latkes
CRISP, FRIED PANCAKES

For American Jews of Eastern European ancestry, these delicious *latkes* (Yiddish for "pancakes") have become the quintessential culinary symbol of Hanukkah. However, they are a relatively recent addition to Jewish cuisine. The potato originated in South America, and was not eaten in Europe until after the sixteenth century, when it was first brought back from the New World by early explorers.

The easy-to-grow and inexpensive potato soon became a staple in Ashkenazic cooking. In early winter, when the geese fattened during the previous summer and fall were slaughtered, pancakes made from potatoes and onions were fried in rendered goose fat (schmaltz). The melted fat came to symbolize the oil in the Hanukkah miracle, and the latkes became a favorite holiday food. Today, most potato latkes are actually fried in oil, not schmaltz, making them even more appropriate for the holiday.

There are about as many variations of these pancakes as there are Jewish cooks who make them. Some prefer to sauté the onions before adding the potato shreds; most use raw onions. Some insist on matzah meal as a thickener; others use flour.

And each latke-maker seems to favor a certain kind of potato shredder or grater, as well as a specific size of shred. Some mavens even insist that the latkes won't be authentic until one's knuckles are grated right along with potatoes. Modern cooks, however, are finding that a food processor fitted with a shredding blade does a very satisfactory job in a minimal amount of time.

After many years of experimenting with these latkes, I have developed a food processor technique that takes very little time (see below). Also, I now use an electric peeler to peel the potatoes, and an electric skillet (with controlled temperature) to fry the latkes, producing consistently delectable results with little fuss. I've also learned that the latkes taste better and require much less salt if the salt is sprinkled on them *after* they are cooked, and not added to the raw potatoes.

Although potato latkes should be eaten as soon as they are made for best taste and texture, no cook wants to be stuck in the kitchen while everyone else is having dinner or noshing at a buffet. Therefore, I've included an excellent way to reheat the latkes on the day they are made so that they taste almost as good as new. They may also be frozen and reheated if desired.

NOTE: The size of the potato and onion shreds is a matter of personal taste. Coarse shreds, which are my personal choice, produce lacier latkes with rough edges. Fine

shreds or grated potatoes produce denser, smoother latkes. If your food processor has only a coarse shredding blade but you prefer finely shredded potatoes, return the coarse shreds to the food processor fitted with the steel blade, and pulse-process just a few times until the potatoes are the desired consistency.

2½ pounds Idaho (russet) baking
    potatoes (5 large ones), peeled
2 medium onions, peeled
3 large eggs or ¾ cup pareve egg
    substitute
¼ teaspoon ground black pepper
About ¼ cup matzah meal
Salt to taste

FOR FRYING
Canola oil

TO SERVE (OPTIONAL)
Applesauce and/or sour cream

For the food processor: Cut the potatoes and onions just small enough to fit in the feed tube. Insert a shredding blade in the food processor and shred the potatoes and onions, alternating them to help keep the potatoes from darkening. Put the shreds into a large colander sitting over a very large bowl. After each piece of potato or onion is put through the food processor, remove any leftover bit that does not get properly shredded, and reserve it.

When all the potatoes and onions have been shredded, press any liquid out of the shreds into the bowl. Discard the liquid; then transfer the shreds to the drained bowl. (Reserve the unwashed colander.) Remove the shredding blade from the food processor, and insert a steel blade. Put all the reserved unshredded potato and onion bits into the food processor bowl along with the eggs and black pepper. Process until the mixture is completely puréed. Pour the puréed egg mixture over the shreds, and mix well until all the shreds are coated with egg. Then mix in the matzah meal. Set the mixture aside while you heat oil in a skillet. Just before you are ready to fry the potato mixture, transfer it back to the colander (so it can drain) and set it over the bowl again.

For a hand grater: Shred or grate the potatoes and onions, placing all the shreds into a large colander sitting over a very large bowl. Press any liquid out of the shreds into the bowl. Discard the liquid; then transfer the shreds to the drained bowl. (Reserve the unwashed colander.) Beat the eggs with the pep-

per, and pour the egg mixture over the shreds. Mix well until all the shreds are coated with egg. Then mix in the matzah meal. Set the mixture aside while you heat oil in a skillet. Just before you are ready to fry the potato mixture, transfer it back to the colander (so it can drain) and set it over the bowl again.

To fry the latkes: Spread several layers of paper towels on a large platter or over a large piece of heavy-duty foil or freezer paper spread on the counter. In a large skillet over medium-high heat, or in an electric frypan set at 325 degrees, heat oil that is about ⅛ inch to ¼ inch deep until it is hot but not smoking. (If the heat is too high, the latkes will brown on the outside before the inside is completely cooked. When using a stovetop skillet, carefully adjust the heat as needed.)

To form each latke, put some potato mixture into a large mixing or serving spoon, and press the shreds with your fingertips, pushing out any excess liquid. Carefully use your fingers to slide the compacted potato mixture off the spoon into the oil; then flatten the mixture slightly with the back of the spoon so that it is not too thick in the center. The latkes should be 2½ to 3 inches in diameter. Continue forming latkes until the skillet is full, leaving some space between each one (six is usually the maximum that will fit).

Fry the latkes until they are well browned on the bottom; then turn them carefully with a slotted pancake turner. Fry the latkes until they are browned on the second side and crisp around the edges, and the inside of each is soft and completely cooked. (Taste a finished latke to be sure that they are done.) Drain them well on the paper toweling (which should be replaced periodically), and immediately sprinkle them lightly with salt. Repeat the process until all the latkes are fried, adding oil to the skillet as needed.

For the very best taste and texture, serve the latkes as soon as possible. To reheat them for serving later in the same day, arrange them in one layer or slightly overlapping in a large shallow roasting pan lined with heavy-duty aluminum foil (for easy cleanup). The latkes in the pan may stay at room temperature for a few hours. Heat them uncovered in a preheated 400-degree oven for about 6 to 8 minutes, or until they are hot and crispy.

To freeze the latkes, let them cool to room temperature; then put them in the freezer in a single layer for about ½ hour or just until they are frozen. You may then store them in airtight freezer bags. Reheat the latkes in a single layer

in the roasting pan as described above, but turn them once and continue heating them until they are hot throughout and crispy.

Latkes are typically served with applesauce and/or sour cream on the side.

Makes about 30 2½- to 3-inch potato pancakes.

Ricotta Latkes
LIGHT AND THIN CHEESE PANCAKES

Both cheese and latkes are very traditional foods for Hanukkah. In fact, the custom of eating latkes made from cheese predates the more popular one of dining on potato latkes.

The following latkes are much more delicate and "refined" than the potato type, and make a tasty breakfast or even a nice dessert, especially when topped with a good jam or fresh fruit. As an added bonus, these pancakes are high in protein.

Many years ago, when I first discovered my love for ricotta cheese, I developed the recipe for these tender flat latkes. They quickly became a year-round family favorite. As the unusual latkes seemed to be especially appropriate for Hanukkah, I put them on the table at our holiday open-house buffets, where they have always been a very popular selection.

After I wrote the first edition of this cookbook, this recipe became one of my top choices whenever I was asked to teach a cooking class or do a demonstration for a store or TV show. It is quick and easy, and practically "no fail." But I'll never forget the Midwest talk-show host who thought that my ricotta latkes weren't cooking fast enough. On live TV, he turned up the gas flame so high that it almost set the studio on fire! When our producer gasped in horror, I quickly turned down the heat and flipped the latkes just in the nick of time.

In another interesting turn of events, these latkes seem to have become a Hanukkah classic. Since the recipe was published in my first edition, adaptations of it have appeared in other cookbooks and national magazine articles about Hanukkah. It's nice to know that Jewish cooking is still evolving, and that my book has had a hand in adding to the collection of what others consider to be traditional for a holiday.

NOTES: I highly recommend preparing these latkes on a *nonstick* griddle, which requires very little grease. I personally prefer to cook the latkes in butter because this adds to their flavor. The small amount of butter in the batter also improves the taste of the latkes, which is why I do not suggest substituting margarine.

BATTER
1 (15- to 16-ounce) container part-
    skim ricotta cheese
4 large eggs or 1 cup egg substitute
2 tablespoons sugar
½ to 1 teaspoon vanilla extract
2 tablespoons butter, melted and cooled
½ cup all-purpose flour

FOR FRYING
Butter or margarine or canola oil

TO SERVE (OPTIONAL)
Jam, applesauce, plain or vanilla yogurt,
    and/or chopped fresh fruit

In a food processor fitted with a steel blade (or in a blender in batches if necessary), put the ricotta cheese, eggs, sugar, and vanilla extract. Process until combined. Add the melted butter, and process briefly. Add the flour, and process until the batter is very smooth, like thick cream. Scrape down the sides of the container a few times during processing. (The batter will be thinner than most pancake batters.)

Preheat a griddle or shallow skillet, preferably nonstick, over medium heat (not hotter). An electric frypan set at 325 degrees also works very well. Lightly grease the griddle. (You can use a stick of cold butter to make 3-inch circles on the griddle.) For each latke, spoon a 1½- to 2-tablespoon measure of batter (no more) onto the greased preheated griddle. The batter will spread to form an approximately 3-inch-diameter latke. Keep the latkes at least ½ inch apart from each other.

Cook for about 3 minutes, or until a few bubbles have risen to the surface of the pancakes, the tops are beginning to look dry, and the bottoms are golden brown in a sort of "splotchy" pattern. The latkes will not rise at all. Carefully use a pancake turner to turn the latkes once. (If the bottoms of the latkes brown before the tops are dry enough to turn them, the heat is too high.) Cook the latkes briefly on the second side just until they are golden brown. Repeat until all the batter is used, greasing the griddle between batches.

Serve the pancakes warm or at room temperature, with your choice of accompaniment. They can be very easily reheated in a microwave oven, or they may be kept warm for a short while in a 200- to 250-degree conventional oven.

Makes about 24 to 30 (2½- to 3-inch-diameter) latkes.

Variation

NO-FAT RICOTTA LATKES

D

Although I prefer the original recipe, the following changes will work for those on restricted diets. Use *nonfat* ricotta cheese and egg substitute. Omit the melted butter in the batter. Use 1 teaspoon vanilla extract. When cooking the latkes, use a nonstick griddle that has been coated with nonstick cooking spray before preheating. Make sure that the heat is not too high.

Quick Blini

THIN BUCKWHEAT PANCAKES

These small, delicate pancakes are becoming common in Israel, having been introduced there by its many Russian immigrants. There are probably as many different versions of blini as there are Russian cooks. The following blini are "quick" ones because the yeast batter rises for only 30 minutes. Most traditional batters must rise at least 3 hours, and some take as long as overnight. Furthermore, I have simplified the technique of mixing the batter.

For those who are really in a hurry, a variation uses baking powder instead of yeast, and requires no rising at all. Though this version does not have the yeasty flavor that is characteristic of most blini, it is nevertheless quite tasty.

Buckwheat flour can be found in most health food or gourmet specialty stores, as well as in some supermarkets. It can be stored in the freezer for a year or longer. Beige-colored, light buckwheat flour produces a blini with a mild, deliciously subtle flavor. Dark buckwheat flour is much stronger, and should be used only when a very intense buckwheat flavor is desired.

Blini are customarily served with sour cream and caviar or smoked salmon. However, they also make a nice Hanukkah breakfast with a little pancake syrup on top.

1 packet (2¼ teaspoons) fast-acting dry yeast (see the Glossary of Ingredients)

¾ cup plus 2 tablespoons warm (105 to 115 degrees) water

1 tablespoon honey

¾ cup light buckwheat flour

¼ cup unbleached flour

¼ cup instant nonfat dry milk powder

2 tablespoons sour cream or plain yogurt

1½ tablespoons butter, melted and cooled

2 large eggs, separated

Pinch of salt

FOR FRYING

Butter, canola oil, or nonstick cooking spray

TO SERVE (OPTIONAL)

Sour cream or plain yogurt

Caviar

Very thinly sliced smoked salmon

Pancake syrup

In a medium bowl, combine the yeast, water, and honey. Let the mixture rest for about 5 minutes or until the yeast is totally softened. Stir in the buckwheat flour, white flour, milk powder, sour cream, butter, and egg yolks. Cover the bowl with plastic wrap, and let the batter rest for 30 minutes. It will not rise very much, but will form bubbles on the surface.

In a separate clean bowl, beat the egg whites with the salt just until they form stiff peaks; do not overbeat them, or they may be difficult to fold. Gently, but thoroughly, fold the beaten whites into the batter.

Preheat a griddle or large skillet over medium-high heat and lightly grease it. Spoon 1½- to 2-tablespoon measures of the batter onto the preheated griddle. When bubbles have formed on the surface of the pancakes, and the bottoms are browned, turn them once and cook just until lightly browned on the second side.

Serve the blini with the desired accompaniments.

Makes about 30 2½- to 3-inch blini.

Variation

EVEN-QUICKER BLINI

Omit the yeast. In a medium bowl, combine the buckwheat flour, white flour, milk powder, and ½ teaspoon baking powder. Stir in the water (which should be at room temperature), sour cream, honey, melted butter, and egg yolks. In a separate clean bowl, beat the egg whites with the salt just until they form stiff peaks. Gently but thoroughly fold the beaten whites into the batter. Cook the blini as directed above.

Spiced "Seafood" Croquettes

Though they use seasonings and a technique like Maryland crab cakes, these fish croquettes are completely kosher. They are made with poached cod or haddock. The patties are fried in oil, making them great candidates for a Hanukkah dinner.

NOTE: Fresh bread crumbs may be made in a food processor fitted with a steel blade. Remove the crusts from a few slices of bread, tear the bread in pieces, and pulse-process it until fine bread crumbs are formed.

1 pound skinless thick fillets of cod or haddock
2 large eggs or ½ cup egg substitute
¼ cup low-fat or regular mayonnaise
1 teaspoon dry mustard powder
¾ teaspoon salt
½ teaspoon celery seed
½ teaspoon Worcestershire sauce
¼ teaspoon black pepper
Pinch of ground cloves

Pinch of mace
Pinch of cayenne pepper, or more to taste
1 cup fresh white or whole wheat bread crumbs (see Note)
Canola oil

TO SERVE (OPTIONAL)
6 to 8 pieces of toasted bread or English muffin halves

Arrange the fillets in one layer in a large skillet. Cover them with water, and bring it to a boil. Immediately lower the heat, and gently simmer the fish

until it is tender and just beginning to flake, about 10 to 15 minutes depending on the thickness of the fillets. Remove the fillets from the skillet with a slotted spoon, draining them well. Chill the fish in the refrigerator. When it is cool, flake it into ¾-inch pieces.

In a medium bowl, beat together the eggs, mayonnaise, mustard powder, salt, celery seed, Worcestershire sauce, black pepper, cloves, mace, cayenne pepper, and bread crumbs. Let the mixture rest for about 5 minutes so that the bread crumbs can absorb some of the moisture. The mixture should be rather stiff. Gently stir the flaked fish into the bread crumb mixture, being careful not to break up the lumps of fish.

In a large skillet over medium-high heat, put oil that is ⅛ to ¼ inch deep. Heat the oil until it is hot but not smoking. Form the fish mixture into ½-inch-thick patties using about ⅓ cup for each, and place the patties in the skillet. Fry the croquettes until they are well browned on both sides. Blot well on paper towels. If desired, serve each croquette on a piece of toasted bread or an English muffin half.

Makes about 6 to 8 fish croquettes.

Bubby Rose's Farfel-Potato Dairy Soup

This was one of the first soups that my mother ever prepared—something she learned from her maternal grandmother and favorite cooking teacher, my great-grandmother Rose Dublin Levine.

Though Mom used to serve this soup quite often when I was younger, I had completely forgotten about it until she and I had a conversation about the culinary prowess of Bubby Rose. Mom gave me the recipe, and I promptly tried it in my own kitchen. To my amazement, just one taste of the delicious farfel-potato soup was enough to bring wonderful gustatory recollections of my early childhood to mind.

This quick and easy soup has become so well liked in my own family that it is now a regular staple in my culinary repertoire. We especially enjoy it on cold winter evenings, such as those that inevitably occur during Hanukkah. I have modified the original recipe only slightly by chopping the onion and sautéing it in butter (Bubby left it whole and removed it when the soup was done). Also, I use milk powder instead of milk to avoid

the possibility of scorching while cooking the potatoes. Real butter adds significantly to the flavor of this soup, so I don't recommend substitutes.

NOTE: The "farfel" in this soup is actually plain, barley-shaped egg pasta, which is often called simply "egg barley." It is usually available with the pasta or in the "Jewish" section of most supermarkets. I've given a range for the amount because you can vary it depending on your taste; more makes the soup thicker. If you double the recipe, however, use no more than 1 to 1¼ cups (1 8-ounce box) egg barley, or the soup may become too thick.

2 medium to large "new" potatoes or
    all-purpose potatoes
1 medium onion
3 cups water
2 tablespoons butter
½ to ⅔ cup (4 to 5 ounces) uncooked
    plain "egg barley" (see Note)

¾ to 1 teaspoon salt
⅛ teaspoon ground white or black
    pepper
1 cup instant nonfat dry milk powder
1 cup cold water

Peel the potatoes and cut them into ½-inch cubes. You should have 1½ to 2 cups of cubes. Peel and finely chop the onion. Put the 3 cups water in a kettle, and bring it to a boil.

Meanwhile, melt the butter in a 3- to 3½-quart saucepan over medium-high heat; then add the onion and sauté it until it is tender. Stir in the boiling water, potato cubes, egg barley, ¾ teaspoon of the salt, and pepper. Lower the heat and simmer the soup, covered, for 20 minutes, or until the potatoes are tender.

While the soup is cooking, put the milk powder into a 2-cup measure or similar cup. Add a small amount of the cold water, and stir until smooth. Then add the remaining water, and stir until all the milk powder is dissolved.

When the potatoes are tender but not mushy, stir the dissolved milk powder into the hot soup, and continue heating and stirring about 2 to 3 minutes, until the soup returns to a simmer. Adjust the salt and pepper to taste. Serve the soup hot.

(This soup gets thicker upon standing. When reheating leftovers, stir in some milk or water if the soup is too thick. A microwave oven is excellent for warming this soup.)

Makes 4 to 5 servings.

Spas

RUSSIAN-STYLE YOGURT-BARLEY SOUP

This tangy soup is wonderfully thick and rich-tasting—perfect for a cold winter night. It's also nourishing and satisfying enough to be a meatless main dish, particularly if you really like the taste of barley, as I do. A friend of mine often serves it as the introductory course for dairy Shabbat dinners with guests.

2½ cups water
1 cup uncooked (medium) pearl barley
2½ tablespoons butter
½ cup very finely minced onion
2 tablespoons all-purpose flour
3¼ cups milk, any type
2 cups plain yogurt
1 large egg, lightly beaten, or ¼ cup
   egg substitute

1 teaspoon salt

TO SERVE (OPTIONAL)
Chopped fresh chives or thinly sliced
   scallions, including green tops, or
   chopped fresh parsley

Bring the water to a boil in a 2½-quart saucepan over high heat; then stir in the barley, cover the pan tightly, and lower the heat. Simmer the barley for about 45 minutes, or until the water is absorbed and the barley is tender but not mushy. Set it aside. (The barley may be cooked up to a day ahead of the soup. If the barley is cooked more than a few hours in advance, refrigerate it.)

Melt the butter in a 4- to 5-quart pot over medium-high heat; then sauté the onion until it is tender. Stir in the flour, and cook for 1 minute, stirring constantly. Then very gradually (so that the flour does not form any lumps) stir in the milk. Continue to cook, while stirring, until the mixture thickens slightly and comes to a boil. Stir in the cooked barley; then cover the pan, lower the heat, and simmer the mixture for 10 to 15 minutes, or until it is very thick.

Meanwhile, stir together the yogurt, egg, and salt. Remove the pan from the heat, and stir in the yogurt mixture. Return the soup to low heat, and cook it, stirring, until it is completely heated. (If the soup comes to a boil, it may look curdled but it will still taste fine.) If desired, keep the soup warm over very low heat.

Hanukkah

To serve, ladle the soup into bowls, and sprinkle some chopped chives or scallions over each serving.

Makes about 8 servings.

Mejedrah

LENTILS AND RICE WITH BROWNED ONIONS

This side dish is eaten by Near Eastern and Middle Eastern Jews on festive occasions, and is also traditional for the meatless "Nine Days" that precede the solemn fast day of Tisha B'Av (usually occurring in August). This simple combination of rice, lentils, and well-fried onions is also called *enjadara, mejadarra, mjudrah,* and several other similar variations on the Arabic name. It is very popular in Israel, where it is even available in packaged mixes. These can sometimes be purchased in American kosher supermarkets.

Iraqi Jews enjoy a slightly different lentil-and-rice dish known as *ketchri,* which features *red* lentils and is highly seasoned with garlic, cumin, black pepper, and tomato paste. It also usually calls for a large amount of melted butter. *Ketchri* typically is steamed in the same lengthy manner as Iraqi rice so that it forms a tasty "crust" on the bottom of the pan.

The following adaptation of *mejedrah* calls for brown rather than white rice because the cooking time for brown rice is about the same as that for lentils, and the nutty flavor of brown rice stands up well to brown lentils. What's more, brown rice is more nutritious than white.

The combination of lentils and brown rice provides complete, high-quality protein, so this dish can be served as a vegetarian main course. For a dairy meal in the Sephardic style, accompany *mejedrah* with yogurt and Huevos Haminados (page 354).

3 large onions, peeled
4 tablespoons good-quality olive oil, divided
3 cups water
1 cup uncooked long-grain brown rice

1 cup dry brown lentils, rinsed and sorted
1 teaspoon ground cumin
¾ teaspoon salt
¼ teaspoon ground black pepper

ADDITIONAL GARNISH (OPTIONAL)
2 to 4 tablespoons pine nuts
1 tablespoon good-quality olive oil

TO SERVE (OPTIONAL)
Plain yogurt

Cut the onions in half through the root end; then thinly slice them. Put 3 tablespoons of oil into a 3½- to 4-quart saucepan over medium heat. Add the onions and cook them, stirring frequently for 20 minutes, or until they are greatly reduced in volume and are richly browned and very aromatic. (Do not let them burn.) While the onions are cooking, bring the water to a boil. When the onions are ready, remove half, and set them aside to use as a garnish. Add the remaining 1 tablespoon oil and the rice to the onions in the saucepan and cook them, stirring, for about 2 minutes. Then stir in the lentils, boiling water, cumin, salt, and pepper.

Bring the mixture to a boil; then cover it, and lower the heat. Simmer the mixture for about 30 to 35 minutes, or until all the water is absorbed and the lentils and rice are tender. If the water is absorbed and the lentils or rice is still not tender, add a little more water, and cook a few minutes longer.

If a pine nut garnish is desired, while the rice and lentils are cooking, sauté the pine nuts in the olive oil until they are toasted. Set aside.

When the mejedrah is done, fluff it gently with a fork, stir in about half of the reserved brown onions. and add seasonings to taste, if needed. Spoon it into a serving dish, and top it with the remaining onions and pine nuts (if used). Serve it hot or at room temperature. If desired, serve yogurt on the side.

Makes about 8 side-dish servings; about 4 main-dish servings.

White Beans and Pasta Skillet

This quick dish is a favorite dairy dinner in my home. It is high in fiber and low in fat, particularly when low-fat cheese is used. Please feel free to vary the herbs to use whatever you already have on hand.

8 ounces uncooked corkscrew or similar
   pasta or about 3½ to 4 cups
   cooked pasta
2 (15- to 16-ounce) cans plain white
   beans, such as navy, great
   northern, or cannellini
3 tablespoons good quality olive oil or
   canola oil
2 medium onions, finely chopped

About 1 teaspoon dried basil leaves
About ½ teaspoon dried thyme leaves
½ teaspoon salt
⅛ teaspoon ground pepper
½ cup milk, any type
About 8 ounces regular or reduced-fat
   grated Cheddar or similar cheese
   (do not use nonfat cheese)

Cook the pasta according to the package directions. Drain well and set it aside. Drain the canned beans, and rinse them well in a colander. Set aside.

Put the oil into a 4- to 5-quart Dutch oven or similar pot over medium-high heat. Add the onion and sauté it until tender. Stir in the basil and thyme (or other herbs of your choosing), salt, and pepper. Add the milk and drained beans, and stir gently until the beans are heated through. Add the pasta, and stir to mix it with the beans. Add the grated cheese, and continue stirring until the cheese melts. Serve immediately.

Makes about 6 main-dish servings.

Black Beans and Rice Casserole

This tasty combination is frequently enjoyed by Jews who live in the American Southwest. Unlike many foods from that region, this vegetarian main dish complies to the rules of kashrut. I consider it appropriate for this chapter because it has the requisite cheese and it's perfect for a Hanukkah open-house luncheon or dinner. I have used it often for that purpose, as well as for potluck dairy buffets with our Havurah (friendship group), where it has been quite popular.

This casserole is very quick and easy to prepare once the rice has been cooked, and it provides an excellent balance of complementary protein. Although the dish is typically layered in a manner like lasagna, I find it easier and tastier when prepared as directed below.

2 cups water

1 cup uncooked brown rice

2 (15- to 16-ounce) cans black beans

1 small onion, very finely chopped, or 2
tablespoons instant minced onions

2 garlic cloves, finely minced or pressed

2 (3- to 4-ounce) cans chopped green
chilies

1 (15-ounce) container nonfat or part-
skim ricotta cheese (about 2 cups)

1 large egg, beaten, or ¼ cup egg
substitute

8 to 12 ounces grated regular or
reduced-fat Cheddar or similar
cheese (do not use nonfat cheese)

In a medium saucepan, bring the water to a boil. Add the rice, and stir. Cover the saucepan, and lower the heat so that the water simmers. Cook the rice for 30 to 40 minutes, or until the water is absorbed and the rice is tender. There should be about 2½ cups cooked rice. (The rice may be made ahead of time, and refrigerated.)

While the rice is cooking, drain the beans in a colander and rinse them well with cool water.

Preheat oven to 350 degrees. Stir the beans, onions, garlic, and chopped chilies into the cooked rice. In a small bowl, combine the ricotta cheese and egg. The mixture should be soft and creamy. Gently stir it into the beans and rice mixture along with all but ⅔ cup of the Cheddar cheese.

Coat a 9 by 13-inch baking dish well with nonstick cooking spray or grease it well. Evenly spread the bean–rice–ricotta mixture in the dish. Sprinkle the reserved Cheddar cheese on top.

Bake at 350 degrees for about 35 minutes, or until completely heated through. Serve hot or lukewarm. (This dish can be made ahead, and refrigerated. Reheat it, covered, in a microwave or conventional oven.)

Makes about 8 main-dish servings, or about 15 side-dish or buffet servings.

Chili con Queso

CHEESE, TOMATO, AND CHILI PEPPER DIP

This Tex-Mex dip makes a perfect snack, buffet, or party dish, and it takes only a few minutes to prepare. It looks like a chunky cheese fondue. Several years ago, when our local Jewish Federation planned a special program about those Jews who arrived in the United States through Galveston, Texas, I was asked to do a cooking demonstration. I could not imagine what recipe to cook, until this warm dip came to mind. It was easy to demonstrate, and everyone present had a great time sampling the results.

NOTE: Reduced-fat cheese may not melt properly in this recipe. Do not use nonfat cheese.

1 pound shredded regular Cheddar, longhorn, or Monterey Jack cheese (see Note)
2 tablespoons all-purpose flour
2 tablespoons olive or canola oil
1 large onion, finely chopped
2 garlic cloves, minced
1 (14- to 16-ounce) can tomatoes, including juice, finely chopped

1 (3- to 4-ounce) can chopped green chilies
¼ cup chopped ripe black olives (optional)

TO SERVE
Corn chips, nacho chips, or broken taco pieces

Toss the cheese with the flour, and set it aside momentarily.

Put the oil into a large saucepan over medium-high heat; then sauté the onion and garlic until they are very tender. Add the tomatoes with their juice, and the chilies. Heat, while stirring, until the sauce gently boils. Gradually add the shredded cheese, stirring constantly. Continue to stir over medium to medium-high heat for 5 to 10 minutes, or until the cheese is completely melted and smooth, and the mixture just comes to a boil. Stir in the olives (if used). Remove the mixture from the heat, and let it cool, stirring occasionally, about 5 minutes, so it can thicken slightly. Serve the warm *chili con queso* in a chafing dish, fondue pot, or deep bowl, with your choice of accompaniments for dipping.

Makes about 4½ cups of dip.

Cheese Coins

Savory Cheese Wafers

During Hanukkah, it is traditional for Ashkenazic parents to give their children small gifts of *gelt* (Yiddish for "money"), usually in the form of shiny coins. The following recipe produces golden disks of edible Hanukkah gelt. With them, one is sure to get a good return on any "dough" invested in the project. And the holiday game of chance played with a *dreidel* (Yiddish for "spinning top") will take on an added dimension when the winnings are so tasty.

I did not originate the name for this appetizer or snack, which is adapted from a variety of classic British recipes for cheese wafers. The ingredient proportions vary from recipe to recipe, but the names—such as cheese coins, cheese pennies or ha'pennies—invariably have something to do with money. As cheese is traditionally eaten on Hanukkah, these coins would be very appropriate for this holiday. And, you can quip to friends, "Gelt's in your mouth—not in your hands!"

8 ounces finely grated sharp Cheddar
    cheese (about 2 cups, packed) (do
    not use reduced-fat or nonfat)
½ cup butter, softened
1 cup all-purpose white flour

1 teaspoon Worcestershire sauce
2 tablespoons instant minced onions
Pinch of cayenne pepper (optional)
Sesame seeds

In a medium bowl, combine all the ingredients except the sesame seeds. Mix well by hand or with a heavy-duty mixer until a dough is formed. Divide the dough in half, and shape each half into a log that is 1 inch in diameter and about 12 inches long. Roll the logs in sesame seeds to completely coat the outside (so that each sliced wafer will be rimmed with seeds). Wrap each log tightly in plastic wrap; then chill several hours or overnight. (The logs may be frozen at this point; thaw them in the refrigerator before using.)

To bake the wafers, preheat the oven to 375 degrees. Carefully cut each log crosswise into ¼-inch-thick slices. Place the slices on parchment-lined or nonstick-spray-coated baking sheets, and bake them at 375 degrees for 10 to 12 minutes, or until lightly browned and firm. Let the wafers cool slightly; then use a metal spatula or pancake turner to carefully remove the wafers from

the baking sheets, and cool them completely on wire racks. Store the "coins" in an airtight container to keep them crunchy.

Makes about 80 small wafers.

Sweet Couscous with Dried Fruit and Nuts

The sixth night of Hanukkah is also *Rosh Hodesh,* or the "New Moon." It marks the end of a month on the Hebrew calendar and the beginning of the next one. Many Jews observe Rosh Hodesh of every month as a joyous semiholiday. During Hanukkah, Moroccan Jews often gather with relatives and friends on the evening of the sixth candle for a festive celebration, which usually includes a special meal followed by several desserts. These may include Zvingous (page 257), Zelebi (page 250), or a rich, sweet couscous like that which follows. When served with a dairy dinner or as a midday snack, it is usually accompanied by yogurt or buttermilk.

1 recipe Quick Couscous made with 1 1/2
   cups dry couscous (page 126)
4 tablespoons butter or margarine,
   melted
1/2 cup chopped pitted dates
1/2 cup dark raisins
1/4 cup sugar
2 tablespoons orange juice or sweet
   wine
1 teaspoon grated orange peel, colored
   part only (optional)

1/2 cup finely chopped blanched almonds
1/2 cup finely chopped walnuts or
   pistachios
1/4 teaspoon ground cinnamon
Extra ground cinnamon, for garnish

TO SERVE (OPTIONAL)
Plain yogurt or buttermilk

Prepare Quick Couscous as directed in the recipe, and set it aside until shortly before serving this dessert. (It may be refrigerated.)

Stir 2 tablespoons of the melted butter into the prepared couscous, using a fork to break up any lumps and fluff up the couscous. Stir in the dates,

raisins, sugar, orange juice, and orange peel (if used). Heat the couscous in a microwave oven or conventional oven, as when preparing it the first time. Use a fork to fluff it up as before. Toss in the remaining 2 tablespoons melted butter, almonds, walnuts, and ¼ teaspoon cinnamon until well distributed.

Lightly mound the Sweet Couscous onto a large serving platter so that it forms a mountainlike cone (as is customarily done by Moroccans). Decorate it with a few stripes of ground cinnamon radiating from the center to the perimeter. For best taste, serve immediately. To serve, spoon into individual bowls. If desired, accompany the dessert with yogurt or buttermilk in small cups.

Makes 5 to 6 servings.

Chocolate-Chip Mandelbrot

ALMOND COOKIE SLICES

The original recipe for these *mandelbrot* ("almond bread," in Yiddish) was given to me long ago by my cousin, Gail Sandler Nathanson, and I have adapted it. Gail has made these mandelbrot for many years, and she never "double bakes" them as I usually do. They are actually quite good either way. The extra baking makes them a little crunchier, if you like that texture.

When her children were young, Gail often gave these chocolate-chip mandelbrot as a holiday gift for public school teachers. She'd slice up one or two baked logs, and neatly arrange the overlapping slices in a tissue-lined cardboard box. She would then sprinkle them with sieved confectioners' sugar. In those days, many of the teachers had never heard of mandelbrot, so they would effusively thank her for the "delicious Jewish pastry." I still remember how it made Gail smile to think of her homespun mandelbrot as fancy pastry.

Before I sampled Gail's mandelbrot, I had never seen this cookie made with chocolate chips. The "modern" innovation is quite tasty, making these the most popular mandelbrot among the children at our table. I make them often for Shabbat, as well as for Hanukkah and other holidays. And sometimes I even use them as holiday gifts for my children's teachers!

Hanukkah

³/₄ cup canola oil

1¹/₄ cups sugar

3 large eggs or ³/₄ cup pareve egg
  substitute

2 teaspoons vanilla extract

1 teaspoon almond extract

1 tablespoon baking powder

3³/₄ cups all-purpose flour

¹/₂ to 1 cup slivered or sliced almonds

1 to 1¹/₂ cups regular or miniature
  chocolate chips or morsels

COATING (OPTIONAL)

Confectioners' sugar or superfine sugar

Put the oil, sugar, and eggs into a large bowl and beat them with an electric mixer until they are very light and fluffy. Beat in the extracts and baking powder. Add the flour, and mix it in slowly by hand or heavy-duty electric mixer until it is completely combined. Finally, stir in (or use a heavy-duty mixer at its lowest speed) the almonds and chocolate chips. Transfer the sticky dough from the bowl to a large sheet of plastic wrap; then wrap the dough, and press it into a large disk. Chill the dough at least 1 hour, or until it is somewhat firm.

Line two large baking sheets with cooking parchment or coat them with nonstick cooking spray or grease them. Set them aside. Preheat the oven to 350 degrees.

Unwrap the dough and divide it into four equal parts. Transfer one part to a floured surface, and coat the entire surface of the dough lightly with flour. (Return the remainder of the dough to the refrigerator.) Form the chilled dough into a log that is 2 inches in diameter and about 10 to 11 inches long, using additional flour as needed. Brush off any excess flour on the dough log. Immediately transfer the log to one long side of a prepared baking sheet. Repeat to make another log. Keep the two logs parallel and at least 2 inches apart, as they expand a lot during baking. Press in the sides of each log with both your hands to even the width of the logs along their entire length.

Bake the logs at 350 degrees for about 25 to 30 minutes, or until they are lightly browned. (Do not be concerned about cracks that form on the logs.) Loosen them from the baking sheets with a metal spatula, but leave them in place to cool to at least lukewarm. When the first two logs are almost done baking, form the remaining two logs on another baking sheet, and then bake and cool them as directed.

When the baked logs are cool, carefully slide them, one at a time, off the

baking sheets onto a cutting board. Use a sawing motion with a serrated bread knife to crosswise cut each log on the diagonal into ⅜-inch-thick to ¾-inch-thick slices (thinner slices may fall apart). (Save the odd-shaped ends for a nosh; they will quickly disappear!)

For softer mandelbrot, cool the slices completely and serve them as is. If desired, sprinkle the slices lightly with sieved confectioners' sugar.

For crunchier mandelbrot, stand the cut slices back on the baking sheet so there is about ½ inch between each of them. Do not lay the slices on their cut sides, or the chocolate will ooze out. Carefully, so the slices don't fall over, put the baking sheet back into the 350-degree oven. Toast the mandelbrot for 8 to 10 minutes. (They will crisp even more as they cool.) Remove the baking sheet from the oven. If a coating is desired, put some superfine sugar into a small bowl. Sprinkle both sides of each warm mandelbrot slice with the superfine sugar, shaking the excess back into the bowl. Cool the slices completely by standing them up on a wire rack. Store the mandelbrot in airtight containers at room temperature for up to a week, or freeze for longer storage.

Makes about 50 mandelbrot slices.

Cinnamon-Walnut Mandelbrot
CRISP COOKIE SLICES

After tasting the cinnamon-walnut combination in store-bought mandelbrot, I decided to try and work out a recipe of my own. Following is the delicious result—a personal favorite. The irony of these cookies is that they are technically not *mandel*brot, as they do not contain a single *mandel,* that is, "almond." However, they do have a little almond extract, so hopefully that allows them to qualify!

Ashkenazic mandelbrot are similar to Italian *biscotti* (which means simply "cookies") in that both begin as a loaf that is baked, sliced, and "double-baked" to produce dry, crisp cookie slices. But they are different in that mandelbrot have much more oil in the dough than biscotti. The result is that mandelbrot are much more tender and crumbly than biscotti, which tend to be very hard and often must be dipped into hot tea or coffee to soften them.

Both are dried in the oven so that they will stay fresh at room temperature for a long time, and not spoil. In *my* kitchen, keeping mandelbrot around for a long time has never been an issue; my family and guests make them disappear before I know it!

²/₃ cup canola oil

1¹/₃ cups sugar

4 large eggs or 1 cup pareve egg substitute

1¹/₂ teaspoons vanilla extract

1 teaspoon almond extract

¹/₂ teaspoon ground cinnamon

1 tablespoon baking powder

4 cups all-purpose flour

1¹/₂ to 2 cups walnut pieces

COATING

¹/₃ cup sugar

1 tablespoon ground cinnamon

Put the oil, sugar, and eggs into a large bowl and beat them with an electric mixer until they are very light and fluffy. Beat in the extracts, cinnamon, and baking powder. Add the flour, and mix it in slowly by hand or heavy-duty electric mixer until it is completely combined. Finally, stir in (or use a heavy-duty mixer at its lowest speed) the walnuts. Transfer the sticky dough from the bowl to a large sheet of plastic wrap; then wrap the dough, and press it into a large disk. Chill the dough at least 1 hour, or until it is somewhat firm.

Line two large baking sheets with cooking parchment or coat them with nonstick cooking spray or grease them. Set them aside. Preheat the oven to 350 degrees. Make the coating by mixing the sugar and cinnamon together very well in a small bowl. Set the coating aside.

Unwrap the dough and divide it into four equal parts. Transfer one part to a floured surface, and coat the entire surface of the dough lightly with flour. (Return the remainder of the dough to the refrigerator.) Form the chilled dough into a log that is 2 inches in diameter and about 10 to 11 inches long, using additional flour as needed. Brush off any excess flour on the dough log. Immediately transfer the log to one long side of a prepared baking sheet. Repeat to make another log. Keep the two logs parallel and at least 2 inches apart, as they expand a lot during baking. Press in the sides of each log with both your hands to even the width of the logs along their entire length.

Bake the logs at 350 degrees for about 25 to 30 minutes, or until they are lightly browned. (Do not be concerned about cracks that form on the logs.)

Loosen them from the baking sheets with a metal spatula, but leave them in place to cool to at least lukewarm. When the first two logs are almost done baking, form the remaining two logs on another baking sheet, and then bake and cool them as directed.

When the baked logs are cool, carefully slide them, one at a time, off the baking sheet onto a cutting board. Use a sawing motion with a serrated bread knife to crosswise cut each log on the diagonal into ⅝-inch-thick to ¾-inch-thick slices (thinner slices may fall apart or become too hard when toasted). (Save the odd-shaped ends for a nosh; they will quickly disappear!)

To toast the cut slices, stand them up on the baking sheet so there is about ½ inch between each of them. For best results, do not lay the slices on their cut sides. Carefully, so the slices don't fall over, put the baking sheet back into the 350-degree oven. Toast the mandelbrot for 8 to 10 minutes. (They will crisp even more as they cool.) Remove the baking sheet from the oven, and sprinkle both sides of each warm mandelbrot slice with some prepared cinnamon-sugar, shaking the excess back into the bowl. Cool the coated slices completely by standing them up on a wire rack. Store the mandelbrot in airtight containers at room temperature for up to a week, or freeze for longer storage. (I often keep extra mandelbrot in the freezer for last-minute company. They defrost very quickly on a serving tray.)

Makes about 50 mandelbrot slices.

Rugelach
RICH NUT HORNS OR ROLLS

This recipe uses a basic cream cheese dough that is quite delectable, but often difficult to work with because it is so rich. However, these traditional rugelach (pronounced with a guttural "ch") should be relatively easy to prepare if you carefully follow the directions below. The recipe has been worked out to make the mixing and rolling of the dough as foolproof and quick as possible. The soft dough is rolled inside a plastic bag (or between two sheets of heavy plastic wrap) so that extra flour is not needed. The sheet of dough is then chilled, and the cookies are formed from very cold rolled dough.

This is one recipe where I use no substitutes for the butter and cream cheese. I bake rugelach only for very special occasions, such as our annual Hanukkah open-house celebration, and they have the best flavor and texture when made in the classic way. Be forewarned: These fill the kitchen with an absolutely divine aroma when they are baking, which makes them very hard to resist!

You may notice there is no jam in the filling, as with some rugelach. I have personally found jam to be messy and not that desirable. However, if you want to use jam, I recommend trying the Log-Style Rugelach variation.

FILLING AND TOPPING	DOUGH
1¼ cups walnut pieces	1 cup butter, softened (2 sticks) (no substitutes)
¾ cup sugar	
2 teaspoons ground cinnamon	1 (8-ounce) package regular cream cheese, softened (no substitutes)
1 egg white, beaten lightly with a fork, or a few tablespoons of egg substitute	1½ tablespoons sugar
	2 cups all-purpose flour

For the filling, put the walnuts, sugar, and cinnamon into a food processor bowl fitted with a steel blade, and pulse-process just until the nuts are very finely and evenly chopped but still have some texture. Remove the filling from the food processor and set it aside in a small bowl. (If you do not have a food processor, very finely chop the walnuts and then mix them with the sugar and cinnamon in a small bowl.)

For the dough, put the butter, cream cheese, and sugar into the bowl of a heavy-duty electric mixer or the food processor bowl. Beat or process until the ingredients are completely mixed together. Add the flour in thirds, beating or processing until it is completely incorporated and the dough is smooth. If the mixer is not strong enough, mix the dough by hand.

Divide the dough into four equal pieces (they can be measured on a kitchen scale for accuracy, if desired). Form each dough piece into a flattened ball, and put each one into a separate large (approximately 12-inch square) clear plastic food storage bag (the type without a zipper). Lay one of the bags flat on the counter, with the dough in the center of the bag. Roll out the dough inside the bag to a very round 9-inch-diameter circle of even thickness.

HINT: This is most easily done if you first draw a circle of the correct size on a sheet of white paper, and place the paper under the clear bag so that the drawn circle is visible. Simply roll out the dough to fill the circle, making sure the edges are not thinner than the center. The paper pattern can be used repeatedly.

Roll all four pieces of dough in the same manner, leaving the dough circles in the bags. Stack the dough circles in the refrigerator to chill for 1 hour or up to overnight, until they are quite firm.

NOTE: If plastic storage bags are not available, use two sheets of heavy plastic wrap—one under and one on top—for each piece of dough.

While the dough is chilling, line several sturdy shiny metal baking sheets (preferably the insulated type) with baking parchment, or coat them lightly with nonstick cooking spray or lightly grease them. Set them aside. Preheat the oven to 375 degrees.

Before continuing, have the nut filling ready along with the following equipment: a ¼-cup measure, a pair of kitchen scissors, a cutting board large enough to hold one dough circle, a 12-inch-long sheet of wax paper, a rolling pin, and a pastry (or pizza) cutting wheel or sharp knife.

Remove one of the dough circles from the refrigerator. Work quickly and efficiently to keep the dough cold. Use the scissors to cut open both sides of the plastic bag, and peel the top of the bag off the dough circle. Sprinkle a very small amount of the nut filling on a cutting board (to help keep the dough from sticking); then turn over the circle of dough on the filling. The other side of the plastic bag will now be on top. Peel off the rest of the plastic bag, and discard it. Sprinkle ¼ cup of the filling evenly over the top of the dough. Lay the wax paper over the circle; then very gently pass a rolling pin over the circle once to lightly press in the filling. (Both sides of the circle will now have some filling, with most of it on top.) Remove the wax paper, and set it aside to use again.

Leave the dough in place during the following procedure. Use the pastry wheel or knife to cut the dough circle in half to form two semicircles; then cut both semicircles in half to make fourths. Cut each fourth into three equal triangles, working from the perimeter into the center, the way a pizza is cut.

You should have twelve triangles. Roll each triangle from the outside perimeter of the circle to the center. Repeat until all the triangles have been rolled. Pick up one rugelach, and dab a bit of beaten egg white inside the point of the triangle so it won't unroll. Dip the opposite side of each rolled rugelach into the egg white and then into the filling mixture. Place the rugelach point-down onto the baking sheet. Repeat with all the cookies, keeping them at least 1 inch apart on the baking sheet.

If there is still room on the baking sheet, repeat the process with another dough circle until the baking sheet is filled. Immediately bake the rugelach at 375 degrees for about 18 to 22 minutes or until lightly browned. Carefully transfer them to wire racks to cool. If any baking sheets are used a second time, be sure they are cooled off first. When the rugelach are completely cool, store them in an airtight container for a few days, or freeze for longer storage. They freeze very well.

Makes 48 cookies.

Variation

LOG-STYLE RUGELACH

These compact rolls look more like the rugelach often found in supermarkets and some bakeries. All the ingredients are the same. Do not roll out the dough into circles, but into four 12 by 5½-inch rectangles instead. (If desired, spread a very thin layer of seedless raspberry jam on the dough, keeping it ½ inch away from both long edges.) Apply the nut filling as directed above; then roll up the dough like a jelly roll, beginning at a long edge. Use the egg white to seal the edge of the roll. Refrigerate the logs for about 10 minutes. Use a very sharp knife to cut the chilled logs into twelve 1-inch slices, then coat the top of each cookie with egg white and filling as directed above. Bake as directed above, seam side (*not* cut side) down.

Makes 48 cookies.

Hanukkah Butter Cookies

ROLLED COOKIES CUT IN HANUKKAH SHAPES

When I was a child, my mother often made delicious buttery sugar cookies as a special treat for my younger sisters and me. She almost always used the same set of four cookie cutters. Each cutter looked like a symbol for one of the suits in a deck of cards: hearts, diamonds, clubs, and spades. And she always topped the cookies with colored sprinkles—never with colored sugar or icing. I grew up assuming that this was the only way to make rolled cookies. I remember thinking that any other shape or topping must not be "Jewish."

When I later told this to Mom, she thought it was rather humorous. You see, she used her favorite cutters all the time simply because they fit together well on the dough with few scraps, and the basic shapes didn't break easily. And she just happened to prefer multicolored sprinkles to sugar or icing.

The sprinkles bring back good memories and are pretty, so I tend to use them on my butter cookies, too. However, I prefer a wide assortment of shapes. At Hanukkah, my children and I have great fun using cookies cutters to make a small *hanukkiyah,* flask of oil, Judah Maccabee, Star of David, and, my favorite, a very plain dreidel, which (come to think of it) looks an awful lot like the cookies my mother used to make!

NOTE: I highly recommend using real butter in this recipe for the best taste and texture. These cookies have very few ingredients, and butter adds significantly to the wonderful, rich taste.

1 cup butter, softened (2 sticks) (no substitutes)	¼ teaspoon salt
	3 cups all-purpose flour
1½ cups sugar	
2 large eggs or ½ cup egg substitute	TOPPING (OPTIONAL)
2 teaspoons vanilla extract	Multicolored sprinkles
1 teaspoon baking powder	Colored sugar (blue is sort of "Jewish")

In a large mixer bowl, use a heavy-duty electric mixer to cream the butter with the sugar until light. Beat in the eggs, one at a time, then the vanilla extract, baking powder, and salt. Finally, beat in the flour, adding 1 cup at a time and beating until it is incorporated. Divide the dough into two, and

place each half on a large piece of plastic wrap. Use the wrap to press each piece of sticky dough into a flat, round disk. Wrap the dough well, and chill it for 1 hour or up to overnight, until it is cold and firm.

Preheat the oven to 375 degrees. Line several sturdy shiny metal baking sheets with baking parchment (for the nicest-looking cookie shapes), or coat them with nonstick cooking spray, or grease them lightly. Set aside.

Remove one piece of dough from the refrigerator, and coat all the surfaces with flour. Tap the dough with the side of a rolling pin to soften it slightly; then roll it out on a floured surface to a little more than ⅛ inch thick, turning it over occasionally to make sure it is not sticking. (If the dough has been refrigerated for longer than 1 hour, it may be too stiff to roll or it may crack a lot at the edges when it is rolled. Let it rest at room temperature for a few minutes to warm it slightly; then roll it out.)

Brush any excess flour off the top of the dough. Use cookie cutters (your choice of Hanukkah designs, or others) to press out shapes in the dough, keeping the shapes very close together to minimize scraps.

Use a large metal spatula or dough scraper to transfer the cookies to the prepared baking sheets, keeping them at least 1 inch apart. Gently collect all scraps into a ball without too much handling, and reroll and cut the dough using less flour than the first time. If the dough becomes too soft to handle, chill it again. (For tender cookies, try not to reroll scraps too many times.)

If sprinkles or colored sugar is desired as a decoration on the cookies, use a small spoon to put a little topping on each cookie so it looks attractive. Try not to get any topping on the baking sheet, or it may stick (not a problem with parchment). Don't worry about the topping staying on the cookie; during baking, it should soften and stick to the cookie.

Bake the cookies at 375 degrees for about 7 to 10 minutes (depending on the exact thickness of the dough and the size of the cookies), or until they are lightly browned at the edges. Cool on the baking sheets for 2 minutes, then use a clean metal spatula to transfer the shapes to wire racks to cool completely. (While the first batch is baking, roll and cut the second half of the dough, and proceed as above. Be sure to let the baking sheet cool before using it a second time.) When the cookies are completely cool, store them in an airtight container at room temperature for several days, or freeze them for longer storage.

Makes 25 to 50 cookies, depending on the size of the cutters used.

"G" Cookies

CHOCOLATE AND VANILLA SWIRLED PINWHEELS

When I was a child, my mother occasionally baked these refrigerator cookies as a special treat for Hanukkah and other occasions. To make them, a sheet of chocolate dough is placed on top of a sheet of vanilla dough, and the two are rolled together like a jelly roll. After the log has been refrigerated, cookies are sliced from the log and baked.

"*G*" *Cookies*—as my mother always called them—were among my favorites for two reasons: they tasted great, and Mom created them especially for me. Or at least I thought so. Each cookie *did* have my first initial clearly visible in the chocolate part of the dough.

It was only when I was much older and saw the same cookies in other places that I realized my mother had been making classic pinwheel cookies. Mom gave them a "personal" name just to please me, when she happened to notice that an uppercase "G" was rolled into every cookie.

As it turns out, my own children love "G" Cookies for almost exactly the same reason that I did. They say that the "G," which mysteriously forms in each delicious cookie, stands for our family's last name!

In the following recipe, I have worked out a technique to make these cookies as quick and easy as possible. Read it through before beginning.

NOTES: The easiest way to melt unsweetened chocolate is to put it in a small Pyrex cup in a microwave oven at high (full) power. After the first minute, check it every 30 seconds to see if it has melted. One ounce should not taken longer than 2½ minutes. The chocolate may not look melted until it is stirred.

Or put the cup of chocolate into a small saucepan of hot water and stir occasionally until the chocolate is completely melted. Be careful that no water gets into the chocolate.

This is another cookie recipe in which I prefer to use butter for its wonderful taste.

½ cup butter, softened (1 stick) (no substitutes)	*¼ teaspoon salt*
	1 teaspoon baking powder
1 cup sugar	*1¾ cups all-purpose flour*
1 large egg (or ¼ cup egg substitute)	*1 ounce unsweetened chocolate, melted (see Notes)*
1 teaspoon vanilla extract	

In a medium mixing bowl, use an electric mixer to cream the butter with the sugar until very well mixed and light. Beat in the egg until light and fluffy. Beat in the vanilla extract, salt, and baking powder. Then, at low speed, beat in the flour to form a very stiff dough. Scrape all the dough into the bottom of the bowl, then remove half of it to a large sheet of wax paper or heavy plastic wrap. (Reserve the remaining dough in the bowl.)

Collect the dough into a ball; then press the dough into a thick rectangle on the paper or plastic. Place another piece of paper or wrap on top, and roll out the dough between the two pieces of paper or wrap to a 10 by 7-inch rectangle of very even thickness. Be careful not to get too many wrinkles in the paper or wrap, and try to make sure that you have a rectangle and not an oval. If necessary, remove the top piece of paper or plastic, and cut off uneven sections of the dough and move them to corners where they are needed. Replace the top piece of paper, and transfer the whole sheet of dough to the refrigerator to cool while you prepare the chocolate dough.

Melt the chocolate as directed in the Notes above. Add it to the dough remaining in the mixing bowl, and beat the dough until the chocolate is completely incorporated and there are no streaks of white. Transfer the chocolate dough to a large sheet of wax paper or plastic wrap, and repeat the same process as for the vanilla dough. Chill the sheet of dough for about 10 minutes, or until the top piece of wax paper or plastic wrap can be peeled off easily.

Remove the light dough from the refrigerator. Peel off the top piece of paper. Lay it back on the dough, and turn over the whole sheet of dough so that the loose paper is on the bottom. Peel off the piece of paper that is now on top. Remove the slightly firm chocolate dough from the refrigerator. Peel off the top piece of paper. Very carefully turn over the chocolate dough directly on top of the vanilla dough so they are lined up with matching edges. Use a rolling pin to very gently push the chocolate dough down onto the vanilla dough without changing the thickness. Remove the piece of paper on top of the chocolate dough.

Let the two sheets of dough rest together for a few minutes until they come to room temperature and soften. (If they are too cold, they will not roll easily and might crack.) Using the loose piece of paper under the light dough as an aid, begin at a long (10-inch) edge and tightly roll up the dough layers as if making a jelly roll. (Do not roll the paper into the cookies!) Smooth the

245

remaining 10-inch edge of dough tightly against the log. Roll the log in a very small amount of flour to smooth the surface and make the log even. Wrap the log well, and refrigerate it for 1 hour, or up to overnight.

When ready to bake the cookies, preheat the oven to 350 degrees, and line a shiny metal sturdy baking sheet with cooking parchment or lightly grease or spray it with nonstick cooking spray. Remove the log from the refrigerator, and use a narrow sharp knife to cut it into ¼-inch slices. (For even slices, notch the top of the log at ½-inch intervals, using a ruler to measure. Make slices on each notch and halfway between notches.)

As each slice is cut, put it on a prepared baking sheet, keeping the cookies at least 1 inch apart. For a "G" to show on top (not essential, of course), be sure to lay the cut slices on the correct side, or the "G" may be backward. (Put remaining dough back into the refrigerator.) Bake at 350 degrees for about 12 to 14 minutes, or until the cookies are barely browned at the edges. Cool the cookies for about 2 minutes on the baking sheets; then transfer them to wire racks to cool completely. The cookies will get crisper as they cool. Repeat the process until all the dough has been used. (If using any baking sheet a second time, be sure to cool it first.) Store the cookies in an airtight container for several days, or freeze for longer storage.

Makes about 40 cookies.

Wacky Cake

MILK-FREE, EGG-FREE CAKE

I have found this unusual recipe to be quite convenient for serving to people who are allergic to eggs and/or milk, or who are limiting their saturated fat intake. Also, it does not need to be prepared with an electric mixer—hand stirring is quite sufficient—and it can be mixed up in just 5 minutes.

When my children were very young, I made this tasty cake with their classmates at our Jewish nursery school. The preschoolers could mix and lick the foolproof batter all they wanted, and they loved the name of the cake. It is called "Wacky" because there are no eggs in it—but there is vinegar! By the end of class, the iced cake was ready to eat in honor of the birthday of one of my children.

This recipe is quite versatile. The basic 8-inch-square Wacky Cake is chocolate with chocolate icing. That's my favorite combination, but I also developed some variations because my husband (and some friends) can't eat chocolate. The nonchocolate variations below include Rainbow Wacky Cake and Spiced Wacky Cake. I've also included directions for vanilla icing, cupcakes, a two-layer cake, and a large rectangular cake. Any version of Wacky Cake would be great fun for a Hanukkah celebration, and you can even let the kids make it.

CHOCOLATE CAKE BATTER
1½ cups all-purpose flour
1 cup sugar
1 teaspoon baking soda
¼ cup plain cocoa
1 cup water
⅓ cup canola oil
1 teaspoon vanilla extract
1 tablespoon white vinegar
Confectioners' sugar (optional)

CHOCOLATE ICING FOR WACKY CAKE (OPTIONAL)
2 cups confectioners' sugar, or as needed
⅓ cup plain cocoa (use a little more for a richer chocolate flavor)
¼ cup (4 tablespoons) softened pareve stick margarine
½ teaspoon vanilla extract
About 1½ to 2 tablespoons pareve milk substitute or water

FOR THE CAKE

Preheat the oven to 350 degrees. Coat an 8-inch-square baking pan with nonstick cooking spray or grease it.

Measure the flour, sugar, baking soda, and cocoa onto a piece of wax paper; then put them through a sifter into a medium bowl. Mix until combined. Add the water, oil, and vanilla extract to the bowl, and mix slightly. Then add the vinegar, and mix well until the batter is very smooth with no lumps. Immediately pour the batter into the prepared pan.

Bake at 350 degrees for 30 to 35 minutes, or until a wooden pick comes out clean and the top bounces back when lightly touched. Cool the cake in the pan on a rack. If desired, sprinkle the top with sieved confectioners' sugar. Or top the cake with chocolate icing as follows.

FOR THE ICING

Put the confectioners' sugar, cocoa, margarine, and vanilla extract into a bowl, and mix well by hand or electric mixer. (An electric mixer will produce

fluffier icing, but it is not necessary.) Add the milk substitute or water about a teaspoon at a time, mixing well each time, until the icing is creamy smooth and the desired consistency. If too much liquid is inadvertently added, just add a little more confectioners' sugar. Use a metal spatula to spread the icing on the cooled cake.

NOTE: This makes enough to cover one 8-inch-square cake. For a two-layer cake or 9 by 13-inch cake, double the icing recipe.

Makes 1 single-layer 8-inch-square cake.

Variations

RAINBOW WACKY CAKE

Omit the cocoa, and prepare the batter as above. Pour the batter into the pan, and scatter about 1 teaspoon colored sprinkles on top. Bake as usual; the sprinkles will sink into the cake during baking.

SPICED WACKY CAKE

Omit the cocoa, and add ½ teaspoon cinnamon, ¼ teaspoon allspice, and ⅛ teaspoon cloves with the dry ingredients in the basic recipe. Prepare as directed above.

VANILLA ICING

Omit the cocoa, and increase the confectioners' sugar to 2¼ cups. For an almond flavor, add up to ½ teaspoon almond extract with the vanilla extract. (For best flavor, use a milk substitute or milk, but not water.)

CUPCAKES

Line about 15 cupcake tins with paper cups, and add batter until they are one-half to two-thirds full. Bake at 350 degrees for about 25 to 30 minutes, or until a wooden pick comes out clean. Makes about 15 cupcakes.

TWO-LAYER OR RECTANGULAR CAKE

For a two-layer cake, double the recipe, and use two 9-inch round pans; bake as directed above. For a large oblong cake, double the recipe, and use one 9 by 13-inch pan; bake for about 40 minutes or until the cake tests done. (If using icing, double that recipe also.)

Soofganiyot

JELLY-FILLED DOUGHNUTS

In Israel, these light jelly doughnuts are the favorite treat eaten during Hanukkah. They may be made at home or purchased at almost any bakery during the holiday. *Soofganiyot* are also sold year-round at informal outdoor kiosks, where they are eaten out-of-hand by Israelis who love to snack. In fact, my husband and I once patronized an extremely popular stand in Haifa that offered only *soofganiyot* and *g'leeda* (ice cream) for sale.

This treat came to Israel via Jewish-German immigrants, according to John Cooper in his fascinating history of Jewish food, *Eat and Be Satisfied*. Large groups of these immigrants arrived during the 1930s, bringing with them the custom of noshing jelly doughnuts on Hanukkah. Cooper says that the new Hebrew word *soofganiya* ("doughnut") was derived from the Greek word for "sponge."

This following version of *soofganiyot* is relatively easy, and requires very little kneading. However, the dough takes a few hours to rise. The time can be filled with holiday activities such as games of spin the dreidel.

3¹/₂ to 4 cups unbleached flour

¹/₃ cup sugar

¹/₃ cup instant nonfat dry milk powder

2 packets (4¹/₂ teaspoons) fast-acting dry yeast (see the Glossary of Ingredients)

1 teaspoon salt

¹/₃ cup butter, melted and cooled, or canola oil

1 cup hot (120 to 130 degrees) tap water (no hotter than this or it will kill the yeast)

2 large eggs or ¹/₂ cup egg substitute

About ¹/₂ cup thick jam (your choice of flavor)

FOR FRYING AND COATING

Canola oil

Granulated or confectioners' sugar

In a large mixing bowl, combine 2½ cups of the flour, sugar, milk powder, yeast, and salt. Stir in the melted butter and then the hot water. Finally, mix in the eggs. Using a wooden spoon or a heavy-duty electric mixer, beat the batter until it is well combined and smooth. By hand or heavy-duty mixer, mix in enough additional flour to make a soft dough.

Scrape down the dough on the sides of the bowl; then cover the bowl loosely with plastic wrap and a dish towel. Let the dough rise in a warm place about ½ to 1 hour, or until doubled in bulk.

Turn the dough out onto a lightly floured surface, and knead it about 2 to 3 minutes, or until it is very smooth. Let the dough rest, covered, for 5 minutes; then roll it out to a ⅜- to ½-inch thickness. Cut out 2-inch-diameter circles.

Place the dough circles on a very lightly floured cookie sheet with space between them, and let them rise in a warm place until almost doubled in size (about 30 minutes). Put enough oil into a large saucepan or electric skillet so that it is at least 2 inches deep. Heat the oil until it is moderately hot, about 325 to 350 degrees. Gently drop a few of the doughnuts (they will be very soft and puffy) into the oil so they are not too crowded. Fry them for about 1½ to 2 minutes on each side, until they are puffed and golden brown, and cooked completely through. If they are browning too fast, lower the heat slightly. Drain them well on paper towels; then coat the warm doughnuts with granulated or confectioners' sugar. Repeat until all the doughnuts have been fried and coated.

To fill the doughnuts, put the jam into a decorating (icing) bag with a long pastry-filling tube attached, or use a special doughnut-filling device, and squeeze some jam into each doughnut. Or cut a slit into the side of each doughnut and use a small (baby) spoon to insert the jam.

For the best flavor and texture, serve the doughnuts within a few hours after they are fried.

Makes about 30 small doughnuts.

Zelebi or Zlabia

FRIED ROSETTES DIPPED IN HONEY SYRUP

These crisp honey-coated pastries, which are made by squeezing narrow strips of loose yeast batter into hot oil, are quite popular among Yemenite Jews and others in Israel. There, they are usually known as *zelebi*. Jews from the Near East, Middle East, and North Africa typically call them *zlabia,* while Iraqi Jews may use the name *zangoola.* In some places, they are sold by street vendors who make them as eager patrons wait. Interestingly, an almost identical pastry called *jalebi* is made in India. The names are so similar that one is probably derived from the other.

Composed of the most basic ingredients, *zelebi* are a very ancient pastry. In fact, there is a mural in the tomb of the Egyptian pharaoh Ramses III depicting their preparation. Before the advent of packaged yeast, the batter was left to ferment on its own for several hours or overnight. Also, since purified sugar was not commonly available in the past, the syrup was often made using only honey.

Zelebi have become my children's favorite Hanukkah treat. It is the first thing that they ask for when they see me decorating our home for the holiday. Not only do they enjoy eating *zelebi,* but they also love to make some themselves. By using an electric fry-pan with a controlled heat setting for the oil, this family cooking project is safe and fun.

To easily squeeze the batter into the oil, we use inexpensive soft plastic ketchup or mustard bottles that have extra-large openings in the nozzle tops. (Sharp scissors can cut the nozzle off lower than usual.) A large funnel with a wide spout that fits into the top of the bottles makes quick work of filling them with batter.

Although I have seen recipes that suggest *zelebi* should be formed into a spiral, I've

found that it's hard to control this shape, as it tends to expand all over the oil. Instead, we start with a large closed circle, which stays in place, and then put spirals and other shapes inside that are connected to the big circle.

SYRUP
1⅔ cups sugar
1 cup water
2 tablespoons honey
1 tablespoon lemon juice
2 cinnamon sticks (optional)
1 to 2 teaspoons rose water (optional)

BATTER
1 packet (2¼ teaspoons) active dry
    yeast (see the Glossary of
    Ingredients)

½ teaspoon sugar
1¾ cups warm (105 to 115 degrees)
    water
2 cups unbleached flour
¼ teaspoon salt

FOR FRYING
Canola oil

First, prepare the syrup so it will have plenty of time to cool. Put the sugar, water, honey, lemon juice, and cinnamon sticks (if used) into a 2-quart (or similar) saucepan. Slowly bring to a boil over medium-high heat, stirring only until the sugar dissolves. Lower the heat slightly and boil the syrup, uncovered and undisturbed, for 15 minutes. If rose water is desired, stir it in during the last minute of boiling. Remove the syrup from the heat, and set it aside to cool to room temperature before using. (The syrup may be made several days ahead. After it has cooled, refrigerate it, covered. Before using it, let it come to room temperature.)

For the batter, mix the yeast and sugar with the warm water in a mixer bowl or a food processor, and let the mixture rest for 5 to 10 minutes, or until it is foamy. Add the flour and salt, and mix with an electric mixer or process until very smooth and creamy, like very thick cream. Cover the bowl loosely, and let the batter rise for 45 to 60 minutes, or until it is very light and frothy. (If desired, the batter may be refrigerated overnight, loosely covered. Make sure the container has room for it to rise. Before using the batter, let it come to room temperature.) Beat the risen batter by hand for about 2 to 3 minutes, and let it rise another 10 minutes. Then beat it briefly. It will be very elastic.

Hanukkah

Put enough oil into an electric frypan, deep skillet, or a large saucepan so that it is 1½ to 2 inches deep. Heat the oil until it is very hot, about 375 degrees. Give the batter a quick stir to deflate any large bubbles. Scoop some of it into a pastry bag that has a round tip with a ³⁄₁₆-inch opening or a soft plastic ketchup or mustard bottle that has had the nozzle cut to that size (see comments above). Each time the pastry bag or plastic condiment jar needs to be refilled, first stir the batter in the bowl to deflate large bubbles.

Squeeze out the batter in a narrow strip into the hot oil and bring it around to form a circle that is approximately 4 inches in diameter; then squeeze out a little more batter back and forth across the circle to make zigzags, squiggles, or other design. The design should be connected together, but the zelebi should have an open, lacy look. If the pan is large enough, make one or two more zelebi in the same manner, being careful that they do not touch each other or they will stick together. In a large electric frypan, you can fry four zelebi at a time, one in each corner.

Fry the zelebi, turning them once with tongs, about 1½ to 2 minutes on each side, or until they are browned and very crisp. The dough strips should puff up and become rounded; if they are flat, either the oil is too shallow or not hot enough. If the zelebi brown very fast but are soft inside, the oil is too hot. Just-right zelebi should be a rich golden color, and completely crisp and crunchy throughout.

When each zelebi is done, lift it from the oil using tongs, and drain it briefly on paper toweling. Immediately drop it into the cooled syrup. Use different tongs (so the syrup will not get oily) to turn the hot zelebi over in the syrup so both sides are coated; then lift the zelebi out of the syrup and let the

excess syrup drip back into the pot. Put the zelebi on a rack over a large plate or bowl to catch any dripping syrup, which may be reused if necessary. Repeat the frying and dipping process until all the batter is used.

Pile the coated, drained zelebi on a large platter. While they are best when fresh, the finished zelebi should stay crisp and delicious for a day or two. Store them loosely covered with aluminum foil at room temperature. Do not refrigerate them.

Makes about 25 4-inch-diameter zelebi.

Koeksisters
FRIED BRAIDED PASTRIES DIPPED IN SYRUP

This South African specialty looks like glistening, miniature challah breads. Of all the fried, syrup-dipped pastries in this chapter, *koeksisters* are the most attractive, and one of my favorites. They are fun to make, and are also very popular when I use them in cooking classes. Children enjoy braiding the little pieces of easy-to-work dough.

Though *koeksisters* are so popular in South Africa that they are eaten throughout the year (particularly at tea time), I've put them in this chapter because they seem to be particularly appropriate for Hanukkah.

The following version of *koeksisters* has been adapted from a recipe I found in a popular South African–Jewish cookbook called *The Singing Kettle,* which was published in South Africa by the Port Elizabeth Branch of the Union of Jewish Women. While not originally a Jewish pastry, *koeksisters* obviously have been adapted into the cuisine of the South African Jews.

SYRUP

1²⁄₃ cups sugar

1 cup water

2 tablespoons honey

1 tablespoon lemon juice

1 or 2 cinnamon sticks (optional)

DOUGH

2 cups unbleached flour

1³⁄₄ teaspoons baking powder

Pinch of salt

2 tablespoons butter or margarine,
*   softened*

²⁄₃ cup milk or water

1 large egg yolk

FOR FRYING

Canola oil

First, prepare the syrup so that it will have sufficient time to chill. Put the sugar, water, honey, lemon juice, and cinnamon sticks (if used) into a 2-quart saucepan, and slowly bring to a boil over medium-high heat, stirring only until the sugar dissolves. Lower the heat slightly, and boil the syrup, uncovered and undisturbed, for 15 minutes. Remove the syrup from the heat, and let it cool to room temperature; then chill it in the refrigerator.

To make the dough by hand: Put the flour, baking powder, and salt into a medium bowl, and cut in the butter with your fingers or a pastry blender until the mixture looks like fine meal. Add the milk and egg yolk, and mix to form a soft, slightly sticky dough. Turn the dough out onto a lightly floured surface, coat it very lightly with flour, and knead it for 5 to 10 minutes, or until it is very smooth and pliable. Wrap it in plastic, and let it rest at room temperature for 30 minutes to 1 hour.

To make the dough in a food processor fitted with a steel blade: Put the flour, baking powder, and salt into the bowl, and pulse-process once or twice to mix. Add the butter, and pulse-process until the mixture looks like coarse meal. Add the milk and egg yolk, and process to form a ball; then process the ball for about 30 seconds to knead it. Remove the dough from the food processor, wrap it in plastic, and let it rest at room temperature for 30 minutes to 1 hour.

On a very lightly floured surface, roll out the dough to a very neat 9-inch square about ¼ inch thick. Use your hands to help shape the square if necessary. Measure and mark the dough with a clean ruler; then use a pastry wheel or sharp knife to divide the square into three equal sections that are each 3 inches by 9 inches. Cut each section crosswise into nine equal 1-inch strips,

for a total of twenty-seven strips, each measuring 1 by 3 inches. (To make the cutting easier, first press the edge of the ruler into the dough to mark it; then cut on the marked lines.)

For each pastry, cut a strip lengthwise into three equal, narrow "tails" that are joined together at the top. Braid the tails compactly, and pinch the ends together very tightly so the braid will not unravel during frying.

Put enough oil into a large saucepan or electric frypan so that it is 1½ to 2 inches deep. Heat the oil until it is very hot, about 375 degrees. Gently drop a few of the braids into the oil so they are not too crowded; they will quickly puff up. Fry them about 2 minutes on each side, or until they are browned and crisp.

Use a slotted spoon to remove them from the oil, and drain them briefly on paper toweling. Immediately drop them into the cooled syrup. Use a different spoon or tongs (so the syrup will not get oily) to turn the koeksisters in the syrup so they are completely coated; then quickly lift them up, and let the excess syrup drain off. Put the koeksisters on a large plate. Repeat the frying and dipping process until all the dough has been used.

The finished koeksisters can be stored for several days in a loosely covered container at room temperature.

Makes 27 koeksisters.

Hanukkah

Hanukkah Bimuelos

FRIED HONEY PUFFS

This is the most traditional Hanukkah treat for Sephardic Jews who come from Turkey. *Bimuelos* (or *burmuelos*) is the pastry's Judeo-Spanish name. Sephardic Jews actually use the name *bimuelos* for a number of foods in addition to this one. For instance, it can also mean pancakes or fried patties, or even a type of baked muffins.

The following *bimuelos* are irregularly shaped, yeast-raised puffs that are dipped into a honey syrup. Occasionally, they are coated with confectioners' sugar instead of syrup.

NOTES: If desired, the honey puffs may be fried shortly in advance, and coated with hot syrup just before serving. Some Sephardic cooks prefer to stir about 1 teaspoon cinnamon into the syrup, and then let each guest pour a bit of syrup over his or her own serving of puffs. In some households, purchased pancake syrup is used. Another easy alternative is: 1 cup honey mixed with ¼ to ⅓ cup water and heated just until blended and hot. Use it while it is warm to drizzle over the puffs.

BATTER

1 packet (2¼ teaspoons) active dry
    yeast (see the Glossary of
    Ingredients)
1 cup warm (105 to 115 degrees) water,
    divided
½ teaspoon sugar
1 large egg or ¼ cup pareve egg
    substitute
2 cups unbleached flour
¼ teaspoon salt

HONEY SYRUP

1 cup sugar
¾ cup water
½ cup honey
1 tablespoon lemon juice

FOR FRYING AND GARNISH

Vegetable oil
Ground cinnamon (optional)

For the batter, mix together the yeast, ½ cup of the water, and the sugar in a medium bowl. Let the yeast mixture rest for about 5 minutes, or until frothy. Stir in the remaining batter ingredients until smooth. The batter should be very loose and sticky. Cover the bowl loosely and let the batter rise for 1 hour, or until about doubled in bulk.

While the batter is rising, prepare the honey syrup. Mix together all the ingredients in a 2-quart (or similar) saucepan, and slowly bring to a boil over medium-high heat, stirring only until the sugar dissolves. Reduce the heat slightly, and boil the syrup, uncovered and undisturbed, for 5 minutes. Remove it from the heat, and set it aside to cool to room temperature.

When the batter has risen, stir it down. Put enough oil in a large saucepan or electric frypan so that it is 1½ to 2 inches deep. Heat the oil until it is very hot, about 375 degrees. Dip a teaspoon into the oil, and then use the spoon to scoop up a portion of the batter. Gently drop the batter into the oil. (Keep your opposite hand lightly moistened with water, in case you need to nudge the batter off the spoon. The batter will not stick to wet hands. Be careful not to splash water into the hot oil.) The dollop of batter will quickly puff up to almost twice its original size. Make more puffs in the same manner, but do not crowd the pan. Fry the puffs, turning them occasionally with a slotted spoon or tongs, about 3 minutes, or until they are browned on all sides and very crisp, and also cooked in the center. (If the oil is too hot, they will brown before the inside is cooked.)

Drain them briefly on paper toweling. Then drop one or two at a time into the cooled syrup. Use a *different* spoon or tongs (so the syrup will not get oily) to turn the hot puffs in the syrup so they become completely coated with it. Lift the puffs up, and let the excess syrup drain off. Put the syrup-coated puffs on a large plate. Repeat the frying and dipping process until all the batter is used. Then sprinkle the puffs very lightly with cinnamon, if desired. For best taste and texture, serve them as soon as possible.

Makes about 36 honey puffs.

Zvingous
FRIED PUFFS IN HONEY SYRUP

Greek Jews often serve these *zvingous* on Hanukkah, and sometimes call them *loukoumades*. North African Jews have very similar treats, which are usually called by their French name, *beignets*. (The French, however, prefer serving this type of beignet with warm jam, rather than dipping it in syrup.)

Though the finished puffs look very similar to Bimuelos (page 256), and are some-times even called by that name, they are made with a totally different dough—one that is not leavened with yeast, but that contains more eggs. When this dough is put into a pastry bag and squeezed through a notched metal tip directly into hot oil, it produces narrow, ribbed, holiday pastries called *tulumbas,* which are dipped in the same syrup and served in the same way as *zvingous.*

A very similar batter, called *pâte à choux* in French, is baked to produce hollow cream puffs and eclairs. During Pesach, it may be prepared with matzah cake meal (in place of flour) to produce *Pesadik* "rolls."

HONEY SYRUP
1 cup sugar
³/₄ cup water
¹/₂ cup honey
1 tablespoon lemon juice
¹/₄ teaspoon ground cinnamon

DOUGH
2 tablespoons olive or canola oil

³/₄ cup water
¹/₄ teaspoon salt
1¹/₄ cups all-purpose flour
4 large eggs (no substitutes)

FOR FRYING AND GARNISH
Canola oil
Finely chopped walnuts, to taste

For the syrup, mix together all the ingredients in a 2-quart saucepan, and slowly bring to a boil over medium-high heat, stirring only until the sugar dissolves. Turn the heat to low, and simmer the syrup, uncovered and undis-turbed, for 10 minutes. Remove it from the heat, and set it aside to cool to room temperature.

For the dough, put the oil, water, and salt into a large saucepan and bring to a boil over high heat. Immediately remove the saucepan from the heat, and add all the flour at once. Stir the mixture with a wooden spoon until it leaves the sides of the pan and forms a ball. Turn down the heat on the burner, and return the saucepan to low heat. Stir the dough, mashing it against the sides of the pan, for 1 minute. Remove the pan from the heat and use an electric mixer to beat in the eggs, one by one, adding the next egg only after the pre-vious one has been completely incorporated.

Put enough oil in a large saucepan or electric frypan so that it is 1½ to 2 inches deep. Heat the oil until it is very hot, about 375 degrees. Dip a tea-spoon into the oil, and then use the spoon to scoop up a portion of the

batter. Gently push the batter into the oil. Keep your opposite hand moistened lightly with water, as the batter will not stick to wet hands. (Be careful not to splash water into the hot oil.) The dollop of batter will quickly puff up to almost twice its original size. Make some more puffs in the same manner, but do not crowd the pan. Fry the puffs, turning them occasionally with a slotted spoon, until they are browned and very crisp. Drain them briefly on paper toweling.

Drop one or two puffs at a time into the cooled syrup. Use a different spoon or tongs (so the syrup will not get oily) to turn the hot puffs in the syrup so they become completely coated with it. Lift the zvingous up, and let the excess syrup drain off. Put the zvingous on a large plate. Repeat the frying and dipping process until all the batter is used. Sprinkle the coated zvingous lightly with walnuts. For best taste and texture, serve the zvingous as soon as possible.

Makes about 36 zvingous.

Sesame Seed Candy

For many Sephardic families, this crunchy confection—which they generally call *susam,* meaning "sesame"—is a must at Hanukkah time. They typically add almonds to the mix (see Variation below).

Jews from all over the Middle East also make this ancient sesame candy. In Israel, where sesame seeds are a national favorite, these *sukariyot soomsoom* (Hebrew for "sesame candies") are also enjoyed on many other holidays, including Rosh Hashanah, Yom Ha'atzmaut (Independence Day), and Pesach. On Purim, Greek Jews mockingly dub this treat "Haman's Fleas."

The following version (which contains nontraditional brown sugar and spices) is very easy, and the candy looks and tastes even better than "store-bought." For best results, try to make it on a cool, dry day. Large quantities of hulled sesame seeds may be available from bulk bins at supermarkets, at health food stores, or at Middle Eastern specialty groceries.

Canola oil or nonstick cooking spray,
   for the pan
2 cups hulled sesame seeds (about 12
   ounces) (see the Glossary of
   Ingredients)

¹/₂ cup honey
¹/₂ cup packed dark or light brown sugar
¹/₂ teaspoon ground cinnamon
¹/₂ teaspoon ground ginger

Lightly coat a 9-inch square baking pan or dish with oil or nonstick cooking spray. Do the same to a metal spatula. Set both aside. Put some very cold water into a bowl. Set aside.

Put the sesame seeds into an ungreased 10-inch skillet (preferably nonstick), and stir them over medium-high heat for about 5 to 10 minutes, or until they are lightly browned and aromatic. Temporarily transfer the seeds (they will be hot) to a bowl, making sure that none are left in the skillet. Set aside.

Put the honey, brown sugar, cinnamon, and ginger into the skillet, and mix them well with a wooden spoon. Slowly bring the mixture to a boil over medium heat, stirring constantly. As soon as the entire mixture comes to a full rolling boil, cook it vigorously while stirring for exactly 2 minutes. Remove the skillet from the heat, and immediately stir in the sesame seeds until well mixed. Quickly turn out the hot mixture into the prepared pan. Immediately dip your hand into the cold water, and use your wet hand to press the candy into a very even layer. To further smooth out the candy, press it down with the prepared metal spatula.

Cool the candy in the pan for 15 minutes, until it is solid but still luke-warm. Run the spatula around the edge of the candy to loosen it. Then turn out the whole slab of candy onto a cutting board. Keep it upside down so that the attractive smooth bottom is now on top. Use a large, sharp knife to cut the large square of warm candy into tiny squares, rectangles, or triangles. To do this easily, cut the slab into equal fourths. Then cut each fourth into fourths. Finally, cut each small square into four tiny squares, four rectangles (by cutting lengthwise strips), or four triangles (by cutting two diagonals). You should have sixty-four small candies.

Cool the candies completely; then store them in an airtight container at room temperature. If a professional look is desired, roll each candy in a small piece of stiff cellophane and twist the ends.

Makes about 64 small candies; about 1 pound.

Variation

SESAME SEED CANDY WITH ALMONDS

For a special Sephardic touch, replace ⅔ cup of the sesame seeds with an equal amount of coarsely chopped blanched almonds. Follow the directions as indicated above.

Iced Cinnamon Buns

These marvelous cinnamon buns have become a favorite treat around my house for holidays, brunches, and even special meetings of my children's Jewish youth groups. They are not that difficult to prepare, and everyone really loves them. I learned the technique by watching the young bakers in the cinnamon bun shop at our local shopping mall. I figured if teens could shape the buns, so could I!

The dough is adapted from my favorite challah recipe, and is very easy to handle. The entire recipe, from start to eating, should take a novice less than 2 hours, and possibly only 1½ hours for those with more yeast dough experience. Every now and then, I follow in my Grandpa's steps (see the comments with Grandpa's Challah, page 39) and wake up earlier than the rest of my family to surprise them with this special breakfast treat. It's so wonderful to see the looks on their faces they come downstairs to the most incredible aroma wafting out of the oven.

This recipe makes eighteen big buns, which should be enough to satisfy anyone's sweet tooth for a while. They would be great to serve at a Hanukkah brunch or open house.

NOTES: The whole wheat flour adds to the flavor and texture of the dough; however, additional unbleached flour may be used instead.

For more details on yeast and on kneading dough with a mixer and by hand, see the recipe for Gloria's Glorious Challah (page 32).

DOUGH

About 3½ to 4½ cups unbleached flour

2 cups all-purpose whole wheat flour or additional unbleached flour

⅓ cup granulated sugar

2 packets (4½ teaspoons) fast-acting dry yeast (see the Glossary of Ingredients)

1½ teaspoons salt

2 large eggs or ½ cup pareve egg substitute

¼ cup canola oil

¾ cup milk or pareve milk substitute

¾ cup water

FILLING

Softened butter or pareve stick or tub margarine (not diet margarine) to taste

Dark brown sugar to taste

Ground cinnamon to taste

ICING

3 cups confectioners' sugar

¼ cup softened butter or pareve stick margarine (½ stick)

1 teaspoon vanilla extract

2 to 4 tablespoons milk or pareve milk substitute

In a large mixing bowl, combine 2 cups unbleached flour, the whole wheat flour, sugar, yeast, and salt. Add the eggs and oil, and mix by hand using a spoon or the dough hook that comes with some heavy-duty mixers.

In a bowl in the microwave or in a small saucepan on the stove, heat the milk with the water to 130 degrees (hot to the touch, but not burning your finger). (If the milk was refrigerated and the water is cool, this will take about 2 minutes in a microwave oven on "high.") Add the milk mixture to the bowl, and beat with an electric mixer, using the dough hook if available, until mixed. With a dough hook, continue to knead, adding flour as necessary, until the dough holds tight to the hook and cleans the sides of the bowl. Knead a total of about 5 to 8 minutes, or until the dough is very smooth and not sticky.

By hand, turn the dough out onto a floured board and knead it, adding flour as needed, for about 10 minutes, or until it is very smooth and elastic and not sticky.

In either case, cover the kneaded dough loosely with plastic wrap, and let it rest for 10 minutes at room temperature to relax the gluten (and make it easier to roll). Meanwhile, for easy removal of the baked buns and easy cleanup, line two 9-inch square (*not* 8-inch; they're too small) shiny metal baking pans with baking parchment or aluminum foil so that it comes up the sides of the pans. If using foil, coat it with nonstick cooking spray or grease it. (This is not necessary with parchment.) Have the pans handy.

Divide the dough evenly in half. Press one-half of the dough out into a neat rectangle with your fingertips, then use a rolling pin to roll it to a 16 by 10-inch rectangle of even thickness. (Keep the other half covered.)

Use a butter knife or metal spatula to completely cover the dough, except for a 1-inch border along one long edge, with a thin layer of soft butter. Use your hands to sprinkle an even layer of brown sugar over the margarine. Sprinkle a little cinnamon, right from the can, over the brown sugar. (The amount of butter, brown sugar, and cinnamon used is not critical to the success of this recipe.) Beginning at the long edge of the dough that does *not* have the clean 1-inch border, tightly roll up the dough like a jelly roll. When you get to the clean edge, pinch it tightly against the log so it cannot unroll.

Gently roll the log under both your hands to even out the diameter and lengthen it slightly. The log should be 18 inches long; use a ruler to measure it. Then use the ruler to mark off 2-inch increments on the log. Cut the log at the marks with a sharp knife. As each bun is cut, place it into the pan with a cut edge facing up. The nine buns should fit like the squares of a tic-tac-toe board, with equal spaces around them.

Repeat the entire process for the second half of the dough. When both pans of buns are ready, turn the oven on to 200 degrees for exactly 1 minute; then turn it off. Put the uncovered pans in the warm, turned-off oven, and let the buns rise for 20 minutes, or until they have almost doubled. Leave them in the oven, and turn it on to 375 degrees. Bake them for about 30 minutes, or until they are lightly browned and firm.

While the buns are baking, make the icing. Mix the confectioners' sugar, butter, and vanilla together until almost combined; then very gradually stir in just enough milk to make a very thick, smooth icing. When the buns are done baking, remove them from the oven. Use the parchment or foil to lift each whole set of nine buns out of its pan (the buns will be stuck together), and put each set of buns on a wire rack, leaving it on the parchment or foil. Use a butter knife or metal spatula to thickly ice the tops of the buns while they are still hot and stuck together. The icing will melt a little and get soft, and seep into the crevices of the bun.

To serve the buns, pull them apart and, for very best taste, eat them warm. They are also delicious at room temperature (do not refrigerate them), and will stay tasty for at least a day. (They probably can be frozen, although we have never had any around long enough to find out!) The buns can be

warmed, one at a time, for a short time in a microwave oven. (If they are microwaved too long, the icing will completely melt and the buns will get hard.)

Makes 18 large cinnamon buns.

Soft Pretzels for Hanukkah

Making chewy pretzels shaped like Judaic and Hanukkah symbols can be an enjoyable project for parents and children. As the dough is formed, the story of Hanukkah can be told, and the experience can be very satisfying and educational at the same time.

Offered here are recipes for two types of pretzels. The basic dough for both contains a bit of olive oil to remind us of the miraculous oil that burned for eight days in the Holy Temple of Jerusalem (and it also helps keep the pretzels fresh). One type features cheese as a reminder of the story about the heroic Judith. And both types use whole grains, a good way to show children that nutritious snacks also can be delicious.

Preparation of the dough requires only a few minutes of kneading (which can be done with a heavy-duty mixer or food processor, if desired), and there's no rising or boiling in water (as with some other pretzels).

The basic recipe that follows is for Whole Wheat Pretzels (with Cheese). Also included is a variation called Caraway-Rye Pretzels.

DOUGH FOR WHOLE WHEAT PRETZELS
(WITH CHEESE)

2 cups whole wheat flour

1 packet (2¼ teaspoons) fast-acting dry yeast (see the Glossary of Ingredients)

1 teaspoon salt

4 to 6 ounces (1 to 1½ cups, packed) coarsely shredded sharp Cheddar cheese (optional)

1 tablespoon honey or sugar

1 tablespoon light or flavorful olive oil

1½ cups hot (120 to 130 degrees) tap water (no hotter than this or it may kill the yeast)

2 to 2½ cups white bread flour or unbleached flour

GLAZE AND TOPPING

1 large egg plus 1 teaspoon water or ¼ cup egg substitute

Coarse kosher salt

Hulled tiny seeds such as sesame, poppy, or caraway

FOR THE DOUGH

In a large mixing bowl or in a food processor fitted with a steel blade, put the 2 cups whole wheat flour, yeast, salt, cheese (if used), honey or sugar, and olive oil. Mix well by hand to combine, or use an electric mixer or food processor. Add the hot water and beat by hand or mixer, or pulse-process to form a loose batter. Add about 2 cups of the bread flour or enough to make a soft dough.

If mixing by hand or with a regular electric mixer, turn the dough out onto a lightly floured board, and knead it for 5 to 10 minutes, or until it is smooth and just a bit tacky. Add small amounts of flour as needed to keep the dough from sticking.

If using a heavy-duty mixer or food processor, knead the dough by machine according to the manufacturer's directions, adding flour as directed above. (You will probably have to knead with the mixer about 5 minutes or the food processor about 1 minute.)

Line some heavy, shiny metal baking sheets with cooking parchment, coat them with nonstick cooking spray or grease them. Preheat the oven to 425 degrees.

TO SHAPE THE PRETZELS

To make the pretzel shapes, pinch off a piece of dough; then roll it on a flat surface until it forms a rope that is ⅜ inch to ½ inch thick. Shape the pretzels on a flat surface as directed below; then transfer each one to a prepared baking sheet as soon as it is made. Keep the pretzels at least 1 inch apart.

For a large, standard-shaped pretzel, make a rope that is about 20 inches long. Bend the rope into a *U* shape. Cross over the arms of the *U* to form an approximately 4-inch-diameter circular loop at the bottom. Then cross over the arms once more at the point where they intersect, so that they intertwine and each arm comes back to the side where it first began. Finally, press the end of each arm down against the bottom curve of the *U.* The completed pretzel will be upside down.

For a *hanukkiyah* (Hanukkah menorah) with candles, first make a rope that is about 24 inches long. Form a very large *U* and double twist it into a 4-inch-diameter loop as if beginning a standard-shaped pretzel (see above). Move the extended arms of the *U* outward to become the top of the *hanukkiyah,* where the candles will be placed. Bend the loop into a flat-bottomed triangular base for the *hanukkiyah.* For the candles, make a second rope that is about 19 inches long. Cut it into nine pieces—eight 2-inch lengths, and one about 3 inches long. Set the longer piece in the center above the twisted part of the triangular base, as the *shamash* candle (the one used to light the others). Evenly place four shorter candles on both sides of it. If desired, press a whole blanched almond into the top of each candle for a "flame."

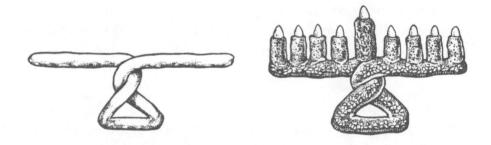

For the spinning top known as a *dreidel* (*sevivon,* in Hebrew), make a rope that is 6 to 15 inches long, depending on the size of dreidel desired. Shape it into an inverted triangle, which points downward and has a flat top. Then make a short rope (about 1 or 2 inches) and attach it to the flat top of the dreidel as a handle. If desired, form another short rope into one of the traditional Hebrew letters—*nun, gimel, hay,* or *shin*—and put it inside the dreidel, attaching it to the sides so it will not fall out when the dreidel is baked.

For a six-pointed Star of David, make two equal ropes, each 12 to 20 inches long. Directly on the baking sheet, form one rope into a triangle that points upward. Then weave the second rope over and under the arms of the first one, pinching its ends together to form an inverted triangle. If weaving is too confusing or difficult, then form the second rope into a separate triangle that points downward, and simply place it on top of the first triangle to form a star. Press the ropes together at the six places where they intersect.

Use your imagination to create additional shapes, such as the battle shields carried by the Maccabees, an oil flask, a stemmed wine cup, or the Hebrew word *chai* (spelled with a guttural *chet* and a *yud*), meaning "life."

TOPPING AND BAKING

For the glaze, beat the egg with the water or use plain egg substitute. Brush the top of each pretzel with some of the egg glaze; then immediately sprinkle it with a little coarse salt and your choice of seeds. For an interesting and attractive look, vary the seeds used on the different parts of a single pretzel. For instance, decorate the *hanukkiyah* with sesame seeds and the candles with poppy seeds, or coat the two triangles of a star with different seeds.

Bake them immediately, without rising, at 425 degrees for 15 to 20 minutes, or until they are browned and well done. (They will rise slightly in the oven.)

Immediately remove the pretzels from the baking sheets (gently loosening them with a metal spatula if necessary), and cool them completely on wire racks. (If parchment was used, they may be cooled right on the parchment on a rack. Or the parchment may be used again for another batch.) Store the cooled pretzels in an airtight container for a day or two. Freeze them for longer storage.

Makes about 16 large, standard-shaped pretzels;
the number of pretzels in holiday shapes depends on their size.

Variation

CARAWAY-RYE SOFT PRETZELS

Substitute light or dark molasses for the honey, rye flour for the whole wheat flour, and 2 tablespoons caraway seeds for the cheese in the dough. The remaining ingredients and the technique are the same as for Whole Wheat Pretzels.

Tu B'Shevat

 *ROSH HASHANAH L'LLANOT*—THE "NEW YEAR OF THE TREES"— is a minor but joyous festival that is commonly known as *Tu B'Shevat,* the Hebrew abbreviation for its date on the calendar, the fifteenth day of the month of Shevat. (Each Hebrew letter has a numerical value. "Tu" is the pronunciation of the numeral 15, which is written with the Hebrew letters *tet,* 9, and *vav,* 6.) According to Jewish law, the fruit of a new tree may not be eaten—or, in biblical times, counted for the tithe—until the tree's fifth year. To avoid confusion, it was decided that every tree's "birthday" is on Tu B'Shevat.

Though the date usually falls in late January or early February, when most Americans are enduring the worst of winter's chill, it is approximately the time when the sap begins to flow in Israel's fruit trees. In fact, more than two thousand years ago, the great sage Rabbi Hillel is said to have moved the date of this botanical "new year" from the first of Shevat to the fifteenth just so it would be more likely to coincide with this seasonal occurrence.

To celebrate the "New Year of the Trees," it has become customary for Jews worldwide to eat fruits and nuts indigenous to ancient Israel, such as almonds, carob, dates, figs, grapes, citrus, and pomegranates. Because, in many areas of the Diaspora, it was once difficult or even impossible to obtain fresh fruit at this time of year, dried fruit became the popular choice for the holiday.

In Ashkenazic households, fifteen different types of fresh and dried fruits and nuts, symbolic of the date, are displayed and eaten throughout the day. Sephardic Jews—who sometimes call the holiday *Las Frutas* in Judeo-Spanish (or "Feast of Fruits")—may have as many as fifty varieties.

Another custom involves late-night studying of passages from Jewish texts that refer to trees, fruit, and the fertility of the earth. Between sessions, it is traditional to snack on the fruits and nuts discussed. In honor of the holiday, Jews of the Diaspora donate money to the Jewish National Fund's reforestation program in Israel. Some children use little blue-and-white JNF boxes to save coins all year long for this purpose. On Tu B'Shevat, many saplings are planted by Israeli children, who proudly march out to the fields wearing garlands of flowers.

For the holiday, homes are often decorated with fresh flowers and foliage clippings. Some Turkish and Greek Jews, as well as other Sephardim, set out an elaborate assortment of dried fruit and nuts for guests. Children are usually allowed to take some of the treats home—sometimes in special, handmade drawstring bags.

It is also traditional for many Sephardim to read from a Ladino translation of an ancient kabbalistic manual called, in Hebrew, *P'ri Etz Hadar* ("Fruit of the Goodly Tree"), and to perform its ritual steps for eating various types of fruit. The kabbalists believed that trees were symbolic of human beings, and that eating a variety of fruits on Tu B'Shevat was a way of improving our spiritual selves. They also thought that all trees represented the Tree of Life, which carries divine blessings into the world.

Recently, it has become increasingly popular for American Jews of all backgrounds to follow the sixteenth-century custom of a systemized ritual meal called a Tu B'Shevat Seder. While most modern-day ceremonies are based on ideas from *P'ri Etz Hadar,* they also include readings from the Talmud, poems, and/or parables related to trees and the fruitfulness of spring.

At a typical Tu B'Shevat Seder, four different types of wine (or fruit juice) are drunk, and fifteen to thirty different fruits—fresh, dried, and sometimes canned—are tasted. The fruits are often divided into three categories of "ascending spirituality," based on how much of the fruit is edible. The three kinds of fruit can also symbolize the different ways that people relate to one another.

Each fruit is cut into small pieces, and arranged on platters to be passed around. The Seder usually begins with the blessing for "new experiences" that is said on the first day of every holiday. During the Seder, alternating samplings of wine and fruit are interspersed with selected readings. The kabbalists believed that chewing the fruits very well

and saying blessings over them would increase the holy "sparks" of divine energy released by the Seder.

The first cup of wine (or grape juice) is white, and possibly chilled, to symbolize winter, when nature is slumbering and all is dry and cold. It is followed by the "lowest level" of fruit, that which has an inedible covering (such as pomegranates, almonds and other nuts, sunflower and pumpkin seeds, coconuts, pineapples, avocados, bananas, melons, oranges, and kiwifruit) and represents the simple physical being—a body "covering" a soul. Also, some people have a hard outer "shell" and find it hard to feel close to others.

The second cup of wine is very lightly colored (such as golden sherry or very light rosé, or white wine with a little red wine mixed into it), and it signifies the early thaw as the sun beats down upon the earth, and the sap begins to rise in the trees. Next comes fruit that is edible except for a pit, stone, or large center of seeds (such as plums, prunes, dates, apricots, peaches, olives, papayas, mangoes, and cherries), which symbolizes that the heart is protected or inaccessible. Also, some people are open and feel close to others, but only to a point; they keep certain feelings deep inside themselves.

The third cup of wine is more deeply colored (such as dark rosé, or white with more red mixed into it), and is symbolic of blooming trees and seeds being sown. It is followed by the highest level of fruit, which can be eaten in its entirety except perhaps for a few tiny seeds (such as carob, blueberries, strawberries, pears, apples, figs, grapes, and persimmons) and is closest to pure spiritual creation or emanation. Also, some people are completely open with others.

The fourth and final cup of wine is richly red or purple, and represents the fertility of trees abundant with fruit, as well as crops ready to be harvested.

Some of the foods eaten on Tu B'Shevat have their own special symbolism, according to Jewish interpretation. The brightly colored apple, for example, represents the magnificent splendor of God. The almond shows how swiftly God punishes sinners, because the first tree to blossom in Israel is the almond, and also because it is written in the Torah that God made Aaron's staff sprout almonds as a warning to those who might challenge his right to be high priest.

The three textures of nuts—soft, medium, and hard—signify that there are three "textures" of Jewish character. Pomegranates and figs stand for peace, prosperity, and fertility. And the carob—sometimes referred to as "poor man's bread"—is the symbol of humility and repentance. (See the recipes for Rich Carob Brownies, page 279, and Carob Layer Cake, page 281, for more information.)

There are only a few holiday dishes prepared particularly for Tu B'Shevat, including the wheat pudding called Kofyas (below). Many Sephardim serve the same sort of pastries eaten on Purim and Rosh Hashanah, especially those containing fruit and nuts. However, there is no particular Jewish cuisine that is traditional for Tu B'Shevat *meals.* Therefore, I have taken the liberty of including in this chapter a variety of nontraditional recipes that use many different types of dried (and fresh) fruits and nuts as well as carob powder. Please feel free to also use recipes in other chapters that are appropriate.

Kofyas
WHEAT BERRY PUDDING

Sephardic Jews from Turkey often eat this dessert on the evening of Tu B'Shevat, and say the prayer in which we thank God for wheat. Similar wheat puddings called *suffah, prehito, mustrahanah,* and *trigo kotcho* may also be prepared by Sephardim for this holiday. Often, chopped dry fruits are added to the basic, sweetened wheat mixture.

Some Greek Jews make an almost identical wheat pudding called *assurei* or *kolliva,* which they may also serve on the first evening of Rosh Hashanah because the honey symbolizes a sweet year and the expanding wheat grains represent the growth and sustenance of life. This may be garnished with pomegranate seeds.

Occasionally, either bulgur or cracked wheat is substituted for the whole grains of wheat known as "wheat berries." (A variation using bulgur wheat follows below.)

Because the wheat berries resemble tiny teeth, *kofyas* is also served to celebrate the appearance of a baby's first tooth. Sometimes, the "lucky" person who discovered the new tooth prepares the pudding. For this same occasion, Syrian Jews make *slihah,* a sweet wheat pudding that contains raisins, caraway seeds, and pistachios or walnuts. And some North African Jews make a very similar wheat or barley pudding called *belila,* which features pine nuts, almonds, and pistachios, and is flavored with rose water.

NOTES: Whole wheat berries are available at most Greek or Middle Eastern groceries, as well as health food stores. They must be cooked for a long time to become tender. Other chopped nuts, such as almonds, pine nuts, or pistachios, may be mixed with the walnuts.

1 cup whole wheat berries (about 8 ounces) (see Note)

4 cups water

¼ to ½ cup honey, or to taste

½ to 1 teaspoon ground cinnamon

½ cup raisins, plumped in water (optional)

½ cup chopped dates (optional)

1 cup coarsely chopped walnuts (see Notes)

Put the wheat berries and water into a large saucepan, and bring them to a boil over high heat. Cover tightly, lower the heat, and simmer the wheat berries for 2 to 3 hours, or until they have split open and are only slightly chewy. Drain off any excess water. Add the honey, cinnamon, raisins (if used), and dates (if used) to the cooked wheat berries, and stir over low heat for about 2 minutes. Remove from the heat and stir in the walnuts. Serve warm or at room temperature.

Makes about 4 to 6 servings.

Variation

For a much quicker wheat pudding that has a similar taste but a completely different texture, substitute 1 cup bulgur wheat for the wheat berries. Simmer the bulgur in only 2 cups boiling water for about 12 minutes, or until all the water is absorbed. Then continue as above. (Cracked wheat may also be used, it will take slightly longer than bulgur to cook.)

Picadillo
SPICY GROUND BEEF WITH FRUIT AND ALMONDS

The flavorful mixture known as *picadillo* (pronounced "pee-kah-'dee-yoh,") is very popular all over Latin America, particularly in Cuba and Mexico. It is sometimes used as a stuffing for green chili peppers, *empanadas* (turnovers), and *enchiladas*. And it is eaten alone as a main course.

In our household, we always serve this family favorite with pita bread, for a Mexican dinner with an Israeli touch. Each diner is given several small pita halves in which

to stuff the *picadillo*. Although we often eat this during the year, it has become a specialty at our Tu B'Shevat Seder, where it always delights guests.

While not a particularly Jewish dish, *picadillo* has always seemed to me to be quite appropriate for this holiday. Apparently others agree, for since I put this recipe in the first edition of my cookbook, it has been featured in other cookbooks and articles relating to Tu B'Shevat.

2 pounds lean ground beef	$^1\!/_8$ to $^1\!/_4$ teaspoon ground cumin
1 large onion, finely chopped	$^1\!/_2$ teaspoon salt
2 to 3 garlic cloves, minced	$^1\!/_8$ teaspoon ground black pepper
1 (14- to 16-ounce) can tomatoes, including juice, finely chopped	$^2\!/_3$ cup pimiento-stuffed green olives, cut crosswise in half
2 medium apples, peeled (if desired) and diced	$^1\!/_2$ cup slivered almonds
1 medium green pepper, diced (optional)	To Serve (Optional)
$^1\!/_2$ cup raisins	Hot cooked white or brown rice
$^1\!/_2$ teaspoon chili powder	Several loaves of whole wheat or white
$^1\!/_2$ teaspoon ground cinnamon	Pita bread (page 454)
$^1\!/_4$ teaspoon ground cloves	

In a very large, deep skillet or a Dutch oven over medium-high heat, cook the meat with the onion and garlic, breaking up the meat with a fork or an *S*-shaped potato masher. When the meat has browned and the onion is tender, drain and discard all excess fat from the pan. Add all the remaining ingredients, except for the olives and almonds.

Lower the heat slightly, and simmer, uncovered, stirring occasionally, for about 30 minutes, or until most of the liquid has evaporated from the pan. Add the olives and almonds, and stir about 2 minutes longer, or until they are heated through.

Serve hot, with rice or pita bread if desired. Cut pita loaves in half to form semicircular "pockets," and let diners fill them with the *picadillo* mixture.

Makes about 6 servings.

Oaf Tapoozim
ISRAELI-STYLE ORANGE CHICKEN

This quick and easy main course uses three foods that are quite popular in Israel—chicken, oranges, and almonds. This dish can be prepared ahead, and is excellent the next day.

Oranges are one of the few fresh fruits now often eaten on Tu B'Shevat because they are available in the winter, and they are a reminder of the wonderful citrus crop grown in modern Israel (including the world-renowned Jaffa orange).

Almonds are eaten because the almond tree, which needs little water, is the first tree in Israel to wake from winter dormancy and bloom, while the other trees are still bare. Thus, the Hebrew root word for almond, *shahked,* also means to be awake, diligent, or alert. This metaphor for the almond is used in the Bible.

3 large navel oranges	*1 1/2 to 2 pounds boneless, skinless*
1 1/2 tablespoons cornstarch	*chicken breast halves*
1/2 teaspoon ground cinnamon	*Salt and freshly ground black pepper*
1/4 teaspoon ground ginger	*2 tablespoons canola oil*
Scant 1 1/4 cups orange juice	*1/2 cup slivered or sliced almonds*
3 tablespoons dry white wine	
2 tablespoons honey, or more to taste	To Serve
2 teaspoons soy sauce (optional)	*Hot cooked white or brown rice*

Use a grater to remove about 2 tablespoons rind (orange part of the peel) from one of the oranges. Set it aside. Peel the oranges, cut them crosswise in half; then separate the halves into small sections. You should have about 2 cups of sections. Set them aside.

In a 2-cup liquid measuring cup, combine the cornstarch, cinnamon, and ginger. Stir in a small amount of the orange juice to make a paste with the cornstarch mixture; then add juice to the 1¼-cup mark on the measuring cup, and stir well so that the cornstarch is all suspended. Stir in the white wine, honey, soy sauce (if used), and reserved grated orange peel. Set aside.

Cut the chicken breasts into 1- to 1½-inch squares and sprinkle the pieces lightly with salt and pepper. Put the oil into a large skillet over medium-high heat; then brown the chicken on all sides. Stir the reserved juice mixture well;

then pour it into the skillet with the chicken. Continue heating, stirring occasionally, until the sauce thickens and comes to a boil. Cover the skillet, and lower the heat. Simmer the chicken, stirring occasionally, for about 10 to 15 minutes, or until it is cooked through and very tender.

When the chicken is ready, stir the orange sections and almonds into the sauce. Raise the heat, and simmer the mixture, stirring often, for about 2 to 3 minutes longer, or until the oranges are heated through.

(Hint: If this dish is being made ahead of time and you like fresh-tasting oranges and crunchy almonds, do not add them to the sauce at this point. Refrigerate the chicken and sauce in a covered container. Shortly before serving, stir the oranges and almonds into the sauce, and reheat the chicken mixture in a microwave oven, a conventional oven, or on top of the stove, stirring often.)

Serve the chicken mixture over hot cooked rice.

Makes about 6 to 8 servings.

Meat, Fruit, and Peanut Curry

The unusual mélange of people in South Africa—native Africans, Malaysians, Indians, Dutch, British, French, and Ashkenazic Jews—has produced an intriguing selection of unusual local dishes. For an example, try this stew, which is quite appropriate for Tu B'Shevat. South African Jews eat similar curries throughout the year.

2 tablespoons canola oil

1 medium onion, finely chopped

1 ½ pounds chuck or other beef stew
    meat or boneless lamb shoulder,
    trimmed of all excess fat and cut
    into ¾- to 1-inch cubes

1 ½ cups water

2 tablespoons lemon juice or apple cider
    vinegar

1 tablespoon curry powder

½ teaspoon salt

¼ teaspoon ground ginger

¼ teaspoon ground cinnamon

1 (8-ounce) package mixed dried fruits
    (such as dried apples, prunes,
    apricots, peaches, pears)

½ cup raisins

2 small, just-ripe, firm bananas

½ cup roasted peanuts or cashews,
    preferably unsalted

To Serve
Hot cooked white or brown rice

Put the oil into a very large, deep skillet or in a Dutch oven over medium-high heat; then sauté the onion until tender. Push the onion to one side of the pot, and add the meat cubes. Brown them on all sides. While they are browning, combine the water, lemon juice, curry powder, salt, ginger, and cinnamon in a large measuring cup. When the meat has browned, add the liquid mixture to the skillet along with the mixed dried fruits and raisins. Stir so that the onions, meat, and fruit are evenly distributed.

Bring the liquid to a boil; then lower the heat so that the liquid just simmers. Cook the curry, covered, stirring occasionally, for about 1 hour, or until the meat and fruits are very tender, and just about all the liquids have formed a thick sauce. (If the skillet cooks dry before the meat is tender, add a bit of water.) Dice one of the bananas, and gently stir it into the curry.

Transfer the curry to a large serving platter. Cut the second banana into thin slices, and put the slices around the curry as a garnish. Sprinkle the peanuts on top. Serve the curry with hot cooked rice.

Makes about 6 servings.

Dried-Fruit Lokshen Kugel

NOODLE CASSEROLE

Lokshen kugel—"noodle pudding" in Yiddish—is popular for Askenazic Jews throughout the year, but this delectable one is especially appropriate for Tu B'Shevat because of the dried and fresh fruit. It is not overly sweet, and makes a perfect side dish for a holiday dinner or buffet meal. I serve it often, and it always receives compliments.

1 (8-ounce) package medium-wide
    noodles

4 tablespoons canola oil, divided

4 large or extra-large eggs or 1 cup
    pareve egg substitute

$1/3$ cup sugar

$1 1/4$ cups orange juice

$1/2$ teaspoon ground cinnamon

$1/4$ teaspoon ground ginger

$1/4$ teaspoon salt

1 cup diced mixed dried fruits (such as
    figs, dates, apricots, prunes)

$1/4$ cup dark or light raisins

1 medium apple, peeled (if desired) and
    diced (about 1 cup)

Cook the noodles according to the package directions. While they are cooking, coat a 9 by 13-inch baking dish with nonstick cooking spray, or grease it well. Set it aside.

Drain the noodles well; put them back into the pot (off the heat) and toss them with 2 tablespoons of the oil to keep them from sticking together. Set them aside to cool slightly. Preheat the oven to 350 degrees.

In a medium bowl, use a fork to beat the eggs with the sugar until well mixed. Beat in the remaining 2 tablespoons oil. Then beat in the orange juice, cinnamon, ginger, and salt. Stir in the mixed dried fruit, raisins, and apple. Add the mixture to the cooked noodles in the pot, and stir until all the ingredients are evenly distributed. Transfer the noodle mixture to the prepared baking dish.

Cover the casserole with aluminum foil, and bake the kugel at 350 degrees for 40 minutes. Remove the foil, and continue baking the kugel, uncovered, for 10 to 20 minutes longer, or until it seems to be firm and set. Let it cool slightly before cutting it into squares to serve. Serve the kugel warm or at room temperature.

Makes about 12 servings.

Brown Rice, Fruit, and Nut Salad

This interesting salad would make nice fare at a Tu B'Shevat Seder.

$2 1/4$ cups water

$1 1/4$ cups uncooked brown rice

$1/2$ cup coarsely chopped pitted whole
    dates

½ cup pecan or walnut pieces

¼ cup thinly sliced scallions

2 to 3 tablespoons finely chopped fresh
parsley

1 to 2 teaspoons dried mint leaves

3 tablespoons lemon juice or cider
vinegar

3 tablespoons flavorful olive oil

¼ teaspoon ground cinnamon

⅛ teaspoon ground ginger

1 cup peeled and coarsely chopped
navel orange or 1 (approximately
11-ounce) can drained and rinsed
mandarin oranges

In a medium saucepan, bring the water to a boil. Add the rice, lower the heat, and gently simmer it, covered, for about 30 to 40 minutes, or until all the water is absorbed. Transfer the cooked rice to a large bowl, and set it aside to cool to room temperature. Meanwhile, prepare all the remaining ingredients.

When the rice is cool, add the dates, walnuts, scallions, parsley, and mint. In a small bowl or jar, combine the lemon juice, oil, cinnamon, and ginger. Pour over the rice mixture, and toss with a fork until all is mixed. Add half of the oranges and mix gently, so they are not broken up. Put the remaining oranges on top, as a garnish. If the salad is not to be served immediately, refrigerate it, covered. Serve it at room temperature or slightly chilled.

Makes about 6 servings.

Rich Carob Brownies with Icing

While in Israel many years ago, I made a determined search for whole carobs, and finally found some of the dark brown, dried pods at the Arab market in Jerusalem. Since then, I have seen them occasionally at kosher grocery stores in the United States around the time of Tu B'Shevat.

Carob pods come from an evergreen tree that is indigenous to the Mediterranean area but also found in many other parts of the world. The dried pods are usually six to seven inches long and about one inch wide, and are flat and leathery-looking. They are edible, but rather hard to chew. Each pod contains several tiny, inedible seeds. My children and I think that carob pods have an intriguing taste, but my husband, like many other people, has reservations (although he loves carob brownies and cake).

Carob became very traditional on Tu B'Shevat for Jews in Eastern European shtetls because it was one of the few "fruits" from Israel that was available during midwinter. In the wonderful stories of Yiddish writer Sholom Aleichem, dried carob pods were the *bokser* that young children, particularly yeshiva boys, often enjoyed as special treats.

Since dried carob pods keep for a very long time in the freezer, I store several there, and take out a few each year just for Tu B'Shevat. However, I have found that most people prefer to eat baked goods made from carob powder, which is available at most health food stores. For the most part, the darker the carob powder, the more intense the flavor. There is much variety in different brands, so you might want to experiment until you find a suitable carob powder.

Following is a recipe for rich, moist, fudgy carob brownies that are sure to delight everyone. But, please, don't compare them to chocolate brownies! Carob has a unique flavor that should be enjoyed on its own merits.

NOTE: For higher, smaller brownies, bake them in an 8-inch square pan for about 30 to 35 minutes, following the directions below.

BROWNIES
½ *cup butter or pareve margarine*
1 cup sugar
2 large eggs (no substitutes)
1 teaspoon vanilla extract
⅓ *cup carob powder, preferably dark*
 (sifted, if lumpy)
½ *cup all-purpose flour*
½ *cup coarsely chopped walnuts*
 (optional)

CAROB ICING
3 tablespoons butter or pareve
 margarine, softened
3 tablespoons carob powder
1 tablespoon light corn syrup or honey
½ *teaspoon vanilla extract*
1 cup confectioners' sugar
1 to 2 tablespoons milk, water, or
 pareve milk substitute

Coat a 9-inch square baking pan with nonstick cooking spray or grease it. Preheat the oven to 350 degrees.

For the brownies, melt the butter or margarine in a medium saucepan on the stove or in a medium glass bowl in the microwave oven. Take the pan off the heat and stir in the remaining ingredients in the order listed, except the walnuts, and mix until very well combined. Then stir in the walnuts until evenly distributed. The batter will be very thick.

Turn out the batter into the prepared pan, and spread it evenly. It will not be very deep. Bake at 350 degrees for about 20 to 25 minutes, or just until the center of the top is firm and a wooden pick comes out clean. (For moist, fudgy brownies, do not overbake them.) Cool the brownies in the pan on a wire rack; then top them with icing as follows.

For the icing, combine the butter or margarine, carob powder, corn syrup, vanilla extract, and confectioners' sugar. Gradually add the liquid by teaspoons, while constantly stirring, until the icing has a thick, yet spreadable consistency. Spread it on top of the cooled brownies in the pan. Let it set for a short while. Cut the brownies into squares.

Makes 16 large brownies.

Carob Layer Cake with Carob Icing

This luxurious dairy dessert is a perfect treat for celebrating the "New Year of the Trees." If desired, the top can be decorated with some of the dried fruits, nuts, and seeds eaten on Tu B'Shevat.

The carob is a very ancient fruit. In fact, according to tradition, it was one of the fruits in the Garden of Eden. Also, the word we use to measure the weight of gems—the "carat"—probably came from the Greek word for carob.

The Talmud says that Rabbi Shimon bar Yochai and his son lived solely on a diet of carobs while they hid from persecution by the Romans. The carobs grew on a tree outside the cave where they lived. The impoverished have often been sustained by carobs, giving rise to the sobriquet "poor man's bread." The following "rich" cake certainly belies this former appellation.

NOTE: Carob powder can vary greatly. For the best flavor, use an intensely flavored, dark carob powder. For more information on carob, see the recipe for Rich Carob Brownies (page 279).

CAKE BATTER

¹/₂ cup butter, softened

1¹/₄ cups granulated sugar

2 large eggs or ¹/₂ cup egg substitute

1 teaspoon vanilla extract

³/₄ cup carob powder, preferably dark
    (sifted, if lumpy)

2¹/₄ cups all-purpose flour

1 teaspoon baking powder

1 teaspoon baking soda

¹/₄ teaspoon salt

1¹/₂ cups buttermilk (no substitutions)

CAROB BUTTERCREAM ICING

¹/₃ cup butter, softened

3¹/₂ cups sifted confectioners' sugar

¹/₂ cup carob powder, preferably dark
    (sifted, if lumpy)

¹/₃ cup hot milk

¹/₂ teaspoon vanilla extract

Coat with nonstick spray or grease two 8- or 9-inch round cake pans. Line the bottom of each pan with a circle of wax paper or parchment, then spray or grease the paper (not necessary with parchment). Set the pans aside. Preheat the oven to 350 degrees.

For the batter, put the butter and sugar into a large mixing bowl, and use an electric mixer at medium speed to cream them together until they are light and fluffy. Add the eggs, one at a time, beating well after each addition. Beat in the vanilla. In a separate bowl (or on a large piece of wax paper), combine the carob powder, flour, baking powder, baking soda, and salt. Sift the carob-flour mixture together, making sure any lumps have been pressed out of the carob powder. Add the carob-flour mixture to the butter-egg-sugar mixture alternately with the buttermilk, mixing after each addition. Beat briefly until all the ingredients are combined completely.

Divide the batter evenly between the prepared pans, and smooth the tops with a rubber spatula. Bake the cakes at 350 degrees for 25 to 35 minutes, or until a wooden pick inserted in the center of each cake comes out clean. Cool the cakes in the pans on wire racks about 5 minutes. Turn out each cake onto a rack, remove the wax paper, and invert the cake by holding a second rack against the bottom of the cake, and turning the two racks together. Let the cakes cool completely before icing and assembling them.

For the icing, use an electric mixer to beat the butter until light and fluffy. Then add the remaining ingredients, and beat for several minutes, or until they are completely mixed and the icing does not taste or feel gritty. (If it is too thin, beat in a small amount of confectioners' sugar; if it is too thick, beat in a few more drops of milk.) Spread the icing between the cake layers, and

over the exterior of the cake. Use the back of a spoon to make peaks and swirls in the icing, if desired.

Makes 1 large layer cake; about 10 to 12 servings.

Cookie-Pudding "Dirt" with Seeds

This is not actually a "recipe," but more of an edible miniproject to keep children (and some adults) happy at your Tu B'Shevat Seder. I came up with the idea (loosely based on other cookie "dirt" recipes that I had heard about over the years) for our Seder at Beth Shalom Congregation in Columbia, Maryland, a few years ago. As the author and leader of our synagogue's first Tu B'Shevat Seder, I had to consider ways to keep almost a hundred people of different ages attentive while we read through the innovative text.

During the Seder, we sang a variety of songs including a Hebrew version of "Happy Birthday to the Trees," tasted lots of dried fruits and nuts, and drank four cups of grape juice. And about halfway through, just when some of the children were starting to squirm, we joined together in a rousing rendition of *Artzah Alinu*—the Israeli pioneers' planting song—and then helped the youngsters to "plant" sunflower seeds in cookie-dirt cups. While the kids noshed on the results, the adults read an English translation of the Jewish National Fund's Planters' Prayer.

The dirt cups were such a success that some adults suggested I have *everyone* make them at our next Tu B'Shevat Seder!

The quantities of the following ingredients will depend on how much "dirt" you want to make, and the proportions that you use:

Chocolate sandwich cookies, crushed

Prepared chocolate pudding (at room temperature or chilled)

Edible "earthy creatures," such as gummy worms or gummy bugs, or dark raisins (for bugs!)

Hulled sunflower and/or sesame seeds

For Each Person

In a small, clear 6- to 8-ounce cup (plastic or glass) that approximates the short, wide shape of a flowerpot, mix together crushed cookies and choco-

late pudding in equal quantities (or use any proportions desired). This is the "dirt." Gently stir a few "creatures" into the dirt. "Plant" several seeds in the top of the dirt. Talk about why we plant seeds on Tu B'Shevat. Eat the dirt, seeds, and, yes, even the creatures!

Dried-Fruit Strudel P

Most of the filling ingredients for this delectable treat have been specifically chosen because of their association with Israel, where this type of strudel is a very popular Tu B'Shevat dessert.

However, other nuts and dried fruits, such as chopped dried apricots, prunes, papaya, pineapple, and apples, can be substituted. Some of the dried fruit-nut mixtures available in bulk at many supermarkets and health food stores would be suitable. Whatever the choice, the combination of chopped dried fruit, nuts, and coconut should measure 5½ to 6 cups.

This recipe uses the classic method of stretching dough, which is explained in detail below. If the directions are carefully followed, even those who have never tried this technique before should be successful and produce very satisfying results.

NOTES: For best results, be sure to use unbleached flour in this recipe. All-purpose bleached flour might not have enough gluten to stretch properly.

Strudel is sometimes made with purchased "filo dough" or "strudel leaves." For a strudel using this technique, see the recipe for Easy Apple-Nut Strudel (page 197). That strudel would also be appropriate for Tu B'Shevat.

DOUGH
1 large egg (no substitutes)
¼ teaspoon salt
½ cup tepid water
2 tablespoons canola oil
Approximately 2 cups unbleached flour (see Notes)

FILLING
1 cup dark or light raisins or currants
1 cup chopped dates
1 cup chopped dried figs
½ cup chopped candied citrus peel (orange, lemon, or grapefruit) or 2 tablespoons grated fresh citrus peel, colored part only

1 cup shredded or flaked coconut

1 cup slivered or chopped almonds

½ cup chopped walnuts or pecans

⅓ cup orange juice or sweet wine

Canola oil or olive oil cooking spray as needed, (See Notes with Pastilla, page 179)

¼ cup graham cracker crumbs, dried cookie or cake crumbs, or plain bread crumbs

4 large egg whites

¼ teaspoon cream of tartar

½ cup sugar

GARNISH (OPTIONAL)

Confectioners' sugar

For the dough, use a fork to beat the egg with the salt, water, and oil. Gradually add the flour, while stirring with the fork, until a soft dough forms. Begin kneading the dough in the bowl, adding a little extra flour if the dough becomes sticky.

Turn out the dough onto a lightly floured surface, and continue kneading, occasionally lifting the dough and slapping it down hard against the surface. After about 10 to 15 minutes, the dough should lose all stickiness and become very smooth and elastic. It may also have some blisters under the surface. Form the dough into a smooth ball, and wrap it in plastic. Cover the dough with an inverted bowl, and let it rest, in a warm place if possible, for about an hour.

Meanwhile, begin to make the filling. Put the raisins, dates, figs, candied or fresh peel, coconut, almonds, and walnuts into a large bowl, and mix. Then add the juice, and mix again. Line a very large, sturdy shiny metal baking sheet with parchment, or coat it with nonstick cooking spray, or grease it. Set aside.

Cover a large surface (such as a kitchen table) with a smooth tablecloth or clean sheet, and flour the cloth lightly. Using a rolling pin, roll out the scantily floured dough as thinly as possible into a square. Brush or spray the top of the dough with oil. Remove all jewelry from your hands, and lightly flour your fists.

With your palms facing down, reach under the dough, and very gently stretch it from underneath using the backs and bent knuckles of both your hands, but not your fingertips. Continuously work all around the dough, starting in the center and moving toward the edges, trying to keep the thickness of the dough even. (Don't be concerned about the slightly thicker edge that tends to form around the perimeter of the dough.) Pinch the dough promptly to patch any small holes before they are stretched into larger ones.

Tu B'Shevat

You should be able to stretch the small piece of dough into a translucent 2½- to 3-foot square. Use kitchen shears or a sharp knife to trim off any very thick edges.

Lightly brush or spray the entire surface of the dough with oil. Evenly sprinkle the crumbs over the dough. Let the dough rest briefly while you complete the filling. Preheat the oven to 375 degrees.

In a large, very clean mixing bowl, beat the egg whites with the cream of tartar until frothy; then gradually add the granulated sugar, and continue beating until the whites form stiff, shiny peaks. Fold the whites into the fruit-nut mixture until combined. Heap the filling in a 3-inch-wide strip along one edge of the stretched dough square, keeping it about 4 inches from that edge and about 2 inches from the three remaining edges.

To roll the strudel, use both hands to lift up the cloth so the uncovered 4-inch margin of dough flips over the filling, enclosing it. Continue lifting the cloth so that the strudel evenly rolls up away from you. Tuck under the two ends of the roll so that the filling cannot come out.

Carefully transfer the strudel, seam side down, to the prepared pan, gently bending the roll into a horseshoe so it can fit on the baking sheet. Brush or spray the outer surface of the strudel with oil.

Bake the strudel at 375 degrees for about 35 minutes, or until the top is browned and crisp.

Let the strudel cool on the baking sheet until it is lukewarm, then cut it into 2-inch sections. If desired, sprinkle the top with sieved confectioners' sugar just before serving. Serve warm or at room temperature. Leftovers may be reheated in a 375-degree oven just until warmed through and crisp. (A microwave oven may soften the crust.)

Makes about 15 pieces.

Old-Fashioned Date Bars

Dates are a popular dried fruit for Tu B'Shevat because they are widely grown in Israel. The country's luscious dates are so naturally sweet that when ancient Israel was described in the Torah as "a land flowing with milk and honey," the word "honey" actually referred to a syrup or juice extracted from dates, according to most scholars. Layered

date bars—the type with date filling sandwiched between oat crusts—have always been a favorite of mine. An easy and delicious version of these classic bars follows below.

This recipe makes a lot of bars, which can be prepared ahead and frozen until needed.

NOTE: Dates are available already chopped, or you can finely chop whole pitted dates. For the best results, the chopped dates should be soft and easy to chew.

FILLING	CRUST
1½ cups chopped dates (8 ounces) (see Note)	½ cup walnut pieces
½ cup water or orange juice	1½ cups all-purpose flour
3 tablespoons granulated or light brown sugar	1¼ cups quick-cooking rolled oats
	1 cup packed dark or light brown sugar
¼ teaspoon ground cinnamon (optional)	¼ teaspoon salt
1 teaspoon vanilla extract	¾ cup butter or margarine, softened

For the filling, combine the dates, water or juice, sugar, and cinnamon (if used) in a medium saucepan. Cook over medium heat, stirring constantly and mashing the dates with the back of a spoon, for about 5 to 7 minutes, or until the dates are "melted" and form a thick paste. (If the dates are very dry, a few additional tablespoons of liquid may be needed to soften them.) Remove the date filling from the heat, and stir in the vanilla extract. Set aside to cool.

Coat a 9 by 13-inch baking pan with nonstick cooking spray, or grease it. Set it aside. Preheat the oven to 350 degrees.

The crust can be made in a food processor fitted with a steel blade or by hand.

For a food processor: Put the walnuts, flour, oats, brown sugar, and salt into the bowl, and pulse-process a few times to mix everything and finely chop the walnuts. Cut the butter or margarine into small pieces, and add it to the bowl. Pulse-process very briefly, just until crumbs are formed. The mixture should *not* form a dough.

By hand: Put the flour, oats, brown sugar, walnuts, and salt into a medium bowl, and mix well to combine. Cut in the butter or margarine with two knives, a pastry blender, or your fingertips to make coarse crumbs.

Tu B'Shevat

When the crumbs are ready, set aside 2 cups for the topping. Use your hands to press the remainder of the crumbs into the bottom of the prepared pan. Evenly spread the date filling over the bottom crust. Sprinkle the reserved crumbs on top so the dates are completely covered, and press the crumbs down gently with your fingertips so the top "crust" adheres to the filling.

Bake at 350 degrees for about 25 to 30 minutes, or until the top is lightly browned. Cool completely in the pan on a wire rack; then cut into rectangular or square bars. These freeze very well.

Makes about 24 bars.

Date-Walnut Squares

These dense treats are crunchy and delicious, yet they take just a few minutes to prepare if you buy chopped dates and walnuts—a great combination for Tu B'Shevat. This unusual recipe contains no butter, oil, or similar fat, and very little flour. It is mostly just the dates and walnuts held together with eggs.

Walnuts are eaten on Tu B'Shevat because they have a hard, inedible outer shell that must be removed to get to soft food inside. Kabbalistic tradition says that this symbolizes our need to peel away outer boundaries so that we can achieve inner spirituality.

Also, there is a commentary that compares the People of Israel to a pile of walnuts. If one walnut is removed, it says, every walnut will be shaken. Similarly, if one person sins, the whole community will suffer.

3 large eggs (no substitutes)
½ cup sugar
½ teaspoon vanilla extract
¼ cup all-purpose flour
1½ to 2 cups chopped pitted dates
    (about 8 to 12 ounces)

2 cups chopped walnuts (about 8
    ounces)
Confectioners' sugar (optional)

Coat a 9-inch square baking pan with nonstick cooking spray or grease it well. Preheat the oven to 350 degrees.

In a medium bowl, beat the eggs with the sugar and vanilla until thick and light. Stir in the flour, then the dates and walnuts. Spread the mixture (it will be very thick) in the prepared pan. Bake at 350 degrees for about 30 minutes, or until a wooden pick inserted in the center comes out clean. Cool in the pan on a rack until lukewarm; then cut into 16 squares, and remove the squares from the pan to cool completely. If desired, sprinkle the tops with sieved confectioners' sugar just before serving.

Makes 16 squares.

Creamy Date Pudding with Walnuts

$\boxed{\text{D}}$

Dates give this very easy and nutritious dessert a delicious, sweet taste.

2 cups water
²/₃ cup instant nonfat dry milk powder
1 large egg (no substitutes)
Generous ¹/₂ cup pitted dates, cut in half (about 4 ounces)

2 tablespoons honey
2¹/₂ tablespoons cornstarch
¹/₂ teaspoon vanilla extract
¹/₄ cup finely chopped walnuts

Put all the ingredients, except the walnuts, into a blender or a food processor, and process until the dates are finely chopped. Pour the mixture into a 2½-quart saucepan, and place it over medium heat. Cook the pudding, stirring constantly, until it thickens and just comes to a boil. Remove it from the heat, and pour it into individual small bowls. Sprinkle the walnuts on top. Cool the pudding slightly at room temperature; then refrigerate it. Serve chilled.

Makes about 5 servings.

Orange-Date Muffins

These very low-fat muffins are adapted from a recipe originally developed by my friend and fellow food writer, Nancy Baggett, for a cookbook we wrote together several years ago called *Don't Tell 'Em It's Good for 'Em*. They are among my all-time favorite muffins. Everyone loves the flavor, but no one can guess that some of it comes from a carrot. A whole orange is used in this recipe, including the skin, to give the muffins a rich orange taste and aroma. They would make a wonderful Tu B'Shevat breakfast.

NOTE: Use soft whole pitted (dried) dates for this recipe, not prechopped dates, which are sometimes very hard or have sugar added to them.

1 small thin-skinned juice orange (not a navel orange)
1 medium carrot, peeled, or about 5 peeled baby carrots
1 cup all-purpose white flour
⅔ cup all-purpose whole wheat flour
¼ cup instant nonfat dry milk powder
1 teaspoon baking powder
1 teaspoon baking soda

¼ teaspoon ground cinnamon
⅛ teaspoon ground nutmeg
½ cup sugar
2 tablespoons canola oil
½ cup water
1 large egg or ¼ cup egg substitute
1 teaspoon vanilla extract
⅓ cup dates (see Note)

Spray twelve cups in a standard-sized muffin tin with nonstick cooking spray, or lightly grease them or fit them with paper liners. Set aside. Preheat the oven to 400 degrees.

Scrub the outside of the orange very well; then cut the orange into eighths and remove all the seeds. Leave the peel intact. Set the orange aside. Cut the carrot into 1-inch lengths. Set the carrot pieces aside.

Combine the white and whole wheat flour, milk powder, baking powder, baking soda, cinnamon, and nutmeg in a medium bowl. Stir until thoroughly mixed, then set aside.

Put the reserved orange and carrot into a blender or a food processor (fitted with a steel blade) along with the sugar, oil, water, egg, and vanilla. Blend on medium speed or process for 30 seconds. Scrape down the sides of the blender or processor bowl, and blend or process for 1 minute longer, or until the mixture is completely puréed and smooth.

With the blender or processor running, add the dates to the puréed mixture. Process for about 15 seconds, or until the dates are finely chopped. Pour the puréed mixture into the dry ingredients in the bowl, and stir only until the dry ingredients are moistened.

Divide the batter evenly among the prepared muffin cups. Bake at 400 degrees for 20 to 25 minutes, or until the muffins are lightly browned and the tops are springy to the touch. Cool the muffins in the pan for 5 minutes, then remove them and cool on a rack. Serve warm or at room temperature.

Makes 12 muffins.

Apricot-Fig Bars

Fruit and nut filling tops the crunchy base of these rich squares, which make a great holiday snack or dessert. The fig is eaten on Tu B'Shevat because it is one of the fruits most associated with the Land of Israel.

Jewish sages have compared the fig to the Torah. The fruit of most trees is picked all at once, while that of a fig must be collected bit by bit. Likewise, the Torah cannot be learned all at once; a Jew must study the Torah a little at a time. Interestingly, the fig is one of the few foods that is frequently mentioned in the text of the Torah.

A ripe *fresh* fig is a delicious wonder, but it is usually available only in summer. For Tu B'Shevat, we generally use dried figs, which are quite tasty and naturally sweet. They are also very high in fiber. Dried figs have been popular since ancient times, when this dietary staple was made into cakes to be used as winter sustenance. In modern times, fig-filled commercially baked cookies seem to be the only way that most people eat dried figs. Try the following for a more interesting way to enjoy them: complemented with another delectable dried fruit, the apricot.

NOTE: For best results, use soft dried fruit that is easy to chew.

Tu B'Shevat

BOTTOM CRUST
1 cup all-purpose flour
¼ cup sugar
⅓ cup butter or margarine, softened

TOP LAYER
½ cup all-purpose flour
¼ cup packed dark brown sugar
2 large eggs or ½ cup pareve egg
    substitute

1 teaspoon vanilla extract
½ teaspoon baking powder
½ cup finely chopped light-brown
    (Calimyrna) dried figs
½ cup finely chopped dried apricots
½ cup slivered almonds
Confectioners' sugar (optional)

Preheat the oven to 350 degrees. For the bottom crust, combine all the in-gredients in a mixing bowl or a food processor fitted with a steel blade, and mix or pulse-process until they are completely combined and crumbly. Press the mixture into the bottom of an ungreased 9-inch square baking pan. Bake the crust at 350 degrees for about 15 minutes, or until it is very lightly browned.

Meanwhile, prepare the top layer. In the same bowl used for the crust, combine the flour, brown sugar, eggs, vanilla extract, and baking powder. Beat or process until very well mixed. Add the dried fruits and almonds, and mix by hand just until they are stirred in.

When the bottom crust is ready, remove it from the oven, and evenly spread the fruit-nut mixture over it. Return the pan to the 350-degree oven, and bake for about 25 minutes longer, or until the top layer is firm. Remove from the oven, and cool completely in the pan on a wire rack. When it is cool, cut into squares. If desired, sprinkle the squares lightly with sieved con-fectioners' sugar before serving them.

Makes 16 squares.

Pear-Walnut Quick Bread

Dried pears are often overlooked, but they are really a tasty treat. They are soft and sweet, and delicious in quick breads and other baked goods. The following low-fat bread makes a perfect accompaniment to a Tu B'Shevat meal. It keeps quite well for several days, and actually tastes best the day after it is made. It also slices very neatly, and each

slice has a very attractive cross section. Be sure to use soft dried pears that are easy to chew.

8 ounces dried pear halves (about 8)	$\frac{1}{2}$ teaspoon ground cinnamon
3 tablespoons canola oil	$\frac{1}{2}$ teaspoon ground ginger
1 cup boiling water	$1\frac{1}{4}$ cups all-purpose white flour
$\frac{3}{4}$ cup sugar	1 cup all-purpose whole wheat flour
1 large egg or $\frac{1}{4}$ cup pareve egg substitute	1 teaspoon baking soda
	1 cup coarsely broken walnut halves

Use a small, sharp knife to carefully remove any hard parts or seeds from the inside of each dried pear half. Cut the pears into ½-inch pieces, and place them in a large bowl. Add the oil and the boiling water, and stir to make sure all the pears are in the water. Let the mixture cool to tepid. Meanwhile, preheat the oven to 350 degrees. Coat an 8½ by 4½-inch loaf pan with nonstick cooking spray or grease it well. Set aside.

When the pear mixture has cooled, add the sugar, egg, cinnamon, and ginger to the bowl. Stir very well by hand until completely mixed. Measure out the white flour, whole wheat flour, and baking soda into a small bowl, and combine them by stirring. Add the flour mixture to the pear mixture all at once, and stir briefly just until all the flour is moistened. Stir in the walnuts, using as few strokes as possible. (Overmixing at this point can ruin the texture of this type of quick bread.)

Turn out the batter into the prepared pan. Bake the loaf at 350 degrees for about 55 to 60 minutes, or until a wooden pick inserted in the center comes out just slightly sticky. Cool in the pan on a wire rack for about 30 minutes. Run a knife around the edge of the pan, and remove the loaf, which should come out easily. Let the loaf cool completely on a wire rack before wrapping it well for storage. Store it at room temperature for up to 3 days, or freeze it for longer storage. Cut the loaf with a serrated knife.

Makes about 8 to 10 slices.

Fruit-Nut Confection Balls

Several of the dried fruits and nuts flavored on Tu B'Shevat are featured in this easy un-cooked treat, which is loved by young and old alike.

½ cup dried apricots	½ cup walnut pieces
½ cup pitted dates	¼ cup shredded coconut (optional)
½ cup dried figs	2 tablespoons honey, or as needed
½ cup pitted prunes	Granulated sugar (optional)

Finely chop the apricots, dates, figs, prunes, and walnuts in a food processor fitted with a steel blade, or put them through the coarse blade of a food grinder (the nuts will help push the sticky fruit through). Or, if desired, finely chop them by hand.

Stir in the coconut (if used) and honey, and mix until well combined. If the mixture seems very crumbly, add honey as needed, but do not use too much or it will become very sticky.

Use your hands to mold walnut-size portions of the mixture into compact 1-inch–diameter balls and, if desired, roll each one in sugar to coat. Store in the refrigerator, but serve at room temperature for best taste.

Makes about 36 balls.

Purim

WHEN IT COMES TO HAVING LOTS OF LIGHTHEARTED, GOOD-natured fun, Purim is one holiday that really stands out! Young and old alike enjoy the masquerade and mockery that highlight the day, as well as the delicious food gifts exchanged among family and friends.

Purim celebrates the triumph of ancient Persian Jews over their archenemy, Haman, as related in the *Megillat Esther* (meaning "Scroll of Esther"), or simply the *Megillah,* as it is called in the vernacular. It is incumbent upon all Jews to listen to the *Megillah* being read aloud on this holiday, and to raucously "blot out" the name of Haman with hissing, foot stomping, and grating noisemakers called *groggers* in Yiddish.

Haman was an ambitious and conniving minister who gained increasing power by taking advantage of the easily influenced King Ahasuerus. When the king commanded that everyone in the kingdom must bow down to Haman, a man named Mordecai refused because he was a Jew and so would bow only to God. This infuriated the anti-Semitic minister, who convinced the king that all the Jews were disloyal and should be exterminated on a date determined by the casting of "lots" or, in Hebrew, *purim.*

Neither Haman nor the king knew that the king's wife, the beautiful and beloved Queen Esther, was a Jew and also Mordecai's cousin. When Esther learned of the plot, she prepared a great feast for the king and Haman. After they had eaten, at risk of her own life, she told the king why Haman wanted to have her and all her people killed.

The king finally recognized that Haman was the real danger, and had him hanged on the gallows that Haman had prepared for Mordecai. The king also allowed the Jews to defend themselves and take vengeance on their enemies on precisely the date set for their destruction—the thirteenth day of Adar. On the following day, the Jews in most of Persia rejoiced over their deliverance. But in Persia's capital city, Shushan, fighting continued for another day, and so celebration there did not occur until the fifteenth.

It has become customary for most of the world's Jews to celebrate Purim on the fourteenth day of the Hebrew month of Adar (which usually occurs in March). However, those who live in cities that were surrounded by walls in ancient times celebrate on the next day, which is called "Shushan Purim."

Thus, Israelis living in Jerusalem are supposed to have their Purim festivities a day later than those in, say, Tel Aviv. Actually, the holiday is such a major event in Israel that many people celebrate *both* days, just in case their homes may have once been inside a walled city!

On Purim, a huge carnival and parade called *Ad'lo'yada* is held in Israel. The name, meaning "until he did not know," comes from the Talmudic suggestion that one should drink enough wine on Purim so as not to be able to distinguish between "Blessed is Mordecai" and "Cursed be Haman." During the celebration, it has become popular for costumed merrymakers to use colorful plastic mallets to tap each other. The compressible mallet delivers a silly chirping sound as it meets its mark, and can be quite ridiculous when one is somewhat tipsy.

Worldwide, there are many ways that Jews enjoy the happy and jovial spirit of this holiday. Both children and adults dress in masquerade, thereby having a "mistaken identity"—a recurrent theme in the *Megillah*. Many participate in hilarious spoofs or plays called *Purim shpiels* in Yiddish, which often parody the story of the *Megillah*. Not even the sacred texts are exempt from the humor, as ludicrous interpretations called "Purim Torah" are presented, sometimes by rabbis who are bedecked for the occasion. Costumed cantors join the charade by chanting traditional hymns to the melodies of modern music.

A wide variety of food is eaten and shared on Purim, not just the eponymous Hamantaschen (page 308) that are so familiar to Ashkenazic Jews. For breakfast, a bread fritter moistened in milk and coated with beaten egg, sometimes called "Queen Esther's Toast," is eaten by some Sephardim. Quite similar to what Americans call "French toast," this fritter is also served throughout the year to new mothers.

On the afternoon of the holiday, a Purim *Se'udah* (festive meal) is held. Merriment

is the keynote of this banquet, and singing, joking, and silliness are encouraged just this once, making it a particular favorite among youngsters.

Kreplach (page 112) are often on the menu, as they are for the prefast Yom Kippur dinner and for Hoshanah Rabbah. The challah bread is often shaped into a long braided loaf called a *keylitsh,* which symbolizes the rope used to hang Haman. Sometimes, the length of the loaf may be six feet or longer!

Purim is also a time to give charity and exchange edible presents, because the *Megillah* proclaims that the holiday should be observed as "a day of feasting and gladness, and of sending portions, one to another, and gifts to the poor." Because the words "portions" and "gifts" are plural, the tradition is to send at least two portions of ready-to-eat food (usually sweets) to each relative and friend, and also give some money to at least two less-fortunate people.

Before the evening reading of the *Megillah,* a basket may be passed in the synagogue to collect the customary half-shekel (an Israeli coin), half-dollar, or comparable amount per person, based on the fee required in ancient times to maintain the Holy Temple. This money is donated to the poor.

The custom of "sending portions"—in Hebrew, *mishloach manot* (or *shalach manos* in the vernacular)—requires that the food gifts be at least two different types, such as baked goods and fruit. That way, the recipient can have the honor of performing at least two *mitzvot*—religious obligations—by saying the proper blessing over each category of food. Popular items include: cookies, pastries, small cakes, wrapped kosher candies, unshelled nuts, fresh or dried fruit, and a small bottle of wine or juice.

In some places, *shalach manos* are delivered on beautiful platters wrapped in rich cloths. On display at the Israel Museum in Jerusalem is a magnificent nineteenth-century silver plate from Austria that was used only for this purpose. It is designed in the shape of a fish, symbolic of the month of Adar. More commonplace nowadays are cardboard boxes or paper plates decorated specifically for Purim food exchange or with a general Jewish theme. Sometimes, inexpensive small baskets are used, with the basket being an additional gift for the recipient.

I sometimes use an attractive plastic or paper plate lined with a lacy doily glued in the center (so it doesn't slide). After neatly filling the plate with an assortment of goodies, I place it in the center of two long sections of colored plastic wrap that have been spread out like a "plus" sign. I bring the four ends up over the plate, and tie them together tightly with a bright ribbon or yarn. Attached to the tie is a colorful holiday note from our family. The enclosed plates of goodies can be assembled a day or two before delivery.

Friends have sent me *shalach manos* in a paper plate folded to resemble a basket, a clear plastic "shell," and an attractive (reusable) foil tray, to name just a few innovative ideas. (Hint: Do not mix unwrapped moist cake and crunchy cookies in one package, or the cookies will get soft. To be on the safe side, wrap pieces of moist cake separately in plastic wrap before putting them with other baked goods.)

In my suburban community, the practice of sending food gifts is relatively rare (though it is on the increase). But in some places, particularly in Israel, it is a major undertaking, with the preparation of baked goods beginning several weeks ahead of the holiday. This is considered the perfect opportunity to use up flour and other baking supplies before the house must be thoroughly cleaned for Pesach.

Many of the sweet treats featured in this book for Rosh Hashanah and Hanukkah are also popular for Purim. These may include, for instance, *zvingous,* which are sometimes called "Purim puffs," *tayglach* or *pinyonati, hadgi badam,* and *zelebi.* In addition, Iraqi Jews make a dry, rolled type of Baklava called *malfoof* and a star-shaped coconut macaroon known as *masafan.*

Several Purim specialties mock various parts of Haman's body. For instance, there are Sephardic fried pastries known as *orejas de haman* or "Haman's ears," very fine egg noodles called *caveos di aman* or "Haman's hair," Turkish sweet rolls called *folares* that are shaped like Haman's feet, Greek sesame candy known as *psires tou amman* or "Haman's fleas," Sephardic walnut bars called *dentes de hamman* or "Haman's teeth," and evil-looking Gingerbread Hamans cookies, baked by some Dutch and Scandinavian Jews.

Costumed children often have the "chore" of delivering *shalach manos.* They are frequently rewarded for their labors with special holiday goodies. Among many Sephardic Jews, these treats may include *huevos de haman,* hard-cooked eggs that are each baked inside a pastry basket that may be decorated to depict some aspect of the Purim story.

The recipes in this chapter include several baked goods that are ideal for gift-giving, and also some dishes for a jovial Purim *Se'udah.* Many are served on Purim because of additional holiday symbolism, which is described with the specific recipe. In addition, the other chapters of this book contain many recipes for cookies and small cakes that would be perfect for *shalach manos.*

Turkey Schnitzel, Israeli-Style

Turkey is traditionally eaten on Purim because it represents King Ahasuerus. The turkey, considered to be the most foolish fowl, is called *tarnegol hodu* in Hebrew, which literally translates as "cock of India." Likewise, it is written that the oft-foolish King Ahasuerus "reigned from India unto Ethiopia."

In the following recipe, turkey looks and tastes remarkably like veal. In Israel, where turkey is plentiful and less expensive than most other meats, restaurants are much more likely to offer this version than the "authentic" wiener schnitzel. And many people actually prefer it. Indeed, turkey schnitzel was one of my children's favorite choices when we took them on a family trip to Israel in the mid-1990s. Israelis also prepare turkey schnitzel at home throughout the year. During Pesach, the bread crumbs are replaced with matzah meal.

NOTES: For best results, the turkey breast cutlets used should be no more than about ½ inch thick. They can be purchased presliced at some supermarkets, or a butcher can cut them from a whole turkey breast.

For a more Middle Eastern taste, season the bread crumbs with cumin, turmeric, and paprika. Sometimes, Israelis will season the raw turkey slices before they are coated with flour, and then use plain bread crumbs on the outside coating.

To prepare turkey schnitzel for Pesach, substitute matzah cake meal for the flour and matzah meal for the bread crumbs.

About ⅓ cup all-purpose flour

2 large eggs beaten with 1 tablespoon water or ½ cup pareve egg substitute

About 1¼ cups fine dry plain bread crumbs seasoned to taste with salt, black pepper, chopped parsley leaves, and other herbs or spices as desired (see Notes)

1½ pounds thinly sliced, boneless turkey breast cutlets (see Notes)

Canola oil, for frying

TO SERVE

Sprigs of fresh parsley leaves

1 lemon, cut into wedges

Put the flour into a wide shallow bowl or a platter with raised sides. Do the same with the eggs, and with the bread crumbs. Put the three bowls in a row in that order.

Place the turkey cutlets between two sheets of heavy plastic wrap and gently pound them with a rubber mallet, meat mallet, or rolling pin, until they are about ¼ inch thick. Be careful not to tear the meat.

Lightly coat each turkey cutlet on both sides with flour, shaking off any excess. Dip each turkey cutlet into the egg mixture, and let the excess drip off. Then immediately coat the cutlet well with the seasoned bread crumbs, and set it aside on a large platter or a piece of wax paper. Do not stack the cutlets. (If necessary, they may be refrigerated at this point, and fried several hours later.)

In a large skillet, put oil that is ⅛ to ¼ inch deep, and heat it over medium to medium-high heat until it is hot but not smoking. In batches, brown the cutlets on both sides. This will take only 2 to 3 minutes on each side; do not overcook the cutlets, or the meat may toughen. Drain the cutlets on paper towels. Then transfer them to a serving platter, and garnish them with the parsley and lemon wedges.

Makes about 6 servings.

Saloona

SALMON AND VEGETABLES IN SWEET-SOUR SAUCE

Sweet-and-sour dishes are sometimes eaten on Purim because of the dual nature of this holiday. When Haman announced to the Jews that they were to be killed, there was much sadness and grief. However, when the tables were turned, and Haman was hanged instead, the Jews were able to celebrate with great joy.

The following delectable "sweet-and-sour" recipe is from Bella Ini, an Iraqi Jew who now resides in my community. After Israel achieved statehood, life became difficult for many Jews living in Arab countries. Such was the case for Mrs. Ini, her husband, and young children, and so they left their native Iraq and immigrated to Israel in 1951. A further move in 1975 brought Mrs. Ini to the United States.

To this day, she still prefers to cook the Iraqi-Jewish cuisine she learned as a young bride. Though she now lives alone, Mrs. Ini often prepares whole Iraqi-style meals, which she shares with her very appreciative children and grandchildren. *Saloona* is one of her specialties.

NOTES: Various types of fish can be used in the recipe, but Mrs. Ini prefers salmon because its flavor goes well with the sauce. When several vegetables are used, this dish is hearty enough to be a main course; however, only the tomato and onions are essential.

If preferred, the sauce, fish, and vegetables may be placed in a 10-inch square (or equivalent) casserole, and baked, uncovered, in a 400-degree oven for 20 to 25 minutes, or until most of the sauce has been absorbed.

SAUCE
½ cup plain canned tomato sauce
3 tablespoons granulated white or packed brown sugar
3 tablespoons white vinegar or apple cider vinegar
2 tablespoons lemon juice
1 garlic clove, finely minced
1 teaspoon curry powder

FISH AND VEGETABLES (SEE NOTES)
1 pound skinless salmon fillets or about 1¼ pounds salmon steaks

All-purpose flour for coating
Canola oil for frying
2 medium onions, peeled, halved, and thickly sliced
1 medium green pepper, cut into strips
1 medium carrot, very thinly sliced on the diagonal
1 celery stalk, thinly sliced
1 large or 2 small cooked potatoes, cut into thin slices
1 small eggplant, peeled and cut into ½-inch-thick slices
1 large tomato, thinly sliced

Combine all the sauce ingredients in a small bowl, and mix well. Pour about 2 tablespoons of the sauce into the bottom of a very large, deep skillet or an electric frypan (see Notes). Set the remainder of the sauce aside.

Lightly coat the fish with flour. In another large skillet over medium-high heat, heat a few tablespoons of oil until hot. Fry the fish until lightly browned on both sides. Lay the fish on top of the sauce in the first skillet. (If salmon *steaks* are used, remove the bones from the cooked fish before adding the fish to the sauce.)

Add a bit more oil to the skillet used for the fish, and heat it until hot. Add the onions, pepper, carrot, and celery, and cook, stirring, until the vegetables are tender but not browned. Spread the vegetables on top of the fish. Spoon about 2 more tablespoons of the sauce over the vegetables; then cover them with the potato slices.

Lightly coat the eggplant slices with flour; then fry them in a small amount of oil just until lightly browned. Lay the eggplant slices over the other vegetables. Put the tomato slices very neatly on top. Pour the remaining sauce evenly over the tomatoes.

Cover the pan tightly, and bring to a simmer over medium heat. Reduce the heat to low, and gently simmer the fish and vegetables about 30 minutes, or until most of the sauce has been absorbed.

Makes about 4 servings as a main course, or more as an appetizer.

Sambusik

IRAQI-STYLE CHICKEN OR MEAT TURNOVERS

Years ago, when Rachel Muallem Gabes was a child in Baghdad, her family used to begin preparing foods for Purim two to three weeks ahead of time. Sometimes, she would help her mother make the many sweet and savory pastries that they would serve to holiday guests or offer as *mishloah manot*—food gifts.

Mrs. Gabes recalled Purim as being particularly joyful and fun for children. The men would read the *Megillah* aloud at her home, and hired musicians would play cheerful melodies. Young girls like her were told to wash carefully on that day so that they would "have the beauty of Esther."

Following is one of Mrs. Gabes's favorite savory pastries that her family served on Purim. It is filled with a spicy mixture of chicken and chickpeas. Other Iraqi Jews make a very similar filling for *sambusik* using ground beef instead of chicken (see Variation below).

Chicken and beef *sambusik* are customarily deep-fried. However, they may be baked, if preferred, using the directions that follow. The baked *sambusik* are not as crisp as the fried ones, but they are still very tasty.

NOTE: Some Middle Eastern and North African Jews have a nonyeast pastry called *sembussak* or *sanbusak,* which is made from a dough that is more like the one for Borekas (page 492), and is always baked.

DOUGH

1 packet (2¼ teaspoons) active dry yeast (see the Glossary of Ingredients)

1 cup warm (105 to 115 degrees) water

1 teaspoon sugar

1 cup whole wheat flour

1¾ to 2¼ cups white bread flour or unbleached flour

½ teaspoon salt

¼ cup pareve margarine, softened

2 tablespoons canola oil

1 large onion, finely chopped

2 cups cooked, skinned, boned, and diced chicken

1 (15- to 16-ounce) can chickpeas (garbanzo beans), drained

¼ cup water

¼ teaspoon ground cumin

⅛ teaspoon ground turmeric

Pinch of ground ginger

½ teaspoon salt

⅛ teaspoon black pepper, preferably freshly ground

CHICKEN FILLING (FOR MEAT FILLING, SEE VARIATION)

2 tablespoons canola oil

GLAZE (ONLY FOR BAKED TURNOVERS)

1 egg, beaten with 1 teaspoon water

For the dough, mix the yeast, water, and sugar in a small bowl, and let the mixture rest for about 5 minutes, or until it is frothy.

In a medium bowl, combine the whole wheat flour, 1 cup of the white flour, and the salt; then cut in the margarine until the mixture resembles crumbs. Add the oil and the yeast mixture, and stir for about 2 minutes or until very well combined. Stir in just enough additional white flour to make a very soft, slightly sticky dough. Cover the dough with plastic wrap, and let it rest for 15 minutes (so the whole wheat flour can absorb some moisture and become less sticky). Turn the dough out onto a lightly floured board, and knead it for about 5 minutes, or until it is very smooth and only slightly tacky. Put the dough into a lightly oiled bowl, and turn it so it is coated with oil. Loosely cover the bowl with plastic wrap and a dish towel, and let the dough rise until doubled, about 1 hour.

Meanwhile, prepare the filling. Put the oil into a large, deep skillet over medium-high heat; then sauté the onion until tender. Add the remaining

ingredients, and mix well. Reduce the heat slightly, and stir the mixture for about 15 minutes, or until all the liquid has evaporated, and the flavors have blended. Use the back of a large spoon or a fork to mash the chickpeas with the chicken so the mixture holds together. Set the filling aside to cool.

When the dough has risen, punch it down, and divide it into twenty-four equal pieces. Form each piece into a ball. One at a time, roll out each ball into an oval, about 4 inches by 5 inches. Put a generous tablespoon of the filling on one side of the oval; then fold it in half crosswise to cover the filling. Pinch the edges together very tightly to form a crescent-like shape. Repeat until all the dough pieces are filled.

To fry the turnovers, put oil about 1½ to 2 inches deep in a large saucepan, deep skillet, or electric frypan; then heat it to 375 degrees. Deep-fry the turnovers, a few at a time so they are not crowded, until they are well browned on both sides. Drain them very well on paper toweling.

To bake the turnovers, preheat the oven to 400 degrees. Put the turnovers about 2 inches apart on parchment-lined or greased or nonstick spray-coated baking sheets. Brush the tops with the egg glaze; then prick each turnover with a fork so steam can escape. Bake them at 400 degrees for 15 to 20 minutes, or until they are well browned.

Serve the turnovers warm. Leftovers of either type may be reheated in a 350-degree oven until warmed through.

Makes 24 chicken turnovers.

Variation

BEEF-FILLED SAMBUSIK

For beef filling, omit the oil and the chicken, and cook the chopped onion with 1 pound raw, lean ground beef, breaking up the meat with a fork, until the meat has browned and the onion is tender. Drain off and discard all excess fat. Add all the remaining filling ingredients, and proceed as above.

Chickpeas and Rice Fit-for-a-Queen

We are told that when Queen Esther lived in the palace of King Ahasuerus, she ate only vegetarian fare, particularly peas and beans, so as not to break the dietary laws of kashrut by partaking of nonkosher meat. For this reason, chickpeas—*nahit* in Yiddish; *humus* in Hebrew—have become very traditional for Purim.

The following dish uses herbs and spices common in Middle Eastern cuisine to give ordinary beans and rice a wonderfully exotic flavor and aroma. Furthermore, it is a great way to use up leftover rice, and a perfect pareve side dish for any meal. It is similar to a pilaf.

The mixture can even be stuffed into pita bread for a light vegetarian main course— my family's favorite way to partake of it. When beans and brown rice are eaten together, as in this dish, they actually provide high-quality protein.

I have often used this recipe for cooking classes, and it always seems to surprise my students that such a simple combination can be so deliciously satisfying *and* healthful. Please keep in mind that all the seasonings can be adjusted to your taste.

NOTE: You may use 2 cups leftover plain cooked rice in place of the uncooked rice below. For a more colorful version of this dish, see the Variation.

1 ½ cups water	½ teaspoon dried marjoram leaves
¾ cup uncooked long-grain brown rice	½ teaspoon dried basil leaves
3 tablespoons extra-virgin olive oil	¼ to ½ teaspoon ground cumin
1 large onion, finely chopped	¼ teaspoon ground turmeric
2 garlic cloves, minced	½ teaspoon salt
½ cup warm water	⅛ to ¼ teaspoon ground black pepper
1 (15- to 16-ounce) can chickpeas	
(garbanzo beans), drained	TO SERVE (OPTIONAL)
¼ cup finely chopped fresh parsley	Several loaves of whole wheat or white
leaves or 2 tablespoons dried leaves	Pita (purchased or see page 454)

Put the 1½ cups of water into a small saucepan and bring to a boil. Stir in the rice and cook about 30 to 40 minutes, or until all the water is absorbed. You should have about 2 cups of cooked rice. Set aside. (This can be done several hours in advance, and the rice refrigerated.)

Purim

Put the oil into a large skillet or saucepan over medium-high heat; then sauté the onion and garlic until they are tender. Stir in the ½ cup warm water, cooked rice, chickpeas, parsley, marjoram, basil, cumin, turmeric, salt, and pepper until all are well combined. (Warning: The turmeric may tint a plastic cooking spoon. It changed my blue spoon to green!)

Lower the heat so that the mixture just simmers, and cover the pot. Simmer the mixture, stirring occasionally, for 15 to 20 minutes, or until the flavors have blended. Serve hot or at room temperature. The mixture can be reheated, covered, in a microwave oven.

For a satisfying main course, cut pita loaves in half to form semicircular "pockets," and let diners fill them with the hot chickpea-rice mixture.

Makes about 6 to 8 servings as a side dish; about 3 to 4 servings as a main course.

Variation

SPICED CHICKPEAS AND RICE WITH VEGETABLES

Add to the rice and chickpeas about ½ cup carrot slivers (1-inch carrot sections cut lengthwise into very small "sticks") and about ½ cup frozen green peas. Cook as directed above.

Mock "Spaghetti" and "Meatballs"

This main dish, which contains neither pasta nor meat, reminds us not only of the jocular nature of Purim, but also that Queen Esther chose to be a vegetarian while she lived in the court of King Ahasuerus to ensure that her diet was kosher. According to tradition, her meals included many beans, such as lentils. Although it is highly unlikely she ever ate anything like the dish that follows, it would still be fun to serve it at a Purim Se'udah. That way, both the guests and the food will be in "masquerade"!

What's more, unlike most spaghetti and meatball dinners, this version may be sprinkled with cheese even by those who observe kashrut.

NOTE: The meatless balls can be served with real pasta, if preferred.

MEATLESS BALLS

½ cup dry brown lentils, sorted and
    rinsed

¼ cup uncooked long- or medium-grain
    brown rice

1½ cups cold water

1 large egg or ¼ cup pareve egg
    substitute

½ cup seasoned bread crumbs

¼ cup finely ground pecans or walnuts

1 small onion, grated

¼ teaspoon garlic powder

¼ teaspoon dried oregano leaves

½ teaspoon soy sauce or Worcestershire
    sauce

2 tablespoons chopped fresh parsley
    leaves

"SPAGHETTI"

1 (3- to 4-pound) spaghetti squash

SAUCE AND CHEESE TOPPING

Pareve spaghetti sauce (homemade or
    store-bought)

Grated Parmesan (or similar) cheese
    (optional)

For the meatless balls, put the lentils, rice, and water into a medium saucepan, and bring to a boil over high heat. Lower the heat, and simmer, covered, for 30 to 40 minutes, or until the lentils and rice are very tender. While they are cooking, line a baking sheet or jelly roll pan with baking parchment, or coat it with nonstick cooking spray, or grease it. Set it aside.

Remove the cooked lentils and rice from the heat, and let them rest in the pan for 10 minutes. Meanwhile, preheat the oven to 400 degrees. When the lentils and rice have rested and cooled slightly, use a fork or potato masher to mash them with any remaining water. Add the remaining ingredients to the lentils and rice, and mix very well. Shape the mixture into about thirty 1-inch balls. Place the balls on the prepared baking sheet or pan, keeping them about 1 inch apart. Bake the balls at 400 degrees for about 20 minutes, or until they are firm.

Meanwhile, cook the spaghetti squash. For firm-textured, "pastalike" strands, it is best to cook the squash whole. Pierce it deeply three or four times with a small knife. Bake it in a microwave oven on high for about 20 minutes, rotating it often; then let it rest for 5 to 10 minutes. Or put it into a large pot, and cover it almost entirely with water. Cover the pot, and simmer the squash about 45 minutes. Or bake it in a preheated 350-degree oven for about 1½ hours. In all cases, the squash is done when its surface gives to pressure. If the squash is undercooked, the strands will not come out easily. But if it is overcooked, the strands will be mushy, and not like spaghetti.

Cut the cooked squash in half crosswise, and carefully scoop out and discard the seeds in the center. Then use the tines of a fork to gently pull out and separate the spaghettilike strands.

To serve, arrange the spaghetti squash in a large platter. Top it with meatless balls and spaghetti sauce. If desired, sprinkle grated cheese on top.

Makes about 4 servings.

Classic Cookie Hamantaschen

The record on how hamantaschen came to be a Purim specialty is quite confusing. Some say that poppy-seed-filled pastries called *mohntaschen* were already popular in Ashkenazic cuisine—*mohn* meaning "poppy seeds" and *taschen,* "pockets." Because the word *mohntaschen* sounded so much like the Yiddish pronunciation of *hamantaschen,* the renamed cookies became associated with Purim.

Others say it happened completely the other way around—that Purim cookies called *hamantaschen* came first. These cookies were eventually filled with poppy seeds just because *Homen* (Yiddish for "Haman") and *mohn* sounded so similar.

Whatever their origin, hamantaschen are said to resemble Haman's tricornered hat (although it is unlikely that Persians wore such hats), or perhaps his pockets filled either with bribes or the lots used to decide which day the Jews would be killed. The triangular shape is also supposed to represent the three patriarchs of Judaism—Abraham, Isaac, and Jacob—who spiritually inspired Queen Esther and gave her inner strength.

Israelis eat these same filled cookies for Purim, but call them *oznai haman,* which is Hebrew for "Haman's ears." (See also the recipe for Orejas de Haman, page 316.)

After much experimentation, I developed this recipe for a delicious pareve hamantaschen dough that has a sweet taste and texture that is very similar to the type often produced in Jewish bakeries. The light crust is tender but firm, and it holds its shape well during baking.

This dough is also very easy to mix and use. When made ahead and refrigerated as directed, it is a cinch to roll, cut, and shape. In fact, my children really enjoy helping me prepare these hamantaschen. (The dough can even be rolled out right after it is made. However, it will need more flour so it is not sticky, it will be a little harder to work with, and the resulting cookies will not be quite as tender.)

A pleasant surprise is that this excellent dough is made exclusively with heart-healthy monounsaturated oil, and it works quite well with egg substitute. Because egg substitute is pasteurized, there is no need to worry about young helpers touching or eating the raw dough.

While I've included an easy, flexible recipe for Fruit Filling (page 311), I find that many canned fillings produce delicious hamantaschen. Generally, I am a purist about cooking from "scratch," but this is one case in which I don't mind using a good convenience product in a pinch. I have a few caveats, however. Personally, I prefer not to use *pie* fillings because they are too soft and loose. Fillings made specifically for pastries and cookies tend to be thicker and drier (though not always). If the filling is too thin or soft, the resulting hamantaschen will be flat rather than high—a problem I have had with plain apricot filling. Please feel free to "enhance" canned fillings with chopped dried fruit, chopped nuts, light or dark raisins, lemon juice, etc.

In general, it's best to try baking a few cookies with a filling you have not yet tried before using it for a whole batch.

NOTES: For best results, be sure to use large (*not* extra-large) eggs, and measure the flour by spooning it into the appropriate cups and then leveling the top with a knife.

A very clean, empty tuna can with both ends and the label removed makes a perfect cutter. I have used the same one for years. Or for a decorative look, use a round cutter with a crimped edge.

DOUGH

4 large eggs or 1 cup pareve egg
    substitute
1⅓ cups sugar
¾ cup canola oil
2 teaspoons vanilla extract
1 tablespoon baking powder
½ teaspoon salt
4¾ cups all-purpose flour (see Notes)

FILLING SUGGESTIONS

"Your Choice" Hamantaschen Fruit
    Filling (page 311) or about 1½ to 2
    (12-ounce) cans pastry filling, such
    as poppy seed, prune, or cherry
Poppy Seed Filling for Honey
    Hamantaschen (page 313)

In a large bowl, by hand or with a heavy-duty mixer, beat the eggs with the sugar until well combined; then beat in the oil and vanilla extract. Beat in the baking powder and salt. Add the flour gradually, blending well after each

addition. Continue mixing the dough well until it is completely combined. It will be stiff but somewhat sticky. Turn out half the dough onto each of two sheets of plastic wrap. Using the wrap, press each piece of dough into a thick disk and wrap it well. Refrigerate the dough for several hours or overnight, until it is very cold and firm.

(To use the dough immediately, without refrigeration, turn it out onto a floured board and knead it gently, adding flour as needed, just until it smooth and not sticky. Then roll out the dough as directed, using only a little flour. Do not roll the dough too thin, or it will be too soft to shape.)

To bake the hamantaschen, preheat the oven to 350 degrees. Line several large shiny baking sheets (preferably insulated or thick aluminum) with baking parchment or coat them with nonstick cooking spray.

Take one of the chilled disks of dough from the refrigerator, and remove the wrap. Completely coat the dough on all sides with flour. Roll it out on a well-floured flat surface (I use a scrupulously clean countertop) until it is slightly less than ¼ inch thick. Try to keep the thickness of the whole piece of dough as even as possible, and use additional flour if necessary to keep the dough from sticking.

  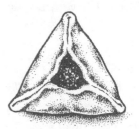

Use a 3-inch cutter to cut out as many circles as possible in the dough (see Notes). Use a pastry scraper or metal spatula to loosen a dough circle then put a very generous teaspoon of filling in its center. Fold up the edges of the circle in thirds around the filling to form a pocket with a triangular base, and pinch the edges together, leaving a small opening in the center of the hamantasch where the filling can be seen. (Hint: First fold two edges up and pinch them together to form a sort of cornucopia around the filling, then fold up the third edge [the opening of the cornucopia], and pinch it on each side to the other two edges.) If you are having trouble getting the edges to stick

together easily, dip your index finger into a cup of water and lightly moisten any edges that won't stick. Or moisten the whole perimeter of each flat dough circle just before you fold it.

As each hamantasch is made, place it on the prepared baking sheet, keeping the hamantaschen at least 1 inch apart. Repeat until all the circles cut from the first piece of dough are filled. Then collect the dough scraps, gently combine them without handling the dough too much, and roll, cut, and fill them as above (using much less flour), until all the dough is used. Repeat the whole process for the second refrigerated half of the dough. Bake the first batch of hamantaschen while forming the remainder.

Bake the hamantaschen at 350 degrees for about 20 to 25 minutes, or until they are firm and very lightly browned. Cool them on the baking sheet for 2 to 3 minutes, then transfer them to a wire rack to cool completely. (If using parchment, you can slide the whole piece of paper with the hamantaschen on it to a cooling rack, and let them cool on the paper if desired. Or remove the hamantaschen from the parchment and use it again for another batch.) Store the hamantaschen in an airtight container at room temperature. They will stay fresh for several days, or freeze for longer storage.

Makes about 30 large hamantaschen.

"Your Choice" Hamantaschen Fruit Filling

My family is very particular about hamantaschen filling. They want only poppy seed! They are not interested in apricot or raspberry, *lekvar* (prune butter), or *povidl* (plum butter). Poppy seed is my favorite, too, but sometimes I get in the mood for variety. I want to see a medley of colors and textures peeking out of the hamantaschen on my *shalach manos* platters. Some canned fruit fillings work well, but when I feel like really being creative, the following flexible recipe is very easy and quick.

Furthermore, it makes a lovely textured filling in which you can taste little pieces of dried fruit. I happen to like that, but if it doesn't please you, simply put the cooked filling into a food processor and process to the smoothness you desire.

Because the moistness and sweetness of dried fruit varies tremendously, this recipe

should be used as a basic guideline. Please don't hesitate to change the quantities of liquid and sweetener to suit your particular needs. I have assumed that most cooks will want to make more than one type of filling, so I have kept the proportions small. The recipe can be doubled if desired.

NOTE: Some suggestions for dried fruit include prunes, apricots, pears, peaches, or possibly pitted cherries. You can use all the same kind of fruit, or a mixture of two for an unusual taste. "Fresh" dried fruit that is soft and tender is the easiest to chop and will work best in the filling; tougher dried fruit may need more liquid and time to cook to the right texture.

BASIC FILLING
8 ounces soft dried fruit (see Note)
¾ to 1 cup orange juice, or as needed
¼ cup mild-flavored honey
2 tablespoons sugar, or to taste
1 tablespoon lemon juice

OPTIONAL ADDITIONS
¼ cup finely chopped walnuts or
  almonds, or to taste
Ground cinnamon or ginger to taste
¼ cup soft light or dark raisins

Use a cutting board and a large, sharp knife to very finely chop the dried fruit. If the fruit is soft, this should not be difficult. The fruit does not need to be cut in neat, even pieces. Press the chopped fruit gently into a glass 2-cup measuring cup; it should measure about 1½ cups.

Put the dried fruit, ¾ cup of the juice, honey, sugar, and lemon juice into a small (1½- to 2-quart) saucepan, preferably nonstick, and mix them well. Place the saucepan over medium-high heat, and bring the mixture to a boil. Lower the heat, and simmer, stirring often, for 5 minutes. Then continue heating, while stirring constantly, for an additional 7 to 10 minutes, or until the fruit is very soft and all the juice has been cooked into the fruit. The filling should have the consistency of very thick preserves, and the fruit should be quite soft. If necessary, add additional juice and continue stirring and cooking to soften the fruit sufficiently.

Remove the filling from the heat and let it cool slightly. Carefully taste the hot filling, and stir in additional sugar if it is needed. Be sure to stir until the sugar is completely dissolved. (If the fruit is still not soft enough, you can stir in additional juice and return the filling to the heat to cook it into the fruit.)

Let the filling cool to lukewarm, stirring occasionally. If nuts, cinnamon, ginger, and/or raisins are desired, stir them in to suit your taste. The fruit filling may be used as is if a coarse texture is desired, or it may be briefly processed in a food processor to make it smoother. Let the filling cool to room temperature before it is used. It may be chilled in the refrigerator, and can be used when chilled. (It will thicken more when chilled.)

The fruit filling can be made up to a week ahead, and refrigerated, tightly covered, until needed. Or it may be frozen for several months.

Makes about 1¼ to 1½ cups fruit filling; enough for 24 to 36 hamantaschen.

Honey Hamantaschen with Poppy Seed Filling

FILLED TRIANGULAR COOKIES

For me, Purim simply wouldn't be Purim without hamantaschen bulging with rich, dark, moist poppy seed filling—perhaps the "original" filling. In fact, my family and I enjoy them so much that I make them year-round.

The following cookie dough contains honey and brown sugar, making it quite different from most hamantaschen recipes. The cookie "crust" is quite tasty, and goes very well with a poppy seed filling; however, it does tend to soften after baking. If you prefer a crunchier cookie, try the Classic Cookie Hamantaschen (page 308). Both recipes produce a dough that is easy to roll and shape.

The filling directions suggest grinding the poppy seeds. I have had the most success doing this with an electric coffee bean grinder. I bought an inexpensive one that I use exclusively for poppy seeds. A blender also works, though not as easily. A food processor swirls the seeds around but does not grind them properly, unless you have a mini-bowl attachment, which may work.

If the homemade filling is too much trouble, use one of the delicious canned poppy seed fillings available at many supermarkets. Of all the flavors of canned filling, poppy seed is probably the best, and I often use it to save time.

DOUGH

½ cup butter or margarine, softened

¼ cup packed light or dark brown sugar

¼ cup honey

2 large eggs or ½ cup pareve egg
substitute

1 teaspoon vanilla extract

1 teaspoon baking powder

½ teaspoon baking soda

2½ cups all-purpose flour (may be half
whole wheat)

POPPY SEED FILLING

1 cup (about 5 ounces) poppy seeds

⅔ cup milk or water

¼ cup honey

3 tablespoons granulated sugar, or to
taste

¼ cup raisins or currants

2 tablespoons butter, margarine, or
canola oil

2 teaspoons lemon juice

For the dough, use an electric mixer at medium speed to cream the butter with the brown sugar and honey in a medium bowl until light and fluffy. Beat in the eggs and vanilla. Then mix in the baking powder, baking soda, and flour until very well combined. The dough will be slightly sticky. Divide the dough in half, and wrap each half in plastic; then press it into a thick disk. Refrigerate the disks for several hours or overnight, until firm and very cold.

Meanwhile, make the poppy seed filling. Grind the poppy seeds in a blender, a very clean coffee grinder, or a food processor with a minibowl, until most of the seeds are broken up. (If the seeds cannot be ground, they may be used whole; however, the texture of the filling will not be as fine and the flavor not as rich.)

Put the ground poppy seeds into a small saucepan with the remaining filling ingredients. Cook over medium heat, stirring frequently, for about 10 to 12 minutes or until the mixture is very thick and almost all the liquid has been absorbed. Stir constantly toward the end of the cooking period. Remove the filling from the heat, and let it cool slightly; then taste it, and stir in additional sugar if needed. Stir until any added sugar is completely dissolved. Chill the filling before using it. (The filling may be made ahead, and refrigerated, covered, for several days.)

To bake the hamantaschen, preheat the oven to 350 degrees. Line two large, shiny baking sheets (preferably insulated or made of thick aluminum) with baking parchment or coat them with nonstick cooking spray.

Take one chilled disk of dough from the refrigerator, and remove the wrap. Completely coat the dough on all sides with flour. Pound it gently with

the side of the rolling pin to flatten it slightly; then roll it out on a floured flat surface (I use a scrupulously clean countertop) until it is slightly more than ⅛ inch thick. Try to keep the thickness as even as possible, and use additional flour if necessary to keep the dough from sticking.

Use a 3-inch cutter to cut out as many circles as possible in the dough. (Hint: A very clean, empty tuna can with both ends and the label removed makes a perfect cutter. I have used the same one for years.) Use a pastry scraper or metal spatula to loosen a dough circle; then put a very generous teaspoon of filling in its center. Fold up the edges of the circle in thirds up around the filling to form a pocket with a triangular base, and pinch the edges together tightly, leaving a small opening in the center of the hamantasch where the filling can be seen. (Hint: First fold two edges up and pinch them together to form a sort of cornucopia around the filling, then fold up the third edge [the opening of the cornucopia], and pinch it on each side to the other two edges.) If you are having trouble getting the edges to stick together easily, dip your index finger into a cup of water, and use it to lightly moisten any edges that won't stick. Or moisten the whole perimeter of each flat dough circle just before you fold it.

As each hamantasch is made, place it on the prepared baking sheet. Repeat until all the circles are filled, keeping the hamantaschen at least 1 inch apart on the baking sheets. Then collect the dough scraps, gently combine them without handling the dough too much, and roll, cut, and fill them as above until all the dough is used. Repeat with the second disk of dough. Bake the first batch of hamantaschen while forming the remainder.

Bake the hamantaschen at 350 degrees for about 15 to 18 minutes, or until they are very lightly browned and firm. Cool them on the baking sheet for 2 to 3 minutes, then transfer them to a wire rack to cool completely.

Makes about 24 hamantaschen.

Orejas de Haman
SEPHARDIC-STYLE "HAMAN'S EARS" COOKIES

P

During Purim, different parts of Haman are symbolically cooked and eaten as a way to mock this wicked enemy of the Jews. For instance, Ashkenazic Jews in the Diaspora always nosh on hamantaschen, which represent his hat or pockets. In Israel, the same triangular filled cookies are usually called *oznai haman,* Hebrew for "Haman's ear," implying that the man had pretty strange ears. Actually, the appellation probably came about because it was an old custom to cut off a condemned criminal's ears before execution.

Jews from many other countries also eat "Haman's ears," but these are usually made of deep-fried twisted noodle dough, which does resemble that designated part of Haman's anatomy. All are quite similar to the Sephardic *orejas de haman* that follow, though some are shaped in a slightly different manner. Among these Purim treats are North African *hojuelos de haman,* Greek *aftia tou amman,* Dutch *hamansooren,* German *hamman-mutzen,* Italian *orecchi di aman,* Swiss *schunzuchen,* and Austrian *heizenblauzen.* Some are traditionally coated with a sugar-honey syrup like that used with many fried Hanukkah treats. Others are simply sprinkled with confectioners' sugar, as is done in the recipe below.

Interestingly, Jews from Persia, where the story of Esther took place, eat no hamantaschen or "Haman's ears" of any type for Purim, but rather an assortment of other rich cookies.

2 large eggs	Pinch of salt
2 tablespoons canola oil	About 2 cups unbleached flour
3 tablespoons water	Canola oil for deep frying
3 tablespoons granulated sugar	Confectioners' sugar for coating
1 teaspoon baking powder	

In a medium bowl, use a fork to beat together the eggs, oil, water, sugar, baking powder, and salt. Gradually beat in enough flour to make a soft, slightly sticky dough. On a lightly floured board, knead the dough for 2 to 3 minutes, adding sprinkles of flour as needed, or until it is very smooth. Wrap it in plastic, and let it rest 30 minutes to 1 hour. (The dough may be made in advance and refrigerated overnight. Let it warm to room temperature before using it.)

On a lightly floured cutting surface, roll out half of the dough until it is very thin and translucent, no more than 1⁄16 inch thick. If it becomes resistant, cover it with plastic wrap so that it doesn't dry out, and let it rest a few minutes; then continue to roll it out. (Keep the unused dough wrapped.)

In a saucepan, deep skillet, or electric frypan, heat oil about 1½ to 2 inches deep until it is hot, about 375 degrees. While the oil is heating, cut out the cookies as follows.

For the easiest cookies, use a pastry wheel (one with a fluted edge gives an attractive look) or a sharp knife to cut the dough into strips that are 1 to 1½ inches wide and about 4 inches long, or into random shapes approximating that size. Then pinch each strip in the middle or twist it, for an interesting "earlike" look.

For cookies that more closely resemble ears, cut out 3-inch-diameter circles of dough (a very clean, empty tuna can be used); then cut each circle in half. Pinch up a pleat across the radius of each half-circle to form a raised bump.

Or use the side of a round 3-inch-diameter cookie cutter to cut large crescent shapes from the edge of the dough. Pinch each crescent in the center like a bow tie, to form earlike shapes.

NOTE: Because these cookies also look like a pair of little "leaves," they are sometimes called *hojuelos* in Judeo-Spanish, which means "leaflets."

Another technique is to cut long, narrow strips, about ¾ inch by 6 inches, and bring the ends together in the center to form two open loops. Pinch the middle tightly (or moisten the dough very lightly) to make sure the dough sticks together.

Gently drop the formed cookies into the oil. Fry only a few cookies at a time, so that they are not crowded. They will puff considerably as soon as they are in the oil. Turn the cookies with tongs or a slotted spoon so that they cook evenly. As soon as they are lightly browned and very crisp (about 1 minute), remove them from the oil, and drain them well on paper toweling. Roll out the second half of the dough, and repeat the cutting and frying. When all the cookies have been fried, coat them well with sieved confectioners' sugar. Store them in an airtight container.

Makes about 50 to 70 cookies, depending on their size.

Gingerbread Hamans (or Esthers)

Mean-looking gingerbread men that represent the wicked Haman are baked by Dutch and Scandinavian Jews for Purim. Like many other treats of this holiday, these cookies mock Haman, as children delight in biting off his head and limbs. The kids also have great fun cutting and baking these cookies, and then decorating them with scowling or grimacing faces.

In the interest of fairness to children of *both* genders (including my only daughter), I also bake "gingerbread ladies," which we decorate as the beautiful Queen Esther (most little girls' favorite character in the story). Of course, these lady cookies are adorned with smiles and lovely hair. And I hope that the Queen Esther cookies are eaten in a more respectful fashion than the Hamans!

This gingerbread dough handles very easily and holds its shape well when cutting little arms and legs. I use a set of four plastic cookie cutters that includes a large man-and-woman pair, which are each 5 inches tall, as well as a miniature pair that are only 2 inches tall. I like to make some gingerbread people of each size. The larger ones are much easier to decorate, but the smaller ones go farther. Both look great on *shalach manos* platters.

NOTES: For a strong spicy flavor (or if your spices are not very fresh), use the larger amounts of ginger and cinnamon.

Measure the flour by spooning it into the cup, and then leveling the top with a knife. Unbleached flour will make slightly flatter, chewier cookies than regular all-purpose, but the latter can be used if desired.

As with most spiced cookies, these have better taste and texture the day after they are made, when they have had some time to mellow.

DOUGH

½ cup canola oil

½ cup light or dark molasses

⅔ cup sugar

1 large egg or ¼ cup pareve egg substitute

1½ to 2 teaspoons ground ginger (see Notes)

½ to 1 teaspoon ground cinnamon (see Notes)

½ teaspoon ground nutmeg

½ teaspoon salt

1 teaspoon baking soda

3 cups unbleached or all-purpose flour (see Notes)

Icing for Decorating
About ½ cup confectioners' sugar
Water

For the dough, put the oil, molasses, and sugar into a mixer bowl, and beat with an electric mixer until completely combined. (Hint: If the same measuring cup is used first for the oil, and then for the molasses, the molasses will slide right out.) Add the egg, and beat until it is completely incorporated. Add the ginger, cinnamon, nutmeg, salt, and baking soda, and beat just until they are mixed in. Finally, add the flour, 1 cup at a time, beating until each addition of flour is mixed in. The dough should come away from the sides of the bowl, and not be very sticky. Gather it into a ball, and knead it gently a few times or until it is very smooth. Divide the dough in half, and place each half on a large piece of plastic wrap, and press it into a thick disk. Wrap the dough, and chill it in the refrigerator at least 1 hour, up to overnight, until it is firm.

Preheat the oven to 350 degrees. Line several sturdy shiny metal baking sheets with parchment (for the nicest-looking cookie shapes), coat them with nonstick cooking spray, or grease them lightly. Set aside.

Remove one piece of dough from the refrigerator, and coat all the surfaces with flour. Firmly tap the dough with the side of a rolling pin to soften it slightly; then roll it out on a floured surface to ³⁄₁₆ inch thick, turning it over occasionally to make sure it is not sticking. (If the dough is too stiff to roll out easily or it cracks, let it warm slightly and try again.)

Brush any excess flour off the top of the dough. Use large and small "people" cookie cutters to press out shapes in the dough, keeping the shapes very close together to minimize scraps.

Use a large metal spatula or dough scraper to transfer the cookies to the prepared baking sheets, keeping them at least 1 inch apart. Collect all scraps into a ball, and reroll and cut the dough, using less flour than the first time.

Bake the cookies at 350 degrees for about 8 to 11 minutes (depending on the size of the people), or until the tops are firm and a fingertip pressed very lightly on a cookie doesn't leave an imprint. If you like the cookies chewy rather than crunchy, be careful not to overbake them. Cool the cookies on the baking sheets for 2 minutes, then use a clean metal spatula to transfer the shapes to wire racks to cool completely.

For the icing, put the confectioners' sugar into a small bowl, and add water a few drops at a time until a thick icing is formed. Spoon the icing into a small plastic freezer bag, seal the top, and cut a tiny hole in one corner. Squeeze the icing through the hole in a thin line, and use it to draw a face and maybe clothes on each cookie. (Hint: Try squeezing the icing on wax paper first. If the icing is too thick to squeeze, add a drop or two of water. If it spreads too easily, stir in some more confectioners' sugar.)

To give Haman a scowling look, have his eyebrows point in and downward and draw his mouth in a frown. Put a happy smile on Queen Esther, and add hair around her face and pretty designs on her gown. Let the icing dry completely before serving or storing the cookies. Store them in airtight containers for several days. For best taste and texture, serve a day or two after they are made (if you can wait!).

Makes about 70 tiny people cookies, or about 18 to 20 large people cookies, or an assortment, the number depending on the size of the cutters.

Baklava

MANY-LAYERED PASTRY WITH NUTS AND HONEY

This luscious flaky dessert is a Purim favorite of Sephardim from many lands. It is also very popular during the Days of Awe, because it contains honey, and thus signifies a hope for a sweet year.

Each group of Sephardim uses a slightly different filling and honey syrup for the pastry. The following version is based on that of Turkish and Greek Jews, who typically call it *baklava* (with a *v*).

Those from the Middle East often prefer pistachio nuts in the filling, and rose water in the syrup. Iraqi and Persian Jews usually use ground almonds spiced with cardamom in their filling, and they also like rose-water-flavored syrup. Jews from Arabic countries generally call the dessert *baklawa* (with a "w"), its Arabic name.

Though the recipe is a bit time-consuming, it makes a lot of baklava, which will keep for at least a week at room temperature or can be frozen for several months.

321

NOTE: This dessert is made with filo. See the Glossary of Ingredients for details on purchasing and using this thin pastry.

FILLING
4 cups (about 1 pound) finely chopped walnuts (or a mixture of walnuts and blanched almonds)
¼ cup sugar
2 teaspoons ground cinnamon
¼ teaspoon ground allspice
¼ teaspoon ground cloves

PASTRY
½ cup unsalted butter or margarine
3 tablespoons canola oil
2 tablespoons hot water

1 (1-pound) package filo sheets (about 20 to 22 sheets), at room temperature (see Note)

HONEY SYRUP
1 cup water
1 cup sugar
Shredded peel from 1 medium lemon, yellow part only
½ cup plus 2 tablespoons honey
Juice of 1 medium lemon (about 2 tablespoons)

For the filling, mix together the chopped nuts, sugar, cinnamon, allspice, and cloves. Set aside.

HINT: If a food processor fitted with a steel blade is used to chop the nuts, have the nuts at room temperature and chop them with all the other filling ingredients. This will keep them from becoming pasty.

In a small saucepan over medium-low heat or in the microwave oven, slowly melt the butter or margarine; then stir in the oil and hot water. Cover the pan, and keep the mixture warm over very low heat until it is needed. Preheat the oven to 350 degrees.

Remove the filo from its plastic package, and unfold it so it lies flat. Keep it covered with a slightly damp cloth. Dip the tip of a large pastry brush into the butter-oil mixture, and use it to grease the bottom and sides of a sturdy 10 by 15 by 1-inch jelly roll pan or slightly larger pan. (Do not use a nonstick pan with a coating that cannot be cut with a knife, as the baklava must be cut in the pan.)

Use a sharp knife or scissors to trim the stack of filo so that the sheets are slightly larger than the pan. (Discard the trimmings or reserve them for another use.)

Purim

Spread out one sheet of filo in the bottom of the pan. Brush it lightly with the butter-oil mixture. Cover with another sheet, and butter that one. Repeat the procedure until there are five stacked, buttered sheets. Sprinkle about ⅔ cup of the nut filling evenly over the filo, making sure that some goes to the edges of the pan. (Use your hand to smooth out the filling so the nuts are not piled in any spots.)

Stack two more sheets on top, buttering each; then sprinkle with another ⅔ cup of the filling. Repeat this process—that is, stack two sheets and sprinkle them with filling four more times, using up all the nut filling. Top with the remaining sheets of filo (there should be at least five), buttering each, including the top. Score the pastry (to allow it to absorb syrup and be cut after it has baked) by using a small, sharp knife to cut *halfway* down the layered sheets.

To make the traditional diamond shapes, cut a large *X* across the pan from corner to corner; then make parallel cuts about 2 inches wide following the main arms of the *X*. (There will be little triangles in the corners and along the edges, but the rest of the pieces will be diamonds.)

For triangles, make three lengthwise parallel cuts and five crosswise parallel cuts to make large rectangles; then cut the rectangles diagonally in half so each forms two triangles.

The pastry may instead be cut into small squares or rectangles, about 2½ to 3 inches on a side.

Sprinkle any remaining butter mixture on top; then sprinkle on a few drops of water or spray the top lightly with a water mister. Bake the baklava at 350 degrees for 1 hour. (If the top is browning too rapidly, cover it loosely with a piece of foil.)

As soon as the baklava is in the oven, prepare the syrup. In a medium saucepan, combine the water, sugar, lemon peel, and ½ cup of the honey. Slowly warm the mixture over medium heat, stirring occasionally, until the sugar completely dissolves. Then bring the syrup to a boil and gently boil it, uncovered and undisturbed, for 10 minutes (or until it reaches 212 degrees on a candy thermometer). Remove the syrup from the heat, and stir in the remaining 2 tablespoons honey and the lemon juice. Set the syrup aside to cool at room temperature.

When the baklava is done baking, remove it from the oven, and immediately pour the cooled syrup evenly over the top. Cut all the way through the scored lines to separate the pieces. Leave the baklava in the pan, and let it rest, loosely

covered with aluminum foil, at room temperature for at least 4 hours (preferably overnight) before eating. Store at room temperature for up to 1 week. After the syrup has been absorbed, the baklava may be covered more securely.

(For a longer period, wrap the baklava well and freeze. Thaw it in the refrigerator, then store at room temperature.)

Makes about 40 to 50 pieces, depending on how the baklava is cut.

Menenas

DATE-FILLED COOKIES

I first learned about *menenas* from Lily Livne, an Israeli Jew who was born in Egypt. Because Mrs. Livne had a bit of difficulty with English, her teenage daughter acted as interpreter during our interview. As soon as I mentioned Purim, the young girl insisted that her mother give me the recipe for these cookies, a family favorite.

Further research turned up a variety of similar date-filled cookies that other groups of Sephardic Jews traditionally prepare for Purim. For instance, there are Persian *klaitcha,* Syrian *ras-ib-adjvah,* and Middle Eastern *ma'aroot* and *ma'amool.*

The cookies all use a shortbread dough, which is sometimes made with semolina, and may or may not include an egg. They are filled with dates that have been gently cooked until they "melt" into a soft paste. Chopped walnuts and cinnamon are often added to the filling, and occasionally also nutmeg and cloves.

The cookies are formed in a variety of different ways. Often, the dough is rolled out and cut into circles, or shaped into walnut-sized balls that are each patted out into a circle. A small ball of date filling is put on the center of each circle. The dough is then brought up around the filling to enclose it, and the filled cookies rolled in the hands to form smooth balls. The cookies may be left as balls. They also may be formed into egg shapes or flattened into disks. For *ma'amool,* each round ball is usually pressed against a wooden mold called a *tabi,* to give it an ornate surface design.

Sometimes, the date filling is shaped into tiny "sausages," which are laid across the circles of dough. The dough is folded over the log to form a semicircle, and the edges pinched tightly closed. Or the dough may be rolled around the "sausage," and then bent into a crescent shape.

For the easiest cookies of all, a portion of the dough is rolled out into a long, narrow rectangle, and part of the date filling is formed into a large log. The dough is brought up around the log to enclose it. Cookies are cut from this large roll. Details for this technique follow below. (A further variation of this method involves spreading the date paste in a thin layer over the dough rectangle, and then rolling up the dough as with a filled jelly roll.)

Menenas are now a favorite in my own family; in fact, I usually double the recipe when I make them. And I often put them on my *shalach manos* platters. I find it easiest to mix up the dough and cook the filling on one day, and then fill and bake the cookies the day after. That way, this recipe is not very time-consuming or tedious.

NOTE: This recipe is easily doubled. Simply use twice the amounts of all the ingredients, and make four rolls instead of two as directed below.

DOUGH
½ cup butter or margarine, softened
½ cup granulated sugar
1 large egg or ¼ cup pareve egg
*   substitute*
½ teaspoon vanilla extract
1¾ cups all-purpose flour

FILLING
8 ounces pitted dates, chopped
2 tablespoons butter or margarine
¼ cup water
½ cup finely chopped walnuts
¼ teaspoon ground cinnamon (optional)

TO SERVE (OPTIONAL)
Confectioners' sugar

First, prepare the dough. Put the butter and sugar in a mixing bowl, and use an electric mixer at medium speed to cream them together. Beat in the egg and vanilla. Then stir in the flour to make a stiff dough. Wrap the dough in plastic wrap, pressing it into a rectangle, and refrigerate for at least 1 hour, or overnight, until firm.

Meanwhile, prepare the filling. Combine the dates, butter, and water in a medium saucepan. Stir the dates constantly over low heat, mashing them with the back of a spoon, until they soften considerably and form a thick paste. (If the dates are very dry, a little more water may be needed.) Remove the date mixture from the heat, and stir in the walnuts and cinnamon (if used). Refrigerate the date mixture, stirring it occasionally, until it is very stiff and cool enough to be handled, about 20 minutes. (If desired, the date mixture may be refrigerated overnight. In that case, it will not need to be stirred.)

Preheat the oven to 350 degrees. Line a large shiny metal baking sheet with baking parchment, coat it with nonstick cooking spray, or grease it. Set it aside.

Divide the chilled dough in half, and roll out each half into a 10 by 4-inch rectangle of very even thickness. Check the measurements with a ruler, and if necessary cut pieces of excess from one edge and attach them to another to get the right size. There should be no leftover dough.

Divide the date filling in half, and use moistened hands to form each half into a log about 9½ inches long. Place one log lengthwise on each rectangle, and bring up the dough over the log to enclose it (as if wrapping a package). Pinch the long edges of the dough together, and pinch the ends tightly closed.

Put the filled rolls seam side down on the prepared baking sheet, keeping them about 2 inches apart. Bake them at 350 degrees for about 25 minutes, or until the bottoms are lightly browned and the tops are firm but still white. Cool the rolls for 5 minutes on the baking sheet; then carefully transfer them to a wire rack to cool to room temperature.

Put the cooled rolls on a wooden board or other cutting surface, and use a sharp knife to cut them crosswise (or diagonally) into ½- to ¾-inch slices. If desired, sprinkle the cookies with sieved confectioners' sugar before serving them.

Makes about 24 to 36 cookies, depending on the thickness of the slices.

Variation

SPIRAL MENENAS

With this version of *menenas,* the date filling has a spiral look. To make them, prepare the dough as directed above. Prepare the filling as directed above, but omit the walnuts. Cool the filling at room temperature (or let it warm to room temperature, if it was chilled) so that it is soft enough to spread. Roll out each half of the dough to a 10 by 7-inch rectangle using the above directions. Use a spatula to spread half of the filling evenly over each rectangle, keeping it ½ inch from all edges. Roll up the dough like a jelly roll, beginning at a long edge. Pinch the edge and ends tightly closed. Bake and slice the filled rolls as directed above.

Travados
WALNUT-FILLED CRESCENT COOKIES

P

This is another of the delectable sweet pastries made by many Sephardic Jews especially for Purim. The oil-based dough is similar to that used for savory Borekas (page 492). After baking, the cookies are traditionally dipped into hot sugar-honey syrup, but confectioners' sugar may be used instead.

FILLING
1 cup very finely chopped walnuts
3 tablespoons sugar
1/4 teaspoon ground cinnamon
1/8 teaspoon ground cloves
1 1/2 tablespoons honey

DOUGH
1/2 cup canola oil
1/4 cup water
1/4 cup sugar

1/4 teaspoon baking soda
2 cups all-purpose flour

SYRUP (OPTIONAL)
2/3 cup granulated sugar
1/3 cup water
2 tablespoons honey
1 teaspoon lemon juice

COATING (IF SYRUP IS NOT USED)
Confectioners' sugar

Preheat the oven to 350 degrees. Line a large shiny metal baking sheet with baking parchment, coat it with nonstick cooking spray, or grease it. Set it aside.

For the filling, combine all the ingredients, and mix them well until they hold together. If the walnuts are still quite dry and crumbly, add a bit more honey. Set aside.

For the dough, mix the oil, water, and sugar in a medium bowl. Add the baking soda and flour, and stir to make a soft, nonsticky dough. If the dough is very sticky, add a bit more flour; if it is crumbly, add a little water. Gather the dough into a smooth ball. Do not knead it or mix it too much. Form the dough into small circles using either of the following techniques.

For the more traditional method, shape the dough into about twenty-five walnut-size balls; then, on a lightly floured surface, either pat out each ball with your fingertips or roll it out to an approximately 2½-inch-diameter circle that is ⅛ inch thick. (Usually, with this technique, each circle is filled as soon as it is flattened out.)

For very uniform circles, roll out all the dough on a lightly floured surface until it is ⅛ inch thick. Use a 2½-inch circular cookie cutter to cut out circles. Reroll any scraps, and cut them out. There should be about twenty-five circles.

To fill the circles made by either method, put a teaspoon of the filling on each circle, then fold it over to form a half-moon or crescent. Pinch the edges tightly together. Put the cookies about 1 inch apart on the prepared baking sheets and bake them at 350 degrees for about 25 to 30 minutes, or until they are lightly browned. Remove them from the baking sheets and cool on wire racks.

If syrup is desired, make it while the cookies are cooling. Put the sugar, water, honey, and lemon juice into a 1½- to 2-quart saucepan and slowly bring the mixture to a boil over medium-high heat, stirring only until the sugar dissolves. Lower the heat, and boil the syrup, uncovered and undisturbed, for 10 minutes. Use tongs or a slotted spoon to dip each cookie in the hot syrup, draining it well. Then let the cookies cool on a platter before storing them.

If the syrup is not used, lightly coat the cookies with confectioners' sugar. Store the cookies in an airtight container.

Makes about 25 cookies.

Mohn Kichelah

QUEEN ESTHER'S POPPY SEED COOKIES

Many Ashkenazic Jews eat these light, crunchy poppy seed cookies throughout the year, but they are particularly favored during Purim. They are sometimes called "Queen Esther's cookies" to remind us how she eschewed the nonkosher food in King Ahasuerus's palace and lived instead on ordinary beans and seeds, including poppy seeds.

The cookie dough may be used to make "drop" cookies, or rolled out and cut into shapes. Occasionally, these cookies are cut to look like the characters in the *Megillah*.

¹/₂ cup butter or pareve margarine,
   softened
¹/₂ cup sugar
1 large egg or ¹/₄ cup pareve egg
   substitute
1 tablespoon water

¹/₂ teaspoon vanilla extract
¹/₄ teaspoon almond extract
¹/₄ to ¹/₃ cup poppy seeds
¹/₂ teaspoon baking powder
2 cups all-purpose flour

For the dough, put the butter and sugar into a medium mixing bowl and use a heavy-duty electric mixer or a wooden spoon to cream them together until they are light and fluffy. Beat in the egg, water, vanilla extract, and almond extract. Then mix in the poppy seeds and baking powder. Add the flour, and mix to form a very stiff dough. The dough may now be used for the traditional, rolled-out cookies, or it may easily be made into drop cookies. For both types, line a large shiny metal baking sheet with baking parchment, coat it with nonstick cooking spray, or grease it. Set it aside.

For rolled cookies: Form the dough into a thick disk, wrap it in plastic or wax paper, and refrigerate it for several hours up to overnight, or until it is quite firm. Preheat the oven to 350 degrees. Roll out the chilled dough on a lightly floured surface until it is about ⅛ inch thick, and cut it into any desired shapes. Squares, circles, and triangles are most common; however, cookie cutters may be used for more elaborate designs. Reroll the scraps and cut out more cookies until the dough is completely used. Refrigerate any dough that becomes difficult to handle.

Use a large metal spatula or pancake turner to carefully transfer the cut-out cookies to the prepared baking sheets, leaving about ½ inch between each cookie. Bake the cookies at 350 degrees for about 10 to 12 minutes, or until they are firm, with lightly browned edges. Remove the cookies from the baking sheets with the metal spatula or pancake turner, and cool them on wire racks.

Drop cookies can be made as soon as the dough is mixed; chilling is not necessary. Preheat the oven to 350 degrees. Drop teaspoonfuls of the dough onto the prepared baking sheets; then flatten the mounds slightly with a floured fork, your fingertips, or the bottom of a glass. Bake the cookies at 350 degrees for about 15 minutes, or until they are firm, with lightly browned edges. Remove the cookies from the baking sheets with a metal spatula, and

cool them on wire racks. (Drop cookies will be smaller and thicker than the rolled-out ones.)

Makes about 30 to 50 cookies, depending on the size.

Marzipan "Petits Fours," Moroccan-Style
ALMOND PASTE CONFECTIONS

Many Jews enjoy marzipan during Purim, when it may be called "the bread of Morde-cai." The following dainty "petits fours" (a French term meaning small sweets) feature nuggets of golden marzipan stuffed into dried fruits or sandwiched between nut halves. The completed confections are beautiful and delicious, and are not very difficult to make. In fact, children can help with the project. And the petits fours are truly an excellent choice for *shalach manos* food gifts. They never cease to impress!

Marzipan—also called *masapan* or *almendrada* by Sephardim—is a rich almond-egg paste that can be prepared in many different ways. A pure white type made with egg whites is a must at many Sephardic weddings and prenuptial receptions, and is also offered to new mothers. Sometimes, it is painstakingly shaped into delicate woven bracelets as a gift for the bride-to-be.

Traditionally, most Moroccan Jews prefer to use egg yolks rather than whites in the paste, and they sometimes tint the paste with various food colors (see Notes). Also, Moroccans do not cook the paste before shaping it, as do some other Sephardim. Moroccan Jews enjoy marzipan not only on Purim but also during Pesach and *Mimouna*—the Moroccan-Jewish holiday that immediately follows Pesach.

The technique for the following confections is adapted from a recipe taught to me many years ago by Ginette Spier, an excellent Moroccan-Jewish cook.

NOTES: As raw egg yolks may contain salmonella bacteria, which can cause severe food poisoning, this recipe calls for pasteurized egg substitute instead. It gives the marzipan its traditional pale yellow color and works very well in this recipe.

When the marzipan paste is first made, it may taste coarse and sugary. For best flavor and texture, it should be allowed to "ripen" overnight. Thus, the petits fours can be shaped as soon as the marzipan is prepared but, for best taste, they should not be eaten

until the next day. This marzipan will never be as smooth as commercial marzipan paste. That's part of its charm: its slightly rough, chewy texture is very pleasing.

If desired, the marzipan can be made ahead of time and refrigerated for a few weeks. It should be allowed to come to room temperature before being shaped. The completed petits fours may also be refrigerated for a few weeks. However, they taste best at room temperature, so allow them to sit out for a while before serving.

The petits fours look particularly attractive when each one is placed in a tiny, fluted paper cup designed for candies. These are available in gourmet cookware stores and some supermarkets.

10 ounces (scant 2 cups) whole blanched almonds or 10 ounces (about 2⅓ cups) slivered blanched almonds

¾ cup granulated sugar, plus extra for dipping

1 1-inch-square piece lemon peel, yellow part only

Scant 2 tablespoons pasteurized pareve egg substitute (see Notes)

1 teaspoon almond extract, or to taste

1 teaspoon fresh lemon juice

3 to 4 ounces each of the following (or your choice, to total about 1 pound):

Whole pitted dates

Whole pitted prunes

Dried whole Turkish apricots

Perfect walnut halves

Perfect pecan halves

In a food processor fitted with a steel blade, grind the almonds with the sugar and square of lemon peel until the almonds are very fine and powdery. (If the almonds have been refrigerated or frozen, let them come to room temperature before grinding.) Add the egg substitute, almond extract, and lemon juice, and process until the ingredients are very well combined and beginning to form a cohesive mass. Test the marzipan mixture by squeezing a tablespoon of it in the palm of your hand. It should feel slightly tacky, but should press together into a ball. If the mixture is too dry, mix in enough additional egg substitute—adding it drop by drop—until the marzipan is the proper consistency. Continue processing the marzipan for about 30 seconds, or until it forms a relatively smooth paste. It will not be as smooth as commercially made marzipan.

Wash your hands very well. Turn out the marzipan into a shallow, wide bowl, and gather it into a ball. Gently knead it for 3 to 5 minutes, or until it

is smooth and malleable, like a very stiff dough. It will feel slightly sticky. Make the assorted "petits fours" as follows.

For each date petit four, use a small, sharp knife to lengthwise slit open a pitted date along one side. Pinch off a piece of marzipan about the size of a cherry, and mold it into an ovoid shape. Gently pry open the date with your fingers, and pres the marzipan in place. Close the date around the marzipan, but do not completely enclose it. Decorate the top of the marzipan by pressing it with the tines of a fork along the length of the date.

For each prune or apricot petit four, mold a cherry-sized piece of marzipan into a ball. Press it tightly in place over the indentation in the center of the prune or on top of the apricot. Decorate the top of the marzipan by pressing the tines of a fork in perpendicular directions (as when making peanut butter cookies).

For each walnut or pecan petit four, mold a cherry-sized piece of marzipan into a cube or ball, and squeeze it between two nut halves to form a "sandwich." If desired, press the exposed surfaces of the marzipan with the fork.

Gently dab the marzipan surface of each petit four in a small bowl of granulated sugar to give it a pretty "crystalline" look. To serve, place each finished petit four into a tiny fluted paper cup, or arrange several of them on a doily-covered tray. The petits fours can be stored for a few weeks in an airtight container in the refrigerator. For best flavor, let them warm to room temperature before serving.

Makes about 40 assorted petits fours (about 1 pound of marzipan filling).

Israeli Mock "Marzipan"

This recipe comes from Israel's early "austerity years," when culinary luxuries, such as large quantities of almonds for marzipan, were not available. It is an example of the clever recipes that Jews have devised over the years to make something seemingly mundane into a special treat.

And it is quite fitting for Purim because one ingredient (oats) "masquerades" as another (almonds). While this uncooked treat doesn't taste *exactly* like marzipan, it is quite

delicious nevertheless. And it is high in healthful oat fiber. Include it on your *shalach manos* gift platters, and keep the recipients guessing!

NOTE: The easiest way to make this is in a food processor fitted with a steel blade. If you do not have a food processor, you can use a blender to finely grind the oats in small batches. Transfer the ground oats to a bowl, and stir in the remaining ingredients except the confectioners' sugar.

2 cups quick or regular rolled oats
(about 3 ounces)
⅓ to ½ cup sugar, or to taste
3 tablespoons canola oil or melted
butter

3 tablespoons milk or pareve milk
substitute
1 teaspoon almond extract
Confectioners' sugar (optional)

Put the oats into the bowl of a food processor fitted with a steel blade, and process until they are finely ground. Add the sugar and continue processing until the mixture is very fine. Add the oil, milk, and almond extract, and process until the mixture holds together and is doughlike. Put about 1 tablespoon in your hand and try to roll it into a ball. If it is very crumbly, add a few more drops of milk. Let the mixture rest about 5 minutes for the oats to absorb the moisture, then form it into balls or other shapes. If desired, roll the balls in confectioners' sugar.

Store the balls in the refrigerator but, for best taste, serve them at room temperature or slightly chilled.

Makes about 24 balls.

Peanut Butter and Chocolate Mock Hamantaschen

This easy no-cook confection is made from a honey-sweetened peanut butter mixture that can be easily molded into various shapes. The combination of peanuts and milk provides a nutritionally complete protein, making this a healthful and tasty snack. The "crust" mixture is light brown, while the chocolate-flavored filling is very dark. (If you

prefer, chocolate morsels or chips can be used as the filling.) This is a great recipe to do with children, who can eat the "dough" without a care!

NOTE: The instant dry milk powder for this treat should be fine and powdery. A few brands are coarse and will not mix well into the dough. If this is the case, process the milk powder in a food processor or blender until it is fine.

"CRUST" DOUGH
1 cup instant nonfat dry milk powder
   (see Note)
⅔ cup smooth (creamy-style) peanut
   butter (6 ounces)
⅓ cup mild-tasting honey

CHOCOLATE "FILLING" DOUGH
½ cup instant nonfat dry milk powder
   (see Note)
1 tablespoon plain cocoa
⅓ cup chunky or crunchy-style peanut
   butter (3 ounces)
¼ cup mild-tasting honey

For the crust dough, put the ingredients into a bowl in the order listed, then mix well. Use your hands or a wooden or sturdy metal spoon to gently "knead" the mixture until it forms a smooth and malleable dough. It should be very slightly sticky. If it is too sticky to shape, add a small amount of milk powder. If it is too dry and crumbly, add a bit more honey. If time permits, chill the dough for easier handling.

For the filling, combine the milk powder and cocoa in a bowl; then add the remaining ingredients and follow the above directions to make a stiff, lumpy (due to the peanut pieces) dough.

To make a hamantasch, take a piece of crust dough about the size of a walnut and roll it into a ball; then press it out on a piece of wax paper into a circle that is about ¼ inch thick. Take a small piece of filling dough (about half the size of the first piece), and roll it into a ball. Place in the center of the circle. Fold up three sides to form a triangle, letting the filling show in the open center.

These imitation hamantaschen can be eaten immediately or stored for gift-giving. To store, place in an airtight container so that none of the hamantaschen is touching one another, and keep in the refrigerator up to a week or more.

Makes about 10 to 12 small hamantaschen confections.

Variation

PINWHEEL SNACKS

These look like miniature pinwheel cookies. On a piece of wax paper, press out a piece of the "crust" dough into a rectangle about ⅛ inch thick. Make a similar rectangle with the darker "filling" dough. Place the filling dough on top of the crust dough, and roll them together like a jelly roll. Cut slices about ½ inch thick and turn them on their sides so the spiral shows.

Poppy Seed Pound Cake

This impressive and delectable cake freezes quite well, so it can be made way ahead to have on hand for *shalach manos* during Purim. A friend of mine divides the batter into miniature loaf pans, and puts a whole small loaf on each of her gift platters. If you are putting this cake on a platter with crunchy cookies such as hamantaschen, wrap the moist cake separately so that it does not soften the cookies.

FILLING
½ cup sugar
1 tablespoon ground cinnamon

2½ cups all-purpose flour
2 teaspoons baking powder
1 teaspoon baking soda

BATTER
⅓ cup poppy seeds
1 cup buttermilk
1 cup butter (2 sticks)
1¼ cups sugar, divided
4 large eggs, separated
1 teaspoon vanilla extract
½ teaspoon almond extract

GLAZE
1 cup confectioners' sugar
½ teaspoon vanilla extract
½ teaspoon almond extract
Milk or water as needed
1 to 2 teaspoons poppy seeds for
    sprinkling

Preheat the oven to 350 degrees. In a small bowl, combine the sugar and cinnamon for the filling. Set aside.

For the batter, mix the poppy seeds and buttermilk in a small bowl. Let the mixture rest for 5 minutes.

Meanwhile, in a large mixing bowl, use an electric mixer at medium speed to cream the butter with 1 cup of the sugar until light and fluffy. Beat in the egg yolks, vanilla extract, and almond extract. Combine the flour, baking powder, and baking soda, and add them to the batter alternately with the buttermilk–poppy seed mixture. Mix until well combined.

In a clean bowl, with clean beaters, beat the egg whites until foamy; then gradually add the remaining ¼ cup sugar, and beat until the whites form stiff peaks. Fold the beaten whites into the batter. Pour half of the batter into a nonstick-spray-coated or greased and floured 12-cup fluted tube pan (such as a Bundt pan) or a plain tube pan. Sprinkle the batter with half of the reserved sugar-cinnamon filling mixture. Cover with the remaining batter. Sprinkle the remaining filling on top.

Bake the cake at 350 degrees for 55 to 60 minutes, or until a toothpick inserted in the center comes out clean. Cool the cake in the pan on a wire rack for 10 to 15 minutes; then turn it out onto the rack to cool completely.

For the glaze, put the confectioners' sugar into a medium bowl, and stir in the vanilla extract and almond extract. Add milk, 1 teaspoon at a time, stirring after each addition, until the glaze has a "drizzling" consistency. Drizzle the glaze in a zigzag pattern over the top of the cake. Sprinkle the glaze lightly with poppy seeds while it is still wet.

Makes about 16 servings.

Streusel-Topped Gingerbread Gems

These attractive, miniature muffins make very palatable presents for *shalach manos,* and would also be perfect for a Purim party. If you are putting them on a platter with crunchy cookies such as hamantaschen, wrap the moist muffins separately so they do not soften the cookies.

STREUSEL
2 tablespoons butter or margarine
1/4 cup all-purpose flour
2 tablespoons sugar
1/8 teaspoon ground ginger
1/8 teaspoon ground cinnamon

BATTER
3/4 cup all-purpose flour (sifted, if at all lumpy)
3/4 cup whole wheat flour or white all-purpose flour

1/4 cup sugar
1/2 teaspoon baking soda
1 teaspoon ground ginger
1/2 teaspoon ground cinnamon
1/4 teaspoon ground nutmeg
1/4 teaspoon ground cloves
1/4 cup canola oil
1/2 cup light molasses
1/3 cup hot water
1 large egg, lightly beaten, or 1/4 cup pareve egg substitute

Preheat the oven to 350 degrees. For the streusel topping, use your fingertips or a pastry blender to combine all the ingredients in a small bowl. The streusel should resemble coarse bread crumbs. Set it aside.

In a medium bowl, mix together all the batter ingredients except the egg; then beat in the egg until it is completely combined. Spoon the batter into twenty-four gem-size (2-inch diameter), paper cup–lined (or nonstick-spray-coated) muffin tins, using about 1 tablespoon batter for each muffin. Sprinkle a scant teaspoon streusel over the batter in each cup, and use the back of a spoon to gently press it into the batter.

Bake the muffins at 350 degrees for about 15 minutes, or until a toothpick inserted in the center of one comes out clean. Remove the muffins from the pans, and cool them on a wire rack.

Makes 24 miniature (gem-size) muffins.

Pesach (Passover)

PESACH (WITH A GUTTURAL "CH") BEGINS ON THE FIFTEENTH day of the Hebrew month of Nisan—which usually occurs in late March or in April—and lasts for seven days in Israel (eight days in the Diaspora), based on biblical commandment. It is a special time, when relatives and friends, young and old, gather to share in the joy of our ancestors' redemption from slavery.

In fact, this freedom festival is probably the most widely observed and best loved of all the Jewish holidays. Unlike most of the others, it is home-based: its main service, the Seder, takes place at the family dinner table, not the synagogue. Also, food plays a pivotal role at Pesach, not just a peripheral one, as with most holidays. Indeed, the entire celebration revolves around the partaking of or prohibition of specific foods.

When the Holy Temple in Jerusalem was in existence Jews made pilgrimage there for the Pesach festival, to offer young lambs and other sacrifices. The lambs were then roasted over an open fire and eaten along with unleavened bread, bitter herbs, and other foods at a ceremonial family meal. After the Second Temple was destroyed, the holiday and its ritual meal became home oriented.

Pesach, like most Jewish holidays, has more than one name. Because the festival is biblically linked with the Israelites' deliverance from bondage in Egypt three thousand years ago, it has been called *Zeman Herutenu,* or the "Season of Our Liberation." In the

Torah, it is referred to as *Hag Ha'Aviv,* or "The Spring Festival," describing the time of year in which it takes place. (The lunar Hebrew calendar contains adjustments to ensure that Pesach always takes place in spring.)

The predominant name for the holiday, however, is *Pesach,* meaning "Passover." It comes from the double use of this Hebrew word (with slightly different vowel sounds) in chapter 12 of Exodus, where the holiday is ordained. In this chapter, God tells Moses and Aaron that each Israelite family must mark its doorposts with the blood of a sacrificial lamb (a *pesach* in Hebrew) as a signal for God to "pass over" when striking down all first-born Egyptian sons.

Each family is instructed to roast the lamb over a fire, and eat it with bitter herbs and unleavened bread. God also says that this day of "passing over" shall be celebrated as "a festival to the Lord throughout the ages," and the people shall eat unleavened bread and completely remove all leaven for seven days or "be cut off from Israel."

In verses 12:25–27, which are often quoted at the Seder, Moses explains to the elders that when they enter the Promised Land, they shall observe the rite of the sacrificial lamb. He tells them: "And when your children ask you what is meant by this rite, you should say, 'It is the passover sacrifice [*pesach*] to the Lord, Who "passed over" [*pasach*] the houses of the Israelites in Egypt when smiting the Egyptians, but saved our houses.' " (It was this plague—the last and most devastating of ten sent down upon the Egyptians—that finally persuaded the pharaoh to free the enslaved Israelites.)

The unleavened bread (*matzah* in Hebrew) of the festival came to represent both the "bread of affliction" eaten by Israelite slaves, and the "bread of liberation" that did not have time to rise because it was so hastily prepared and baked by the freed Israelites as they fled Egypt. And the leaven that was to be completely removed from every Jewish household came to symbolize the *yetzer ha'ra* or "evil inclination" in all of us that we constantly struggle to remove. (It has been said that the *yetzer ha'ra* "puffs us up" with false pride just as leaven "puffs up" bread.)

The modern Pesach *Seder* (a Hebrew word for "order") is held on the first night of the holiday and repeated on the second night throughout the Diaspora. It follows a specific order of service that dates back at least to the Mishnaic period of the early second century in the Common Era. Each of the numerous steps of the Pesach Seder has a name, which together form a mnemonic rhyme that may be sung aloud by all Seder participants. Repetition of the tune helps to tie all the parts of the Seder together.

The prayer book delineating the components of the Seder is called a *Haggadah,* which means "story" or "narrative." The Pesach Haggadah, which is often richly illustrated, was first produced in book form in the thirteenth century. In Diaspora commu-

nities, it is printed not only in Hebrew but also in the local vernacular to be sure that everyone present (including young children) can clearly understand its message. While every Haggadah contains the same order of service, each community customizes details of the text to suit its own needs, resulting in thousands of different *Haggadot* (plural) produced over the years.

At the Seder, the story of the Exodus is retold, and symbolic foods on the holiday table are explained and usually sampled. Representative portions of most of these foods are displayed on a special ceremonial platter, or "Seder plate" (*k'arah* in Hebrew), which may be ornately designed specifically for this purpose. The following five foods are on all Seder plates:

Zeroah—a roasted shank bone or other meaty bone (or possibly a roasted poultry neck or wing, or a beetroot or "meaty" mushroom for vegetarians)—represents the ceremonial paschal lamb (*paschal* is the Greek cognate of *pesach*) that was always sacrificed in the Holy Temple for the Pesach festival and then roasted over an open fire for the main meal.

Because the Jewish sacrificial system was abandoned after the Second Temple was destroyed, some modern-day Jews do not eat lamb or any kind of roasted meat at the Seder meal. On the other hand, certain Sephardim specifically partake of it, in remembrance of the paschal sacrifice. (NOTE: Uncovered meat baked in a modern oven is not *roasted* in the biblical sense, even though it may be called "roast beef" or "roasted chicken." Some modern-day Jews avoid it anyway due to the vague similarity.)

Baytzah—a roasted or baked egg—is symbolic of an offering always brought to the Holy Temple for festivals, and considered to be a second sacrifice on Pesach. The egg is also a symbol of the life cycle and the renewal of spring. (Because its continuous cylindrical shape symbolizes eternal life, an egg is eaten by mourners. Some say its presence on the Seder plate shows that the loss of the Holy Temple is still lamented by Jews. For this same reason, many Jews partake of a hard-boiled egg, often in a bowl of salt water, symbolizing tears, as their first course of the Seder dinner.)

Karpas—a mild (nonbitter) vegetable or green, such as fresh parsley or celery (or possibly a root vegetable, such as a cooked potato)—is the hors d'oeuvre of the Seder. At the beginning of the ceremony, it is dipped into salt water or vinegar and sampled. This is to recall that formal meals once began with such dipped hors d'oeuvres. Green karpas may also symbolize the new growth of spring. Ashkenazim who lived in northern climates where Pesach came too early for fresh greens adapted the custom of using root vegetables (which could be stored over the winter) instead.

Salt water, preferred by Ashkenazim for the dip, represents the tears shed by enslaved

Israelites. Vinegar is the more traditional dip for most Sephardim, while others use salt water with fresh lemon juice added to it.

Maror—a bitter herb, or a leafy green that is said to become bitter, usually horseradish among Ashkenazim, and romaine lettuce, endive, or escarole among Sephardim—symbolizes the intense bitterness endured by the Israelites during their slavery. The Talmud suggests using a type of lettuce because this plant starts out soft, but the core eventually becomes hard. Also, the bitter taste is not so obvious at first. Likewise, the Israelites' sojourn in Egypt was "soft" and agreeable at first, but ultimately became hard and bitter when they were forced into slavery. (Horseradish—a root that stores well over winter—is probably used by Askenazim for the same reason that potatoes are used for *karpas*.)

Haroset (pronounced with a guttural "h")—most often a sweet spread made from fresh and/or dried fruit, nuts, and wine—represents the mortar and mud bricks used by Israelite slaves as they labored to build the pharaoh's cities. The bitter herb is dipped into haroset (the second "dipping" of the Seder). The sweet taste of the haroset is supposed to temper the sharpness of the bitter herbs as an expression of eternal Jewish optimism.

Jews from various communities make their haroset in a wide variety of ways, as can be seen by the selection of recipes in this chapter. Most haroset mixtures are quite delicious and are highlights of the Seder. However, one Sephardic family that I met, who used a thick syrup made only with puréed raisins and water, insisted that haroset should be "as plain as the mud" it symbolizes.

In addition, the following food is on many Seder plates:

Hazeret (pronounced with a guttural "h")—a second bitter herb or green that is said to become bitter, such as romaine lettuce, watercress, or possibly even horseradish—is also on many Seder plates. Some say it is included because, in conjunction with Pesach, the Torah uses the plural word for "herbs" with regard to the paschal meal, indicating there should be more than one type or portion. The hazeret, which is often considered to be optional, may be used in the *korekh* or "sandwich" of matzah and bitter herbs that is eaten during the Seder ceremony. (Ashkenazim have sometimes used potatoes for the same reason as with karpas—that is, no greens were available in early spring.)

Also on the Seder table are three stacked and covered *matzot* (the plural of *matzah*), which are said to symbolize the three religious divisions of the House of Israel—Kohen, Levite, and Israelite. Actually, two of the matzot serve the same purpose as the two loaves of bread that are generally on the holiday table—to represent the double portion

of manna that fell on Shabbat. Some suggest that the third matzah shows the joyous nature of the holiday; others say it symbolizes the "bread of affliction." Mostly, it is needed for the afikomen (see below).

At the Seder, matzah made with only flour and water is supposed to be used—not the type that is enriched with eggs, juice, or other extra ingredients—to clearly represent the "bread of affliction." Some prefer *matzah shmurah* ("watched matzah" or "guarded matzah"), which is made from wheat that was carefully observed from harvesttime until baking to be absolutely certain that it had no chance to leaven. (Usually, the grain used for matzah is scrutinized only after it has been ground into flour.) Shmurah matzah, as it is called in the vernacular, may be handmade into rough circles that are reminiscent of our ancestors' unleavened bread.

During the service, the middle one of the three stacked matzot is broken in two. (In one Greek-Jewish family that I met, the leader now announces, "This is how the Red Sea parted.") The larger piece of matzah is designated the *afikomen,* a Greek word meaning "dessert" (or, according to the above family, "that which is eaten later"). It is wrapped in a napkin or specially designed cloth, and set aside in some manner. The afikomen is later retrieved and divided among all the participants, and is supposed to be the last bit of food eaten during the Seder.

Different customs regarding the afikomen help keep the children at the table alert. In many Ashkenazic families, the leader of the Seder hides the afikomen, and then offers a gift to the children who find it, so the Seder can be completed. Sometimes, the children are expected to "steal" the afikomen away from the leader, and hold it for "ransom" in a hiding place.

In some Sephardic households, a young child holds the wrapped afikomen on his or her shoulder to represent the "burden" carried by the Children of Israel when they wandered in the desert after the Exodus. The child is asked a series of questions to which there is a set response. "Where do you come from?" The child answers, "From Egypt." "Where are you going?" "To Jerusalem." "What provisions do you have for the way?" At this, the child points to the afikomen.

Among other Sephardim, the father or leader of the Seder takes the role of the wanderer instead of a child. Often, everyone at the table is given the opportunity to briefly "carry the burden" on his or her shoulder.

Another interesting Sephardic custom takes place in the early part of the Seder. The leader lifts the Seder plate above the center of the table, and all participants help support the platter together as a way of acknowledging its importance. Children stand on chairs

Pesach (Passover)

if necessary. Sometimes, the Seder plate is held briefly over the head of each participant instead.

One Sephardic Seder custom that my own Ashkenazic family has adopted takes place during the singing of *Dayenu.* As we join together in a lively rendition of the tune, we gently "flog" each other with "whips" of scallion (green onion) to recall our ancestors' treatment when they were slaves. This always wakes up any inattentive children, and also the adults! (For another enjoyable Sephardic custom that we have adopted, see the recipe for Huevos Haminados on page 354.)

As with most Jewish ceremonies, wine plays an important part in the Seder. Four glasses of wine (or pure grape juice) are drunk by each participant during the service—two before the festive meal, one during the holiday "Grace after Meals," and a final cup just before the concluding prayers and songs.

After the third cup of wine is drunk and the fourth cup is filled, most Ashkenazim and some Sephardim set out a special cup of wine for the great prophet Elijah. It is said that Elijah never died, but was carried up to heaven in a fiery chariot, and he will return to announce the Messianic Age. The door is opened to symbolically welcome Elijah, and legend has it that his spirit visits every Jewish household and takes a minuscule sip of wine. At this late point in the Seder, weary children often become alert just to scrupulously observe Elijah's cup.

It is a religious obligation, or *mitzvah,* to eat matzah at the Seder. For the remainder of the holiday, however, matzah is considered to be optional. Nevertheless, "leaven" or *hametz* (pronounced with a guttural "h" in Hebrew) is strictly forbidden at all times during Pesach. According to the Jewish law, hametz is flour made from wheat, rye, oats, barley, or spelt (an ancient kind of wheat making a minor comeback) that may have had any conceivable chance of fermenting (and, thus, leavening). To avoid even the slightest possibility of eating leaven, all foods made from these grains—with the exception of matzah—are prohibited. (Note: Baking powder and baking soda are *not* leaven; see the end of this introduction for more details.)

Matzah, however, *must* be made from one of the aforementioned grains to fulfill the commandment of eating unleavened bread at Pesach. By Jewish law, the entire process of matzah preparation—from mixing the flour-water dough until the matzah is completely baked—can take no longer than eighteen minutes, because once flour has been exposed to water, this is the minimum amount of time considered necessary for fermentation to begin.

After the matzah has been fully baked, no further leavening of the grain is thought to be possible. Thus, matzah is commercially ground into powdery "matzah cake meal"

(or "matzah flour") and into coarser "matzah meal," which are often used for holiday baking and cooking in place of regular flour or bread crumbs.

However, certain pious Jews, particularly among the Hasidim, prefer not to mix matzah or matzah products with any liquids during Pesach, just in case any part of the matzah may not have properly baked and could possibly ferment. They call such "mixed" foods *gebroks,* and partake of them only on the eighth day of the holiday—a day that was added in the Diaspora by rabbinic injunction and is not observed in Israel.

During the post-Talmudic period, Ashkenazic religious authorities decided to prohibit additional foods during Pesach because "flour" ground from them might be confused with flour from one of the specific five grains. Called *kitniyot* (Hebrew for "legumes"), these foods include actual legumes (beans and peas) of all types, as well as "lesser grains" such as rice, millet, corn, and buckwheat (kasha). The rabbis were concerned that *kitniyot* flour might be used to make unacceptable matzah, or, conversely, that a cook might use prohibited hametz flour during Pesach, assuming it was *kitniyot.* To be certain that there was no confusion whatsoever, *kitniyot* were banned in all their forms. For many centuries, this ban has been Ashkenazic *minhag* (with a guttural "h"), or compelling community custom.

However, most Sephardim never adopted this custom because their cuisine was dependent on *kitniyot.* Therefore, they generally permit these foods during Pesach, though actual Sephardic *minhag* varies considerably from place to place. For instance, some Sephardim eat lesser grains but not legumes, whereas others have the reverse preference. And in some communities, fresh peas and beans are acceptable, but not dried ones.

Many Sephardic families feel that it is traditional and thus essential to have rice, or possibly fresh beans, on the Seder table. Curiously, one Jew of Near Eastern birth told me that when she was young, her family ate all legumes during Pesach except for chickpeas (garbanzo beans) because they were called *humus* in the local vernacular, which sounds like *hametz.*

In modern Israel (and sometimes in the Diaspora as well), the adjunct restrictions on *kitniyot* have caused strife within families of "mixed" marriages between Ashkenazim and Sephardim. Also, Israeli processed foods are often labeled *"kosher l'Pesach"* based on Sephardic standards. A few contemporary Ashkenazic rabbis have therefore suggested that perhaps it is time for a more relaxed attitude toward *kitniyot,* at the very least in Israel. Though *kitniyot* have never been considered in the same category of prohibition as actual hametz, this is still quite controversial, particularly among the Orthodox.

Furthermore, there are discrepancies about exactly what falls into the category of *kitniyot.* For instance, some Ashkenazic authorities says peanuts—technically a legume, but grown under the ground—are not *kitniyot,* others say they are. There is similar confusion

Pesach (Passover)

about *fresh* green beans. And some consider peanut *oil* to be acceptable for the holiday, but not the nuts or peanut butter. Regarding corn and corn products, a few authorities now say that this relatively modern plant, first grown in the Americas, has been mistranslated from biblical and Talmudic sources, and should probably not be prohibited as once thought.

While some communities have lessened dietary restrictions based on modern knowledge about *kitniyot,* certain ultra-Orthodox groups have added to the prohibited list such foods as mustard seed, sunflower seeds and oil, safflower oil, cottonseed oil, garlic, and spices because they grow like grains or for other reasons.

Over the years, certain culinary customs have evolved for the holiday. It was once common for many Ashkenazim to set aside crocks of cleaned beetroots with water shortly after Purim, so that the beets and liquid could naturally ferment over a period of weeks into *rossel.* This was then used for all sorts of Pesach dishes, ranging from borscht to red horseradish. And an alcoholic beverage called *med* or *mead* was fermented from honey. Some say these practices came about as a reaction against those who claimed that *all* fermented foods, not just grains, should be prohibited during Pesach.

Also prepared ahead of time were many sweets, such as jams, candied fruits, and syrups. Among Egyptian Jews, for instance, coconut jam has long been a holiday favorite because its whiteness symbolizes purity. And some Ashkenazic Jews have enjoyed candy made from such sweet vegetables as beets and carrots.

During Pesach, the rice eaten by certain Sephardim is thoroughly sorted from three to seven times—the number depending on local convention—to be absolutely certain that there is no foreign matter or errant kernels of proscribed grains in it. Some Sephardim do not eat rice primarily to avoid this time-consuming procedure.

For the Seder dinner, seasonal spring vegetables, such as asparagus or, among some Sephardim, fresh fava beans in the pods, are usually on the menu. Recipes for many other Seder specialties, and also several midholiday favorites, are included in this chapter. (Although these recipes come from many Jewish cultures, all have been adapted to follow the Ashkenazic custom of avoiding *kitniyot* during Pesach.)

The conclusion of Pesach is observed by Moroccan Jews as a special holiday called *Mimouna,* which is considered a testimony of their faith in God. According to many Moroccans, the name of the holiday comes from *emounah,* a Hebrew word for "faith" or "belief." Others suggest that it commemorates the death in Fez of Rav Maimon, the father of the great Jewish scholar Moses Maimonides, who lived in the twelfth century.

In the evening when Pesach has ended, Moroccan families hold joyous Mimouna open house celebrations for their friends and relatives. Several years ago, Rabbi Joshua Toledano told me how he dressed in finery and visited grandparents on both sides of his

family when he was a youth in Morocco. Because his paternal grandfather was a great rabbi, the congregation always flocked to that home immediately after evening services. The visitors kissed the elderly rabbi's hand, and he blessed them and presented them with dates, almonds, and walnuts.

At Rabbi Toledano's maternal grandparents home, the table was set with a platter containing a huge raw fish, the symbol of fertility, which was surrounded by fresh flour. In the flour were coins, representing the hope for a prosperous year. The table was decorated with green wheat stalks, fresh peas in the pods, and beautiful flowers. Muslim friends came to visit, and brought with them freshly baked bread, honey, yeast, milk, and yogurt. Dairy products were included among the gifts because these were not *kosher l'Pesach,* and so were abstained from during the holiday.

At modern Mimouna open houses, traditional *muflita* are typically served along with a multitude of sweet cakes and pastries. *Muflita* are very thin pancakes that are spread with plenty of butter and honey, and then eaten out-of-hand.

The celebration of Mimouna continues the next morning with community-wide outdoor picnics. This practice has been carried to Israel, where many Moroccan families meet in a huge park in Jerusalem. Together, they enjoy abundant delectable foods and spend the day in jubilant singing and dancing. It is a joyous time for all, and a fitting epilogue to the great festival of Pesach.

NOTE: There are many recipes in other chapters of this book that follow the dietary laws of Pesach, and would be quite appropriate to serve on this holiday. Be sure to take a look!

A Candle, Feather, and Wooden Spoon: The Search for Hametz

Soon after nightfall on the evening before the first Seder, the Jewish family does a ritual search for hametz left around the house. It is customary to turn down the lights and use a single candle to focus the search. A blessing regarding the biblical commandment to remove hametz is said before the search begins. So that the blessing is not "wasted" when the home is already thoroughly cleaned for Pesach, some small pieces of leavened bread (often ten) are strategically placed beforehand.

While carrying a feather, wooden spoon, and small paper bag, the family searches for the bread as well as any other stray hametz. (My children really enjoy this task; it's the only time they actually want to help "clean up"!) As each piece of bread is located, the

feather is used to brush all crumbs into the spoon so they can be carried to the paper bag. When every bit of bread is found and collected in the bag, a head of the household declares that any hametz not seen or removed or known about is nullified and owner-less. (This does not include any hametz specifically reserved for the next day's breakfast.) The bag of hametz is put aside until morning.

After the last hametz in the house is eaten in the morning, the bread collected during the previous evening's search is typically destroyed by burning, though it may be disposed of in another specified manner, such as tossing it into running water or throwing it to the wind. A head of the household then proclaims on behalf of the whole family, "All leavened grain that is in my possession, whether I have recognized it or not, whether I have seen it or not, whether I have removed it or not, is hereby nullified and ownerless like the dust of the earth." At this point, visible hametz is forbidden on the premises. (Matzah, however, is not eaten until the designated point of the Seder.)

Special "kits" that contain a candle, feather, and wooden spoon in a paper bag decorated specifically for the Search for Hametz (*Bedikat Hametz,* in Hebrew) may be purchased at Jewish bookstores. In some families, a dried lulav palm branch saved from Sukkot is used instead of a feather to brush up the bread crumbs, or it may be used to start the fire that burns the hametz.

Special Notes on Pesach Ingredients

There is much confusion about the use of baking powder, baking soda, and cream of tartar during Pesach. While it is the custom of many to avoid these products because they help baked goods to "rise," the products themselves are not made with grains and are not *hametz*. They cannot cause leavening. Most baking powder, however, contains cornstarch, which generally is considered to be *kitniyot* by Ashkenazim. And it may contain cream of tartar, which is derived from grapes during the wine-making process and therefore requires kashrut certification. Baking powder (which is different from baking soda in that it contains as least *two* chemical rising agents) can be produced that is *kosher l'Pesach*.

Baking soda is a pure chemical (sodium bicarbonate) that is not prohibited in any way for Pesach, and is actually used by many commercial companies for kosher holiday baked goods. According to most authorities, it does not even need special certification (as with coffee, tea, and sugar) if it is purchased before Pesach. Nevertheless, many home cooks continue to avoid baking soda (and baking powder) in an effort to produce home-made Pesach baked goods that are different from those eaten during the rest of the year.

In that spirit, I have not included any chemical rising agents in the following Pesach recipes. I have also not called for confectioners' sugar, as it usually contains cornstarch.

Most flavoring extracts, such as vanilla and almond extract, as well as nonstick cooking and baking sprays, are made with grain alcohol, and are therefore forbidden. Special Pesach substitutes that have been produced following holiday restrictions may be available. In past years, there have been Pesach flavorings and a cooking spray made with extra-virgin olive oil. Sometimes, vanilla sugar (which has been infused with flavor from a vanilla bean) is used in place of vanilla extract.

Regarding oil, the one most easily available that is labeled for Pesach tends to be cottonseed oil, which is high in saturated fat and thus not heart-healthy. According to many authorities, other oils that may be used for the holiday, and are very low in saturated fat, include olive oil (some say that it must be "extra-virgin" or "virgin"), canola oil, safflower oil, and, peanut oil.

"Pareve egg substitute" may not be available kosher for Pesach. However, I have listed it as an alternative ingredient in the following chapter because those who prepare these recipes year-round may want to have that choice. For Pesach, you can use the whole egg or egg white alternative, as desired.

Ashkenazic-Style Haroset, My Way

Unlike Sephardim, who have many different types of haroset made with a wide variety of ingredients, Ashkenazim usually limit the mixture to apples, nuts, and red wine, possibly flavored with cinnamon, and sugar or honey. The apples are said to be a reminder of pious Israelite women who went into the apple orchards to give birth so that their babies would not be killed by the Egyptians.

There are so many minor variations of this type of haroset that I would never say any particular one was the *right* one. The following recipe is simply the way I make it, and a guide for those who have never done it before.

Until I decided to include this recipe here, I had never measured the amounts of ingredients, especially since I have always enjoyed adjusting them to taste. So, please feel free to do the same yourself. And keep in mind that the consistency of the haroset is also a matter of personal preference. Some make it very coarse, almost like fruit salad; while others completely purée it. My favorite haroset is somewhere in between.

By the way, though a food processor is great for making haroset, it is not essential.

Once, in a pinch when we were away from home during Pesach, I bought an inexpensive nut chopper (the kind with a plunging *X* blade on a spring) at a supermarket and used it to make plenty of excellent haroset (in very small batches) for our whole family. My kids had a great time helping out. Haroset can even be made the *really* old-fashioned way, with a knife and a cutting board.

NOTES: I generally use Golden Delicious apples for this haroset because they are sweet, they don't get mushy, and they have a light-colored peel that doesn't show up in my haroset (I don't peel the apples). Sometimes, I use a mixture that includes one tart Granny Smith apple for an interesting contrast of textures and tastes. You can use other apples, if you prefer.

Although I have always used walnuts in my haroset and consider them to be essential, others prefer almonds or hazelnuts (or even pecans). The choice is yours.

*3 large, firm Golden Delicious apples
    (see Notes)*
1 to 1½ cups walnut pieces (see Notes)

*About ⅓ to ½ cup sweet red Pesach
    wine (any type)*
1 to 2 teaspoons ground cinnamon
1 tablespoon honey, or to taste

Cut the apples into eighths, and remove the core from each piece, but do not peel the apples. Put the apples and nuts into a food processor fitted with a steel blade, and pulse-process two or three times until they are very coarsely chopped. Add the remaining ingredients (using the smaller amounts first), and pulse-process a few more times, or until the apples and nuts are finely chopped, and the mixture forms a rather rough wet paste. Do *not* purée the haroset; there should be some discernible pieces of nuts when the haroset is tasted. If it is dry, stir in a little more wine by hand. If more cinnamon and/or honey are desired, stir them in.

If a food processor is not available, very finely chop the apples and nuts by hand, or use a spring-style nut chopper (see the comments above). Then transfer them to a medium bowl, and stir in the remaining ingredients to taste.

Put the haroset in a shallow serving bowl and refrigerate it, covered, until needed. It will stay fresh and delicious for several days in the refrigerator.

Makes about 2½ cups.

Turkish-Style Haroset

When I demonstrated this recipe at a Hadassah meeting several years ago, one of the older members delightedly exclaimed that it tasted just like the haroset she remembered from her childhood in Turkey.

This haroset has become a family favorite that I make every Pesach. It has a texture similar to Ashkenazic haroset, though it is moister, with a lovely citrus flavor. It is also lighter in color due to the lack of cinnamon and because the orange juice helps the apples retain their light color. Dates naturally sweeten it, so honey is not needed.

15 pitted dates
*1 large apple, such as a Golden
    Delicious*
1 medium navel orange
*1 cup light or dark raisins (or a
    mixture)*
½ cup walnut pieces

½ cup slivered almonds
*About 2 tablespoons sweet red Pesach
    wine (any type)*

GARNISH (OPTIONAL)
*1 medium navel orange, thinly sliced
    and each slice cut in half*

Cut the dates in half. Cut the apple into eighths, and remove the core from each piece. (You do not need to peel the pieces.) Peel the orange, then cut it into chunks.

Put the dates, apple, orange, raisins, walnuts, and almonds through the coarse blade of a food grinder, or coarsely grind them together in a food processor fitted with a steel blade (in batches, if necessary). Add the wine, and mix or process to form a soft, slightly coarse mixture.

Transfer the haroset to a shallow bowl, and garnish it with semicircular orange slices around the edge of the bowl. Refrigerate the haroset, covered, until needed. It will stay fresh and delicious for several days in the refrigerator.

Makes about 3 cups.

Moroccan-Style Haroset

During a summer vacation to Canada several years ago, my family and I were delighted to find a kosher Moroccan restaurant on Bathurst Steet in the "Jewish neighborhood" of Toronto. At Le Marrakech, we had one of the best meals of our entire trip.

Some inquiries led us to the owners, Ralph and Suzanne Ohayon and their son, Yves. The Ohayon family had moved to Canada from Morocco in 1968 with the assistance of the Hebrew Immigration Aid Society. In Toronto, they found it difficult to get the type of kosher cuisine to which they were accustomed. They thought that others might have the same gustatory desires, and so, in 1983, they finally opened a Moroccan restaurant, with Yves as manager.

Actually, everyone in the family seemed to love cooking, including Ralph Ohayon, who generously shared some family recipes with me. Though we talked for hours about many delicious dishes, his eyes really glowed when he described the following haroset, which he annually prepared in very large quantities for family and friends. I have kept his proportions, but cut down the amounts.

Unlike most haroset, this delectable dried fruit–nut mixture is formed into little balls, which will keep for weeks in the refrigerator. I like to serve them in tiny paper cups designed for candy.

NOTE: For best results, use dried fruit that is soft and fresh.

25 pitted dates, halved

10 large, brown (Calimyrna) dried figs,
    stems removed and quartered

20 dried apricots, halved or quartered

10 large, pitted prunes, halved or
    quartered

2 cups walnut pieces

1 cup blanched slivered or whole
    almonds

1/2 cup shelled pistachios (optional)

1/4 cup sweet red Pesach wine, or as
    needed

Ground cinnamon (optional)

Cut up all the dried fruit as directed, and put it into a large bowl with all the nuts. Mix well. Put all the nuts and dried fruit through the fine blade of a food grinder, or finely grind them together in a food processor fitted with a steel blade (in batches, if necessary). Mix in just enough wine to make a smooth paste that is soft and malleable, but not sticky.

Form the mixture into 1-inch balls, with moistened hands if necessary. If desired, sprinkle the balls lightly with cinnamon. Store the balls in a tightly covered container in the refrigerator for up to 2 weeks. For best flavor, let the balls come to room temperature before serving.

Makes about 70 1-inch balls (about 3 cups of haroset mixture).

Israeli-Style Haroset

Many immigrant Israelis continue to make the haroset of the countries in which they once dwelled. However, *sabras* (native-born Israelis) often prefer to use ingredients more typical of their own country. The following delicious haroset is of the latter type. A Jaffa orange from Israel would be particularly appropriate for this recipe, though it is not necessary.

1 medium navel orange
10 pitted dates, cut into thirds
*½ cup slivered or whole blanched
    almonds (or possibly peanuts,
    among Sephardim)*
*1 large apple, peeled (if desired), cored,
    and cut in large pieces*
1 large or 2 small bananas
1 tablespoon fresh lemon juice

1 tablespoon sugar
1 teaspoon ground cinnamon
¼ cup sweet red Pesach wine
About ⅓ cup matzah meal

GARNISH (OPTIONAL)
*1 medium navel orange, thinly sliced
    and each slice cut in half*

Scrub the orange well. Use a grater to remove most of the outer, colored part of the orange peel. Reserve the grated peel. Remove and discard the white pith from the orange. Cut the orange into pieces. Put the reserved grated orange peel, orange pieces, dates, almonds, apple, and banana through the fine blade of a food grinder, or finely grind them together in a food processor fitted with a steel blade. Stir in the lemon juice, sugar, cinnamon, and wine. Then stir in enough matzah meal for the desired consistency. (The mixture will get a bit thicker as it sits.)

Transfer the haroset to a shallow bowl, and garnish it with semicircular orange slices around the edge of the bowl. Refrigerate the haroset, covered, and serve it chilled. It will keep fresh for about 2 days in the refrigerator.

Makes about 2½ cups.

Date Haroset

Haroset made primarily from dates is used by many different groups of Jews, including those from North Africa, Iraq, Persia, Afghanistan, and Calcutta, India. It may be called *dibis* or *halek* (with a guttural "h") or several other names.

The haroset is made by cooking dates with water to produce a paste or a thick syrup. This technique was developed in ancient times. In fact, it is generally understood that date syrup is the "honey" repeatedly mentioned in the Torah. Some use plain date syrup for haroset. Others add chopped walnuts and/or almonds. The nuts may be mixed into the paste or syrup, or sprinkled on top.

Occasionally, the date paste is flavored with cinnamon. Sometimes, the paste is made thick enough to be formed into small balls, which might be coated with edible, dried, rose petals by Moroccan Jews.

The following version of date haroset is an amalgam of several of these types. For best results, use dried dates that are soft and fresh.

1 pound chopped pitted dates
2 cups water
½ to 1 cup finely chopped walnuts
and/or almonds

½ to 1 teaspoon ground cinnamon
(optional)

Put the dates and water into a medium saucepan, and let them soak for 1 hour. Then bring them to a boil over high heat. Lower the heat, cover the saucepan, and slowly cook the dates, stirring them often and mashing them with a spoon, for 1 hour, or until they are very soft and form a paste.

To smooth out the paste, press it through a sieve, colander, or food mill, or purée it in a food processor. If the purée is too thin for your taste, return

it to the saucepan and simmer it down to the desired consistency, keeping in mind that it will thicken slightly more as it cools.

Let the date paste cool to room temperature. Stir in the nuts and cinnamon (if used). Store the paste in the refrigerator for up to 2 weeks. For best flavor, let it come to room temperature before serving.

Makes about 2 cups.

Yemenite-Style Haroset

Yemenite Jews like spicy food, and their haroset is no exception. It has an intriguing sweet-hot flavor that is worth trying. Yemenites generally use very little sweetener in their cooking, and might not use honey in the following haroset. However, those with more Western tastes will probably prefer to include it. For best results, use dried fruit that is soft and fresh.

6 large light brown (Calimyrna) dried figs, stems removed and quartered
6 pitted dates, halved
2 tablespoons sesame seeds
About 1 teaspoon honey

1/2 teaspoon ground ginger
1/8 teaspoon ground coriander seed
Pinch of cayenne pepper (optional)

Put the figs and dates through the fine blade of a food grinder, or finely grind them together in a food processor fitted with a steel blade, to make a very firm, sticky paste. Mix in the sesame seeds, honey, and spices, adjusting the latter to taste. Store the haroset in the refrigerator for up to 2 weeks. For best flavor, let it come to room temperature before serving.

Makes about 2/3 cup haroset mixture.

Pesach (Passover)

354

Huevos Haminados

SEPHARDIC-STYLE LONG-COOKED EGGS

P

These delicious, long-cooked eggs, which appear to be uniquely Jewish, are a must at just about all Sephardic holidays and functions, including funerals and the Shabbat dairy brunch known as *Desayuno*. The eggs are virtually identical to those included in Shabbat stews that are cooked overnight, such as Dafina (page 52), and Sephardic *hamin*. In fact, their Judeo-Spanish name—*huevos haminados*—is derived from the name of that Sephardic "hot pot." The technique has been modified to conveniently cook many eggs at once, yet still tint the shells brown as when they are baked with the stew. *Beid hameen* is the term used by Jews from Arabic countries. In Israel, they may be called simply *haminados* or *hameen*.

Huevos haminados are simmered on the stove or in the oven for at least 8 hours, up to overnight, which turns the albumen brown, darkens the yolk slightly, and gives the entire egg a creamy texture and deliciously rich "smoky" flavor. The eggs are often cooked with onion skins (or coffee grounds), to give the shells their characteristic mottled brown hue. They are usually served warm or at room temperature, and taste best that way.

In Israel and in American cities with large Israeli populations (such as Los Angeles), *huevos haminados* are often sold with Borekas (page 492)—cheese-filled flaky turnovers—in cafés and at outdoor kiosks, where they are displayed in glass warming ovens. The combination makes a great breakfast or lunch for those on the go.

During Pesach, *huevos haminados* are on most Sephardic Seder tables. Before eating them, some families, like the Danas from Istanbul, use the unshelled eggs for a friendly competition. Each Seder guest taps the pointed end of his or her egg against those of the other participants until only one egg with an intact shell remains—and its owner is declared the winner. The eggs are then served with Bimuelos de Massa (page 363), as the first course of dinner.

My own family has adopted the egg-tapping contest, and it has become a highlight of our Seder. We compete just before the main meal. After the tapping is concluded, we shell our own eggs and eat them dipped in salt water—thereby combining a Sephardic custom with an Ashkenazic one.

My children like these eggs so much that I make them frequently during the holiday, using a slow-cooker so that they are no trouble at all. I also sometimes prepare them for special brunches at other times in the year.

NOTES: To keep eggs from cracking while cooking—use a pin to prick a tiny hole in the round end (side with the air pocket) of each egg so that the heated air can escape, start the eggs in cold water and bring the water slowly to a boil, and do not let the water boil too fast or the eggs will crash into each other. For hard-boiled eggs that are easiest to shell, use eggs that are at least 3 days old.

Do *not* use an aluminum pot (even the hard-anodized type) or any easily stained pot for this recipe, as the onion skins (or even plain long-cooking eggs) may tint the pot an unattractive color.

Many recipes for *huevos haminados* suggest putting a layer of oil on top of the water to help keep it from evaporating. I used to do this, but it made the eggs greasy for the tapping contest. So I tried leaving the oil out, and it didn't seem to matter that much. Be sure you do have plenty of water and that it does not boil too fast.

Any number of raw eggs in their shells   *Dry brown skins from several onions*
(optional)

Prick the round end of each egg with a pin to help prevent cracking (see Notes). Put the eggs into a large nonaluminum pot or an electric slow-cooker, and cover them several inches over with cold water. If desired, add onion skins to the water to tint the shells muted shades of brown. If the onion skins are put in the water under the eggs, they may help to cushion the eggs and keep them from breaking. (Onion skins are not necessary to tint the egg albumen brown. This happens because of the very long cooking.)

Slowly bring the water to a boil over medium-high heat, or turn the slow-cooker to "high" for about 30 minutes. Then cover the pot tightly, and lower the heat on the stove, or turn the slow-cooker to "low," so that the eggs simmer very gently. If desired, the eggs may be simmered in a 200- to 225-degree oven.

Simmer them for at least 8 hours up to 12 hours. (If cooking the eggs overnight, be sure there is plenty of water in a tightly covered pot, and that it is very gently simmering. (A slow-cooker is best for overnight cooking.) With or without onion skins, the egg water may produce a slightly strange odor and become tinted brown.

For easiest shelling, remove the eggs with a slotted spoon, and immediately plunge them into a large bowl of ice water. Let the eggs soak until they can be handled. Serve the eggs warm (for best taste), at room temperature, or chilled.

Store the eggs in the shell in the refrigerator for up to a week. Or remove the shells, and store the eggs submerged in a container of cold water for a few days. Eggs in the shell may be reheated, if desired, by boiling them for 3 to 5 minutes.

Special "Light" Knaidlach

LOW-FAT HERBED MATZAH BALLS

These knaidlach (pronounced with a guttural "ch") are a year-round family favorite. In fact, I serve them so frequently for Shabbat and holidays—afloat in golden chicken soup—that I have to stop making them about a month before Pesach just so my family will appreciate them at our Seder meal!

My knaidlach are light in that they contain very little fat and no cholesterol. I often serve these delicious matzah balls to company, and no one ever misses the traditional egg yolks or schmaltz. The herbs give the balls a wonderfully different flavor, so they are not at all bland like most other versions.

My knaidlach are *not* light with regard to their density. My family and I prefer a substantial ball with some bite. We do not consider "fluffy" a positive attribute when it comes to matzah balls.

NOTES: Because I make knaidlach often, I use a #40 ice cream disher to scoop up the matzah meal batter quickly and easily. However, I still roll the balls in my wet hands to smooth the outside, as directed below.

Prepared herb mixtures, with names like "salad herbs" or "herbs de Provence," are available in the spice aisle of most supermarkets. They are a wonderful convenience. Just be sure that they contain *only* herbs—with no salt, garlic products, or other additives.

¼ cup canola oil
6 extra-large egg whites or 1 cup pareve
    egg substitute (see page 347)
1½ to 2 teaspoons of a prepared herb
    mixture (see Notes) or a mixture of

dried tarragon, basil, thyme,
    marjoram, mint, and/or parsley.
¾ teaspoon salt
Generous ⅛ teaspoon ground black
    pepper

¾ *cup cold water*
1½ *cups matzah meal*

To Serve
My Mother's Incredible Chicken Soup
(page 41)

Put the oil and the egg whites (or the egg substitute) into a medium bowl, and beat with a fork until well combined. Use the fork to beat in the herbs, salt, and pepper, and then the water. Stir in the matzah meal until it is completely moistened. Press plastic wrap against the top of mixture, and chill it for at least 1 hour.

Put water into a 5-quart or larger pot so that it is two-thirds full. Bring it to a boil over high heat. Wet your hands and a spoon in cool water. Use the wet spoon (see Notes) to scoop a walnut-size lump of the matzah meal mixture into your wet hands. Roll the mixture into a smooth ball. Drop the ball into lightly boiling water (lower the heat so that the water doesn't boil too fast, or it may break up the balls). Repeat until all the mixture is used, keeping your hands very wet so that the mixture doesn't stick.

Run a spoon through the pot to make sure that none of the balls have stuck to the bottom. Cover the pot, but tilt the lid so some steam can escape. Gently boil the balls for about 30 minutes, or until the balls are slightly puffed and cooked through. Remove them from the pot with a slotted spoon. The cooked balls may be transferred directly to a pot of hot chicken soup (this will help to keep the balls puffed). Or they may be left in their hot cooking water, off the heat, for up to an hour (they will deflate a little). Or they may be placed in a container at room temperature for several hours or refrigerated, covered, for a longer period (they will deflate somewhat and be more dense). They may be reheated in chicken soup if desired. The balls may be left in the chicken soup in the refrigerator for 2 or 3 days with no loss of flavor or texture. They may even be frozen in chicken soup and thawed with it in a microwave oven.

Makes about 24 matzah balls; about 12 servings.

Pescado con Agristada

Fish in Egg-Lemon Sauce

Among some Sephardim from Turkey and Greece, this is the most traditional fish course for the Seder dinner on the first night of Pesach. It is also often served on Shabbat. *Agristada* is the Judeo-Spanish term for a lemony, egg-thickened sauce that is popular in Sephardic cuisine. This fish dish is also frequently called *pescado con huevo y limon,* with many variant spellings of the phonetically transliterated Judeo-Spanish. It means simply, "fish with egg and lemon."

As with many other Sephardic fish dishes, this one may be made ahead and chilled before serving, making it particularly convenient for a Seder meal. The recipe is based on one I learned several years ago from Ida Dana, an excellent Turkish-Sephardic cook.

NOTE: Any type of firm-flesh fish may be used in this dish. Some Sephardic favorites are flounder, salmon, haddock, and striped bass. Fillets are recommended for convenience in serving; however, fish steaks may be used if desired.

POACHING LIQUID AND FISH
1 ½ cups water
2 tablespoons olive or canola oil
Juice of ½ of a medium lemon (reserve the other ½ lemon for the sauce)
2 tablespoons finely chopped fresh parsley leaves
½ teaspoon salt
Pinch of ground black pepper

2 pounds skinless firm-fleshed fish fillets, cut into serving-size pieces (see Note)

SAUCE
2 large eggs, well beaten (not substitutes)
Juice of ½ lemon
1 tablespoon matzah cake meal
About 3 tablespoons water

To poach the fish, combine the water, oil, lemon juice, parsley, salt, and pepper in a wide skillet. Add the fish fillets, in one layer if possible. Bring the liquid to a boil; then lower the heat and cover the skillet. Gently simmer the fish for 5 to 10 minutes, or until it is just cooked through but not falling apart. Use a slotted spoon to transfer the fish to a serving platter with raised sides (to contain the sauce) or a wide shallow bowl. Reserve the broth.

For the sauce, beat the eggs and lemon juice together in a medium bowl.

In a small bowl, mix the cake meal and water to make a creamy paste. Stir the paste into the egg-lemon mixture. Then gradually stir in about ½ cup of the hot fish broth. Stirring constantly, add all the egg-lemon mixture back to the remaining fish broth, and stir over low heat until the sauce has thickened. Adjust the seasonings. Pour the sauce over the fish. Serve hot or, as is more customary, refrigerate the fish and sauce, covered, and serve them chilled or at room temperature.

Makes about 8 servings as a first course.

Keftes de Pescado
"SALMON CROQUETTES" IN TOMATO SAUCE

Fried fish patties like those that follow were a favorite of mine when I was a child. My mother always served "salmon croquettes," as she called them, as the main course of a special dairy dinner.

As an adult, I learned that virtually the same dish (with a Judeo-Spanish name) is often served by Turkish and Greek Jews as a first course on Shabbat night and for Pesach Seders. The Sephardim add a light tomato sauce to their *keftes de pescado.* For extra convenience, the fish patties can be fried ahead of time, and reheated in the sauce just before serving.

Interestingly, some South African Jews make similar croquettes called *frikkadels,* which are often seasoned with ginger and nutmeg instead of parsley and lemon.

NOTES: It is not necessary to remove the bones and skin from canned salmon; both are hardly distinguishable in the cooked croquettes. Furthermore, the bones are a good source of dietary calcium and the skin contains heart-healthy fish oils.

If desired, you may add 1 teaspoon dried dillweed or 2 teaspoons chopped fresh dillweed to the fish mixture for an appealing variation.

Before frying the patties, some Sephardim prefer to coat them lightly with additional matzah meal (or matzah cake meal) and then with beaten egg. This egg coating is traditional for many types of *keftes,* such as Keftes de Prassa y Carne (page 364), and is quite tasty.

Leftover croquettes that have not been cooked in tomato sauce are quite tasty when eaten cold.

1 (15½-ounce) can salmon, including liquid (see Notes)

2 large eggs or 3 large egg whites or ½ cup pareve egg substitute (see page 347)

1 small-to-medium onion, grated

3 tablespoons finely chopped fresh parsley leaves

1 to 2 tablespoons lemon juice (optional)

⅛ teaspoon ground black pepper

About ½ cup matzah meal

Canola, safflower, or other oil for frying

SAUCE

1 (8-ounce) can plain tomato sauce (about 1 cup)

1 to 2 tablespoons lemon juice

¼ cup finely chopped fresh parsley leaves

1 garlic clove, finely minced

Salt and ground black pepper to taste

For the croquettes, put the salmon into a medium bowl and mash it well with a fork. Add the eggs, onion, parsley, lemon juice (if used), and pepper. Stir in enough matzah meal to hold the mixture together. Let it rest about 5 minutes for the matzah meal to absorb some of the moisture.

In a large skillet, add oil to a depth of ⅛ to ¼ inch. Heat the oil over medium-high heat until hot. Form the salmon mixture into ½-inch-thick patties, using about ¼ cup for each one, and put each patty into the oil as it is formed (see Notes). (If the mixture is too soft to be shaped, stir in more matzah meal.)

Fry the patties in the oil until they are well browned on both sides. Drain them on paper towels. Pour any leftover oil out of the skillet, and wipe it out.

In the skillet, combine all the sauce ingredients, and mix well. Over medium-high heat, bring the sauce to a simmer. Arrange the browned croquettes in the sauce and simmer them, covered, for about 5 minutes. Baste them occasionally with the sauce. Transfer the croquettes and sauce to a serving dish, and serve them hot or at room temperature.

To make this ahead and then serve it hot, wrap and refrigerate the plain fried croquettes. Shortly before the keftes de pescado is to be served, heat the sauce as directed above and warm the croquettes in the sauce for about 10 minutes, or until they are heated through.

Makes 9 to 10 2½-inch-diameter croquettes.

Gefilte Fish Loaf with Horseradish Sauce

In the early 1980s, when Tulkoff's, the giant in the horseradish industry, had just moved to their new headquarters near the Baltimore harbor, vice-president Martin Tulkoff gave me a personal tour of the sprawling plant, while he recounted his company's interesting history. Though Tulkoff's eventually became one of the largest processors of horseradish in the world, Mr. Tulkoff explained that the business actually began as a sideline.

Back in the late 1920s, Harry Tulkoff, the patriarch of the family, was a fruit and vegetable vendor, as were many other Russian-Jewish immigrants. The work was very difficult, and competition was tough. To attract more customers, Harry Tulkoff began grinding fresh horseradish root for his customers, on the side. In that era, the pungent concoction was rarely sold bottled.

One day, as Martin Tulkoff told me, his father had a brainstorm. Harry Tulkoff abruptly announced to his wife, "We're going into the horseradish business." Her reply: "You're *meshuggeh!* How are we ever going to make a living?"

In the old days, Harry and Lena Tulkoff scrubbed the gangling roots one by one, and ground them in a hand-cranked wooden grinder, which collected the horseradish in a drawer. Then they mixed the ground horseradish with vinegar and salt in large wooden barrels, and bottled, capped, and labeled it—all by hand. The original bottles were octagonal, with a label that said, in Yiddish lettering, "*Chrain,*" (with a guttural "ch") which means, simply, "Horseradish."

Gradually, specialized equipment, most of it custom-designed by family members, took over each task. The modern plant is almost completely automated. And Tulkoff's brand horseradish products are known throughout the world. However, a special Pesach horseradish mixture is still produced each year just for the holiday, and is very popular among Jewish customers.

After all, virtually every Ashkenazic Seder plate includes some horseradish. And most Ashkenazim prefer to eat their holiday gefilte fish with horseradish in some form.

Following is a recipe for an innovative gefilte fish dish with a delectable sauce, based on horseradish, to accompany it. (Of course, purists may prefer their horseradish "straight.")

Any firm-fleshed, light-colored fish can be used in the loaf; however, a combination of pike, whitefish, and/or carp will give it an old-fashioned, authentic flavor. Garnished with strips of pepper and carrot circles, the loaf is quite attractive and can be served either warm or cold.

HORSERADISH SAUCE
¾ cup mayonnaise
¼ cup plain prepared horseradish
⅓ cup ketchup
A few drops lemon juice or apple cider
    vinegar to taste
Ground black pepper to taste

FISH LOAF GARNISH
½ medium green pepper, seeded and cut
    into strips
1 small carrot, peeled and cut crosswise
    into thin circles

FISH LOAF
1 pound skinless fillets of firm-fleshed,
light-colored fish, such as pike,
    whitefish, cod, carp, and/or
    haddock (may be a combination;
    see comments above)
1 medium onion
1 medium carrot
1 large egg or 2 large egg whites or ¼
    cup pareve egg substitute (see page
    347)
1 tablespoon canola or safflower oil
2 tablespoons water
¼ cup matzah meal
3 tablespoons finely chopped fresh
    parsley leaves
½ teaspoon salt
⅛ to ¼ teaspoon ground black pepper

For the horseradish sauce, combine all the ingredients in a small, covered bowl, and refrigerate the sauce several hours to give the flavors a chance to blend. Preheat the oven to 350 degrees.

For the fish loaf garnish, grease an 8 by 4-inch loaf pan well. Line the bottom of the pan with a rectangle of wax paper cut to fit; then grease the paper. Use the green pepper strips and carrot circles to form an attractive design on top of the wax paper. For instance, arrange the strips of pepper so they form parallel crosswise stripes, then put two or three carrot circles between each stripe. The design will be inverted when the loaf is turned out of the pan, so put the "good" sides of the vegetables facing down.

To make the fish loaf, use a food grinder or a food processor fitted with a steel blade to grind or chop the fish, onion, and carrot until they are very finely minced. (If desired, the onion and carrot may be grated by hand, instead.) Add the egg, oil, water, matzah meal, parsley, salt, and pepper, and mix until very well combined. (If the food processor bowl is large enough, all this may be mixed in it.)

Gently spoon some of the fish mixture around and over the vegetable design in the pan, being careful not to disturb the vegetables. Press it into place, leaving no air spaces. Then add the remaining fish mixture to the pan, spread-

ing it evenly. Cover the fish mixture with another rectangle of wax paper that has been greased on the side facing the loaf.

Bake the loaf at 350 degrees for about 50 minutes, until it is firm. Remove the pan from the oven, and let it rest about 10 minutes. Peel off the wax paper on top; then run a knife around the sides of the loaf to loosen it. Invert the loaf onto a serving dish, and lift off the pan. If the second piece of wax paper is attached to the loaf, peel it off. Serve the loaf lukewarm, at room temperature, or chilled, cut crosswise into slices.

Offer the horseradish sauce on the side.

Makes about 8 servings.

Bimuelos de Massa
MATZAH MEAL PANCAKES

These Sephardic pancakes are virtually identical to the more familiar Ashkenazic matzah meal latkes. Some Sephardim include them as part of the Seder meal. Others prefer to serve them for breakfast, accompanied by sugar, yogurt, and possibly *arrope*—a thick syrup made from raisins, which is also used as haroset in some households.

Sometimes, Pesach *bimuelos* are made from matzah farfel or crumbled matzot, which are soaked in water to soften them.

NOTE: If these are to be served for breakfast, 1 or 2 tablespoons sugar may be stirred into the batter.

4 large eggs or, for "flat" bimuelos only, 1 cup pareve egg substitute (see page 347)
1 cup water

½ teaspoon salt
1 cup regular or whole wheat matzah meal
Canola, safflower, or other oil for frying

For "flat" *bimuelos,* use a fork to mix the eggs, water, and salt in a medium bowl. Stir in the matzah meal. Let the mixture stand about 10 minutes to thicken slightly.

For "light" bimuelos (my personal preference), separate the eggs. In a medium bowl, combine the egg yolks, water, and salt. Stir in the matzah meal. In another bowl, use an electric mixer to beat the egg whites until they are stiff but not dry. Mix the beaten whites with the matzah meal mixture.

For either type, heat oil that is about ⅛ inch deep in a large skillet over medium-high heat. Spoon 2- to 3-tablespoon portions of batter into the oil. Fry the pancakes until they are golden brown on both sides.

Makes about 15 to 20 pancakes.

Variation

BIMUELOS DE MASSA Y QUESO
(MATZAH-MEAL PANCAKES WITH CHEESE)

For these, use either of the above methods to make the *bimuelos,* but substitute milk for the water. Add ½ cup finely grated cheese to the batter just before frying the pancakes. If desired, the pancakes may be fried in melted butter mixed with a little oil.

Keftes de Prassa y Carne

LEEK AND MEAT PATTIES

These Turkish-Jewish *keftes,* which are also served by some Greek Jews, are one of the most popular items at my Seder each year because they are so unusual and delicious. This dish seems to be a particularly Jewish based on the ingredients, technique, and name. For instance, after the formed patties are coated with matzah cake meal, they are dipped into egg, and placed directly into the hot oil. This odd technique makes a light crust on each kefte. Sephardic Jews often use it throughout the year, with flour replacing the matzah cake meal. The name of the dish is a curious combination of Turkish and Spanish words that is uniquely Sephardic.

Although I have slightly changed the following recipe, I first learned how to make the leek *keftes* many years ago from Ida Revah Dana. In 1969, Mrs. Dana, her husband, and their two children emigrated from their native Istanbul to the United States.

Over the years, the Danas welcomed increasingly large numbers of family and friends to their Pesach Seders, up to fifty people, and Mrs. Dana would make the entire meal herself.

Many Sephardic holiday favorites have always been on the Danas menu. For instance, there are Huevos Haminados (page 354), Bimuelos de Massa (page 363), and Pescado con Agristada (page 358), and the following delectable leek-meat *keftes*, served with stewed meat or poultry.

Mrs. Dana would prepare these *keftes* ahead of time, and refrigerate or freeze them. Shortly before serving, she would top them with cooking juices from the stewed meat or chicken, and warm them in a 350-degree oven for about 20 minutes or until heated through.

NOTES: These *keftes* have a large proportion of leeks to meat. They are made small to be used as one of many dishes, not as a main course.

In the traditional version of this recipe, the leeks are not sautéed, just boiled. After several years of experimentation, I have found that sautéing the leeks brings out much more of their splendid flavor; the subsequent simmering in a minimal amount of water then softens them sufficiently for the recipe.

PATTIES
*8 fresh leeks, each ¾ to 1 inch in
    diameter (about 3 to 4 pounds)*
*3 tablespoons olive, canola, or safflower
    oil*
¾ cup hot water
1 pound very lean ground beef
2 large eggs, beaten
*About ¼ cup matzah meal or matzah
    cake meal*
1 teaspoon salt
¼ teaspoon ground black pepper

FOR FRYING
*About ½ cup matzah cake meal, for
    coating*
3 large eggs
Canola or safflower oil

TO SERVE (OPTIONAL)
*About ¼ to ⅓ cup juices from stewed
    beef or chicken*

To clean the leeks, cut off and discard the roots and all but 1 to 2 inches of the green tops. Slice the leeks lengthwise into quarters, and rinse them very well to remove any grit. Finely chop or very thinly slice the drained leeks, and set them aside.

Put 3 tablespoons oil into a large skillet over medium to high heat; then sauté the leeks for about 4 minutes. They should not brown. Add the water, cover the skillet, and lower the heat so the water just simmers. Steam the leeks for about 15 minutes, or until they are very soft. Stir them occasionally, and add water if they are becoming too dry. When the leeks are soft, remove the cover from the saucepan, and cook the leeks, stirring, to evaporate almost all of the moisture. Be careful that they do not get browned.

Remove the leeks from the heat and let them cool to room temperature. Use your hands to squeeze out any remaining liquid. In a medium bowl, combine the cooked leeks with the ground beef, 2 eggs, ¼ cup matzah meal, salt, and pepper. Repeatedly squeeze the mixture through your fingers to blend it very well. The mixture should be soft, but firm enough to be molded into patties as directed below. If necessary, add a bit more matzah meal.

To fry the patties, put the ½ cup matzah *cake* meal into a shallow bowl. Spoon a 2 to 3-tablespoon portion of the meat mixture into the matzah cake meal, and coat it on all sides with cake meal. Then use your hands to form the coated meat mixture into a very small patty that is about 2 to 2½ inches wide and ½ inch thick. Repeat until all the meat mixture is used, arranging the patties in one layer on a large platter or pan (for easy cleanup, line the platter with wax paper or foil). In a small bowl, beat the 3 eggs until they are slightly frothy.

Put oil about ¼ inch deep into a large skillet (or electric frypan), and heat it over medium-high heat until it is quite hot. One at a time, dip a patty into the beaten egg to coat it, and let the excess drip off; then immediately place the patty into the hot oil. Fill the skillet, but do not crowd the patties. Fry the patties until they are golden brown on the bottom; then turn them once with a slotted spatula, and brown them on the second side. They should be cooked through completely. If they are browning too quickly, lower the heat.

Drain the fried keftes well on several layers of paper towels to remove any excess oil. Repeat the coating with egg and frying until all the patties have been cooked, adding oil to the skillet as needed. Put the fried keftes into a large casserole, neatly arranging them in layers.

If the keftes are not to be served immediately, refrigerate them covered. To serve the keftes in the Turkish-Greek manner, spoon juices from stewed meat or chicken over the keftes just before reheating them. Reheat them, covered,

at 350 degrees for about 20 minutes, or until they are heated through. They should absorb the juices. (They may be reheated without stewing juices, if desired.) Serve them as one of many courses at a Seder or at a Sephardic-style meal.

Makes about 30 to 40 small patties; to serve 10 or more as one of many courses.

Ground Beef and Potato Casserole, Israeli-Style

In this very appealing dinner casserole, sliced potatoes surround a filling of cinnamon-spiced ground beef and spinach. The recipe has been adapted from *The Art of Israeli Cooking* by Chef Aldo Nachum, who calls the dish *karikh basar*, which simply means "meat sandwich."

NOTE: For an easy way to defrost spinach in the microwave oven, see the Glossary of Ingredients.

About 4 pounds all-purpose or "new" potatoes

2 (10-ounce) packages frozen chopped spinach, thawed and very well drained (see Note)

2 pounds lean ground beef

1 large onion, grated

4 to 5 scallions, including green tops, thinly sliced

2 medium tomatoes, cored and finely chopped

¼ cup chopped fresh parsley

1 to 1½ teaspoons ground cinnamon, or to taste

1 teaspoon salt

¼ to ½ teaspoon black pepper, or to taste

3 large eggs or 5 egg whites or ¾ cup pareve egg substitute (see page 347)

Olive or canola oil

Paprika

Salt and pepper to taste

Peel the potatoes and cut them into ⅜-inch-thick slices. Put the slices into a large saucepan with about 1 to 2 inches of water. Cover, bring to a boil, and

steam the potatoes for about 10 to 15 minutes, or until they are barely tender. Drain the potatoes well, and cool them while preparing the meat layer.

Grease well or coat with nonstick cooking spray a 9 by 13-inch baking dish. Set aside. Preheat the oven to 375 degrees.

For the meat layers, squeeze any remaining liquid from the spinach. In a large bowl, mix the spinach with the ground beef, onion, scallions, tomato, parsley, cinnamon, salt, pepper, and eggs. Knead the mixture with your hands, or mix with a fork, until it is very smooth and well combined.

In the bottom of the prepared pan, arrange half of the potato slices in one layer. Cover with all the meat mixture, pressing it compactly into place. Top the meat with the remaining potato slices. Brush (or spray) the potatoes lightly with oil; then sprinkle them with paprika and a light sprinkling of salt and pepper.

Cover the baking dish with foil, and bake the casserole at 375 degrees for 20 minutes. Then uncover it, and bake for another 20 minutes, or until the top is golden brown.

Makes about 8 to 10 servings.

Mahshi or Dolmas

MEAT-STUFFED VEGETABLES

This type of dish is very popular all over the Middle East as well as North Africa, Iran, and the Balkans. The idea of stuffing meat into vegetables probably originated in Turkey (the word *dolma* is Turkish for "to stuff"), and spread during the time of the Ottoman Empire. Because of its opulent nature, it is likely to have been developed in the court of a sultan. However, it was eventually adopted by the lower classes, and became a dish for all the people, including the Jews, who lived in these lands.

The basic ground beef or lamb filling may be slightly varied with the addition of pine nuts, raisins, or tomatoes. Jewish cooks often extend the meat with matzah meal instead of the more conventional rice.

All the vegetables listed below can be "mixed and matched" in one meal. Also, you can adjust the herbs and spices to suit your own taste.

NOTE: A metal melon-baller or serrated grapefruit spoon is very helpful for scooping the centers from the vegetables. If desired, the edible scooped-out parts of the vegetables may be chopped up and added to the sauce.

VEGETABLES (4 TO 6 TOTAL)

Green peppers, small zucchini, miniature Italian eggplants (about 5 to 7 inches long), and/or potatoes

STUFFING

1¼ pounds very lean ground beef or lamb

1 small onion, grated or very finely chopped

2 tablespoons finely chopped fresh parsley leaves

1 teaspoon salt

½ teaspoon ground cinnamon

¼ teaspoon ground nutmeg

¼ teaspoon black pepper, preferably freshly ground

⅛ teaspoon ground allspice (optional)

1 large egg

About ½ cup matzah meal

SAUCE

1 (14- to 16-ounce) can tomatoes, including juice, chopped

2 to 3 garlic cloves, minced

½ cup water

¼ teaspoon ground black pepper

Pinch of cayenne pepper (optional)

To prepare the vegetables, cut each one in half lengthwise. For green peppers, remove the stems, seeds, and ribs. For zucchini, cut off the stem, then carefully scoop out a depression in the center of each half, leaving a ½-inch shell. (If necessary, you can use larger zucchini that have been first cut in half crosswise.) For eggplants, scoop out a depression in the center of each half, leaving a ½-inch shell. For potatoes, peel them, and scoop out a depression in the center of each half, leaving a ½-inch shell.

To prepare the stuffing, place all the stuffing ingredients in a bowl; then mix it with your hands, a fork, or a food processor until very well combined and smooth. Add just enough matzah meal so the stuffing is neither sticky nor dry. Press the stuffing into the prepared vegetables, rounding the mixture on top so that it extends ½ to ¾ inch above each vegetable.

For the sauce, put the tomatoes and their juice into a large deep skillet or Dutch oven. Stir in the remaining sauce ingredients. Gently place the stuffed vegetables in the sauce, stuffing side up. Bring the sauce to a boil; then immediately lower the heat and simmer, covered, for 30 to 40 minutes, or until all the vegetables are tender and the meat is cooked through. (Or, if preferred,

the vegetables and sauce may be placed in a 9 by 12-inch baking pan, covered with foil, and baked in a 350-degree oven for about 40 to 50 minutes.) Occasionally use a spoon to gently move the vegetables around so they do not stick to the bottom of the pan. After the mahshi have cooked about 20 minutes, baste them periodically with the sauce.

Use a slotted spoon to remove the stuffed vegetables from the sauce. If the vegetables have given off a lot of juice during cooking and the sauce is thin, boil it down for a few minutes to thicken it. Pour a little sauce over the vegetables, and serve the remainder on the side.

Makes 8 to 12 pieces; 4 to 6 servings.

Mina de Carne or Mayeena

MEAT-POTATO MATZAH "PIE"

*M*ayeena is the Egyptian-Jewish equivalent of a Sephardic *mina* made with meat and mashed potatoes. This *mina* is sometimes served as part of a Sephardic Seder dinner. It can also stand on its own as a main course for a midholiday meal. This dish is a great way to use up leftover mashed potatoes. The Egyptian version is seasoned with cinnamon and allspice instead of garlic, celery, and dillweed.

NOTES: It is necessary to soak the matzah to soften it so that the *mina* can be easily cut and eaten. Regular matzah holds together very well when it is softened by soaking, but egg matzah disintegrates into mush.

If only oil is used to grease the bottom of the pan, the matzah tends to stick. By using margarine and then oil, the matzah crust gets crispy but does not stick.

1½ pounds all-purpose or "new" potatoes

Salt and ground black pepper to taste

2½ to 3 square sheets of plain whole wheat or white matzah (see Notes)

Pareve margarine for the pan (see Notes)

1 to 2 tablespoons olive, canola, or other oil, for the pan

1 pound lean ground beef

1 medium or large onion, finely
    chopped
1 to 2 garlic cloves, minced
2 celery stalks, finely chopped
2 tablespoons finely chopped fresh
    parsley leaves

1 teaspoon chopped fresh dillweed or 1/2
    teaspoon dried dillweed (optional)
3 large eggs or 3/4 cup pareve egg
    substitute (see page 347)

First make the mashed potato topping. Peel the potatoes, and cut them into quarters. Put them into a 2½- to 3-quart saucepan, and add water to cover. Bring to a boil; then simmer them, covered, for about 20 minutes, or until they are soft. Drain the potatoes; then use a potato masher or fork to mash them in the pan. Season them to taste with salt and pepper. Set them aside to cool.

Put some warm water into a 9-inch square baking dish, then add the whole sheets of matzah and let them soak for 2 to 3 minutes, or until they are soft and flexible but not falling apart. Carefully lift each sheet of matzah out of the water, and place it flat on paper towels to drain. Completely dry the baking dish. Grease the baking dish well with margarine; then add 1 to 2 tablespoons oil and tilt the pan so that the bottom is covered. Set it aside.

In a large skillet, over medium-high heat, brown the ground beef with the onion, garlic, and celery, breaking up the meat with a spoon or fork. When the meat has browned, and the vegetables are tender, drain off and discard any excess fat. Remove the meat mixture from the heat, and stir in the parsley and dillweed (if used). Season the meat mixture with salt and pepper.

Add 2 of the eggs (or ½ cup egg substitute) to the mashed potatoes and mix until well blended. Stir about ¼ to ½ cup of the mashed potatoes into the meat to help hold it together. Set the meat mixture and remaining mashed potatoes aside. Preheat the oven to 375 degrees.

Beat the remaining egg and pour it into a large platter that has a slightly raised edge. Coat both sides of a softened matzah lightly with egg, lifting it so that all the excess egg drips off. Place the matzah in the bottom of the greased and oiled baking dish. Use part of a second egg-coated matzah to fill in any spaces so that the bottom of the dish is completely covered. (You can easily cut softened matzah by following the dotted lines.) Repeat to make a second layer of matzah over the first one. Reserve any leftover egg.

Pesach (Passover)

Spread the meat mixture on top of the matzah in the dish. Spoon the mashed potato mixture on top, and spread it so that it completely covers the meat. Pour any leftover beaten egg on top.

Bake the *mina* at 375 degrees for about 30 minutes, or until the top is lightly browned and the filling is firm. Remove the *mina* from the oven, and let it stand for 5 minutes before serving. Cut it into large squares to serve.

Makes about 4 servings as a main course, or more as a part of a multicourse meal.

Orange-Glazed Chicken Breasts

This has become one of my favorite Seder main dishes. It is easy to prepare, it can be assembled ahead of time, it makes a lot of servings in a minimum of space, and it looks and tastes great! The lightly "breaded" (with matzah meal, of course) chicken has a delectable sweet-tart flavor, and it is very easy to serve and eat because there are no bones. Orange marmalade is generally available kosher for Pesach.

1½ cups matzah meal
3 tablespoons finely chopped fresh parsley
1½ teaspoons ground ginger
¾ teaspoon salt
¼ teaspoon ground black pepper
3 to 4 extra-large egg whites or 2 large eggs or ½ cup pareve egg substitute (see page 347)

3 to 4 pounds boned and skinned chicken breast halves, about 12
1 (12-ounce) jar orange marmalade
1 cup white table wine (the type is your choice)
3 tablespoons canola or safflower oil

Line a very large roasting pan (or two smaller pans) with heavy-duty aluminum foil (for easy cleanup); then grease the foil so that the chicken won't stick to it. Preheat the oven to 350 degrees.

In a medium bowl, combine the matzah meal, parsley, ginger, salt, and pepper. Put the egg whites into another bowl, and lightly beat them until they are frothy. Dip each chicken breast half into the egg white, and then coat

it completely with the matzah meal mixture. Arrange the coated chicken breasts close together in the prepared pan so that none overlap.

Put the marmalade, wine, and oil into a small saucepan or a microwave-safe bowl, and mix them well. Over medium heat, or in the microwave oven, slowly bring the mixture to a brief boil. Spoon the mixture over the chicken breasts so all tops are moistened and there are some orange slivers on each breast.

Bake at 350 degrees, uncovered, for about 35 to 40 minutes, or until the chicken is cooked through but is not dry. If not serving the chicken immediately, wrap the chicken well, and refrigerate or freeze it. Defrost it before reheating it in a covered pan. Do not reheat for too long, or the glaze may harden and the chicken can become dry and tough.

Makes about 10 to 12 servings.

Baked Chicken with Fruit-Nut "Stuffing"

For the greatest ease in preparing and serving this dish, the chicken is cut up and placed on top of the stuffing in the pan. The stuffing gets flavor from the chicken, but there is no messy carving.

NOTES: For an alternative "stuffing" that is not as sweet, see the recipe for Mushroom-Onion Farfel Kugel (page 377).

"Matzah farfel" (tiny pieces of broken matzah) is usually available in boxes at the supermarket or kosher grocery. If you cannot find it, break plain white matzah into rough ½-inch pieces, and use as directed.

Pesach (Passover)

STUFFING

3 tablespoons olive or canola oil

2 medium onions, finely chopped

3 celery stalks, thinly sliced

4 cups matzah farfel (see Notes)

1 cup raisins

1 cup diced mixed dried fruits

⅔ cup walnut pieces

1 (approximately 10½-ounce) can
   condensed clear chicken soup

1 cup water

½ teaspoon cinnamon, or to taste

Salt and ground black pepper to taste

3 large eggs or 1 large egg plus 3 large
   egg whites, lightly beaten or ¾ cup
   pareve egg substitute (see page
   347)

CHICKEN

1 large (about 5-pound) roasting
   chicken or capon, cut into 8 pieces,
   or 2 smaller chickens, cut into 4
   pieces

Olive or canola oil

1 medium onion, grated

Paprika, salt, and ground black pepper

Grease well a 10 by 15-inch baking dish or roasting pan. Preheat the oven to 350 degrees.

Put the oil into a very large skillet or Dutch oven over medium-high heat; then sauté the chopped onion and celery until they are tender. Remove the skillet from the heat, and stir in the matzah farfel, raisins, dried fruit, and walnuts. Add the chicken soup and water, and stir to mix in evenly. Stir the mixture gently for a few minutes until the moisture is absorbed. Then mix in the cinnamon, salt, and pepper to taste. Finally, stir in the beaten eggs.

Spread the stuffing in the bottom of the prepared pan. Clean the chicken very well, removing any giblets and lumps of fat. Arrange the chicken pieces, skin side up, very close together on top of the stuffing. Brush the skin of each piece lightly with oil, then spoon some grated onion on each piece, and sprinkle them all lightly with paprika, salt, and pepper.

Bake the chicken at 350 degrees for about 1 to 1¼ hours, or until the chicken is golden brown and completely cooked through (thighs will take longer than breasts). Serve each piece with some stuffing.

Makes about 8 servings.

Chicken Breasts in Spiced Sauce

The aromatic Moroccan-style spices in this easy dish penetrate the chicken as it cooks, giving it a wonderful flavor. The chicken breasts are "stewed" in a small amount of liquid, keeping the meat very moist and tender. After the chicken is done, its well-seasoned broth becomes a tasty low-fat sauce. Adjust all the seasonings below to taste.

NOTE: In a pinch, individually frozen boneless, skinless chicken breasts may be used in this dish without defrosting. Simply cook them about 10 minutes longer than indicated below, or until they are cooked through.

1 cup water
1 tablespoon olive or canola oil
¾ cup chopped fresh parsley
1 large onion, grated
¾ to 1 teaspoon ground ginger
¾ to 1 teaspoon cinnamon

½ teaspoon ground turmeric (optional)
¼ to ½ teaspoon black pepper
½ teaspoon salt
About 2 pounds boneless, skinless
  chicken breast halves

Put all the ingredients except the chicken into a large, deep 12-inch skillet or a Dutch oven. Put the pot over medium-high heat, and bring the sauce ingredients to a simmer. Simmer the sauce, uncovered, for about 2 minutes, then add the chicken breasts. Spoon some sauce over each piece. Simmer the chicken covered for about 15 to 20 minutes, or until it is cooked through and tender. Occasionally turn the chicken pieces so that each side is immersed in the broth for part of the cooking period.

Remove the chicken pieces from the pot onto a serving platter. If the sauce remaining in the pot is too thin, then bring it to a boil and slightly reduce it to the desired consistency. Pour the hot sauce over the chicken pieces.

Makes about 6 to 8 servings.

Pesach (Passover)

Tagine of Chicken with Prunes and Almonds M

This delectable dish is quite popular with Moroccan Jews, who sometimes substitute boned, cubed lamb for the chicken. Those Sephardim who do not abstain from eating rice during Pesach may serve it with this *tagine* (pronounced "tah-'jheen")—a general term for any slowly simmered Moroccan stew. The word also means the special type of ceramic casserole usually used in Morocco to cook these stews.

1 cup whole blanched almonds

3 tablespoons olive, canola, or safflower oil

2 medium onions, finely chopped

About 3½ pounds meaty chicken pieces (skin removed, if desired) or about 2 pounds skinless, boneless chicken breasts or thighs

1 cup water

1 to 3 teaspoons ground cinnamon, to taste

½ teaspoon ground ginger

¼ to ½ teaspoon ground black pepper, to taste

Pinch of salt

10 to 12 ounces (about 2 cups) pitted prunes

1 tablespoon honey or sugar (optional)

First, toast the almonds. Spread them in a shallow pan and place them in a 350-degree oven for about 10 minutes, stirring them occasionally, until they are very lightly browned. Set them aside. (The almonds can be toasted ahead and stored in an airtight container when cool. To keep them crunchy, do not add them to the *tagine* until just before serving.)

Put the oil into a very large skillet or a Dutch oven over medium-high heat; then sauté the onion until it is tender. Push the onion to the perimeter of the skillet. Add the chicken to the skillet, and lightly brown it on all sides.

Mix the water with the cinnamon, ginger, pepper, and salt, and pour it over the chicken. Bring the liquid to a boil. Cover the skillet tightly, lower the heat, and simmer the chicken pieces for 25 minutes (or the boneless breasts for 5 minutes; boneless thighs for 10 minutes), turning the chicken occasionally. Add the prunes and honey or sugar (if used) to the skillet, evenly distributing the prunes among the chicken pieces, and making sure they are covered with liquid. Simmer the chicken and prunes together in the covered skillet for about 15 minutes, or until both are very tender. If the sauce becomes too dry and begins to stick to the bottom of the skillet, stir in additional water as needed.

Use tongs or a slotted spoon to remove the chicken to a serving platter. Stir about half the almonds into the prune sauce remaining in the pot; then spoon the sauce mixture over the chicken. Use the remaining almonds to garnish the top.

If preparing the *tagine* ahead of time, transfer the cooked chicken and prune sauce to a covered casserole, and refrigerate. Shortly before serving, reheat it, covered, in a 325-degree oven, stirring occasionally, for about 30 minutes, or until completely heated through. Stir about half the almonds into the *tagine,* and sprinkle the remainder on top.

Makes 6 to 8 servings.

Mushroom-Onion Farfel Kugel

I created this kugel especially for my second-born son—a picky eater, particularly during Pesach. As this dish contains two of his favorite foods—mushrooms and fried onions—he found it hard to resist. After just a few bites, he proclaimed it to be delicious, and definitely a "keeper" for this book.

The fragrant mixture may be used as stuffing for a turkey or other fowl, if desired. It can then be prepared ahead up to the addition of the eggs. Add the eggs just before stuffing and roasting the fowl.

3 tablespoons olive or canola oil
3 medium onions, finely chopped
2 garlic cloves, finely minced
4 celery stalks, thinly sliced
1 pound fresh mushrooms, cleaned and sliced (about 5 cups)
3½ cups matzah farfel (see Notes on page 373)

1 (approximately 10½-ounce) can condensed clear chicken soup
1 cup water
1 teaspoon dried thyme leaves
Salt and ground black pepper to taste
3 large eggs or ¾ cup pareve egg substitute (see page 347)

Grease well a 9 by 13-inch baking dish, and set it aside. Preheat the oven to 350 degrees.

Pesach (Passover)

Put the oil into a 5-quart or larger pot, and place it over medium heat. Add the onion and garlic, and sauté them until the onion is soft. Stir in the celery, and sauté about 2 minutes longer. Then stir in mushrooms, and sauté an additional minute or two. Add the farfel, and stir just until it is mixed in well. Turn off the heat. Add the chicken soup and water, and stir to mix in evenly. Season the mixture with the thyme, salt, and pepper.

After the seasonings are adjusted to taste, beat the eggs lightly and stir them into the farfel mixture until completely combined. Transfer the mixture to the prepared baking dish, and smooth the top. Bake the kugel, uncovered, at 350 degrees for about 45 to 50 minutes, or until the top is firm and dry.

If you are not serving the kugel immediately, cover the baking dish tightly and refrigerate or freeze the kugel. Defrost the kugel before reheating it in a covered dish.

Makes 12 or more servings.

Carrot Soufflé Kugel

This sweet, moist kugel has a deliciously surprising taste, almost like a very light pumpkin pie. The last thing people usually suspect is that it is made from carrots. It is really a nice change from some of the heavier side dishes that we have at Pesach, and the interesting flavor and vivid orange color go far to liven up everyone's palate and plate.

The Carrot Soufflé Kugel is lightest right after baking, but it can be refrigerated and reheated if desired. It deflates a bit, but is still somewhat fluffy. As it is too soft to cut into squares, it is served with a spoon directly from the baking pan, like spoon bread.

I developed this recipe after *lots* of experimentation; however, I first got the idea for a spiced cooked-carrot kugel from my good friend and excellent cook, Susan Groman. She pointed out to me that convenient canned carrots taste almost exactly the same as fresh-cooked in this kind of kugel.

NOTES: A food processor is needed to purée the carrot mixture for this recipe.

If desired, the kugel may be further "spiced up" with the addition of ½ teaspoon ground nutmeg or ginger and ¼ teaspoon cloves. It will have a more intense "pumpkin pie" flavor.

3½ cups fresh or frozen peeled carrot slices or 2 (14- to 16-ounce) cans of cooked sliced carrots
¾ cup sugar, divided
3 large eggs, 2 of them separated
¼ cup canola or safflower oil
1 teaspoon ground cinnamon
⅓ cup potato starch

If you are using fresh or frozen carrots, cook them in a small amount of water until they are very soft. Drain them well, and let them cool to room temperature. If you are using canned carrots, drain them in a colander, rinse them lightly with cool tap water, and drain completely. Set the carrots aside.

Grease well an 8- or 9-inch square baking dish or pan that is at least 1¾ inches deep. Preheat the oven to 325 degrees.

Put the reserved carrots into a food processor fitted with a steel blade. Pulse-process to coarsely chop the carrots. Add ½ cup of the sugar, 1 whole egg, 2 egg yolks, the oil, and cinnamon. Process until the mixture is completely puréed and smooth, scraping down the sides of the container as necessary. Add the potato starch, and process until it is mixed in. Set aside.

Put the 2 egg whites into a medium mixing bowl, and beat with an electric mixer at medium speed until the whites are frothy. Then slowly add the remaining ¼ cup sugar, and beat the whites at high speed until they form stiff peaks. Add the carrot mixture to the whites, and fold them together until the whites are completely mixed in (don't worry if the mixture deflates a little). Be sure there are no lumps of whites.

Pour the batter into the prepared baking dish. Bake the kugel at 325 degrees for about 60 to 65 minutes, or until the top seems firm and a small knife inserted in the center comes out almost clean. The kugel may be served immediately, or it may be allowed to cool in the pan on a rack until lukewarm. (It will deflate somewhat, but still tastes great.) To serve the kugel, scoop out servings with a large spoon. The kugel will be very moist and soft.

To make the kugel ahead, let the kugel cool to lukewarm, then refrigerate it. Reheat it, covered, in a microwave oven or in a low conventional oven just until it is heated through. The kugel will not be as high as when it was first made.

Makes about 9 servings.

Pesach (Passover)

Lemony Sesame Asparagus

 OR

Asparagus, a popular spring vegetable, is often on the Seder table. This is one of my favorite ways to serve it. The lemon juice reflects Sephardic influences, while the sesame seeds are an Israeli touch. This takes only a few minutes to prepare, but it looks and tastes quite elegant.

2 pounds fresh asparagus spears, each spear approximately ½ inch thick
3 tablespoons sesame seeds
3 tablespoons butter or pareve margarine

2 tablespoons lemon juice
⅛ teaspoon salt (for use with unsalted butter or margarine)

Wash the asparagus well; then gently break off the tough white part at the bottom of each stem, and discard. Lay the asparagus spears in a large skillet, and cover them with water. Cover the skillet, and bring the water to a boil over high heat. Reduce the heat, and gently simmer the asparagus spears just until they are tender, about 7 to 10 minutes. Do not overcook the spears or they will become mushy and stringy.

Meanwhile, toast the sesame seeds, stirring them constantly in a small skillet over medium heat until they are golden brown and aromatic. Set them aside.

Melt the butter or margarine in a small saucepan over medium heat, or in a small bowl in the microwave oven. Remove from the heat, and stir in the lemon juice and salt (if used). Drain the cooked asparagus very well; then carefully transfer the spears to a serving platter. Pour the lemon-butter sauce on top of the spears; then sprinkle them with the toasted sesame seeds.

Makes about 8 to 10 servings.

Spinach with Pine Nuts and Raisins

ITALIAN-STYLE SAUTÉED SPINACH

Spinach provides a glorious green for a Pesach menu, with pine nuts and raisins adding an intriguing Italian-Jewish touch to this side dish. I have used frozen spinach because it is convenient and very tasty; however, you may choose to use fresh spinach that has been stemmed, washed well, and briefly cooked in a minimal amount of water. You may use chopped or whole spinach leaves, whichever you prefer.

NOTE: For more information on pine nuts, see the Glossary of Ingredients.

2 (10-ounce) packages chopped or
    regular frozen spinach
3 tablespoons olive oil
1 medium onion, finely chopped
2 to 3 tablespoons pine nuts (pignoli)

¼ cup soft fresh raisins
Salt and ground black pepper to taste
Nutmeg to taste (optional)

Defrost the frozen spinach by stabbing a few holes in the top of each box, and then putting the boxes, one at a time, on some paper towels (for drips) in a microwave oven set on high for 3 to 4 minutes. Or, if you prefer, remove the spinach from the boxes and cook it briefly as directed on the package just until thawed. Drain excess liquid from the spinach, but do not squeeze it dry. Set the spinach aside.

Put the oil into a large saucepan over medium heat; then sauté the onion and pine nuts until the onion is soft and the pine nuts are lightly browned. Add the spinach and raisins, and stir for 1 minute. Cover the top, and steam the spinach mixture about 2 minutes to plump the raisins, then uncover and stir constantly until all the excess liquid has evaporated. Season to taste with salt, pepper, and nutmeg (if used). Serve hot or lukewarm.

Makes about 6 servings.

Vegetarian Tzimmes
VEGETABLE-FRUIT CASSEROLE

P

Most Ashkenazic households have at least one dish similar to this on the Seder table. It can be made ahead and reheated shortly before serving.

4 large sweet potatoes,
1 medium butternut squash
4 medium apples
7 to 8 ounces pitted prunes (about 24)
1/3 cup sweet red Pesach wine or orange
  juice

1/3 cup water
About 1/2 cup sugar, or to taste
1 1/2 teaspoons ground cinnamon
1/2 teaspoon ground ginger

Grease a 9 by 13-inch baking dish well. Preheat the oven to 375 degrees.

Peel the sweet potatoes, and cut them in ¾-inch cubes. Do the same with the squash, discarding all seeds and fibers. Cut the apples into fourths, and remove the seeds. If desired (it is not necessary), peel the apples. Then coarsely chop them.

Put the sweet potatoes, squash, and apples into a large bowl with the prunes. In a small bowl or glass measuring cup, combine the remaining ingredients. Pour the mixture over the fruit and vegetables, and mix everything very well so all is coated with the liquid.

Turn the mixture into the prepared dish. Cover the dish tightly with foil, and bake the tzimmes at 375 degrees for about 1 hour, or until the sweet potatoes and squash are tender.

Stir the tzimmes before serving, to evenly distribute the sauce and slightly mash the apples.

Makes about 8 servings.

Mom's Best Potato Kugel

POTATO-ONION CASSEROLE

When I was growing up, this delicious kugel was a staple on our holiday table throughout the year, and a family favorite. There was only one minor problem; we all wanted the crunchy corners. My mother learned to put extra oil on the top of the kugel so that the whole crust would become brown and crisp, while the inside stayed soft and moist.

Mom used to grate the potatoes and onions with a hand-cranked grinder, but she was delighted to switch to a food processor as soon as those devices became available. The following directions reflect that change. Of course, this kugel can be made by hand, if preferred, and those directions are included.

This kugel contains no matzah meal. It's just a simple mixture of potatoes, onions, eggs, and seasonings.

NOTES: The baking dish is coated with margarine *and* then layered with oil because the oil browns the bottom of the kugel, but does not keep it from sticking.

I always buy an extra potato just in case one is rotten inside and can't be used.

Pareve margarine for the pan
4 to 5 tablespoons canola or safflower oil, divided
3 to 3½ pounds russet baking potatoes (about 6 or 7)
2 medium-to-large onions

4 large eggs or 2 large eggs plus 3 egg whites or 1 cup pareve egg substitute (see page 347)
2 teaspoons salt
Generous ¼ teaspoon ground black pepper

Coat a 9 by 13-inch baking dish with margarine; then pour about 2 table-spoons oil into the bottom, and tilt the pan so that the bottom is entirely covered with oil. Preheat the oven to 400 degrees. Peel the potatoes and the onions.

For the food processor: Cut the onions into fourths or eighths (depending on the size of the onions), and remove the root end from each piece. Set aside. Grate the potatoes using the small-holed grating blade of the food processor. Reserve any small potato ends that don't get properly grated. Transfer all the grated potatoes, including any liquid, to a very large bowl.

Pesach (Passover)

Remove the grating blade from the food processor, and replace it with the steel "chopping" blade. Put the reserved potato ends, onions, eggs, salt, and pepper into the food processor bowl, and process until the mixture is puréed. Pour the puréed onion-egg mixture over the potatoes, and mix well.

By hand: Finely grate the potatoes and whole onions into a large bowl, alternating them to help keep the potatoes from darkening. Beat the eggs with the salt and pepper, and mix well into the potato and onion shreds.

For both: Pour the potato mixture into the prepared pan and smooth the top with the back of a large spoon. Very carefully use the spoon to layer about 2 to 3 tablespoons more oil over the potato mixture so the entire top is covered.

Bake at 400 degrees, uncovered, for about 1 hour, or until the top is browned and crisp. Cool slightly on a rack before serving. The kugel may be made ahead and reheated, covered tightly with foil, in a 300- to 325-degree oven until warmed through. It may be reheated in a microwave oven, but it will not be as crisp.

Cut into large squares to serve.

Makes about 12 to 14 servings.

Roasted Potatoes with Onions

The simplicity of this recipe makes it hard to believe how delicious and popular this dish is. It is the hit of the meal every time that I serve it. One of my tricks is to toss the potato-onion mixture in a huge plastic bag with a zipper closing. That way, I can use a minimal amount of oil and get it to coat every potato surface.

For this recipe, I highly recommend using a roasting or baking *pan* and not a glass baking dish. Glass does not conduct heat very well, and will not "roast" and brown potatoes as well as metal. A nonstick pan is ideal for easy cleanup, but be sure the nonstick surface can withstand the high oven temperature. If the pan is not nonstick, you may want to line it with heavy-duty foil for easy cleanup.

3 pounds red potatoes (such as Red
   Bliss)
3 medium or 2 large onions
¼ cup extra-virgin olive oil, canola oil,
   or safflower oil

1 teaspoon dried thyme leaves
2 to 3 garlic cloves, finely minced or
   pressed
Salt and ground black pepper

Lightly oil a 9 by 13-inch metal baking pan or roasting pan (see the comments above). Set it aside. Preheat the oven to 425 degrees.

Clean the potatoes very well, removing any marks or bad spots on the surface, but do not peel them. Cut them into chunks that are about 1½ inches on a side. Put them into a jumbo-sized (2-gallon) heavy-duty plastic food storage bag with a zipper (or use a large bowl). Peel the onions. Cut them in half through the root end, and then crosswise into ¼-inch slices. Separate the "rings," and put the onions with the potatoes. If you are using a bag, add the oil to the bag, and zip it tightly closed so there is an air pocket in the bag. Shake the bag vigorously to evenly distribute the oil. (If you are using a bowl, add the oil, and mix with a spoon or your hands to evenly distribute it.)

Open the bag, and add the thyme, garlic, and generous sprinkles of salt and pepper. Seal the bag, and shake again as before. (Or mix everything in the bowl.)

Transfer the seasoned potatoes and onions to the prepared pan. Bake for about 1 hour, or until the potatoes and onions are very soft and browned. Very gently stir the potatoes 3 or 4 times during the cooking period to be sure that they are cooking evenly and are not sticking to the pan.

Makes about 8 servings.

Baked Potatoes with Spinach and Tomatoes

I created this Sephardic-style combination as another way to use the delicious filling from the Mina de Espinaca y Tomat (page 388). The topped baked potatoes make a very satisfying low-calorie and low-fat vegetarian main dish that I prepare all year round. They can also be used as a great side dish. If desired, tuna may be added to the filling

and/or the filled potatoes may be topped with grated cheese. This recipe is easily doubled if desired.

NOTE: For an easy way to defrost spinach in the microwave oven, see the Glossary of Ingredients.

About 4 large russet (baking) potatoes
2 tablespoons olive or canola oil
1 medium onion, finely chopped
1 to 2 garlic cloves, minced
1 (14- to 16-ounce) can tomatoes, including juice, chopped
1 (10-ounce) package frozen chopped spinach, thawed and very well drained (see Note)

1 teaspoon dried basil leaves or 2 teaspoons finely chopped fresh basil
Salt and ground black pepper to taste

OPTIONAL "EXTRAS"
1 (6- to 7-ounce) can solid white tuna, drained
About 4 ounces (1 cup) grated mild cheese, such as Muenster, Swiss, mozzarella, or Parmesan

Scrub the potatoes very well, cutting away any "eyes" or green patches; then dry them. Use a fork to pierce the top of each potato several times to allow steam to escape. Place the potatoes directly on the rack of a preheated 400- to 425-degree oven, and bake for about 50 to 60 minutes, or until the potatoes feel soft when pressed and are tender all the way through when pierced by a fork. Remove the potatoes from the oven, but do not cut them open. They will stay hot for 15 minutes or longer. They can be left in the turned-off hot oven to stay warm even longer.

When the potatoes are almost done baking, make the spinach and tomato topping. Put the oil into a large skillet over medium-high heat; then sauté the onion and garlic until they are tender. Add the tomatoes and their juice, along with the drained spinach and basil. Cook the mixture, stirring occasionally, for about 5 minutes or until most, but not all, of the liquid has evaporated. Season the mixture with salt and pepper to suit your taste; then remove it from the heat. If tuna is desired, flake it into large pieces, and gently mix them into the spinach.

Split each potato in half lengthwise, and open it onto a serving platter. Use a fork to loosen and "fluff up" the inside of each potato, leaving it in the potato skin. Spoon the spinach mixture (including juices) on top of each

potato, dividing it evenly. If cheese is desired, sprinkle it over the potato mixture. Serve as is, or put the potatoes briefly under a broiler to melt the cheese. The potatoes may be eaten in their entirety, or the insides may be scooped out of the skins.

Makes about 4 main-dish servings; about 8 side-dish servings (¹⁄₂ potato each).

Fritada de Espinaca
SPINACH-CHEESE CASSEROLE

Although I often see this popular Sephardic dish, which is sometimes called a *quajado*, described as a spinach soufflé, it is not really puffy and light. And it certainly isn't fried in a skillet and then broiled (to finish the top) like the similarly named Italian frittata. Actually, a *fritada* most resembles an Ashkenazic kugel or perhaps a crustless quiche.

While the following tasty spinach *fritada* is perfect for Pesach, Sephardim might serve it year-round at dairy meals. It makes a nice main course for a light lunch or dinner, or a small part of a multicourse meal. I like to serve it at dairy buffets.

NOTES: For an easy way to defrost spinach in the microwave oven, see the Glossary of Ingredients.

The combination of hard cheeses is based on general Sephardic preference; please feel free to vary the combination as you desire.

2 (10-ounce) packages frozen chopped
    spinach (see Note)
Butter or margarine for the pan
4 large eggs or 1 cup pareve egg
    substitute (see page 347)
¹⁄₂ cup matzah meal
8 ounces mild cheese, such as Swiss,
    Muenster, mozzarella, or
    kashkaval, grated (2 cups, packed)

¹⁄₄ cup grated Parmesan or Romano
    cheese (or more of the same cheese
    as above)
1 (7¹⁄₂- to 8-ounce) package soft
    curd–style farmer cheese or 1 cup
    small-curd cottage cheese
About ¹⁄₄ teaspoon salt
¹⁄₄ teaspoon ground black pepper

Defrost the spinach and drain off excess liquid, but do not squeeze the spinach dry. Set it aside.

Use butter or margarine to generously grease a 9- or 10-inch square (or equivalent) baking dish. Set it aside. Preheat the oven to 375 degrees.

In a large bowl, beat the eggs until they are well blended. Add the reserved spinach, and all the remaining ingredients except for about ½ cup of the grated mild cheese (i.e., not the Parmesan or Romano) to use on the top of the *fritada*. Mix all the ingredients well. Evenly spread the spinach mixture in the prepared pan, and smooth the top. Sprinkle the reserved grated cheese on top.

Bake the *fritada* at 375 degrees for about 40 to 45 minutes, or until it is firm. Let it rest for about 5 minutes before serving it. Or let it cool longer, and serve it at room temperature. If desired, it may be easily reheated in a microwave oven.

Makes about 6 main-dish servings, or about 16 squares for buffet serving.

Mina de Espinaca y Tomat
SPINACH-TOMATO MATZAH "LASAGNA"

During Pesach, Sephardic Jews, particularly those from Turkey and Greece, enjoy many different types of *minas* (pronounced "'mee-nahs"). Each "pie" has a base and often a top of softened matzot, with various fillings sandwiched in between. Sometimes, as in the recipe that follows, there is a third layer of matzah inside the pie.

Dairy versions, such as this one and the Mina de Prassa con Queso (page 391), are usually served for brunch or a light evening meal. A *mina* made with meat, such as Mina de Carne (page 370), may be part of the Seder dinner.

Minas are particularly convenient in that they can be made ahead, and reheated. They are cut into squares for serving. Following is one of my family's favorite *minas,* which I prepare often during the holiday.

I have also demonstrated this dish frequently in cooking classes, where it is invariably dubbed "matzah lasagne" by my students. Frankly, I think that this *mina* is much more elegant than that, but there is a certain similarity.

Authentic *minas* are frequently made with large quantities of oil, both in the pan and on top of the pie. I have eliminated most of it. Consequently, this *mina* is not as crisp as some made by Sephardim, but it is lighter and quite tasty. Because less oil is used, it is necessary to "grease" the bottom of the pan with another fat (butter or margarine) that prevents sticking better than oil.

For another use of this delicious filling, see the recipe for Baked Potatoes with Spinach and Tomatoes (page 385).

NOTES: To double this recipe for about 8 main course servings, use a 9 by 13-inch baking dish and follow the same directions. Use twice the amount of each ingredient. You will need a total of seven sheets of matzah—two whole ones in each layer and one that is torn to fill in gaps—but only 3 eggs to coat the matzot. Bake the *mina* about 30 to 35 minutes.

It is necessary to soak the matzah to soften it so that the *mina* can be easily cut and eaten. Regular matzah holds together very well when it is softened by soaking, but egg matzah disintegrates into mush.

If only oil is used to "grease" the bottom of the pan, the matzah tends to stick. By using butter or margarine and then oil, the matzah gets crispy but does not stick.

For an easy way to defrost spinach in the microwave oven, see the Glossary of Ingredients.

Regarding the cheese in this *mina*, you may use any kind or combination of relatively "mild" cheese, such as Muenster, Swiss, mozzarella, etc. A little Parmesan is fine, but do not use all Parmesan cheese. Sephardim might use some kashkaval or kasseri; for more information on these cheeses, see the recipe for Borekas (page 492).

3½ to 4 square sheets plain whole wheat or white matzah (see Notes)

Butter or margarine for the pan (see Notes)

3 to 4 tablespoons olive, canola, or other oil, divided

1 medium onion, finely chopped

1 to 2 garlic cloves, minced

1 (14- to 16-ounce) can tomatoes, including juice, chopped

1 (10-ounce) package frozen chopped spinach, thawed and very well drained (see Notes)

1 teaspoon dried basil leaves or 2 teaspoons finely chopped fresh basil

Salt and ground black pepper to taste

2 large eggs, beaten

4 to 6 ounces (1 to 1½ cups, packed) mild grated cheese (see Notes)

Pesach (Passover)

Put some warm water into an 8- or 9-inch square baking dish, then add the whole sheets of matzah and let them soak for 2 to 3 minutes, or until they are soft and flexible but *not* falling apart. Carefully lift each sheet of matzah out of the water, and place it flat on paper towels to drain. Completely dry the baking dish. Grease the baking dish well with butter or margarine; then add 1 to 2 tablespoons of the oil and tilt the pan so that the bottom is covered. Set it aside.

Put the remaining 2 tablespoons oil into a large skillet over medium-high heat; then sauté the onion and garlic until they are tender. Add the tomatoes and their juice, along with the drained spinach and basil. Cook the mixture, stirring occasionally, for about 5 minutes or until most, but not all, of the liquid has evaporated. Season the mixture with salt and pepper to suit your taste; then remove it from the heat. Set it aside to cool slightly. Preheat the oven to 375 degrees.

Pour the beaten eggs into a large platter that has a slightly raised edge. Coat both sides of a softened matzah lightly with egg, lifting it so that all the excess egg drips off. Place the matzah in the bottom of the greased and oiled dish. Use part of a second egg-coated matzah to fill in any spaces so that the bottom of the dish is completely covered. (You can easily cut softened matzah by following the dotted lines.)

Spoon half the cooked spinach mixture (including any juices) over the matzah in the dish, and spread it evenly. Sprinkle a third of the grated cheese over the top. Put another egg-coated matzah on top of the cheese, filling in any spaces as before. Then top that with the remaining spinach mixture, and another third of the cheese. Finally, cover with another layer of egg-coated matzah, and sprinkle the remaining cheese directly on top of the last matzah layer.

Bake the mina at 375 degrees for 20 to 25 minutes, or until the cheese is melted and the casserole is bubbly. Remove it from the oven, and let it stand for 5 minutes before serving. Cut it into large squares to serve.

Makes about 4 servings as a main course, or more as a side dish.
To double this recipe, see the Notes above.

Mina de Prassa con Queso

LEEK-CHEESE MATZAH "PIE"

Turkish and Greek Sephardim usually cook leeks by simmering them in water; however, I think they have a richer flavor if they are sautéed in a little butter first, as in the tasty *mina* recipe that follows. It is one of my personal favorites.

NOTES: It is necessary to soak the matzah to soften it so that the *mina* can be easily cut and eaten. Regular matzah holds together very well when it is softened by soaking, but egg matzah disintegrates into mush.

If only oil is used to "grease" the bottom of the pan, the matzah tends to stick. By using butter or margarine and then oil, the matzah "crust" gets crispy but does not stick.

4 medium fresh leeks, each about ¾ to 1 inch in diameter (about 1½ to 2 pounds)

2½ to 3 square sheets plain whole wheat or white matzah (not egg matzah; it's too soft)

Butter or margarine for the pan (see Notes)

1 to 2 tablespoons olive, canola, or other oil, for the pan

3 tablespoons butter or olive oil

1 medium onion, finely chopped

¼ cup water

1 (7½- to 8-ounce) package curd-style farmer cheese or 1 cup ricotta cheese

Salt and ground black pepper to taste

3 large eggs or ¾ cup egg substitute (see page 347)

About 6 ounces mild-type cheese (such as Muenster, Swiss, mozzarella, kashkaval, etc.), cut into thin slices or grated

To clean the leeks, cut off and discard the roots and all but 1 to 2 inches of the green tops. Slice the leeks lengthwise into quarters, and rinse them very well to remove any grit. Finely chop the drained leeks, and set them aside.

Put some warm water into an 8- or 9-inch square baking dish, then add the whole sheets of matzah and let them soak for 2 to 3 minutes, or until they are soft and flexible but *not* falling apart. Carefully lift each sheet of matzah out of the water, and place it flat on paper towels to drain. Completely dry the baking dish. Grease the baking dish well with butter or margarine; then add 1 to 2 tablespoons oil and tilt the pan so that the bottom is covered.

Pesach (Passover)

Melt the 3 tablespoons butter in a large skillet over medium-high heat; then sauté the leeks and onion for about 4 minutes. (They should not brown.) Add the water, and cover the skillet. Steam the leeks and onions for about 5 minutes, or until they are tender. Remove the cover, and cook the mixture, stirring, to evaporate any moisture. Remove the mixture from the heat, and let it cool until lukewarm. Stir in the farmer cheese, and season to taste with salt and pepper. Add 2 eggs (or ½ cup egg substitute), and mix until well blended. Preheat the oven to 375 degrees.

Beat the remaining egg and pour it into a large platter that has a slightly raised edge. Coat both sides of a softened matzah lightly with egg, lifting it so that all the excess egg drips off. Place the matzah in the bottom of the greased and oiled dish. Use part of a second egg-coated matzah to fill in any spaces so that the bottom of the dish is completely covered. (You can easily cut softened matzah by following the dotted lines.)

Spread about two-thirds of the sliced or grated cheese over the matzah. Top it with all of the leek-cheese mixture. Cover the mixture with a second layer of egg-coated matzah, and top that with the remaining sliced or grated cheese.

Bake the mina at 375 degrees for about 30 minutes, or until the cheese is melted and the filling is firm. Remove the *mina* from the oven, and let it stand for 5 minutes before serving. Cut it into large squares to serve.

Makes about 4 servings as a main course, or more as a side dish or as part of a multicourse meal.

Matzah Brei

FRIED MATZAH-EGG "PANCAKES"

There are many different versions of this Ashkenazic "fried matzah," which is sort of like French toast made with crumbled pieces of matzah. The cinnamon-flavored variation below is one of my family's favorite Pesach breakfasts (and is a great way to use up matzah as the end of the holiday draws near). Even with cinnamon, this type of matzah brei (pronounced to rhyme with "cry") is somewhat bland, so I usually cook it in real

butter to give the exterior a wonderfully rich flavor. And I always cook matzah brei as flat "pancakes," rather than mixing it up like scrambled eggs as some others do. Since I find that most Jews tend to have rather strong opinions as to which style of matzah brei they prefer, I have given both techniques below.

Matzah brei can also be prepared as a savory dish. Onions and possibly mushrooms may be browned in a little fat, and then stirred into the matzah-egg mixture, which is generally seasoned with plenty of salt and pepper. Savory matzah brei is usually fried in oil to keep it pareve for serving with a meat meal.

NOTE: If desired, the matzah pieces in the following recipe may be soaked in milk, rather than water, to soften them.

4 sheets matzah, any type, or 2 cups matzah farfel (see Notes on page 373)
Cool water (see Note)
4 large eggs or 2 large eggs plus 3 egg whites or 1 cup pareve egg substitute (see page 347)
¼ teaspoon ground cinnamon, or to taste (optional)

¼ teaspoon salt, or to taste (optional)
Butter, margarine, or oil for the skillet

To Serve (Optional)
Jam
Granulated sugar or cinnamon-sugar
Pancake syrup

Break the sheets of matzah into very small pieces about ½ inch in diameter (or use matzah farfel). Put the matzah pieces into a medium bowl, and add water to cover. Let the matzah soak for a minute or two, or just until it is softened but not at all mushy. Drain it well.

In a small bowl, beat the eggs with a fork until they are completely blended. Beat in the cinnamon and salt (if used). Add the egg mixture to the wet matzah pieces, and mix well. Let the matzah-egg mixture rest for about 5 minutes while you preheat the skillet over medium to medium-high heat.

For smaller, individual matzah brei "pancakes," use a 7-inch skillet; for larger pancakes, or for the scrambled type of matzah brei, use a 10-inch skillet. Melt butter in the hot skillet to cover the bottom. Spoon in enough egg-matzah mixture for a thin layer that fills the bottom of the pan.

For the small and large "pancakes," let the matzah brei cook until one side is browned and the top is dry. A small pancake may be flipped over with

Pesach (Passover)

a wide spatula. For a large pancake, slide it out of the skillet onto a plate, and add a small amount of butter to the skillet; then carefully invert the matzah brei back into the skillet. (Wash the plate before using it to serve the matzah brei.) If using a plate is too much of bother, simply cut the large pancake into four equal sections, and flip each one separately. In any case, cook the pancake on the second side until browned.

For "scrambled" matzah brei, use a nonstick skillet if possible, and begin to gently stir the egg-matzah mixture after it has cooked briefly in the pan. Continue cooking and stirring until the matzah brei is completely cooked through. This technique is quicker than the pancake method.

Serve warm with your choice of accompaniments.

Makes about 4 servings.

"Greene-ola" for Pesach

Many years ago, before it became easy to buy commercial granola, I used to make my own on a regular basis. As a sort of family joke, we called it "Greene-ola," and it was one of our breakfast staples. Eventually, we started buying boxed cold cereals, and I stopped making my own granola. However, when my husband and children constantly *kvetched* about the boxed cold cereal available for Pesach, I decided to dig out my old recipe and adapt it for the holiday.

This granola is good not only for breakfast, it also makes a great snack and can be packed in small bags for an on-the-go treat.

NOTES: Please feel free to add other items to this granola if you wish. For instance, diced dried fruits, sunflower seeds, dried coconut, and other nuts may be added. Do not add any dried fruit to the mix until after the granola has baked, or the fruit will get too hard.

To make this more like sugar-coated cold cereal, sprinkle a few more tablespoons of sugar onto the granola immediately after baking it. For a "cinnamon-crunch" kind of cereal, add a little cinnamon to the sugar. The recipe is quite versatile.

5 cups matzah farfel (see Notes on page
   373)
1 cup slivered almonds
1 cup walnut pieces
1 ½ to 2 teaspoons ground cinnamon,
   or to taste
⅓ cup canola or safflower oil

⅓ cup honey
2 tablespoons water
2 tablespoons sugar (or more to taste,
   see Notes)
1 ½ cups dark or light raisins, or to
   taste

Line a 10 by 15-inch jelly roll pan with heavy-duty foil, and set aside. Preheat the oven to 350 degrees.

Put the matzah farfel, almonds, walnuts, and cinnamon into a large bowl and mix to combine. Put the oil, honey, and water into a microwave-safe bowl or cup, or into a small saucepan. Heat the mixture in a microwave oven for about 30 seconds, or over low heat on a stove, until it is slightly warmed and the honey has thinned. Mix it well, and pour it over the farfel mixture. Use a large spoon to stir the granola well until all pieces of farfel are moistened. Sprinkle the sugar over the granola, and mix until it is evenly distributed.

Spread the granola evenly in the prepared pan. Bake at 350 degrees for about 15 to 20 minutes, or until it seems to be dry. (The granola will get crunchier as it cools.) Remove it from the oven, and, while it is still warm, stir it in the pan to break it up and loosen it from the foil. Let it cool in the pan on a rack. When the granola is cool, sprinkle the raisins on top. Lift up the foil, and use it to transport the granola to a plastic container with a lid (or a similar container). The granola should keep fresh for the entire week of Pesach (or longer) if stored in the airtight container. Use it as breakfast cereal with milk, or as a snack.

Makes about 8 cups granola.

Stuffed Baked Apples

These are very simple to prepare, but always seem to be a hit. If the apples are to be served at a dairy meal, use butter for its better flavor, rather than margarine. Each apple contains only a very small amount of fat.

I have chosen Golden Delicious apples because they have an excellent sweet flavor, hold their shape well during cooking, and do not darken easily. However, other firm baking apples may be used. The amounts in this recipe are not critical, and may be adjusted to taste. By the same token, the recipe can be easily adapted for any number of apples desired.

NOTES: These apples may be baked in a microwave oven. Arrange them in a circle in a large round dish, and follow the directions below. Microwave them on "high" for about 9 to 11 minutes, or until almost done, turning the dish and basting them twice during the cooking period. Let the apples rest for at least 2 to 3 minutes before serving, to complete the cooking.

Although the baked apples taste best when warm, leftover whole apples are also good chilled. They may be briefly reheated in a microwave oven.

6 large Golden Delicious apples

½ cup orange juice

3 tablespoons raisins or dried currants,
    or as needed

3 tablespoons butter or margarine

¼ cup honey

Ground cinnamon (optional)

1½ cups apple cider or richly flavored
    apple juice

TO SERVE (OPTIONAL)

Vanilla ice cream

Core each apple through the top (stem end), being careful not to cut all the way through the bottom. The cavity left in each apple should be about 1 inch wide at the top. Peel only the top third of each apple (the remaining peel helps the apple keep its shape). Use a fork to prick several holes in the peeled part of the apple. Preheat the oven to 375 degrees.

Stand the apples in a baking dish that is just large enough to hold them all with a little extra space. Sprinkle the orange juice into the cored cavity and over the cut part of each apple (this will help to keep them from darkening). Fill each apple cavity with raisins, then top each cavity with 1½ teaspoons of

butter. Drizzle about 2 teaspoons honey into the cavity and over the peeled part of each apple, so that some goes into the fork holes. If desired, sprinkle each apple very lightly with cinnamon. Finally, pour the apple cider around the apples.

Bake uncovered at 375 degrees for 40 to 50 minutes, basting the apples well every 10 minutes or so with the juices in the baking dish. The apples are done when they are fork-tender but not mushy. For best flavor, serve immediately or when lukewarm. Put each apple into a small bowl with some of the baking juices. If desired, top each hot apple with a small scoop of vanilla ice cream.

Makes 6 servings.

Poires Bourguigonne
PEARS POACHED IN RED WINE

This simple but elegant French dessert is a perfect light ending to a Pesach meal. The wine tints the outside of each pear a lovely, rosy-red color, but the inside stays white. The pears can be served warm, at room temperature, or chilled.

6 medium firm, ripe pears	*2 teaspoons grated orange peel, colored*
1 ½ cups sweet red Pesach wine	*part only*
⅓ cup honey or generous ⅓ cup sugar	*2 3-inch cinnamon sticks or ½*
1 ½ tablespoons lemon juice	*teaspoon ground cinnamon*

Peel the pears and cut them in half lengthwise. Carefully scoop out the seeds from each half while leaving it intact. In a large saucepan, combine the remaining ingredients, and bring to a boil over medium-high heat. Add the pear halves, and cover the pan. Lower the heat, and simmer the pears for 10 to 20 minutes, basting them often with the wine syrup. The pears are done when they are tender but not mushy. The exact time will depend on the type of pear.

Pesach (Passover)

Cool the pears in the wine syrup. Serve them lukewarm, at room temperature, or chilled, with a little of the cooking syrup poured over each pear.

Makes 6 servings.

Pan de Espanya
PASSOVER SPONGE CAKE

This is probably one of the most popular cakes made on Pesach by both Ashkenazic and Sephardic Jews. The latter call it *pan de espanya* (or a variant spelling of that), which means "bread of Spain" and harks back to earlier, pre-Inquisition days.

For me, sponge cake and Pesach are tightly linked; I simply must have one with the other. As far back as I can remember in my childhood, there was always homemade sponge cake on our Pesach table, and I carried on the tradition when I married.

I inherited a nice sponge cake recipe from my mother. It has a delicious citrus flavor and is moister than many other sponge cakes; however, it still seemed dry at times. After my mother and I both had problems with the original recipe (which was published in the first edition of this book), I decided to experiment. I took a clue from chiffon cakes, and added some oil to the recipe. I also changed the technique slightly. Following is the wonderfully moist result.

Although this cake really needs no garnish, I developed the recipe for Orange or Apricot Fluff Frosting as an optional way to "gild the lily." Another alternative is to top each slice with defrosted frozen strawberries or raspberries in syrup, or fresh berries, and possibly a dollop of whipped cream for a dairy meal.

NOTE: For best results, do not omit any ingredients that are not optional; each serves a purpose. For instance, the lemon juice beaten with the egg whites acidifies them, thus helping to make the egg white foam more stable. Also, follow the detailed directions exactly as they written.

1 1/4 *cups sugar, divided*
2/3 *cup potato starch*
1/3 *cup matzah cake meal*

1/4 *teaspoon salt*
9 *large or 8 extra-large eggs*
2 *tablespoons lemon juice*

½ cup orange juice

1 tablespoon grated orange rind,
   colored part only (optional)

¼ cup canola or safflower oil

TOPPINGS, CHOOSE ONE (OPTIONAL)

Apricot or Orange Fluff Frosting (page 400)

Quick Chocolate Mousse (page 406)

Sliced fresh strawberries or whole raspberries

Defrosted frozen berries in sugar syrup

Have an *ungreased* very clean 10-inch tube pan ready, preferably the two-piece type with a removable tube insert. (This will make it easier to remove the cake from the pan.) Preheat the oven to 350 degrees.

In a small bowl, combine ½ cup of the sugar, the potato starch, cake meal, and salt. Stir with a spoon or fork. The sugar should keep the other dry ingredients from lumping. If there are any lumps, put the entire dry mixture through a sifter or sieve. Set aside.

Separate the eggs, putting the whites into a very large mixing bowl and the yolks into a medium bowl. It will be easiest to cleanly separate the eggs if they are cold. Each white should be first separated into a small bowl to ensure that it contains no yolk (or blood spots), and then the white added to the large bowl.

Beat the egg whites with the lemon juice until foamy; then, slowly but deliberately, add the remaining ¾ cup sugar in about a minute or so, and continue to beat the whites just until they form stiff peaks. This may take several minutes.

Use the same beaters (or a fork) to beat the egg yolks with the orange juice, orange rind, and oil for about a minute, or just until completely combined. (They should not be "light" or fluffy.) Pour the yolk mixture over the whites, and gently fold them together, leaving some streaks of white.

Sprinkle about half of the reserved dry ingredients on top, and fold in. Repeat with the rest of the dry ingredients, so that all ingredients are thoroughly folded together.

Pour the batter evenly into the tube pan, and smooth the top with a rubber spatula. Hold the pan with both hands, and gently tap the bottom once or twice against the countertop so that any large air bubbles in the batter will rise to the surface. (If using a pan with a removable tube insert, be sure to press the tube down with your thumbs as you tap, so it does not lift up and allow batter to seep out the bottom.)

Pesach (Passover)

Bake the cake at 350 degrees for 55 to 60 minutes, or until the top springs back when lightly pressed with a fingertip and any cracks are dry. Remove the pan from the oven, and immediately invert it on its "legs" or fit the tube over the neck of a wine bottle to cool the cake upside down.

When the cake is *completely* cool, run a knife around the tube and the outer edge of the pan. If you are using a two-part tube pan, lift out the tube insert and run a knife under the cake, then invert it onto a serving plate. With a one-piece pan, invert the cake onto a platter and tap the bottom of the pan to release the cake.

If desired, cover the cake with frosting, or serve it with chocolate mousse or berries on the side. (See the comments above.) To avoid squashing the cake when cutting it, use a serrated knife and cut with a sawing motion.

Makes about 12 servings.

Apricot or Orange Fluff Frosting
FOR SPONGE CAKE OR OTHER CAKE

This pareve cake topper is a new variation of the old-fashioned seven-minute frosting, with a texture that is reminiscent of "marshmallow fluff." Instead of using sugar, it calls for apricot preserves or orange marmalade, which are generally available *kosher l'Pesach*. The orange icing is a bit more tart than the apricot due to the bits of orange peel, but both are quite tasty.

The egg whites are beaten with very hot preserves or marmalade, and then placed over simmering water so that they "cook," destroying any salmonella bacteria that may be present. This recipe requires only two ingredients. Read the instructions and have all the equipment ready so that you can proceed through the recipe without stopping. It will take about 15 to 20 minutes, depending on the speed of your portable electric mixer. If your mixer has a sturdy whisk attachment, it may be used for this recipe.

NOTE: Pasteurized dried egg whites reconstituted with water (see the Glossary of Ingredients and the recipe for Quick Chocolate Mousse, page 406) may be substituted for the raw egg whites. In that case, this frosting does not need to be beaten over simmering water. After the hot preserves or marmalade is added to the whites as directed below, just continue to beat until the frosting forms very stiff peaks and has cooled somewhat.

2 large or extra-large egg whites from
    fresh unblemished eggs, completely
    free of yolk (see Note)

1 (12-ounce jar) apricot preserves or
    orange marmalade

Put the egg whites into a large, deep metal mixing bowl that will sit in the top of a saucepan (like a double boiler). Put water that is about 2 inches deep in the saucepan, and heat it to simmering. It will be used as a water bath to complete the beating (and cooking) of the egg whites.

Remove the preserves or marmalade from the jar, put it into a small (1 quart) saucepan, and bring it to a gentle boil. Boil gently, stirring occasionally, for 5 minutes. Use a spoon to break up any large pieces of apricot or orange peel. Remove the pan from the heat.

Use a portable electric mixer to beat the 2 egg whites just until they form very soft peaks, then stop the mixer. Be careful not to overbeat. Return the saucepan with the preserves or marmalade to medium-high heat and quickly bring it to a full boil. Immediately pour the very hot liquid into the softly beaten egg whites while constantly beating at high speed. (You will need to beat with one hand, and pour with other other.) For best results, pour the hot liquid against the inside of the bowl, not into the beaters. Continue to beat at high speed for 2 minutes longer, then place the bowl over the simmering water bath. Continue to beat at high speed at least 4 to 6 minutes longer, or until very stiff peaks form.

Remove the bowl of frosting from the water bath, and continue beating until the frosting has cooled and is a spreading consistency. For the lightest, fluffiest frosting, use it immediately. If the frosted cake is not to be served shortly, store it in the refrigerator (as a precaution, in the unlikely event any salmonella is still present).

The frosting does not need to be used immediately, and may be refrigerated for up to 2 days. Before using, stir the chilled frosting vigorously with a spoon for a minute or two until it is creamy. The frosting will deflate somewhat and be denser and "creamier" than when first made, and will also have a more intense flavor. Some people actually prefer this to the freshly made fluffier frosting.

Makes enough frosting for a sponge cake, a 9 by 13-inch single layer, or an 8- to 9-inch two-layer round cake.

Pesach (Passover)

Hazelnut-Chocolate Viennese Torte

This magnificent flourless torte is the ultimate dessert for dark-chocolate lovers. Since the first edition of this book was published, I have received more comments and compliments on this recipe (along with its alternative chocolate mousse topping) than any other one in this book. It has also been reprinted in many media, including the Internet. That has been very satisfying to me, as I spent many difficult weeks in originally developing the recipe. The torte continues to be a staple of my own Seders, and it always gets raves.

The round cake, which is specked with bits of chocolate, is blanketed with an incredibly shiny chocolate glaze and then beautifully garnished. It stays moist and delicious for several days, and has best flavor and texture if made a day ahead of serving. Although ground hazelnuts are my preference for the recipe, it is also wonderful with walnuts or almonds, or even pecans (which give a Viennese torte an American touch).

NOTES: The recipe is not difficult, but it is time-consuming. If desired, it can be simplified in several ways. For instance, you can forgo the wine and the jam coating, as well as the ground nuts on the outside of the torte. (I highly recommend keeping the decoration of chocolate curls, however, as they make a fantastic impression and are very quick to do.) Also, the cake can be baked several days (or longer) ahead of when it is glazed. (See the directions.)

For the quickest torte, omit the wine, jam, and chocolate glaze, and instead top the torte with a thick layer of Quick Chocolate Mousse (page 406) and chocolate curls. This has become the favorite version of many of my readers (including one who suggested using bottled "raspberry syrup" under the mousse, to replace the wine and jam).

For this torte, I recommend using eggs right out of the refrigerator (and not at room temperature) for two reasons. First, it is easier to separate cold eggs without breaking the yolk. Second, cold whites are less likely to get overbeaten, which could ruin the torte. Be sure to use large, not extra-large, eggs.

The ground nuts and grated chocolate in the torte batter replace flour, and thus must be very fine and powdery. You can use a food processor to grind the nuts; however, be sure not to overgrind them or they may get oily and pasty. For best results, have the nuts at room temperature, and process them in quick pulses. Another alternative that works well for walnuts and pecans (but not harder hazelnuts or almonds) is a nut grinder with a plastic holding chamber screwed on top of a glass jar to catch the nuts after they are

chopped. If I turn the handle on mine toward me (rather than away, as is more natural), it makes a rather fine grind.

Prior to Pesach, many kosher groceries stock ground nuts just for holiday baking. These are a great convenience and work quite well in this torte. A 7-ounce package contains just about 2 cups of nuts. Finely ground walnuts, almonds, or pecans may be substituted for the hazelnuts (which are sometimes called "filberts"). Whichever type, there should be at least 2½ cups of powdery ground nuts.

For grating the chocolate, I highly recommend using a small barrel-style rotary hand grater (available at most supermarkets and kitchen-supply stores). It is inexpensive, and one can be reserved for Pesach use. A food processor may be used; however the grating blade on most brands will not work with hard dark chocolate. Therefore the steel blade must be used to finely *chop* the chocolate instead of grating it. (Do not substitute milk chocolate bars in this recipe.)

Easy Chocolate Curls: To easily make chocolate curls for garnishing the torte, hold the extra ounce of bittersweet or semisweet bar chocolate in the palm of your hand for a few seconds to warm and soften it slightly. Then run a sharp vegetable peeler slowly across the edge of the chocolate, letting the peeled slice curl up. Let the curls fall directly onto the torte, or onto a piece of wax paper. If not using the loose chocolate curls immediately, chill them until they are needed.

FOR THE PAN
Pareve margarine (do not use oil)
Potato starch or sugar

BATTER
6 large eggs, 5 of them separated (see
Notes)
Pinch of salt
2 teaspoons lemon juice
¾ cup sugar, divided
2 teaspoons freshly grated lemon peel,
yellow part only
3 ounces very finely grated pareve
bittersweet or semisweet bar
chocolate (see Notes)
2½ cups (about 8 ounces) very finely
ground unblanched hazelnuts (or
"filberts") (see Notes for
alternatives)

FOR THE TORTE (OPTIONAL, SEE
NOTES)
¼ cup sweet Pesach wine, sherry, or
flavored brandy (optional)
About ½ cup apricot or other preserves

CHOCOLATE GLAZE (OR SUBSTITUTE
QUICK CHOCOLATE MOUSSE, SEE
NOTES)
⅓ cup water
3 tablespoons canola or safflower oil
(not peanut oil)
1 cup sugar
½ cup plain cocoa powder (sifted, if
lumpy)

GARNISH (OPTIONAL)
About 1 cup ground hazelnuts (or an
alternative), for the sides of the torte
1 ounce semisweet bar chocolate (for
chocolate curls, see Notes)

Grease the bottom and sides of a 9-inch springform pan well with margarine; then coat it with potato starch or sugar, tapping out any excess. Set the pan aside. Preheat the oven to 325 degrees.

For the batter, put the 5 egg whites, salt, and lemon juice into a large mixing bowl, and beat them with an electric mixer until they are foamy. Then very gradually add ¼ cup of the sugar, and continue beating the whites just until they form stiff, but not dry, peaks. Be careful not to overbeat the whites.

Use the same beaters and another bowl to beat the 5 egg yolks and the additional whole egg with the remaining ½ cup sugar and the lemon peel until they are very light and fluffy. Gently, but thoroughly, fold the beaten whites into the beaten yolk mixture. Then fold in the grated chocolate and ground hazelnuts. Turn out the batter into the prepared pan, and smooth the top with a spatula.

Bake the torte at 325 degrees for 50 to 55 minutes, or until the top

springs back when gently pressed with a fingertip. The torte will not rise very much. Leave the torte in the oven, turn off the heat, and open the oven door slightly. After 10 minutes, remove the torte from the oven. Run a knife around the edge of the torte to release it from the pan rim; then cool the torte 30 minutes longer in the pan. Remove the pan rim, and cool the torte completely on the pan bottom. (The center of the torte will settle slightly.)

While the torte is cooling, make a base for it by covering a 9- or 10-inch cardboard circle with heavy-duty foil or freezer paper, or use a cake platter. Invert the cooled torte onto the prepared base or platter, and remove the bottom of the pan. You may need to slide a knife between the torte and the pan bottom.

(The torte can be prepared to this point, wrapped airtight, and refrigerated for up to 2 days or frozen for up to a month. Thaw in the refrigerator before proceeding.)

If the wine is desired, sprinkle it evenly over the torte. This gives the torte a mysterious "European" flavor and makes it even moister; however, the torte is also wonderful without it.

If the chocolate glaze will be used, heat the jam in a small saucepan on the stove, or in a small heatproof bowl in the microwave oven, until it is thinned. Then brush or spread the thinned part of the jam all over the torte. Do not use any large pieces of fruit. The jam not only adds flavor, but also evens out the surface of the torte so the chocolate glaze will be perfectly smooth.

For the chocolate glaze, combine the water, oil, sugar, and cocoa in a small saucepan, and mix very well. Cook the mixture over *low heat,* stirring constantly, for about 10 to 14 minutes, or until the glaze thickens slightly and is very smooth and shiny. For best flavor and texture, it should not boil. Remove the glaze from the heat, and stir it constantly for several additional minutes, or until it cools considerably and gets much thicker. (This process can be expedited by setting the pot in a large bowl of ice water. Be sure that no water gets into the glaze.)

Pour all the glaze in the center of the torte, and immediately use a metal or rubber spatula to evenly spread it all over the top and sides. Wipe up any drips from the cardboard base or serving platter.

If the garnish is desired, let the torte rest for a few minutes until the glaze begins to set. Press handfuls of ground nuts all over the sides of the torte, but

do not put any on the smooth top. When the glaze is completely cooled, heap some chocolate curls (or coarsely grated bar chocolate) in the center of the torte, where it may have settled a bit. (See the Notes for directions for easy chocolate curls.)

Refrigerate the uncovered completed torte for several hours or, preferably, overnight so that the glaze can set, and the flavors and textures can "mellow."

Once the glaze has set, the torte can be frozen for up to 3 weeks. Freeze it uncovered; then wrap it in plastic wrap or aluminum foil. Unwrap it before defrosting so the glaze will not stick to the wrapper, and let it defrost for several hours in the refrigerator. (The glaze may be a little less shiny than when first made.)

For best flavor and texture, remove the torte from the refrigerator a few hours before serving.

Makes about 12 servings.

Variation (see the Notes):

Omit the chocolate glaze, and top the torte with a thick layer of Quick Chocolate Mousse. Garnish the mousse with chocolate curls (or coarsely grated chocolate). Do not freeze the torte with the mousse on top.

Quick Chocolate Mousse

This delectable mousse is especially quick and easy to prepare because the chocolate is "automatically" melted as it whirls with boiling water in a food processor or blender. A bit of coffee serves to heighten the flavor of the mousse. Unlike most recipes for chocolate mousse, this one is pareve and contains no whipped cream. On its own, it is a wonderful dessert, especially when garnished with easy yet impressive chocolate curls. Or it can be used as a cake topping, such as for Hazelnut–Chocolate Viennese Torte (page 402) or Pan de Espanya (page 398).

In the first edition of this book, my recipe for chocolate mousse called for raw eggs.

This has become a food-safety issue due to the increased risk of raw eggs being contaminated with salmonella bacteria, which can cause severe food poisoning. Egg yolks are most likely to harbor the bacteria, while egg whites seem to be a bit more resistant, according to some reports. The contamination gets worse when food is allowed to sit for hours at room temperature, as it might at a Seder.

To avoid any potential problems, I considered omitting Chocolate Mousse from this book. However, based on responses from many readers of the original edition, it seems to have been one of my most popular Pesach recipes! Therefore, I decided to include the mousse, but not to use raw eggs.

I had to do much experimentation, and made about a dozen different versions of the mousse. (My kids were delighted to be "tasters.") I replaced the raw yolks with some oil and additional liquid. To replace the raw egg whites, I used a product generically known as "pasteurized dried egg whites." This white powder is reconstituted with warm water following the package directions, and then is beaten exactly like fresh egg whites. The foam produced by the pasteurized whites is actually more stable than with fresh whites, so the chocolate mousse holds its shape especially well. (In my area, an excellent brand of pure dried egg whites [with kashrut certification] is available in supermarkets. For more information on this product, see the Glossary of Ingredients.)

I have made the "winning" chocolate mousse recipe (printed below) many times, and no one can tell the difference between my "new" (cholesterol-free) mousse and the one that I used to make with raw eggs. They love it just as much, if not more!

NOTES: The mousse can be refrigerated so that it stays light and fluffy, or it can be served frozen for a texture that is like melt-in-your-mouth soft chocolate ice cream. The technique is exactly the same. The frozen mousse can be defrosted, though the texture might not be exactly the same as before it was frozen.

If additional servings of the mousse are desired, just repeat the whole recipe. For best results, do not double the amounts of the ingredients in one batch.

If a slightly sweeter mousse is desired, increase the sugar beaten with the egg whites to ½ cup.

Chocolate chips or morsels may be used instead of bar chocolate—6 ounces equal 1 cup.

6 ounces pareve bittersweet or
   semisweet bar chocolate, broken
   into small pieces (see Notes)
¹/₂ teaspoon instant coffee granules
   (optional)
¹/₃ cup boiling water
2 tablespoons canola or safflower oil
¹/₄ cup sweet Pesach wine or Pesach
   liqueur or orange juice

Pasteurized dried egg white powder
   reconstituted in warm water to
   equal 4 egg whites (see the
   comments above)
¹/₃ cup sugar

GARNISH (OPTIONAL)
1 ounce kosher l'Pesach pareve bittersweet or semisweet bar chocolate

Put the 6 ounces of chocolate and instant coffee granules (if used) in a food processor fitted with a steel blade, or a blender, and process for several seconds until the chocolate is very finely chopped. With the machine running, pour the boiling water in through the top, and continue processing for several more seconds until the chocolate is completely melted. Add the oil and wine, and process until well mixed and completely smooth.

Put the reconstituted pasteurized dried egg whites into a large mixing bowl. Use an electric mixer to beat the dissolved egg whites until they are foamy; then gradually add the sugar and continue beating for several minutes until the whites form very stiff shiny peaks.

Gently but thoroughly fold the chocolate mixture into the whites until no streaks of white remain. Turn out the mousse mixture into an attractive 6- to 8-cup serving bowl or about eight individual bowls. If desired, a rubber scraper or spatula can be used to swirl the top of the mousse in an interesting design.

To easily make chocolate curls for garnishing the mousse, hold the extra ounce of bittersweet or semisweet bar chocolate in the palm of your hand for a few seconds to warm and soften it slightly. Then run a sharp vegetable peeler slowly across the edge of the chocolate so that each peeled slice curls up. Let the curls fall directly onto the top of the mousse in the serving bowl or dishes, or onto a piece of wax paper. If not using the loose chocolate curls immediately, chill them until they are needed.

If preferred, the bar chocolate may simply be grated over the top of the mousse.

Chill the mousse for several hours or until it is firm. Or it may be frozen for taste and texture like very soft ice cream.

Makes about 8 or more servings.

Tishpishti

SEPHARDIC-STYLE WALNUT CAKE

This is a Pesach version of a very popular cake that is served by Turkish and Greek Jews throughout the year. As with many other Sephardic desserts, the cake is soaked in a sugar-honey syrup after it is baked. For best flavor and texture, *tishpishti* should be made at least one day ahead. It will stay tasty for several days.

NOTE: This new version of *tishpishti* is much lighter than the one that appeared in the first edition of this book.

CAKE
7 large eggs (no substitutes)
1 cup sugar
¼ cup canola or safflower oil
1½ teaspoons ground cinnamon
¾ cup matzah cake meal, sifted
2 cups (8 ounces) finely chopped
    walnuts, or almonds, or a
    combination

SYRUP
1¼ cups water
1¼ cups sugar
3 tablespoons honey
2 teaspoons lemon juice

For the cake, grease and coat lightly with matzah cake meal a 9 by 13-inch baking dish or pan. Preheat the oven to 350 degrees. In a large mixing bowl, use an electric mixer to beat the eggs with the sugar until the eggs are very light and thick, and significantly increased in volume. This will take several minutes. Beat in the oil and cinnamon. By hand, fold in the sifted cake meal and then the walnuts. Pour the batter into the prepared pan, smoothing the top. Bake at 350 degrees for about 45 minutes, or until the top is nicely browned and a wooden pick inserted in the center comes out clean.

As soon as the cake is in the oven, prepare the syrup so it has time to cool. In a heavy saucepan, put the water, sugar, honey, and lemon juice. Bring to a boil while stirring to dissolve the sugar; then lower the heat and boil the syrup, uncovered and undisturbed, for 10 minutes. Set it aside to cool at room temperature.

When the cake is done, remove it from the oven and slowly pour the lukewarm syrup over the top so the entire surface is moistened with syrup. Let the cake cool, uncovered, in the pan on a wire rack, and do not cut it for several hours so that the syrup can be completely absorbed. (For the best taste and texture, allow the cake to rest overnight, covered.) To serve, cut the cake into squares or diamonds. It may be served directly from the pan, or the pieces may be arranged on a platter. Store, covered, at room temperature for several days.

Makes about 20 pieces.

Chocolate-Orange Torte

This rich, fudgy cake is based on recipes used both by Austrian Jews and North African Jews for Pesach. Like some other baked goods in this chapter, it contains no matzah products, but relies instead on ground nuts for substance.

NOTES: Packaged ground almonds are often available at kosher groceries for the holiday. The packages usually contain 7 ounces of very finely ground nuts, which provides the 2 cups needed for this recipe. For this recipe, be sure to get *blanched* ground almonds, as the unblanched ones can have a harsh taste. (For more information on almonds, see the Glossary of Ingredients.)

For ease in separating the eggs and to help avoid overbeating the whites, use chilled eggs (directly from the refrigerator) for the torte.

Chocolate chips or morsels may be used instead of bar chocolate—6 ounces equal 1 cup.

6 ounces pareve bittersweet or
*   semisweet bar chocolate (see Notes)*
1 cup sugar, divided

1 tablespoon grated fresh orange peel,
*   colored part only*
3 tablespoons fresh orange juice

8 large eggs, separated (see Notes)
2 cups (about 8 ounces) ground
blanched almonds (see Notes)

About ¾ cup orange marmalade
2 navel oranges, peeled and thinly
sliced crosswise into circles

Grease the bottom and sides of a 9-inch springform pan, and set it aside. Preheat the oven to 350 degrees.

Break the chocolate into small pieces, and put them into a medium saucepan (about a 2-quart) with ½ cup of the sugar, the orange peel, and juice. Put the saucepan over low heat, and stir constantly until the chocolate is melted. (Or use a microwave oven to melt the chocolate with the other ingredients.) Remove the pan from the heat, and let the chocolate mixture cool to tepid. Add the egg yolks to the pan, and stir until they are completely combined with the chocolate.

Put the egg whites into a large mixing bowl, and beat them until foamy. Slowly add the remaining ½ cup sugar while continuing to beat. Beat the whites just until they form stiff, shiny peaks. Vigorously stir about one-fourth of the whites into the chocolate mixture in the saucepan to lighten it. Then gently but thoroughly fold all the chocolate mixture back into the whites. Finally, fold in the ground almonds. Turn out the batter into the prepared pan.

Bake the torte at 350 degrees for about 45 to 50 minutes, or until a wooden pick inserted into the center comes out almost, but not completely, clean. (If the torte is overbaked, it will be dry and crumbly, not fudgy.) Turn off the heat, but leave the torte in the oven, with the door slightly ajar, for 10 minutes. Remove the torte from the oven, and run a small, thin knife around the top edge of the torte to release it from the pan rim. Cool the torte in the pan on a wire rack for 30 minutes. Then remove the rim, and cool the torte completely on the pan bottom. Slide a thin knife or metal spatula between the pan bottom and the torte to loosen the torte, and invert it onto a serving platter.

(The torte can be prepared to this point, wrapped airtight, and refrigerated for up to 2 days or frozen for up to a month. Thaw in the refrigerator, unwrapped, before proceeding.)

Heat the marmalade in a small saucepan or in a bowl in the microwave oven until it is thinned. Brush or spoon the marmalade over the top and sides of the torte. Arrange the orange slices in a circle around the top of the torte so that they overlap each other slightly. Brush the orange slices with more of

Pesach (Passover)

the thinned marmalade to glaze them. Store the torte, uncovered, in the re-
frigerator. (The torte may be stored in this fashion up to 24 hours.)

Serve the torte chilled or, for best flavor, let it come to room temperature.

Makes about 10 servings.

Apple-Nut Cake

This recipe uses far fewer egg yolks than most Pesach cakes, and has a wonderful flavor.
It would be nice for a brunch as well as a Seder dessert. For added fiber, do not peel the
apples.

FILLING

½ cup finely chopped walnuts or pecans

¼ cup sugar

1 teaspoon cinnamon

*1 large Golden Delicious or other firm
    baking apple*

BATTER

2 large eggs, one separated

1 cup sugar, divided

⅓ cup canola or safflower oil

¼ cup orange juice

¾ cup matzah cake meal

2 large egg whites

Grease an 8-inch square baking pan, and set it aside. Preheat the oven to
350 degrees.

For the filling, combine the walnuts, sugar, and cinnamon, and set aside.
Peel the apple (if desired), core and thinly slice it. Set it aside.

For the batter, combine 1 whole egg and 1 egg yolk (reserve the white) in
a medium mixing bowl, and use an electric mixer to beat them until thick.
Gradually add ¾ cup of the sugar, and beat until light. Beat in the oil and orange
juice until well combined. Then, at slowest speed, mix in the matzah cake meal.

Put the remaining 3 egg whites into a clean mixing bowl and use clean
beaters to beat them until frothy. Gradually add the last ¼ cup sugar, and beat
the whites until they are stiff but not dry. Fold the whites into the matzah
cake meal mixture, mixing completely.

Pour half of the batter into the bottom of the prepared baking pan, and use
a spatula to spread it evenly. Sprinkle with two-thirds of the nut mixture.

Arrange the apple slices in one layer on top of the nuts. Cover with the remaining batter, and then sprinkle the remaining nut mixture on top. Bake at 350 degrees for 40 to 45 minutes, or until a wooden pick comes out clean. Cool completely in the pan on a wire rack, and cut into squares or rectangles to serve. The cake may be wrapped well and frozen; defrost it wrapped before using it.

Makes about 9 servings.

Caramel-Coated Orange Flan

BAKED CUSTARD

This elegant, light dessert has been adapted from a classic that is common to Spanish, Mexican, and French cuisines. *Flan* or *crème caramel,* as it is called by the French, uses milk or cream in the custard, which would be unacceptable at a Seder where meat is served. Therefore, I developed this pareve "Jewish" version, which uses orange juice instead. It can be made up to 2 days ahead of time, and refrigerated. However, it should not be removed from its baking pan until just before serving time.

With this dessert, "caramelized" (melted) sugar is used to coat the pan before the custard mixture is added. Some of the caramel is absorbed into the outer layer of the custard, and the rest is mysteriously transformed into a wonderful syrup that bathes the dessert when it is inverted after being chilled. Though it may sound tricky, it is not very difficult when the directions are carefully followed.

NOTE: The following recipe makes a flan that will serve about 6 people. If you wish to have more servings, do not increase the amounts, or the custard may not mold properly. Rather, make two or more flans by repeating the recipe.

CARAMEL COATING FOR MOLD
½ cup sugar
3 tablespoons water

ORANGE CUSTARD
5 large eggs (no substitutes)
⅓ cup sugar

2 cups orange juice, heated until lukewarm, or ½ cup thawed orange juice concentrate plus 1½ cups hot tap water

GARNISH (OPTIONAL)
About 2 tablespoons finely grated orange peel, colored part only

Pesach (Passover)

Have nearby some pot holders and an ungreased 1-quart ovenproof casserole dish that can withstand high heat.

To make the caramel coating, put the ½ cup sugar and water into a small, heavy saucepan. Bring the mixture to a light boil, swirling the saucepan gently by its handle to help dissolve the sugar. When the syrup is clear, boil it rapidly, swirling the saucepan occasionally, until the syrup caramelizes, that is, thickens and turns a light, golden-brown color. Watch the syrup carefully and do not let it get dark brown, or it may have a burned taste.

Immediately pour the syrup into the ovenproof casserole. *Be careful—the syrup will be extremely hot!* Quickly pick up the casserole with the pot holders, and carefully tilt it in all directions, letting the syrup coat the bottom and sides, until the syrup solidifies, in about 30 seconds. Set the casserole aside. (The saucepan and any spilled syrup can be cleaned up with hot water. To keep the saucepan from warping, let it cool before immersing it in water.)

The custard must be baked in a hot water bath. Use any pan that is several inches wider than the casserole and almost as deep as the casserole. Bring a kettle of water to a boil, so that it will be ready to be poured into the pan. Preheat the oven to 325 degrees.

For the custard mixture, use a fork to beat the eggs in a medium bowl until they are well blended; then beat in the ⅓ cup sugar. Beat for a minute or two to make sure the mixture is well combined, but not frothy. Slowly add the warm orange juice to the eggs, beating constantly. Pour the orange custard mixture into the caramel-coated casserole.

Set the casserole into the larger pan; then add enough boiling water to the larger pan so that it comes about halfway up the outside of the casserole. Bake at 325 degrees for 50 to 55 minutes, or until a small knife inserted near the center of the custard comes out clean.

Remove the casserole from the water, and cool it on a rack at room temperature for 30 minutes. Then refrigerate the flan for at least several hours or up to 2 days. The flan should be completely chilled before it is unmolded shortly before serving.

To serve the chilled flan, unmold it onto a flat serving platter that has a raised rim to hold the caramel syrup. To unmold, carefully run a knife around the top edge of the custard to loosen it from the casserole. Invert the serving platter over the casserole. Hold the two tightly together, and reverse them.

Lift off the casserole. The syrup from the casserole will flow over and around the flan. If desired, sprinkle freshly grated orange peel on top of the flan.

Serve immediately, using a very large spoon to dish out portions of the flan. Include some of the caramel syrup with each serving.

Makes about 6 servings.

Not-to-Pass-Over Fudge Brownies

I tested many batches of brownies to get to this recipe. I "passed over" those that were dry or gritty or matzah-mealy or just unattractive. I wanted brownies that tasted *and* looked great without any nuts or other "fillers" to disguise their texture or flavor. I also hoped to have my brownies be as healthful as possible, considering the limitations.

After several tests, I gave up on trying to use cocoa (lower in fat) instead of chocolate; it just didn't work with matzah cake meal. But I was able to successfully substitute monounsaturated oil for the usual margarine, which tends to be especially high in saturated fat during Pesach, because it is often made with cottonseed oil. Finally, I found that 4 egg whites with only 2 yolks (for a minimum of cholesterol) worked really well for height and texture.

To make my brownies even smoother, I let the batter rest for a few minutes so that the cake meal could absorb some of the moisture from the egg whites.

The result of my culinary experimenting is the following delicious fudge brownies. They are moist and soft and high, they look wonderful, and they stay fresh-tasting even after being stored for several days. They quickly became a family favorite when I was testing this recipe, even though it wasn't Pesach. In fact, my son said that I should not save the recipe just for the holiday; rather, I should bake these brownies "all the time."

For the best results, carefully follow the directions below. In the directions, I have provided a clever technique for baking the brownies that not only makes them easy to cut, but also keeps the baking pan clean.

NOTES: My children prefer these fudge brownies to be plain, without "things" in them. However, you may add up to ¾ cup coarsely chopped nuts to the batter if desired.

Chocolate chips or morsels may be used instead of bar chocolate—6 ounces equal 1 cup.

6 ounces pareve bittersweet or
    semisweet bar chocolate, broken
    into small pieces (see Notes)
1/2 cup canola or safflower oil
1 cup sugar

1/4 teaspoon salt
2 large eggs (no substitutes)
2 large egg whites
3/4 cup matzah cake meal

Put the chocolate and oil into a 4-cup microwave-safe bowl or in a medium saucepan. Melt the chocolate with the oil in a microwave oven (about 1½ minutes on "high") or over very low heat on the stove. Remove the mixture from the heat, and stir until the melted chocolate and oil are combined. If the mixture has become hot, let it cool until it is tepid.

By hand, use a sturdy spoon to stir the sugar and salt into the chocolate mixture until combined. Use a fork to beat the eggs and egg whites together in a small bowl until they are well blended. Add the beaten eggs to the chocolate mixture, and stir until they are completely incorporated. Add the matzah cake meal to the chocolate mixture, and gently stir for 2 to 3 minutes. (The batter will be very thick.) Then let the mixture rest for 5 minutes. Meanwhile, preheat the oven to 350 degrees, and prepare the baking pan.

Use an 8-inch square shiny metal pan (or two 8-inch square disposable foil pans nestled together to be more sturdy). Line the pan with a piece of aluminum foil that is large enough to reach to the top of both sides. Be sure to press it into the corners. (The foil will be used to lift out the baked brownie cake, leaving behind a clean pan.) Grease the foil. When the brownie batter has rested 5 minutes, stir it briefly and spread it into the prepared pan, smoothing the top. Bake it at 350 degrees for 35 to 40 minutes, or just until the center of the top is puffed and a wooden pick comes out clean. For the fudgiest brownies, do not overbake them.

Cool the whole "brownie cake" in the pan on a wire rack. Use the foil to lift the cake completely out of the pan, and leave it on the foil. If it still feels warm on the bottom, let it cool longer on the rack. When the cake is cooled to room temperature, use a metal spatula to loosen it from the foil; then lift the entire cake off the foil, and put it on a cutting board. Use a large, sharp knife to evenly cut the cake into 16 brownies. (Hint: For the neatest-looking brownies, wipe the knife after each cut.) Store the brownies in an airtight container for up to 3 or 4 days, or freeze them for longer storage.

Makes 16 brownies.

Marunchinos
CHEWY ALMOND COOKIES

These popular, marzipanlike Sephardic treats have long been the favorite Pesach cookie of my Ashkenazic family. In fact, I make *marunchinos* year-round and have also used them in Purim *shalach manos* baskets. The off-white cookies look very plain, so I have always topped each one with a whole unblanched (brown) shelled almond—my own innovation. Only recently did I discover that some Sephardim do the same with an almond half or piece of slivered almond.

As blanched almonds tend to taste somewhat bland, the almond extract in the recipe below adds significantly to the flavor of these cookies. Bakers used to include a few "bitter almonds" in their cookie dough to improve the almond flavor and aroma. But bitter almonds contain a potentially toxic chemical, so they are now illegal for consumer use in the United States. However, they are still used to make almond extract or flavoring. If you can't find this for Pesach use, you may omit it. (Or try the *hadgi badam;* this Iraqi-Jewish variation flavors the cookies primarily with cardamom.)

NOTE: A food processor makes this recipe very quick and easy. However, it is not necessary with packaged ground almonds, which are often available at kosher groceries for the holiday. The packages usually contain 7 ounces of very finely ground nuts, which provide the 2 cups needed for this recipe. Cookies made with packaged ground nuts tend to be softer and less chewy than those made with nuts ground in a food processor. Be sure to get *blanched* ground almonds, as the unblanched ones can have a harsh taste. To use ground almonds in this recipe, see the directions below. (For more information on almonds, see the Glossary of Ingredients.)

8 ounces whole or slivered blanched almonds (about 2 cups) (see Note)
²/₃ cup sugar
2 large egg whites
¹/₂ to 1 teaspoon kosher l'Pesach almond extract or flavoring, or to taste

FOR TOPS OF COOKIES (SEE THE COMMENTS ABOVE)
24 unblanched or blanched whole almonds

Line two large baking sheets with baking parchment paper. Or grease the sheets, then coat them with matzah cake meal or potato starch, tapping off the excess. Set aside. Preheat the oven to 325 degrees.

Pesach (Passover)

With a food processor: Put the almonds and the sugar into the bowl fitted with a steel blade. Process until the almonds are very finely ground. Add the egg whites and almond extract, and process to form a very thick, stiff paste.

Without a food processor: Use a 7-ounce package of ground almonds (see Note above). In a medium bowl, beat the egg whites just until they are broken up and frothy. Stir in the sugar and extract until combined. Then stir in the ground almonds to make a thick, stiff paste.

With either method, use wet hands (or a very small #70 ice cream disher) to form the paste into 1- to 1¼-inch-diameter balls, and arrange the balls about 2 inches apart on the baking sheet.

(Egg sizes within 1 carton can vary considerably. If the almond paste is very loose and cannot be formed into balls, add more ground almonds or a small amount of potato starch. Or chill the paste until it is firmer. Or just use a teaspoon to "drop" rounded spoonfuls of the paste onto the cookie sheet as when making drop cookies.)

Press a whole almond into the top of each ball or mound of almond paste, flattening it slightly. Bake the cookies at 325 degrees for 15 to 20 minutes, or just until they are firm to a gentle touch. They should not brown. Use a metal spatula to remove the cookies from the baking sheet and cool them on a wire rack. (For cookies baked on parchment, simply slide the parchment with the cookies still on it to a wire rack to cool. When the cookies are cool, peel the parchment off them.) Store the cookies in an airtight container at room temperature.

Makes about 24 cookies.

Variation

HADGI BADAM FOR PESACH
(CARDAMOM-FLAVORED ALMOND COOKIES)

Iraqi Jews prefer this variation. Use only ¼ to ½ teaspoon almond extract or omit it. Add ½ teaspoon ground cardamom to the batter. Follow the above directions.

Mustachudos
Walnut Cookies

These chewy, Sephardic cookies are quite easy to make. They are similar to macaroons in that they have no flour or matzah products; however, the entire egg, not just the white, is used. Sephardim sometimes shape the dough into crescents instead of balls, and they frequently sprinkle the baked *mustachudos* with confectioners' sugar.

NOTES: Confectioners' sugar that contains cornstarch is prohibited by Ashkenazic custom on Pesach.

While not traditional, pecans also work well in this recipe, and make very delicious cookies.

Mustachudos are made with basically the same technique as Marunchinos (page 417). However, due to different ingredients and proportions, they do not look or taste alike. Actually, they complement each other rather well.

7 ounces (about 1¾ cups) walnut pieces	*½ teaspoon ground cinnamon*
½ cup sugar	*1 large egg*

Line one large or two smaller baking sheets with baking parchment paper. Or grease the sheets; then coat them with matzah cake meal or potato starch, tapping off the excess. Set aside. Preheat the oven to 325 degrees.

With a food processor: Put the walnuts, sugar, and cinnamon into the bowl fitted with a steel blade. Process until the walnuts are very finely ground. Add the egg, and process to form a very thick, stiff paste.

Without a food processor: Use a nut grinder to very finely grind the walnuts. You should have 1½ cups ground walnuts. (Or use 1½ cups packaged ground walnuts.) In a medium bowl, beat the egg with a fork until the white and yolk are blended. Stir in the sugar and cinnamon until combined. Then stir in the ground walnuts to make a thick, stiff paste.

Use wet hands (or a very small #70 ice cream disher) to form the paste into 1- to 1¼-inch-diameter balls, and arrange the balls about 2 inches apart on the baking sheet.

If the walnut paste is very loose and cannot be formed into balls (egg sizes

within a carton can vary considerably), add more ground walnuts or a small amount of potato starch. Or chill it until it is firmer. Or just use a teaspoon to drop rounded spoonfuls of the walnut paste onto the cookie sheet, as when making drop cookies.

Bake the cookies at 325 degrees for about 15 to 20 minutes, or just until they are firm to a gentle touch. They should not brown. Use a metal spatula to remove the cookies from the baking sheet and cool them on a wire rack. (For cookies baked on parchment, simply slide the parchment with the cookies still on it to a wire rack to cool. When the cookies are cool, gently peel the parchment off them.) Store the cookies in an airtight container at room temperature.

Makes about 20 cookies.

Light Nut Cookies

Low-fat cookies similar to these delectable meringuelike nut cookies have been appearing on the market for Pesach. It's very easy to make your own if you use the very finely ground nuts available in many kosher groceries around Pesach. These cookies can be made with walnuts, pecans, or hazelnuts. (For a similar recipe with almonds, see Amaretti, page 421.)

The almond extract or flavoring will intensify the "nut" flavor of these cookies; however, it may be omitted if desired.

2 large egg whites
1 teaspoon lemon juice
³⁄₄ cup granulated sugar
About ¹⁄₂ teaspoon kosher l'Pesach almond extract or flavoring (see comments above)

1 (7-ounce) package very finely ground walnuts, pecans, or hazelnuts (2 cups)
1 tablespoon potato starch, sifted

Line two large baking sheets with baking parchment paper. Or grease the sheets; then coat them with matzah cake meal or potato starch, tapping off the excess. Set aside. Preheat the oven to 350 degrees.

In a medium bowl, use an electric mixer to beat the egg whites with the lemon juice until they are foamy; then gradually beat in the sugar and almond flavoring, and continue beating for several minutes until the whites form very stiff, shiny peaks. Stir in the ground nuts and potato starch until well combined.

Drop generous tablespoonfuls of the batter into small mounds about 2 inches apart on the prepared baking sheets.

Bake the cookies at 350 degrees for 17 to 22 minutes, or until they are firm and very lightly browned. Use a metal spatula or pancake turner to remove the cookies from the baking sheet, and cool them on wire racks. (For cookies baked on parchment, simply slide the parchment with the cookies still on it to a wire rack to cool. When the cookies are cool, gently peel the parchment off them.) Store the cookies in an airtight container at room temperature.

Makes about 30 cookies.

Amaretti

ITALIAN-STYLE ALMOND MERINGUES

These crunchy, meringuelike cookies are very popular in Italian cuisine. Sometimes, slightly stale amaretti are crumbled and used as a filling for baked apples or baked pear halves.

As most almonds taste relatively bland, almond flavoring is usually added to amaretti to give them a more intense almond taste. (For more information on almond flavoring, see the recipe for Marunchinos, page 417.)

NOTE: The almonds may be ground in a food processor fitted with a steel blade, or with a hand grater. If the almonds were frozen, let them come to room temperature before using them, and be careful that they do not become pasty from overgrinding. Prior to Pesach, many kosher groceries stock ground almonds just for holiday baking. The packages usually contain 7 ounces of finely ground almonds, which provide the 2 cups needed for this recipe. Be sure to get ground *blanched* almonds, as the unblanched ones can have a harsh taste. (For more information on almonds, see the Glossary of Ingredients.)

2 large egg whites

¾ cup granulated sugar

1 to 1½ teaspoons kosher l'Pesach almond extract or flavoring, or to taste

2 cups (7 to 8 ounces) very finely ground blanched almonds (see Note)

1 tablespoon potato starch

Line two large baking sheets with baking parchment paper. Or grease the sheets; then coat them with matzah cake meal or extra potato starch, tapping off the excess. Set aside. Preheat the oven to 325 degrees.

In a medium bowl, use an electric mixer to beat the egg whites until they are foamy; then gradually beat in the sugar and almond extract, and continue beating for several minutes until the whites form very stiff, shiny peaks. Stir in the ground almonds and potato starch until well combined.

Drop generous tablespoonfuls of the batter into small mounds about 2 inches apart on the prepared baking sheets.

Bake the cookies at 325 degrees for 25 to 30 minutes, or until they are firm and very lightly browned. Turn off the oven, and let the cookies dry in the warm oven for 1 to 1½ hours, or until they are quite crunchy. Use a metal spatula or pancake turner to remove the cookies from the baking sheet, and cool them on wire racks. (For cookies baked on parchment, simply slide the parchment with the cookies still on it to a wire rack to cool. When the cookies are cool, gently peel the parchment off them.) Store the cookies in an airtight container at room temperature.

Makes about 30 cookies.

Mandelbrot for Pesach

These sliced nut cookies are ideal for using up extra matzah cake meal because everyone seems to like them, even if they are tired of other Pesach foods. The recipe is adapted from one kindly given to me by my friend Jacalyn Ely, who bakes several batches of the mandelbrot each year.

4 large eggs or 1 cup pareve egg
    substitute (see page 347)
1½ cups sugar
1 cup canola or safflower oil
2 cups matzah cake meal
⅓ cup potato starch
1 tablespoon lemon juice

1 cup coarsely chopped almonds or
    walnuts

CINNAMON-SUGAR COATING
½ cup sugar
1 tablespoon ground cinnamon

Put the eggs, sugar, and oil in a large bowl, and beat them until well combined. Stir in the cake meal, potato starch, and lemon juice until completely moistened. Stir in the nuts. Chill the dough at least a few hours or overnight, so that it is stiff enough to handle without sticking very much.

Preheat the oven to 350 degrees. Grease two large baking sheets. Divide the dough into fourths, and form each fourth into a log that is about 10 inches long. (Use a very small amount of extra matzah cake meal, if necessary, to keep the dough from sticking to your hands.)

Place the logs lengthwise on the prepared pans, and bake them at 350 degrees for about 35 minutes, or until golden. Cool the logs for 5 minutes; then cut them on the diagonal (a serrated knife is best) into ¾- to 1-inch slices. (Hint: If the slices are too thin, they may fall apart.)

Coat both cut sides of each slice with a mixture of the sugar and cinnamon; then stand up the slices on baking sheets, and return them to the 350-degree oven for about 8 to 10 minutes, or until they are toasted and firm. Be careful that slices do not burn. Cool them completely before storing. Store in airtight containers.

Makes about 40 cookies, depending on their thickness.

Cinnamon Balls
British-Style Almond-Cinnamon Cookies

This British-Jewish variation of the nut cookies so popular at Pesach uses ground almonds and lots of cinnamon. The nut dough is rolled into balls, and the baked cookies are customarily coated with confectioners' sugar.

NOTE: Confectioners' sugar that contains cornstarch is prohibited by Ashkenazic custom on Pesach.

1 (7-ounce) package very finely ground blanched almonds (see Note on page 421)
⅔ cup granulated sugar, divided
1 tablespoon ground cinnamon

2 large egg whites
Kosher l'Pesach confectioners' sugar (optional; see Note)

Line two large baking sheets with baking parchment paper. Or grease the sheets; then coat them with matzah cake meal or potato starch, tapping off the excess. Set aside. Preheat the oven to 350 degrees.

In a small bowl, mix together the almonds, ⅓ cup sugar, and cinnamon. Set aside. In a medium bowl, use an electric mixer to beat the egg whites until they are foamy; then gradually add the remaining ⅓ cup sugar and continue beating only until the whites form *soft* peaks. Stir in the almond mixture until well combined. You should have a sticky dough.

Use wet hands to form the dough into approximately 1¼-inch-diameter balls. (Or use a very small #70 ice cream disher to make the balls, then smooth them with wet hands.) Arrange the balls about 1 inch apart on the prepared cookie sheets.

Bake the cookies at 350 degrees for about 15 minutes, or until they are firm on the outside and still slightly soft inside. The cookies tend to get harder after they are baked, so don't bake them too long. Use a spatula to remove the cookies from the baking sheet. Cool them completely on wire racks. Coat them with confectioners' sugar if desired. Store the cookies in an airtight container. Or freeze them for longer storage.

Makes about 24 cookies.

Rocks

FARFEL COOKIES WITH A VARIETY OF FILLINGS

These lumpy cookies look like their name, but fortunately they don't taste like it! They are really very good, with a crunchy interior of farfel and nuts.

Depending on the additional filling ingredients that you put into these cookies, they will have a different taste. Chocolate chips give them a sort of Toll House cookie flavor, while raisins make them more like oatmeal Hermits.

NOTE: Matzo "farfel" is simply plain matzah broken into very small pieces. You can purchase it ready-made, or break up sheets of plain or whole wheat matzah to very small, about ½-inch pieces. The matzah should not be crumbled into "meal." One sheet of matzah yields about ½ cup farfel.

2 large eggs or 3 extra-large egg whites
    or ½ cup pareve egg substitute (see
    page 347)
⅓ cup canola or safflower oil
⅔ cup granulated sugar or brown sugar
1 cup matzah meal (not cake meal)
¾ teaspoon ground cinnamon (optional
    with chocolate chips)

¼ teaspoon salt
1 cup matzah farfel
¾ cup dark raisins or pareve chocolate
    chips or morsels
½ cup coarsely chopped walnuts

Line one very large shiny metal baking sheet or two smaller sheets with parchment, or grease them well. Set aside. Preheat the oven to 350 degrees.

Put the eggs into a medium bowl, and use a fork to beat them well with the oil. Beat in the sugar until completely combined; then the matzah meal, cinnamon, and salt. Stir in the farfel, raisins or chocolate chips, and walnuts.

Drop by tablespoons onto the prepared baking sheets, and bake at 350 degrees for about 20 to 25 minutes, or until lightly browned on top. Transfer the cookies to wire racks to cool completely. Store them in an airtight container.

Makes about 24 to 30 cookies.

Yom Ha'Atzmaut and Yom Yerushalayim

ISRAEL'S INDEPENDENCE DAY
AND JERUSALEM DAY

 ON MAY 14, 1948, THE FIFTH DAY OF IYAR IN THE YEAR 5708 on the Hebrew calendar, the modern-day State of Israel was established. Annually, on the Hebrew anniversary of that date (with certain exceptions),* Israelis, and also many Jews throughout the Diaspora, joyously celebrate the rebirth of the Jewish state. A major milestone for the young democracy was its recent fiftieth birthday.

Each year, *Yom Ha'Atzmaut* is immediately preceded by *Yom Ha'Zikaron* (Memorial Day), when Israelis solemnly honor those who have given their lives for the country. The proximity of this somewhat somber holiday to the very happy one seems to be in keeping with the Jewish philosophy that we must not forgot the sorrowful times in our history, even as we celebrate the good ones.

Sirens sound throughout Israel on the evening of Yom Ha'Zikaron and again the next morning. Everyone and everything, even traffic, immediately stops to observe a few moments of silence. At nightfall, twelve torches (one for each tribe of ancient Israel) are lit on Mount Herzel in Jerusalem to signify that Memorial Day has ended and Independence Day is about to begin. (Each "day" on the Hebrew calendar begins and ends

---

* When the fifth of Iyar happens to fall on a Friday or Saturday, the celebration of Yom Ha'Atzmaut is moved up to the preceding Thursday, so that the laws of Shabbat will not interfere with the merrymaking that typifies the holiday.

at sunset.) A gun salute honors modern Israel's existence with a round fired for each year.

Because the chief rabbinate of Israel has decreed that Yom Ha'Atzmaut be observed as a break in the Omer period of semimourning between Pesach and Shavuot (as is the holiday Lag B'Omer), all sorts of jubilant festivities can take place. Israelis typically celebrate Yom Ha'Atzmaut with plenty of proud flag-waving, parades, fireworks, music festivals, and family barbecues.

At Dizengoff Square in the heart of Tel Aviv, special platforms are set up for theatrical groups, musicians, comedians, and other types of entertainment. There are food and drink for all, and the mayor of the city may personally greet visitors.

Throughout the country, there is much exuberant singing and dancing in the streets, sometimes all through the night and the next day. Often, friends get together for *kumzitz* ("come and sit") around neighborhood bonfires. At their cookouts and picnics, many Israelis enjoy an abundance of favorite local foods. Several of the same outdoor foods eaten on Lag B'Omer (see that chapter) are also quite popular for Yom Ha'Atzmaut.

Although the holiday is definitely more patriotic than religious, many Jews throughout the Diaspora celebrate it simply because of a strong sense of identification with the Land of Israel. For the first time in almost two millennia, there is once again a Jewish homeland. Furthermore, it is likely that at least one member of every extended Jewish family can well remember those frustrating and very difficult years after World War II that culminated in the critical UN vote for partition in Palestine and, ultimately, in Israel's Declaration of Independence.

In some American cities, special parades and other celebrations are held in honor of Yom Ha'Atzmaut. And Jewish communities throughout the world have lively sessions of Israeli folk dancing and songfests, which always include the national anthem of Israel, *Hatikvah* ("The Hope"). Delicious samplings of typical Israeli foods are usually prominent at Diaspora celebrations of Yom Ha'Atzmaut. Thus, this chapter features many dishes that are either indigenous to Israel or have become very much associated with it. (Some additional Israeli dishes are scattered throughout other chapters of this book.)

These same foods are also very appropriate for *Yom Yerushalayim,* or "Jerusalem Day," which takes place on the twenty-eighth day of the Hebrew month of Iyar (about three weeks after Yom Ha'Atzmaut). This Israeli national holiday celebrates the anniversary of Jerusalem's reunification after the Six-Day War in 1967, a monumental occurrence ranking second in importance only to independence itself. After a two-thousand-year hiatus, the entire city of Jerusalem, including the Temple Mount and Western Wall, was finally under Jewish control.

Yom Ha'Atzmaut and Yom Yerushalayim

As the modern State of Israel is a melting pot, with citizens ingathered from numerous countries around the world, many other international dishes in this cookbook have also become commonplace in that country and are considered a part of its cuisine. They, too, would be quite suitable for both Yom Ha'Atzmaut and Yom Yerushalayim. Especially ideal would be those dishes with Middle Eastern and North African origins, which have had the greatest influence on modern Israeli cuisine.

NOTE: For those of us in the Diaspora, the recipes in this chapter would be perfect for any type of "Israel" celebration or event, even if it is not to celebrate an Israeli national holiday. For instance, on behalf of my synagogue's sisterhood, I have held a very popular "Israel Day" brunch as a closing event for the year. I display posters from the Israeli embassy, offer booklets of information about Israel, and show videos and share photos of trips to that country. And, of course, I offer a sampling of many different Israeli foods, including several featured in this chapter.

Falafel, Israeli-Style

TINY CROQUETTES MADE WITH DRIED CHICKPEAS

Of all the street foods in Israel—and there are many—falafel is without a doubt the most popular. In fact, it's probably the food most often identified with Israeli cuisine.

Falafel is sold at outdoor kiosks that almost always have large "salad bars." (And we Americans think we invented that idea!) When a falafel sandwich is ordered, the vendor places a few freshly fried falafel balls (and, possibly, some French fries) inside a split loaf of pita, and hands it to the purchaser, who then adds his or her own choice of salads and dressings.

Israeli teens are masters at skillfully stuffing so much into their pita sandwiches that the doughy pocket seems on the verge of bursting. They push in the salad with a vengeance, until the falafel balls themselves are a mere pittance, squashed almost into oblivion.

Most amazing is that these teens then partake of such meal-size sandwiches while walking and chatting, losing nary a lettuce leaf in the process. Tourists, on the other hand, sparsely fill their own loaves, but still leave behind a telltale trail of chopped vegetables and dressing.

While visiting Israel in the early 1980s, I sampled the wares of several outdoor kiosks. Upon returning home, I tested numerous falafel recipes until I was finally satisfied with one that I thought tasted authentic. I found that cumin, a spice often used in Middle Eastern cooking, is responsible for much of the distinctive flavor of falafel. Dried chickpeas and bulgur wheat give the falafel a really nice texture.

I knew I had truly hit the mark when my spicy chickpea balls garnered much praise from an Israeli family temporarily situated in the United States. Before the sampling, they had greatly missed "real" falafel but had no idea how to make it. As falafel is always so inexpensive and easily available in Israel, they explained, it is rarely prepared at home.

NOTES: Falafel vendors in Israel often use a cleverly designed metal gadget to quickly mold the chickpea mixture into 1-inch-diameter croquettes. When the gadget's plunger is released, a perfectly shaped croquette is ejected. "Falafel makers" come in single and double styles (to make two croquettes at once), and are nice souvenirs from Israel. However, falafel can also be molded by hand.

This recipe begins with dry chickpeas, as is usually done by those who make falafel from scratch in Israel. For a version that calls for *canned* chickpeas, see the recipe for Quicker Falafel (page 431).

Falafel has become so popular among American Jews that kosher grocery stores often carry frozen falafel or falafel mix. While not as good as freshly made falafel, they are quite satisfactory in a pinch.

The amounts of herbs and spices in the following recipe should be adjusted to taste, particularly where a range is indicated.

1 cup dry chickpeas (garbanzo beans)
1/3 cup bulgur wheat
2 to 3 tablespoons lemon juice
2 large eggs or 1/2 cup pareve egg
    substitute
3 tablespoons water
2 to 3 garlic cloves, chopped
1 to 1 1/2 teaspoons ground cumin
1/2 teaspoon ground turmeric
2 tablespoons finely chopped fresh
    parsley leaves or 1 tablespoon dried
    leaves

1/4 to 1/2 teaspoon each dried basil and
    marjoram leaves
1/4 to 1/2 teaspoon ground coriander seed
1/8 teaspoon cayenne pepper
1 teaspoon salt
1/2 to 1 cup fresh bread crumbs
    (preferably made from pita in a
    food processor), or as needed
Canola oil for frying

Yom Ha'Atzmaut and Yom Yerushalayim

To Serve
*Several loaves whole wheat or white
 Pita (purchased, or see page 454)*

Israeli Salad (page 432)
Tahina (page 434) (optional)

Sort and wash the dry chickpeas well; then put them into a small saucepan with about 3 cups water. Bring them to a boil over high heat; then lower the heat, and boil them, covered, for 10 minutes. Turn off the heat, and let the chickpeas rest in the covered saucepan for 1 to 3 hours.

Meanwhile, soak the bulgur wheat in water to cover for about 20 minutes; then drain it very well. (The easiest way to do this is to put the bulgur into a large sieve; then lower the sieve into a bowl of water until the bulgur is covered. To drain the bulgur, simply lift up the sieve and press out any excess water.)

Drain the partially cooked and soaked chickpeas, and put them into a food processor (fitted with a steel blade) along with the lemon juice, eggs, water, and garlic. Pulse-process until the chickpeas are very finely chopped but not puréed. (Alternatively, very finely chop the chickpeas with a food grinder, and then mix them with the other ingredients.)

Put the chickpea mixture into a bowl, and mix in all the herbs and seasonings until well combined. Add the drained bulgur. Stir in enough bread crumbs so that the mixture holds together well. Cover the mixture, and let it rest for 15 to 30 minutes to firm up slightly.

Shape the mixture into 1-inch-diameter balls by hand or use an Israeli "falafel maker" (see Notes). Set the balls aside on a platter, not touching one another. When all the chickpea mixture has been shaped, put enough oil into a large saucepan or electric frypan so that it is 1½ to 2 inches deep. Heat the oil until it is very hot, about 375 degrees. Put several of the balls into the oil, but do not crowd them. Fry them, turning them occasionally, until they are well browned on all sides and cooked through. Drain them on paper towels. Repeat until all the falafel balls have been fried.

To serve the falafel, cut open the loaves of pita, and place several falafel balls inside each pocket. Top the falafel with salad and, if desired, *tahina* dressing.

Leftover falafel balls freeze well. Reheat them, uncovered, in a 350-degree oven until they are crisp and heated through.

Makes 50 to 60 1-inch-diameter falafel balls.

Quicker Falafel

TINY CROQUETTES MADE WITH CANNED CHICKPEAS

The use of canned chickpeas in this falafel makes it quicker, though not quite as "authentic," as the recipe for Falafel, Israeli-Style (page 428). This version is also slightly less spicy, and it makes fewer balls.

Be careful not to overprocess the canned chickpeas in this recipe because they can easily turn to mush, and falafel tastes best if it has some texture.

(For more information about the making and eating of falafel in Israel, please see the comments with the recipe for Falafel, Israeli-Style.)

¼ cup bulgur wheat

1 (15- to 16-ounce) can chickpeas
(garbanzo beans), well-drained

1 to 2 garlic cloves, coarsely chopped

1 tablespoon lemon juice

1 large egg, lightly beaten or ¼ cup
pareve egg substitute

2 tablespoons finely chopped fresh
parsley leaves or 1 tablespoon
dried leaves

½ to 1 teaspoon ground cumin, or to
taste

¼ teaspoon ground turmeric

¼ teaspoon ground coriander (optional)

½ teaspoon salt

⅛ teaspoon ground black pepper

½ to 1 cup fresh bread crumbs
(preferably made from pita in a
food processor), or as needed

Canola oil for frying

TO SERVE

Several loaves whole wheat or white
Pita (purchased, or see page 454)

Israeli Salad (page 432)

Tahina (page 434) (optional)

Soak the bulgur wheat in water to cover for about 20 minutes; then drain it very well. (The easiest way to do this is to put the bulgur into a large sieve; then lower the sieve into a bowl of water until the bulgur is covered. To drain the bulgur, simply lift up the sieve and press out any excess water.)

Put the drained bulgur and chickpeas into a food processor (fitted with a steel blade), and pulse-process just until the chickpeas are finely chopped but not puréed. If the chickpea mixture sticks to the perimeter of the bowl, use a rubber spatula to push it back into the center. (Alternatively, use a food grinder with a coarse blade to grind the chickpeas and softened bulgur together.)

Yom Ha'Atzmaut and Yom Yerushalayim

Transfer the mixture to a bowl, and stir in the garlic, lemon juice, egg, parsley, and seasonings until well combined. Then stir in enough bread crumbs so that the mixture is not sticky. Let the mixture rest for 15 to 30 minutes to firm up slightly.

Shape the mixture into 1-inch-diameter balls by hand or use an Israeli "falafel maker" (see Notes on Falafel, Israeli-Style, page 428). Set the balls aside on a platter, not touching one another. When all the chickpea mixture has been shaped, put enough oil into a large saucepan or electric frypan so that it is 1½ to 2 inches deep. Heat the oil until it is very hot, about 375 degrees. Put several of the balls into the oil, but do not crowd them. Fry them, turning them occasionally, until they are well browned on all sides and cooked through. Drain them on paper towels. Repeat until all the falafel balls have been fried.

To serve the falafel, cut open the loaves of pita, and place several falafel balls inside each pocket. Top the falafel with salad and, if desired, *tahina* dressing.

Leftover falafel balls freeze well. Reheat them, uncovered, in a 350-degree oven until they are crisp and heated through.

Makes about 40 1-inch-diameter falafel balls.

Israeli Salad
KIBBUTZ-STYLE CHOPPED FRESH VEGETABLES

Israel is well known for its outstanding vegetables, which are grown in three major crops during the year. In fact, most Israeli families have gorgeous farm-fresh produce on the table daily. The following salad—widely known simply as "Israeli Salad" or *Salat Yisraeli* in Hebrew—is eaten throughout the country. It first became popular at farm cooperatives called *Kibbutzim*.

Many *kibbutzniks*—those who live and work on *kibbutzim*—help grow some of the succulent vegetables they eat. In the *kibbutz* dining room, vegetables are served in many different dishes, both raw and cooked. At most kibbutzim, this raw vegetable salad is offered at virtually every meal, including breakfast. The ability to chop vegetables to the

smallest, most perfect dice for this salad is considered a mark of status among many kibbutz cooks.

In the dining room, a colorful selection of whole salad vegetables may be strategically placed for kibbutzniks to cut up and dress as they choose. Typically, there is also a large bowl of assorted homemade pickles on every table, and there may even be some cooked (and chilled) vegetable salads, such as the Salat Hatzilim (page 437) in this chapter.

At kibbutzim and throughout all of Israel, a salad such as the following one is surely on the menu for Yom Ha'Atzmaut. The recipe is meant only to be a guide; please feel free to vary the proportions of all the ingredients to taste. Tomatoes, cucumber, and scallions or onions are considered to be characteristic of this salad, but other diced or shredded salad vegetables, such as peppers, lettuce, cabbage, carrots, or radishes, may be added. Just don't put them all in the same salad! For the best flavor, prepare the salad just before serving it.

3 large tomatoes, preferably vine-ripened, diced

2 to 3 medium cucumbers, peeled (if desired) and diced

4 scallions, including green tops, thinly sliced or 1 small onion, peeled and finely diced

1 to 2 medium green or red bell peppers, diced

¼ cup finely chopped fresh parsley

3 tablespoons fresh lemon juice, or to taste

3 tablespoons full-flavored olive oil

Salt and freshly ground black pepper to taste

Put the tomatoes, cucumbers, scallions, peppers, and parsley into a large serving bowl. In a small bowl, mix together the lemon juice and oil. Pour over the vegetables and toss them well. Season the salad to taste. Serve immediately, as a side dish, or in a pita loaf as an accompaniment to falafel.

Makes about 6 to 8 servings.

Yom Ha'Atzmaut and Yom Yerushalayim

Tahina

LEMONY SESAME DIP OR DRESSING

Tahina (pronounced "tah-'chee-nah," with a guttural "ch") is very popular in Israel—on its own as a dip with Pita (see 454), and also as a topping or dressing with many different foods, particularly Falafel sandwiches (see pages 428 and 431).

Its main ingredient is *tahini*—a pure paste ground from hulled sesame seeds just as peanut butter is made from peanuts. Tahini is available at most health food and specialty stores, as well as many supermarkets. Once opened, it will keep for several months in the refrigerator if the plastic lid is tightly resealed on the can. A newly opened can of tahini should always be stirred very well before using it, to resuspend any separated sesame oil. This task is most easily done in a food processor. The refrigerated tahini should then stay well mixed for quite a while. (Never discard any separated oil, or the tahini will be much too dry.)

In Israel, both the pure sesame seed paste and the "dip" made from it are called *tahina*—the only difference being that the latter is sometimes described as *prepared tahina*. To avoid confusion, I have designated the pure paste *tahini* (with a final *i* instead of an *a*), as it is usually labeled in the United States.

The following tahina dip is fun to make with children, not only because it is so simple, but also because fascinating physical changes take place during its preparation. Pure tahini looks much like very thin peanut butter. When a little water is mixed in, however, it mysteriously becomes extremely stiff and hard to stir. Then, as more water is gradually added, it lightens considerably in color, and becomes smooth and creamy like mayonnaise.

¹/₂ cup tahini (pure sesame paste) (see comments above)
About ¹/₂ cup water
2 to 3 tablespoons fresh lemon juice
Salt and freshly ground pepper to taste
About 1 tablespoon finely chopped fresh parsley leaves (optional)

Other herbs and seasonings to taste, such as finely chopped dillweed or garlic (optional)

TO SERVE (OPTIONAL)
Several loaves whole wheat or white Pita (purchased, or see page 454)
Raw vegetables for dipping

Put the tahini into a small bowl, and add the water in a slow stream, stirring constantly until the mixture eventually becomes very smooth and

velvety. (At first, the mixture will become very stiff; then it will thin out and become lighter in color.) Stir in the remaining ingredients, adjusting the amounts as desired for taste and consistency. If the tahina is too thick, add more water; if it is too thin, stir in a bit more tahini.

If possible, refrigerate the tahina a few hours to give the flavors a chance to blend. (It gets slightly firmer when chilled.) Before using the tahina, let it come to room temperature, and stir it again. Serve it as a dip with pieces of pita or cut-up raw vegetables. (For use as a dressing, the tahina should be thinner than when using it as a dip.) If tightly covered and refrigerated, tahina will stay fresh for several days up to a week.

Makes about 1 cup.

Humus
CHICKPEA DIP

This thick purée—called *humus b'tahina* in Hebrew (meaning "chickpeas in sesame paste") or, more often, simply *humus* (pronounced "'choo-moos," with a guttural "ch")—is one of my favorite appetizers, and it's so easy to prepare that I serve it often. It keeps in the refrigerator for up to a week, and can even be frozen. Although humus is quite tasty with crackers and even cut-up raw vegetables, it is customarily eaten on small triangles of pita.

Chickpeas are a staple in Israel. They are used most often in humus and falafel. Many salads also include cooked chickpeas. The most popular is the simplest: drained, cooked (or canned) chickpeas tossed with olive oil, lemon juice, chopped fresh parsley, salt, and pepper—all in amounts to taste.

Chickpeas are also frequently used in Israeli *hamin*—the Shabbat meal-in-a-pot that is quite similar to *dafina* and cholent.

NOTES: Tahini is a pure paste made by grinding sesame seeds. Sesame seeds naturally contain a lot of oil, which tends to separate out of the paste. The oil must be stirred completely into the paste before using it, or it will be much too dry. A food processor

Yom Ha'Atzmaut and Yom Yerushalayim

may be used for this task, and can be used to mix the entire can of tahini. If the stirred tahini is refrigerated, it should stay suspended for a while. For more information on tahini, see the recipe for Tahina (page 434). If a newly stirred can of tahini is used for this recipe, remove most of the tahini from the food processor and return it to the can, leaving behind about ¼ cup; then add the remaining ingredients to the food processor as directed below.

Although I frequently use chopped fresh garlic that comes in jars for my cooking, this is one recipe that really requires *fresh* garlic cloves. The same is true for the lemon juice. Most Israelis prefer this with lots of garlic; adjust the amount to your own taste. Start out with the lower amount, and add more later if desired. You may do the same with the lemon juice.

¼ cup tahini (pure sesame paste) (see Notes)

1 (15- to 16-ounce) can chickpeas (garbanzo beans), drained

3 tablespoons extra-virgin olive oil

2 to 4 fresh garlic cloves, coarsely chopped (see Notes)

About 2 to 3 tablespoons fresh lemon juice, or to taste (see Notes)

2 to 3 tablespoons water

Salt and freshly ground pepper to taste

GARNISH (OPTIONAL)

Sprigs of fresh parsley

Whole pitted ripe (black) olives, cut in half

Additional extra-virgin olive oil

1 tablespoon pine nuts (pignoli), lightly toasted

TO SERVE

Several loaves whole wheat or white Pita (purchased, or see page 454)

Put the tahini, chickpeas, oil, garlic, lemon juice, and water into a food processor (fitted with a steel blade) or a blender. Process until smooth, scraping down the sides of the container a few times. (With a blender, it may be necessary to add 1 to 2 tablespoons more water to avoid clogging the blades.) Add the seasonings to taste.

Transfer the humus to a small, shallow bowl. If desired, put some sprigs of parsley on the center of the humus, and olive halves around the perimeter of the dish.

Refrigerate the humus for several hours to give the flavors a chance to blend. (It will get a bit firmer during refrigeration.) Before serving, let it come to room temperature. If desired, just before serving, sprinkle the top of the humus with a few teaspoons of olive oil, as is the Middle Eastern custom,

and scatter the pine nuts on top. Cut the pita into small triangles, as a pizza is cut. Accompany the humus with pita triangles for dipping. If tightly covered and refrigerated, humus will stay fresh for several days up to a week.

Makes about 2 cups of humus.

Salat Hatzilim
ISRAELI-STYLE EGGPLANT SALAD

Eggplant is extremely popular in Israel and all the other Middle Eastern countries, as well as in North Africa and the countries of the Mediterranean area. In these places, it is prepared in hundreds, possibly thousands, of different ways.

For salads such as this one, which is really more of a dip, eggplant is cooked over a gas flame or under a broiler until the skin is charred. In some places, eggplants are still roasted over open campfires, as they have been for centuries. The charring gives the eggplant a characteristic smoky flavor. A modern gas or charcoal grill gives very similar results.

This is one of the salads that may be put inside a falafel sandwich on top of the falafel balls and chopped vegetables.

SALAD
2 medium eggplants (about 1 to 1½ pounds each)
1 to 2 fresh garlic cloves, pressed or very finely minced
2 to 3 tablespoons extra-virgin olive oil
1 tablespoon fresh lemon juice

3 tablespoons finely minced fresh parsley leaves
Salt and pepper to taste

TO SERVE
1 ripe tomato, cut into thin wedges
Several loaves whole wheat or white Pita (purchased, or see page 454)

Prick each eggplant in several places with a fork. (If you don't, they may explode!) Put them on a heavy, foil-lined baking sheet about 6 inches under a heated broiler element. Broil the eggplants, turning them often, for 20 to 30 minutes, or until the skin is blistered and charred, the eggplants have shriveled

somewhat, and the completely cooked pulp is soft and juicy. (If desired, the eggplants may be roasted on a grill in the more traditional manner; be sure to turn them frequently.)

Cut open the eggplants, and let them cool until they can be handled. Remove and discard any large clusters of seeds in the center. Peel off and discard the skin and stem.

Chop up the eggplant pulp, and put it into a medium bowl. Add the garlic, olive oil, lemon juice, and parsley, and stir until well combined. Season with salt and pepper. Refrigerate the salad for several hours, or until the flavors have had a chance to blend. Readjust the seasonings, if necessary. Garnish the salad with the tomato. Serve it with the pita cut into small triangles, as one would cut a pizza. Spoon small amounts of salad onto the pita, or use the salad as a thick dip. (It tastes best at room temperature.)

Makes 4 to 6 servings.

Variation

ISRAELI EGGPLANT SALAD, ASHKENAZIC-STYLE

Ashkenazic Jews in Israel use mayonnaise in this salad for a different flavor and texture. To make it, substitute mayonnaise to taste for the oil and lemon juice. If desired, a chopped or grated Spanish onion or some thinly sliced scallion may be substituted for the garlic.

Baba Ganoush
EGGPLANT-SESAME DIP

This delicious appetizer dip of Arabic origin is very popular in Israel, as it is all over the Middle East, where it is sometimes said that a cook's worth is equal to how many eggplant dishes he or she can prepare. The combination of ingredients in *baba ganoush* makes the dip quite interesting. In fact, it's hard to tell that the main ingredient is eggplant—a bonus for those who think that they dislike that vegetable!

NOTE: Tahini is a pure paste made by grinding sesame seeds, just as peanut butter is made from peanuts. Sesame seeds naturally contain a lot of oil, which tends to separate out of the paste. The oil must be stirred completely into the paste before using it, or it will be much too dry. A food processor may be used for this task, and can be used to mix the entire can of tahini. If the stirred tahini is refrigerated, it should stay suspended for a while. For more information on tahini, see the recipe for Tahina (page 434). If a newly stirred can of tahini is used for this recipe, remove most of the tahini from the food processor and return it to the can, leaving behind about ⅓ cup; then add the remaining ingredients to the food processor as directed below.

2 medium eggplants (about 1 to 1½ pounds each)
2 fresh garlic cloves, finely minced or pressed
⅓ cup tahini (pure sesame paste) (see Note)
2½ tablespoons fresh lemon juice
2 tablespoons water
1 tablespoon extra-virgin olive oil
2 tablespoons finely chopped fresh parsley leaves

½ teaspoon salt
⅛ teaspoon ground black pepper
Pinch of cayenne pepper (optional)

GARNISH (OPTIONAL)
Sprigs of fresh parsley

TO SERVE
Several loaves whole wheat or white Pita (purchased, or see page 454)

Prick each eggplant in several places with a fork. (If you don't, they may explode!) Put them on a heavy, foil-lined baking sheet about 6 inches under a heated broiler element. Broil the eggplants, turning them often, for 20 to 30 minutes or until the skin is blistered and charred and the completely cooked pulp is soft and juicy. (If desired, the eggplants may be roasted on a grill in the more traditional manner; be sure to turn them frequently.)

Cut open the eggplants, and let them cool until they can be handled. Remove and discard any large clusters of seeds in the center. Peel off and discard the skin and stem.

If a food processor with a steel blade is available, put the eggplant pulp into the bowl, along with the remaining dip ingredients (see Note). Pulse-process the mixture until it is almost smooth, but not completely puréed. Occasionally scrape down the sides of the bowl during the processing.

Yom Ha'Atzmaut and Yom Yerushalayim

If a food processor is not available, chop the eggplant pulp very finely by hand, and put it into a medium bowl. In another bowl, combine the remaining dip ingredients, and stir them until very well blended. Then stir them into the eggplant.

Transfer the *baba ganoush* to a small, shallow serving bowl. If desired, put some sprigs of parsley on the center of the dip. Refrigerate the dip for several hours or, preferably, overnight to give the flavors a chance to blend. Serve it cold or, for the best taste, at room temperature. Cut the pita loaves into small triangles (as if cutting up a pizza), and accompany the *baba ganoush* with pita triangles for dipping.

Makes about 2 cups dip.

"Oven-Fried" Breaded Eggplant

Fried eggplant is very popular in many Israeli dishes. However, eggplant tends to absorb great quantities of oil when it is fried. So I developed this tasty, broiled version of breaded eggplant, which is much lower in fat. It makes a great side dish alone, or it can be used whenever a dish calls for fried, breaded eggplant.

NOTE: If desired, canned Italian-style seasoned bread crumbs may be substituted for the seasoned crumb mixture below. If they include cheese, then this recipe will be "dairy," not pareve.

SEASONED CRUMB MIXTURE
2 1/2 cups coarsely cubed fresh or slightly stale bread (may be part or all whole wheat)
1 1/2 tablespoons dried parsley flakes
2 teaspoons instant minced onions
1 1/2 teaspoons dried oregano leaves
1 teaspoon dried basil leaves
1/2 teaspoon dried marjoram leaves
1/4 teaspoon dried thyme leaves

1/4 teaspoon garlic powder
1/4 teaspoon salt
1/8 teaspoon ground black pepper

EGGPLANT
1 medium eggplant (about 1 to 1 1/2 pounds)
2 large eggs or 1/2 cup pareve egg substitute
2 tablespoons canola oil

For the seasoned crumb mixture, put all the ingredients in a food processor or blender, and process them until fine crumbs are formed. (This may be done in advance, and the crumbs can be stored for months in the freezer. Thaw them before using.)

Lightly grease or coat with nonstick cooking spray one or two large, heavy, shiny metal baking sheets.

Cut off and discard the ends of the eggplant. Cut the eggplant crosswise into ⅜-inch-thick slices. In a small bowl, use a fork to beat the eggs with the oil until well combined. Put the crumbs in another bowl that is wide enough to fit the eggplant slices.

Dip each slice of eggplant into the egg mixture; then let the excess egg mixture drip back into the bowl. Immediately coat both sides of the eggplant slice with the crumb mixture. Lay out the coated eggplant slices on the prepared baking sheets. Turn on the broiler.

Put one filled baking sheet in a preheated broiler about 5 to 6 inches under the heating element. Broil the eggplant slices for a total of 10 to 15 minutes, turning them over once with tongs, until they are browned and cooked through. Turn the pan around during broiling if necessary for even browning. Repeat to broil any remaining slices. Serve hot or lukewarm.

Makes about 6 servings as a side dish.

Gezer Chai
CARROT-CITRUS SALAD

The name of this very easy, tasty salad, *gezer chai* (pronounced with a guttural "ch"), translates literally as "living carrot." It is a relatively new dish, created and made popular in the modern State of Israel, where it is likely to be on the menu of many Yom Ha'Atzmaut picnics. Sometimes, *gezer chai* is served over avocado halves, to provide a beautiful contrasts of colors and textures.

If possible, it would be quite appropriate to use a delicious Jaffa orange, imported from Israel, in this salad.

SALAD

1 pound fresh carrots, peeled (or
    scrubbed) and finely grated

About ¾ cup fresh orange juice

1 to 2 tablespoons fresh lemon juice

1 medium to large navel orange, peeled
    and finely chopped

Sugar or honey to taste

Pinch of salt (optional)

Pinch of ground ginger (optional)

TO SERVE (YOUR CHOICE)

Crisp lettuce leaves

About 6 hollowed-out lemon or orange
    halves

About 3 medium ripe avocados, halved
    and seeded

Sprigs of fresh spearmint (optional)

Mix together all salad ingredients. Refrigerate the salad for several hours or, preferably, overnight, to allow the carrots to absorb the juices and for the flavors to blend. This salad may be kept refrigerated up to 3 days, and actually improves with storage.

Just before serving, stir the salad well and adjust seasonings if necessary. Serve it on lettuce leaves, in lemon or orange "shells," or over avocado halves. If desired, garnish the salad with mint.

Makes about 6 servings.

Couscous and Chickpea Salad

Several summers ago, I created this salad, based on Israeli and Moroccan cuisines, to have something different to take to a neighborhood picnic. It was such a hit that I have brought it again and again to different events, and serve it often at home. It is very easy to prepare using the packaged "ready-to-cook" couscous that is now easily available.

NOTE: The couscous in the following recipe is not the same as the large "Israeli couscous" that resembles large egg barley and is sold is some kosher supermarkets and Jewish specialty stores. This couscous is a very tiny pasta that resembles a grain. For more information about couscous, see the recipe for Quick Couscous (page 126.)

FOR THE COUSCOUS

1½ cups (10 ounces) plain dry "quick-cooking" couscous

1½ cups water

¼ teaspoon turmeric

2 tablespoons extra-virgin olive oil

About ¼ cup warm water (or more as needed)

FOR THE SALAD

3 to 4 tablespoons lemon juice

3 to 4 tablespoons extra-virgin olive oil

1 teaspoon ground cumin

1 teaspoon dried marjoram leaves

1 teaspoon dried basil leaves

½ to 1 teaspoon dried mint leaves or 2 to 3 teaspoons chopped fresh spearmint leaves

⅛ to ¼ teaspoon ground black pepper

¼ to ½ teaspoon salt

2 (15- to 16-ounce) cans chickpeas (garbanzo beans), drained and rinsed

Put the dry couscous into a large bowl. (The couscous will increase in size several times.) In a small saucepan, bring the water to a boil with the turmeric and 2 tablespoons oil. Lower the heat and simmer, stirring, for 1 to 2 minutes, or until the turmeric is dissolved. Add the yellow-tinted water to the dry couscous, and immediately stir with a fork, lifting and separating the grains, for about 5 minutes, or until the water is completely absorbed. Use the fork or your fingers to break apart any lumps. Gradually add warm water 1 tablespoon at a time, stirring with a fork after each addition until it is absorbed, until the couscous is tender with a slight "bite" when it is tasted. If you stir enough, the couscous should be very light and fluffy.

Add the remaining ingredients to the couscous except for the chickpeas, adjusting the amounts to your own taste. Stir in the chickpeas. Refrigerate the salad, covered, several hours or overnight, to allow the flavors to mingle and the couscous to absorb the dressing. Before serving, stir the salad and taste it. If desired, more of the listed herbs and seasonings may be added to taste.

For best taste, serve the salad at room temperature, but store it in the refrigerator, where it will stay fresh for several days.

Makes about 8 cups of salad, about 10 to 12 side-dish servings.

Yom Ha'Atzmaut and Yom Yerushalayim

Marak Teimani

YEMENITE-STYLE MEAT AND VEGETABLE SOUP

M

During our first visit to Israel in the early 1980s, my husband and I had a memorable dining experience in the Yemenite quarter of Tel Aviv. It was at a small, unassuming restaurant frequented mainly by Yemenite Jews who spoke no English. The short menu was scrawled in Hebrew on a blackboard, leaving us confused over what to order.

Looking around, we saw that other diners were partaking of a hearty meat soup, grilled skewered meat cubes (Shashlik, page 446), assorted chopped vegetable salads, and pita. Two types of relish sat in small dishes on each table, and everyone was enthusiastically spooning one or both over each course—even over the bread.

The food looked and smelled absolutely wonderful, and we were ravenous after a long day of sightseeing. But when a young man came to take our order, the language barrier seemed insurmountable. As we frantically tried to communicate with the waiter, a man at the next table saw our problem and kindly offered, in broken English, to assist us. When the food came a short while later, our new friend pointed to the two dishes of relish on our table, and said simply, "Hot. Be careful."

The entire meal was delicious and, thanks to the polite warning, we did not totally sear our mouths on the relishes, but sampled just enough to know that when a Yemenite says hot, he means HOT!

The following soup, which makes a great one-dish meal, is often served ladled over pita. The bread absorbs some of the broth, and becomes deliciously soft. Though the soup does contain a lot of seasonings, it is not very "hot" in the spicy sense. (When Yemenites eat it, they add plenty of *hilbuh,* a relish made with fenugreek and chili pepper. I have omitted this.)

7 cups water

1½ to 2 pounds beef chuck, lamb shoulder, or other soup meat, cut into 1-inch cubes and trimmed of all fat and gristle

1 or 2 marrow bones

1 medium onion

1 large leek

3 large carrots (or use about 15 peeled baby carrots)

1 tomato

1 stalk celery

3 garlic cloves

1 teaspoon salt

¼ teaspoon ground black pepper

1 teaspoon ground cumin

½ teaspoon ground turmeric

¼ teaspoon ground cardamom
(optional)

2 pounds "new" or all-purpose potatoes

½ cup finely chopped fresh parsley
leaves

2 teaspoons dried cilantro leaves or 1 to
2 tablespoons chopped fresh leaves

To Serve (Optional)

6 to 8 small loaves whole wheat or
white Pita (purchased, or see page
454)

Bring the water to a boil in a 5- to 6-quart soup pot or Dutch oven over high heat. Add the cubed meat and the bones, and lower the heat. Gently simmer the meat, uncovered, for 15 minutes while skimming off and discarding all the foam that rises to the top. Cover, and continue to simmer for 45 minutes longer.

While the meat is simmering, prepare the vegetables. Peel the onion, cut it in half through the root end, and then into ¼-inch slices. For the leek, wash it well, and cut off the root and all but about 2 inches of the green top. Peel off one or two outer white layers (which are likely to contain sand), and wash the leek top very well by separating the leaves with your hands and running water between them. Cut the leek into ¼-inch slices.

For the carrots, peel or scrape them and cut them into 2-inch pieces. Core the tomato and cut it into eighths. Cut the celery into 1-inch-long pieces. Finely chop the garlic.

When the meat has simmered for 1 hour, add all the prepared vegetables, along with the salt, pepper, cumin, turmeric, and cardamom (if used). Bring the soup again to a simmer. Gently simmer the soup, covered, for about 1½ hours longer, or until the meat and vegetables are very tender. Meanwhile, peel the potatoes, and cut them into chunks.

Add the potatoes, parsley, and cilantro, and simmer the soup for about 20 to 30 minutes longer, or until the potatoes are tender. Adjust the seasonings if necessary.

To serve in the Yemenite way, put a loaf of pita into the bottom of each soup bowl. Ladle some broth, meat, and vegetables on top.

Makes about 6 to 8 servings as a main course.

Yom Ha'Atzmaut and Yom Yerushalayim

Shashlik

ISRAELI-STYLE GRILLED BEEF OR LAMB CUBES

M

This delicious, skewered and grilled meat is basically what Americans call "shish kebab." In Israel, the term *kebab* usually means skewered *ground* meat, whereas *shashlik* indicates that the meat is *cubed*. The latter name is adopted from the Russian term for such grilled meat.

The dish was probably brought to Israel by Russian Jews from the Caucasus and Georgia, where shashlik is said to have originated. However, it is so similar to certain Middle Eastern kebabs that it is also considered a specialty of Israelis from Yemen.

In Israel, it has become customary on Saturday evenings for many families to patronize restaurants and outdoor cafés especially for shashlik and ground-meat kebab (see the recipe for Mititei, page 473). The grilled meats are usually accompanied with Tahina (page 434), Humus (page 435), and assorted vegetable salads.

Before cooking shashlik, the meat must be marinated for several hours or, preferably, overnight. Oil and vinegar in the marinade help to tenderize the meat, and the seasonings give it a delectable flavor.

NOTE: If any grilled skewered vegetables are desired at the same meal, put them on separate skewers from the meat, as they never seem to take the same amount of time as the meat and don't cook together properly. Also, it is much quicker and easier to assemble skewers that contain only meat *or* vegetables.

MARINADE
1/2 cup red wine vinegar
1/4 cup extra-virgin olive oil
1 medium onion, very finely chopped or
     grated
2 garlic cloves, finely minced or pressed
1/2 teaspoon salt
1/4 teaspoon black pepper, preferably
     freshly ground
1 tablespoon finely chopped fresh
     parsley leaves
1/2 teaspoon dried thyme leaves
     (optional)

1/4 teaspoon dried marjoram leaves
     (optional)

FOR SKEWERS
2 pounds beef or lamb, trimmed of all
     surface fat and gristle, and cut into
     1 1/4-inch cubes

TO SERVE (YOUR CHOICE)
Several loaves whole wheat or white
     Pita (purchased, or see page 454)
Hot cooked plain rice or rice pilaf

In a medium nonaluminum bowl, combine all the marinade ingredients and mix them well; then add the meat cubes and toss them so they are well coated with marinade. Cover the bowl tightly. In the refrigerator, marinate the meat for 4 to 24 hours, stirring it occasionally. The longer the meat is marinated, the more tender and flavorful it will be. Remove the bowl of meat from the refrigerator 30 to 60 minutes before grilling or broiling, to allow the meat to come to room temperature.

Thread the meat cubes onto metal skewers or sturdy disposable wooden skewers that have been soaked in water for several minutes (see the recipe for Teriyaki Chicken, page 475). Discard the leftover marinade.

Grill the shashlik over hot coals or on a preheated gas grill set to medium-high, turning them often with long tongs, for about 10 to 15 minutes, or until the meat is browned on the outside and cooked to the desired doneness. Or, if preferred, broil the shashlik about 4 inches from the heat element, turning them often (with long tongs), for about 10 to 15 minutes, or until the meat is cooked as desired. Use a fork to slide the meat off the skewers. Serve with pita or rice.

Makes about 6 to 8 servings.

Variation

CHICKEN SHASHLIK

Use skinless, boneless chicken breasts. Remove the tenderloin piece from the underside of each breast half. Cut the tenderloin in half, and cut the rest of the chicken breast into 1¼-inch squares. Make the marinade as directed above, except use only ¼ cup wine vinegar and 2 tablespoons oil and add ¼ cup white wine or dry sherry. Proceed as above, but marinate the chicken for no longer than 1 to 2 hours. Chicken will take less time to cook than meat, but it must be cooked through completely.

Makes about 6 to 8 servings.

K'Tsitsat Basar B'Agvaniyot
ISRAELI-STYLE MEATBALLS IN TOMATO SAUCE

A similar dish that was once served at a kosher restaurant in Philadelphia inspired this recipe. It is very easy, and would be nice to serve at home on the evening of Yom Ha'Atzmaut.

MEATBALLS
1 pound very lean ground beef or lamb
1 small onion, grated or very finely chopped
1 large egg
$1/3$ cup matzah meal or plain dry bread crumbs
2 tablespoons finely chopped fresh parsley leaves
1 teaspoon dried mint leaves or 1 tablespoon chopped fresh spearmint leaves
$1/2$ teaspoon dried marjoram leaves
$1/4$ teaspoon each ground cinnamon, nutmeg, and ginger
$1/2$ teaspoon salt

$1/4$ teaspoon ground black pepper

SAUCE
1 (14- to 16-ounce) can tomatoes, including juice, chopped
$3/4$ cup beef broth
1 small onion, finely chopped
1 to 2 garlic cloves, minced
2 tablespoons finely chopped fresh parsley leaves
$1/8$ teaspoon black pepper, preferably freshly ground

TO SERVE
Hot cooked brown or white rice

Combine all the meatball ingredients in a medium bowl, and mix them very well with your hands or a fork. For the smoothest balls, squeeze the meat through your fingers. Set aside.

In a large, deep skillet, combine all the sauce ingredients. Bring the sauce to a simmer over medium-high heat. Form the meat mixture into 1¼-inch balls, and add them to the simmering sauce. When all the meatballs have been formed, cover the skillet, and simmer the meatballs, basting them occasionally, for 45 to 60 minutes or until they are cooked through and firm, and the sauce has a rich flavor.

Serve the meatballs over the rice, spooning some sauce over each portion.

Makes about 4 to 5 servings.

Siniyeh

SPICED MEAT LOAF WITH SESAME TOPPING

This interesting Middle Eastern ground meat dish, which has been adopted by the Israelis, includes unusual spices and the very popular sesame paste known as *tahini*. Yemenite Jews were among those who brought the dish to Israel. In the Galilee region, *siniyeh* has become a popular offering in restaurants, where it is served with an assortment of salads.

This dish is traditionally made with ground lamb, although ground beef is also frequently used. The name, which is similar to the Arabic word for "tray," indicates that the meat is cooked in a shallow pan.

The sesame topping, which is actually a variation on tahina, is also used by Israelis on baked fish.

NOTE: Canned tahini must be stirred very well before it is used. For more information, see the recipe for Tahina (page 434).

MEAT LOAF
2 pounds lean ground beef or ground
    lamb
1 medium onion, finely chopped or
    grated
2 garlic cloves, finely minced or pressed
¼ cup finely chopped fresh parsley
    leaves
½ teaspoon ground cumin
¼ teaspoon ground cinnamon
¼ teaspoon ground allspice
1 teaspoon salt
¼ teaspoon ground black pepper

TOPPING
½ cup tahini (pure sesame paste) (see
    Note)

⅓ cup water
2 tablespoons lemon juice
2 tablespoons finely chopped fresh
    parsley leaves
1 garlic clove, finely minced or pressed
    (optional)
¼ teaspoon paprika (optional)
⅛ teaspoon salt
⅛ teaspoon black pepper, preferably
    freshly ground

GARNISH
About 3 tablespoons pine nuts (pignoli)

Yom Ha'Atzmaut and Yom Yerushalayim

Preheat the oven to 400 degrees. Coat a 9 by 13-inch baking dish with nonstick spray or grease it well.

In a large bowl, combine all the meat loaf ingredients, and mix by squeezing through your fingers until well combined and smooth. Press the mixture into the bottom of the prepared dish. Bake at 400 degrees for about 20 minutes, or until the top is browned.

Meanwhile, prepare the sesame topping. Put the tahini in a small bowl, and slowly add the water, stirring vigorously. (At first, the mixture will become very stiff, then it will thin out and become lighter in color.) Stir in the remaining topping ingredients. Adjust seasonings to taste.

When the meat loaf is browned, remove the dish from the oven, and carefully drain off any excess fat that has been released from the meat loaf. Spread the prepared sesame topping over the meat loaf. Sprinkle the pine nuts on top.

Return the meat loaf to the 400-degree oven, and bake for about 10 minutes longer or until the topping is puffed and lightly browned, and the meat is cooked completely through in the center.

Makes about 6 to 8 servings.

Spiced Ground Beef in Pita

The spices in this quick and easy beef mixture give it an appealing Middle Eastern flavor. And pita turns it into a delicious dinner in a pocket.

This dish can also be used for buffet entertaining. Keep the filling warm in a chafing dish, and accompany it with several miniature loaves of pita that have already been slit open at the top.

NOTE: If desired, 1 (15 to 16-ounce) can chickpeas (garbanzo beans), drained, may be substituted for the rice in the following filling.

FILLING
¾ cup uncooked brown or white rice
1 pound lean ground beef
1 medium onion, finely chopped
2 garlic cloves, minced

1 (8-ounce) can plain tomato sauce
⅓ cup water
½ teaspoon dried basil leaves
½ teaspoon ground cinnamon
⅛ teaspoon ground cloves

¼ *teaspoon salt*
⅛ *teaspoon black pepper, preferably*
    freshly ground
¼ *cup raisins*

TO SERVE
Several loaves whole wheat or white
    Pita (purchased, or see page 454)

Cook the rice according to the package directions. Set aside.

In a large, deep skillet or a Dutch oven over medium-high heat, brown the ground beef, breaking it up into small pieces with an *S*-style potato masher or spoon. Add the onion and garlic, and cook them in the fat from the meat. When the onion is tender, spoon off and discard any excess fat in the skillet. Stir in the remaining filling ingredients, along with the reserved cooked rice.

Reduce the heat, and simmer the mixture, stirring often, for 15 to 20 minutes, or until the filling is thick and the flavors have blended. Cut the pita loaves in half, and fill them with the meat–rice mixture.

Makes 4 to 5 servings as a main course.

Oaf Mandareenot B'Avocado

TANGERINE CHICKEN WITH AVOCADO

In Israel, poultry and citrus fruit are plentiful, and they are often cooked together in a wide variety of dishes. The following recipe includes tangerines (a type of mandarin orange, which explains the Hebrew word for tangerine, *mandareenah*), and also features avocado, another Israeli favorite that is frequently used in unexpectedly delicious ways. With the color contrast of orange and green fruits, this entrée looks as great as it tastes.

This dish may be made ahead of time. If so, do not cut up and add the avocado until reheating it, as avocado tends to darken while standing.

Yom Ha'Atzmaut and Yom Yerushalayim

1½ tablespoons cornstarch

¼ teaspoon ground allspice

⅛ teaspoon ground cinnamon

Scant 1½ cups tangerine juice (made
from frozen tangerine juice
concentrate, if desired) or orange
juice

2 tablespoons honey

2 tablespoons extra-virgin olive oil

1½ to 2 pounds skinless, boneless
chicken breast halves

Salt and ground black pepper

2 cups fresh tangerine sections, seeds
and fibers removed (from about 6
tangerines), or 2 (10- to 11-ounce)
cans mandarin orange segments,
well drained

1 medium-to-large ripe avocado

1 to 2 tablespoons lemon juice

To Serve

Hot cooked white or brown rice

In a 2-cup liquid measuring cup, combine the cornstarch, allspice, and cinnamon. Stir in a small amount of the tangerine juice to make a paste with the cornstarch mixture; then add juice to the 1½-cup mark on the measuring cup, and stir well so the cornstarch is all suspended. Stir in the honey. Set aside.

Put the oil into a large skillet over medium-high heat; then sprinkle the chicken with salt and pepper, and brown it on all sides. Add the juice mixture to the skillet, and continue cooking until the sauce thickens and just comes to a boil. Cover the skillet tightly, and reduce the heat. Gently simmer the chicken, basting it often, for about 20 minutes, or until the chicken is cooked through and tender.

While the chicken is cooking, prepare the tangerine sections, and set them aside. Cut the avocado lengthwise in half, and remove the large pit in the center. Peel each avocado half; then cut it lengthwise into thirds. Cut each piece crosswise into ½-inch-thick slices. Toss the avocado slices with the lemon juice to keep them from discoloring. Just before using the avocado slices, drain off the lemon juice.

When the chicken is ready, stir the drained avocado pieces and the tangerine sections into the sauce. Raise the heat, and simmer the mixture, stirring often, about 2 to 3 minutes longer, or just until the fruits are heated through.

(Hint: If this dish is being made ahead of time and you like fresh-tasting tangerines and avocado, do not add them to the sauce at this point. Refrigerate the chicken and sauce in a covered container. Shortly before serving,

prepare the tangerines and avocado and then stir them into the sauce. Reheat the chicken mixture in a microwave oven, a conventional oven, or on top of the stove, stirring often.)

To serve, arrange the chicken on a bed of rice, and spoon the sauce on top.

Makes about 6 to 8 servings.

Kugel Yerushalmi

JERUSALEM NOODLE "PUDDING"

This unusual *kugel* (a Yiddish word adopted into the Hebrew vernacular) has become a trademark of Mea Shaarim—an ultra-orthodox area of Jerusalem—and of nearby areas. In fact, preparation and distribution of the delicious noodle pudding are the prime means of support for a few of its older residents. Kugel Yerushalmi is served at many Israeli weddings and bar mitzvah celebrations, and even at state functions. The unusual recipe calls for caramelizing sugar in oil, to give the kugel a subtly sweet taste that contrasts perfectly with the large amount of pepper.

1 pound fine egg noodles, vermicelli, or very thin spaghetti broken into 2-inch lengths	*1 teaspoon salt*
¹⁄₂ cup canola oil	*³⁄₄ to 1 teaspoon ground black pepper*
¹⁄₄ cup sugar	*4 large eggs, beaten, or 1 cup pareve egg substitute*

In a 5- to 6-quart pot, cook the noodles in boiling water according to the package directions. Drain them in a colander. Then rinse them with cool water and let them drain very well.

Dry the same pot well; then put the oil and sugar into it. Stir the sugar in the oil over medium-low heat (they will not actually combine) for 5 to 10 minutes, or until the sugar melts and caramelizes, and turns a rich golden brown—the color of caramel candy.

Immediately add all the well-drained noodles to the pot, while stirring them very well, so that the oil and caramelized sugar are evenly distributed. If

Yom Ha'Atzmaut and Yom Yerushalayim

any of the sugar solidifies into chunks, continue stirring the noodles over low heat until the sugar melts. Remove the noodles from the heat, and stir in the salt and pepper. Then let the noodle mixture cool for about 20 to 30 minutes, or until it is lukewarm. Meanwhile, coat a 9- to 10-inch square pan (or equivalent) with nonstick cooking spray or grease it well. Preheat the oven to 325 degrees.

When the noodles are lukewarm, stir the beaten eggs into them completely. Then turn out the noodle mixture into the prepared pan. Bake the kugel at 325 degrees for 1¼ to 1½ hours, or until the top is golden and very crisp. Let the kugel cool for at least 5 minutes before cutting it. Serve it hot or lukewarm. The kugel may be made ahead, and reheated if desired. (It will cut easiest when it is cold.)

Makes about 8 to 10 servings.

Pita

FLAT ROUND "POCKET" BREAD

This bread, which becomes hollow during baking, is a staple in all Middle Eastern countries. In Israel, it is filled with everything imaginable, from falafel to French fries to salads—sometimes all at once! Often, the loaves are cut or torn apart to be used as "dippers" with spreads and salads, such as humus, tahina, and *salat hatzilim.*

In the United States, pita has become increasingly popular due to its good taste, convenience for sandwiches, and low calorie count. In fact, delicious loaves of pita can now be found in most supermarkets. However, it is still an interesting experience to bake pita at home, just to watch the thin pieces of dough puff up into bread "balloons."

Though most bread cookbooks do not admit it, baking pita can be a bit tricky. Commercially, it is made in huge, very hot ovens, where the bread is baked directly on the oven floor, like pizza. It is the blast of high heat that causes the dough to separate and form the characteristic pocket. To simulate this, the home oven and baking sheet must be preheated to a very high temperature.

For best results, it is also important to handle the dough as little as possible, and not to damage the surface once the dough has been rolled out. The dough circles are baked in the same order that they were rolled out, so all are allowed to rise for the same amount of time.

The following recipe is written in detail to help you successfully produce beautiful loaves of pita. It makes a delicious whole wheat version.

1 packet (2¼ teaspoons) active dry
   yeast
1¾ cups warm (105 to 115 degrees)
   water
1 tablespoon honey
1 tablespoon canola or safflower oil

2¼ to 2½ cups white bread flour
2 teaspoons salt
2 cups whole wheat flour
Canola or safflower oil, to coat the
   dough

In a large mixing bowl, combine the yeast, water, and honey. Let the mixture rest for 10 to 15 minutes, or until it is very frothy. Stir in 1 tablespoon oil, 2 cups of the white bread flour, and the salt, and beat with an electric mixer at medium speed (or with a wooden spoon) for about 2 minutes, or until the batter seems to be very elastic. By hand, or with a heavy-duty mixer, mix in the whole wheat flour to make a sticky dough. Scrape the dough down from the sides of the bowl, and cover the bowl with plastic wrap. Let the dough rest for 15 minutes, so the flour can absorb some moisture and become less sticky.

Sprinkle a few tablespoons of white bread flour over the dough in the bowl; then use a rubber scraper to press down around the sides of the dough so flour falls between the dough and the bowl, making removal of the dough easier. Transfer the dough to a lightly floured surface. Knead the dough, adding very small amounts of flour as necessary, about 8 to 10 minutes, or until the dough is very smooth and elastic, yet still a bit tacky. (If you have a mixer with a dough hook, leave the dough in the bowl and, after it has rested, knead with the dough hook.)

On a cutting board, press the dough out to a rectangle of even thickness. Use a sharp knife or dough scraper to cut the dough in half, then cut each half in half, and again twice more, until the dough has been divided into sixteen equal pieces. Using tiny bits of flour, roll each piece in the palms of your hands to form a very smooth ball.

Lightly coat the entire surface of each ball with oil, using your hand or a brush. Then arrange the balls about 2 inches apart on a large sheet of wax paper. Completely, but loosely, cover the balls with additional sheets of wax paper so they will not dry out, and let them rise until doubled, about 1 hour.

Meanwhile, adjust one oven rack to the lowest possible position, and a second one about one-third of the way down from the top. Put a very heavy, ungreased shiny metal baking sheet (*not* the insulated type) on the top rack. When the balls have risen, preheat the oven and baking sheet to 500 degrees, and set a timer for 30 minutes (to help you keep track of the time).

Carefully remove the wax paper covering from a few of the dough balls. (Keep the rest covered until they are needed.) From now on, handle each ball as little as possible. Use a metal spatula, dough scraper, or pancake turner to lift one of the balls from the bottom sheet of wax paper. On a well-floured surface, use your fingertips to gently pat out the ball to a 3-inch circle. Then, use a rolling pin to gently roll it out to a circle approximately 5 inches in diameter and ³⁄₁₆ inch thick. Use as few strokes as possible during the rolling, and make sure the dough does not stick or pull at all. Lightly coat the dough circle with flour, gently brushing off any excess, and set it aside on a large sheet of wax paper.

Repeat with the remaining balls, keeping the dough circles arranged in the order that they were rolled out. Cover all the circles very loosely with wax paper and, if the timer has not already rung, let them rise until it does. (This indicates that the first dough circles have had at least 25 minutes to rise.)

During the following baking procedure, it is important to keep the oven temperature high and stable, so open the oven door as little as possible, and work quickly. Using thick oven mitts, remove the preheated baking sheet from the oven, and set it on top of the stove. (It will be very hot!)

Immediately use a large, well-floured metal pancake turner to transfer—one at a time—the first two dough circles that were rolled out to the hot ungreased baking sheet, keeping them at least 2 inches apart. (Do not bake more than two loaves at once, even if they will fit on the baking sheet.) As soon as the loaves are on the baking sheet, put it on the *bottom rack* of the oven. Bake the dough circles for 2½ minutes (they should puff up); then quickly transfer the same baking sheet and loaves to the *upper rack*. Bake the puffed loaves for an additional 2 to 2½ minutes, or until they are firm and very lightly browned on top.

Quickly use the pancake turner to remove the finished loaves from the baking sheet, and set them on a wire rack to cool. Immediately transfer the next two dough circles to the baking sheet. Repeat, baking the dough circles in the order in which they were rolled out, until all the loaves are baked. Keep the dough circles loosely covered until they are needed.

As soon as the baked loaves are completely cool, *gently* press them down to deflate them (the pockets will remain), and put them into sealed plastic bags. Store them at room temperature. If the loaves are not to be eaten within a day or two, freeze them, as they tend to become stale quickly. If desired, reheat them briefly in a 325-degree oven or a microwave oven; do not heat them for too long, or they will get hard.

Makes 16 5-inch loaves of pita.

Toasted Pita Triangles

The simplicity of these cheesy snacks belies their delicious taste. The triangles can be completed in advance and reheated shortly before serving, making them great party fare. Store them in the freezer or refrigerator. All the amounts can be adjusted to taste.

8 (5- to 6-inch-diameter) loaves whole
    wheat or white Pita (purchased, or
    page 454)
½ cup butter, softened
About 4 teaspoons finely chopped mixed
    fresh or dried herbs, such as basil,

marjoram, thyme, tarragon,
    parsley, etc.
⅓ to ½ cup finely grated Parmesan or
    other hard cheese

Cut around the edges of each pita loaf, separating the top and bottom into two thin circles. Spread the rough side of each circle with ½ tablespoon of butter. Then sprinkle each circle with about ¼ teaspoon of the herbs and 1½ to 2 teaspoons of the cheese. Use a knife and cutting board (or kitchen shears) to cut each large circle into four triangles. Arrange the triangles in one layer on ungreased baking sheets. Toast them in a preheated 375-degree oven for 8 to 10 minutes, or until the cheese is very lightly browned. Serve the triangles warm.

If the triangles are made in advance, reheat them in a 325-degree oven until hot and crispy.

Makes 64 appetizer-size triangles.

Yom Ha'Atzmaut and Yom Yerushalayim

Oogiyot Tahina
Sesame Tahini-Oat Cookies

These treats are packed with protein and other nutrients, as well as good taste. In Israel, tahini and honey are often used in baked goods. The tahini adds a special sesame flavor, and the honey helps keep the cookies soft and fresh for several days.

Another Israeli favorite, sunflower seeds, is also included in the cookies. Israelis particularly enjoy eating toasted, unhulled sunflower seeds out-of-hand. In fact, cracking sunflower seeds (with one's teeth) has been humorously described as one of the country's favorite national pastimes. *Garanim* (or "seeds"), as they are called in Hebrew, are sold and eaten virtually everywhere. The floors of many buses, movie theaters, and athletic stadiums are constantly littered with discarded shells. In the following recipe, be sure to use *shelled* sunflower seeds, or your cookies may be rather hard to chew!

NOTE: For more information about tahini, see the Glossary of Ingredients and the recipe for Tahina (page 434).

1/3 cup tahini (pure sesame paste) (see Note)
1/2 cup honey
1 large egg or 1/4 cup pareve egg substitute
1/2 teaspoon ground cinnamon
1/8 teaspoon ground allspice
1/8 teaspoon salt

1 1/3 cups old-fashioned or quick-cooking rolled oats
1/4 cup finely shredded sweetened coconut
1/3 cup unsalted shelled sunflower seeds, raw or toasted
1/4 cup dark raisins

Line a sturdy, shiny metal baking sheet with baking parchment, or coat it with nonstick cooking spray, or grease it. Preheat the oven to 350 degrees.

In a medium bowl, combine the tahini, honey, egg, cinnamon, allspice, and salt. Stir in the oats, coconut, sunflower seeds, and raisins until well combined. Use wet hands (or a #70 ice cream disher) to form the sticky mixture into 1¼-inch balls, and arrange them about 2 inches apart on the prepared baking sheet. Slightly flatten the top of each cookie with moistened fingertips.

Bake the cookies at 350 degrees for about 12 minutes, or until the cookies are firm and the bottoms are lightly browned. Use a metal spatula to remove the cookies from the baking sheet, and cool them completely on a wire rack before storing them in an airtight container. They will stay fresh for several days.

Makes about 24 cookies.

Oogat Soomsoom
CHEWY SESAME BARS

The Hebrew name of this tasty treat, *oogat soomsoom,* translates literally as "sesame *cake.*" Though we Americans would probably call these "bar cookies," they do not really fit the word *oogiyot* that Israelis use for "cookies." The bars are reminiscent of sesame candy, though they are considerably softer and easier to chew.

These chewy bars are filled with delectable toasted sesame seeds, an Israeli favorite that is frequently used in baked goods. Toasting brings out much flavor in the sesame seeds, and gives the bars a wonderful rich taste.

NOTES: For complete directions on how to easily toast sesame seeds, see the Glossary of Ingredients. Unbleached flour helps to provide the chewy texture of these bars. However, all-purpose bleached flour may be substituted.

For lighter, more "cakelike" bars, use an additional egg.

1 cup hulled white sesame seeds (see Notes)	*1 large egg or ¼ cup pareve egg substitute (see Notes)*
½ cup granulated sugar	*1 teaspoon vanilla extract*
½ cup packed dark brown sugar	*¼ teaspoon salt*
½ cup canola or safflower oil	*½ teaspoon baking powder*
¼ cup honey	*1¼ cups unbleached flour (see Notes)*

Toast the sesame seeds (see Notes), and set them aside to cool.

Yom Ha'Atzmaut and Yom Yerushalayim

Line a 9-inch square pan with aluminum foil so the edges hang over slightly at the top; then coat the foil with nonstick cooking spray or grease it. Set it aside. Preheat the oven to 350 degrees.

In a medium bowl, combine the granulated sugar, brown sugar, oil, and honey. Use a spoon to mix the ingredients well. Add the egg, and beat the mixture with the spoon until it is smooth. Mix in the vanilla extract, salt, and baking powder. Then mix in the flour until the batter is smooth. It will be very thick. Stir in the cooled, toasted sesame seeds until they are completely blended into the batter.

Turn out the batter into the prepared pan, and use a rubber spatula to smooth the top. Bake the cake at 350 degrees for about 35 minutes, or until the top is browned and a wooden pick comes out clean. Cool the cake in the pan on the rack for 30 minutes to 1 hour. Then lift the foil so the entire cake comes out of the pan. Cool it completely on the foil on a rack.

When the cake is cool, lift it off the foil to a cutting board. Use a large, sharp knife to cut it in half lengthwise and crosswise to make four squares. Cut each square in fourths in the same manner. Then cut each small square in half to make small bars.

Store the squares in an airtight container for several days, or freeze them for longer storage.

Makes 32 small bars.

Lag B'Omer

 FOR MANY PIOUS JEWS, *LAG B'OMER* (OR *LAG L'OMER,* AS GEN-
erally preferred by Sephardim) is an island of happiness and jubilation
within a sea of solemn weeks. It takes place on the eighteenth day of the
Hebrew month of Iyar, which usually occurs in May.

Omer is a Hebrew word meaning "measure" or "sheaf" of grain. In biblical times,
the Jewish people were predominantly agriculturally oriented. On the second day of the
Pesach pilgrimage festival, they celebrated the commencement of the grain harvest by
bringing to the Temple priest an offering of their first omer (about one-tenth of a
bushel) of barley. They then counted seven complete weeks (i.e., forty-nine days) from
that one and celebrated Shavuot on the fiftieth day by offering two loaves of bread made
from the first wheat crop. This process is delineated in the Torah (see Leviticus 23:9–17).

Although there have been no grain (or other) offerings since the destruction of the
Second Holy Temple in Jerusalem, the "Counting of the Omer" (*Sefirat Ha'Omer,* in
Hebrew) still takes place in modern-day synagogues on each day of the omer interval.

Orthodox Jews also observe the *Sefirah* as a period of semimourning. During most
of this time, therefore, they do not have haircuts or listen to music, and festivities such
as weddings are not permitted. This is to commemorate a tragic episode in Jewish history, which took place during the counting period.

In the year 70 of the Common Era, the Second Holy Temple was destroyed by the

Romans, and the city lay in ruins. About sixty years later, Shimon bar Kochba and his followers despaired of ever rebuilding the Jewish city while it was under Roman rule, and so they revolted in an effort to regain national independence.

At first, the Jews were victorious and, some say, even began to build the Third Temple. But, in the end, Roman military might prevailed. Bar Kochba, as well as several of the foremost scholars of the day, including the famed Rabbi Akiva, met their deaths. The fighting and a concurrent epidemic also took the lives of thousands of Rabbi Akiva's students and disciples.

On the thirty-third day of the counting, however, the epidemic is said to have miraculously abated, and the rebellion was briefly successful. In celebration of these happier occurrences, all prohibitions of the Sefirah are suspended on Lag B'Omer, and it is celebrated with much joyfulness. (Some Jews discontinue mourning practices *after* Lag B'Omer, as well.) The name of the holiday comes from the numerical values assigned to the Hebrew letters *lamed* (thirty), and *gimmel* (three). "Lag" is simply the pronunciation of the *numeral* thirty-three.

The day also has special significance because of other events that occurred during the Roman rule of Judea. It is said the learned Rabbi Shimon bar Yochai defied decrees against the study of Torah, and bravely continued to teach his pupils. When this endangered his life, he fled with his son to a cave in the mountains of Galilee. There, they lived and studied for thirteen years and allegedly wrote the *Zohar,* a book that is the basis for the Jewish study of mysticism called the *Kabbalah.*

According to tradition, Rabbi Shimon bar Yochai's students visited him each year on Lag B'Omer. In order to mislead the Roman soldiers, the students often disguised themselves as hunters carrying bows and arrows. It is further said that the rabbi died on Lag B'Omer, but that his last request was for the anniversary of his death to be observed with joyous celebration, not mourning. Also, he is said to have revealed many wonderful secrets to his pupils on that day.

Israeli children have no school on this holiday, which has also been designated a national "scholars' day" because of its many associations with great Jewish teachers. In imitation of Rabbi Shimon bar Yochai's pupils, the youngsters often play a bow-and-arrow game of "Jews and Romans." They also engage in all types of sports, races, hikes, and other athletic events. Israeli soldiers sometimes have marksmanship contests on Lag B'Omer.

To honor Rabbi Shimon bar Yochai, tens of thousands of Jews make pilgrimage to Meron, an Israeli village near Safed, where he is buried. Many pitch tents, and spend the early part of the evening chanting psalms, singing Hasidic melodies, and studying the *Zohar.*

At sundown, huge communal bonfires are lit near the rabbi's tomb, and people gaily sing and dance around the fire until morning. Some three-year-old Hasidic boys have their first haircut on this day, and the clipped locks are tossed into the bonfire.

All over Israel, Lag B'Omer is celebrated with campfires and other outdoor events like those at Meron. Many friends gather for *kumzitz* ("come and sit"), and enjoy barbecues and picnics, just as on Yom Ha'Atzmaut. Treats made with carob are sometimes eaten on Lag B'Omer, because a carob tree is said to have grown outside Rabbi Shimon bar Yochai's cave, and sustained him while he dwelled there. (For the same reason, carob is eaten on Tu B'Shevat. See that chapter.)

In the United States and other countries of the Diaspora, community cookouts, complete with outdoor games and sporting competitions, are popular for Lag B'Omer, just as in Israel. The dishes in this chapter are deliciously appropriate for such a celebration. For several additional ideas, see the chapter on Yom Ha'Atzmaut.

Ensalata de Avicas y Enginaras

Herbed White Bean and Artichoke Salad

This tasty combination of two popular Sephardic salads is great for a picnic, or any time. Sephardim from Turkey and many parts of the Middle East serve such salads at almost every main meal, as part of the *mezzeh* (or *meze*).

Mezzeh is an appealing assortment of appetizers, hors d'oeuvres, dips, salads, pickled vegetables, and possibly smoked or pickled fish, which is served as a first course. Each selection is set out in its own serving dish, and diners help themselves to their choices.

The following salad and most of the other Sephardic vegetable salads and dips in this cookbook might be among *mezzeh* selections, as well as such delicacies as rice-stuffed grape leaves (page 466). Foods for *mezzeh* are almost always prepared in advance, and served chilled or at room temperature.

The *mezzeh* has gained increasing popularity in Israel, where it is sometimes simply called *salatim,* meaning "salads."

The following salad is a personal favorite that I often bring to pot-luck picnics and similar events. It is very quick and easy to prepare, I can make it a day ahead of time, and the ingredients are flexible. I never hesitate to adjust the amounts to my taste or to use whatever salad vegetables I happen to have on hand. Best of all, it is always one of the most popular selections on the table.

NOTES: Canned small white beans may be found in the ethnic food or Hispanic sections of some supermarkets. If small white beans (such as navy beans) cannot be found, larger white beans (such as cannellini or great northern beans) may be used, although they are softer and not as delicate as the smaller beans. Be sure to use *plain* canned beans, not those that contain other foods such as pork. About 3 cups cooked dry white navy beans can be used to replace the canned beans (1⅓ cups dry beans will produce about 3 cups cooked ones).

If a very low-fat salad is desired, about ½ to ⅔ cup bottled low-fat or nonfat pareve Italian salad dressing may be used to replace the oil and vinegar below.

2 (15- to 16-ounce) cans plain small
    white beans (see Notes)
1 can (about 8 ounces, drained weight)
    water-packed whole or quartered
    artichokes
⅔ to 1 cup diced sweet red or green bell
    pepper or celery (or a combination)
½ cup coarsely chopped or sliced pitted
    ripe (black) olives
¼ cup finely chopped red or Spanish
    onion or thinly sliced scallions
¼ cup chopped fresh parsley leaves

1 teaspoon dried mint leaves or 2
    teaspoons finely chopped fresh
    spearmint leaves
¾ teaspoon dried basil leaves or 1½
    teaspoons finely chopped fresh basil
    leaves

DRESSING (SEE NOTES)
⅓ cup good-quality olive oil
¼ cup red wine vinegar
Salt and freshly ground pepper to taste

Put the beans into a colander, and rinse them well with cool water until there is no foam. Make sure they are completely drained. Put them into a medium bowl.

Drain the artichokes well, and if whole ones are used, cut them lengthwise into fourths through the bottom so that the leaves do not fall apart. Add them to the beans along with the bell pepper or celery, olives, onion, parsley, mint, and basil. Gently stir all the ingredients so that they are evenly distributed.

In a small bowl or jar, stir or shake together the oil and vinegar; then toss the dressing with the bean mixture (or use bottled Italian dressing; see Notes). Season the salad with salt and pepper to taste.

Refrigerate the salad for several hours or overnight, stirring occasionally, to allow the flavors to blend. Serve the salad cold or at room temperature.

Makes about 8 servings.

Variation

WHITE BEAN AND ARTICHOKE SALAD WITH PASTA

Sometimes, for variety or to feed a larger crowd, I add pasta to this salad. Cook about 4 to 8 ounces of any small pasta (such as small shells, macaroni, or twists), drain it well, and stir it into the salad. Increase the amounts of herbs, dressing, and seasonings to your taste.

Tabouleh

BULGUR WHEAT AND VEGETABLE SALAD

This nutritious salad (sometimes spelled *tabouli*) is popular among Jews from many Middle Eastern countries. The main ingredient is bulgur—precooked wheat kernels that have been dried and cracked into small pieces. For tabouleh, the bulgur (which is also called *burghul*) is softened in water, and needs no cooking.

Tabouleh is customarily served with large lettuce leaves, which are rolled around the salad when it is eaten. It is also delicious with pita.

Sometimes, diced cucumbers and/or bell peppers are added to this salad. While not as traditional, feel free to add these if you wish.

1 ½ cups bulgur wheat	1 to 1 ½ teaspoons salt, or to taste
3 to 4 medium tomatoes, preferably vine-ripened, diced	¼ cup finely chopped fresh spearmint leaves or 2 tablespoons dried mint leaves
1 cup finely chopped fresh parsley leaves	
1 cup thinly sliced scallions, including green tops	TO SERVE (YOUR CHOICE)
½ cup flavorful olive oil	Large lettuce leaves
⅓ to ½ cup lemon juice	Several loaves whole wheat or white Pita (purchased, or see page 454)

Soak the bulgur wheat in warm water to cover for about 30 minutes; then drain it very well, squeezing out the excess water. (An easy way to do this is to put the bulgur into a very large sieve; then lower the sieve into a large bowl

of water until the bulgur is covered. To drain the bulgur, simply lift up the sieve, and press out any excess water.)

While the bulgur is soaking, core and dice the tomatoes, and put them in a large bowl with the chopped parsley leaves and scallions. In a small bowl, beat together the olive oil, lemon juice, salt, and mint leaves (or shake them together in a small jar). Set the dressing aside.

Add the soaked and drained bulgur to the tomato mixture in the bowl, and stir to combine. Add the oil–lemon juice dressing, and mix the salad well. It may seem a bit wet, but the bulgur should eventually soak up most of the liquid.

Refrigerate the salad overnight so the flavors can blend, and the bulgur can soften and absorb the dressing. Stir the salad occasionally during this period, and once again just before serving.

To serve the tabouleh, heap it on a bed of lettuce leaves. Or put it into a serving bowl, and accompany it with lettuce leaves and/or pita cut into halves or triangles.

Makes 8 to 10 servings.

Dolmas or Yaprakes
VINE LEAVES FILLED WITH MINTED RICE PILAF

Among Jews from Greece, Turkey, and other Balkan countries, stuffed grape (or "vine") leaves, which look like miniature cabbage rolls, are very popular. They are usually called *dolmas* or *dolmades* in Greek, or *yaprakes* in Turkish. The leaves are typically filled with either rice or meat.

When an herbed rice mixture is used, as here, the stuffed grape leaves are served chilled, as part of a salad, or as hors d'oeuvres. Turkish Sephardim frequently include them in the salad buffet called *mezzeh*. When a meat mixture is used, they are served hot and often topped with an egg-lemon sauce.

The rice-filled grape leaves are one of my favorite hors d'oeuvres. This recipe makes a lot, and they keep well for a long time in the refrigerator. So, I may use them for several different meals, sometimes as an accompaniment to a salad. They are also wonderful on a buffet table, and have been quite popular at sisterhood brunches at my home.

NOTES: The brine-preserved "vine" leaves used in this recipe are sold at most gourmet stores and Greek or Middle Eastern groceries, as well as at many supermarkets in the gourmet or ethnic section. Two or three bunches of tightly rolled leaves are usually packed into each jar. Before buying the leaves, make sure that the liquid in the jar is clear, not cloudy.

Either medium-grain or long-grain rice may be used in the filling; however, I have found that the stickier medium-grain rice (which is less traditional) holds together better, making it easier to use.

Dried currants, which look like miniature raisins, are made from a small berry. They are usually called simply "currants." Their tiny size and delicate flavor make them perfect for this filling. Boxes of currants are available at most supermarkets.

In a pinch, slivered almonds maybe substituted for the pine nuts; however, the latter give a very special taste. For more information on them, see the Glossary of Ingredients.

1 (16-ounce) jar preserved grape (or "vine") leaves in brine (see Notes)

4 tablespoons extra-virgin olive oil, divided

2 medium onions, finely chopped

1 cup uncooked white rice (see Notes)

2 cups boiling water

½ teaspoon salt

Pinch to ⅛ teaspoon ground black pepper, or to taste

½ cup currants (see Notes)

¼ cup pine nuts (pignoli) (see Notes)

¼ cup finely chopped fresh parsley leaves

1 tablespoon dried mint leaves or 2 tablespoons finely chopped fresh spearmint leaves

2 teaspoons lemon juice

½ cup cold water

To Serve

2 lemons, cut into wedges

Drain the grape leaves, unroll them, separate them, and soak them for 10 minutes in a large bowl of cool water to get rid of the brine taste. Carefully rinse the leaves, one at a time, under cool running water. Spread out the leaves in layers on paper towels, with the dull, thickly veined side (the back of the leaves) facing upward. Trim off and discard any thick stems.

For the filling, put 3 tablespoons of the oil into a medium saucepan over medium-high heat; then add the onions and sauté them until they are tender. Add the rice and cook, stirring, for 2 to 3 minutes longer, or until it is well coated with oil and slightly toasted. Add the boiling water, salt, and pepper.

Stir the rice once, cover the pan tightly, and reduce the heat. Simmer the rice until it is tender and all the liquid is absorbed, about 15 to 20 minutes. Remove the rice from the heat, and stir in the currants, pine nuts, parsley, mint, and lemon juice.

Arrange about 10 of the smallest grape leaves and any torn leaves in the bottom of a heavy 3-quart (or similar) saucepan. To fill each of the remaining grape leaves (you should have about 40), place it on a flat surface, dull side up, so that the stem end is toward you. In the center, place 1 heaping teaspoon to 1 heaping tablespoon of rice mixture (the exact amount depends on the size of the leaf). Fold over the lower left point of the leaf to cover the rice filling; then overlap it with the lower right point. Begin to roll up the leaf from the stem end. Fold in the upper left and upper right points of the leaf, and continue rolling to the uppermost point of the leaf. (This is much easier to do than to read about!)

Each completed dolma will look like a miniature log about 2 inches long and about 1 inch in diameter. As each dolma is formed, put it, seam side down, into the leaf-lined saucepan. Keep the dolmas close together, and stack them when it becomes necessary.

When all the leaves are filled, sprinkle the dolmas with the remaining 1 tablespoon oil and the cold water. Cover the saucepan very tightly, and put it over high heat for *only* 3 minutes; then turn the heat to *low,* and steam the rolls

for 50 minutes. Uncover the saucepan, and let the dolmas cool to room temperature. Carefully transfer the dolmas to a covered container and refrigerate them. They will keep in the refrigerator for a week or longer.

Serve the dolmas chilled or at room temperature. They should stay compact and not unroll easily. Attractively arrange the dolmas on a serving platter, and garnish them with the lemon wedges. If desired, use one or two of the lemon wedges to squeeze a little fresh lemon juice over the dolmas.

Makes about 40 dolmas.

"Confetti" Rice Salad

Oranges, dates, and sunflower seeds make this salad unusual and appealing. For a pareve salad, omit the sour cream and use all mayonnaise instead. Adjust the amount to taste.

3 cups cooked white or brown rice
1 large apple, cored and diced
1 large navel orange, peeled and diced
²/₃ cup chopped walnuts
²/₃ cup diced celery
¹/₂ cup diced pitted dates

¹/₄ cup unsalted sunflower seeds (raw or toasted)
¹/₄ cup sour cream
¹/₄ cup mayonnaise
3 tablespoons orange juice
¹/₄ teaspoon ground ginger

In a large bowl, combine the rice, apple, orange, walnuts, celery, dates, and sunflower seeds. In a small bowl, mix the sour cream, mayonnaise, orange juice, and ginger. Stir into the rice mixture until combined. Chill, covered, for several hours or until serving time, to allow the flavors to mingle.

Makes about 8 servings.

Coleslaw for a Crowd

Here's an easy recipe that is perfect for a Lag B'Omer picnic. This recipe makes quite a bit of coleslaw, but it tends to go quickly, and any leftovers can be stored up to five days in the refrigerator. For ease in preparation, shred the vegetables in a food processor or with a rotary grater.

1 large or 2 medium heads white cabbage, finely shredded	¾ cup pareve mayonnaise
4 to 5 medium carrots, finely shredded or grated	¼ cup cider vinegar
	¼ cup sugar
1 small onion, grated	About 1 teaspoon salt
	Ground black pepper to taste

In a large bowl, combine the cabbage, carrots, and onion, and mix well. Then add the mayonnaise, vinegar, sugar, salt, and pepper. Adjust the amounts to taste, if necessary. Refrigerate the coleslaw for several hours or overnight to allow the flavors to blend. Stir well before serving.

Makes about 9 cups.

Chicken and Apple Salad

M

This wonderful chicken salad combination makes a satisfying meal when served inside pita pockets, and would be perfect for a Lag B'Omer picnic. The salad could also be served on large lettuce leaves.

NOTES: For quick, cooked chicken with little mess, line an 8-inch square (or similar) microwave-proof baking dish with heavy plastic wrap. Arrange 3 large raw bone-in chicken breasts (total of about 2 pounds) in the dish, and cover with another piece of plastic, leaving a hole for steam to escape. Microwave on "high" for about 8 to 10 minutes, turning occasionally, until completely cooked through. Cool the chicken; then remove the skin and bones, and cut the chicken meat into cubes. Makes about 3 cups.

Crystallized (or candied) ginger has a delicious "bite" that adds a wonderful, distinctive flavor to this salad. It can be found in the supermarket with the gourmet spices or in specialty groceries. It may be omitted if desired.

2 large Granny Smith apples

3 tablespoons orange juice

3 cups cubed cooked chicken (see Notes)

1 cup thin celery slices

1 cup coarsely broken walnuts

²/₃ cup pitted dates, each sliced crosswise into thirds, or 1 cup grapes, halved

2 to 3 tablespoons finely chopped crystallized ginger (optional, see Notes)

About ¹/₂ cup pareve mayonnaise or similar salad dressing

TO SERVE

Pita and/or lettuce leaves

Cut the apples into fourths, and remove the seeds but not the peel. Cut each fourth into ½-inch pieces. In a large bowl, toss the apples with the orange juice. Add the chicken, celery, walnuts, dates, and crystallized ginger, and toss to combine. Stir in just enough mayonnaise to moisten all the ingredients. Chill, covered, for several hours or until serving time. To serve, line pita bread pockets with lettuce leaves and fill them with salad. Or mound the salad on a bed of lettuce.

Makes about 6 servings.

Grilled Vegetables

My family and guests always enjoy vegetables grilled in the following manner. In fact, many people who claim that they do not like zucchini gobble it down when it is prepared this way. I find that grilling the vegetables directly on the grate gives much better results than when they are strung on a skewer, kebab-style.

This is not exactly a recipe, as I do not give specific amounts, but more of a technique. If your grill has widely spaced grates through which the vegetables may fall, you may wish to purchase a metal grill tray that is specifically designed to hold smaller pieces of food.

I have given directions for the vegetables that are favorites of my family and guests; however, you can also use this simple technique with other vegetables. Grilling gives them a wonderful smoked flavor and aroma that is very appealing to most people.

NOTES: Olive oil now comes in a spray can to be used for cooking. This spray is a very quick and easy way to coat the vegetables with oil.

There are many nice prepared dried herb combinations now available in jars in supermarkets. Try to choose those that contain *only herbs,* with no added salt, MSG, dried garlic, or other additives. You can also make your own combination of mixed dried herbs.

If you are using your grill for meat or other foods during the meal, grill these vegetables first and serve them lukewarm. Or reheat them briefly in a microwave oven. They are even good cold, and are great inside a sandwich.

Small or medium zucchini

Green and/or red bell peppers

Extra-virgin olive oil or olive oil cooking spray (see Notes)

Salt and ground black pepper

Your choice mixed dried herbs (see Notes)

Wash the vegetables well. Cut each small zucchini lengthwise into ¼-inch-thick slices, leaving them attached at the stem end. Carefully fan out the slices. For each medium zucchini, cut off the stem end, then cut the zucchini lengthwise into ¼-inch-thick slices.

For the peppers, carefully remove the stem and attached seed pod. Cut each pepper in half down through the stem end. Remove any remaining seeds and thick interior membranes.

Lay the vegetables in one layer on a foil-lined (for easy cleanup) baking sheet or other flat surface that will be used to transport them to the grill. Put some olive oil into a small cup and lightly brush it on the top surface of each vegetable, or spray the top surface of the vegetables with olive oil cooking spray. Sprinkle them lightly with salt and pepper, and then with the mixed herbs. Turn each piece over, and repeat the oil-seasonings-herbs process on the reverse side.

Grill the vegetables in one layer over hot coals or on a preheated gas grill set at medium-high. Turn the vegetables once with long tongs.

Zucchini will take only a few minutes on each side; be careful not to overcook it or it may be too soft to easily remove from the grill. (In that case,

use a long-handled metal spatula.) Red pepper will take a little longer, but it cooks faster than green pepper. The pepper skin may blacken slightly; if it is getting too dark, finish cooking the peppers skin side up. If the grill has a cover, you may close it briefly during the grilling to speed up the cooking of the vegetables.

Serve the vegetables hot, lukewarm, or at room temperature.

The number of servings depends on the amount of vegetables used.

Mititei or Carnatzlach

GRILLED GROUND-MEAT KEBABS

My children describe *mititei* as "hamburgers-shaped-like-hot-dogs." Interestingly, with their garlicky taste, they are reminiscent of their lower-class cousins, but so much better. They are one of our favorite summer grills, and also very popular with guests. Leftovers are even delicious when reheated. That is why I have doubled this recipe since it was published in the first edition of this cookbook; there is no point in making any less!

The Romanian name of these wonderful "skinless sausages"—*mititei* (pronounced "meh-tee-'tay," according to an acquaintance of Romanian-Jewish descent)—literally means "very small," and describes their petite size. In Yiddish, they are known as *carnatzlach* (with a guttural "ch"). Romanian Jews always use a very generous amount of garlic in the meat mixture, and serve *mititei* with red and green chili peppers, dill pickles, and plenty of wine or beer.

Jews from the Middle East and North Africa have a very similar dish called *kofta kebab* or *kefta*. This is usually made with ground lamb instead of beef, and onion instead of garlic, and is served over a bed of rice.

Many Israelis serve their version inside pita, and top it with tahina. And they may call the grilled ground meat *keftedes,* or simply *kebab.* The latter term often confuses American tourists, who tend to think it means skewered cubes of meat. In Israel, however, that dish is known as Shashlik (page 446).

The delicious meat mixture below is seasoned in the Romanian fashion. For a Middle Eastern or North African flavor, use less or no garlic and add a small grated onion. The herbs and spices differ everywhere this dish is served, but usually include at least a

few of the following: parsley, mint, marjoram, thyme, oregano, coriander, cumin, cinnamon, allspice, cloves, ginger, and paprika, in various combinations depending on the whim of the cook.

NOTES: Although ground beef with more fat may produce juicier *mititei,* I always use extra-lean meat for health reasons. The water in the mix helps retain moisture. If the meat has too much fat, it will drip out and cause the grill to flare up and burn the outside of the *mititei* before the inside is cooked. Ground beef must always be cooked completely, with no pink remaining, to eliminate possible bacterial contamination.

Mititei and similar kebabs are often shaped and grilled on metal skewers. I think the following technique is easier, and it works just as well.

2 pounds lean ground beef (see Notes)
4 to 6 garlic cloves, pressed or very
   finely minced
½ teaspoon ground allspice
¼ teaspoon ground cloves
½ cup finely chopped fresh parsley
   leaves or ¼ cup dried parsley leaves

2 teaspoons dried marjoram leaves
½ teaspoon dried oregano leaves
1¼ teaspoons salt
¼ teaspoon ground black pepper, or
   more to taste
½ cup water

Put all the ingredients in a medium bowl, and mix them very well. For the mititei to have the proper texture, the meat combination must be mixed until it is soft and almost pasty. To do this, knead the meat with your hands and repeatedly squeeze it through your fingers.

With wet hands, form ½-cup portions of the meat mixture into 9 or 10 finger-shaped sausages, about 4 to 4½ inches long and about 1½ inches in diameter. They will shrink a lot during grilling; if they are too narrow, they may dry out.

(If desired, the formed mititei may be refrigerated overnight, wrapped, to allow the seasonings to better permeate the meat. Be sure to wrap the mititei very well or your entire refrigerator will smell like garlic. Remove the sausages from the refrigerator ½ hour before cooking them.)

Grill the mititei over very hot coals or over a preheated gas grill set to medium-high. Be sure to arrange the mititei *across* the grate of the grill, which should keep them from falling into the coals and also give them attractive grill lines crossing the meat. Turn them often with long tongs so that

all sides face the coals for a while, and grill them until they are cooked completely through, about a total of 6 to 8 minutes. Or broil them about 4 inches from the heat source for about 4 to 5 minutes on each side. They should be well browned and cooked through.

Serve the mititei hot or lukewarm. (When necessary, I have made these ahead of time on my outdoor grill, and then reheated them, covered, in a casserole in the microwave oven.) They can be refrigerated or frozen, and reheated as above or covered in a conventional oven. They go very well with rice pilaf.

Makes about 9 to 10 mititei; *about 6 servings.*

Teriyaki Chicken Skewers

Though they aren't at all Jewish, these delicious Japanese-style grilled "kebabs" are perfect for a Lag B'Omer cookout. My children call this dish, a favorite of theirs, "chicken on a stick."

The easiest way to grill the chicken is on disposable wooden skewers made especially for this purpose, which are available in cooking stores and supermarkets. There are several different types. Those that are too long and thin will burn at the ends where they are not covered with chicken. Slightly shorter, heavier sticks work much better. All should be soaked in water for at least ½ hour before using.

MARINADE
½ cup soy sauce
⅓ cup dry sherry or dry white table wine
2 teaspoons canola oil
2 teaspoons honey or sugar
2 to 3 garlic cloves, finely minced or
* pressed*

½ teaspoon grated fresh gingerroot or
* ¼ teaspoon ground ginger*

SKEWERS
1½ to 2 pounds skinless, boneless
* chicken breasts*

Combine all the marinade ingredients in a rectangular baking dish or plastic container that is just as long as the skewers. Cut the chicken lengthwise into strips about ½ to ¾ inch wide (the tenderloin on the back of each breast

half may be used as a strip). Thread the strips on the wooden skewers (as when sewing a basting stitch), using two or three strips of chicken on each skewer, depending on their size. The strips may be bunched a little like gathered pleats.

Place the filled skewers in the dish with the marinade, turning each one so that it is coated with marinade. The skewers may be slightly stacked in the dish if necessary. The amount of marinade may seem skimpy, but it is enough.

Cover the dish or container with plastic wrap or a lid, and refrigerate the skewers for 30 minutes or up to several hours. Occasionally turn them so all are coated with marinade. Or if the plastic wrap or lid is very tight, shake or carefully invert the dish or container to distribute the marinade.

Grill the drained chicken strips over hot coals or on a preheated gas grill set to medium-high for about 3 to 5 minutes on each side, or until the chicken is cooked completely through. Use long tongs to turn them. Or, if preferred, broil the chicken strips about 4 inches from the heat source, for about 3 to 5 minutes on each side or until cooked through.

Serve the hot chicken strips on the skewers for diners to remove individually or eat right off the sticks.

Makes about 6 to 8 servings.

Klops

MEAT LOAF WITH HARD-BOILED EGGS

Jews of Germanic background brought this tasty meat loaf to Israel, where it has become very popular. It is often prepared in advance and then chilled, so it can be served at picnics on such festive occasions as Lag B'Omer and Yom Ha'Atzmaut. Potato salad and assorted pickles usually accompany the meat loaf.

When cut into slices, the following version of klops is particularly attractive, as each slice features a golden and white cross section of hard-boiled egg.

NOTE: This recipe may be doubled and baked in a 9 by 5-inch loaf pan. Use only 4 or 5 hard-boiled eggs in the center.

1 pound extra-lean ground beef

1 medium onion, grated

1 to 2 garlic cloves, minced or pressed

1 medium carrot, grated

1 large egg or ¼ cup pareve egg
   substitute

½ cup matzah meal

⅓ cup plain tomato sauce

¼ cup finely chopped fresh parsley
   leaves or 2 tablespoons dried
   parsley leaves

½ teaspoon salt

⅛ teaspoon ground black pepper

Pinch of ground nutmeg

4 hard-boiled eggs, shelled

Coat with nonstick cooking spray or grease an 8 by 4-inch loaf pan. Preheat the oven to 375 degrees.

In a medium bowl, mix all the ingredients, except the hard-boiled eggs, with your hands or a fork until very well combined. For an especially smooth loaf, squeeze the mixture between your fingers as you mix it. (If the klops will be served chilled, increase the seasonings slightly, as their flavors will not seem as intense.)

Press a little less than half of the meat mixture into the bottom of the prepared loaf pan. Arrange the hard-boiled eggs, ends pointing toward each other, lengthwise at even intervals across the top. Pat some additional meat mixture around the eggs to hold them in place; then top them with the remainder of the meat, smoothing the top.

Bake the klops at 375 degrees for about 1 hour, or until it is browned and shrinking slightly away from the sides of the pan. Hold the pan with pot holders, and carefully tilt it over the sink to drain off any released fat. Cool the klops in the pan for about 5 minutes, then unmold it. To unmold, cover the loaf pan with an inverted plate; then invert the two together, and lift off the pan. To turn the klops upright, repeat the process with another plate. Serve the klops warm, at room temperature, or chilled. To serve, cut the klops into thick slices. It slices best when chilled.

Makes about 5 servings.

Glorious Oatmeal Cookies

I make this family favorite very often for cookouts and picnics. The scrumptious oatmeal cookies hold up well outside, and are always a hit with the adults as well as the kids. They are chewy and sweet, with plenty of oatmeal to give them an old-fashioned taste.

NOTES: Rolled oats can be purchased in several styles, including quick, old-fashioned, and instant. Quick-cooking oats are simply rolled oats that have been broken up so that they cook faster.

My family likes the cookies with only coconut; however, raisins, soft chopped dates, coarsely chopped walnuts, or chocolate chips may be added to the dough (or any combination of these).

Be sure the brown sugar is soft, with no lumps at all, or your cookies will have little holes of melted sugar.

1 cup butter or margarine, softened
1 cup packed dark brown sugar (see Notes)
1 cup granulated sugar
2 large eggs or ½ cup pareve egg substitute
2 teaspoons vanilla extract
1 teaspoon baking soda

1¾ cups all-purpose flour
3 cups quick-cooking rolled oats (see Notes)
1 cup sweetened shredded coconut, raisins, coarsely chopped walnuts or dates, or chocolate chips (or a mixture)

Line several sturdy shiny metal baking sheets with parchment, or coat them with nonstick cooking spray, or grease them. Preheat the oven to 375 degrees.

Put the butter, brown sugar, and granulated sugar into a large mixing bowl, and use an electric mixer to cream them together until very smooth and light. Beat in the eggs, one at a time, and the vanilla until very smooth. At low speed, beat in the baking soda and then the flour, just until combined. With a spoon or a heavy-duty mixer, slowly mix in the oats and any additional ingredients.

Use lightly moistened hands to form the dough into 1½-inch-diameter (walnut-sized) balls. (Or use a #40 ice cream disher to make the balls.) Place

the balls about 2 inches apart on the prepared baking sheets. Flatten each ball very slightly with your fingertips or a glass dipped in flour.

Bake at 375 degrees for about 10 to 13 minutes, or until an imprint does not remain when a cookie is very lightly pressed. (Cookies get much firmer as they cool. For chewy cookies, be careful not to bake them too long.) Cool the cookies on the baking sheet about 2 minutes, then transfer them to a wire rack to cool completely. Store in an airtight container for several days or freeze for longer storage.

Makes about 35 approximately 3-inch-diameter cookies.

Carob Drop Cookies

Carob is eaten on Lag B'Omer because the great scholar Rabbi Shimon bar Yochai is said to have been miraculously sustained by a carob tree while he hid in a cave for thirteen years. These cookies would be great for a dairy picnic or holiday hike.

These cookies, which have a soft, cakelike texture, form perfectly smooth, rounded tops as they bake. When they are completely cool, the flat bottoms of half the cookies can be spread with your favorite icing, and paired with the remainder to form filled cookie "sandwiches."

NOTE: Carob powder can have many variations. For the best results, use an intensely flavored dark-style carob powder. For more information on carob, see the recipe for Rich Carob Brownies (page 279).

½ cup butter softened
⅔ cup sugar
1 large egg or ¼ cup pareve egg
    substitute
½ teaspoon vanilla
½ cup buttermilk
½ cup water

½ cup carob powder, preferably the
    dark style (sifted, if lumpy) (see
    Note)
1 teaspoon baking soda
½ teaspoon baking powder
¼ teaspoon salt
2 cups all-purpose flour

Line one large or two smaller baking sheets with parchment, or coat them with nonstick cooking spray, or grease them. Preheat the oven to 400 degrees.

Put the butter and sugar into a medium mixing bowl, and use an electric mixer to cream them together well. Beat in the egg and the vanilla extract. Add the buttermilk, water, and carob powder, and beat until well combined. Add the baking soda, baking powder, salt, and flour, and beat until completely incorporated into the batter.

Using a measuring tablespoon of batter per cookie (or a small, #70 ice cream disher), drop the batter into rounded mounds about 2 inches apart on the prepared baking sheets. Bake at 400 degrees for 8 to 10 minutes, or until the top of a cookie springs back when very lightly touched in the center. Let the cookies cool for 2 minutes on the baking sheets, then use a metal spatula to remove the cookies from the baking sheet, and cool them completely on a wire rack.

Makes about 24 cookies.

Shavuot

Shavuot is the wedding anniversary of the Jewish people, and the Torah is
the marriage certificate between the Jews and God.

—*A kabbalistic interpretation*

 LIKE THE TWO OTHER BIBLICALLY MANDATED PILGRIMAGE FESTI-
vals of ancient times—Pesach and Sukkot—Shavuot has agricultural
connections. Celebrated on the sixth and seventh days of the Hebrew
month of Nissan (only on the sixth in Israel), which usually occur in late
May or June, it once celebrated the onset of the wheat harvest. One of the three names
given to it in the Torah is *Hag Ha'Katzir,* or "Festival of the Harvest." Among the
thanksgiving offerings taken to the Temple in Jerusalem were always two loaves baked
from new wheat.

Offered, too, were the *bikurim,* or choicest "first fruits" of the season, including
those representing the "Seven Species" for which ancient Israel was famed: barley,
wheat, figs, grapes, pomegranates, olives, and dates. Thus, the holiday is also referred to
as *Yom Ha'Bikurim,* or "Day of the First Fruits."

Because it comes at the end of the seven-week period during which the omer is
counted, it was called *Hag Ha'Shavuot,* meaning "Festival of Weeks." Our modern
name, *Shavuot,* is derived from this. Since the holiday occurs on the fiftieth day after the
counting begins, it is occasionally referred to as *Pentecost,* a Greek word meaning "fifty."

The holiday also came to be traditionally known as *Zeman Matan Toratenu,* or "The
Time of the Giving of our Law," because rabbinic scholars calculated that the Revelation at Mount Sinai, when God appeared to Moses and gave the Torah to the Jewish

people, took place on the sixth of Sivan. This monumental event became the dominant theme of Shavuot after the destruction of the Second Holy Temple.

The foods usually served on this holiday are related to both its agricultural and religious facets. One of the oldest and most prevalent culinary customs worldwide is the eating of cheese and other milk products. The simple agrarian explanation for this custom is that Shavuot occurs in the season when grazing animals give birth and find lush pastures; thus, there is an abundance of milk.

However, with their usual ingenuity, Jewish scholars have determined several symbolic reasons, all pertaining to Revelation, for partaking of dairy foods on Shavuot. A popular one is that the Law was given in "a land flowing with milk and honey" (as ancient Israel is described in Exodus). Also, it is written in the Song of Songs that "honey and milk are under thy tongue," implying that the words of the Torah are as sweet as honey and as nourishing as milk. (It is generally believed that, in biblical times, the word "honey" referred to the juice or a syrup of dates, one of the "Seven Species.")

Furthermore, some reasoned, the Jewish people did not know about kashrut until they received the Torah. As they did not have time to prepare kosher meat, they had to eat dairy dishes instead.

Others said that the people fasted prior to receiving the Torah, and became so ravenous that they could not wait for a meat meal to be cooked. Still others deduced that while the people were waiting, their milk curdled, and so they immediately made it into cheese.

Mystics construed meaning in the fact that the total numerical value of the letters in the Hebrew word for "milk" (halav) is forty, which equals the number of days that Moses spent on Mount Sinai. And, some noted, the infant Moses would take milk only from a Hebrew wet nurse. It is also said that even the wisest scholars are like suckling babes when it comes to true comprehension of the Torah.

Primary among the dairy foods favored for Shavuot are those in which a sweet or savory cheese filling is encased in some sort of dough. Ashkenazic Jews enjoy blintzes, kreplach, strudel, knishes, pirogen, and a pastry known as *topfen.* Sephardic favorites include flaky turnovers called *borekas,* as well as ravioli–like *calsones.*

Among the dairy holiday specialties of Kurdistani Jews are wheat cooked in clabbered milk and dumplings filled with cheese and butter. And many modern American Jews identify Shavuot with New York–style cheesecake.

Another reason why milk products are eaten on Shavuot is that they are usually white, and thus symbolize the purity of the Torah. Other white foods, particularly rice, are also traditional for many Sephardim. Often, the rice is cooked with milk for a special holiday dish, such as *soutlach,* a favorite among Turkish Jews.

The New Jewish Holiday Cookbook

Certain Near Eastern and Middle Eastern Jews flavor their Shavuot rice with rose water or garnish it with rose-petal jam, because they consider the holiday to be, among other things, the "Feast of Roses." At the synagogue, they may scatter rose petals on the scrolls of the Torah or sprinkle rose water on members of the congregation.

Ashkenazim from Russia and nearby areas often eat *schav,* a cold soup made from sorrel, an herb that flourishes during late spring. Chilled fruit soups are also popular for this holiday.

In some communities, it is customary to mix milk or yogurt with the last matzah from Pesach, as a reminder that Shavuot was once considered to be the conclusion of the Pesach holiday season, and also that the Revelation at Mount Sinai was the culmination of the Exodus.

Prominent among holiday desserts are cakes and cookies shaped like the Two Tablets of the Ten Commandments, as well as conelike cakes resembling Mount Sinai. Some Sephardim take particular pride in baking *siete cielos* (Judeo-Spanish for "seven heavens"), round, seven-layered cakes or seven-tiered breads that are filled with fruits and nuts and decorated with symbols of the Revelation. The number of layers corresponds to the weeks of the omer period that precedes Shavuot, as well as to the seven "spheres" of heaven that God is said to have traversed in order to present the Torah to the Jewish people.

Other holiday foods include a pair of extra-long loaves of bread to symbolize the measure of the Law, which, according to Job, "is longer than the earth," and also to recall the ancient Shavuot bread offerings at the Temple in Jerusalem. Sometimes, the breads are decorated with ladders, because the numerical value of the Hebrew word for "ladder" is the same as that for "Sinai," and also because a ladder represents Moses' ascent and descent of Mount Sinai. The ladders often have seven rungs for the same reasons that the *siete cielos* has seven layers.

The agricultural side of Shavuot is also specifically recalled in certain aspects of its celebration. For instance, fresh fruits, particularly those that are new to the season, are often included in meals and table centerpieces. In addition, lush foliage and flowers are used to adorn many homes and synagogues, and the scrolls of the Torah may be crowned with garlands.

In modern-day Israel, the custom of collecting "first fruits" is being revived at many kibbutzim and farming towns. The *bikurim* are brought to central points, and then distributed to the needy or other worthy groups.

In Eastern Europe, it was once customary for Ashkenazic Jews to begin their children's Jewish education on Shavuot. To make the introduction to Torah especially

"sweet" and memorable, the children were given honey cakes or candies decorated with Hebrew letters, or the letters on a child's slate were dabbed with honey for the child to lick off.

Other Shavuot customs include reading the Book of Ruth, and an all-night study session known as *Tikun Leil Shavuot,* during which a small section of every part of Jewish law is studied and discussed. In America, Shavuot has also become the time when many religious schools hold confirmation and graduation ceremonies.

The recipes in this chapter emphasize dairy and fresh fruit dishes, and include a wonderful assortment of hors d'oeuvres, soups, main dishes, and desserts. Many are perfect for buffet entertaining. It would be particularly appropriate to serve them from a holiday table decorated with seasonal greenery, fruit baskets, and freshly picked flowers.

Also, see the chapter on Hanukkah for many more dairy food recipes.

"First Fruits" Rainbow Salad

In ancient times, Jews brought their finest "first fruits" or *bikurim* to the Temple in Jerusalem as a special offering for Shavuot. In remembrance of this, many now serve fresh fruit on the holiday, particularly "new" fruits not yet eaten that season. Sometimes, whole fresh fruits are arranged in a pyramid-shaped centerpiece to represent Mount Sinai.

Following is a simple but delectable fruit salad—composed primarily of fruits mentioned in the Torah or found in modern-day Israel. Feel free to adjust amounts or omit some fruits. Of course, other fruits may be added, such as mango and papaya (tropical fruits now gaining popularity in Israel), avocado, pomegranate, melons, pears, pineapple, dates, and so forth. You can use ten different types to symbolize the Ten Commandments.

2 large pink or white grapefruit	*2 medium bananas*
3 large navel oranges	*¹/₂ cup each seedless green and red*
1 or 2 tangerines	*grapes*
2 medium apples	*3 fresh figs (optional)*
2 medium pears	*1 cup blueberries and/or raspberries*
1 pint strawberries	*¹/₂ cup coarsely chopped walnuts*

½ cup slivered almonds

2 to 3 tablespoons mild honey

2 to 3 tablespoons sweet sherry or table
wine or fruit juice

Peel the grapefruit and oranges, and cut them into ¾-inch chunks, removing all seeds. Peel and section the tangerines, removing all "strings" and seeds. Wash the apples well, cut them into fourths, and remove the stems and seeds; then dice the apples. Do the same with the pears. Wash the strawberries very well, remove the hulls (leaves and stem), and cut the berries in half. Peel the bananas and cut them into slices. Wash the grapes well, and remove them from the stems. Wash the figs (if used) very well, and cut them into fourths.

Put all the prepared fruit into a large serving bowl along with the berries and nuts. In a small bowl, or in a blender, combine the honey and wine or juice. Pour over the salad. Refrigerate for several hours to allow the flavors to blend.

Makes 8 to 10 servings.

Har Geveenah

MOUNT SINAI FRUIT-AND-CHEESE "BALL"

King David's psalms are read on Shavuot because it is traditionally considered to be the anniversary of both his birth and death. In one of his psalms, Mount Sinai is described as, among other things, *har gavnunim,* or "a mountain of peaks."

Scholars have interpreted the similarity between the Hebrew word for "peaks" and that for "cheese" (*geveenah*) as another of the many reasons why dairy foods should be eaten on Shavuot.

Foods that look like the "mountain of peaks"—that is, cone-shaped cakes, cookies, and confections—are also often served on Shavuot. Sometimes, they are topped with jam or nuts to represent the dark cloud that is said to have hovered over Mount Sinai at the time when the Tablets of the Law were given. Or a perfect walnut half may be used instead, to symbolize the stone Tablets themselves.

The following appetizer/snack—which combines both the custom of eating cheese and that of eating foods shaped like Mount Sinai—is completely my own creation. The whimsical Hebrew name literally translates as "mountain of cheese," and is a play on the words of David's psalm. The cheese "ball" is molded to resemble a mountain, and it is coated with finely chopped almonds (to represent the snow that may have been on the peak) and/or chopped parsley (to symbolize the oasis that is said to have surrounded the base of Mount Sinai). Its summit is topped with either a prune (for the dark cloud) or a perfect walnut half (for the Tablets).

In addition, the cheese mixture includes fruits and nuts indigenous to Israel, which may have been among those offered as *bikurim* during the ancient Shavuot pilgrimage.

This cheese mountain is served as a spread for crackers. I find it particularly fitting to use any matzah crackers (or pieces of matzah) left over from Pesach, as Shavuot is the conclusion of the seven "weeks" of counting that began at Pesach.

I have often used this recipe in cooking demonstrations as a way to teach about the customs of Shavuot. During the class, I dramatically place a beautiful walnut half on my *har geveenah* to represent the Tablets of the Ten Commandments. Interestingly, the entire mountain may disappear at the tasting that always follows my demonstrations, but no one ever dares to eat the Ten Commandments!

1 (3-ounce) package cream cheese, softened
2 tablespoons sour cream
About 2 tablespoons sweet or dry red table wine
8 ounces finely grated Cheddar or similar cheese (2 cups packed)
1/2 cup slivered almonds
1/3 cup finely chopped dates
1/3 cup finely chopped dried figs
1/3 cup dark or light raisins

COATING AND GARNISH
Finely chopped blanched almonds
Finely chopped fresh parsley leaves (optional)
1 perfect walnut half or 1 large prune

TO SERVE
Crackers, such as matzah crackers, or small cocktail bread slices

In a large bowl, beat the cream cheese with the sour cream until light and fluffy; then beat in the 2 tablespoons wine. Add the remaining cheese and fruit mixture ingredients, and mix very well. Use the back of a spoon to press the mixture against the sides of the bowl to help it form a coherent mass. If the cheese mixture seems to be very dry, add small amounts of wine as needed.

In the center of a large platter, form the cheese mixture into a mountain-like cone shape, and drizzle the chopped almonds over the outside (to symbolize snow). If desired, parsley may be sprinkled around the base of the cone (to symbolize grass). To represent the Two Tablets of the Law, stand the perfect walnut half upright near the peak. Or, for the dark cloud that hovered over Mount Sinai, horizontally set the prune on top of the summit.

Serve immediately or, for best flavor, chill the "cheese mountain" several hours or overnight to allow the flavors to blend and the cheese mixture to firm up. Arrange crackers or bread slices around the mountain, and provide a small knife for spreading the cheese mixture.

Makes 1 large cheese "ball."

Spring Salad
COTTAGE CHEESE AND VEGETABLE SALAD

For many Ashkenazic Jews, this easy salad has long been a favorite way to enjoy some of the special culinary delights of spring. In fact, it is often considered a must for the Shavuot holiday table.

For as long as I can remember, the following version of spring salad has been one of my mother's favorite dairy dishes. Though she eats it all year round, Mom insists, and I agree, that it tastes the very best at Shavuot time, when the first luscious vine-ripened tomatoes of the season are just becoming available.

A very similar salad is often served in Israel, where wonderful produce is almost always in season. Israelis usually make the salad with *leben* or the richer *lebeniya,* cultured milk products that are similar to yogurt. These products are available in some American supermarkets, as are wonderful cherry tomatoes imported from Israel.

Feel free to adjust all the amounts in this salad to taste. Low-fat or nonfat dairy products may be used in this salad if desired.

1 (1-pound) carton cream-style cottage
  cheese (about 2 cups)
1 (8-ounce) container sour cream
  (about 1 cup)
1 bunch scallions (4 to 5 medium)
1 large tomato, preferably vine-ripened,
  or several cherry tomatoes

1 medium cucumber
3 to 4 radishes
Salt and ground black pepper to taste

To Serve (Optional)
Lettuce leaves

In a large bowl, combine the cottage cheese and sour cream. Cut up the vegetables as follows, and add them to the bowl.

Wash the scallions well; then cut off and discard the roots and about ½ inch of the tops. Cut the scallions, including the green tops, into ¼-inch slices. Core the tomato, and cut it into ¾-inch to 1-inch chunks. If using cherry tomatoes, cut them in halves or fourths, depending on their size. Peel the cucumber, and cut it in fourths lengthwise; then remove the seeds if desired. Cut the cucumber into ½-inch slices. Slice the root and stem end off the radishes; then thinly slice them or cut them into small pieces.

Mix in all the vegetables; then season the salad with salt and pepper to taste. If desired, serve the salad on a bed of lettuce leaves.

Makes 5 to 6 servings.

Cherry Soup, Hungarian-Style

This delicious chilled soup, a favorite of Jews from Hungary and Czechoslovakia, makes an elegant beginning for a Shavuot meal. Or it may be served as a light dessert.

2 (16-ounce) cans tart red cherries in
  water
⅓ to ½ cup sugar, or to taste
Pinch of ground allspice
Pinch of ground cloves
1 tablespoon cornstarch

½ cup sweet red wine, fruit-flavored
  wine, or cream sherry (or use dry
  wine and add more sugar to taste)
⅓ cup sour cream

Garnish (Optional)
Additional sour cream

Drain the liquid from the cherries, reserving it. Add enough water to the liquid to make a total of 2⅔ cups. Put this into a large saucepan with the cherries, sugar, allspice, and cloves. Cover, and bring to a boil over high heat. Lower the heat, and simmer the cherry mixture for 5 minutes.

Put the cornstarch into a small bowl, and slowly stir in the wine until the cornstarch is completely suspended in it. Add the wine-cornstarch mixture to the cherries, and cook, stirring, until the cherry soup thickens slightly and comes to a boil. Simmer about 1 minute. Remove it from the heat, and cool it to tepid. Stir about ¼ cup of the liquid part of the soup into the ⅓ cup sour cream to soften it. Add this back to the rest of the soup, and stir well until it is completely mixed in.

Refrigerate the soup for several hours or overnight, or until it is completely chilled. Serve the soup chilled. If desired, garnish each serving with a dollop of sour cream.

Makes about 6 servings.

Light-and-Easy Strawberry Soup

Strawberries are usually at the peak of their season during Shavuot, and this chilled soup makes a delicious use of them.

⅔ cup cold water

1 cup orange juice

¼ cup sugar

⅛ teaspoon ground allspice

⅛ teaspoon ground cinnamon

4 cups hulled fresh strawberries

1 tablespoon cornstarch

½ cup sweet red wine, fruit-flavored
    wine, or cream sherry (or use dry
    wine and add more sugar to taste)

1¼ cups very fresh buttermilk

In a large saucepan, combine the water, juice, sugar, allspice, and cinnamon. Bring to a boil over high heat. Add the strawberries, and cover the pan. Lower the heat, and simmer the strawberries for about 5 minutes, or just until they are tender. Transfer the contents of the pan to a food processor (fitted

with a steel blade) or a blender, and process until the strawberries are completely puréed.

Return the strawberry purée to the saucepan. Put the cornstarch into a small bowl, and slowly stir in the wine until the cornstarch is completely suspended in it. Add the wine-cornstarch mixture to the strawberry purée. Stir over medium-high heat until the soup thickens slightly and comes to a boil. Simmer about 1 minute. Remove it from the heat, and let it cool to tepid. Stir in the buttermilk.

Refrigerate the soup for several hours or overnight, or until it is completely chilled. Serve the soup chilled.

Makes about 4 servings.

Turban of Sole with Sole Mousse

In this magnificent turban, an attractive ring of fish fillets is wrapped around luscious, spinach-flecked fish mousse. Though it is quite impressive and very delicious, it is not that difficult to prepare. In fact, the mousse filling is made in just seconds using a food processor.

Furthermore, the entire turban may be assembled up to a day ahead of time, and then baked shortly before it is served—making this dish especially convenient for company meals at Shavuot and other times during the year.

NOTE: If you do not like mushrooms, simply pour hot melted butter all over the top of the ring.

2 1/2 pounds thin, skinless sole fillets
3 large eggs or 3/4 cup egg substitute
1/4 cup butter, melted and cooled to tepid
    (1/2 stick)
1/4 teaspoon ground nutmeg
3/4 teaspoon salt
1/4 teaspoon ground black or white
    pepper

1/2 cup whipping cream
2 ounces fresh, trimmed spinach leaves,
    washed, well drained, and coarsely
    chopped (about 1 cup, tightly
    packed) (Do not use frozen
    spinach.)

GARNISH

¼ cup butter

8 ounces fresh mushrooms, cleaned and finely chopped or thinly sliced (see Note)

Coat a 6½-cup ring mold well with butter or nonstick cooking spray. Choose 1½ pounds of the nicest, most evenly sized sole fillets. Line the mold with these fillets (smooth, darker, skinned-side up) positioning them so that they go across the ring like the spokes of a wheel. The narrow end of each fillet should point toward the center and possibly overhang the inside rim of the mold, and the wider end should overhang the outside rim.

For the mousse, put the remaining 1 pound of sole fillets into a food processor fitted with a steel blade. Pulse-process until the fillets are puréed. Add the eggs, melted butter, nutmeg, salt, and pepper, and process until well mixed. With the machine running, slowly add the cream through the chute and process a few seconds longer to be sure it is incorporated into the fish. Turn off the machine, add the spinach, and pulse-process only until the spinach is finely minced and flecked throughout the mousse.

Use a rubber spatula to put all the mousse mixture into the fillet-lined mold, filling in all the spaces. Smooth the top of the mousse, then fold the overhanging ends of the fillets over the top of the mousse. Chill the assembled turban very well, covered, for at least 3 hours or up to overnight.

To bake the turban, preheat the oven to 350 degrees, and bring some water to a boil. Put the uncovered ring mold into a slightly larger pan, and add boiling water to the outer pan so that it comes two-thirds up the outside of the ring mold. Bake at 350 degrees for about 40 minutes, or until the turban is firm. (If dinner is delayed, the turban can stay in the warm, turned-off oven for up to 15 minutes.)

When the turban is almost done baking, make the mushroom garnish. Melt the butter in a large skillet, and quickly sauté the mushrooms until they are barely cooked. Do not overcook them or they will become rubbery.

To unmold the turban, run a rubber spatula around the edges of the ring mold to loosen the fish fillets. Cover the mold with an inverted serving platter; then over a sink, invert the two, holding them together. Tilt the plate slightly to allow all the excess liquid from the mold to drain off into the sink. Carefully lift the mold off the turban, which should beautifully hold its circular shape. Sprinkle the sautéed mushrooms and their buttery pan juices over

the turban; then serve it immediately. To serve it, cut it into thick slices. Each slice will have green-flecked mousse encircled with baked sole fillet.

Makes 6 to 8 servings.

Borekas

SEPHARDIC SAVORY PASTRIES FILLED WITH CHEESE AND VEGETABLES

Also spelled *burekas* (and several other ways), these are probably the best known of the wonderful savory pastries favored by Sephardim with Turkish, Greek, and similar backgrounds. The Judeo-Spanish name was likely adapted from the Turkish word for a similar filled pastry, *borek*. Jews from Syria and other Middle Eastern and North African countries make very similar pastries called *sanboosak* or *sembussak*.

The same rich dough is also used for miniature pot-shaped "tarts" called *pasteles* or *pastelicos,* which are usually filled with meat.

In Israel, very large triangular *borekas* made with a crust of flaky multilayered puff pastry or, possibly, filo dough are popular street food, and can even be purchased as a convenience food from the freezer section of supermarkets. When eaten on-the-go, *borekas* are almost always accompanied by warm Huevos Haminados (page 354), long-cooked whole eggs.

Borekas are made with a variety of fillings, each usually including a vegetable and cheese. The favorite vegetables are potato, spinach, and eggplant. And the cheeses most often used are kashkaval, Parmesan, Romano, and feta. Other choices of cheese include Swiss, Muenster, Monterey Jack, Cheddar, and a firm type of farmer cheese. When cheese is added to the dough as well as to the filling, the pastries are often called *borekitas,* especially when an eggplant-cheese filling is used.

Kashkaval (also called *kaskaval*), a Balkan cheese made from sheep's milk, has become commonplace in Israel, although it still tends to be a specialty cheese in the United States. Very similar cheeses that are sometimes used are Greek *kasseri* and Italian *caciocavallo.* According to *Eat and Be Satisfied: A Social History of Jewish Food,* by John Cooper, the word *kaskaval* is derived from *caciocavallo.* Cooper says that this cheese was so popular with Near Eastern Jews that the Greeks called it *casheri* (*kasseri?*), meaning "kosher" cheese!

Most Sephardim serve *borekas* and other delectable cheese-filled pastries, such as

Spanakopitas (page 496) and Bulemas (page 499), on Shavuot as well as on many other festive occasions, particularly for *Desayuno*. Though this Judeo-Spanish word literally translates as "breakfast," the Sephardim use it to mean specifically a special dairy brunch that they often enjoy after morning synagogue services on Shabbat and holidays.

In addition to pastries, *Desayuno* customarily includes a selection of cheeses, yogurt, *huevos haminados,* vegetable-cheese casseroles such as Fritada de Espinaca (page 387), olives, homemade preserves, seasonal fresh fruits, and possibly the rice pudding called Soutlach (page 512).

NOTE: The following "rich" boreka dough includes butter and is specifically designed for dairy fillings. Another popular boreka dough that has only oil can be used with meat fillings as well (see Variation). Originally, only olive oil was used in the dough; but in relatively recent times, other types of oil have become more common.

RICH DOUGH (SEE NOTE)
½ cup butter, melted and cooled to tepid
½ cup canola or safflower oil
½ cup lukewarm water
½ teaspoon salt
3½ cups unbleached flour

POTATO-CHEESE FILLING
1¼ cups plain mashed potatoes
4 ounces (1 cup, packed) finely shredded kashkaval, kasseri, Monterey Jack, Muenster, Swiss cheese, or Cheddar cheese
½ cup finely grated Parmesan or Romano cheese
2 large eggs or ½ cup egg substitute
Generous pinch of freshly ground black pepper

EGGPLANT-CHEESE FILLING
1½ cups eggplant pulp from approximately 2 large, broiled

eggplants (for directions, see the recipe for Salat Hatzilim, page 437), drained of excess moisture in a colander or large sieve
1 cup finely shredded kashkaval, kasseri, or finely grated Parmesan or Romano cheese
2 large eggs or ½ cup egg substitute
¼ teaspoon salt
Matzah meal (optional; use a small amount only if the filling is very wet)

SPINACH-FETA FILLING
Use the same filling as for the Spanakopitas (page 496)

GLAZE AND TOPPING
1 large egg beaten with 1 teaspoon water or ¼ cup egg substitute
Sesame seeds (optional)
Grated cheese (optional)

Shavuot

For the dough, combine the melted butter, oil, water, and salt in a medium bowl and mix well. Gradually stir in the flour to make a soft, slightly greasy dough. Mix only until the dough comes away from the sides of the bowl; do not overmix. Gather the dough into a ball, and wrap it with plastic wrap. Let it rest for 15 to 30 minutes while the filling is prepared. (Do *not* refrigerate the dough. It can rest at room temperature for up to an hour if necessary.) Each filling recipe is sufficient to fill one batch of dough.

For the potato-cheese filling or the eggplant-cheese filling, combine all the ingredients to make a soft, stiff paste. For the spinach-feta filling, follow the directions in the recipe for Spanakopitas (page 496).

To make the borekas, have a filling ready and several heavy, shiny metal baking sheets. They may be left ungreased, or they may be lined with baking parchment for easy cleanup. Shape the dough into about 36 balls, each approximately the size of a small walnut. For each boreka, use your fingertips to flatten one of the balls on a board or other flat surface until it forms a thin oval approximately 3 by 4 inches. Put 1 tablespoon of the filling on one side of the oval; then fold it in half crosswise to cover the filling, and form a half-moon shape.

Pinch the edges together and secure them with the tines of a fork. Or, to form a decorative, ropelike ("festoon") edge, as most Sephardim do, hold the pastry in one hand, and use the thumb and index finger of the opposite hand to squeeze a bit of the edge and then fold it up toward the pastry on a slight angle. Begin at one side of the pastry and move continuously around to the other. As each boreka is made, put it on the prepared baking sheet, keeping the borekas about 1 inch apart.

While making the borekas, preheat the oven to 375 degrees. Before baking the borekas, brush the top of each one with the egg glaze. If desired, sprinkle the tops lightly with sesame seeds or grated cheese. (When making borekas with more than one type of filling, Sephardim use a different topping for each

type to make later identification easy.) Prick each boreka once with a fork to allow steam to escape. Bake the borekas at 375 degrees for 30 to 35 minutes, or until they are golden brown and crisp.

If desired, borekas may be frozen before or after baking. Freeze them in a single layer; then pack them into airtight bags or containers when frozen. If the borekas were frozen *before* baking, do not thaw them, just bake them as above for an extra 10 minutes, or until they are done. If they were frozen after baking, reheat them, frozen, in a 375-degree oven until hot throughout. Sephardim usually keep a supply of unbaked borekas in the freezer, ready to bake at any time for unexpected guests or family snacks.

Leftover borekas may be refrigerated for a few days, and reheated in a 375-degree oven (or even a toaster oven) for a short time. A microwave cannot be used to reheat a boreka, as it will soften the crust.

Serve the borekas hot or at room temperature.

Makes about 36 3-inch borekas.

Dough Variations

BOREKA OIL DOUGH

This is a very popular dough that is used by Sephardim for all kinds of *borekas* and other pastries. Sometimes warm water is used, sometimes the water and oil are brought to a boil, and sometimes just the water is boiled, as below. It differs from the dough in the main recipe above in that it contains no butter or margarine, and it has a lower proportion of total fat to flour.

¾ *cup boiling water*
¾ *cup canola, safflower, or olive oil*
¾ *teaspoon salt*

3¾ *to 4½ cups unbleached flour, or as*
needed

Put the water in a medium bowl with the oil and salt, and mix well. Gradually add the flour while mixing with a fork. When the dough becomes too stiff to mix, and is beginning to come away from the sides of the bowl, turn it out onto a board. Knead it for about 5 to 10 minutes, adding flour as needed, until it is very smooth and pliable. It may be rolled out immediately, or it may be allowed to rest, wrapped in plastic wrap, for up to an hour. The

dough may be formed into borekas as described above, or it may be rolled out until it is ⅛ inch thick and cut into 3½-inch circles with a cutter. The scraps should be rerolled immediately. Fill, fold, and bake the borekas as described above.

FILO BOREKA WRAPPERS

Follow the directions for the filo wrappers with the recipe for Spanakopitas (below), but use the above fillings.

Spanakopitas or Ojaldres
SPINACH AND CHEESE IN FLAKY PASTRY

Sephardic Jews, particularly those from Greece and Turkey, make a variety of savory pastries that are wrapped in an ultra-thin dough known as *filo.*

Spanakopitas is the Greek name for filo pastries that are filled with spinach and cheese, and folded into triangular shapes or rolled into narrow cigarlike cylinders. (Occasionally, all the filling is baked between layers of filo, to form a sort of pie.) When the filling contains cheese, but no spinach, the same pastries are called *tiropitas.*

Ojaldres is the Sephardic name for the same pastries, which may be made with the favorite Sephardic cheeses, kashkaval and kasseri, rather than feta. *Ojaldres* are typically formed into triangles.

Bulemas (see Variation) are Sephardic pastries that are often made with filo dough and contain fillings similar to *ojaldres.* For *bulemas,* though, the filling is rolled inside a large filo tube, which is then twisted into a coil. (More traditional *bulemas* may be made with a stretched yeast dough instead of filo.)

These pastries are often included among those served at the Sephardic holiday dairy brunch known as *Desayuno.* They also make excellent hors d'oeuvres for entertaining at any time.

NOTES: For an easy way to defrost spinach in the microwave oven, and for details on using filo, see the Glossary of Ingredients.

For extra ease in forming these pastries, use a can of olive oil cooking spray instead of butter (which must be brushed on). The pastries will not taste "buttery," but they will still be quite delicious.

SPINACH-FETA FILLING
2 tablespoons extra-virgin olive oil
1 medium onion, finely chopped
1 (10-ounce) package frozen chopped
    spinach, thawed and very well
    drained (see Notes)
8 ounces feta cheese, crumbled
1 cup part-skim or regular ricotta
    cheese
2 large eggs, lightly beaten or ½ cup
    egg substitute
2 tablespoons plain or seasoned dry
    bread crumbs

1 teaspoon dried dillweed
⅛ teaspoon nutmeg
Generous pinch of ground black pepper

FILO WRAPPERS
10 or 11 filo sheets (about ½ pound) at
    room temperature (see Glossary)
About ½ cup butter (preferably
    unsalted), melted (1 stick) (see
    Notes)

For the spinach-feta filling, heat the oil in a skillet over medium-high heat; then sauté the onion until it is tender. Add the spinach and lower the heat. Cook, stirring, until almost all the moisture has evaporated from the spinach. Remove the spinach-onion mixture from the heat, and let it cool until tepid. Stir in the feta, ricotta, eggs, bread crumbs, dillweed, nutmeg, and pepper.

Line several heavy, shiny metal baking sheets with baking parchment, coat them with nonstick cooking spray, or grease them. Set them aside. Preheat the oven to 375 degrees.

There are two basic ways to shape spanakopitas. For either one, cut a large sheet of filo crosswise into fourths, to make four strips. (If desired, cut the stack of sheets together, and collect the strips into one pile.) Use a slightly damp (not wet) dish towel to cover the unfilled filo sheets so they do not dry out.

For rolls, or *cigaras,* as they are sometimes called, brush one strip of filo very lightly with melted butter. Place 1 tablespoon of filling in a thin line along one narrow edge of the strip. Fold over the edge to cover the filling; then fold in each long edge of the strip ½ inch. Roll up the strip, beginning at the end with the filling, to form a tight cylinder. Repeat with the remaining dough strips and filling.

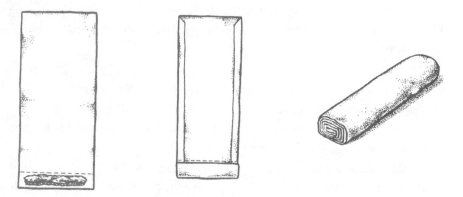

For triangles, brush one strip very lightly with butter; then fold it in half lengthwise and brush the top surface with butter. Put 1 tablespoon of filling about 1 inch from a narrow edge. Diagonally fold the end of the strip over the filling so that the narrow edge meets the side of the strip and forms a right-angle triangle. Fold the triangle forward, and then on the diagonal, just as when folding an American flag. Continue to the end of the strip. Repeat with the remaining strips and filling.

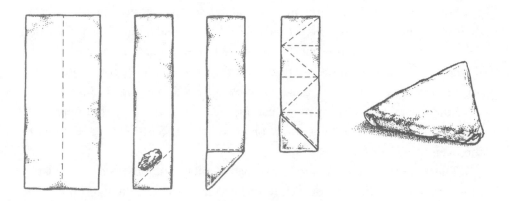

Put the pastries about 1 inch apart on the prepared baking sheets, and brush the tops well with butter. Bake them at 375 degrees for 25 to 30 minutes, or until golden brown. Serve warm. (Freeze if desired, in a single layer; then pack into airtight bags or containers when frozen. To serve, reheat the frozen pastries at 375 degrees until warmed through.

Makes 40 to 44 hors d'oeuvres.

Variation

BULEMAS (Coiled, Filled Flaky Pastry)

Brush one large sheet of filo very lightly with melted butter; then fold it in half lengthwise, and brush the top with butter. Put 3 to 4 tablespoons of filling in a thin line along one of the long edges. Fold each of the shorter sides in 1 inch. Then fold over the long edge to enclose the filling, and continue rolling up the filo like a jelly roll to form a log. Use both hands to push the ends of the log toward the center to "pleat" the log a bit so it will bend more easily. Gently curl the log into a snakelike coil. Repeat with the remaining dough and filling. Place the coils on parchment-lined or greased baking sheets, and brush the tops well with melted butter. Bake the *bulemas* in a preheated 350-degree oven for about 40 to 45 minutes, or until they are golden brown.

Makes about 10 large pastries.

Cheese Kreplach

TRIANGULAR NOODLE DUMPLINGS

Three-cornered, cheese-filled kreplach are eaten by many Askenazic Jews on Shavuot because the number "three" has several connections with the holiday. The Law is *three*-fold, comprising Torah, Prophets, and Writing. It was given to Moses, the third child born of his parents, on the sixth day (two times three equals six) of the third month of the Hebrew calendar. Moses brought it to the Jewish people, who formed three groups: Kohen, Levite, and Israelite.

Cheese *varenikes* are almost identical to cheese *kreplach,* the only difference being that the dough is cut into circles, not squares, and folded into half-moons.

SAVORY FILLING

2 (7$\frac{1}{2}$- to 8-ounce) packages curd-style
    farmer cheese

2 tablespoons sour cream

1 large egg or $\frac{1}{4}$ cup egg substitute

1 tablespoon instant minced onions

Salt and ground black pepper to taste

SWEET FILLING

2 (7$\frac{1}{2}$- to 8-ounce) packages curd-style
    farmer cheese

2 tablespoons sour cream

1 large egg or $\frac{1}{4}$ cup egg substitute

$\frac{1}{4}$ cup sugar, or more to taste

$\frac{1}{2}$ teaspoon vanilla extract

$\frac{1}{4}$ teaspoon ground cinnamon (optional)

DOUGH

2 cups unbleached flour

$\frac{1}{2}$ teaspoon salt, or $\frac{1}{4}$ teaspoon, if a
    sweet filling is used

2 large eggs

2 to 4 tablespoons water

TO SERVE

Melted butter

Grated cheese to taste, with savory
    kreplach (optional)

Cinnamon-sugar to taste, with sweet
    kreplach (optional)

Butter for frying (optional)

For the savory or sweet filling, combine all the listed ingredients until well mixed. Cover and refrigerate while making the dough.

For instructions on how to make the dough, roll it out, cut it, form the kreplach, and boil them, see the directions for the recipe for Meat Kreplach (page 112). The only difference with the cheese kreplach is that the dough should be divided into only two pieces when rolling it out by hand or into three pieces for a pasta machine. (Also, do not warm these kreplach in chicken soup!)

Toss the hot cheese kreplach with melted butter, and, if desired, sprinkle them with some grated cheese or cinnamon-sugar, depending on the filling. Or, if desired, heat some butter in a large skillet over medium-high heat, and fry the kreplach until they are golden brown on both sides. Serve them hot as a side dish or appetizer.

Makes about 24 kreplach.

Mom's Best Cheese Blintzes

It is very traditional for Ashkenazic Jews to eat blintzes on Shavuot. Not only are they filled with the customary cheese, but two of them placed next to each other look like the two Tablets of the Ten Commandments that were given to Moses on Mount Sinai.

Cheese blintzes have always been a favorite of mine, and they were one of the first "Jewish" dishes that I learned to cook. When I was a teen, I loved to watch (and occasionally help) my mother to prepare the delicate crêpelike blintz wrappers that never seemed to tear. (And, oh, how I sometimes wished they would, because then I'd be allowed to nosh on the delectable fragments.) Mom also taught me how to neatly fill and fold the blintzes, so they would look as wonderful as they tasted.

While I was in college, French-style crêpes suddenly became very popular and I was the only one of my peers who actually knew how to make them (thanks to my mom's blintz lessons). As crêpe restaurants were rather expensive (at least on impoverished students' budgets), my apartment kitchen became the site of some very interesting meals with friends.

To this day, I still prepare blintzes (and crêpes) the way my mom, Helene "Hindy" Kaufer, showed me. Following is her easy, no-fail recipe.

BATTER FOR BLINTZ WRAPPERS
4 large eggs (no substitutes)
1 cup all-purpose flour
1 cup milk
1 tablespoon sugar (optional)

CHEESE FILLING
4 (7½- to 8-ounce) packages curd-style
    farmer cheese
3 large eggs or ¾ cup egg substitute
1 to 3 tablespoons sugar, or to taste

FOR FRYING
Butter
Canola or safflower oil

TO SERVE
Applesauce
Sour cream or plain yogurt
Fruit preserves or jam

For the blintz wrappers, put all the batter ingredients into a blender (or a food processor fitted with a steel blade), and process until very well combined. Scrape down the sides of the container once or twice during the processing. The batter will be very thin, similar to the consistency of cream. Let it rest for about 30 minutes for the flour to absorb some of the liquid.

Shavuot

Meanwhile, prepare the filling. Combine all the ingredients, and mix very well. Set the filling aside.

To make the blintz wrappers, preheat an 8-inch skillet with sloping sides (and, preferably, a nonstick surface) over medium-high heat. Very lightly grease the hot pan by running a stick of cold butter over the surface. Give the batter a brief stir to resuspend the ingredients. Then pour enough batter into the hot pan to completely cover the bottom about ¼ inch deep. Let the pan sit on the heat only about 5 seconds; then immediately lift the pan by the handle, and pour all the excess batter out of the pan and back into the original container. The small amount of batter that remains in the pan will make a very thin, perfectly smooth blintz wrapper, about 6½ inches in diameter. It will have a little "extension" on the edge where the batter was poured out.

Cook the blintz wrapper about 30 seconds, or until it is dry on top and cooked through. The bottom does not have to brown very much. Do not flip it over in the pan; it is browned only on one side. (Crêpes are cooked on both sides because they are eaten as soon as they are filled. However, filled blintzes are fried with the nonbrowned side out.)

Use a dull knife or small spatula to loosen the edge of the blintz wrapper. Turn the blintz wrapper out of the pan onto a table or countertop covered with paper towels. The browned side should now face upward. (If the wrapper does not come right out of the pan, pull on it gently to release it.) Repeat with the remaining batter, arranging the cooked blintz wrappers next to each other, but not overlapping each other. If space is very limited, they may be stacked in one pile; however, it is easier to evenly divide the filling when all the wrappers are spread out.

NOTE: Do not be concerned if the first few wrappers do not come out right—be patient and you will get the hang of it.

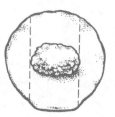 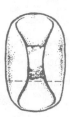 

Spoon about 3 tablespoons of the filling onto the center of each blintz wrapper, dividing the filling evenly among them. To form each blintz, fold two opposite sides of a wrapper over the filling so that they almost meet in the center. Then fold up the two remaining sides so that they overlap, completely enclosing the filling and forming a rectangle about 2½ by 3 inches. Turn all the formed blintzes over so that the loose edge is on the bottom. The un-cooked side of the shell should be on the outside of each blintz.

The blintzes may be made ahead to this point, and refrigerated or frozen. Arrange them next to each other on a platter or in a freezer container. If the blintzes need to be stacked, place a sheet of wax paper between each layer.

To cook the blintzes, melt an equal amount of butter and oil in a large skillet over medium to medium-high heat so that the bottom is completely covered. Beginning with their loose edges down, fry the blintzes in batches, turning them once, until they are golden brown on both sides and the filling is cooked through. (The frying should seal the loose edge of the wrappers tightly closed.) If they are browning too quickly, lower the heat slightly. If the blintzes have been frozen, do not thaw them before cooking; simply fry them at a lower temperature for a longer time to make sure the cheese filling is cooked through.

(If desired, uncooked blintzes may be baked instead of fried; however, they are not as rich-tasting as the fried ones and they do not "brown." To bake the blintzes, melt a few tablespoons of butter in a casserole dish; then put in the blintzes, and turn them so they are lightly coated with butter. Bake them, seam side down in a single layer, uncovered, in a 400-degree oven for about 15 to 20 minutes, or until they are cooked through and hot. Bake frozen blintzes in a 350-degree oven for about 35 to 40 minutes.)

Serve the blintzes with your choice of accompaniments.

Makes about 20 blintzes; about 4 to 5 servings.

Quick-and-Easy Cheese Blintz Casserole

THREE-LAYER SQUARES

Though cheese blintzes rate as an all-time favorite in my family, I don't always have the time to prepare them in the usual fashion. Therefore, I created the following casserole, which has a fantastic flavor very similar to blintzes (some say it's even better); yet it takes only a few minutes to prepare. In fact, I make it often throughout the year.

It is quite different from the popular cheese blintz casseroles made with frozen commercial blintzes. For my version, a layer of cheese filling is baked between two light layers of a special blintz-type batter. The casserole is then cut into squares for serving, making it a perfect choice for a dairy buffet and great for Shavuot.

Since the first edition of this book was published, this layered blintz casserole has proven to be one of its most popular recipes. The dish is served at the famous Moosewood Restaurant in Ithaca, New York, where it has become a favorite brunch offering under the name "Easy Cheese Blintz Puff." And the recipe has appeared in a number of books and magazines. Like some of the other "creative" recipes in this book, this one appears to be on its way to becoming a classic of "new" Jewish cooking.

NOTES: The types of cheeses in the filling were determined after much experimentation with various mixtures. It is the best combination to produce the desired results of separate layers.

The top of this casserole is rather plain. If desired, it may be sprinkled lightly with cinnamon or cinnamon-sugar before the casserole is returned to the oven for the final baking.

BATTER

4 large eggs (no substitutes)

1¼ cups milk

2 tablespoons sour cream

¼ cup butter, melted (for best flavor, no substitutes)

¾ teaspoon vanilla extract

1⅓ cups all-purpose flour

1 to 2 tablespoons sugar

1¼ teaspoons baking powder

FILLING (SEE NOTES)

2 (7½- to 8-ounce) packages curd-style farmer cheese

1 (15- to 16-ounce) container ricotta cheese, any type

2 large eggs or ½ cup egg substitute

2 to 3 tablespoons sugar

2 tablespoons lemon juice

To Serve

Sour cream

Plain or vanilla yogurt

Applesauce

Sliced fresh strawberries or other fruit

Preheat the oven to 350 degrees. Butter a 9 by 13-inch baking dish or coat it with nonstick cooking spray.

In a blender or a food processor (fitted with a steel blade), combine all the batter ingredients. Process until very smooth, scraping down the sides of the container once or twice. Measure out 1½ cups of the batter, and pour it into the bottom of the prepared baking dish. Bake at 350 degrees for about 10 minutes, or until it is set.

Meanwhile, combine all the filling ingredients in a large bowl, and mix them well. When the bottom layer has set, remove it from the oven and spread the filling over it, smoothing the top. Give the remaining batter a brief stir to resuspend the ingredients; then very slowly pour it over the cheese filling so the filling is completely covered. Carefully return the casserole to the 350-degree oven, and bake it an additional 35 to 40 minutes, or until the top is puffed and set.

Let the casserole rest for about 10 minutes before cutting it into squares. Serve with your choice of accompaniments.

Makes about 8 servings as a main course, more as a side dish or buffet dish.

Rich-and-Fruity Lokshen Kugel

SWEET NOODLE "PUDDING"

Dairy lokshen kugel is traditional for Ashkenazic Jews on Shavuot because of the milk products it contains. This one is especially appropriate because it also features lots of fruit (Shavuot is the time of the "first fruits").

The kugel is so luscious and attractive that it could almost be served as dessert. (In fact, I once included it in a cooking series that I taught called "International Desserts.") It can be baked ahead and reheated just before serving, making it convenient for enter-

taining. This kugel has become a regular at my dairy buffets, and I often prepare it for our Yom Kippur "break-fast" and Hanukkah open-house celebrations. It is always very popular with guests.

NOTES: Over the years, the sizes of the cans containing the fruits seem to keep getting smaller in minute increments. Use the closest size you can find; it is not critical to the recipe.

I have found that mandarin oranges canned in syrup hold their shape better than those canned in juice. For this recipe, all the syrup is drained off.

For best results, do not use nonfat sour cream or cream cheese in this recipe. Low-fat or reduced-fat products work well, though the kugel will be less rich-tasting.

TOPPING
2 tablespoons sugar
1 teaspoon ground cinnamon

KUGEL
8 ounces medium-width egg noodles (²/₃ of a 12-ounce package)
1 (16-ounce) can pitted dark sweet cherries in syrup (see Notes)
1 (10-ounce) can mandarin orange segments in syrup (see Notes)
1 cup sour cream (see Notes)

1 (8-ounce) package cream cheese, softened and cut into small pieces (see Notes)
½ cup sugar
2 teaspoons vanilla extract
4 large eggs or 1 cup egg substitute
1 (8-ounce) can crushed pineapple, including juice

For the topping, put the sugar and cinnamon into a small bowl, and mix them well. Set the topping mixture aside.

For the kugel, cook the noodles in a 5-quart or similar pot following the package directions. While the noodles are cooking, drain the cherries and mandarin oranges in a colander, and rinse them slightly with cool water. Set them aside to drain completely. When the noodles are done cooking, drain them well, and return them to the pot off the heat. Set aside.

Preheat the oven to 350 degrees. Coat a 9 by 13-inch baking dish with nonstick cooking spray or grease it well.

In a food processor (fitted with a steel blade) or a blender, combine the

sour cream, cream cheese, sugar, vanilla, and eggs. Process until the mixture is completely smooth, about 1 minute or longer, scraping down the sides of the container once or twice. Pour the mixture over the noodles; then stir the noodles gently with a large spoon so that the cream-cheese mixture is evenly distributed. Add the drained cherries and mandarin oranges, along with the pineapple, and gently stir so that the fruit is evenly distributed.

Transfer the noodle-fruit mixture to the prepared baking dish. Smooth the top, pushing down any cherries that have floated to the top. Sprinkle all the reserved cinnamon-sugar topping over the top of the kugel.

Bake the uncovered kugel at 350 degrees for 1 hour, or until it is set. Let it rest for at least 10 to 15 minutes before cutting it. Serve warm or at room temperature, cut into squares.

If the kugel is made ahead, let it cool to room temperature. Then cover the top tightly with plastic wrap, and refrigerate or freeze the kugel. Defrost it, covered, in the refrigerator for several hours or overnight. Shortly before serving the kugel, reheat it, covered, in a microwave oven or a 350-degree conventional oven until it is warmed through.

Makes about 16 or more servings.

Mamaliga

ROMANIAN-STYLE CORNMEAL WITH CHEESE

One of the staples of Romanian-Jewish cuisine is *mamaliga,* cornmeal mush that is cooked until it is so thick it can be molded into a "cake." It is then sliced with a heavy white thread (never a knife!). For dairy meals, the slices are usually fried or baked with cheese.

Most Romanians prefer to use brinza cheese with their *mamaliga.* However, almost any kind of cheese—Muenster, mozzarella, kashkaval, Parmesan, feta, Monterey Jack, mild Cheddar—works well. It is simply a matter of taste.

Mamaliga is virtually identical to the Italian dish called *polenta,* which Italian Jews make on Shavuot using white cornmeal, rather than the customary yellow, because white symbolizes the purity of the Torah.

I adapted the following recipe from one given me by a "Romanian-Jewish friend," who asked that I not identify her by name. Though Romanian Jews love this dish and serve it often to their own families, it seems they consider it to be such unrefined "peasant" fare that they would rather not publicly admit to making it!

BASIC MAMALIGA
2 cups yellow cornmeal (or white
    cornmeal, if preferred for Shavuot)
4 cups cold water, divided
1 teaspoon salt
3 tablespoons butter

FOR FRIED MAMALIGA
1 to 2 large eggs, beaten
1 to 2 cups very finely grated Parmesan
    or similar cheese
Butter for the pan
Sour cream to serve (optional)

FOR BAKED MAMALIGA
About 2 cups grated or thinly sliced
    cheese (see comments for
    suggestions)
Butter to taste

For the basic mamaliga, combine the cornmeal and 1½ cups of the water in a medium bowl. (This softens the cornmeal, and helps to prevent lumps in the mamaliga when the cornmeal is cooked.)

In a large saucepan over high heat, bring the remaining 2½ cups water to a boil. Lower the heat to medium, and add the moistened cornmeal while stirring constantly with a wooden spoon. (Romanians prefer to use a 1-inch-thick wooden dowel that they keep on hand just for this purpose.) Adjust the heat so that the mixture just simmers, and stir it constantly. It will become very thick and stiff. Stir in the salt and butter. Continue stirring constantly for about 10 minutes.

Then cook the mamaliga over very low heat, stirring occasionally, for 10 to 15 minutes longer, or until it seems to pull away from the sides and bottom of the pan. Use a spoon or a spatula that has first been dipped in water to push all the cornmeal mixture from the sides of the pan, forming a mound in the center. Let the mixture sit on the heat for 1 to 2 minutes, undisturbed, so that steam can loosen it from the bottom of the pan. Lift up the pan by the handle, and immediately invert it onto a wooden board or platter in one quick movement. The mamaliga should fall out into a sort of "cake." If it does not,

use a spoon or spatula to remove it from the pan. Smooth out the surface of the "cake" with the back of a wet spoon or a wet knife, and, if necessary, shape it into a neat mound. If plain mamaliga is desired, let it cool only slightly, and serve it as is. Cut it in the Romanian style with a long thread held taut between your hands, or use a knife.

For baked or fried mamaliga: Let it cool completely. (It may be refrigerated overnight, if desired.) Then use a knife or thread to cut it in ¼- to ½-inch-thick slices.

To bake: Preheat the oven to 375 degrees. In a buttered or nonstick-spray-coated casserole, alternate slices of mamaliga with grated cheese and bits of butter, ending with cheese on top. Bake, uncovered, in a 375-degree oven for about 20 minutes, or until the cheese is melted and bubbly and the top is lightly browned.

To fry: Dip each slice into beaten egg and then into finely grated Parmesan cheese. Heat a large skillet over medium-high heat; then melt a generous amount of butter in it. Fry the slices until they are browned on both sides and heated through. If desired, serve the fried mamaliga with sour cream.

Makes 6 to 8 servings.

Challah "Bread Pudding"

Jews began "recycling" long before this practice became commonplace in modern-day America. It is a Jewish tradition not to throw away an object used for ceremonial purposes, but to somehow recycle it into something else holy. Jewish cooks have brought this custom into the kitchen by turning leftovers from one meal into something scrumptious for the next. For example, stale challah may be made into a savory kugel for the following Shabbat.

Another way to recycle challah is into the delectable sweet "bread pudding" that follows, which is really a kugel of sorts. It is dairy, making it perfect for Shavuot brunch or dessert.

½ cup granulated sugar

¼ cup light or dark brown sugar

1 teaspoon ground cinnamon

¼ to ½ teaspoon ground nutmeg

3 large eggs, lightly beaten, or ¾ cup
    egg substitute

2½ cups milk, any type

2 tablespoons butter, melted

1 teaspoon vanilla extract

6 cups ½-inch-square challah cubes,
    crust removed

¾ cup raisins

To Serve (Optional)

Vanilla ice cream

In a large bowl, combine the granulated sugar, brown sugar, cinnamon, and nutmeg. Reserve 2 tablespoons of the mixture. Add the eggs to the mixture remaining in the bowl, and mix well.

Stir in the milk, melted butter, and vanilla. Toss the challah cubes with the raisins, and add to the milk mixture. Mix with a large spoon so that all the cubes are moistened. Let the cubes rest about 15 minutes, stirring occasionally, so they can absorb the moisture.

Meanwhile, coat with nonstick cooking spray or grease well a 9-inch square baking dish. Set aside. Preheat the oven to 325 degrees. When the cube mixture has rested, transfer the cubes and all their liquid to the prepared baking dish. Sprinkle the top with the reserved 2 tablespoons of sugar mixture.

Bake at 325 degrees for about 1 hour, or until puffed and set. Remove the bread pudding from the oven, and let it cool a few minutes before serving it. For best taste, serve it warm (it may be reheated in a microwave oven). Spoon it out or cut into squares to serve. If desired, top each piece with a small scoop of vanilla ice cream.

Makes about 8 servings.

"Light" New York-Style Cheesecake

Shavuot often brings to mind a huge "New York–style" cheesecake that is delicious—but also too rich, too heavy, and too much for a family to eat. The following "light and easy" cheesecake is adapted from a recipe created by my friend and fellow food writer Nancy Baggett for a cookbook that we wrote together called *Don't Tell 'Em It's Good for 'Em.*

Nancy is a whiz at making low fat taste scrumptious. This "light" cheesecake contains only about a third of the fat that is in most conventional recipes, yet it has a wonderful flavor and creamy texture. You'll never have to tell any Shavuot guests that this cheesecake is, relatively speaking, "good for 'em"!

NOTES: For best results, this cheesecake should be refrigerated overnight, so plan to bake at least 1 day ahead of when you need it.

To make strawberry "fans" to garnish this cake, rinse ripe but firm, large strawberries, but do not cut off the leaves. Use a small knife to cut several very thin slices in each strawberry from the point end of the strawberry up to, but not through, the leaves. Fan out the slices, leaving them attached at the leaves. Arrange several fans around the perimeter of the top of the cheesecake.

CRUST
⅔ cup graham cracker crumbs
1½ tablespoons slightly softened butter
1 tablespoon sugar

FILLING
1 small lemon
1 (15- to 16-ounce) container part-skim ricotta cheese (about 2 cups)
1 cup plain low-fat yogurt
1 cup sugar

2½ tablespoons all-purpose flour
1 (8-ounce) package regular cream cheese, softened
2 large eggs
2 large egg whites
2 teaspoons vanilla extract

GARNISH
Fresh strawberries

Preheat the oven to 350 degrees. Have ready an 8½- to 9-inch-diameter round springform pan. Set aside.

For the crust, combine all the crust ingredients in a food processor fitted with a steel blade. Pulse-process until the crumb mixture is well blended. Put all the crumbs into the bottom of the springform pan, and press them with your fingertips to form a bottom layer (only) of even thickness. Bake at 350 degrees for 15 minutes, or until the crust is crisp and lightly browned. Set aside on a wire rack to cool. (Do not turn off the oven.)

Meanwhile, wash the lemon well; then use a grater to remove the yellow part only of the peel. Reserve the grated lemon peel. Cut the lemon in half, and squeeze out all the juice into a small cup, removing any seeds.

In the same food processor fitted with a steel blade (just wipe out the bowl; washing is not necessary), combine the ricotta cheese, yogurt, sugar, flour, reserved grated lemon peel, and lemon juice. Process for about 1 minute, or until the mixture is completely smooth. Cut the cream cheese into eight pieces. With the food processor running, add them one at a time through the feed tube. Process for about 1 to 1½ minutes longer, or until there are no lumps of cream cheese in the batter, and it is perfectly smooth. Add the eggs and extra egg whites along with the vanilla extract, process for only about 10 to 15 seconds longer, or just until blended.

Pour the cheesecake batter over the prepared graham cracker crust. Bake at 350 degrees for 15 minutes. Then lower the temperature to 325 degrees, and bake for 1 hour and 15 minutes (75 minutes) to 1 hour and 20 minutes (80 minutes) longer, or until the cheesecake center is slightly puffed and seems "set" when the surface is lightly tapped. Place it in the pan on a wire rack to cool to room temperature. Then refrigerate the cheesecake in the pan until it is thoroughly chilled (preferably overnight) before serving it. It may be stored in the refrigerator, wrapped after it is cool, for several days.

Just before serving the cheesecake, remove it from the springform pan. Garnish the top with fresh strawberries, which are whole, sliced, or cut into fans (see Notes). Or serve the strawberries on the side.

Makes about 8 servings.

Soutlach

CREAMY SMOOTH RICE PUDDING

This delicate, tasty pudding is a favorite of those Sephardic Jews who hail from Turkey and nearby areas. It is served on Shavuot and other Jewish festive occasions, and is often accompanied with other dairy foods such as sweet cheese-filled pastries. Sometimes, it is eaten as Shabbat breakfast.

In some households, a family member's initial or first name is inscribed on top of each individual portion using drizzled ground cinnamon. Those Sephardim who consider Shavuot to be a "Feast of Roses" flavor a similar pudding with rose water, and serve it with rose-petal jam.

I first tasted *soutlach* in 1982 when I visited Istanbul. It was offered in small square bowls at just about every restaurant and cafeteria. Sometimes, the cooked pudding was baked in a low oven for several hours until the top caramelized and formed a brown skin.

The following version of *soutlach* is simplified and modernized by the substitution of Cream of Rice cereal for the customary ground rice or combination of cooked rice and rice flour. Unlike custard-type rice puddings, it does not contain eggs but relies instead on the starch in the rice to congeal it.

6 tablespoons uncooked Cream of Rice cereal
½ cup sugar
4 cups milk, any type

1 teaspoon vanilla extract or rose water
Ground cinnamon for sprinkling, to taste

In a large saucepan, combine the Cream of Rice cereal and sugar. Slowly add the milk, stirring constantly so that no lumps form. Set the saucepan over medium-high heat, and cook, stirring constantly, for 5 to 10 minutes, or until the pudding begins to thicken and comes to a boil.

Lower the heat so that the pudding just simmers, and cook it, stirring often, for 15 to 20 minutes longer, or until the pudding thickens considerably and heavily coats the spoon. The rice granules should be very soft and mostly disintegrated.

Remove the pudding from the heat, and stir in the vanilla or rose water. Pour the pudding into six small individual bowls or one large shallow serving bowl. Lightly sprinkle cinnamon on top. Serve the pudding warm, or refrigerate it and serve it chilled.

Makes about 6 servings.

Strawberries and "Cream"

This strawberry compote is wonderful for Shavuot when large fresh strawberries are just coming into season. The "cream" is a puréed ricotta cheese mixture that tastes rich and thick, but has much less fat and fewer calories than the usual whipped heavy cream.

If desired, the cream topping may be used as a dip for whole strawberries. To serve it that way, put the cream topping in a small bowl, and place the bowl in the center of a large platter. Surround the "cream" with large, ripe strawberries that have been rinsed but still have their leaves. Use the leaves to hold each strawberry as it is dipped into the "cream."

BERRIES
4 cups sliced fresh, hulled strawberries
3 tablespoons granulated sugar
2 to 3 tablespoons orange juice

"CREAM" TOPPING
1 ½ cups part-skim ricotta cheese

½ teaspoon vanilla extract
¼ cup confectioners' sugar
½ cup regular or low-fat vanilla yogurt

GARNISH
About 6 perfect whole strawberries

About 2 to 3 hours before serving time, toss the sliced berries with the granulated sugar and orange juice. Cover and refrigerate the berries, stirring occasionally.

For the "cream" topping, put the ricotta cheese, vanilla extract, and confectioners' sugar into a food processor fitted with a steel blade, and process until the mixture is completely smooth and creamy, scraping down the sides of the bowl once or twice. Transfer the mixture to a small bowl. By hand, fold in the vanilla yogurt (the food processor will make it watery). Refrigerate the "cream" in a covered bowl until it is well chilled.

To serve, divide the sliced strawberries with a little of their juices into about six dessert cups or stemmed glasses. Top the berries with dollops of "cream," dividing it equally among the servings. Place one whole strawberry on top of each serving.

Makes about 6 servings.

INDEX

In order to make this book especially useful for year-round menu planning, recipes are listed in this index by course: Appetizers and First Courses, Main Dishes, Side Dishes, and Desserts. There are also categories for types of dishes: Bars and Bar Cookies, Breads, Breakfast or Brunch Fare, Cakes, Candies and Confections, Casseroles, Challah, Cookies, Dumplings, Fish, Fried Foods, Icings, Kugels, Pastries, Puddings, Salads, Soups, and Stuffed Foods.

For the convenience of those who observe Jewish dietary laws, the heading for Main Dishes is divided into three categories: Dairy, Meat, and Pareve. In addition, within the other headings for courses and categories, the recipes are marked (D) for dairy, (M) for meat, and (P) for pareve ("neutral"). Where "(D) or (P)" is indicated, the category depends on the exact choice of ingredients that you use in preparing the dish.

Pasta *(cont'd)*:
   and White Bean Skillet, 227–28
   see also Couscous; Noodle(s)
Pastilla (Chicken and Almond Pie in Filo), 179–83
Pastries:
   Baklava (Many-Layered Pastry with Nuts and
      Honey) (D) or (P), 320–23
   Borekas (Sephardic Savory Pastries Filled with
      Cheese and Vegetables) (D), 492–96
   Bulemas (Coiled, Filled Flaky Pastry) (D), 496,
      499
   Fruit-and-Nut-Filled Yeast (Raised-Dough
      Cake) (D), 199–201
   Koeksisters (Fried Braided Pastries Dipped in
      Syrup) (D) or (P), 253–55
   Rugelach (Rich Nut Horns or Rolls) (D),
      237–40
   Sambusik (Iraqi-Style Chicken or Meat
      Turnovers) (M), 302–4
   Spanakopitas or *Ojaldres* (Spinach and Cheese in
      Flaky Pastry) (D), 496–98
   Travados (Walnut-Filled Crescent Cookies) (P),
      326–27
   Zelebi or *Zlabia* (Fried Rosettes Dipped in
      Honey Syrup) (P), 250–53
Pea, Split, Bean, and Barley Soup, Meaty
   (*Mitzapuny*), 168–69
Peanut(s), 343, 344
   Butter and Chocolate Mock Hamantaschen,
      332–34
   Meat, and Fruit Curry, 276–77
   oil, 344, 347
Pear(s):
   -Cran-Apple Sauce, 189–90
   "First Fruits" Rainbow Salad, 484–85
   Poached in Red Wine (*Poires Bourguignonne*),
      397–98
   Raspberry Tart, 159
   and Sweet Potato Casserole, Layered, 140–41
   Walnut Quick Bread, 292–93
Pepper(s) (bell):
   Grilled Vegetables, 471–73
   Israeli Salad (Kibbutz-Style Chopped Fresh Veg-
      etables), 432–33
   Mahshi or *Dolmas* (Meat-Stuffed Vegetables),
      368–70
   Roasted, and Tomato Salad (*Ensalada de Pimiento
      y Tomat*), 73–74
   Steak, 58

Stuffed, Freda's, 173–74
Pesach (Passover), 337–425, 483
   dietary restrictions at, 16, 342–44, 346–47
   history of, 338
   matzah and, 338, 340–41, 342–43
   names for, 337–38
   recipes for, 347–425
   search for Hametz and, 345–46
   special notes on ingredients for, 346–47
   see also Seders
Pescado con Agristada (Fish in Egg-Lemon Sauce),
   358–59
Pesce all'Ebraica (Italian-Style Sweet-and-Sour Fish),
   117–18
"Petits Fours," Marzipan, Moroccan-Style,
   329–31
Picadillo (Spicy Ground Beef with Fruit and
   Almonds), 273–74
Pies:
   Apple Crumb, 155–57
   Chicken and Almond, in Filo (*Pastilla*), 179–83
   see also Minas
Pilafs:
   Brown Rice, 79
   Kasha-Mushroom, Herbed, 79–80
   Lamb and Brown Rice, 122–23
Pineapple, Mashed Sweet Potatoes with, 141–42
Pine nuts, 20
   Meat Loaf with Bulgur Wheat and (*Kibbeh*),
      175–77
Pinwheel Snacks, 334
Pinyonati (Crunchy Dough Nuggets in Honey),
   146–48
Pita (Flat Round "Pocket" Bread), 454–57
   Triangles, Toasted, 457
Plum Knedliky or Knaidlach (Fruit-Filled Potato
   Dumplings), 192–94
Poires Bourguignonne (Pears Poached in Red Wine),
   397–98
Pomegranates, 101, 271
Poppy seed(s), 21
   cakes
      Pound, 334–35
      Yeast, 95–97
   Cookies, Queen Esther's (*Mohn Kichelah*),
      327–29
   Filling, Honey Hamantaschen with, 313–15
Potato(es):
   Baked, with Spinach and Tomatoes, 385–87

ABOUT THE AUTHOR

GLORIA KAUFER GREENE, former food editor of the *Baltimore Jewish Times,* has written several cookbooks and hundreds of articles for newspapers and magazines. She frequently lectures and teaches cooking classes on Jewish cuisine. She lives in Maryland with her husband and children. Gloria Kaufer Greene can be found on the Internet at **www.jewishcuisine.com**.